The BREATH of KINGS

The BREATH of KINGS

Gene Farrington

Frederick Muller Limited
London

First published in Great Britain in 1982 by Frederick Muller Limited,
Dataday House, Alexandra Road, London SW19 7JZ.

Published in the USA by Doubleday & Company Inc., Garden City,
New York.

Copyright © 1982 Gene Farrington

All rights reserved. No part of this publication may be reproduced, stored in a retrieval system, or transmitted, in any form or by any means, electronic, mechanical, photocopying, recording or otherwise, without the prior consent of Frederick Muller Limited.

ISBN 0 584 31161 3

Farrington, Gene
The breath of kings
I. Title
813'.54(F)　　PS3556.A773

ISBN 0-584-31161-3

Printed in Great Britain by
Billing & Sons, Ltd., Worcester

To Donald for his patience

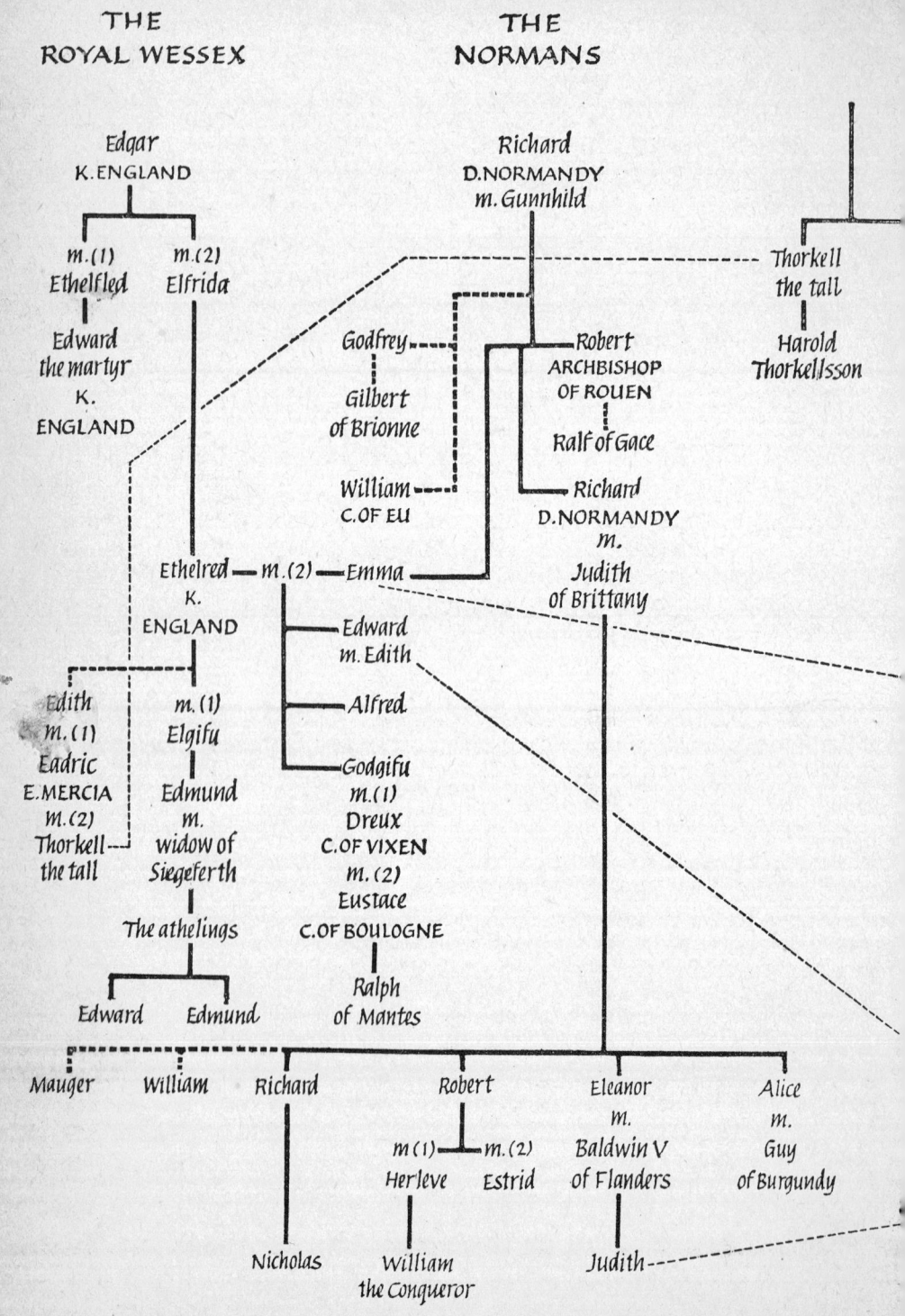

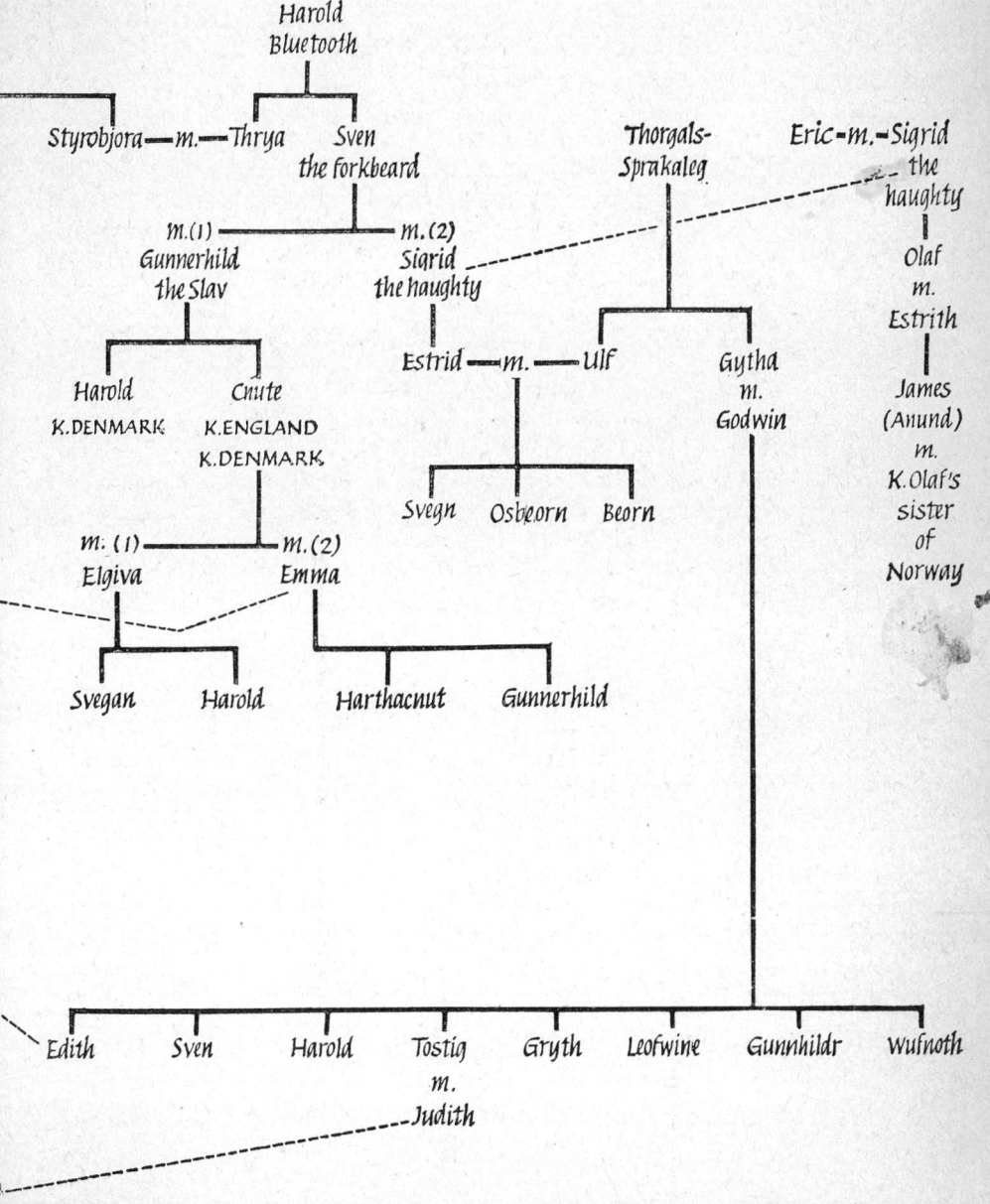

The BREATH of KINGS

BOOK ONE

The Atheling

CHAPTER 1

Corfe, England, 1012

A HAZE OF YELLOW SMOKE HUNG IN THE LONG HALL. IT LIFTED FROM THE hearth, but seemed inert in its rise to the hole overhead. It obscured and distorted. It distanced the heavy timbers above, and the figures in the tapestry seemed in a fog, and the gray walls of lime, earth and dung, already made a vile green in the light of the torches, paled to acceptable indistinction. Yet the smoke did nothing to soften the voices—voices of thegns and slaves, of clerics and ladies, the voice of an earldorman, the voice of a bishop, the voice of a King's son and the voice of the King—voices which loudened as ears were deafened by flowing mead and the din of other voices. But there was no voice of the Queen, for Emma sat silent. She was weary of all the hate and she wondered if she was now ready for death. There seemed little left but hate. Fight was ebbing away. Why, when she did not even like her own nine-year-old son, Edward, did she continue to fight that the throne might be his? Was it instinct which drove her to battle Edmund, King Ethelred's son by that pagan witch? Her eye caught a rat as it darted over the fetid straw floor. From the corner it scurried the length of the table, which stretched the distance of the hall. The rat vanished into the darkness, and Emma looked up. At the far end of the table near the heavy doors she could see a young thegn she did not recognize. His hair was the color of torches. She sensed pleasure and a moment of respite from the hate. Yet she shuddered, for despite her thoughts and the fire, a sea-cold chilled her and she tightened the cinch of her bliaut.

Next to her, Ethelred was in his cups. He leaned toward her, spilling the wine from the bowl. The liquid formed in gilted coins on the table. His drunken breath was like a dragon's, warm and sour, and she turned away in disgust.

"The Danes are pig dung." Ethelred turned back to the earldorman beside him and belched loudly. "They can be bought."

The young man at the end of the table looked up as if he had been hit. Emma realized he was a Dane, the son of Thorkell the Tall.

"Give them enough silver and if the bastards' ships don't sink from the weight they'll go home." He spilled more wine.

"It's not the same with Sven." It was Edmund, seated beyond the earldorman, who spoke.

Edmund was right. Sven the Forkbeard was no Viking marauder come to plunder and disappear. He was a Dane King who would be King of England as well. Ethelred was deceiving himself with drunken talk. Sven would not be content with Danegeld, he wanted the country and, while Ethelred drank and hunted and whored and gorged, the Dane chieftain was taking it. Ethelred was a coward, but Sven wasn't, and worse, he was clever as well as fearless. He would be supported in the North as well as the English Danelaw. Edmund could see it. She counted Edmund a bastard, hated him, but never underestimated him, and Edmund was right: the kingdom was slipping away. "There are traitors submitting to him all through Anglia and Mercia."

"I know what to do with traitors. There was Aelfric of Hampshire and . . ."

It was the repetition of a tale the King had told a hundred times. He had taken Aelfric's young son and had his eyes burned out. She listened to the story with disgust, but her disgust for her husband was not limited to the cruelty of his tale nor this evening's drunken stupor. It was constant and intense. She had meant to love Ethelred. At seventeen she had boarded the ship for England with a sense of excitement, her adventurous Viking blood, no doubt aroused by the sea, speeding in anticipation. She was to be a queen. But she had despised him from the moment she stepped from the boat and looked up into his cruel eyes, more when he first entered her body, shoving his penis into her as if he were mortally wounding an enemy with a lance. She hated Ethelred. She hated the three living brats she had borne him. She hated the dead ones. She hated the aborted masses of semideveloped things, a part of him, which she had dropped from her womb. She hated sitting at this table with him. She hated the gross leg that now brushed against her gown. She smiled at the young Dane. He dropped his eyes. A juggler walked down the center of the long table tossing balls into the air, stepping into plates of food. A burly Wessexman stood and whacked him across the ass. The wooden balls went flying, scaring roosting doves from perches overhead. Ethelred stopped in the middle of a story, leaned back away from the table and vomited. Near the end of the long table a housecarl fell from the bench and landed atop a sleeping pig. The young thegn helped the man to his feet amid laughter and pig squeals.

Emma stood, pulling her gown up with her forearm. The ladies started to arise, but she motioned them to sit.

The King stopped vomiting. "Where are you going?" His words were slurred and belligerent.

"Must I even get my lord's permission to waste my water?"

She raised her chin, moved around the end of the head table and without looking down stepped to the lower level. She could hear his silent rebuke: "Your goddamn Norman airs." Her skirt swept over the matted, fetid straw as she walked toward the heavy doors. Her eyes veered only once, when she looked at the young thegn, commanding him with a single glance to meet her outside. An attendant with a torch preceded her from the room, but she ordered him back inside.

The sea waved against the rock below; she could hear it and it drowned the voices within. She moved from the giant shadow of the timbered hall, her skirt train sweeping the wet grasses and leaving them flat behind. She walked in the brightness of a full-faced moon to the brink where earth dropped, as if sliced away, into the sea. She stared down to the black water and saw death, a constant moving death, eluding itself, broken by white where the force of the sea met itself. She was attended by neither dread nor hope, and though her life was ruled by the dictates of faith, she secretly sensed a finality, an end, in death. The idea of end was comforting.

She felt an intrusion and swung around to see the approaching silhouette. He was even taller than his father, a thin giant shadow moving in vital strides of youthfulness. She turned from him to the sea but knew when he had come up behind her.

"It is dangerous for you to be here," she said, still without looking at him. "You must go back to your place at the table. Tomorrow do not join the others in the hunt. I will wait for you in the chapel in the morning."

His large hands moved to her shoulders. "No." Her voice was the command of the Queen. "Go back now." The hands fell away.

This place was called Corfe. She preferred being here, perhaps because Normandy and home lay straight across the channel at the end of the path of the moon, or perhaps because of the sea itself, its power somehow being the source of her own. Escape always seemed nearest at Corfe.

She turned and walked without haste back toward the noise of the hall.

Morning. Emma pushed back the boards of the window. The cold of night had given way to the warmth of bright day. The yard below was a sea of confusion. The yelp of dogs intermingled with the yelling of men whose voices betrayed their places of birth. She could sense the lust for blood, the urgency and tension in both packs, man and dog.

She looked at Ethelred. They told that from the window where she now stood, he, at ten, had stood and watched as his mother's retainers had killed his thirteen-year-old brother, the King. That event thirty-five years ago in the yard below had come back to haunt Ethelred. They raised the dead boy King from his grave. "No corruption," they claimed. They venerated; they enshrined the body; they spoke of miracles over those skin-covered bones. The stories of wonder grew, swelled in telling like air blown in an animal's bladder, transforming an inept boy king into the figure of a saint—Edward the Martyr. As the cult grew, so grew the accusations of Ethelred's complicity, no matter the denials, no matter Ethelred declared a festival day in March to honor his dead brother. "The King is dead. Kill the King." The earldorman and thegns and bishops and clergy used it as their excuse to turn to Sven. And Edmund would use it, skillfully, when the time seemed appropriate. Emma doubted not at all what Edmund would do. And when the hour came and Sven or Edmund slew Ethelred, what was to become of her? She did not fear death, but it angered her to think of life being stolen from her.

She watched as men and dogs made their way down the steep incline into the hamlet. Beyond the huts and hovels was a wide field and between it and the sky stood the black height of forest. The diminishing figures disappeared into the woods as a distant hunting horn called out of the black trees. The yard below was now desolate except for animals and two camp followers who were swearing, pulling at each other's hair and fighting over something one had apparently concealed in her hand. Emma closed the boards.

She made her way carefully down steep steps into the lower chamber where her children were supposed to be having their morning porridge. What she found was her six-year-old daughter terrorizing a slave woman with a large dangling snake and the youngest, Alfred, painting the wooden floor with his porridge and wine, using bread for an applicator. There was no sign of the older boy.

"Godgifu!" Emma yelled.

The girl let the snake sail through the air and out the window. The child is an ugly little thing, Emma thought. But no matter how ugly she grew to become she would never surpass her older brother. The boy was grotesque. She knew it was unnatural to find such revulsion in ones own offspring, but she was repulsed by the sight of her son. She would have suffocated him at birth, as barbarians did when a monster was born among them, had it not been that he was a legitimate Christian heir to the throne and her uncertainty whether or not she would bear another. She shunned him, but he followed her as if he were some penance she was meant to endure for having given birth to him. Yet, he remained her hold on England. Edward was her tenuous link to power, to control of the throne and the kingdom. "Where is he?"

"Hiding," Godgifu told her. "He's hiding. He was afraid of the snake."

"Don't bring those odious creatures in."

She stepped out into the yard. One of the camp followers who had been fighting had apparently killed the other and now the empty yard was filled and there was a commotion among the slaves and workers.

"Madam."

Emma turned to see the slave woman, Aesval, standing in the doorway. She had a blue cloak in her arms.

"There is still a morning chill." The large woman held out the garment. Aesval was as constant as a shadow, mothering and sensing Emma's wants.

Emma let the woman put it over her shoulders, ignored the camp followers and made her way to the chapel. The chapel had a stone undercroft and she entered from below and up a ladder rather than through the entrance at the front. She was surprised to find the Dane already there. He stood nervously inside. Light from the arched loft encircling the room illuminated his yellow hair. Emma took command. She barred the main door, crossed to the rear and threw a bar across that door as well.

"Here? Here in the chapel?"

"We would be seen going to my chamber. It is natural for me to closet myself here in prayer."

"But in the chapel?"

"What is done before God will be confessed before God."

He was near perfect, flawed only by the missing fingers on his right hand. The thumb and little finger were all that remained.

He saw her look to his hand. "King Sven," he said, "cut them off. He would have killed me but Cnute stopped him."

"This son of Sven's is so weak he will not see his father's enemies punished?"

"Cnute is my friend."

"But your father is traitor to his father."

"My father was right. Sven's men should not have killed the Archbishop of Canterbury. God will punish Sven for such a sin."

"God will punish us all for our sins," she said. She softened the hard wood with her cloak and, taking his left hand, pulled him down to the floor. There was a tenseness in his lean hard body.

"There is nothing to fear," she whispered. "Be calm. They are all hunting elsewhere." His tension eased as she touched him. Slowly enjoying the moment, they revealed piecemeal their bodies to each other. She opened her bodice and let her breast rest in the hand with the missing fingers. It was a strange sensation, the stubble of the fingers against her flesh. With his left hand he further unlaced her garment, revealing her abdomen, in which had been carried the dead and living children of Ethelred. The stretch marks of pregnancy had mostly disappeared in the climbing of the narrow steep steps. She was twenty-seven years old and sometimes it seemed to her most of those years had been spent with a swollen belly. There were ways and herbs to be taken and she vowed next time she would not endure the long months of carrying another being. The Dane's arms and chest were muscled from struggling with the heavy weapons and his body was hard and smooth like the polished stone about his neck and she ran her tongue down his chest, touching his navel where light pubic hair met her lips. They felt and held, extending the moments, sometimes gently, at others intensely savage. Now nude, they rolled and turned and twisted upon the spread cloak until it lay wrinkled and bunched beneath her back. She fastened her legs about his waist and her eyes were held tightly shut. Gasping in the ecstasy of release, she threw back her head and opened her eyes to look straight up to the loft where two pink eyes stared at her in terror. In anger, she winched, made one spastic move, freeing herself from the young Dane's penis, stood up facing the boy at the rail above and screamed, "YOU DIRTY LITTLE MONSTER!"

He began to wail. It was a "No" he was crying over and over but it sounded inhuman, like the pain of a wounded wild animal. The Dane covered himself, staring frantically at what he must have thought some apparition. Emma's oldest child was an albino. His white skin was topped with white thin strands of long colorless hair.

"Come down from there!" Emma yelled. "COME DOWN . . ."

The boy continued only to wail.

"Down! Or I'll drag you down."

She picked up her cloak and moved to unbar the door. The boy fled down the ladder on the outside and before she could get the door fully open he was wailing through the yard. She stood in the doorway of the chapel with nothing covering her but the cloak, which was open in the front. Slaves and a priest stopped their chores and gaped. The boy sped down the hill toward the hamlet. He flew with the deftness of a young fawn being hunted. She could only watch him. He stumbled once, but quickly recovered and flew across the open field, the whiteness of his hair visible against the gold of the ripened grasses. The Dane, fully clothed, stood in the doorway behind her. She turned and looked up into his frightened face. "Flee," she said. "Flee for your life, son of Thorkell."

And he was gone.

She took her gown from the floor and rolled it up into a bundle. Fastening the cloak about her, she came down the steps from the chapel leaving the door open behind her. Work within the yard ceased as she crossed. She could feel their eyes. Among them, both the free and the slaves, there would be concern. For what happened in the chapel would bring change, and change was disruptive. Insects gathered on the corpse of the camp follower who had been knifed and would continue to collect on the open dead flesh until an authoritative voice returned from the King's hunt and pronounced: death and guilt and death. One fat breast was exposed and bruised and she still had the knife stuck in her abdomen. The dirt about her was muddied by the blood.

The sun, so promising earlier, hid behind a growing drift of charcoal clouds. Near the chamber house Godgifu was attempting to poke a chicken's eyes out. The chicken pecked her hand and freed itself; the girl let out a yelp. Emma went by, seeing it all and saying nothing.

The heavy breath of Aesval followed her up steps to her chamber. Emma turned at the top and looked at the woman, who paused to suck in air. She was probably young, but her size and the habit of toil left her without age, neither a hint of youth nor distinction of years. Emma sent her away and dressed herself in fresh clothes. Then she took out her relics. From the cupboard she removed the tiny wooden box with the glass lid.

The box contained a tooth of St. John Chrysostom and had been given her by her mother when she was eleven. They had been playing in the old tower at Rouen. The tower built by her great-grandfather, Rolf the Viking. She had torn her gown as she led her brothers in an imaginary battle against the dark foes who held the tower. "I should lead," her brother Richard said. "No, I am the great warrior queen," Emma told him and pushed him out of the way. It was then she had torn her gown. It was an old aunt, she was mostly French, who said it was "unseemly" and a needle had been thrust in Emma's hand and she was not allowed to go any longer to the tower to play with her brothers. She sat in the dim light pushing the needle through the tapestry fabric, her old aunt scowling across from her, and when Emma cried her mother brought her the tooth in the glass-lid box.

Ritual. She took all her relics and placed them, spaced evenly, in a circle about her: the stone from the cell of St. Anthony, tiny bones of St. Monica, a scrap from the veil of St. Brigid, a fingernail of St. Martin de Tours, St. Hild's tiny cross of iron, a plain ring worn by St. Itte and her daughter Gertrude, a link of chain said to have been St. Cuthert's, broken chips of wood from the crozier of St. Botulf and a cap once worn by St. Dunstan, faded and frayed. But the most treasured of her relics was a bone needle used by St. Irene in exile. It was St. Irene among all whom Emma admired. Wise and with skill, even at the necessity of imprisoning and blinding her own son, she had ruled not as empress but as the Emperor of the great Byzantium.

Sitting in the circle of relics, Emma could see out the open window. The sky was getting darker. They would come and Ethelred would have her killed. More than death, it was losing which disturbed her. All the years of enduring the filthy body of Ethelred would have been worthless.

She had earned the right to have her son king and control England. It began to rain; the clouds twisted and rolled. Sometimes a breath of rain pricked her cheeks. She heard the dogs first, then the noise of men. It drowned the sounds of rain as the men moved into the yard and, unlike other days after other hunts when stags and boars were carried in on long stakes, today's sounds were not of triumph but of anger. Emma picked up the relics and returned them to the cupboard.

She was not alarmed when they broke into her chamber. There were two of them and they were Edmund's men; she knew them both. One was called Heljer and he had a cockeye that turned off as if to look where a piece of his ear was missing. The other's name she did not remember. His face, hands, and arms were covered with hundreds of small lumps of flesh all about the size of acorns and as if formed from the same mold. Heljer, pulling her from the bench, pressed his body against hers, and the other man rubbed his hand over her breast as he tore off a gold brooch she wore. They dragged her from the room, pawing her body as they pulled her through the yard. The yard was a wallow of mud and it clung to her gown and limbs. She ached from the hold the men had upon her but refused to cry out. The dead camp follower had not been dealt with and was soaked with rain and the mud. The doors to the great hall were held open and the pair dragged Emma in, letting her fall to the straw clumped with mud from the feet of the men who filled the room. They had dropped her near the carcass of a dead boar and her hands and her face rested in blood from the beast.

Ethelred stood, legs apart, on the raised table at one end of the hall; his arms were crossed, and when they threw her down on the floor beneath him, he spit on her. "Bring the boy in."

It was Edmund who pulled Edward into the hall. She looked up at the quaking figure of her son with not the slightest plea.

Ethelred roared at him. "Repeat what you have told Edmund."

But Edward did not speak. He began to shriek wildly, long piercing wails, then with hands outstretched his entire body began vibrating and the words came; garbled, rolling sounds that meant nothing. Emma watched in horror, unable to remove her eyes from him. From the corners of his mouth, froth began dripping and he fell to the floor, his body leaping in spastic lurches.

The men all stood silent, transfigured by the strange contortions of Emma's son. Then, as if he alone were free of the spell, Ethelred's chaplain flung his body over Edward's. "He is possessed of the devil," he said. In Latin he began canting softly and as he spoke the boy seemed to calm; then he lifted Edward and took him in his arms from the hall.

Emma stood up. The blood of the boar smeared her face and she made no attempt to wipe it away.

"I accuse her of adultery." Edmund's voice was almost a whisper. "Of treason against the King."

"Lady"—Ethelred was as indifferent as if she were some stranger—"you have been accused of treason. You will be thrown in the river. If you do not rise to the surface you will be adjudged innocent of this affair. Edmund, she is yours."

Emma's voice betrayed no fear. "Is it not enough that Edmund here traitorously conspires for your throne and that the King of Denmark rules most of your kingdom? Would you also have my brother, Richard, bring the wrath of Normandy upon you?"

"Your brother would not tolerate your vileness. No man would tolerate what you have done in God's chapel, whore."

"My brother would give the accused the fairness of trial by ordeal and leave such judgments in the hands of God, not to the lying tongue of a son who conspires against his father."

"My Lord"—Edmund's voice was angry—"I found Edward terrified in the forest. I came up on him thinking it was some wounded animal. She did this to him. Because of her he is mad and possessed."

"The only one who has heard the boy is Edmund?" Emma felt the wet blood on her face. "And who is Edmund? A conspirator who sees Emma as a threat because Emma has a son whose throne he will steal."

No one replied.

"Ethelred, you have held the kingdom together for thirty years, buying off the Danes, killing off your enemies, but kill me without trial and the wrath of the house of Normans will rent this kingdom apart. Do as you wish. I care not."

Emma's eyes fell to the carcass of the wild boar, its life removed so easily. The rain beat upon the roof. It was the only sound. Then Archbishop Wulfstan went forward and spoke quiet words to the King, who listened with anger written in his eyes.

Emma looked across at Edmund. He was watching Wulfstan and Ethelred. His face was hard as if carved in ice.

"No!" Ethelred yelled. His chin quivered.

Emma could hear Wulfstan's voice but not the words. She continued watching Edmund. As if sensing her gaze, he turned. There was a sneer of triumph as he looked directly at her.

"No," Ethelred repeated, but even Edmund must have sensed Ethelred's "No" lacked conviction, for the sneer betrayed apprehension.

Ethelred swung around, but he did not look at Emma as he spoke. His voice was angry. "You will stand trial by ordeal."

"No!" Edmund yelled. "It is a ruse."

Emma had won, but it was not enough. The trial had to be held in her brother's demesne. "The trial to be at Rouen."

"Here." Ethelred turned from her.

"My brothers will never believe the trial was fair. At Rouen."

Edmund rushed toward her. The boar's blood dripped over her eye and she could scarcely see him. "Your brother is Archbishop of Rouen. What sort of trial would that be?"

She did not flinch from Edmund's threatening stance. "Robert, unlike you, Edmund, is a man of principles. A man of God."

"This is trickery!"

"No one would ever have cause to question my death when I fail to walk on hot coals and am found guilty by my own brothers. Think, Ethelred, put me to death here and I might well turn out to be St. Emma, like your martyred brother. I should like being a saint, I think. Would be better than this life."

The archbishop started to say something, but Ethelred cut him off. "So be it. We will take this lady to Normandy. Now lock her away lest she flee the country on her own."

"My Lord . . ." Edmund began.

"Lock her away."

CHAPTER 2

Corfe, 1012

THERE WAS A GREAT RAIN. EDWARD SLOPPED THROUGH THE PUDDLES TOWARD the pit. He looked down through the grating and, though he could not see her, he could see the aura of light about her. "Mother," he whispered loudly. There was no answer and the light moved farther back from the opening. The floor of the pit was like looking into a dirty well. "Mother," he called again, but there was no answer.

A thegn came over to him. "You best be gone from here, lad."

Edward walked away, but as he did he heard the thegn say to a soldier, "He is an ugly child."

It hurt Edward. No matter how often he heard it, it hurt. His father said he was the ugliest of God's creatures. "See yourself," Ethelred with the mean eye said, "as others see you with white skin and pink beady eyes and a few wispy strands of white hair. You might as well face the truth. The world loves beauty and shuns ugliness." Ethelred's eyes seemed meaner when he spoke.

Tears came to Edward's eyes and as he looked up they mingled with the rain. A boy on the roof of the great hall was repairing a hole in the thatch and Edward watched him through wet eyes and then pulled his hood and cloak about him as if to hide within it and went out of the wind into the cold of the great hall.

The hall was crowded, but despite clerics and thegns gathered there a cloud of quiet hung over the room and the rain and the scratching sound of the boy on the roof could be heard. Yesterday had been the feast of the great St. Bice, but there had been no celebration. There had not even been a mass in the chapel for the doors were barred and nailed and a soldier with a spear stood at the entry. Soldiers of the King had marched through the Danelaw and had cut off the heads of all the Danes. They whispered at Corfe that the great Sven's sister had been among those killed and that now Sven the Forkbeard would rage England with his armies and they would all be killed.

Ethelred's mean eye looked at him and Edward hid deeper in his cloak and went over to the fire and stood looking into the flame. The King sat at the far end of the room and Edward could feel him there though he did not turn about and look at him. He always saw his own ugliness reflected in the King's mean eye.

In other years there had been great feasts on St. Bice's day, but none yesterday. He had had another fit and had fallen in the yard near the pit where his mother was kept and they said a dragon had been seen in the forest and a great bear had come in the night to Corfe and its tracks were in the mud—and out to sea was said could be seen, although he had seen nothing in the direction where they pointed, a flaming ship of a dead Viking warrior on his way to Valhalla. "A good omen," the Thegn of Urgler had said and the other had nodded, but nothing good seemed to happen.

He wished there was a way to help his mother in the pit. The grate was too heavy and chained. If only she would answer him. He had been terrified by the pain Thorkellsson had been inflicting upon her in the chapel, but he had not meant to say anything to Edmund. He hated Edmund. It had just come out. Now he must find a way to get her out of the pit, for she would die in all this rain down in that dark hole. If only she would speak to him.

The doors banged open and Edward turned about to see a soldier shoving a priest, three servants, a slave and an old beggar linked together with a rope.

"These are them, my Lord," the soldier said. "These are the men which looked upon the Queen. There is one other, but he ran off during the night, but we'll find him, rest assured, my Lord."

"What say you?" The King's voice was weary, as if he didn't really care.

There was no answer. They all stared down except the priest, who looked without emotion directly at the King, stared right up into the King's mean eye. Edward wondered why he wasn't afraid.

"Saw you the Queen's nudity?" The King's tone indicated neither anger nor interest.

"Nothing. I saw nothing," the old beggar pleaded. "Please, my Lord, I saw . . ."

"It is so," a servant said without looking up. "We saw nothing."

"Priest?" It was the archbishop who asked the question.

"Yes," the priest answered and when he talked it was almost as if he were singing. "The Queen stood in the door of the chapel. The front of her cloak open, her body exposed. I saw the Queen thus."

"Poke out their eyes," the King said.

The rope binding the men together was cut.

"Please, my Lord King," one of the servants pleaded, but Edward knew by his voice he expected no mercy.

The King's man lifted a hot poker from the fire. Edward watched, horrified, but unable to turn away, as the soldier held one of the servant's eyes wide open with his fingers, until it looked like his eyeball would fall out, and then the King's man who held the poker slowly raised it and with a quick thrust shoved it into the socket. The cry was a piercing wail and the cry, more than the act itself, was terrible to Edward. When the soldier let loose of the blinded man, he fell to the floor, covering his eye sockets with open hands. He cried out like a wounded fox and blood seeped through his hands. Edward had not remembered the man's name at first, but watching him, head down and seeing the open sore on the back of the man's neck, he realized it was the swineherd who had made him a whistle from a hollow twig on a hot summer day.

The old beggar yelled and tried to escape and finally wiggled loose from his capturer. He leaped for the door and a sword rent open his back and he fell dead upon the straw.

Edward pulled the hood of his cloak tighter, as if to muffle the screams of the other two servants and the slave, as each in turn, with a ritualistic sameness, lost his sight. It did no good for the sound was the same, muffled or otherwise. It was the priest's turn. They took the crucifix from his waist. The poker was raised and jabbed into the socket. He flinched, but made no sound. And in some ways the silence was even more frightening than the crying had been. The poker was shoved into his other eye, but there was hardly the sound of his breath. He stood, even as they let him loose; an eyeball had been pulled back out on the poker and dangled from the socket. Edward knew when he became king he would never order a man's eye poked out.

The soldiers lifted the blind men to their feet, whirled them about and then gave each a shove. The sightless men collided and groped and Edward thought of the children's game he had seen played in the yard. The priest stumbled forward and lurched in the direction of the archbishop; Wulfstan pulled away, but not quite quickly enough, for the blinded priest grasped his robes and clung to them.

"Away from me." The archbishop yanked free the clutching fingers at his garments. "You have sinned exceedingly."

"Get them out of here!" the King's voice boomed.

"God forgive you." The priest's words were barely audible.

Edward wanted to cry, but he knew he mustn't, and the soldiers opened the doors and shoved the blind and bleeding-faced men into the rain. A brown dog sniffed at the swineherd and ambled into the hall before the doors closed. The wind had carried the wetness into the room and Edward could feel it dabbing his cheeks. He went back to the hearth and sat on the stone.

Why did men see? Edward wondered how he would know if anything was, if he couldn't see it? What if everything was but a vision and nothing existed but himself? What if God and he were all that was? But he knew it was not so. His mother was in the pit. His father stood there angrily with his mean eye. The archbishop paced, speaking to no one. The priest was without eyes, yet he existed. Edward knew it was all someway separate from himself and he did not understand it. He watched the movements of the flame. Why was fire and where did it come from? The archbishop came toward him. "Why is there fire?" Edward asked him.

"Because we need to keep warm and cook our food."

"But where does it come from?"

"It is a gift from God," the archbishop said.

"Is the sun made of fire?" Edward asked.

"Of course not. Don't be so silly and ask such stupid questions." He walked away.

What was the sun made of? Where did it go when it rained? Edward looked back into the fire. He kicked the brown dog away as the animal lifted his leg and was about to pee on his cloak. The hall had become quiet again and there was the sound of the rain and the scratching of the boy on the roof.

The doors burst open and Edmund came riding into the hall. His horse was wild and feisty and would not stand still though Edmund tugged on the reins. The animal's mane and tail dripped water and Edmund's mail, as well, seeped drops of rust. "What in God's name idiocy did you do yesterday?" he cried out at the King, pulling the horse back as he spoke.

"Get off that horse. I am the King and I do as I do." The King stopped talking for a moment as if he were choking. "Get off that horse!"

But Edmund made no move to get down. "You have destroyed us all. You are a fool!"

The thegns in the hall moved back lest they seem to stand between the King and his son.

"One more word," the King answered, "and I'll be done with you. Now, get down from there and get the beast from my hall."

Edmund raised his leg over the animal and lifted himself to the floor. The wind howled as the doors opened and a ceorl tugged the reluctant horse out into the wind.

"Was it not enough," Edmund screamed at his father, "that you taxed us to death, turning thegns into beggars, wasting geld to buy off the

Danes? You might as well have thrown it in the sea, for whatever little good it might have done, it is for naught. You have destroyed us with this . . . this massacre . . . this bloodbath . . . you are a stupid, ignorant—"

"Hold your tongue. Dare you talk to me thus?"

"And who else will? Who else will tell you what a damnable fool you are?"

"I'll have your head!"

Edward pulled his cloak tighter about him as if to make himself smaller and less conspicuous. Ethelred was said to have sent his soldiers into the Danelaw and slaughtered the Danes. All the Danes, Edward had heard a soldier say to a whore as he showed her the dried blood on his sale.

Edmund stood, his feet planted apart. "Women, dogs, babes, whatever moved, your idiot soldiers killed. The St. Bice's day massacre they call—"

"I'll part you at the neck . . . you insolent—"

"I am not afraid of you, King Ethelred," Edmund yelled back at his father. "Touch a hair of this head and Eadric of Mercia and the nobles of the north will march upon Wessex until all you are is but a pile of earth. That is if Sven doesn't have you first. Among those you had butchered was his sister."

To Edward it seemed Ethelred almost looked frightened. "A lie—"

"You would wish it was, but one of your fine soldiers killed her first and then raped her. Sven will unleash an army on you, Ethelred. If ever—"

Edward looked up as the roof gave way; the boy came crashing down into the hall and screamed as he fell with a thump upon the hard mat of straw. Edmund hardly seemed to notice. "Why?" he said to the King, "Just tell me why?"

"The boy," Edward yelled. Two housecarls had run over to the crumbled groaning mass of flesh. Edward was sickened by his own helplessness as he stood unable to take his eyes from the boy. The boy's own eyes begged for help.

"Am I responsible to you?" The King's voice was louder even than Edmund's. "Must I account to a rash, brazen—"

"But the boy," Edward cried out.

"Rash? You dare call me rash after what you've done?"

The boy's wailing grew louder and the housecarls attempted to move him.

"Get that wailing baggage out of here," the King ordered.

The boy let out a fierce cry as they picked him up. His voice revealed the terrible pain as they struggled to get him to the door. Edward followed after.

"Stay here, Edward," the King ordered.

Edward turned, helpless, and faced the mean eye of his father.

The King came down to where Edward stood. "Hear this, all of you." His hands dug painfully deep through the cloak into Edward's bony shoulder. "This Atheling, Edward, shall rule after me. Not that loathsome thing who stands there among you. THE ATHELING EDWARD WILL BE KING HEREAFTER."

Ethelred turned and took from the wall the great sword of Edgar. The handle contained dazzling stones which reflected the light from the fire as the King carried it over to Edward. "This is the sword of Bedwig of Sceaf, the son of Noah, who came to the land of Saxons after the Great Flood. He was the father of the god, Woden, and for him he made this magic sword, and with it raised before him Woden led the Valkyries into battle. The sword has been handed down to Cerdic, to Alfred and to my father, but I could not use this sword for it came to my martyred brother, Edward, and though I can give it to my son, I was not able to raise it before any man less God strike me dead."

Edmund stared at Edward, the fire reflecting in his eyes as well as upon the sword. "It is mine. The sword of Bedwig is for me, the eldest."

"The sword of Bedwig is for my Christian son, the rightful heir, not for an ingrate who calls his father a fool." The King brought down the heavy sword upon Edward's shoulders and Edward nearly fell beneath the weight. Edward knew he would be King and when he was King he would not put out the eyes of men, nor let the broken bodies of children be left in pain. He would be a saint as well, like Edward the Martyr, and saints could cure the crippled and the sick.

"No man in England would have this monstrous, ugly boy as its king," Edmund said and he banged open the doors and left the hall.

"After him," Ethelred yelled out, but no one went and the hall fell into silence and the sword was placed back on the wall and the King sat drinking mead and the men drifted away, but Edward knew he would be King and he went up and looked at the sword of Bedwig and could see his own reflection in its polish.

Edward went back out into the rain. It was getting dark as evening seeped in beneath the clouds. A muddy ooze ran down from the yard into the pit. An old woman with sores on her hand pushed wads of soggy bread down through the opening in the grating. Edward stood above searching for his mother in the blackness. All he saw was the aura of light and he spoke to the light. "I'm going to be King," he said, but she didn't answer.

The old woman stuffed the remainder of the soggy bread from the pot into her own mouth and went away.

"I will find a way to get you out," he whispered into the grating. "I did not mean for Edmund to know . . . I did not mean to tell Edmund . . . I . . ."

"Go away, Edward." The voice from the pit was tired. She said nothing else, but he did not go away but sat there in the rain beneath his hood thinking of the wondrous things he would do when he was King.

CHAPTER 3

Normandy, 1012

SHE TURNED; THE STRAW OF THE BED SCRATCHED AT HER CHEEK. THERE WAS no day yet; the window was a square of black night, not a hint of morning. Still morning lingered near, for the cant of women's voices echoed through the stone walls of the nunnery with monotonous unison. It was a strange order, these nuns into whose keeping she'd been thrust. She was a queen, yet the abbess had not welcomed her, nor made any attempt to see her, and the quarters were not those befitting a queen but hardly better than a peasant's hovel. Except for Aesval and the novice she saw no one. The novice, a frail thing with a poxed face and a hunched back, for two weeks and three days had been the only contact with the world of the nunnery and beyond. Rouen had been but a short ride, not a half day's distance, yet she had heard no word from either of her brothers, the duke or the archbishop, nor anything from Ethelred. She had come to Normandy ready to face trial and death, not this isolation. Her thoughts turned to St. Irene, torn from the seat of power of an empire and left to the drudgery of sewing on her exiled island. Emma dozed.

"Outside it is burning hot," Aesval said.

Emma opened her eyes to face the square light of day in the window. Aesval, free to come and go, had brought wine and bread and a bowl of cold water. Emma splashed the water on her face and washed the sleep from her eyes. The novice had told Aesval that God had not meant for women to bathe and that these nuns never washed but the tips of their fingers.

"What is wrong with this place," Aesval scolded, "is that there are no trees."

Emma dried her face on a linen. "Did you see any of the nuns?" It was a question she placed every morning in the English that Aesval understood. How ironic that these days spent in her Norman homeland she spoke only the language of the Saxons.

"If I did not hear them I would not believe there were any nuns here but Geravesta, the novice." It was the same answer she had given each day.

Emma sipped the wine and stuffed some bread in her mouth. She offered the bread to Aesval. At first the woman had been reluctant to be so familiar with her mistress, but it had become routine. They had only each other for company. Some days they sat silently embracing the cool cellar air and sped their needles, Emma not too patiently, in and out of the stiff fabric of a developing tapestry and Aesval repairing a tear or loose hem in one of Emma's garments. But mostly they talked.

"When I was a little girl I wanted to be the Pope when I grew up," Emma told her.

"That's silly."

"Very silly. Women give birth to the world, but do not rule it." Emma folded the linen cloth and gave it to Aesval. "How did you come to be a slave?" Emma could not remember when Aesval had first come into Ethelred's household. She was one of the bodies, faces, there to command, and at some point Emma had come to rely upon, to trust her judgment and skills above the others. Aesval had not been selected, she had simply flowered like a blossom in a weed patch.

"My husband was caught stealing from a thegn . . . the thegn of another village."

"What did he steal?"

"Two books. Great Latin words. I saw them on the pages."

"Amazing. Where did he learn to read?"

Aesval lowered her voice to a whisper. "He came from far away. He was a monk and he . . ." She stopped short.

"Go on," Emma urged.

"I say too much."

"Hardly. Yours is the only voice I hear. Please . . ."

"I should not. There is still danger to him."

"I will take your secret to my grave and that as you know may not be long off."

The woman still hesitated.

"Go on . . . go on."

"He came from the place called Ireland. From a great monastery by the sea."

"Why did he leave?"

She paused. "In search of the books. He was charged of magical practices, he said, and when he was ordered to repent or be called with heresy, he ran away. He was learned and knew of things which I don't understand. He had papers with drawing on them that get you from somewhere to somewhere else. He came to Sussex."

"To your village. In search of the books."

"Aye, to our village, but the books were not in our village, but belonged to the thegn of the next village and were kept in the church there where everyone could see them. We had heard of the books. My sister's husband had once seen them in the church."

"So this monk comes to your village and there is a great romance. He is much taken with you."

"No. I doubt he was taken with me at all, but I told you how my father was villein who held a great acreage, nearly forty-five acres, and how he had eleven daughters and no sons. And what does a villein with eleven daughters and a great acreage do?"

"He marries them off fast, I would not wonder."

"Indeed, Madam, he does. I was ready to marry off and this fellow comes along. We did not know he was a monk; still, he was not made welcome to our moot and none would have him about save my father, who would have taken dwarf, giant, mute or monster if he had two arms and a pair of legs and was willing to marry one of his daughters. This man would have me, and though he talked hard to understand I found him to my liking. It was later when he told me about being a monk and about the books. 'The books are a great wonder,' he said and he had to get them."

"What were the books about?"

"Magical things. The secrets of he who my husband called Ibrahim ibn Adham. There is written there how to swallow fire and glass, to walk upon water or burning flames, to fly through the air and to be transported over many miles in the blink of an eye and such things as you cannot believe . . ."

"How did such books get to your village?"

"Not our village, but the next village. They said the grandfather of the thegn had taken them as booty in some battle against the Moors. A monk who had once passed through Sussex had been shown the books by the priest there. It was he, over in Ireland, who had told my husband of them and how they contained magical things and such and terrible heresies."

"If they were such heresy why did the priest have them in the church?"

"He could not read and neither could the thegn. Only my husband knew what was in the books. One night late when our village was asleep my husband got up and dressed. I was frightened and urged him not to, but he went through the forest. I knew I should never have seen him alive again for the forest had not only wolves and bears, but there was a strange monster lived deep in the center. A husband of one of my sisters had once seen the beast. But before morning my husband was back and he had the two books, which he buried in the floor of our hut."

"Wasn't there an uproar . . . ?"

"A great row, I'll tell you, through the whole hundred, but it died down. Everybody said how it must the Devil, hisself, had took the books, and even some said, would you believe, how there was cloven tracks leading inside the church."

"Did he tell you what was in the books?"

"Yes, and sometimes he would do the things he read about and it would scare me. I cried so once when he ate the fire and another time he cut hisself but didn't bleed, and when I had the sickness and was thought to die of fever, he but touched my head and it went away."

"He had the touch?" Only saints and devils had the touch. What sort of fellow was this husband of Aesval?

"A quiet man, but soon he was healing people in the village. Just a little at first. Still, word got around. He used to make like a great ball of nothing in his hands. Over and over he would turn this invisible ball and even though there was nothing there it was so hot you couldn't put your hand near it . . . and he would take the ball and touch the sick person and take the illness right out of them."

"You saw this?"

"Yes, often, but I begged him to stop for I knew there would be trouble. There were already those, even those he helped, whispering that he consorted with evil spirits. He had built a door on our hut so as to read by the fire at night. The men of the thegn of our village came and broke down the door one night and found my husband there with the books."

"Did they charge him witchery?"

"They were to bring him before the hundred, taking him off with the books, but on the way he cast a spell on them, took the books and ran off. They burned my hut to the ground and sold me into bondage to make good the stealing of the books."

Emma poured herself some wine into the bowl. "He was a coward."

"Nay, they would have cut off his hands or worst his head. And I am no the badder off as a slave in the house of a king, I can assure you, than being a widow or the wife of a man without hands to labor. I am the better the fed, I am sure . . ."

"I will not argue the point, Aesval, but have you never heard nor wondered where he is?"

"From time to time I have had word. He was tutor some years ago among the Bulgars. Is that a far place?"

"Yes, very far. How did you hear from him?"

"A traveler brought word to my sister. But a fortnight ago a man came saying that he was in Rouen. I was hoping, maybe when we came to here, I might see him. I have no idea where to look and I am but a slave. I mayn't go about as if I were free."

"At the present, Aesval, your freedom is greater than mine. Still, I will help you find him."

"Aye," Aesval sighed.

"Nay, Aesval. You need not resign yourself to defeat. My brothers will not leave me locked in this convent of isolation for long. We will find this husband of yours. What's his name?"

"He is called Felim MacBoru."

"We will find this Felim MacBoru."

Emma wished she was as certain of her brothers as she pretended to be. It was unlike either Richard or Robert, both of whom had always doted upon her, to abandon her like this. Surely, neither was that horrendously offended by her adultery. They might not be able to save her life, but neither would pass moral judgment upon her.

Emma was alone in the cell on the next afternoon, bored and sewing. Aesval had gone off to gather some fresh berries and perhaps trap a rabbit or a hen, anything to supplement the sometimes moldy bread, bland porridge and tasteless stews served up by the unwashing nuns. Emma heard the footsteps of the hunchbacked nun as she limped along the loggia toward the cell. Someone was with her. The steps were heavy, those of a man.

"Madam." The tall youthful Norman stooped to get through the low doorway.

"Goddy. My lovely Goddy. How did you ever get in this convent?"

She stood up and hugged him. The novice limped away, leaving them alone.

"When you are a half brother to the archbishop, Emma, dear, there is not a convent door in the land closed to you." He kissed her and kept an arm slung about her shoulders.

"You'd not want any of these, Goddy. I am told they never wash. And don't even mention our brother archbishop; I've enough of him. I have been here these—"

"Two weeks—"

"And four days and I have not heard a word, a sound from either him or Richard."

"For a purpose, dear sister, for a purpose. The duke has led Ethelred to believe you have escaped. No one knows you are here, not even the nuns, save the lady abbess and that hunched novice. Richard and Robert have been careful not to contact you lest one of your husband's spies should learn of it."

"But you came . . ."

"Nobody pays any attention to the bastards in the family."

"I do. You'll always be my favorite, Godfrey."

"You've always had a weakness for a good-looking man, Emma."

"Is there a note of sarcasm in that?"

"None, Lady. A bad choice of words under the circumstance, but I came to find out what you need."

"What I need is Ethelred dead. Why doesn't Richard have it done?" Emma sat down and looked up at her lanky half brother. "We can put my ugly boy on—"

"I wish you would not talk about your children that way."

"I can't help it if I don't love Ethelred's horrid offspring."

"But they're yours as well."

"I need no reminding, Goddy." She looked directly at him. "Why doesn't Richard kill Ethelred? We can have Edward crowned and I shall rule England."

"Because you'd never get the boy on the throne, not now. Edmund is more firmly entrenched than ever, and if the King of England died in Normandy, they'd never let you back again."

"Let Edmund be the one to die. Ethelred should kill him."

"It's not just Edmund. Sven the Forkbeard is about to destroy England."

"Let Ethelred go drive the Dane out. And may he die in the process and then I can put Edward on the throne."

"Dreams, Emma. Dreams."

Emma walked toward the door. There was no sound of Aesval returning. "Goddy, my woman, Aesval, has a husband somewhere in Rouen. I want you to find him."

"Emma, you shift the conversation like the channel wind."

"His name is Felim MacBoru."

Goddy looked directly at her. "I've heard the name." His voice was soft and slow.

"Find him and bring him here."

"They say of this MacBoru that he consorts with—"

"He's a magician and I may have use of him."

"What do you know of him, Emma?"

"Can you find him?"

"Yes, though I suspect he is careful not always to be found. Tell me what you know of his witchery."

"I know nothing. Bring him to me."

"Do you think it wise? The fewer ears that know your whereabouts the fewer mouths to speak."

"Please. Just do . . ." Emma stopped short as Aesval came trudging into the room.

"I found a milch cow wandering loose and I got this jug . . ." She looked across, obviously surprised to see the tall man standing there.

"My brother, Aesval. Godfrey."

Aesval set down the bowl of milk and put berries from her overskirt onto a table. "My Lord." She held open her hands, which were stained from the berries.

"Goddy is going to find your husband for you, Aesval."

"His name is Felim MacBoru," Aesval told him.

"Yes," Godfrey said. "Felim MacBoru."

It rained. For two days it rained and now the ceiling of the cell dripped water. Aesval had gone in search of the novice to see if something couldn't be done about the puddle forming in the corner. Lightning erratically split the gray sky in the frame of the open window. Emma turned away. The storm disturbed her. Peeled daubing flaked to the floor as a sharp crack of thunder shook the already water-damaged walls. She lowered her head and looked at the puddle of water forming in the corner, as if transfixed. It was while she was watching the black circle of water that she sensed the presence. Turning, she breathed a quiet cry in fright as she saw the dark-hooded figure in the window set against the eerie gray sky.

Her voice was uneasy. "Who are you?" She touched the knife hidden beneath the fabric of her bliaut at the waist.

"I am Felim MacBoru, Lady." The voice was deep and soft, almost not to be heard.

She breathed somewhat easier and tried to see his face, shadowed by the hood. It was somewhat disappointing. He seemed a plain man, his eyes holding no great mystique, nor gave indication of great secrets beyond them. "You gave me a start, Felim MacBoru. What are you doing at the window?"

"Your brother thought it better if I did not come into the cell." He spoke in Norman-French, but the accent of the Celt was obvious in his speech.

"Aesval should be returning in a little while, but you'll catch your death in the rain."

"I wished also to see you," he said. "Your brother, Godfrey, has told me of the charges against you. However, need I say, few in Rouen have not heard. They say if you are found you are to face trial by ordeal."

"Yes. As long as Ethelred lives I'm destined either to hiding or to trodding the burning coals."

"Should you choose the trial I can teach you to endure the walk and suffer no pain or burns. There would be no sign upon your body." Water dripped down from his hood.

"Felim MacBoru, I am guilty of the adulterous charge. I gave myself to the son of Thorkell in the chapel at Corfe. I am afraid—"

"No matter, Lady," he interrupted. "I can teach you to walk over the burning embers without pain to your feet."

"You do not believe in God? You do not believe in his justice, in divine retribution?"

"I believe in God's mercy, Madam. God has given me a rare gift. I can see things others cannot. There is an aura about your body which I am able to control or teach you to control. I can help you, Lady Queen."

"By magic."

"Not magic I think—an understanding of the unknown. The Sufi of Islam knew it. I have walked on hot coals and have not felt the pain nor burned my feet. I have had red iron laid across my hands and felt nothing and no flesh has burned. I will show you how this is done."

"And what do you want of Emma, Queen of England, in return?"

"To be tutor to her son, the heir."

"To Edward?"

"Yes. To Edward."

Emma heard the footsteps. More than one person was coming. Emma moved back from the window as Aesval came into the cell. The novice was not with her, but Godfrey was.

"You have heard what MacBoru says, Emma?" he asked.

"I have heard."

"What think you?"

"I have yet to see a miracle. Still I have nothing to lose but burned feet and my life. Robert? Is he a party to this?"

"The archbishop has heard tales of MacBoru and says this, Emma. If you are confident of Felim's powers and wish trial by ordeal he will order it set. If it succeeds he will offer the magician his protection. If it fails he will be burned as a heretic."

"So," Emma said, "Felim MacBoru and Emma are both to live or both to die. How say you to that, MacBoru?"

"We shall live."

"And in Normandy for a time, sister," Godfrey told her. "Sven has landed in the Midlands with an army of Danes."

All the while Aesval had stood staring at the man, saying nothing.

"Well, Aesval," Emma coaxed.

"You are looking well, Felim," Aesval said.

"And you healthy," he said, shaking loose the water on his hood.

Emma laughed at the formality of their reunion. There was an awkward silence. "Why do you want to be tutor to my son?" she asked.

"Your brother has said some things about him which interest me."

"He is ugly," Emma told him, "and given to having fits."

"Yes," Felim said and then vanished from the window.

CHAPTER 4

Normandy, 1013

Edward scoured his hands by rubbing them tightly against one another as if he could press the water into his skin.

"It is pagan to be so clean," Hilder said. Hilder was his grandmother and very old. Her head and her hands shook. She had a long thin nose. "The Romans were clean . . . always bathing, they said . . ." Hilder wandered off.

He was not frightened of Hilder; she never touched him. There was nothing wrong with being like the Romans. They knew things, great secrets which they kept in Latin, and he would learn Latin and learn the secrets.

His hands, white like thin sticks with the bark peeled away, were caressed by the gentle water. Solids frightened him. His uncle's huge palm gripping his shoulder pained him to tears. Edward was ten, and the touch of another being, even an animal, was agony. He loved his mother; she seldom touched him. And he loved God. He loved the elusive image of God. God knew he had meant his mother no harm. He had cried at his mother's pain, not at the sin, which he did not understand, but at the torture of the heavy man's body pushing against hers, against her very insides. Edmund had tricked him into telling. Edmund was evil and had raised a great army in England to use against Ethelred when he returned. Edmund was trying to steal the throne, but God would smite him for it.

"Edward." It was Godgifu who called. He scrumpled himself into a recess at the base of the stone wall. All the walls of Normandy seemed of rock, hard and impregnable. The walls at home were of mud, dung, straw and timber, and though the great timber looked heavy and mighty, it burned like a field of straw. Godgifu had set fire to a chamber house at Winchester. The lambent of the flame had fired his cheeks and his eyes had burned from the smoke. But rock was damp and cold and lived forever. Like God.

"Edward!" she called again. She would bite him. Sometimes she did. She called him "ugly" and "freak" and when she said it the words didn't hurt, but when she harrowed her teeth into his flesh he cried with the hurt. She went away and he crawled out of the hiding place and looked at his hands. They were dirty and he pushed them back into the basin of water. Edward hated the touch of dirt.

A priest came in. "Edward, we sent your sister for you and have been looking everywhere. Your uncle the archbishop wants you."

Edward didn't know the priest. He wiped his wet hands on his tunic.

"Your mother, the Queen, has been found."

He trembled and knew it was going to happen. A fit. They called it a fit, but he never remembered—only the beginning. "*Your mother, Edward,*" Edmund had said, "*is guilty of treason and must die.*" His head began to shake and his eyes lost their focus. He was aware of the priest, but could no longer see him. "*Your mother, Edward, is guilty of a great sin and will burn in hell.*" His eyes rolled back in his head and he could no longer see. "*Ethelred will butcher the Queen.*" His arms flew up and he knew he was falling.

There was a great flash of light. God was light, and Edward thought perhaps in the fits he saw God.

He never knew how long they lasted. He squinted open his eyes. It had ended. He was lying on stone. The man's face leaning over was like that of some giant gentle beast. It was his uncle, the Archbishop of Rouen. His uncle helped him up and he was uneasy on his feet.

"Come sit here." His uncle pointed to an empty faldstool.

"I can stand."

"Certainly you can, but be comfortable."

Edward sat.

"I have news of your mother. She is well and sends you her love. She loves you very much."

"I know that."

The archbishop looked at the floor. "Soon she will rejoin you here."

"No."

"No?"

"The King will kill her. He must not know where she is."

"Understand, Edward, your mother must prove her innocence. She is to face an ordeal—the judgment of God—"

"No," Edward screamed. He stood up trembling. He clutched his fist.
"Nothing is wrong, boy. It will be all right. She is innocent."
"I saw," he yelled.
"You thought you saw. You thought. You thought . . . Edward, listen to me. It was an ugly vision sent you by the Devil—"
"But, I—"
"Like the fit just now. The Devil's work. Even Christ was tempted."
Edward's trembling lessened.
"Do you see how it was just a vision, Edward?"
"Yes." It was a whisper.
"Tomorrow you shall see your mother adjudged innocent by God."
"But in the chapel . . ."
"A diabolic vision. Tomorrow—"
"Tomorrow?"
"At sunrise your mother, before God and man, shall, feet bare, walk over coals of fire and when I call forth, 'Who accuses this woman?' they will bring you before me and you must reply truthfully and say what you saw. What did you see, Edward?"

He made no response.

"You saw, boy, an apparition of evil sent you by the force of evil, Lucifer himself. Isn't that so, Edward?"

He hesitated. "Yes."

"Now you should go pray for your mother." The big hand came toward him and he flinched. A ferule thumb made the sign of the cross on his forehead. His head ached from the pressure and still hurt him as he moved from the room.

He bathed his hands in holy water as he entered the empty chapel and then eased his forehead into the font. The water dripped from his thin white hair over the painful thumb-impressed cross and down his cheeks. The pain vanished.

Light from the only window in the small room focused too intently upon a St. Peter bound in elipses of umber paint. Soldiers beat upon the figure with thin strands of black paint and tore at the pigments of flesh, making it drip rivulets of red dye. He stood before it for hours and the light faded and chains became real and the blood moved and St. Peter seemed in raptured pain. It became too dark to even make out the figure of the saint. Still he stood, forgetting to pray for his mother. He stood the night, staring at the blackness, no longer clearly able to discern where the painting ceased and the wall began but comforted always in knowing it was there.

Morning light eased through the window, cold and gray, and St. Peter's pain was almost colorless. The door of the chapel opened and he turned to see a boy, older than himself, as beautiful a creature as he knew he was ugly. Even in the dimness of the early light he could see the liquid blue eyes staring at him. The face was chiseled like a piece of delicately cut rock. Perhaps he was a vision. A saint.

"It will soon be sunrise," the boy said. His voice was pleasant.

"Who are you?" Edward asked.

"I am called Robin." The boy walked from the chapel. He wore the garb of a monk.

After Edward scrubbed and scoured every inch of his pale body, he donned fresh clothes and walked from the ducal castle. The parvis lay forward in his path, but there was time, and he turned from the direction of the cathedral to the Seine.

Nature was incomprehensible to him. Why did the tide rise or fall? Why were two sides of a leaf the same? or How come sometimes there were more stars in the heavens than at others?

In the distance at the edge of the Seine he could see the rubble of a tower. He dropped a broken branch into the river and it was carried downstream toward the crumbling structure. Rolf had built it, Rolf, the great conqueror. There was conqueror's blood in him, but Edward could think of nothing to conquer. What he knew of the great kingdoms of the world were already in the rule of some kin or another. He followed along the bank of the Robec from where its water slipped into the Seine. Where did all the water go? If all the rivers run into one another and then into the sea, how come the sea never gets filled up and runs over?

A bearded goat leaped, anchoring its hind legs on the rear of a she-goat. As the male goat's pink penis came out of the hair, Edward's fists tightened. From the water he picked up rock after rock, pelting the goat, and when the bearded goat could endure no more it turned from the she-goat and with horns down plowed toward Edward. But he had been ready for him and, grabbing a low branch, lifted himself into a tree. The goat butchered the bark of the trunk with its head until in places the trunk was scaled white. Why did goats give milk but not pigs? Why did some trees lose their leaves but not others? The she-goat had wandered off. The male ran off, forgetting Edward in the tree.

He climbed down and washed the sap from his hands in the river. Across the water a woman flung clothes against wet stones but did not look up at him. The sky began to brighten and he ran a different way than he had come back toward the parvis. He ran between the houses and hovels of the merchants and the workers, the places where the Jews lived and the market and the dealer in wool and a house of physicians and the sign of the master mason under whose direction the stones of the cathedral reached toward heaven. Slop was thrown from doors and chickens pecked at seeds and dogs followed a bitch in heat. He stepped around the horse dung as he reached the parvis. Already a crowd had begun to gather, to mill about in the open square of earth which stretched outward from the wide steps of the unfinished stone cathedral. There was noise and pushing and he made his way through the crowd. At the steps was the bed of burning coals. It was red hot, covered in places with white ash. Here and there small yellow flames sprouted. Edward stood at one end of the smoking bed and looked the distance down which his mother would walk. On the steps were great chairs and stools to rest the feet and overhead was a canopy of gold cloth and embroidery and jewels stitched to the cloth and in two spots bird dung had seeped down the front. He sat on the step breathing the smoke of the fire and looking out over the crowd which was growing in the parvis. The bright morning sun came and the great cathedral cast cool shade over the crowd.

Judith of Brittany, the duke's wife, came with many ladies. She coughed a lot and scratched her thighs. Edward's young cousins, Richard and Robert, named the same as his uncles, stood by her chair. Richard had a pet bird on a chain and tried to give it to Edward but Edward shook his head. Judith coughed some more and a woman brought her a bowl of wine. Young Richard climbed up into the duke's chair with his bird, but his mother stopped scratching and shooed him out of it and spilled wine on her gown and scolded.

Aesval came and she had Godgifu and Alfred and made them sit on stools and Godgifu told Edward she was going to poke out his eyes and Aesval told her to hush. Monks paraded carrying unlit candles and at the end of the parade Edward saw the young monk he had seen that morning in the chapel. Then the duke came, and the archbishop and his father, the King, whose eye looked meaner than ever, and Uncle Goddy and another uncle, the Count of Eu, who everyone called Willie, and there were lots of nobles and thegns; only they called them something different in Normandy, and there were monks and priests, who all looked very stern and sang. A priest entered carrying the Holy Eucharist and Edward blessed himself and was surprised to see Archbishop Wulfstan, who must have come all the way from Wessex.

The people out in the shadow of the great building didn't seem stern at all and some brought food and ate their morning meal and drank wine and they talked and laughed. Some babies cried and the crowd seemed to get louder and the people on the chairs more restless and sterner-looking and then the archbishop moved forward, raised his crozier and quiet came except from the monks, whose chants seemed louder for the stillness. The archbishop began to pray and Edward prayed and then they brought her out of the cathedral.

She was dressed in nothing but a white gown and her feet were bare. It was still chilly and he knew she must be cold in the morning air and he wanted to run and give her his cloak but he knew he must not. His uncle archbishop blessed her and he saw Aesval go over to her with some man he did not know and with them was a nun with a hunched back and poxed face.

"Edward," Ethelred yelled at him. "Stand before His Grace, the Archbishop of Rouen."

Edward went over and the archbishop said, "Who accuses this woman?"

He answered softly, "What I saw—"

"Speak up, Edward!" Ethelred roared.

"What I saw," Edward screamed out, "was a vision the Devil put before me. The Devil showed me a vision of the Queen, but it was not her."

"WHAT NONSENSE IS THIS?" His father came down and shook him.

He looked at his father's mean eye and without flinching yelled back at him, "It was like the fits."

Ethelred took his hand and swung so hard that, when he hit Edward's ear and the side of his head, Edward fell to the steps. He looked up bravely, but the pain was immense. His mother stared at him with indifference.

"King Ethelred." The Archbishop Robert's voice was angry. "This is the business of God and the Church. The boy has spoken his truth here. He is under my protection. Leave him be."

Archbishop Wulfstan, looking rather sour at the King, led him back to his place.

The Archbishop of Rouen raised his hands. "Emma, daughter of Richard, wife of Ethelred, Queen of the English and Wessex, child of Normandy, the charge of adultery is upon you. You are to be tried by God. You will put your feet upon these coals and walk the distance. If you cry out or suffer burns upon your feet you will be adjudged guilty and your head shall be cut from your body. Your heart shall be fed to the dogs and your body left to the street to be consumed by maggots. If God finds you innocent he shall guide your feet and there will be no pain and your body shall suffer no burns and his grace will be upon you. Amen."

Edward began to tremble as his mother moved toward the coals. The man standing next to Aesval came over to him, took his hand. It was strange for he had attempted to pull away, but the man's hand brought no pain to Edward. There was a strange warmth and a tingling sensation. The man whispered, "You are a brave young man, Edward. Now continue so and have not a thought of fear, for your mother will succeed."

The light about her seemed to grow as she neared the bed of smoldering coals. She reached the foot of the long narrow frame and all noise in the square ceased, including the chanting of the monks. She lifted her white gown up slightly with both hands and raised her right foot over the coals and slowly lowered it almost to the burning embers, but she pulled it back and set it again upon the stone of the street.

There was a low "ah" from the crowd, as if it at once had let out its breath.

But then without pausing, she raised her foot and this time rested it on the burning coals.

"God be gracious," a woman called out, but it was the only sound. Everyone seemed to be watching her and the light around her was brilliant and her gaze far off as if she were not really there at all. The crowd seemed to be waiting for her to cry out, but she made no sound and, holding her gown up from the coals, moved step by step down the long, smoking path.

"I've never seen the light about her so bright," Edward said, more to himself than to the man standing at his side.

"You see a light about her?"

"Aye. But never so much light."

"Do I have light about me?"

"Everybody does," Edward told him.

"Yes," he said, "everybody does."

It seemed a great distance and his eyes never left her, even as he spoke with the man.

She reached the end. A loud cry went up from the crowd and she stepped to the ground and people were clapping and cheering and the archbishop, his uncle, tried to get them to pray and Edward knelt and prayed but nobody else seemed to and they were saying "miraculous" and "wondrous" and one man whispered, "The Devil's work, calamity will come upon us all." Edward saw his father rise and go inside the cathedral, but his Uncle Robert went to his mother and led her back to the steps and the cheering grew louder and Edward heard a man near him say, "No woman in the world be as beautiful."

Edward knew this was so. It was her eyes. They were soft brown, and even when she was angriest at him she still looked like a sainted Madonna. She stood before the entrance to the great church and she was the Queen, her back straight, her head poised high, looking up toward the top of the high doors. Her yellow hair dripped down over her shoulders onto the white gown. She turned about to face the crowd and a great cheer went up. She raised her hands and then spoke first in Norman-French to ask God's blessing upon the people and then in Saxon, addressing herself to the slave, Aesval. "Aesval of Wessex, spouse of Felim MacBoru, before God and King henceforth you are a free woman. God go with you." Then she came over to the man who stood beside him. "And you, Felim MacBoru, I will always have open ears to whatever you need of me."

"Thank you, Madam. I will hold you to your promise that the boy here may be my pupil. More than ever I am certain now I want to be his tutor."

Archbishop Wulfstan came up to his mother. "Only two matters are paramount, Madam—God and the Kingdom of England. You have the protection of God and you will have mine as long as your concern is for England."

Before she could answer, he had turned and walked away. Judith coughed and spit the phlegm upon the steps before she spoke. "These Saxons are a strange folk."

Edward slipped away and into the cathedral. Ethelred was prostrate before the altar. He had rent his clothes and looked to be covered with rags for the tears in them.

Edward tipped his fingers into the font of holy water and began rubbing his hands as if to clean them.

CHAPTER 5

Lunduntown, 1014

THEY WERE AN INDEPENDENT BREED, THESE MEN OF LUNDUNTOWN, CAPRIcious and strangely individual. To Emma there was an uncertainty about the town. It could be felt in the dank air, in the gloom of the early afternoon. They came, the deputation wishing to see their King. Emma made her way through the dark shadows of the passageway, brushing a cobweb from her face. Wardrobe Palace was a gloomy place, even the great hall, and she entered looking into a sea of dim faces revealing nothing.

"Men of Lunduntown, the King begs your indulgence. He is prostrate before his God on the chapel floor. A special vigil—"

"We would see the King . . . the King!" the cry went up. "The King."

". . . a vigil that all will go well against the Danes. He will not move from the chapel this night. Come in the morning. He will see and hear you all in the morning."

They grumbled, but agreed and filed out.

Wulfstan coughed and sat on a stool by the fire. "Is he so drunk?"

"Incoherent, your Grace," she said, joining him at the fire. "Tomorrow we will keep the mead from him long enough to let these Lunduners have a look at their King. We need the support and help of these folk, independent as they be."

"More than ever, Lady. Sven's fleet is reported moving south."

"Does he leave the North unprotected? Perhaps we can strike—"

"No, Cnute holds the North for his father." He stirred the fire with a twisted branch and the sparks flickered up. "The young man is said not only to be a ferocious warrior like Sven but a greater charmer of the people."

"A bedeviler, no doubt. These northerners are so easily led to witchery that a boy—"

"He is a man—"

"Have you ever seen him?"

"No, but the Bishop of Coventry has writ me of Cnute, saying he does have grace and a way about him that men look to."

"A barbarian—"

"Still, Christian, and his mother—"

"He is a plunderer and a pirate. He would not find the men of Wessex so easily taken in by Danish sorcery. This is our England. He is an intruder here. He has no right here . . . no right!"

Wulfstan turned the branch in the fire again. "But he is a leader. And who will lead our armies if Sven comes? Ethelred is—"

"Is King. Chosen by God and the Witangemot."

"And in no condition to lead an army. We shall have to turn to Edmund."

"No. He is a traitor. He plots with the Thegns Siegeferth and Morcar and would have himself named King in Ethelred's stead."

"How know you this?"

"The Earldorman Eadric has sent us proof. And after what occurred but two nights ago . . ."

"Edmund did that in anger, Lady."

"Ethelred has disavowed him for it, once and finally. Edward shall be King—"

"That is fine, Madam, and I support you in that, but who leads us now when Sven's butchers rampage through Lunduntown?"

"I."

"You? A woman? It is against God and—"

"In the King's name, of course. From the King's bedchamber. When his mind is mired by mead, what else is to be done? The word will be the King's, in the King's name. But someone—and is there anyone but me?—has to decide how the town is to be defended, the army deployed. Will you stand by me in this, your Grace?"

"But Edmund . . ."

"Has fled."

"Then have I any choice? But what do you know of armies and war?"

"I am the daughter of the great Norman duke and have nursed upon the breast of war. I shall not, dear bishop, sit astride a horse at the head of the King's troops. We have the thegns and chiefs to command their men. Hopefully, as well, the folk of Lunduntown will bear arms beside us.

But I know enough of war to understand its strategy and how to defeat an enemy. Will you stand by me?"

"I shall simply because there is little alternative. I would not, were Edmund here. For I like it not at all. War is not the place of women."

"Thank you, your Grace." Emma arose and went back into the dank passageway. If Edward were a bit older she could have put him at the front of the army. A figurehead, but nonetheless seen to be the leader. Edward was coming along, better than she had hoped. Still ugly, perhaps uglier, for he had grown taller and was gangly. She had brought him a peregrine and he had taken a fancy to hawking. If only he would not insist on dipping his hands into the blood of the prey. Still, he had shown a fancy and a knack for the sport and in that was the makings of a soldier. He was not afraid of death nor blood.

She climbed up a steep wind of stairs. She hated Wardrobe Palace. It smelled of dead rats and urine. At the top she stood at a window.

Edmund had sealed his own fate two nights earlier when, foolishly, he had awakened the King from a drunken stupor with a candle held quite deliberately before him. The King had been beaten by his mother, Queen Elfrida, when but a child. She was said to have hit him relentlessly on the face with a frozen taper until his face ran with blood. There was still a small scar visible just slightly above his eyebrow. The King was deathly afraid of candles. They were never burned anywhere in the royal house or in his presence. The King had gone quite mad that night as Edmund appeared with the candle and screamed throughout the night, but in the morning he had remembered and had had Edmund locked away. She had hoped for his death, but Edmund had friends about the court and had escaped.

"Sven the Forkbeard is at the mouth of the Thames!" The cry was heard all over Lunduntown. The King was in a stupor and from his chamber Emma mobilized the forces. She decided that the best position for the army would be on the bridge. If the Danes landed on either side of the Thames the army would be in position to quickly assemble against them. In the meantime they would be in excellent location if the ships came near the bridge. Missiles could be launched effectively from the bridge on the ships below. Troops could be deployed the length of the span. She decided on four trusted messengers and thought to take unobtrusive command from a vantage view on a nearby hill where she could seem to be simply the Queen observing the events of battle.

"MacBoru, I would have you bring Edward with you and join me in watching the battle. It will be good experience for him."

They walked through the Lundun street. Aesval accompanied the Queen as if it were an ordinary outing. Aesval was uneasy, not of the impending battle, but in her new position of stature as a lady to the Queen.

"There is a stillness," Emma said, "like the wooded creatures before a great storm. Is it a mood of anger or terror, I wonder?"

"I know not, Lady," MacBoru said, "but note there is not one buffoon, juggler or rebec player to be seen in the streets."

"They hide?" Aesval asked.

"They flee," MacBoru told her, "like men of uncommon good sense."

"Or cowardice," Emma added as they walked down the quiet street.

"To avoid death still seems to be a matter of good sense."

"I suspect, Felim, you are right. Survival it is for all of us, particularly a queen."

"Gainsborough," Edward chimed in, his mood seemed to be one of enjoying the event, "has given nine and thirty hostages."

"Where did you hear this?"

"The Abbot of Peterborough told me. And Oxford burns. Lindsay has fallen and—"

"Enough," Emma ordered. "The abbot is an ass and a rumormonger."

They made their way up the hill. Emma blocked the morning sun from her eyes with her left hand and looked down upon the Thames. Everything seemed quiet, almost too quiet. The brown water wound to the east and toward the sea, but even the seabirds had seemed to vanish. Nothing moved on the bridge and across the river Sudwerke stretched a silent cluster of fishermen's hovels and empty small boats lapping against the shore and, beyond, a rise of trees stood dark against the sky. They waited, no longer speaking.

"SHIPS!" Edward called out. "I see the ships."

Emma strained to look but saw nothing.

"There. Those things there."

Emma watched and then saw the strange shapes on the river in the distance. What moved inward from the direction of the sea were not Viking sails but piles of wood taller than ships.

"What are they?" one of the messengers asked.

"I am not certain," Emma replied. "Some trick of Sven's." She dispatched two of the messengers to the thegns commanding the troops near the bridge.

They stood there watching. Emma counted eleven vessels.

"They frighten me," Aesval said.

"The strange always frightens us," Felim told her.

"It is hiding a great sea serpent," Edward said.

"Do you think so, Edward?" Aesval was alarmed.

"Nonsense, Edward," Emma said, but she was not certain herself what was hidden beneath the piles of wood that were becoming more visible and looked the more strange as they approached. They were like houses built over the top of each ship. True, it would offer protection to the ship from any army above, but they would not be in range long enough to warrant building such protection. There had to be another reason for the strange coverings.

The King's soldiers began to move out on the bridge; one of the messengers had obviously reached the bridge commanders. She counted the ships again as they moved like silent ghosts through the brown water—the water cold, formidable—and the ships in an even pace moved toward the bridge. Emma realized these were not houses built over the tops of the ships but cage-like structures hanging over the hulls. Hurdles, one next to the others, with enough space to see men, Viking men, moving beneath, shadows, fearful shadows in the early morning light. The bells of St. Paul's pounded the air, and the people of Lunduntown lined the banks armed with swords, scythes and other tools. More soldiers ran out on the bridge. Closer the ships came. As they neared she could see the hurdles were made of withes and cut wood spaced so that boulders and rocks of any size fired from the bridge could not penetrate. The bell continued to hammer.

And then for a moment it was as if everything stood still except the ships, their oars slapping the water. To the south, Sudwerke bank was empty, not a soul stirred. The north bank was lined with Lunduners, men and women, holding their household weapons. The bridge was a mass of soldiers, perhaps as many as there were room for, solid from end to end. The oars dipped in unison through the water, trailing a white stream of broken water behind each vessel. And then—

The first missile flaunted the air and crashed down upon one of the hurdles over the lead ship.

Edward let out a piercing shriek.

"Stop it!" Emma ordered.

Edward angrily moved away and stood with his back to Emma.

Another rock flew down upon another hurdle, upon another ship, but it did not penetrate, nor the next, nor the barrage which followed. The huge rocks either rested atop the hurdles or splashed into the river.

Edward stood as if sculpted. She had brought him along that he might learn something of battle and she was angry with his attitude. He looked as impregnable as the bridge below.

The ships reached the bridge. Burning brush was dropped down, but it rolled from the hurdles and into the sea. Nothing was to keep the ships from moving upstream, yet suddenly they stopped, moored underneath the wooden structure of the bridge. Why? She stood watching. Nothing moved, and then Vikings dropped from the ships into the water and just as quickly climbed back aboard. She still could not comprehend what in God's name they were about. The army stood above on the bridge. A messenger stood at her side, but she had no message to send. Suddenly, as if on a command, oars beat the water and the eleven ships in a line lurched forward in the direction of the sea. A barrage of rocks fell from the bridge. The oars moved faster and faster, leaving a foam of white water.

"THE ROPES!" Felim yelled.

And she saw them now on the surface of the water, stretching taut, the vessels' oars flapping in the water, the ships no longer racing forward but pulling, straining toward the sea. The bridge began to twist as the ships leaped forward again yanking at the supporting pilings. Finally the bridge gave way.

The screams of men tore the air as the collapsing timber crumpled into the brown water, bodies and wood and rock plummeting down. The river became a swirl of broken timbers and flesh—men seemingly everywhere, floating, drowning, paddling, yelling, confused and dead. It was difficult to distinguish between wood and man being washed in the direction of the sea. Those who reached the bank were pulled out by the extended weapons of the Lunduners, but most did not. Weighted by leather and metal, they sank into the deep of the Thames. What had she done? An army was lost. What would the Vikings do now?

Edward stood frozen, not even moving during the terror as the bridge fell.

"Edward!" she screamed. But he didn't move a muscle.

Men were still being retrieved from the water. The ships moved downstream and then seemed to anchor still in view but at a distance. The Thames was filled with debris. What was she to do now? Was there anything she could do? The Lunduners still lined the bank below. The Vikings would have a bad time landing there. The bridge was gone; if they landed on the south shore, there was no way across. They would have to land downstream and come by land to the city walls. There was little to do but wait.

Afternoon came. Felim left to help below. Aesval brought Emma a chair and some wine. All the while the Viking ships stood at anchor, and Edward stood, not moving. A bird nearly rested on his shoulder, yet he did not flinch. He was an irritating brat, as well as ugly.

A cloud formed over to the west, a strange cloud so red it seemed filled with blood. Some omen portending evil.

"Do you see it?" she asked Aesval.

"Yes. I am feared."

"Find us a seer," Emma told her. "The old man at Eastgate will do. Know you who I mean?"

Emma paced. She kept hearing the sound of the screams as in her mind the bridge fell again into the sea. The red cloud seemed to become deeper and heavier with blood. She expected it to rain great sanguineous drops.

A courier brought word. Edmund and his army held the north bank just east of Lundun. The Vikings would be forced to battle if they landed there. The ships never seemed to move from their position downstream near the southern shore of the river. Damn, it would be her misfortune to be saved by the bastard Edmund. The archbishop, flanked by an entourage of priests and clerics, came slowly up the hill. All the while Edward stood.

"Lady," Wulfstan addressed her.

"I have lost an army through my ineptness," she told him.

"There was little I could see that you or anyone could have done to stop it. Still, I suppose, it is God's retribution for letting a woman command an army."

"I should have understood what they were about. It was so obvious."

"No man on the bridge perceived what they were about. How could a woman?"

It was then she saw the first flames. Sudwerke, across the river, was afire. The Vikings had gone by land on the south shore, the wrong shore. The litter of hovels, taverns and stalls burned like dry grass, and smoke drifted across, carrying the nauseous scent of human flesh burning. The whores and drunks of Sudwerke found hell before they were dead.

Edward stood.

Aesval puffed back up the hill. Felim was with her. "There is no seer in all of Lunduntown. Fled with the actors and jugglers most likely."

She had forgotten the red cloud, now nearly hidden by the smoke lifting to the sky. Fires flamed and reached up as if trying to push above the smoke. She saw them, it seemed, all at once. Vikings. Rows of Vikings amassed at the river's edge. They began making a great clamor as if they expected the river to dry away and the water to drain out to sea. There was a frenzy of yelling and bodies moving closer and closer to the water's edge and then for no apparent reason the first row of helmets, shields and noise marched into the river followed by a second row, and wave after wave they walked right into the river.

"It is madness," Wulfstan said.

Emma stood transfixed by the Vikings walking into the deep river of death. Rocks from the Lunduners were tossed at them, but never reached them. A few of the men tried to swim, but most just walked like rats into the water. The bodies of the Vikings, like the soldiers on the bridge, sunk or rode toward the sea.

Edward stood. Emma could bear it no longer. "Are you mad, Edward?"

"Madam?" he asked softly.

"Are you crazy, standing there like that the day long?"

"I wished the Vikings to walk into the deep river and they did. God has done as I asked."

"That is blasphemy, Edward," Wulfstan said.

"It is because I willed it," Edward said.

"Felim, take this child away," Emma ordered.

She stood there, the screams of the men still in her mind. The smoke rose across the river and the stench continued. Edward was mad; still, she had no answer as to why the Vikings marched into the river and death.

CHAPTER 6

Lunduntown, 1014

EDWARD DID NOT SLEEP. HE STOOD IN THE DARK PEERING THROUGH THE cracks where the boards covering the windows were joined. He had stood there for several hours watching the guards below. Sometimes their laughter crept up, but it was soft and he could not hear their voices. There was only the glow about their bodies that assured him they were there. Horses approached. Voices became audible. Yelling out. A thegn had arrived. His name was Godwin. That much Edward heard. A banging of doors. More horses. Torches were lit. Edward watched as soldiers and servants milled below. Monks and priests scurried. Bundles and baskets were carted out.

The door to his chamber opened.

"Edward, get up and get clothed." It was Felim MacBoru. "Edward, you have naught even gone to bed. What is this?"

The boy did not turn about nor move.

"Edward, no games. No anchorite suffering at this moment, please. Play the saint later. We are off to Rouen."

Edward turned and faced him. "But it will soon be the Nativity."

"Aye and we'll spend it there."

Edward stood.

"Edward, move. The King and Queen will have gathered those of the house in the great hall. And if you keep them waiting they will be angry."

"The relic. My present for the Queen."

"A slave will gather your things. Come along. The King is ired enough without you angering him further."

The King's yelling voice was audible long before they reached the hall. "A BASTARD. Bastard. Bastard. Bastard!"

With Felim ahead, he slipped into the hall as the King was hurling an empty cup across the room. It clanged against the wall near where they had entered.

"Edmund is a bastard. ALL OF YOU HEAR. I am the King and I say Edmund is a bastard. His mother was a sow. Crown him with pig shit. A bas—" He began choking on his words and gagging. His face was deep red and his hands waved about as if he had no control over them.

The Queen eased the King down upon a wooden seat and handed him a full cup of wine.

"Thegns," she said in a loud commanding voice, "good bishops and friends, a thegn here, by the name of Godwin, has brought us word that the Earldorman of Mercia has betrayed the King. Eadric joins Edmund and they march upon Lunduntown. Sven comes from the west with an army and the Lunduners are rightfully afraid. There is rumor they will call Sven their king in our good King's stead. Your Lord Ethelred takes the fleet upon the Thames—"

"The goddamn Dane!" Ethelred interrupted with a bursting yell. He stood up and yelled again and then slipped back onto the seat. "The goddamn Dane," he muttered.

"Thorkell and his army are at Greenwich and will support us but dare not turn back to face Sven before he reaches Lunduntown lest our route to the sea be cut off. Bishop Aelfhun will take the athelings, Edward and Alfred, overland to safety. The kind abbot here will escort me safely along another route. God be with you all."

There was a piercing shriek in the hall, a cry that sounded like a wounded dog. It was Godgifu. "How about me?" she wailed. "They are going to leave me for the goddamn Danes."

"I wonder if they'd ever recover," his mother said and pushed the child over to a slave. "Send her with Bishop Aelfhun."

The night ride was slow. The bishop was an old man. Felim and Edward often outdistanced him and his soldiers and had to wait for them to catch up. A wind arose as they neared the sea and the snow came softly, speckling the dark night air as he and Felim waited at the edge of the road.

Edward could see the shadows of the horses approaching, black in the night, and the aura of the light about each rider. They neared and Edward could hear their voices, and then a horse neighed and snorted and Edward saw its black shape rise up on its haunches and the rider yelled out and the horse stamped its front hoofs and rose again and Edward could see the man's aura rise in the air, being tossed from the beast and falling hard to the earth with a thump.

Felim leaped down from his mount and ran to the man.

"The horse. Get the horse," someone yelled, and the men went running after the beast.

Edward climbed down and went over to where Felim was on his knees over the man. "The light about him is so dim," Edward said.

"Hush, Edward, everyone does not see this glow of light about others."

The man moaned and Felim touched the binding where it was torn and the man cried out in pain. Even in the night's blackness, blood was visible in the open tear. There was a long gash and moist flesh pushed through the ripped skin.

"Keep moving," Felim told the other riders. "I will tend him." The riders continued on. "You must not speak of the light, Edward. It is a gift. And I would say a secret."

"But you see the light, Felim."

"Yes."

"And my mother?"

"I think not."

"What does it mean, Felim?"

"I am not certain, but it is useful and as you grow older I will teach you." With that Felim began to draw down toward his hands all of his own light and then without actually touching the light he wound his hands about, forming the light into a brilliant ball. As Felim moved his hands over the man's leg, the ball of light moved as well and rested where the wet blood oozed and had now wet the rest of his leg wrappings. There seemed a spot of darkness forming in the cluster of light over the man's wound. It was difficult to tell where the man's dim light ended and the ball of light in Felim's hands began. Felim shoved the two clusters of light together and then slowly pulled away. The black spot was drawn up into the ball contained in Felim's open hands. He stood and shook the ball until the black spot vanished as if, like shaking loose the dirt of a wrap, it was made clean. The light about the man once more formed an aura about his body, but the wound had disappeared. There was no opening in the man's flesh. Felim collapsed upon the ground as the light about him, too, returned to surround his body.

After a moment of rest, Felim asked the fallen rider, "Is there any more pain?"

"None," the man answered. "What did you do? I swear my leg was broken."

"It would be better if you did not talk of this," Felim said. "Just say you were not hurt."

The thegn who had come to warn them of the Earldorman of Mercia and Edmund's treachery rode back to them. He was leading the fallen rider's horse. "How bad is he hurt?" the thegn asked. Edward could not remember the man's name.

"He was just stunned," Felim said. "I will give him a hand up on his horse." Felim did, then got back on his own mount and rode off.

"What really happened here?" the thegn asked Edward.

"Nothing. The man was thrown, that was all." Edward knew to keep the secret about seeing the lights. Edward sensed that because of it he was different. He rode to catch Felim. The thegn's name was Godwin. Yes, that was it. As he reached Felim he asked, "Will you show me how, Felim?"

"In time, Edward. In time I will show you how."

That night on the deck of the dark ship, Edward knew that if he could do what Felim had done he would become a great saint and cure great sickness and he would be a great king, too, and kill great numbers of people, including his brother Edmund, the traitor. Edward tried to bring the light about his body into a ball, but this he could not do.

The ship heaved over the rough water.

"Edward." She had crept up on him before he could run away. "Edward," Godgifu cried, "I'm scared and my belly aches. And I'm going to drown."

Edward, who had shied back as she came up to him, looked at her. She was shaking, shivering and tears streamed upon her fat cheeks.

"Here," he said, "sit beside me and this skin will cover us both. She pressed against him and that hurt. She smelled of vomit. "See," he said, "you won't drown."

The girl stopped crying and shortly fell asleep. The ache her body caused against his own became numbness and after a time vanished. For the only time in his life the touch of another body, other than Felim's, caused him no pain.

"Godgifu," a slave woman called.

"Hush," Edward said as she approached.

"The girl ran off."

"She is here sleeping."

"Give her to me."

"Go away, old woman, and let her sleep."

"I . . ."

"Go away."

Edward dozed. Occasionally when the girl moved he would partially awaken. Godgifu snored softly.

Once when he awoke he saw the aura of light standing forward in the bow of the ship and knew it was his mother. The wind lifted her cloak. He fell back asleep.

CHAPTER 7

Rouen, Christmas, 1014

A STORM RAGED, BUT INSIDE THE BOISTEROUS SOUNDS OF CHRISTMAS MADE IT all but inaudible. The Yule log burned, an English custom in deference to the guests. There were the Saxons in exile gathered with the Normans in rows of tables in the great hall at Rouen—rows of counts and thegns, bishops and children, ladies and priests, monks and slaves—and an old man, a stranger, wandered in and sat at the end of one of the long tables.

Edward sat next to Emma and meticulously picked at his food. "Why do they burn the log at Christmas?" he asked.

"It is the custom," she said and turned away. She was tired of his endless questions.

Ethelred, who had been sitting to her other side, crawled up atop the table, singing loudly as he attempted to get to his feet between a plate of larded meal cakes and a bowl of dark, greasy goose. A horn blared a raspy tune and a lute chimed in sometimes, seeming to play the same tune and at others not. Ethelred stood up, pushing his hands into the gravied rabbit, and danced between the piled dishes, occasionally knocking aside stacks of bones or kicking a bowl of wine into a lap as he made his way down the table. He was taunted and teased, encouraged and mocked by the feasters.

"Disgusting," Judith snorted and scratched.

Duke Richard smiled and seemed not to care.

What would be a lovely Christmas gift, Emma decided, was the sudden death of Ethelred right at the table. But it wasn't true. He mustn't die yet, not while England was occupied and divided between Sven and Edmund. Let them kill each other first, then Ethelred could go home and die and Edward would become King. Goddy was teaching the boy soldiering and Felim the boy to read, though neither the duke nor Ethelred approved of the latter occupation. "Are you rearing a king or a cleric?" Richard had asked Emma. Yet, there was power in being able to read and she recognized that. Edward, as ugly as he was, showed some talent in both endeavors, but he had a bad habit of going about asking the most ridiculous questions of people and he turned now to the bishop, on the other side of him, and asked the same question he had just asked his mother about the Yule log.

"To celebrate the birth of the child," the bishop answered.

Ethelred fell from the table onto the hard stone of the floor and let out a horrible cry. He moaned and lay there in apparent pain. Emma sat and sipped her wine, but others got up and looked to him and a bed was brought in for him and he lay on it near the long tables, moaning and consuming quantities of wine until he fell asleep.

The old stranger who had wandered in spoke suddenly, not getting up from where he sat at the end of one of the long tables. "I will tell you a story. . . . Once upon a time, when there was the first Christmas ever, a young man, a Jew, came to the place where the baby Jesus, still wet from his mother's womb, had but entered the world. The young Jew said, 'I will cut the cord that binds this babe,' and so he took his knife and cut the cord and tied it and handed the baby to his mother."

The great hall at Rouen' had grown silent as all turned to listen to the story. Only the old man's words and the snoring of the King broke the silence.

"And the mother said, 'Cry no more, child,' and she sang him a song of sleep and the babe slept and the mother said, 'Young Jew, because you have cut this cord your knife will never let blood. It is holy and you shall be blessed.' On his way down the hill from the town, the young Jew was set upon by highwaymen and when he tried to defend himself the knife would not cut and the highwaymen beat him and robbed him. He lay there a sore night long and when the day came he made his way onward and he hungered. But as his luck would have it he fell upon a wild boar which would have made his feast, but when he tried to attack the boar the knife proved of no use against the boar's hide and the angered boar turned and drove his tusks into the flesh of the young Jew. Pained and bleeding, the young man made his way until he fell upon a tree with ripened fruit. From the tree he knew he would find nourishment, but when he sought to cut loose the fruit the tree would not yield it up. And so in time, beset upon by man and beast and nature, and unable even to dig roots with the knife, the man died alone and was left to the vultures."

"That is the end?" asked Ralph of Tosny, who was said when on crusades in Spain to have boiled the heads of infidels for his table.

"Yes," the old man replied and began to shake.

"It is the silliest story I have ever heard," said the Abbot of Peterborough.

Sweat seeped from the old man's forehead and with little warning he fell over, his head hitting the hard table.

"Quick," Mabel of Montgomery ordered, "look upon his belly."

They propped him up and opened his gown.

"See the black blister there. He will be dead by morrow."

"How know you this?" Judith asked Mabel of Montgomery, who was said to have killed her Norman husbands, one after the other, with poisons.

"It is always thus. See, too, the black lines upon his forehead. It is death coming."

"Take him out. Take him out," Emma cried. "This is not the place for death. Not here on this feast."

"Silliest story I ever heard," the abbot repeated as two slaves the size of giants carried the old man from the room.

"This has been an evil omen," Judith said. "Someone get water with herb of cinquefoil, say over it the Paternoster and scrub this spot where he fell."

"It turns red. The water upon the spot turns red," a monk whispered in a loud hoarse voice.

"What means it?" Emma asked.

"Before St. George's day passes a member of the family of the highest noble among us shall die," Mabel of Montgomery pronounced.

"The King outranks us all," Judith said, obviously quite willing to be outranked. "Ethelred's house, the house of Edgar, shall know someone dead before St. George's day." Judith looked at Emma and smiled.

Emma said nothing. She knew Judith was wrong, and she turned from her.

The feast ended and the guests drifted from the great hall shaking their heads and speaking of the omen they had witnessed. Ethelred's servants came and carried him to his bed.

Edward, who was standing over the red spot where the old man had fallen, turned to Felim. "Why do they burn the Yule log, Felim?"

"It is an ancient custom from pagan times to celebrate the sun, for when the sun stayed the shortest, as it does on this day when the night is long, then the large log allows the light to wax and the fire to burn."

Emma had her own question of Felim. "You are wise in these things. Is what has been spoken of the stranger here the truth?"

Felim came closer to her. "Madam, death comes without asking. Death has it own conscience and relies on neither you nor me for advice. And I think not waits upon portents."

"Know you this stranger? This old man?"

"Nay, Lady."

"So might not he well be the messenger who comes before?"

"And might he well be not," Felim said.

She was left alone in the great hall except for her brother Robert, who sat in voluminous ecclesiastical robes, away from the fire in the dark. Robert was a corpulent man, but he had a large mind as well as body. All the sounds of the storm could be heard now that the revelers were silent, even the dripping from leaks as it fell in rhythmic taps upon the stone. The Seine rumbled below and the sky rumbled above.

"You must forget the old man," her brother-archbishop said. "He was simply a passing stranger, a bit mad perhaps. You cheated death before a crowd of your countrymen that day you walked over those hot coals. It won't take you, not now, not until you are old and ready."

She went to the dying fire, sitting apart from him. She could not see his face in the darkness. "It is not my own death I fear. I am not of the house of Edgar."

"Well, your concern is hardly for Ethelred."

"No." She paused, looking into the embers. "Edward. I know with a strange certainty that within the year Edward will be dead. God is going to punish me—"

"That is nonsense, Emma."

"God is going to punish me because I hate my son. He gave me a relic for Christmas, a bone from the foot of St. Agobard, and he knew it would please me. Yet, I loathe and detest the sight of him."

"And for that," he said, getting up from his chair, "God is going to damn you to hell?"

"No. He is going to deprive me of any purpose in life. If Edward dies I will be locked away in some convent to last out my days without living. I could not endure that, Robert. I fear that more than death. But God will punish me because I am evil."

He came over to her. "You are not evil, Emma."

"The soldiers," she said, looking up at him.

"What soldiers?"

"On Lundun bridge. I brought them death because—"

"You made a decision because your husband, the King, was too drunk to do so. What happened is but the fortune of war. Such events you must learn to accept."

"At night sometimes when I cannot sleep I hear the screams of those soldiers." A draft crept over the fire and the embers flamed, illuminating the face of the man who stood above her. "I, like you, try to blame Ethelred for the dead soldiers. I hate him—"

"And well you should. He is inept and worthless. Like a coward, he feasts himself in Rouen while his land is being overrun by the Forkbeard. You have cause to hate him."

"I have too much hate."

"And love as well, Emma. You have love for me and Richard—"

"Yes and Goddy and Willie, too, but my children—"

He put his arm upon her shoulder. "You gave them life. They can ask for no more. I saw your daughter sitting on the floor with her head resting in her brother's lap but last evening by this very fire. You used to do the same with me."

"They've become suddenly attached to one another. I do not understand the sudden change. Godgifu used to treat him with horror."

"The boy is strange in more than his grotesque ugliness. He stands for hours without moving, sometimes poses the most absurd questions and has a religious fanaticism—"

The voice interrupted from the door. Two men stood there, but it was Duke Richard who spoke. "Is piety a crime, brother Bishop?"

"Nay, Richard, but excessive piety to me always borders upon madness. Show me an anchorite or a flagellant and I will show you a madman. We were speaking of Edward, but what keeps you from your bed?"

"This fellow is a messenger who seeks the King."

"He is abed and will not be disturbed," Emma called across to the man still standing at the door.

"I've told him thus," Richard said, "and so he would seek you out, Lady."

The duke motioned him to come forward, and the messenger, obviously Saxon by his attire, came in toward the fire. His voice was hoarse. "I serve the Thegn Godwin—"

"The same Godwin who helped us flee from Lunduntown?"

"Aye, Lady Queen, the same. The thegn sends you word which he hopes will make your Christmas more joyous." He paused and then in his hoarse voice added, "Sven the Forkbeard is dead."

Silence fell on the room. For a moment only the rain and the leaking water could be heard.

It was Emma who spoke first. "This is certain?"

"Certain, Lady Queen. He died at York but two days ago and took the Christian faith, God rest his soul."

"God rest his soul," the archbishop spoke mechanically, but his face betrayed both delight and surprise.

"The very best Christmas present," Emma said.

"We have heard nothing," the duke said. "How came this Godwin to have such news so soon?"

"My master Godwin served King Ethelred, my Lord, but when the King fled, Godwin did much to oppose the bastard Edmund."

"That does not answer the question, fellow," Robert said.

The messenger looked down into the fire. "He opposed Edmund, your Grace, by serving Cnute."

"He is a traitor!" Emma spat the words out.

"No, Lady Queen. He owes all to the house of Edgar, but he will not serve the betrayer Edmund and so fights against him under the raven banner of the young warrior Cnute."

"Which is worse?" Emma demanded.

The duke touched her arm. "Nonetheless the news he brings bears celebration. Ethelred can return to England and this Thegn Godwin can serve him once again. Wine!" he called out. "We shall drink to the Christian burial of the renowned Dane, Sven the Forkbeard, that he may have a long and happy death."

The wine was brought by a sleepy-eyed slave.

They raised the bowls, the two brothers, the messenger and Emma.

"To Sven, may God have mercy on his murderous soul!" Robert said.

"To Ethelred, may he reign, but not forever." The duke tipped his bowl.

The messenger said nothing and drank.

"To Edward!" Emma said and lifted the bowl to her lips, her joy clouded by the sound of the dying soldiers on the bridge.

CHAPTER 8

Canterbury, 1015

"Death must be like the sea," Felim had said.

Edward did not understand. He looked out into the fog and down into the water, rough and rising in the wind. The ship rose high and fell across the white water. His eyes searched for the English coastline. He saw nothing but the gray dense morning. He was anxious to see land. The sea was frightening. But they were going home to England and he was going to be King. Well, not really King, but King in the King's stead. The Witangemot had declared "no lord dearer to them than their natural Lord Ethelred" and asked him to return and govern more justly than before. But the duke convinced Ethelred it might be a trick and to send Edward first as an envoy. He had heard the duke and his mother talking, though, and knew the trick was really on Ethelred. The duke had said, "It will establish the Atheling's position indisputably." Edward certainly wasn't going to tell Ethelred with his mean eye what the duke had said. Besides, he wanted to be King and hoped Ethelred would die soon.

He knew his being King made his mother happy too. She scolded and scowled less often at him and sometimes these last few days she came and talked to him. "Survival," she told him, but he wasn't certain what she meant. "You must learn to fight to survive. There is nothing else, Edward, but survival. St. George's day will pass you and I by." But he didn't understand at all what she meant. "Fight," she said, but how did one fight the sea, which took men and boys without warning, a sea with monsters, scaled and fierce; how did one survive that? Yet his mother was unafraid of the sea. She stood across from him looking not toward the land but back at the water. The wind caught her loose yellow hair.

The Abbot of Peterborough approached. Edward had first thought him pious and wise, but began to see what a silly man he was. Besides, he was continually farting.

He took hold of Edward's shoulder and the boy cringed and freed himself from the pressured pain of the worn hand, its fingers weighted with rings.

"The sea breeds idle minds," the abbot snorted. "Your tutor should be in attendance upon you these wasted hours, instructing you in all that you should learn. Where is he?"

"MacBoru dislikes the sea. He rests in the tent."

"I shall be your tutor then. I will instruct you, Edward. But in what? What needs an atheling instruction in?" His brow wrinkled and his beady eyes squinted as if thought were a matter of intense pain.

You could teach me how to fart, Edward thought . . . and smiled.

"I have thought upon marriage," the abbot said.

Knowing full well what he meant, Edward replied, "But is it not against the laws for abbots to marry?"

"Mercy God. I meant not. Mercy God, no. I have thought to instruct you in the laws of marriage. I am much knowledged in the laws of marriage."

Edward trembled at the thought of marriage. Pain. The horrible pain of that act he now understood as part of it. Godfrey had explained it to him and he had tried to close his ears. He wanted to run away from the silly abbot and wash himself. He felt the need to wash himself, to feel the touch of water. He looked down into the sea. He would never marry.

It was as if the abbot had read his thoughts. "All kings must marry," he said.

Edward did not yell "Not I" but wanted to.

The abbot went on about God's law and child rearing and pledges and oaths and he went on and on and Edward only half listened. "And wives," he said, "must always be submissive to their husband's demands for women are inferior beings, Edward. They have weakness of mind, are given easily to gossip and temptation. The great St. Cuthbert spoke to no woman, ever. Ever in his life. They tell stories yet of women who dare enter the yard where he is buried. There was Sungeova, the wife of Bevo's son—"

"Land," Edward yelled. White cliffs loomed large ahead as the fog broke apart. "Land."

His mother came across and stood near Edward, looking out at the English cliffs rising high from the sea.

"I've been instructing Edward, Lady," the abbot told her.

"In what?"

Edward answered. "In that women are inferior beings."

"So we must constantly be told," she said angrily, "lest we prove otherwise."

"It was more, Lady, that"—the abbot was flustered—"that I was instructing him in the nature of marriage."

"Good Abbot, when we reach the port at Hastings, you must be allowed to journey on to Peterborough. Too long have we kept you from your duties."

"But, Madam, the King would wish I accompany you on to Canterbury."

"No need."

"But the King—"

"My son is the King's emissary in all now. What say you to this, Edward?"

"The abbot goes to Peterborough."

"My Lord—"

"To Peterborough." Edward loved being able to order the silly old man about and repeated, "Peterborough."

"Lady, he is but a boy. Let me reason with you."

"I am but a woman, an inferior woman. He is the King's representative on a great mission to Canterbury. All the nobles of this land and the great bishops will look to Edward for his words, for before all he will speak for the King."

"And I, Lady?"

"You, Alfsige, will be en route to Peterborough."

The man turned and left, farting as he walked off.

Edward looked up at his mother. Her eyes smiled and then her mouth. "To Peterborough," he whispered.

Hastings smelled of fish. Felim MacBoru was one of the first to leap upon the land. He bent down and kissed the earth.

"Fear you the sea so much, MacBoru?" his mother asked Felim.

"Aye, Madam."

"With all your powers?"

"They seem useless at sea, Lady."

"I fear the land. There is more death about us here."

Edward stood. He felt kingly in the new clothes, yet he would have liked to dip his hands in the bay or splash his feet as he saw two boys doing at the water's edge. He no longer wore the simple tunic of the child but was outfitted with his hose cross-gartered in golden bands, his tunic embroidered at the hem and his cloak lined with a black fur they say came from a far-off land. A large gold amulet with a sapphire center hung on a chain about his neck. He fingered the sharp edge of the stone.

They waited. He was late, but Earldorman Eadric did finally arrive with, as was said, forty soldiers. Eadric bowed to them. "I'm sorry for this tardiness, Madam, but I was detained at Pevensey by the Atheling Edmund."

"Our enemy," she said.

"Nay, Lady. He begs the King's gracious pardon. He asks to be allowed to come to Canterbury."

"Never," Edward answered.

"Lady, I was addressing you."

"The boy speaks the father's will. He knows it well. The King has been deeply wronged by this bastard Edmund. There are those who profess now he is not even the son of Ethelred but that his mother-bitch sired him by another."

"I think this ugly rumor, Madam. And as for wronging his gracious father, have we not all wronged the King?"

"All are not his sons. Or said-to-be sons."

"If we're ever to be united against the Danes, Lady, we must include a lord of such wealth and kinship to the throne as Edmund."

"He may not have either long, Eadric. Speak no more on it. Do you see us to Canterbury, Lord?"

"I do, Lady Queen."

"Then let us be off."

Some mounts had been brought from Normandy aboard ship, others by Eadric. More than a hundred horses with riders lined the road as the entourage began on the route north to Canterbury.

Christ Church seemed to lean. The end pillar of the facade had broken away and the roof sagged at the corner. The weight had pressed the rough-hewn stone blocks into the earth giving the church the appearance of being ready to topple over. Edward had been here before, but he had forgotten how ugly Christ Church was—how old, and brown, and ugly. Edmund had told him that the Jutes used to butcher boys of Edward's age as offering to the Anse gods, but Edmund lied and Edward knew that it was here in this very church that St. Augustine had baptized Ethelbert, the King of the Kentish.

Edward stepped beneath the stone arch and entered the vestibule. It was dank and smelled of mold and a dead rat, but Edward forgot it all as he looked at Bishop Lefing, the Archbishop of Canterbury, waiting robed and jeweled before the altar. It seemed to Edward as they entered the church in great ceremony that the light about the bishop was so bright that it was hard to stare directly at him. Edward, his mother beside him, walked the open nave as the monks sang out, "*Laudamus te—*

glorificamus te—adoramus te." Edward liked being King and he moved deliberately, aware all eyes were on him. He moved, his fingertips pressed together and pointed toward heaven. His mother attempted to quicken the pace, but he held the slow cadence. Even she was under his control. If he were really King he could control them all. He was almost sorry to reach the sanctuary. Here his mother left him, for she was not allowed. He moved up to the throne. He turned. From the side bishops Wulfstan, Godwineth, Eadnoth and Aelfhun approached him. It was Wulfstan who spoke:

"We, for all the people of the kingdom . . ."

Save those of Lindsay, Edward thought, for was said they harbored the dead Sven's son, Cnute, and the people of Lindsay had proclaimed Cnute their king.

". . . we greet this emissary, who comes in the name of our King."

Edward as he listened rehearsed his own lines once more in his head.

". . . we ask in the name of all England that our rightful King return among his people."

"The King, our father"—Edward's voice began weak—"greets all his people. The King, our father, says he will be a gracious lord to them. The King, our father"—the strength of his voice came to him and his words echoed through the stone church and he rather liked the sound—"says he will reform all things which are hated and the King, our father, says all things that had been said and done against him should be forgiven in that all will turn to him in un-a-a"—Edward stumbled over the word—"unanimity and without treachery."

"Then all the people say," Wulfstan spoke, "this our true King, Ethelred, son of Edgar."

Edward knew all did not mean Edmund. It was as if Edmund were more there by not being there. Even as the archbishop spoke, Edward knew what was in his mind. ". . . and the people say all kings of Danes be outlawed and are to be driven from Wessex and all of England forever. The people take this oath that their only King shall be their gracious anointed Lord."

"And the King takes this oath," Edward said as the archbishop gave him a quick nudge, "to reform all things which are hated. This as sovereign Lord of all the people."

"So let it be before God," Wulfstan said.

"So let it be before God," Edward repeated, proud that he had come to the end, having done all as was rehearsed with Archbishop Robert in the ducal palace in Rouen.

The choir sang out. Bells pealed louder than the choir sang and drowned their voices. Edward, sorry now to see it over so quickly, turned and, with what he knew was stately majesty, as he had seen among the Norman court proceedings, walked from the sanctuary.

"*Kyrie eleison*" burst forth from the monks in unison. God was in his majesty, Edward knew, and Edward walked with great pomp beside the Queen, his mother, from the church.

Outside she moved to under a large tree as if to escape the sun, but he stood outside upon the steps awaiting the procession of earls and thegns, but they passed him by to form about the Queen. The priests and monks, the bishops and archbishops too, came out, but they also passed him by.

The nobles parted to allow Archbishop Wulfstan, a head taller than any of them, to approach the Queen.

"Tell the King without Edmund there can be no real peace in the land."

"Treachery!" the Queen responded to Wulfstan. "It is treachery to bear his name before the King."

"Perhaps, but without him there is not the strength to put down Cnute."

"Edmund is the King's sworn enemy."

"Tell the King of what I have said."

Edward looked angrily at them. "I am the King," he spoke softly beneath his breath. "Today I am the King." But he knew it wasn't true. He was but a boy. He wished one of them would fall deathly ill and then, like Felim, he would rid the man of all illness. But even this he knew was dreaming, for Felim had not yet shown him how to make such miracles.

A young man approached him. "Atheling." The young man was dressed in a long green robe and wore a scarf about his head. "You will be King."

Edward looked at the young man, who like himself had no color to his skin and had eyes which seemed pinkish-sore from rubbing.

"But before you and the throne be five kings."

The young man turned and walked off and behind him all the while he had been talking had been standing a dwarf. The dwarf, who had only become visible when the young seer turned away, was of dark skin and with as much color as the young man lacked. The dwarf ran after the youth, trying with his short legs to keep pace with the strides of the other.

Edward simply stood there.

"Where is the thegn they call Godwin?" he heard his mother ask.

"Not among us, Lady Queen. He serves Cnute Svensson and should not be counted as loyal to his King."

CHAPTER 9

Rouen, 1015

EDWARD RODE. THE HOODED PEREGRINE, PROUD AS ANY PRINCE, RESTED ON his glove. The light touch of the bird gave him no pain. "Have you ever hawked?" Edward asked.

"No, my Lord." The young man who walked beside him was the boy-monk with the blue eyes that he had first seen that night in the chapel here at Rouen. "I find the shedding of blood, man's or beast's, not to my liking."

Edward found that strange, for the sight of blood was exhilarating. To dabble one's fingers in the thick red liquid was a sensation that gave pleasure—such a pleasure that Edward could not have described the sensation to Robin of Jumieges if he had wished.

He looked down at the monk. "Will you be my friend?"

"Yes," the monk assured him.

"I am ugly. Ethelred with the mean eye—"

"Your father?"

"Yes. He says I am the ugliest creature he has ever set eyes upon."

"I doubt that is so," Robin of Jumieges said. "And if you are not a beauty at least you are free. The world owns beauty. They say of me, 'He is one of beauty,' maybe it is so, but for this beauty I have paid. I was a favorite of my father and for it my jealous brothers plotted my death. A knight of my father's court saved me. For what? Perhaps you are too young to understand this, but he kept me as a man keeps a whore and used me such. I ran from him and returned to my father. I told him of what my brothers plotted, but not of the knight, because of this I was ashamed. He protected me, but my stepmother tried to seduce me and, when I would not yield, told my father I had attempted to rape her. He gave me to the monks at Jumieges. Even there it was with difficulty, for I became the object of jealous rows and unclean attentions. Your uncle-archbishop arranged that I be brought to St. Ouen. It is better there."

"It hurts to be ugly," Edward said.

"And to be beautiful as well."

"I will be your friend, Robin of Jumieges."

But Robin was often times busy being a monk. Still there was falconry and soldiering and his days were busy as well with Latin and learning. Just knowing Robin was there he had come to feel less isolated in his ugliness, knowing Robin's beauty was as painful for the young monk to bear.

"Am I ugly?" Edward asked his mother.

"Why such a question?"

"Am I ugly?" he asked again.

"Yes."

"Monstrously so?"

"Yes."

And he became conscious and shy of his ugliness and yet he would ask a stranger as well for confirmation of that fact and shy from the answer.

"Will you stop bothering people? Will you stop asking people if you are ugly?" his mother insisted.

"I want to know," he said.

He asked Godgifu. "Am I ugly?"

"You are beautiful."

He asked Uncle Godfrey. "Am I ugly?"

"No. What a stupid idea."

He asked the Abbot of St. Ouen. "Am I ugly?"

"What is ugly?"

He asked the juggler, the archbishop, the gatekeeper, his brother Alfred and the old nun who carried flowers, the Jew in his yellow cap and the beggar by the Seine. No one answer was the same.

He saw the stranger, a simply dressed man walking ahead of him on the north side of the courtyard.

"Am I ugly?" he asked the man.

"No creature of God's is ugly, Edward."

The man, who took long strides, knew who he was; that surprised Edward. He tried to keep up with the man. They came upon a house ceorl who was flaying a slave with a drinking horn. The slave cringed and cowered and tried to cover his head with his hands and the horn cracked across his knuckles.

"Stop it at once," the man with Edward ordered, and even though he spoke with great authority there was a softness in his voice.

The ceorl stopped, but held on to the horn. "He was stealing wine." His voice betrayed a belligerence toward the soft-voiced man, a belligerence above his station.

The man did not seem to mind. "Nonetheless, remember always compassion and forgiveness."

"Yes, my Lord," he answered, but there was little conviction as he turned and walked away.

Edward looked at the man. Surely the slave deserved to be flogged. Why had the man let him loose?

"Edward, child," the man said, "you look disapprovingly at me. Did I not do right?"

"He was stealing wine."

"Indeed a sin, but just as sinful is it to be cruel to our fellows upon this earth. Think you not?"

Edward thought and then proudly put forth, "But when Cnute's men come and steal our lands and plunder and burn surely the King must punish. The slave is like the Danes."

"War breeds war. Killing breeds killing. Flogging breeds flogging. What happens when your father punishes the Danes?"

"At Lindsay, Cnute put out to sea and when he came to Sandwich he let ashore all the hostages given his father and he cut off their hands and ears and noses. Cnute does great atrocities, they say."

"My point, Edward. Violence breeds violence like a yeast in the bin. Do you see?"

He nodded, but he really didn't see at all, although he told the man, "I wouldn't put anyone's eyes out. Still, a king must—"

"I am a king," the man said.

"You, sir?" He surely didn't look like a king. His clothes were plain. He wore no jewels and he certainly didn't act like a king. He had no majesty at all. He was, in truth, if a king, a very unkingly king.

"I'm Robert, son of Hugh Capet."

He was the King of France! The great duke was this King's vassal. Edward was amazed and stared at the man more closely. "And your wife is a wi—" he started to say, but cut himself short.

"A witch? Some say a witch. She is not. Bertha is a woman of great insights, but because, Edward, I listen to the Queen and would take her counsel above all others, men hate her and call her witch. Let me tell you this story of her. There was a piece of land said to belong to France, but the Emperor claimed it as his. For this land, it was said, I should raise armies and go battle my friend Henry. The Queen bade me go take the Emperor a gift. And so I did. And the Emperor was so pleased he said, 'Take the land, for you are my friend.' But I say, 'Nay. It is yours.' And in the end we divided the land but kept our friendship. Remember when you are King, Edward, blessed are the peacemakers for they shall inherit the earth."

"But the Danes?"

"The Danes are men, too. All God's people, and must be dealt with in the true manner of Christ."

Edward thought of all the presents Ethelred had given the Danes. To what use? Sven came and now Cnute. He said nothing, not knowing what should be said, and besides the King didn't cease talking long enough to say anything anyway.

"I tell you this, Edward. For when we go out upon a day, that which we see and hear becomes a part of us. What you have heard today, these words become a part of you. Abide them or not, you will not forget I have said them."

Edward decided the king preached a lot. They had been walking toward the great hall and as they reached it the King motioned for Edward to precede him in. The hall smelled of fresh-baked wheat cake and was crowded with ladies and French and Norman knights. A knight near the door was telling another of a priest of the Burgundians who had an eye of bloodstone. A slave poured wine in the knight's drinking horn.

Edward was startled to see his mother. He had not been told she had arrived from England, yet there she stood beside the duke, and she, like all the others, even the duke, bowed as the man walking with Edward came toward them. A woman Edward did not know took the King's hands and Edward realized that this must be Queen Bertha. She certainly didn't look like a witch. In fact, she looked unremarkably like every other lady.

King Robert turned toward the duke. "I've just been giving your nephew here some pointers in kingmanship."

"Should he have a kingdom to govern, Sire," the duke responded.

"The war goes badly?" Robert questioned.

"Yes, my Lord." His mother seemed pale and she spoke as if tired. "All goes unwell. Since Michaelmas it has been one long battle. No man knows any longer who fights with him or against him, and the treacherous Earldorman Eadric fights with and against them all—"

"Eadric?" the King asked.

"Yes, a Mercian. First he collected an army, went north to join Edmund and betrayed the King, but Edmund, I gather, did not totally trust Eadric, or perhaps the other way around, I am not certain which, and they parted. Eadric then took forty of the Ethelred's ships and went over to Cnute. And so it goes. Cnute and Edmund war. Cnute and the King. The King and Edmund."

"You see, Edward. It is as I've been telling you. War begets war. Peace begets peace."

"I would quarrel with you, my Lord." The duke began to cough. "War begets victors and the victors own the peace."

"I live in peace, Duke Richard."

"Indeed, my Lord, purchased in blood by your great father—"

The duke suddenly fell forward, collapsing on the floor. His wine bowl fell and clanged as wine spilled in a puddle. Everyone moved about the duke at once.

"Stand from him," the Queen of France ordered and, as Edward had seen Felim do so often, she began making a ball from the light about her. Her movements were different from Felim's, but she drew the duke's aura toward her own and she, too, grasped within her light a black spot which she tossed from the light ball away from her. She sank to the floor and the light returned about her.

Edward watched the look of his mother, who seemed to understand what was happening. The others just stared with strange expressions, watching Queen Bertha. Edward realized none of them could see the lights. He often forgot that when Felim came to a man's rescue that others did not see what he saw.

The duke opened his eyes and a servant helped him up. "I could have sworn I had been dead. There was a great light and I could see my body as if I were standing up there above it in midair and then I watched as the Lady Bertha drew a strange black object from me."

"Yes," the Queen of France said. "It is often so."

Later during the evening when Queen Bertha sat, somewhat aside by the fire, Edward went over to her. "I, too, will learn to do that," he told her. "To make the sickness go away."

She smiled.

"When Felim MacBoru teaches me. I see the light Felim calls the aura."

She no longer looked at him as if he were a small child. "You see this about me, Edward?"

"About everyone, even babies."

"Be careful. Never tell this."

"I know," he said. "Felim has told me."

"For people will do great harm to you. Were I not the Queen of France I would be dead already for witchery."

"Why?"

"Because men fear the incomprehensible. The King has been threatened already with excommunication."

"Because you heal the sick?"

"They say it is because the King and I are cousins, that is true, but what they fear are my powers of good."

"Does the King see the aura?"

"Nay, but he knows well I do and understands. King Robert is the greatest of living men, but he is feared because he comprehends God and seeks only goodness, never giving in to evil. When you have mastered that, Edward, then you can become a saint."

CHAPTER 10

Jumieges, Normandy, 1016

"I SAW GOD," EDWARD SAID. HE LOOKED UP FROM THE ORNATE "DEO" scrolled on the parchment before him.

"You saw God?"

"I did, Felim. Yesterday. When I knew I was going to have a fit. When I was shaking all over. I saw him."

"And"—the man's tone was casual—"what did God look like?"

"Kind."

"What sort of description is that? You saw God and all you can tell me is that he looked kind." Felim MacBoru got up and walked to the window. The windows were narrow slits in the thick walls, built as if this room in the abbey were a fortress in need of defending. Edward watched as the man leaned forward into the splay to look out. "The sun is shining out there. It washes the tall yellow grass until it almost is white in the light. Yet, it is as cold and dark in here as the depths of hell."

"I thought hell was hot," Edward told him.

"Who knows what hell is like. If it even exists?" Felim turned back from the window.

"There is a hell." Edward spoke with a positive authoritarian air.

"Yes. There is a hell."

Edward returned for a moment to the parchment. "I did see God. I can't describe him. I'm not sure I saw his face, only the light. There was a great light. Then the fit came and I can't remember any more."

"But you have a gift, Edward. You see a light about everyone. It was probably just someone about you."

"No. It was different. It was God."

"Whatever it was, be careful. I've told you before, use care who you say these things to. There are those would accuse you of sorcery."

Edward thought for a moment. There was quiet except for the buzzing of an insect and the footsteps of someone approaching along the corridor. "What is the difference, Felim, between what is miracle and what is sorcery?"

A voice spoke from the doorway. "The power of the man judging, nephew, and whether or not you are a threat to him."

"Your Grace," Felim said, bowing to the Archbishop of Rouen.

Edward stood up. He was glad to see his uncle and knelt to kiss the ring upon the large man's hairy finger.

"Up." The archbishop withdrew his hand before the boy could take it. "We have no need of such formalities, you and I, Edward. We are friends."

"And sometimes I wonder if the only family he has . . ." Felim's voice seemed weary.

"Know your place, son of Boru. It is not for you to judge noble houses."

"Forgive me, your Grace. My concern was only for the boy."

"That I am glad to hear. The boy will need your help now." He looked down at Edward. "Child, I would have a word with MacBoru. Go and enjoy this countryside. Have you been to the stream that runs beyond the north wall?"

"Yes, Uncle."

"A favorite spot of mine. We will walk there, perhaps, later. I have news for you, Edward."

"My mother?"

"The news is not of her, but she is well and on her way to see you here at Jumieges. Now run along. I envy you your youth and time you can spend by the stream."

Edward bowed his head in a light nod and ran out into the corridor but tripped outside the door, falling upon the hard stone floor. It was agony and as he waited for the pain in his scraped knees to abate, he heard the men speaking. He looked at his hands, which he rubbed across his knees. They were stained with bits of blood.

"Killed in battle?" Felim asked, loud enough for Edward to hear the words.

"No. Died of some disorder. Who knows. Poison is always a possibility."

"And the Witan?"

"No. He is not their choice. And I am not surprised."
"But Sven is dead."
"His son is not."

Edward limped down the corridor. Someone was dead. The air was dank and smelled of sour wine. Who had died? Had they gone to heaven or hell? There was a hell. Felim MacBoru should not say there was no hell. When Edward died he knew he would go to heaven for he was going to be a saint. Now that he had seen God, he was sure of it. Next time, perhaps, God would speak to him. There were saints God talked to.

Outside, the light made his eyes squint and through the thin white strands of hair he felt the sun's hot fingers against his skull. He wished Robin were about, but Robin was no longer at his bidding. Robin was in Rouen. He ran through the yellow grass toward where he knew the stream was hiding beyond the trees. He didn't know why his uncle liked the stream, but Edward liked it to bathe in. He got his garments off, cleaned the blood off his fingers by putting his hands into the water first and then he set his whole body into the cold, sitting upon the stone bottom, the water coming nearly to his shoulders. It was clear and he could see his pale white legs twisted and bent by the depth of the water.

The girl came. By her attire he knew she was a slave, or at best some villein's child. She was taller than he, that he could tell, and filthy. Her clothes were covered with field dirt and, by the looks of the stains, the waste and grease of cooking and eating. She started to undress.

"Go away," he said.

"No," she told him, staring directly at him and continuing to take off her dirty clothing. He started to get up but modesty drove him to submerge himself back into the water.

"Go away," he repeated.

She stood naked at the water's edge. Her chest was large like a woman's and he looked at the nipples, which stuck out. He turned away. His mother in the chapel at Corfe. He tried not to think about the girl's breasts but how dirty her body was. Even from the distance which she stood apart from him, he could see the layered filth on her skin. Her face was young and she walked to the edge of the bank. The little humps of flesh with the open crack between, where her penis should have been, were plainly visible. He had seen Godgifu's. His mother's at Corfe, the mat of hair hiding the opening where the Dane had entered her body. The girl stepped into the water and moved toward him. In the sunlight the aura of light about her was dim and, as she approached, seemed to gather more brightly at the open slit between her legs.

"Go away," he told her and looked down into the water. His mother at Corfe. He washed his hands with a flurry, stirring up the water.

"You can put your hands on my pee-pee place," she told him.

"Go away."

She reached down in the water and touched his penis. The pain was excruciating. He leaped up and ran from the stream.

"I wouldn't let you touch my pee-pee, even if you wanted to," she called.

He picked up his clothes in a bundle and ran toward the abbey.

"You've funny eyes and hair and are ugly and I wouldn't let you put your fingers on me anywhere. You're a witch—a funny-looking witch . . ."

As he ran he barely heard her. All he could think of was his mother at Corfe. Wetness formed in his eyes and he fell into the yellow grass. He lay silent, fought away the tears. Even his breath seemed silent, slow. He wondered if he could just stop breathing if he wanted. At that moment he wanted to, for he did not see the yellow grass, nor the sun, but only the patch of hair on his mother in the chapel at Corfe. He almost didn't see the rat that boldly inched toward him. It did not dart as rats did, but rather would start and stop in his direction. It was this movement, perhaps, that caught his attention. And as he became aware of the animal, he slowly, barely moving, pushed his hand into the bundle of clothing and felt until his hand grasped the handle of the dagger. Godfrey had taught him to handle the weapon. The rat had nearly reached his other outstretched fingers when with one swift thrust he drove the dagger into the gray-skinned rodent. The rat squealed and blood seeped out, into the brown earth, matting the yellow grasses. And with the killing of the rat, the quick act done, his mind again conjured the vision of his mother. He began to shake and quiver. For a moment before he was lost in the fit, when the strong white light engulfed him, he heard the voice. God spoke. "You must keep from evil." He heard as well a piercing scream and realized it was his own voice. And then he remembered no more.

He knew as he came out of the fit that it had ended. He was lifted and carried and felt the cruel pressure of other hands. He did not open his eyes. It seemed less effort to keep them shut. Yet with eyes closed he knew the familiar darkness and felt the damp coolness of the monastery.

What surprised him was the voice of his mother. He was almost afraid to open his eyes for fear she would be naked as she was at Corfe. He lay listening. Soon it was too late to look at them. He was spying on their talk.

At first he thought it Godfrey's voice, that Godfrey had come for their weekly round of soldiery. He had come to enjoy brandishing the heavy sword, but it was the archbishop who spoke. "No, you must leave the boy here in Normandy where he is safe, Emma."

"That dead Saxon pile of dung they called the King had sworn before I ever crossed the channel that my son, my firstborn would be his successor. It was in our marriage contract."

"Be pragmatic, sister. Ethelred is dead . . ."

Edward could hardly keep his eyes closed. His father, Ethelred with the mean eye, was dead! Now he would be King and kill Edmund Ironside.

"No matter what he promised," his Uncle Robert continued, "Edmund now occupies the south of England and Cnute the north. Whoever triumphs will be King."

"Did I endure that gross beast all those years to come to this? No, brother. I will set a son upon that throne."

"And what of Edmund?"

"Men die."

Yes, Edward thought, and by the sword of Edward, king and saint.

"Careful, Emma."

"Have I ever been less than?"

"Yes. We have undergone its consequence. Discretion is not one of your fine points."

"It is not necessary to remind me of my 'indiscretion,' as you wish to call it, Robert."

"I am only warning you to care."

"I shall use care, but I will see this Edmund dead. I shall prostrate myself before him. I will go to his bed if need be."

"I doubt you be asked. He knows you loathe him. Don't you suspect he might be slightly suspicious of this sudden fondness . . . ?"

Edward lay there listening, trying to determine what had happened. Ethelred and his mean eye were dead. Then why was he not King?

". . . Edmund Ironside is no idiot."

"No need to remind me. He is wily like a wolf at Byland and he knows I am as well. I shall be frank with him. I shall allow him to believe I am an opportunist bowing to the inevitable. He knows I have lands and holdings I need protected. There is after all the matter of wealth. A queen, a king's widow, must live. And it's to his advantage not to have a potential heir invading him from the flank. Edmund will see the practicality of an alliance."

"And when he no longer needs you and your alliance?"

"He may not be alive. That family, as has just been proven again, is notoriously short-lived."

"One wonders," the archbishop said, "how much poison eats at their collective bones."

"Hearsay. Any of it remains unproven."

"And, I say, too many opportune dyings to be believed and one more is going to increase suspicion. So care, Emma. I caution you. The death of Edward the Martyr haunted Ethelred until his own. There must be no trace. There must not be the slightest doubt."

"Think me a fool? Men are known to die suddenly, particularly these."

"What e're. You have too much passion within you. Always bursting out. Be ruled by the head, this chance."

"I shall heed your good advice, brother Bishop."

"And my advice about leaving the boy here?"

"No. A show of strength is essential. Edward will lead an army in his brother's cause."

"He's but twelve years old."

"Well, I cannot. Why a woman cannot, I know not. But I cannot. I am certainly more able than this child. There were Saxon queens—"

"We are civilized. Normans, Emma. A woman does not deal in blood."

"A woman lives with blood from the age of twelve. She expends more blood than any man will ever let. I know the color of blood, Robert. It is fetid and flows with death."

"You should listen to this wise brother, nonetheless."

"My brother Duke agrees with me."

"Then Richard, too, is wrong."

"But you, yourself, say the boy commends himself well as a soldier."

"As a child, yes . . ."

"He is a king's son and will be a king."

"A boy."

"A boy, if you insist—but boys have led armies into battle. Edward must go to the aid of his brother against the Dane. That is what I will say to Edmund. It is what princely brothers do. You and Richard can see to the troops and the sailing. Godfrey, I am certain, or Willie, will serve Edward in command. I will get word to Edmund so he doesn't think we've raised an army against him."

He would not be cheated. They had promised he would be King. There was a moment of quiet between them and Edward opened his eyes. Forgetting the folly of finding his mother naked, he saw her fully clothed wearing a scarlet cloak, stained above the breast with an uneven brownish spot that looked like the head of a dog.

She actually seemed to be smiling.

"I will be King," Edward said.

"In time, Edward. In time. Your father is—"

"Dead," he interrupted. "Who killed him?"

"No. He simply died."

It was as Mabel of Montgomery had predicted at the Christmas feast when the old man fell with the mark of death on him. Ethelred died upon the very day, the feast of St. George's. Mabel of Montgomery had said the feast of St. George's.

"I would have thought someone would have killed him," Edward said. The mean eye was closed forever. "I am the King."

"Not yet."

"You promised," he said.

CHAPTER 11

Winchester, 1016

THE HALL AT WINCHESTER ROARED WARMTH. EMMA, WHO HAD TRAVELED from the sea in icy wind, welcomed the flash of heat upon her cheeks. She entered the huge room in a flourish and they stormed in behind her: soldiers, slaves, servants and clerics. It was crowded in the large hall, but the bodies flanked an open path between Emma and Edmund, who stood at the far end on a raised platform. The very idea of "King" Edmund was abhorrent to her. He stood surrounded by the Witangemot of aging men and the younger soldiers who now linked their fortunes with his. Edmund had a natural arrogance that was conveyed even in his stance. There was a king's demeanor about him as he stood at the center point amid his court; a red mantle, the color of blood, hung from his shoulders. He was not an ugly man; he little resembled his father, but the sight of him infuriated her nonetheless.

"Close enough, Queen. We shall not have you too close. Distance will keep us both alive."

"Fear you a humble woman, Edmund?"

"Humble, nay, Widow."

"My emissaries have told you. I come as a friend."

"A friend? A word never used to describe our relationship heretofore and I doubt its applicability now, Lady."

"I am pragmatic . . . King." She had trouble calling him "King." "I have lands and holdings. Without these I am a poor woman. You are besieged by Cnute. I bring you an army. For this I want your protection and assurance that what I have I may keep."

"I trust you not."

"Nor I you, but we're victims of the Danes. Need breeds strange bedfellows."

"Though you are known to many beds, Stepmother, you may keep from mine."

"A mere figure of speech, but would you rather I am here with an army to your cause or would you prefer I lurked across the channel with my troops ready to sail when the Danes have you at a weak position?"

"For years you protested my right to my father's throne. Am I to believe you have so altered?"

"Circumstance has left me thus."

"Yes, Madam, indeed it has." He stiffened, pulling his shoulders up. "Lady, we are wary of your support, but accept it for the peace of our kingdom."

Emma started to walk toward him.

"Stay, Madam. We urge you keep your distance. I have not yet seen enough birthdays to ready myself for death."

"And my holdings?"

"Behave yourself and you may retain your own lands."

"And what assurance have I?"

"What assurance do any of us have, Widow? All is mutable. Where is this army of yours?"

"Coming from the south. Your brother Edward leads them."

"A child? Does he lead an army of children?"

"An atheling . . . King. Men follow their princes, boys or men. Ships, my Lord. I bring you ships and an army of Saxons, Danes and Normans."

"And these are for me?"

"Yes. They will, with the noble lords who lead them, help you drive Cnute from this island kingdom."

"And when he is gone how stands our peace?"

"My question, Edmund. What is to happen to Emma when he is gone?"

"Note this, my Lord Archbishop Wulfstan. We pledge to Emma, Widow of Ethelred, King, my father, that all those lands which she justly claims as hers will have the protection of this King. That is my oath and we will reaffirm your charters."

"Thank you, my Lord."

"But bear this in mind, Lady. The heir to this kingdom will not be thy son Edward, nor Alfred, but the athelings of my own seed, twin boys that Siegeferth's widow, Aldgyth, has newly dropped from her womb."

Emma hoped her disappointment and anger were not betrayed by her face or voice. "Understood," she said as carefully as she was able.

Edmund dismissed her with a wave of his hand and she moved back into a corner. She stood alone except for those in her own entourage. None of those of the court came to console her or to offer a friendly word. Her position would not remain this long, she assured herself.

A soldier burst into the hall. Emma knew the face though not the name. He wore the pointed helmet of the Norman. "My lords . . ." He tried to catch his breath and gasped, "Cnute has struck at . . ." The King and the others, having stopped talking, waited for him to go on as he paused to swallow air. "The army of the Atheling, as it came from the sea—"

"Edward?" Emma was alarmed. "What of Edward and his uncles, Godfrey and the Count of Eu?"

At the same time, drowning out her words with the force of his own, Edmund fired questions at the messenger. "Was he routed? His army? What of his army? Where is Cnute now?"

"Cnute and the Danes was routed, my Lord!"

Wulfstan, standing beside the King, seemed to be the most surprised. "The boy's army has defeated Cnute?"

"Aye, your Grace. Edward, that is Lord Edward, knocked the huge Dane from his mount. They was all talking of it. Would have driven his lance straight through Cnute, they said, had not the thegn they call Godwin rode through the battering swords and lances and lifted the Danish King upon the 'hind of his horse. That part I saw with me own eyes."

Emma was pleased and, as hard as she found the tale to believe, she knew her face was revealing the pleasure.

"He's but a boy," Edmund said.

"A boy he may be, Lord, but he fights like a great warrior. Many is the man there that thought not much of following a child to battle, what would follow Lord Edward to hell now."

"And he was not hurt?" Emma asked, not so much concerned for her son's well-being as interested in the details of his heroics.

"Some say they saw a lance run through his leg and indeed I saw the torn cloth myself. But they say the one called MacBoru came and standed over him, making magical incantations, the wound did vanish. And I saw the boy later and it is true enough there is no wound at all. Not even a scar where there'd be'ed one."

"And you witnessed this? You saw Felim MacBoru conjuring over him?"

"No, my Lord, I but heard; though as I says I saw the boy aft'wards."

Edmund turned to Wulfstan. "This Felim MacBoru practices witchery. Perhaps, Archbishop, the Church need examine him."

"Perhaps, my Lord." But Wulfstan's voice suggested he'd rather not pursue it.

"In Rouen," Edmund said with sarcasm. "They let this MacBoru do his witchery, teaching whores to walk on hot coals, but here in Wessex we reckon more with God and his presence and keep ourselves from deviltry."

"Soldier," Emma asked, ignoring Edmund, "your name?"

"Odo of Bec, Ma'am."

"Yes, Odo. I know thy face. Come have a cup of mead and you will tell me all of my son. My Lord, Edmund, if I may be allowed, could I take this messenger away and have a good report of your brother in battle?"

Edmund paused. "Go thy way, Lady."

She walked toward the tall wooden doors with the soldier following. Edmund, perhaps, was speaking louder than he realized and she heard him as he addressed Wulfstan. "I trust her not. Never have I heard Emma have the slightest concern for Edward except for her desire to have him on the throne. And as for Felim MacBoru . . ." Emma had walked out of earshot and she could no longer hear without having to stop conspicuously to listen. She preceded Odo of Bec from the hall.

"Are you at all able to ride as yet?"

"Certainly, Lady Queen."

"I liked not Edmund's look when he spoke of MacBoru. Ride to Lord Godfrey and tell him MacBoru is to go to Corfe. I will send his wife, Aesval, to join him. Tell my brother also that when he and the Atheling come to Winchester they should deny that Edward had been wounded. Do you understand that Felim MacBoru is in danger?"

"Aye, Lady." He got up and pushed his spur into the horse and the beast lurched forward and was gone.

The archbishop came from the hall. "My Lady Emma," he said.

She turned and looked at the man. He always seemed so solemn. She wondered if he ever smiled. "Your Grace."

"Mean you to be sincere in aiding Edmund?"

"What choice have I?"

"To wage war upon him."

"May we walk?" she asked.

He nodded.

"This army marching behind my son is hardly of strength to defeat the forces of Edmund. They have apparently won a battle. It was no war won."

"Your brother, the duke." It was not a question.

"Richard, your Grace, is an astute ruler. He would hardly with such little assurance of success support Edward's claim to the throne."

"And do you find there would be little success?"

"Little. As long as you and the other counselors of the Witangemot acknowledge Edmund, what claim have we even in victory? And why should you not choose Edmund? He is a man. Edward a boy. And though I would never give Edmund the satisfaction of knowing I truly believe such, he is a far better leader than Ethelred was. I have often found little disagreement with what he said. I do not deny I personally dislike him. Why should I try to hide my feelings to you? In honesty I hate him." To Emma the speech was having just the necessary mixture of truth and what she thought Wulfstan wanted to hear. She had to convince him, if she wanted to convince Edmund of her sincerity. "And what have I to offer in his stead? A mere boy."

"A boy. And that is the truth of it, Lady. The matter was met and discussed. The Witan would have chosen Edward had he been a man because your marriage to Ethelred bore the blessings of the Church and because the Duke of Normandy is a powerful ally. Though we do not look upon Edmund as bastard, as you would call him, we do find Edward the more legitimate choice. But Edmund controlled. Edmund is the King's son. And Edmund is of age." They walked some steps before the archbishop added, "But do you really acquiesce, so easily, Queen?"

"As I indicated, it is not a matter of choice."

"Still you have powerful brothers who could if they wished—"

"And they wish not. Be assured, your Grace, I do not deny requesting their help. It was not granted. Both the Archbishop of Rouen and the Duke of Normandy said it was unwise and they had no desire to become embroiled in entanglements beyond their own insecure borders."

A large raven swooped and perched on the roof of the great hall.

"I hope it is so. The country has been ravaged, the people plundered. The day of the invaders is once again upon us. We must have one king and be one people. I see a time when boundaries shall divide lands and these shall be sovereign. And no man should dare raise his hand against the lawful king. The destruction of the sovereign king is the destruction of a land."

"And now Edmund is the true King?"

"He will be when he is crowned and has been anointed in God's name."

Then, Emma thought, we shall see him dead of poisoning before this divine blessing is set upon him. They had reached the blacksmith's shed and the fire gave off a warmth and Emma turned to absorb the heat. She was looking directly at the archbishop. There was an intenseness about him; she wondered if he weren't a little mad. He certainly was fanatical about the idea of a sovereign land.

"I don't often place much store in dreams," he said, "but I keep having this recurring dream."

"Dream?"

"Yes. In the dream you are once more Queen of England."

CHAPTER 12

The battle of Assandun, 1016

HE PRETENDED TO LEAD THE SOLDIERS AND GODFREY PRETENDED HE LED the soldiers and the soldiers pretended he led the soldiers, but he knew he did not. All knew the leadership lay with Godfrey. It was like being King at Canterbury when the nobles bowed and listened, but they knew what his mother said was more important than his memorizing oaths. Still, he pretended and rode before them flanked by Goddy to one side and his other bastard uncle, Willie, on the other. William was a count, but usually wore the dress of the more simple soldier. Goddy said it was because Willie had so many debts he couldn't afford better. "You're goddamn right," Willie said. "Lend me some money, Edward boy." "Aye," Edward had told him, but Willie knew Edmund had taken all that should have been his and there was nothing to lend. When he became King, Edward knew he would give money to Willie and all who befriended him.

"If I were King, Uncle Willie," he said.

"But you are not," Godfrey said.

"A seer promised me I will be King."

"And perhaps you will," his uncle, Count of Eu, said, "and when you are, promise to lend me some money, for surely by then my debts shall be astronomical."

They fell silent. The bounding of chain mail had a distinct sound unlike all other. From his one and only previous battle he had learned to hear the difference in the sound of marching Danes and his own troops, mainly Norman in their long hauberks and drape of twisted metal. He had not really knocked Cnute from his horse. Goddy had. But Goddy said, "Let the word put out be that you did it. No one will know but you and I and that dead soldier there . . . and Cnute, of course."

"Why?" Edward had asked.

"It is politic."

He had enjoyed being hero even when he knew it was a lie. "It is important," Godfrey had said, "that they believe it was you." His mother had smiled and his brother Edmund had looked like he was smiling. But Edward did not smile back for Edmund had stolen his throne. He did do as his mother had said and told Edmund he had not been wounded, though he had been in great pain and knew he was going to die. Edmund had a way of glaring into you, not Ethelred's mean eye, but looking at you as if he could see deep inside and Edward knew Edmund could see inside and knew that he had not knocked Cnute from his horse and that he had been wounded in the leg. "And Felim MacBoru, did he mend your wounded leg?" But Edward was not to be tricked, for Edmund did not even ask if he had been wounded, only if Felim had healed him. "I was not wounded," he answered, and as Goddy had told him to say, "these were just soldiers' tales." And even though he knew his half brother was aware these were lies, Edward enjoyed telling this "king" what he did not want to hear, because he hated Edmund Ironside and someday was going to kill him.

Someday, Edward had decided, when he had learned to read as well as Felim, he would learn the secrets of Felim's books and surely there would be in such wondrous books all manners and ways of killing Edmund.

The army moved toward the trees. Where the road went into the dark wood the trees bent toward one another like the doorway of the great church in Rouen. It was dark beneath the trees, cold almost, and still except for the chatter of the mail and an occasional Norman word. He would liked to have stayed in the woods and forgotten the battle. He was not afraid so much, well not terribly afraid, not terrified, as he was disappointed. Battle, at least his first battle, had not been what he had thought it would be. Oh, the color of blood was brilliant, the colors of open flesh so bright, so amazingly bright, but the stench of dying—there was no escaping it. The killing he had imagined would be wondrous as it was in stories, glorious like the tales of Havelok or Beowulf, where death was much like the soaring, floating falcon, who like lightning in a stormy sky dived, hit and swooped its prey in the clear blue air. That was death. Death as he imagined it. Death was Jesus, blood, unsoiled, dripping from the high cross. Death was the scarlet-colored robes of a great bishop. Death was like the leaping stag, spinning, a spear in his sides, through the air. Death was the burial of the great Viking kings floating off to Valhalla in the burning ships. This was death and what war was meant to be. But it had not been. It had been the flesh of men rolling on the earth until you could not tell where the wound ended and the earth began. It was bodies thrown aside and the precious spears retrieved, ripping apart the skin, and bowels torn open revealing chunks of brown matter. It was eyeballs parted from sockets and hair matted with blood and sweat. It was arms separated from bodies and legs thrown, unclaimed, aside. It was dead horses. It was men he had once heard laugh, making only the last agonizing groans. The sound—perhaps the sound most frightening—was the cries of men no longer caring to conceal the pain, shrieking out in death.

He longed to stay within the quiet sanctuary of the woods, but already he could see the brilliant sun at the end of the long aisle of trees.

They came to the hill called Assandun and camp was made. And in the Norman fashion great stoves were set up and caldrons boiled with a thick gruel and meat was roasted for the Norman knights and Saxon thegns. And women came and were chased away but came back. Though the army of Edward was the first, soon the hill was a mass of soldiers who belonged in the armies of bishops, earldormen and mighty thegns, and the army of the King, Edmund, was among the last to appear.

"Brother," the King told him, "when last you met the Dane, was said you knocked him from his mount. This time, 'tis my turn. I shall kill the son of Sven. Take care, brother, too, you be not wounded, I see no Mac-Boru about to tend your open flesh." Edmund rode off before Edward could reply.

Today, perhaps, Edmund might die. If Edward were given the chance, he would do the job himself.

The armies of Cnute were like a flood, a roaring tide, for they made great noise as if to frighten the Saxon and Edward's Norman troops. Edward found horror in the terrible sounds. The Raven banner of the Danes, Woden's bird, flailed before. At the last battle Edward heard the soldiers tell how if the wings and feet and bill of the large black-winged creature did move that the Danes knew victory. The soldiers told how once the victory was so great that the bird rose high in the air free of the banner and circled above the dead bodies of the enemy. The first ranks came together in another sound, a crash of one tide hitting another. Swords cut the air and plunged with thumps into human flesh, and banged against the wood and metal of shields. Danes and Saxons crowded at one another. "It is," Goddy said, "as if they all want to occupy the same yard of earth."

The soldiers of Rouen waited, watching, biding the time the cry should move them toward the battle and the cry went up and the Normans in their pointed helmets stood out like pointed spears and Edward could see at his distance as Normans fell. The bowmen from the flank raised their bows and loosed a stream of pelting sticks as Danish riders came toward the battling soldiers.

"Now," whispered Goddy, loudly.

Edward raised the sword of Edgar and yelled the command and, with it, riders on all sides galloped toward the battle. Horses stumbled, battle axes cut at legs, arms and pounded helmeted heads. Riders fell, and horses atop them. The blood of beasts mingled with the blood of men. Edward's eyes did not focus. Blood spat out upon horses from the torn flesh of riders and then his vision cleared and he looked down into the face of the Dane. It was the face of a young man, not as tall, but looking much like the son of Thorkell. He saw the man standing as if nude in the chapel at Corfe. And their eyes met and before the man could strike, Edward, with all his force, brought the heavy sword of Edgar down across the young man's shoulders. The figure reeled and fell among the bodies upon the earth. A horse trampled over the young Dane and he cried out and Edward rode from the man. Yet, he could still hear his cries.

Edward felt the horse give way and it seemed forever to be falling, sliding to the earth. He landed across a headless man and, as he raised himself up in horror, he was struck behind and fell forward again across the man, dazed. He could no longer hang on to Edgar's sword and it slipped from his hands. He could not get up.

"No," he screamed out. It was a Dane who picked him up. "No," he screamed again.

"Quiet, Edward," the man yelled, holding him in front of him on the mount like a sack of meal. And Edward stopped yelling and rode on the horse with the rider, feeling the pain of the man's heavy hand holding on to him. And they rode away from the shapes and sounds of the battle. Yet Edward, still dazed, could not turn to make out the figure riding with him.

"You will be safe here, boy," the man said and let him slide down off the horse into the tall grasses.

Edward looked up and for a moment his vision cleared and he saw the face. It was Thorkell the Tall. "The sword of Edgar," he told the man, but Thorkell had ridden away.

Then Edward began to shake and he knew it was coming, the fit. He was kneeling on the earth and then the brilliant light came and truly it was God, for no light could be watched so bright unless it was God. Then a voice cried out and he thought it God's, but it was the young Dane's. And when the crying ceased he remembered no more.

"Edward," Goddy was saying. Edward first thought it was God again. Yet the sight of his uncle as he opened his eyes was comforting. The man did not shake or touch him. Goddy seemed to understand his pain. "Are you all right, lad?"

"Yes," he said shamefully. He felt somehow he had done wrong by being here when the battle raged.

"You've survived; that is the most important thing."

"Honor," Edward said.

"Yes, I suppose. Still, does it matter when you are dead? Does God ask, I wonder, Edward, 'Was your death in battle honorable?'"

"I lost the sword. I lost the sword of Edgar. I needs find it."

"No, boy. It belongs to the Dane now."

"The battle is lost?"

"Yes. Eadric began the flight. So many of the others, the great Saxons, are dead. Bishop Eadnoth, the Abbot Wufsize, as are the Earldormen Aefric and Godwillian. Athelweald, son of Athelwise, Eulfcetel of East Anglia. And that is just those I know of."

"And Edmund?"

"He readies for Glouchestershire, beaten."

"Not dead."

"I'm afraid not."

"I had wished it."

"No matter, after this day I would say there be very little of the kingdom left to claim."

"It is Edmund's fault."

"Nay, not really," Goddy said. "It was Ethelred's."

CHAPTER 13

Corfe, 1016

She stood in the clearing near the point. The sea was calm and the waves hitting against the rocks below seemed idle, lazy. Flotsam sifted about, having no destination. Sails of two ships, too distant to be recognized, crossed along the horizon. She watched the ships, but her mind was on Edmund. She had meant to kill him. Whether it would have made any difference didn't seem to matter. The point was she had intended to kill him and had not. She was angry with herself, with her failure.

She saw the animal. She had first thought it a dog. It stood in the clearing not far from her. It was not a dog, but a gray wolf. It seemed neither ferocious nor intimidated by her. It was fully aware of her; in fact she sensed it was fascinated somehow by her presence. Perhaps it was not alone. Her hand checked the handle at her waist. Hidden beneath the bliaut, the sharp weapon was habitually a part of her dress; she often forgot it was there.

Not killing Edmund was weakness. Weakness destroyed. The power of any family would dissolve in weakness. Survival depended on power. The Capets were weak. They were melting away. King Robert listened too much to Bertha. He thought too much and acted not enough. That was weakness. She came of better stock. There was a tale her father told of their great Viking ancestor Rolf. It brought a smile as she remembered her father's telling of it. Rolf, rough warrior that he was, was told to pay homage to the French King by kissing his foot. Rolf kissed Charles the Simple's foot all right. He turned the monarch upside down to do it.

The wolf stood his ground.

She visualized Edmund cold dead, white, bloodless and corrupting. There was finality in it. But there was weakness thinking about the finality. The irrevocability of it could cause uneasiness. There had been a dead whore. Here in the yard at Corfe, she had seen a dead whore with a knife stuck in her, but Emma couldn't remember when. Yes, that was weakness, thinking about a lifeless dead whore, as if it mattered.

She saw the wolf leap into the air before she heard him. It was a cry of death. It fell, the spear in its side standing straight up above the tall grass. Edward came out from the trees.

"Why did you do that?"

"He was going to kill you," he said.

"He was not."

"Perhaps he was." Edward went over to the wolf and pulled the spear from the carcass. Blood oozed from the wound and Edward reached down and put his hand to the blood.

"Stop that," she ordered.

"The blood of a wolf protects the hand against sin." He did not look up at her.

"Where did you hear such nonsense?"

"Against the sins of the flesh." He held his blooded hand out to her. "Here."

She pulled back from him. His hand was so pale, so white in contrast to the fresh blood.

He stood up. He seemed to have grown so during the past months. He would soon be taller than she was. But he had no flesh on him and was but bones with pigmentless covering.

"I want to be King," he said.

"Wanting and getting are a long way apart."

"You said I would be King." He raised the hand dripping with blood and shook it. She sensed a threat in the move.

"You'll have to find a way to get it from the Dane first," she said, trying to ignore his actions.

"A seer said I would be King."

"Did he also tell you Edmund would lose that same kingdom at Assandun?"

"It was but a battle. I was there. I know."

"Then you should know it was decisive."

"I will be King."

"Of what?"

He had no answer. He fell to his knees again and examined, without touching, the dead animal. "Why do dead things turn cold?"

She paid no attention to his question.

He now seemed disinterested in the subject of being King and was more concerned with the wolf. He raised the beast's head from the grass and scrutinized its face as if searching for something.

She turned and left the boy and the dead wolf. Edmund must be killed. Powerless or otherwise, he should be gotten out of the way. She walked alongside the cliff. The sea. If like the birds she could but fly. What it must be like to be a bird. The sun had fastened itself behind a cloud. Without the glare of brightness it was easy to look up at the birds drifting as if leaving messages and passing on. There seemed to be a fog growing in the distance. She looked back at Edward. He was an irritating, ugly child, but she would make him King, nonetheless, and she would rule him. The boy stood there immobile. It was getting cold; she turned her back to the sea and walked in the direction of the buildings.

Aesval was coming toward her. The heavy woman held a cloak out to her, but Emma indicated with a slight toss of the head that she didn't need it.

"Put it on," the woman ordered.

"You wait on me more now than when you were a slave," Emma said, letting Aesval wrap the garment about her, "but you are becoming a nag."

"Someone has to look out for you."

"And what of MacBoru, who looks out for him?"

"His books. Why ask me?"

"Aren't you happy?" Emma asked.

"What is happy? I have no hurt and I don't expect much more than that."

Emma mused on what she said. "Perhaps that's my trouble. I expect too much."

"You are the Queen," Aesval said, stepping around dried animal dung in her path.

"Not really. No longer. And I think I miss it."

"You will be Queen again," Aesval said, as if wishing made it true.

"No," Emma said. "But the mother of a king—"

"To be the mother of a king." Aesval made it sound a glorious accomplishment. "Mother of a king."

The sun came out for a moment and then disappeared again.

"Aesval, you must tell Felim to be careful. Edmund has spies everywhere. No doubt he has them here at Corfe—"

"Oh, no, my Lady. I know all at Corfe."

"Perhaps, but tell him still to be careful. It would be wise instead of sleeping in your own chambers that you moved about. The King's bed be empty and there is always room where the children are. It is like Edmund's men to steal in during the night and take him back to Winchester."

"Why?"

"To try him for witchery."

"The books. It is always the books," she said. "It's unnatural and it'll be the death of Felim yet."

They neared the yard and the noise from the compound drifted out.

"Have you never wanted to be a mother, Aesval?"

"Yes, but I am barren, as you see. Felim says it is just as well."

"That is foolish. Sometimes I think those books make Felim a little strange in the head. His skull is getting soft."

"Aye, Lady, you be right. Mind the puddle."

Emma stepped around it. "Did you never want children, Aesval?"

"I found a baby once." Aesval whispered it.

"Found?"

"When I was still a maid. It was at the forest's edge. The babe had an enormous head and where one arm should've been it had but a small fingerlike thing. I took it home, but my mother told me it was a demon's child and to take it back at once."

"She was probably right."

"Aye, but it was hard to leave that poor babe alone in the forest, strange as it was. Poor little thing. It was a boy babe. Head like a dwarf. The cord was still hanging from it. But I left it and when I went back the next morn it was gone."

"The demons," Emma said, "probably came and took it away."

"Or the wolves."

They had reached the chapel. Emma could not look at the door without remembering. Where was Thorkell's son now? He was said with Cnute. What woman was he arousing with the stubble fingers? Emma shivered. She heard the riders coming and looked up as the men on horses came swiftly up the hill. The stance of the lead rider she recognized. No one sat a horse as Godfrey did, holding the reins high in one hand.

He leaped down. Even from a distance she could see the scowl on his face. The chain mail rattled softly as he came toward her in his hauberk.

"Have you come to wage war upon me?" Emma attempted to draw a smile. She was happy to see him.

"I come from Alney." He did not smile.

"And?"

"At Alney, Eadric brought Edmund and Cnute to table."

"With what treachery in mind?" The pitch of her voice rose not just with interest but in apprehension. "What does the traitor of Mercia meddle in now?"

"Peace, as he would call it. Cnute and Edmund have exchanged hostages and have agreed."

"Agreed to what?"

"This news will anger you, sister. They have agreed to a divided kingdom."

"NO!"

"To cease their war and divide England."

"No," she repeated. "No."

"London and the north to Cnute. Wessex and the south to Edmund."

"It is mine. Edward's."

"It is done, Emma."

"It is not done. It will never be done."

"They no longer have each other to contend with. Now they can join if you war against either."

"Edmund gives away that which rightfully is not his."

"By force it is, Lady."

"By hell it isn't."

"It is gone nonetheless."

"Why in God's name . . . ?"

"As he says, he came from Alney with more than he went with."

"The coward, the miserable bastardly coward. Even Ethelred . . ."

"Perhaps he is right, after Assandun."

"I should've killed him."

"Care, thy tongue, sister," he whispered. "God but knows who listens."

"Nonetheless"—but she spoke softly—"I should have. Come to my chamber, where we may talk."

He followed her across the yard and up the steps to the second floor of the wattle and mud building. It was dark and musty in the room.

She opened the window boards. "The fog is coming in."

"Will you return to Rouen?" Godfrey asked her.

"I will yet kill Edmund."

"To what purpose?"

"Damn. Blood and nails. I should not have waited."

"What good—"

"I will have England. I have been a fool, Goddy. With Edmund dead, the Witan will bow to Edward."

"And Edmund's athelings . . . what of them?"

"Children, babes. Besides, twins. There is deviltry there. The Witan will choose Edward. Wulfstan practically admits Edward is the true King."

"And Cnute . . . will he just vanish? Will he be so frightened when you have Edmund buried in the earth that he will run? Emma, be realistic. It is done. Over."

"No. Brother Duke will take care of the Dane."

"If what Richard has offered so far is the support you can expect, then I can assure you it is not going to be enough to rid England of Cnute."

"Richard will aid us in this. He wants a Norman England."

"And the Witan? They are as unpredictable as a storm at sea, and if they even have the least suspicion that you had Edmund killed, they will never accept Edward as King."

"No one shall dare suspect. I have been taught poisons by a woman of Brittany. She has potions which leave no trace and can be given such that I shall be far from Edmund when this event occurs."

"Then all you have to worry about is the woman in Brittany revealing your mastery of the art."

"She is dead."

"Of poisoning no doubt."

Godgifu came into the room.

"What have you got?" Emma yelled.

She carried the wolf's head. Blood still dripped from it.

"Get that out of here."

"Edward gave it to me," Godgifu said.

"Take it out!"

The girl went to the window and tossed the head out.

"Sometimes I think you are as mad as your brother," Emma told her. "Why did you throw it out the window?"

"I threw it out the window," the girl said.

"I know you threw it out the window. What I asked was why?"

"To see it go smush."

"You're a horrible child."

"I'm going down and see it," the girl said and ran out.

"She's a strange child, Emma." Godfrey was watching the girl as she ran out.

"So is the boy. After all, he gave her the head."

"You would have him King."

"I can control him," Emma said with assurance.

"And when he is grown?"

"I will still control him."

"Well, first you have to get him there."

"Are you with me in this?"

"Of course. And you can depend on Willie as well, I'm sure."

"Then get me to Rouen and back quickly," she said. "I need to see Richard and Robert. We will leave quietly. Edmund shan't know I have even left."

"He'll know. Take Edward from this land and he will know."

"We won't take Edward."

"That's dangerous, Emma. What if Edmund hears you are gone and comes down upon Edward?"

"MacBoru will be here. And no one need realize we've gone. I'll let it be known I am ill. Aesval can look as if she attends upon me. Food can be brought to my chamber. My clothes can be aired."

"I don't know, Emma. I would feel better knowing the boy was safe."

"If we all leave, then Edmund will learn of this departure and he will suspect something amiss. We can take Alfred. I'll work things out here so no one knows and you arrange for the ship at a time before sunrise."

"I'll do as you ask, but I have an uneasy feeling about this business."

CHAPTER 14

Corfe, 1016

EDWARD KNEW HE WAS TWO PEOPLE. IT WAS THE OTHER EDWARD, THE ONE inside, who had the fits; it was he who could stand for hours without moving as much as a finger; it was he who had killed the gray wolf; and it was he who now got out of bed in the dead of night and went from the chamber searching for the boy who had fallen through the roof the day the swineherd was blinded. "He lives with the animals," the blind swineherd had told him. Edward saw the boy once with a wolf; his body was twisted and the bones at his hip stuck out as he ran on both his legs and arms. Edward called to him, but in spastic thrusts he vanished with the wolf into the black of trees. "At night," the swineherd said. "He comes out at night and sometimes breaks into the larder and steals food."

The night was black, yet day was not that far away. Edward sat uncomfortably, leaning against the rough wall of the house where the food was stored. Even through the walls Edward could capture the tangy smell of dried meat and fish and the scent of herbs and grain and pungent curds. The boy didn't come. It was cold and he wished he had stayed in bed, but the other Edward wouldn't let him leave, so he sat and finally dozed.

It was more than just noise that awakened him. Perhaps it was the furtiveness of the sounds. The commotion was not ordinary: whispers too loud, attempts at quiet which failed. Day was coming. He stood up and slipped back around the corner as he saw the riders. Even through the dark early morning remnants of fog, the auras of light about them were clearly visible. There were four riders. Another horse, the white mare which his mother often rode, was being led. But she was not there, only the horse, who stamped, swung its tail and moved about as if impatient in the waiting. He shivered. One of the riders was his Uncle Godfrey, who spoke down to Felim MacBoru, who had come out. Goddy was whispering loudly and Edward caught the words: "danger," "Rouen," "ship," "care" and his own name, but Edward could not hear it all. Aesval came out carrying his brother, Alfred. He was bundled and she handed him up to Godfrey. His mother appeared and was helped onto the white mare. Felim handed a parcel to her. The horses turned and began the trek down the hill along the path that went through the hamlet and then to the sea. Aesval and Felim walked beside the riders. The soft gray morning began giving shape to the day.

Edward knew from the scattered words that his mother was off to Rouen. Why hadn't they told him? As the riders vanished down the hill, Edward slipped across to his mother's chamber and went up the steps. It was warm inside and smelled of his mother. He went to the cupboard. The relics were there. It was a certain sign; she would not be gone long. He picked up St. Irene's needle, looked at it and then carefully put it back. He closed the cupboard and went back down the steps. A few slaves were lugging caldrons already in preparation for the morning meal. The blind swineherd was slopping hogs. He wondered how the man knew where the trough was. He spilled nothing.

"It is the Atheling," the blind man said. The aura of light about the swineherd seemed more brilliant than about others.

"Yes," he told the man. "I waited for the boy who fell through the roof, but he never came to the larder."

"He is asleep in the empty stall where the Queen's horse is not to be found."

"How do you know the Queen's horse is gone?"

"Since the day your father had these eyes poked out, nothing moves in or out of this yard of which I am blind."

"And you think the Queen gone."

"To Rouen and you know it as well, Atheling, for you stood at the corner of the larder."

"Why has she gone?" Edward asked him.

"To see the Duke of Normandy."

"But why?"

"If I knew it would probably make no sense, for who, but kings and queens and dukes, understands the way of kings and queens and dukes?"

"How so?"

"The fate of Corfe may well be the fate of this old man. Whether I eat or starve depends on the rain and sun and the lord who stalls his horse here. But what is said at Rouen makes no change in my hours of day.

Wars come and go, and aye, there is a king and the next day there is another or perhaps another and still the hogs must be swilled and eggs stolen from nests and gruels boiled. And it makes no difference to the swine or birds or corn or men of such little consequence as I."

"And when I am King?"

"I will still stand here in the stench of pigs."

Edward began stirring a circle in the dirt with his foot. "Why are you born a swineherd and I an atheling?"

"It is the way of life. We cannot change what is."

"Never?"

"Only in death. There was a priest who stood beside and had his eyes poked from his head."

"I remember," Edward said. "He did not cry out."

"He thought he could change the way things were."

"Is he dead?"

"No. In despair. He does not speak and he does not come out to feel the warmth of the sun. He cannot see, but sulks behind some vats of mead your father, the King, has hidden beneath the chapel croft."

"I have never seen him." Edward spoke as if the swineherd had made up the tale.

"Nor do others. Only an old whore who takes him bread and gruel and sour beer, leftovers taken from the table in the great hall."

"I should like to go see him."

"No," the man ordered. "Leave him in his miserable peace."

"I think it's a tale," Edward said and looked in the direction of the chapel.

"Think as you wish," the blind man said, pouring another bucket of slop into the trough.

Edward ran off. It was the other Edward who was in command and they went in search of the boy who had fallen through the roof. The Edward inside was certain he could make the body of the boy straight and him well again, just as Felim could do. Edward approached the stall stealthfully. The blind swineherd was right: the twisted body was curled in a corner on some straw. Edward moved ever so quietly and as he neared he began turning his hands about to form a ball of his aura, but nothing happened. He attempted to pull the aura from the crippled boy; nothing changed. He strained and tried harder. It was futile. He attempted again and, as he leaned down over the boy, the boy stirred, looked up at Edward with eyes of a trapped animal. He shrank farther in the corner and leaped past Edward and began running on his arms and legs, crying out much like a wolf. Edward fell as the boy leaped by, but he got to his feet quickly and tried to catch the boy, who moved clumsily but swiftly away in the direction of the point.

Edward ran after him, and as he looked back he saw Felim and Aesval walking from the hamlet.

"Edward," Felim called, but Edward pretended not to hear and continued to pursue the boy who had fallen through the roof, but as they neared the point the boy vanished in the dark trees. Edward walked to the cliff edge and sat in the long, dead grass. He watched the sea and the square sail of the ship bearing his mother from Corfe. He sat, his knees pulled under his chin, looking out to sea, perhaps an hour, perhaps longer, and the sail vanished on the horizon. There was no sign of the boy and Edward walked back to the compound.

Aesval's heavy frame appeared at the door of the chamber house where the red bird nested on the roof. "Edward!" Her voice was barely audible above the squeal of the hogs. "Quick, boy. It is Godgifu."

He ran to her. "What is wrong?"

"She is ill and—"

"Felim?" he interrupted.

"I have sent for him. He went into the hamlet. There was an old man fell into a well." The woman paused, but he could tell she was searching for what to say. "Your mother . . ." She stopped and then rushed the other words out. "The Queen is ill, herself, and cannot leave her chamber."

He wondered yet why he could not be told that his mother had gone to Rouen, but it was clear he was not to know.

Godgifu lay upon the straw. Sweat beaded on her forehead and he took her hand. He had come to sense, no longer pain but a pleasantness in her touch as she would cling to his fingers; now, though, her hand seemed on fire and he put his lips to her forehead and that, too, was burning.

"Edward," she whispered.

"Where does it hurt?"

"My belly," she said. "My belly." Tears seeped from her eyes and then she cried out in pain. It was a frightful sound and he thought of the priest who had stood silent.

He clutched her hand more tightly. "Felim"—he spoke almost in a whisper—"will be here soon. Felim will make the pain go away."

"Aye," Aesval said. Her face had a worried look as if she were not certain. "Felim will make you well."

Godgifu cried out again as Felim came into the dark room. Edward saw the worry disappear from Aesval's face. The man bent over her and his big hand took the child's. "Hush, now, wee thing," he said. "It will be gone soon."

"Her belly," Aesval said. "She hurts in the belly."

Felim began to pull the light from around his body into his hands. Edward watched him. "Will you show me, Felim?" he asked. "Will you show me?"

"Now?"

"Yes."

"Aesval," the man ordered, "go outside and keep watch. If anyone comes, stave them off or warn us."

She waddled out without answering and closed the door behind her.

"It is time you were taught."

Godgifu cried out again. Then, still for a moment, she looked up in fear before she burst loose with a piercing fearful cry.

"You must forget Godgifu and her pain," Felim told him. "First, Edward, make your body relax. Close your eyes. Say to yourself, slowly, 'Relax.' Start with your feet. Make your feet relax and your legs and then your torso and your chest and your arms and hands and neck and head. Breathe deeply, slowly, and begin to think of being eased in a bucket into a well and count backwards from ten. Ten-nine-eight . . . keep counting and when you reach one start again with ten and go deeper and deeper into the well and when you near the bottom think of your hands, think about nothing but your hands and draw your light into the hands."

Godgifu cried out again.

"Do not hear it," Felim said. "Pull the light into your hands and then turn it and turn it until it becomes a glowing ball that you can see with your eyes closed. You have seen me do this. Open your eyes after you see the glowing ball and go to the child and place the ball near her belly and pull the illness away, into the ball in your hands. You shall see when you have drawn it away, for there will be a black evil spot in the light, and then take the ball and shake away the black blotch, off into the corner, and when it is gone open your hands and let the light go. Let it return to your body. You will feel weak for a moment. It is natural. Just lie on the floor or sit. Your strength will return."

Again, Godgifu wailed.

"Remember. You must not think of Godgifu. Concentrate. Don't let anything upset your concentration or you will not be able to do this thing. Do not hear her cries; do not acknowledge her pain. Think only of relaxing and the trip down into the dark well."

"That is all I must do?"

"It is all. But think of nothing but what I have told you."

Edward relaxed. He heard Godgifu yell. And then he forced himself not to listen and he concentrated on his body. He felt the tension in his feet and then his legs leave as he ordered his body to relax. He felt peaceful and somewhat limp as he made his shoulders and neck rest.

And then Godgifu yelled out and he heard her and it all vanished and he looked across at Felim.

"You must not hear her. You must not think of Godgifu, Edward."

Edward began again, letting the tension slip away and the limpness return. He breathed slowly as Felim had told him to do. He became no longer aware of the man, nor the child in the room. His mind could not find the well and instead it conjured the sea and his descent on a white rope from End's Point into the dark water. It seemed as though night and a deep blackness. And he counted, ten-nine-eight . . . deeper and deeper he dropped toward the sea. He felt asleep and awake at the same time and there seemed a soothing slap of the waves below him. He reached the bottom and the rocks. It was not hard like rock, but soft, and it was as if he did not control his body but another Edward living deep inside him was in command and he recognized the other Edward. Though his eyes were closed, and he could not see, he could feel as the light was drawn to his hands at the command of the boy inside. He could feel the warmth, the power, the strength that pulled between his hands like giants in a tug of war. He rolled the power into the form of a ball and with his eyes tightly closed could see the glow. He opened his eyes as if he had no control to do otherwise and he was aware of Godgifu's body, the light dim about it, withering to a haze, and he knew Godgifu was going to die.

She was going to die!

With that awareness he could feel himself return to consciousness and the ball of light in his hands begin to slip back toward his body. He tightened his eyes closed and fought consciousness with his fists clinched so tight they hurt. She was going to die. No, he must not think of her. The sea . . . the calm soft sea . . . he slipped down the rope at End's Point . . . and once more felt the warmth of the light forming in his hands. He opened his eyes and began again to form the ball of light. He heard no sound and saw nothing but the aura of light belonging to the child. He moved toward it and brought the ball of brightness in his hands over the belly of the girl. It was with difficulty at first that he pulled. Like a cartwheel not giving way in the mud, he struggled to bring the aura of light about her to the center where he held his own. He grasped tightly and with short moves tugged and then released, tugged and released, but nothing happened. He refused to give up, and again and again and again he persisted, pulling until his arms ached and his shoulders tired, but despite the pain he persisted, pulling and pulling . . . and then slowly, ever so slowly the dim ray of light about her moved toward his own and soon the child was in darkness except for the bright center of light near her waist. He then began drawing back as if pulling something from her and he was aware of the ebony spot, an evil thing, that had neither shape nor form but a grotesque fearful quality about it. He could see the black and ugly thing darkening the edges of his own light. He yanked hard with the little strength he had left and pulled it free of her. Turning from the child, he shook in quick jerks. The ball of light and the black blotching edges drifted free, leaving brilliance of light in his hands. He raised his arms and swung his hands apart and the light fell back around his body and he felt weak and unable to stand. Consciousness began to return to him and he saw the bright light about Godgifu as he collapsed upon the floor. For a moment he stayed there, and then, feeling his strength return, turned and looked up at Felim.

"Are you all right, Edward?"

"Godgifu? How is Godgifu?"

"Well."

"I did it? I really did do this thing?"

"Yes."

Edward lay there listening to his own breath. "There is someone lives inside me," he said.

"Yes. There is someone."

"Is it a demon?"

"It is yourself, Edward. Somewhere within that shell of your body there is the Edward who tells you what to do."

"It is he who killed the wolf," Edward told him.

"The wolf?"

But Edward did not have a chance to explain. Godgifu called out to him. He got up with difficulty, his legs hardly able to hold him, and went over to her.

"I can sit up," she said and did. "I am all well. Edward, you made me all well." She started to get off the bed.

Felim came over. "You lie in bed a bit." His voice was quiet and deep. "Then you can get up." He turned to Edward. "You can use this new gift you have to keep from the fits as well."

"I don't want to."

"That is stupid, Edward."

"It's the time when I see God. I should not see God if I stopped having fits."

"Edward, I have known others who have had the fits and after a while it begins to destroy their minds."

"Why is that?"

"I do not know, but I have seen men who have gone mad after years of having these fits." He went and opened the door. "It is done. You can come back in."

"And Godgifu?" Aesval asked.

"The sickness is gone."

"Edward?"

"Yes."

"I did it, Aesval," Edward said.

"You should tell no one, Edward. It is dangerous." Aesval had a stern look on her face. "Admit to nothing and never brag on this."

"Aesval is right," Felim said.

Edward was sorely disappointed. It seemed silly being able to do these wondrous deeds if no one knew. How could you become a saint if men, particularly men of the Church, did not know how saintly you were?

Later in the day, when the fog was eaten away by the sun, Edward lay in the deep grass and the sun felt warm against the back of his neck and upon his bare arms. The air was cold and winter would come as quick as the bird who appeared overhead, but for now it seemed almost summer in the midday and as if winter were far off. He could smell the corpse of the dead wolf. It was the other Edward, the one inside, who had severed the head from the dead animal. He knew it was him for otherwise he didn't know why he had done it, so it had to be the other Edward, someone else. The Edward inside was a marvelous Edward capable of wonders, like curing Godgifu, but sometimes he did things Edward did not understand. He realized it was "the other" who stood for hours in the dark of night; it was he who spent three days in a cupboard. He raised his head up. The sea was flat and calm as a bowl of wine. Birds drifted and pecked their way along the rocky land below. The waves slapped without excitement upon the shore and slipped back to sea. He felt sleepy and dozed.

It was the shadow over him breaking the warmth of the sun that startled him into awareness. He turned over and looked up into Felim Mac-Boru's face.

"The healing tires," Felim said.

"Aye. Did I do well?"

"Fine, boy. You did just fine. Godgifu is up and about. God knows tormenting who."

"What was wrong with her? The illness?"

"There's no name for it. There comes a great pain in the side and back and then the belly and it gets worse and worse. Sometimes herbs relieve the pain, but usually it is the same . . . death."

"Godgifu would've died?"

"Most likely. I've seen them, young or old, always it seemed the same."

"And is there no potion?"

"I've read what sounds to be the same illness in books of Coptic writings where ancient Egyptians cut open the belly and removed a great inflammation. But the art is lost and no man is skilled to such. Still, we, you and I, have found a better way. Today, lad, you've become a healer."

"But I can tell no one," he said, indicating his disappointment.

"No one. When you do heal, avoid letting others see. What cannot be witnessed can more easily be denied. But come, I forgot my purpose in finding you. There are ships on the horizon. You cannot see them from here, but walk a few feet and look beyond the edge of trees and you will see what seems ships in the distance. Who knows whether friend or enemy? But it will be better if we are all together just in case they are not friendly."

"Perhaps it is only my mother turned back."

"The Queen is said to be ill in her chamber."

"The Queen sailed at first light this morning and you were there, Felim MacBoru."

The man grinned. "How know you this?"

"I saw. My brother, Alfred, went with her and Godfrey and three others. Why did she leave me behind, Felim?"

"Appearances. She figured she alone, with only the boy, would not be missed these few days she will be away, but if you were all gone, spies would certainly report such to Edmund and Cnute."

"Then why not tell me so?"

"Why not indeed? She perhaps forgets sometimes you are growing up."

"I've led an army to battle."

"The Queen hopes to bring you a greater army. An army strong enough to war against Cnute."

"My sword is gone. How will I lead an army? I've lost the sword of Edgar. Cnute has it now."

"You will simply have to win it back."

"Yes," he said. "The ships. I can see them now. There are too many. It is not my mother and Godfrey turned back."

"And perhaps not friendly either. Come, let's go back to the compound."

Felim turned and started moving away from the sea. Edward stood for a while and then ran to catch his tutor.

"Do you know, Felim, there is a blind priest who hides in the cellar of the chapel croft and will not speak?"

"Who told you this?"

"The swineherd. My father had their eyes poked out and some other men's as well for they looked upon the Queen and so did I, but then Uncle Robert, the archbishop, said it was only a vision and not my mother at all, though I suspect the other Edward—"

"The other Edward?"

"The one inside me. He believes differently; he thinks the Queen was really there. Anyway, the others screamed out when the hot poker was put to their eyes, but the priest did nothing. He didn't make a sound."

"And he is said below the croft?"

"Aye. An old whore brings him table scraps to eat."

Felim increased the length of his strides.

Edward hurried to keep up.

CHAPTER 15

Corfe, 1016

EDWARD DECIDED NOT TO SLEEP, AND WITH DAWN BUT A FEW HOURS TO come, he had stood the night at one end of his chamber fully dressed. It was not he, of course, but the other Edward, the one inside, who had not moved but seemed anchored to the same spot on the floor, lost in deep concentration. Edward had first believed he stood for hours in some penance done to attain sainthood, but the other Edward knew it was not so. The other Edward knew it was to concentrate, to dwell upon one thought. To think of nothing but one thought for hours and hours. The other Edward believed that by thinking about something long enough it could be made to happen. It had happened with the Danes walking into the Thames. The other Edward had made that happen, Edward was certain of it. He was there and he saw it happen and the other Edward had said it was going to happen. He wanted to be King and the other Edward would bring it about. The other Edward was capable of doing marvelous, wondrous things, of not being bound by time, of healing and perhaps even seeing God without having a fit. However, so far, he had achieved little success in seeing God. Yet, it didn't matter, for when the other Edward took over, he could escape. He could free himself of his own body and be apart from the pain, and also, what at times was unendurable, his own ugliness. He was able to isolate himself. Yet, he had become aware, except for his two selves, that he was alone in the world. Perhaps he was the only creature in God's creation and all the rest were imaginary, like the paintings in the chapel. He could not be certain he was not alone. Still, the pain they bore him made him real enough. Ethelred had been mean enough and real enough. But, even if they all existed, he was alone in another sense, not simply because as Felim said he was different, but because no one seemed ever to consider him. Godgifu could sometimes reach him, but it was a slender thread which linked them, and it was the child's own aloneness, Edward saw, which drew them together.

It was the silence of the deep night, or his concentration, one or the other or perhaps both, which honed to an acute awareness that something was wrong. The other Edward had only one thought, being King, and yet Edward himself had become aware of the reality of Corfe and knew something was not the same. It was not what he heard, but what he didn't hear. The owl was silent, the night sounds of animals stilled. Not even a dog barked. The other Edward vanished. The ships earlier? It was the Danes; they had come.

He was free of the other Edward. Without creaking a board, he moved the length of the room, picked up his cloak and with patient stealth soundlessly unlatched the door and slid out. There was no moon and a fog heightened the blackness. Edward pressed his body against the wall of dried dung and earth and slipped along the building. At the corner he peered into blackness and ran to the next structure. He pushed his body against the wall and edged to the door. Again he managed a door latch without a sound.

"Godgifu," he whispered, squatting to the floor alongside her bed. "Godgifu."

She stirred and started to speak. He slapped his hand over her mouth and then moved it to make a finger across her lips. She understood with a single slow nod of her head, which he could see in the glow about her. He wrapped the skin around her, and together, she as silent as he, slipped from the chamber into the cold and darkness and its eerie silence. They stayed against the building, hands joining. With as much speed as he was able, still without making a sound, he took sideways steps, his back pressed against the rough texture of the structure. She followed with shorter steps. Inch by inch they moved toward the corner of the building. He froze. A light. Suddenly someone else's aura was behind them at the corner. A hand came over his mouth and with it fear filled his chest, but it was momentary. The familiar smell of pig dung told him the hand belonged to the blind swineherd.

The man must have felt the tension pass for he removed his hand and with it took Edward's and led him and Godgifu from the building. He moved quickly. It was as if he alone could see in the night's blackness. They stopped and Edward felt the grille frame beneath his feet. He tensed. He knew where they had been brought.

"It is the only answer," the blind man whispered.

For a moment Edward hesitated. But the man was right. It was the only answer. He started down the ladder and helped Godgifu, above him, the long distance into the musty coldness. One of the rungs was loosely tied and he nearly slipped. At the bottom he stepped upon the soft mushy earth. The ladder was raised; he barely saw it go up. Dawn was coming. There was a trace of early morning lightness. He pulled his sister back from the opening and they huddled deep in a wet corner of the pit. He had not heard and could not see well enough yet, but assumed the blind swineherd had replaced the grid covering the pit.

A stench of putrid water pervaded. Godgifu started to speak but he hushed her and wrapped the skin more tightly about her and pulled her beneath his cloak as well. He waited for the sounds, the fearful expectant sounds and the wait seemed long. But it finally came; the first shriek pierced the near-day. Followed by another. Another. Another. Horses, the heavy clump of horses on the earth above.

A blast of light. A painful orange light illuminated the cross pattern of the grid over the opening and he wanted to cry. The awful smell of burning, the deathly smell of fire seemed the more fearful trapped in the pit, not knowing what was being devoured. The fire was intense, for the flames began to roar, like some bestial creature. Men yelled out. Banging. Cries. Moans. Metal against metal, against flesh. Animals' groans. Shouts, cursing. Anger, pain, death became a cacophony until barely one sound was distinguishable from the rest.

Godgifu tried to speak again, but he put his hand over her mouth. Moments later he felt the wetness soaking his leg binding as she had peed on herself.

And the natural light of day came, diminishing the color of fire, and with it the sounds of soldiers, laughing, cursing, ordering, quarreling. At first he did not sense the strange familiarity in the noise, but gradually the awareness that these were no Daneland tongues wore upon him. These were not the fearful Viking raiders readying to leave; these were Wessexmen arguing over loot, banding together those being taken in slavery, herding the animals together. There were cries of women. And then heard was the voice near above him and he knew for certain these were not Cnute's men. Godgifu shuddered in her wet cloak.

"There is nowhere left to look," the voice above said.

"He lied to us. There is no other answer." Edward knew the speaker had a cockeye and a piece of his ear missing. "That son of an ogre has lied to us." It was Heljer, Edmund's man.

"But the woman," the other said. His voice was unfamiliar to Edward. "She agreed with everything he said. She swore the Queen was ill and in her chamber and the Atheling was seen in the yard late of the afternoon."

"Never trust a priest, nor a whore."

"Do we take them as slaves?"

"No," Heljer said. "Of what use is a blind priest or a worn-out whore? Kill them both."

"The King . . ." the other spoke.

"Yes, King Edmund must be told. Still, we did take care of the sorcerer."

Felim? Were they talking of Felim? What had happened to him? And Aesval?

"Where is the Queen, if not here?"

"Fled to Normandy, no doubt." Heljer began moving away and it was getting more difficult for Edward to hear what they said.

"But we saw no ships."

"Then think up your own answer, they're not here and if they're not here, then they're someplace else."

The men had moved too distant from the opening and Edward heard only their sound and soon not their voices at all.

Felim and Aesval? Slaves. They would be made slaves to Edmund or worst to Heljer. No matter, Felim would know how to get free. Perhaps, Felim had already found an escape. Yes, he was certain of it. They would not catch Felim, and if they did would not keep him long.

The riders and wagons and the captured moved amid clamor, yelling and swearing. The smell of smoke hung above the grate. The sounds began to move off away from Corfe and, Edward assumed, toward the hamlet and the sea. The noise diminished to almost inaudibility, broken only by the blast of a conch or a faint yell. And then a stillness fell, a silence punctuated by the caw of birds and once a human moan. Light came through the grate, a warm inviting light, but they huddled back in the cold shadows.

Godgifu started to speak. "Not yet," he whispered. He did not wish to frighten her, but wondered how they were to get out of the pit. The sides went up at least five- or sixfold his height and were smooth and dug so as not to be scaled. And even if he were able to reach the top, who was there to lift the heavy grillwork away? Had the hamlet been spared? Was the blind swineherd still alive? It would be days before his mother returned and though he knew he could survive, letting the other Edward take command, the child with him could not.

"I am cold," Godgifu said and Edward pulled her closer to him.

They waited.

Edward told Godgifu stories that Felim had read him from the books. Stories of far-off lands of wondrous magic.

They waited.

It had to be midafternoon when the first flakes of snow drifted down into the grid. Edward collected them in his hands and let Godgifu lick the moisture from his fingers.

They waited and darkness fell and the snow came heavier.

CHAPTER 16

On the sea to Corfe, 1016

GREAT WAVES LIFTED THE SHIP, BATTERING ITS HULL AND SETTING IT DOWN into the sea, only to pick it up again, and cold wind billowed the sail as the vessel moved with great speed across the winter channel. Emma stood in the bow devouring breaths of cold air which burned in her chest. Her brothers had tried to discourage her from sailing. "Wait until it clears." "I must get back to Corfe and my children," she had said, but what she had meant was that she had to get back to England and find a way to kill Edmund.

While her sister-in-law Judith scowled, her brothers Richard and Robert promised her armies. She was to see to Edmund's death and they would give her the forces to raise against Cnute in Edward's name. "It won't be easy to defeat the Dane," Robert had said. "Men are loyal to him." But Edward's army had defeated Cnute in one battle and it could be done again she was certain. "Women should tend their children," Judith said and pulled her two boys into her arms, "and not worry about war." But Judith's children were little more likable than Emma's. The younger, Robert, was a beastly little brat with a vicious streak which his father only laughed at, and the older of the two, the heir, Richard, was a timorous creature afraid even of himself, Emma suspected.

The sky was a rage of dirty gray clouds and the sea reflected its anger. Water splashed upon her face and it was cold, but she felt alive. She was always alive on the sea and from the time she had been a small girl she had sailed with her father, even as he went to war. He would take her on the great Viking ship with the black- and gold- and red-striped sail and she would stand in the bow as they moved north into the cold sea or south beyond the great rock at Gibraltar. "If you were a boy," he told her, "I would build you a great fleet and you could conquer the world." "Build it for me and I will," she told him. He laughed, but she had been serious. He had stories of the great conquerors, of Alexander, of her great-grandfather Rolf, of the Romans and Charlemagne. To rule the world? How many ships would it take? "Emma the Conqueror!" the duke called her. But her mother frowned. "You should not put such thoughts in the child's head. War is the way of men. Women must be pure and holy." Her mother was said to be pure and holy. "Lady H" she was always addressed and she was tall and "stately" they said of her and had yellow hair which hung to her knees and which ladies brushed four times a day. She was known for her great reverence and her love of God, but Emma knew that she was cruel and that her feet stank and that she led the priest with the black curly hair to her bed and Emma did not like her and avoided her. Old Hilder was no longer "stately" but bent and senile and wandered about the ducal house at Rouen muttering and no one paid any heed to her and Emma seldom acknowledged the old woman's existence. She would soon die, for she was beyond the age of living, but her death would mean little for Emma no longer hated the woman. She felt nothing for her. When Emma had been quite young, perhaps but six or seven, she and her cousin of Flanders, a boy of about the same age, had been exploring the strangeness of the other's genitals. Even now she remembered how his penis had dripped with a long dangle of foreskin. "Lady H" had found the two of them exposing themselves and had dragged Emma off by the hair, beat her with a birch branch and locked her in a cupboard in the chapel. "Animals and beasts do those things!" her mother duchess had screamed at her. Emma went to her father and told him about the priest with the black curly hair, but he only said, "You must not say such things of a pious woman like your mother."

But her father was a great and wise man. He was merciful when mercy was demanded and had forgiven a knight sent to assassinate him and made him a loyal guard of his house, but "a duchy cannot exist without order" he maintained. A band of villeins had gathered in a commune, "rule by the people" they called it, and refused to accept the laws of vassalage. They shared the labor and all lived in a compound together and ate, it was said, at a common table and professed to be true followers of Christ. There were priests and those of the Church who upheld their cause, but not the then Bishop of Rouen nor her father. "It undermines the very core of all social order. Chaos would follow when men do not seek to live within God's order and rule. A man owes his life to his liege lord and must do him homage."

She rode with her father on a winter's day as cold as this one at sea. Her mother had dressed her in warm sable and she sat a great black mare as her father rode beside her. He was a big man with enormous hands. They came to the commune, hovels grouped within a timbered barricade, and the duke ordered it burned to the ground. Those who fled the fire were butchered. She watched as two small children, a boy and a girl in rags, were sliced by swords. She buried her head within the fur of her hood. There were tears in her voice as she said softly, "They were little babies." "They are the most dangerous," her father said, "for they do not forget. You must not cry, little wren. One rules or one doesn't rule, but if one is to rule, order must precede or rule cannot follow." They called him a despot. "Despotism tempered by carnage," he had said and he was serious.

She was his darling, but her brothers did not seem to mind and pampered her as well, and then the day came when she had to leave the ducal house at Rouen. "I have made you a match. I have made you a queen," her father told her on a day when the Seine was gray and cold. "It is the best I can do for you." She left with tears on her cheeks but with anticipation at being the great Queen of England. She never told her father how miserable Ethelred was to her. She never wanted him to know. "A queen," he would say. "You are the greatest queen in all of Christendom." And she'd smile and was too ashamed to tell him that her husband was no better than a beast, and on her visits to Rouen she would lie in the chamber of her childhood and weep.

It was done and Ethelred was dead and soon Edmund would be dead and order would be restored and she would rule. She looked into the turbulent sea.

Godfrey came to the bow. "You shall drown in the spray if you stay up here, Emma."

"It purifies me," she said. "The sea is like a baptism."

"We should sight land soon," he said.

"Yes," she agreed, and they did.

The steerboard was raised and the anchor lowered. They led their horses into the cold water.

"I will sit all night by the fire and not move and I wager I will still not be warm," Godfrey told her as they walked from the water.

"Amen to that," one of Godfrey's men said, pulling on the reins of his horse.

Snow had piled in crevices of the black rocks at the sea's edge and covered the trail leading up away from the water. The wind blew the light-falling snow at their faces.

They came up around the big rock to the hamlet road. Emma was first and the first to see. The hamlet was burned to rubble, still smoldering despite the covering of snow. "No!" she yelled and looked up the hill. The great hall was but a charred frame sticking above the battered spike enclosure. For a moment she stopped, stunned, and Godfrey at a gallop flew past her, and then she let out a piercing cry and slapped the flank of the horse and the white beast bolted forward. "Edward," she cried out and she reined the mare inside the gates. A corpse partially buried in snow lay in her path. The head of a woman was mounted on a pike on one side of the gate and that of a man without eyes in the sockets on the other side.

Godfrey ran about the yard. "Edward! Aesval! Felim! Edward!" His calls brought no response.

Emma got down off the horse, and as she did, she looked into the face on the pike. "Edward!" The other riders came in the gate and the servant girl carrying Alfred trudged behind. The smell of dead fire hung in the air. "Edward! Edward!" Emma stumbled toward one of the buildings still standing. "Edward!" There was no need to open the door; it had been torn from its hinges. The chamber on the lower level had been Felim and Aesval's. The room was stripped of its hangings and blood was spattered on the floor and walls. There on the straw bed, stripped of its covers, was the headless body of a man. Felim. The hands were his, yet as if denying the certainty of what blatantly lay in dry blood before her, she searched about for a head to go with the body and found none. His books, his writings, his parchments were gone as well. She went outside and vomited as Godfrey went in. "Edward!" she continued to call and went up the steps to her own chamber. It was empty. Her precious relics gone. The bone needle of Irene, her greatest treasure, was gone.

She came back again into the yard.

"Felim," Godfrey said.

She nodded.

"There is no sign of Edward or Godgifu, nor Aesval. They must have been taken."

"What will Cnute do with him? Will he kill him?"

"They say he is a just young man. Perhaps not."

"Would a just young man do this?"

"You planned to bring an army against him, Emma."

"EDWARD!" It was a wail more than a call and she slumped down on a burned and fallen timber without brushing away the snow.

The servant girl hummed softly and rocked Alfred in her arms, but except for that it was quiet, that and the cawing of the birds. Emma thought she heard a cry, and then again. "Mother." But it was a faint sound. "Mother."

"Did you hear, Goddy?" she asked.

"Yes. Listen."

"Mother." The cry was weak, but it was Edward's voice and Godfrey ran off in the direction of the sound and she got up from the timber and followed.

"Mother." The sound came from the pit.

They stood over it, looking down into the darkness, and she could make out the figures of the two children.

"Mother." And now it was a sob.

Godfrey made a ladder of burned timber and lowered it into the black hole. He tore the girl from Edward's arms and carried her up.

"Is she dead?" Emma asked.

"Nearly," Godfrey said. He turned to one of the men still on horseback. "Go to the ship, fetch skins and food and bring more men." To another he ordered a fire be built in one of the standing chambers. He handed Godgifu to Emma and went back into the pit.

She held the child but was horrified by what was in her arms and wanted to drop her and she smelled of death and reeked of her own urine.

Godfrey came up the ladder bearing Edward.

"I can stand," Edward said.

"NO," Godfrey said, but Edward broke free and stood.

"The other Edward bore the pain," her son said and she knew he was out of his head.

"When did Cnute do this?" Godfrey asked. He took Godgifu from Emma and began walking toward Emma's empty chamber house.

"It was not Cnute," the boy said, and he was quite rational. "It was Edmund's man, Heljer."

"My God," Emma said. "Edmund has lived too long."

Edward's voice was relatively strong. "Take Godgifu inside and I will make her well."

"What?" Godfrey asked.

"Felim taught me," Edward said. "He taught me of healing."

Godfrey carried the girl up the stairs and Edward followed. Emma walked behind. "When?" she asked.

"The day you sailed."

"My God," Godfrey asked, "how did you survive?"

"On snow," Edward said. "A rat I caught and fungus growing on the walls of the pit."

Emma turned and ran back down the stairs. She felt sick and angry and afraid of God and ran to the chapel. She was lying on the floor when Godfrey came to her. The chapel had been stripped and there was nothing left but a bare altar. Emma, her face pressed against the wood of the floor, wept until she knew there could be no more tears within her and yet she still continued to sob.

"Come," Godfrey said. "You must have a bowl of broth and some wine."

"Goddy. I am a woman of evil."

"Come," he said.

"No. Before God I must tell someone this. My children are brought from near death and I think nothing of them. I don't care that they yet breathe, that they have escaped death, only that Edward is alive that I might set him before an army. Am I some monster that I cannot care for Ethelred's children the way I might some abandoned slave?"

"Emma, you are what you are. Accept yourself."

"And the children?"

"They will survive, even you. They have survived this. Edward has a strength that is beyond what is human. And he does have the touch. Godgifu is awake and well."

Emma stopped crying and let Godfrey help her from the floor. "Aesval. Does Edward know where Aesval is?"

"He doesn't; in fact I have not yet told him of Felim. But an old blind man, a swineherd, Edward said it was he who put them in the pit, came wandering into the compound but minutes ago searching for Edward. He had been taken slave by Heljer, had escaped days ago but had gotten lost trying to reach Corfe again. He came back to take the children from the pit. From him I learned all that were not killed were taken to Winchester. Aesval has been taken to Edmund."

"Then we must go north to Winchester."

"We will think on it. We must plan. Willie will come soon with his small army of men and we will plan."

"We will go to Winchester," Emma said and wiped her face on the sleeve of her gown.

CHAPTER 17

North to Winchester, 1016

It was afternoon and they turned north to leave behind the sea. They had followed the sea, the water almost always in sight, since leaving Corfe. The land was autumn-bare; long brown grasses bent brittle from an early frost covered the slopes. The riders had followed the sea trail; sometimes it edged the water, at others was above it on gentle hills or wandered dangerously on cliffs above, which dropped abruptly off, and loosened rocks kicked by the trodding horses flailed the air and fell to the quiet sea below. In the distance the silhouettes of barren trees hid little of a bright sky.

"We will be safer traveling near the sea," his Uncle Godfrey had told his mother before they started.

"But it is so much farther." His mother, Godfrey and Uncle Willie were organizing the caravan, planning the order of march, setting the guard, seeing to the logistics of food and wine.

"But safer. Goddy is right, Emma." The two soldiers, who knew the countryside well, had been in agreement.

"We must reach Winchester before . . ."

"Before what?" Godfrey had asked her.

"Before Edmund be gone from there."

"You must be prepared," Willie had reminded her, "that when we reach Winchester, Edmund may not have been there for some time."

"You said he was there. You said Edmund was at Winchester."

"It was what I heard. Spies are not always reliable."

"He must be there. He simply must be."

"It is going to be a hard journey. It is the worst time of the year and a cold coming we'll have of it. Are you certain, Emma, you want to attempt it?"

"I have never been more certain of anything."

So they had traveled near the sea. When it was not near enough to be visible, it was always close enough to catch on the wind. And now they were turning north, away from the sea's breath.

Edward, too, while never having been that fond of the sea, could appreciate the security it offered, for though they saw no Norman vessels there was always the promise that somewhere in the channel help awaited. Escape was but beyond the water. But now they were leaving it behind and heading into the King's domain.

The riders led the way into the deepening green of the woods, horses moving slowly so as to allow the staggering line of foot soldiers, and not enough of them to feel safe, and servants to keep up. In the woods was said lived fairies and trolls, giants and witches, strange creatures half human, half something else. There were tales of so many that went into the depth of the forest never to return. Sunlight sifted down in open spots like windows in the dark church of St. Ouen. He caught up with his uncles.

"You should've stopped her, Goddy," Uncle Willie was saying. "This is foolhardy."

"And how? Could you? She is determined."

"I suppose you're right. Still it is a foolish thing we do."

"She is set. She will kill Edmund."

"Unless he manages to do us all in first."

"Hope he has no news of our coming."

"Sometimes," Willie said, "I think the very trees have ears."

Edward looked about at the sinister trees, more black than green in the dim light, and as they penetrated deeper into the forest, the gnarled trunks seemed to pull together, closing their very path, and the huge trees leaned over to one another as if whispering, and the rough bark began to take on the appearance of faces, unsmiling, angry faces, and branches like grotesque arms leaned down as if to pick them up and keep them prisoners. He shuddered and knew the trees were listening, and no longer lagged even slightly behind but tried to position himself as often as possible between his uncles. They had to move into a single file, for the winding road had grown too narrow for but one horse.

"Who knows," Willie said, "who lurks ahead bearing news of our coming?"

"The old man could tell," Edward said. "He can hear someone coming from miles off."

"What old man?" Count Willie asked.

"The blind swineherd. He can hear horses long before they come in sight."

"Is he with us?"

"No, Uncle Willie. Mother said he would only slow us down and made him stay behind at Corfe with the red-faced hunchback."

His uncles stopped talking. There was only the rustle of horses' hoofs trampling the brush and dead leaves. The boy came riding up. He had not left Edward's sight very often or for very long since Edward had rescued him from death. It was the boy who fell through the roof the day the swineherd was blinded and Edward had found him on the Point dying. Edward had chased the wolves away and made the boy's body straight and his mind well again. His name was Seven and Edward had seen to it that he had a horse to ride. "Servants can walk," Uncle Willie had insisted. "No. He must have a horse," Edward had said. "And who are you?" "I am to be King." "We are authoritative, aren't we?" And in the end, Edward had gotten the horse for Seven. "What a strange name you have," Edward had said. "It is because my father's children never lived. He soon decided, so he told me, it was no longer worth the effort to name us, so he numbered us. All who came before me died as did Eight, Nine, Ten and Eleven. All dead 'cept I, and if it not bein' for you, me Lord, I be as dead as they." Seven had clung to him, waiting upon him and chasing away any other who would serve him. Now the boy rode directly behind him. Although apparently having little experience with horses, he took to it naturally and handled the beasts without difficulty.

"I keep hearing noises," Willie said. "I wish we had the old blind man you were talking about here, Edward."

"We do, me Lord Count," Seven said. "He walks behind with the soldiers."

"The Queen—" Edward started to say.

"He didn't pay no mind. He wouldn't be left behind."

"Bring him up here," the count ordered and Seven turned back his horse.

They put the old blind man on the horse with Seven and the pair rode ahead. But they heard nothing and saw nothing and the trail became wider and it got lighter and they reached the edge of the forest. They had been climbing and were now high on the ridgeway and behind them was the dense dark green of the trees and beyond it the sea, flickering like polished metal in the sun. The Isle of Wight was visible, pushing out of the water.

"Can we go no faster?" his mother came forward and asked.

"We cannot go without the soldiers and the soldiers can walk no faster."

"Edmund will die of old age before we ever reach him. Godgifu, stop it."

The girl was attempting to squirm away from the man who was carrying her with him on his mount. "He's trying to put his finger in my pee-place," the child said. She was not afraid; she was angry.

"Oh, stop making up stories," the Queen said.

"She can ride with me," Edward said and pulled the girl free from the man's hands. The rider's empty hands were shaking and for a moment he looked at Edward in fear and then turned away.

"I should have your hands cut off," Edward told him and hung tightly on to Godgifu and jerked the reins as he moved his own mount away.

They camped for the night. The day had been unseasonably warm but now the night, high on the ridgeway, was freezing. Snow began to fall, and Edward, like the others, huddled in fur near the open fire. A thegn, one of Ethelred's men, had a house but an hour's ride down to the east, but they knew not how he stood. Barjour, as his name was, was fickle and mercenary and apt to sell them all to Edmund or Cnute, according to Willie. His mother agreed.

"It is the eve of St. Andrew's," Godfrey said, rubbing his hands out to the fire.

"Aye, but it is," the blind man said. "Each month I put small stones for the number of days in my pouch and every night I throw one out before I sleep. Tonight there will be but one stone left."

Uncle Willie was still eating. "Who was St. Andrew, anyway?" he asked, throwing the bone of the fowl into the flame.

"Willie, I'm ashamed of you," his mother said.

"There's so goddamn many saints, anyway, who can keep track?"

"Obviously not you, Count," Godfrey said.

"He was the brother of St. Peter," Edward told them and he thought of the painting in the chapel at Rouen.

"Well 'twas easier I bet," Willie said, "for our Viking forefathers, who didn't have to keep track of them all."

"I shall be a saint," Edward said.

"Don't talk nonsense, Edward," his mother told him. "God will punish you if you talk that way." Then she turned to the others and her voice became mysterious. "I saw once a piece of St. Andrew's cross and was said to cure the scrofula."

"No doubt it cured pilgrims of their pocketbooks."

"Sometimes you sound the heretic, Willie," she admonished her brother. "You shall go to hell if you are not careful."

"So shall we all, Emma. The sons and daughters of Richard of Normandy living in the forest like outlaws. God will mistake us for highwaymen."

"Wayfarers and cutthroats sitting about open fires plotting thievery and murder." Godfrey spoke in a sinister voice.

His mother laughed. "If we spend much more time out in the cold, we might as well be highwaymen; 'twould be more profitable."

We shall not go to hell, Edward thought. Their joking about it made him angry, but he did not voice his opinion for fear she would be upset with him again. He always seemed to make her angry at him.

"I wish it were not so cold," Emma said as the conversation ebbed.

Someone, as if in answer to her statement, threw more wood on the fire. A lean-to of skin was built for her and she bade them night and retired to it. But Edward knew he was expected to sleep as a soldier, finding warmth as best he could about the fire. When he became King he would be certain never again to be cold.

He dozed and awoke to a dying fire and he had to urinate. He forced himself to get up and he pulled the fur coverings tighter. Seven, too, as if waiting for Edward, stood up as well. The boy followed behind. Edward, accustomed to being waited upon, was not embarrassed by the inordinate attention that Seven paid to his well-being. They moved from the dim light of the fire and into the trees.

At first in the shadows of the night, despite the visible auras of light about them, Edward could not see what the two soldiers were doing. One was kneeling before the other, his low legs pillowed in a patch of snow, and then Edward realized the standing soldier had his hard penis stuffed into the mouth of the kneeling figure. The one standing looked at Edward; even in the dark, Edward could see the terror in his eyes and his big hands shoved the kneeling man roughly away, causing him to topple in a ditch. Edward looked down at the ground. He didn't understand, yet was terrified by what he had witnessed. He turned around and Seven stood in his path. He pushed past him.

"I must get to Goddy," he said.

Seven grabbed hold of him and the fur was not enough to shield him from the pain. "No, my Lord. Please don't."

"It is against God," Edward said, not at all certain what and why it was against God. He simply knew it was and had seen the shame in the soldier's eyes.

"They will take these men," Seven told him in a whisper, "and hang each from a tree. Not by his neck, so as he will die fast, but by the wrists, and then they will cut off his pee-prong and leave him to bleed to death."

Edward turned and looked first at the man standing, his eyes pleading, and then down at the soldier still lying in the ditch. He glared up at Edward in scorn.

"Please, Lord Edward, be merciful," Seven begged.

"And what are they to you? Know you them?"

"Nay. But they are men. Men loyal to the count, to the Queen and to you, Lord Edward."

Edward walked back toward the dying fire. He sat down in the cold, colder now and in misery yet, for he had forgotten to urinate.

Seven came up to him. "My Lord—"

"Go away," Edward said. "Just go away."

His bladder paining him, he sat through the night and the snow fell wet and heavy, clinging to the fur and wetting his nose and cheeks. He did not sleep. And in the darkness could see light about the guards who moved in circles around the campsite. Had he been wrong not to report the soldiers? What would Felim have done? He had not thought about Felim and realized for the first time that he would never see the man again. It was a frightening thought. Death became real.

St. Andrew's day came and the snow continued. Riders, horses and foot soldiers turned from the trail on the ridgeway into another forest below.

"Is there not a thegn in the land who would grant us the worth of his hall?" his mother asked.

"Aye," Willie answered, "but who's to know which is he and which is the traitor?"

And so they detoured about lands and main trails and hung to little roads.

"We are in real enemy territory now," Goddy said as their slow pace seemed to move even slower in the late afternoon sun. "We will camp not too far distant and enter Winchester on the morrow."

"And if Edmund is not fooled by our sincerity and believes that we believe Cnute responsible for the burning of Corfe, we shall burn Winchester down and keep warm by the fire." But Edward knew his mother didn't mean that.

Night came and quiet fell on the camp. Seven lay down near where Edward sat. Uncle Willie stretched out back toward the trees and seemed instantly to fall asleep. There was stillness. Edward put his head down on the cold earth; across the fire, he could see Goddy sitting, his arms pulled about his knees. His uncle was staring into the flames as if seeing something important there. The wind came, raising the fire, sweeping the flames up and back, yellow and bright. The guard encircled the sleeping camp, his steps crunching the dried leaves and iced snow. The wind gusted. Edward slid his feet back from the fire. And then the wind began crying out like a wounded beast. Its fierce howl battered the empty trees and Edward shivered more from the sound than the cold. The fire lifted up so brightly it wiped away the shadows, leaving the faces of the sleeping nothing but yellow expressionless masks. Across the flame, Goddy's body had vanished and only his face was visible as if it had risen from the fire, floating free like some bird. The waves of heat shriveled and twisted it grotesquely until it seemed some monster. And then his uncle pulled back from the flame and the night seemed to go on interminably.

The blind swineherd jolted upright. His voice was a hoarse whisper. "A rider is coming."

Godfrey went over to him. "Speak old man," he said softly.

"There is but one," the old man said. "A single horse is coming from the east."

Edward wondered how the blind man knew which way was east. They awoke his mother and Uncle Willie. Soldiers were sent scattering among the trees. Seven crawled over to where Edward lay, remaining silent. It was as if the camp had not awakened, for the only sound was the howl of the wind.

"He is close," the blind man whispered, "and stays upon his mount. He comes not in secret."

Edward listened and heard nothing that did not seem the wind. And then with a crash of the barren brush, he, a lone rider in the garments of a Dane, rode into the camp caring not if there were a thousand soldiers hiding among the trees. Edward looked in horror as he saw the face of the rider in the firelight. The flame lit the yellow hair of the lanky horseman and Edward wanted to scream out!

"Son of Thorkell," his mother hailed the man.

"My Lady Queen." The tall rider dismounted.

"These are my brothers." His mother extended her hand in the direction of Uncle Willie. "The Count of Eu and our good Godfrey."

"I know them by reputation, Lady. They are valiant men and I trust you have been safely in their keeping. I come to grant you aid as well."

"But are you not serving the Danish invader? We journey, Thorkellsson, to seek help of King Edmund." The Queen stared at the man as she spoke. To Edward it did not sound like the lie that it was.

Edward was pained by the sight of the slender tall Dane.

"Why, Lady, would you expect help from Edmund Ironside?"

There were the first trembling signals of the fit coming over him. It was getting lighter and he could feel his hands begin to shake. He concentrated on his hands, as Felim had taught him, forcing his fingertips to stillness and then moving through the bones of his fingers to the palm of his hands. Despite the intensity of his mental focus, he was aware of the conversation going on between his mother and the Dane.

"Edmund is—"

"He went to Corfe to kill you. He burned Corfe to the ground and yet you would seek his aid?"

"How know you this? What makes you certain it was Edmund and not another's doing? Your Lord Cnute, perhaps? And how did you come to find us here?"

"One question at one time, Madam." The Dane raised the hand with the missing fingers.

The sight of it brought trembling to Edward's own hands. "*Your mother, Edward, is guilty of a great sin and will burn in hell.*" He forced his fingers to stillness.

"I can assure you it was not Cnute who had Corfe burned. As to how I knew you were here, Godwin has had a spy among the Count of Eu's men."

"Hear you this, Willie?" Emma cried out angrily.

"It is fair, I suppose," Willie answered, "since I have one in Cnute's court as well. Although I must say he has not been doing a very considerable job as of late."

"It is because we hung him," Thorkell's son said.

Willie only shrugged.

"It is nonetheless my intent," his mother said, "to seek the protection of Edmund."

"You are too late, Lady. I thought the message I bring would be joy to your ears. I have been wrong I see; I bear you bad news. Early on St. Andrew's day, Edmund, son of Ethelred and King of Wessex, died in his bed."

For a moment there was a deathly stillness. Then his mother let out a wail. "NO! No! You lie, Thorkellsson. Not yet. He cannot be dead yet."

"Emma, please," Goddy said and led her back to the fire.

"No," she cried, and falling upon the earth, she beat her fist upon the frozen ground.

"How was Edmund killed?" Uncle Willie asked the Dane. "Was he murdered? Was this Cnute's doing?"

"No. From all it would appear he died at no man's hand."

"And Cnute?"

"Becomes the King of all England. This was the pact between them. Godwin will arrange safe passage for the Queen, the Athelings, and yourself to Normandy."

"The Witan—"

"They will support Cnute in this, I think you will see. Might is right, as the saying goes. And for this night I can offer you warm lodgings. But a short distance is the house of the Thegn Godwin, Guildford. You know he bears the Queen love and would do you all well. You are safe in his keeping." Thorkell's son walked over to where his mother was. "Madam, there is a lady of your house taken by Edmund's men at Corfe. With Edmund's death I took her away from Winchester. She awaits you at the house of Thegn Godwin."

"Aesval? Is her name Aesval?"

"Yes, Lady, that is she."

The wind had died. A wolf howled far off. Soldiers laughed and urinated upon the flame, and when it did no good, dirt was loosed from the hard dormant earth and sifted over the fire to kill it. In the darkness was a confusion of sounds, of horses, of men yelling and then they began the trek down the hill.

It seemed a brief ride. They followed the Dane along the narrow trail in the woods and into the clearing. A short distance beyond light cracked through window boards and smoke rose from a roof. They trooped into the long hall to be hit by the heat of the fire. Their outside voices were too loud for the room and clamorous. The place was afire with bright torchlight and a priest and the two women waiting at one end of the hall seemed not fully at ease with the arrival of such noise. The building itself appeared new and not yet given to cold drafts but blistered in the warmth from the hot fire.

Edward had no doubt who was in command. Godwin stood near the fire, and though a rather common-looking man, there was the strength of authority in his stance that said this is my house and you are here at my grace. At first Edward did not see the other man, alone in the far corner where it was less light. And even when he did see him, it took some time to realize who the fellow was. Edward stared at him and saw the recognition in his eyes. Edward did not scream out, "There is the traitor." But there was no doubt, he was the spy among them. He looked at Edward not with scorn as he had done kneeling in the ditch, but in fact smiled, and Edward turned away to avoid his gaze. Would they be here within these warm walls had Edward ignored the pleading of Seven? He swung around to face Seven, who was, as always, close on his heels.

CHAPTER 18

Guildford, 1016

WHERE WAS AESVAL? SHE HAD BEEN SO CONCERNED ABOUT GETTING WARM she had forgotten Aesval. She must ask Thorkell's son. Or was it a ruse? He stood with her brothers across the room. No, she decided, he would not do that to her. He was no less beautiful than he had been that day over four years ago in the chapel at Corfe. She could almost feel the stubble of his fingers against her flesh. Yet, she could not afford this now, could not become captivated by the young Dane, for she was going to Rouen to raise an army against his lord, Cnute. The throne belonged to her, to Edward, and no invading Dane was to steal it from her. Still, it did no harm to admire the tall young man the distance of the hall and she continued to follow his movements with her eyes. It was pleasant and she must have smiled for her host came up to her.

"You look content, Madam," Godwin said. He was not a handsome man, nor was he ugly. And plain seemed unsuited, for he had bright eyes and a solid face. He was disarmingly comfortable, neither tall nor short, and his hair was a vague sort of brown. He smiled easily, yet Emma sensed there was far more to him than the smile revealed.

"I am warm," she answered. "For these past days sleeping in the snow I have prayed for a warm hall and a roaring fire." She sipped from the cup of heated wine. "It seems almost sinful to feel the flush of fire on my face."

"A face as beautiful as yours, Lady, would seem free of sin."

"You flatter, Godwin, but I shall not stop you. A woman of my age—"

"Age, Madam?" he interrupted in polite anger. "You are yet young."

"Not as young as the Dane you serve."

"No, Lady, Cnute is barely a man . . . twenty-two in all."

"And how is it, Thegn, you serve a king of the north, yet your lands are here in Wessex? Was not Edmund Ironside your lord?"

"Circumstance." He motioned for her to sit down upon a bench. "This land was granted my father by King Ethelred, your husband. My father saved Queen Elfrida. She was abducted by some zealot followers of the sainted King Edward and taken into the marshes, bound and left to die. My father came upon her and rescued her from her plight and the King granted to my father and his heirs these lands in recompense."

"I have heard this story before, Godwin, but was told the tale that the lady, the King's mother, was saved by a swineherd."

"Indeed, Madam, she was. My father was a swineherd. I have had humble beginnings."

"You have risen well, Godwin."

"I am ambitious, Lady. Perhaps it is having lived among the pigs, for I seem able to smell events in time and ride with them."

"And what sense you now in the wind?"

"This, and it shall not be to your liking, but Cnute will be undisputed King of all England."

"And what of my Atheling?"

"It is not my place to say."

"Say," Emma ordered.

"The Witan will go with strength. Not with a . . ." He paused and then added, "A boy."

"You were going to say ugly boy."

"In truth, Lady, I was going to say ugly boy."

"That is a fact enough. He is ugly."

He poured her some wine. "It is wrong, no doubt, but it is easier to look upon a comely face."

"And the young Dane who would be King?"

"An uncommonly comely face."

"You are a blunt man, Godwin."

"It is easier to be devious when you are blunt and straightforward. The victims are less suspecting."

"Am I your victim?"

"Yes, in a way, I suppose you are."

"And then are we to be your prisoners here? Are you to deliver us into the hands of the son of Sven the Forkbeard?"

"No, Lady, though I know not what your contrivances against King Cnute may be, you are yet the widow of our Lord Ethelred and I will see you safe-journeyed to Rouen."

"And were I as blunt as you, Godwin, I might say, I go to Rouen to raise an army to secure the Atheling's throne."

"Then I should have to find a devious manner of stopping you." He stood up. "But enough conjecture. I am not playing the proper host. I have someone waiting to meet you."

"Aesval?"

"Yes, a lady of your house, I believe. She was taken a slave to Winchester from Corfe, I understand."

"How came she to be here?"

"It should not surprise you I have had a spy in Edmund's household. He brought us word immediately of the Ironside's death and Thorkellsson went at once to Winchester. Aesval remembered him and asked if he could help get her to you."

"I thank you for this kindness."

"The woman was tired and distraught when she arrived. She rests yet in a chamber, but will no doubt be comforted by being reunited."

She wondered as she walked from the hall into the cold if Godwin was not too disarming and more devious than he appeared. She followed the torchbearer, the light reflecting upon the snow, and suspected perhaps there was no Aesval and that she was being led to her death. She fingered the blade yet kept in the cinch of her waist.

The torchbearer pushed open the chamber door with his foot. Light and heat emanated from the room. Aesval lay sleeping on the bed.

"Thank you," Emma whispered, but the torchbearer had already closed the door and was gone.

"Aesval," she said. Her voice soft, not wanting to alarm the woman. "Aesval."

The woman opened her eyes and then sat up with a jolt, as best as her huge frame would allow, and then there was recognition and she smiled. "Lady. My dear Lady Emma."

Emma sat down beside her and embraced her, finding comfort in the familiar bulk of the woman, a sense of still having roots and all the cold nights and snow and agony flooded from her eyes. It had been long since Emma had wept, had dared to let herself, but for a moment it was joy to stop fighting and give way, allowing the accumulation of pain to drain down her cheeks. "Felim . . ." She had trouble getting the words out.

"I watched," Aesval said. "Edmund stood there and made me watch."

"Edmund himself? Edmund was there, too?"

"Yes. He came. I knew not a buzzard before to kill its own prey."

"This was terrible for you. I did not know."

"The children?"

"Edward and Godgifu are alive. They are here with me."

"I dared not cry out for them. Edmund had decided they, too, had fled to Rouen."

"An old blind swineherd had hidden them in the pit."

"I know the man." She paused, then as if it was difficult to tell the next: "Edmund," she spoke slowly, "took Felim's head to Winchester. He had it placed on a pike in the great hall and took me to it and made me yell out that it was the head of a devil."

"My dear Aesval."

"It was but a few short days I was there."

"And he is dead. But I have been cheated of his death and now more than ever I am angered to have been cheated so."

"'Tis better for the Atheling you were not a part of it."

Emma was surprised at the woman's understanding. "Yet, Aesval, I spent those long hours to learn all there was to know of poisons for but that one death I was deprived of."

"And taught me as well—"

"Yes," Emma spoke before Aesval had a chance to finish, "and how it could be done undetected. So no man could know."

"Made to look like a death of sickness, so that—"

The recognition came. "AESVAL! YOU!"

"Ssssh."

"Aesval. I don't believe it."

"Believe what, Lady?"

"Believe that you actually managed it. Oh sweet revenge!"

"Madam, I did nothing. King Edmund died at no man's hand. It is so recorded. Bishop Wulfstan said it is so recorded."

"Aesval, you are a wonder."

"I know nothing of such things. I am a simple woman." She smiled.

"A simple genius. But tell me how, tell me."

"I deny all. It is best for us both." Aesval went to a sack on a bench. "And, I have a present for you." She took a cloth bundle and opened it on the bed.

"My relics. Oh, Aesval. My precious relics. Are they all here?"

"All, Madam. Edmund—"

She was stopped by a light rap at the door and Aesval quickly rolled the cloth back up. And, as if still her servant, Aesval went and opened the door. With a sweep of cold air that raised the flame of the fire a Danish soldier stooped down to get through the door. He was a fair man, as well as tall, clean-shaven. He wore no helmet and bits of snow sparkled in his loose blond curls.

"Lady," he said, "I come from King Cnute." His eyes were a pale liquid blue. He closed the door and seemed awkwardly wondering what to do with his hands. "He was hoping to meet with you at Winchester, but had to return to Lunduntown, but assures you of safe passage to Rouen."

"I see," she said. "And that is it?"

"Yes, Lady." He stood looking at her.

If she did not move to invite him to stay, he would be gone. Yet, she was a queen and, as sensual as she found him, he was but a simple soldier. There was Aesval, too, the reunion with Aesval and dead Edmund to discuss and rejoice over and Godwin to contend with and more important a war against Cnute to be in the forefront of her thinking. This was no time for a dalliance with a common soldier. Yet, he was uncommonly attractive. So they stood, the three of them.

"Madam." It was the soldier who broke the silence. "I've been traveling in the cold. Would you mind if I stood by the fire and warmed myself before I go back out?"

"Do," she said, and heard the undisguised pleasure in her own voice and was alarmed by it.

He walked over to the fire. His thighs seemed as big as her waist and his hands were enormous, rough, like the soldier he was, and unadorned by rings.

"Sit if you like," she said.

The bench cracked under his weight. He turned and looked directly up at her and embarrassed her because she had been staring at him with far too much interest; she turned away, certain her face was red, as she felt the flush.

Aesval looked over to her. "Madam," she said, "perhaps I should go and get some wine or—"

"No, Aesval, stay!" She realized there was panic in her words. Why this perturbation over a soldier? She took a deep breath and spoke with what she hoped was calm. "You serve the King?"

"Yes," he said. He spoke the Danish dialect in a deep gentle voice. He was young, perhaps no more than twenty-one or -two. He was not quite shy, but more simply quiet.

"Your King, he is not older than you, I understand."

"No older, Madam."

"And comely, they say."

"I don't know about that, Lady. I am no judge of that."

Neither spoke. Aesval coughed. The fire cracked.

He was the one to speak. "The fire feels good. I was very cold."

"I know what it is to be cold," she said.

"They say how you traveled like a soldier from Corfe."

"Yes. I had great fear of Edmund Ironside."

"He is dead. Now King Cnute is to be King of all England. And this is a good thing."

"And why so?" Emma's voice, she knew, betrayed her irritation.

"Because there will be peace in England."

"Does that matter to you, a Dane soldier?"

"Yes," he said. "It matters."

He seemed tired. She wanted to put her arms about his wide shoulders and comfort him. "Do you have a wife?"

"Yes."

"You seem so young."

"I have a son," he told her.

"Are they in England, in the Danelaw?"

"No. They are home. In Roeskild. But I suppose home is here now."

"You stay with the King?"

"Yes," he said.

She hoped when the time of battle came he was not killed.

There was silence.

"I am warm now," he said. "And have a journey ahead." He stood up, towering over her, then turned and went to the door. As he stooped to go out, he turned back to her. Mixed with the cold wind she heard his words. "I have often heard them speak of your beauty, Lady, but these words were not enough. I shall tell the King you are the most beautiful woman I have ever seen." He went out, closing the door behind him.

CHAPTER 19

Guildford, 1016

IT WAS DAY. THE EARTH WAS DROWNED IN FRESH SNOW. IT SMELLED COLD and clean and the sun reflected on it as if precious gems were sprinkled atop it and it hurt his eyes to look at it. Edmund was dead. He would be King regardless of this Cnute and so, despite the brillance which made him squint, Edward held his head erect and walked not as Ethelred with the mean eye had walked but as great kings would walk, disdaining the people but having great compassion, proudly and moving with grandeur and dignity. But the snow got deeper and as his feet cracked through the hard crust and sank in it was hard to walk like a king. Still he held his head high just as he would do when he led the army against Cnute to win the great victory and go off to be anointed and have the heavy crown put upon his head. And though Ethelred never wore the crown, Edward would wear it always and he would walk in the great hall at Winchester while Wulfstan and the bishops would bow and Godfrey and Uncle Willie and great nobles would come to him bringing gifts. And he would marry Godgifu to a noble and he would treat her with kindness and Edward would dispense his favors to those who came to plead. And Edward would dress his mother in grand robes and she would walk behind him wearing a crown and weighed with jewels she would do as he bade.

A hawk swooped above the trees in the distance, and then soared up and cut a great arc through the sky.

Edward left the snow and went into the hall.

His mother sat on a bench and beside her stood the man called Godwin. These were his lands and Edward did not know whether he liked him or not. He seemed kind and he spoke in friendship, but there was something in his eyes, not evil or cruel, but a distance, as if he looked beyond.

"Edward," Godwin said. "I have a surprise for you. Come here, boy."

Edward went over to the man. Godwin turned to the table behind him and picked up a sword and raised it before his face.

Edward stared at the jewels of the hilt. His. The heavy weapon was his. The sword of Woden—of Cerdic—of Alfred. A king's sword. He spoke with reverence. "The sword of Edgar."

"Yours, I believe," Godwin said.

"Yes."

"Then you must take it."

And Edward took it. "It is well I have this sword again, for I shall now be King."

Godwin looked at him.

"And when I go to battle against Cnute I shall lead the armies with this great sword."

"You go to battle Cnute?" Godwin asked.

"Best, Edward," his mother cautioned, "you do not speak of such here. These are the men of Cnute."

"Yes." Goddy smiled. "It is not polite to tell your host that you plan to war against him."

They were treating it as if it were some joke. It was no joke; his mother had told him his uncles would give him armies to lead against the Danes. Edward scowled. "When do we leave for Winchester?" he asked.

"We don't," his mother told him. "We go to Normandy."

"Wulfstan. We must see the archbishop." His mother had said the archbishop would support him. Edward lifted the sword. He wanted to hear Wulfstan speak. He was surprised at his mother. He must teach her the ways of politics.

"There is no need to journey. The archbishop comes to us here."

Seven came and brought him some wine and took the sword away and wrapped it in a piece of fabric.

"You must thank Thegn Godwin, Edward," Godfrey said, "for recovering the sword."

"It was Cnute who sent you the sword," Godwin told them.

Edward looked up at the man and drank from the cup. "And I shall use it to cut off his head."

"Edward," his mother said. "We've had enough sword waving. Let's keep our counsel."

"You must take care," Godwin said to him, "that you don't show the enemy your hand. Your mother is trying to caution you to discretion."

"Are you the enemy, Godwin?" the Queen asked.

"I would hope not, Lady," he replied.

Cnute was the enemy and Edward would pass the sword of Edgar to the man's neck and his head would tumble away, rolling onto the earth, and the Raven flag would fall limp and the Danes would flee in fright and the armies would kneel to their King—Edward, King of all England. Edward, perhaps it was the other Edward, deliberately let his wine cup fall to the floor. Seven came running over and cleaned up the wine. His mother gave him an angry look.

He bundled up in warm fox pelts and went back outside into the crisp air. When he was King he would not allow his mother to give him angry looks nor to tell him whose head he might or might not have. When he was King they would do as he wished and be silent when he wished and talk when he wished. His eyes became accustomed to the brightness. The wrap of snow stretched clean in every direction. In the distance, like ants trooping across a white altar cloth, an entourage of riders approached. Behind they left a winding dark line through the snow. The large cross on the archbishop's banner wandered in the breeze. When he was King, Edward decided, he would have an enormous flag, so large hardly one man could bear it—blue, perhaps, he loved blue, and with birds, peregrines circling, more frightening than the black raven. Edward climbed up on a snow-covered rock to make himself taller. If those approaching were to prostrate themselves at the feet of their King, he must be ready. The archbishop bounded taller than the rest of the riders, and as they neared, men came out from the hall to greet them.

In the clamor of greeting, the spy, the one for whose life Seven had pleaded, walked by Edward. "I thank you, my Lord," he said, and repeated, "I thank thee for your kindness," and he went away before Edward could consider an answer.

The archbishop did not bow to him nor say to him, "I greet thee, my King." In fact, the archbishop did not even look at him but with wet feet trooped into the hall, to be followed by other wet footsteps, none acknowledging their King, leaving a path of puddles, and Edward, the last, went in after them.

"We were planning to journey to see you, Your Grace," his mother said. "We thank you for coming to greet us here."

"The King is dead," Wulfstan said. It appeared meant as fact, not as news.

"Edmund Ironside is dead," his mother said.

The room, which had become quiet with the entry of the towering man, was stilled more as everyone seemed to be listening to the words of the Queen and Wulfstan.

"The Witan have met," he told her.

"How find they?"

"For peace, Lady. We are weary of wars. We are tired of two kingdoms, where but one should be. We want strength to give us stability, peace to bring rest among the people."

"You are Saxon." Her voice was raised and angry and Edward didn't understand why.

"We are said to be Saxon and Celt and Dane and Angle and Roman and Briton and, as well, Norman, and we are many people, Lady, who together hold this island-earth and we would hold it better in the calm of a firm hand raised above us in the name of God to save us from abroad, protect us and let us go about the business of existing."

"How find you?" There was a weariness, a resignation, in her voice that made no sense to Edward. What was wrong? The Witan would choose him King. His mother had told him so. "Wulfstan is with us, of that I am certain," she had said to Uncle Goddy and more than once on their trek north from the sea.

"Madam, for the good of England. The Witan has chosen Cnute their King."

His mother said nothing. No one in the room said anything. They all seemed to be watching him. He stared about in disbelief and then shrieked as loud as he was able, "I am the King." And he felt the fit coming. His arm began to shake and he could sense his breath vibrating in his mouth and his tongue rolled and he could feel the froth seeping from the corners, dripping from his lips, and then his eyes turned up into the sockets. He did nothing to stop it. He waited for God. He wanted God for no one else cared, only God. And he could see nothing but the brilliant white light that came and was brighter than the snow, more dazzling, and he heard his own anguished voice yelling and then the voice of God yelling incoherent great obscenities and Edward knew he was falling, dropping . . .

CHAPTER 20

To Rouen, 1016

EMMA WAS TIRED. EXHAUSTED. SHE WAS MELANCHOLY AND DISTURBED. Aesval hushed and reassured her, but to no avail. The destruction of Corfe, the long cold march through Wessex, the unexpected death of Edmund, however welcome, the meeting with Godwin, the sudden appearance of Thorkell's son, the unnerving visit by Cnute's young soldier and the Witan's choice of Cnute as King had thrown off her equilibrium. Events were occurring too fast and there was a gnawing in her guts that things had not ended. Nothing that had yet happened, even Edward's condition, would deter her from raising an army and taking the kingdom by strength. But she had a sense of losing control, that fate was depriving her of decision.

She looked forward to her friend the sea.

They bore the litter to Pevensey. Edward had been out of his head since the fit at Guildford. It was the worst she had ever seen him have. He writhed on the floor, foam seeping from the corners of his mouth, and he babbled. She was angry with him. He could have stopped the fit. She knew he could stop the fits. Felim had taught him how. There had been no need. Edward was simply perverse. She had watched other times and she knew when the fit was coming and saw how, despite the shaking hands, the quivering lips, the blinking eyes, he was able to take hold and drive away the madness. What was she to do? What would Richard do when she brought in all their hopes on a litter, babbling and foaming at the mouth? Edward could have stopped it. He had not. He had defied her. He lay there in that suspended state neither dead nor alive, neither asleep nor awake. Sometimes he talked nonsense, rambling about a dead wolf, a spy, about fire, hell, God. Mostly he said nothing and the words were not words at all but sounds garbled in his throat. He was that way now, silent, at Pevensey, a stronghold on the sea which had been Edmund's. In the faces here, despite the polite voices and the deferential bowing, she read their hatred of herself and the boy. Their lord had died or they would not have been even as subservient as they were. There was hostility here and she was anxious to sail but the weather forbade it.

While her thoughts would turn away, they kept returning to Edward. If there were any other way she would forsake the ugly little beast. Alfred was too young; it would be much the more difficult. Still?

The winter raged and sea refused calm.

"Lady, I am sorry. We cannot sail in this. We'd all be killed."

And so they waited.

A priest was brought, a healer said to drive away the madness. In a closed room he stayed with Edward the night through. And there was no cure. So he stayed the day and another night. And there was no cure. She sent him away. The boy called Seven was always near, either in the room or at the door. She wondered when he ate or slept or relieved himself.

The old blind man came to her. "Tomorrow the wind will calm."

"How know you this?"

"I can hear it. I can tell by the sounds. Tomorrow the wind will die."

"And for how long will it be calm?"

"Who's to tell? I do not see the future. I am only a swineherd who knows the sea."

"Send for a seer," she ordered and they brought to her a wee man, stooped and dressed in layers of black rags. He smelled of camphor and even in the snow wore nothing on his feet. He carried a large rock before him in two hands, holding it out with a priestly rituality as if he bore the Holy Eucharist.

"What is the rock?" she asked him.

"I bear the sins of my father. He killed a man with this stone and an angel has bid me, as a reminder for eternity, to bear the instrument of death before me."

"And do you always?"

"When ere I go forth."

"Tell me, Seer, when passes the storm?"

"On the morrow, Lady. It will pass for seven days and come again."

"Make ready," she ordered them all. "We sail on the morrow for the sea will be calm."

"Emma have you looked out?" Godfrey stared at her as if she were as mad as Edward.

"It will pass. We sail comes the morning light."

She buried herself in furs and braved the wind. The sea was carried on it and felt wet against her face. She walked toward the sound of water that beat against itself and hammered the rocks beneath. The sky swirled, gray, like an aroused dragon. Thunder drummed overhead and there were splashes of lightning, yet snow stretched across the land. She stood facing out at the angry water, gray like the sky, lifting and falling, the sight as terrifying as the sound.

The blind man had followed and now stood slightly behind her.

"It is like the end of the world," she said. "If you were able to look upon this, I doubt you could believe it to be calm by the morrow."

"I can see it. In my mind the sounds show me the picture and the years I've seen the sea, thus I promise as I hear it now it will be quiet come the morning."

"But will it last?"

"Only God can say."

Rain, heavy, cold, and dripping with ice, began falling, puncturing the snow and freezing where it made holes. Despite it she stood, her clothing saturated and clinging wet to her skin, and saw through the thick rain the moving, whirling sea. The blind man, seemingly as oblivious to the weather, remained at her side. And when she finally turned and left to go inside, he followed.

Safe from the storm, those in her company gathered in the hall to be served by the unfriendly faces of Edmund's house. Emma sat at the long table and dipped a hard crust of bread into a cup of wine. "It will cease," she said. The rain drummed heavier against the building. Darkness fell. After the meal she sat on the hard seat between her brothers listening to the soft sounds of a boy sing of the wanderings of a Frankish prince. The boy, no more in age than Edward, had large open sores, dripping, on his face. The pounding of the rain stopped. Emma gathered her wraps about her and went out into the cold. The rain had been transformed to ice that clung to barren trees and even in the darkness found flecks of light to reflect and glisten. A soft snow was blown on the wind. She went in. "It is ending," she told Aesval and went to sleep.

A cold sun rose through a broken sky. The sea was quiet, so perhaps it was only the somberness of the day that made it seem ready to fight again. Yet it lapped gently at the shore in the early morning.

"Lady," the blind man came and spoke in a soft voice, "do not sail for another storm comes." She ignored him and ordered all ready to make to sea.

And the navigator came and spoke not softly. "There is a storm ahead."

"You should do as he says, Emma," Godfrey said.

"No. We are boarded. All is ready. We will sail."

A drum pounded the tune of the waves and the giant oars slapped the water, dipped and were raised aloft. The helmsman turned the ship to the wind and the sail was raised and bellowed out shameless as a pregnant whore. The pounding repetition of the oars continued and Emma stood aft watching the lone figure of the blind swineherd on the cliff above vanish in the distance and the cliffs themselves were soon barely visible. And the sea, so calm but moments before, began to churn like a thin gruel ready to boil in the pot and heavy clouds vanquished the sun.

Those were the only warnings; there were no heralds. Without announcement the storm struck, tearing the sea apart and lifting it up over the ship and the water came as if a giant pig trough had been dumped over the ship and there was no relenting and for hours it beat against the wooden vessel, turning it, raising it high on the edge of giant waves, then dropping it, sinking down into the hole between the swells, tossing it like an indifferent juggler, and the slapping of the oars was irregular and the beating drum, its skin wet, muffled the cadence and no man knew in what direction the course lay or into what wind they sailed, but it seemed as if they were being pushed to the north away from Rouen and the smell of the sea, salty, sated the dripping clothes and the giant mast cracked, splintered and brought the sail tumbling onto the deck and two men were knocked beneath the weight of the wood and one was killed and the Atheling, Edward, was tossed from the litter and like a stuffed rag flopped about on the wet decking until Emma had him lashed against a bulkhead and he choked and regurgitated seawater and the boy, Seven, covered with Edward's vomit, stayed close to him and oars splintered and broke away in the water and rowers were left with sticks in their hands and the drum ceased to pound and sharp cracks of lightning cut through the sky and reached down into the water and the helmsman screamed out that there was a giant sea serpent to the steerboard side but Emma saw nothing and a soldier fell overboard and was beaten into the water by the oars and still the water slapped across the deck and the sea would not relent and Emma saw, through the wet hair plastered down her face, a slave girl being thrown to the deck and a soldier picked her up and held her, his rough hands rubbing her wet breasts and then with a sense of urgency groped between her legs and she saw Willie come up behind the soldier and strike him across the back of the neck and the soldier and the girl reeled and slid across the wet footing and Emma edged over to the girl and looked down at her, watching the water wash over her.

"Know you witchery?" Emma yelled out over the wind.

"No, Lady." There was fright in her voice.

"You have talent for nothing," Emma said and moved toward Willie, whose face still fixed with anger. "It will take strong deviltry to safeguard us against this cursed gale."

Yet, the storm diminished nearly as fast as it had arisen and land came in sight, vanished, and then reappeared. The navigator took water swept in from the sea and, dropping his britches, rubbed the wet sample upon his genitals. His scrotum was creased with dirt. "Flanders," he said. "This is the seawater of Flanders."

The land came nearer and the helmsman seemed helpless and the ship searched the land on its own. A battering jolt and the smash of splintering wood and oars fell to the water and sailors, soldiers, horses, all were spewn across the deck and Emma clung to a bulkhead and the ship ceased to move, run aground on the rocks, and they were close in to the coast. But what coast? Was the navigator right, was it Flanders?

The vessel clung precariously on the rocks as if debating whether to disintegrate or return to sea and one by one they carefully left the ship and slipped into the shoulder-high water. A soldier offered to bear Emma in his arms but she declined and made her way on her own toward the shore. The shallow water was spotted with large ragged rocks which at intervals offered an anchor as she pushed through the soaking sea. Loosened chunks of snow slipped from overhanging land, floated and then drowned in the weight of their own wetness. Emma could see six shadows of varied heights that she realized as she approached were human figures: a man, a woman and four children, bundled in dirty rags. A horse being led ashore splashed by. Emma reached the snow-covered ground and she climbed without help up the eroded bank. She shivered, colder out of the water than she had been within. Her hair streamed wet and her clothing stuck to her body and was the temperature of ice. Her possessions in wood staves were lugged ashore, but the clothing within was as wet as that she wore.

"What is this place?" Emma asked the rag figures.

The man pointed inland. "Bruges. There is Bruges." The tongue spoken was decidedly Flemish.

Most of the horses had either been swept ashore or their legs had been broken and they were left aboard to die. But among the four yet able to walk one was brought forward for Emma. Edward's litter was carried to land and laid atop a drift of snow.

Among the last to leave the ship were Godfrey and Willie. They bore Alfred ashore and as they reached land Emma could see boards beginning to break away and, once loose, float in the cold sea.

"Show us to Bruges," Emma ordered the man in the rags, but he stood there as if not understanding.

"We don't need him," Willie said. "I know where we are. It is but a short ride. You can see the tower on the rise and there will be fire and heat and wine and the hospitality of our good Count Baldwin." Willie helped Emma mount the horse. The beast was wet and slippery and she steadied herself against the dripping mane. Emma held back the reins and looked at the entourage of wet, freezing human flesh, alive and seeming not to care. Only Edward was oblivious to it all, a peculiar smile on his face, and in her misery she was angered by his serenity.

As they made their way slowly from the sea, Emma turned back to see the ragged shadows rush into the water and toward the breaking vessel.

"Scavengers," Aesval swore and ran to keep apace with Emma.

The sun appeared. Bruges, in the distance, became a silhoutte set at the end of the glaring stretch of snow. The light about it reminded Emma of some painting she had seen of Jerusalem. Moving toward them from the town was a distorted blurred image. A man. At some point Emma realized he was naked. His hair, long and a dirty yellow, dropped about his face mingling with scraggles of a urine-colored beard. His body was scraped with stripes of blood between patches of dirt and as he continued to approach he made new lines of pain upon his legs with a leather scourge, the ends of which seemed tipped with metal that sparkled in the sunlight. He passed close beneath her, nearly, in his oblivious state, running into the horse, and Emma saw the insipid smile. She looked back at Edward and saw his expression of serenity. The flagellant continued down the road away from them.

Riders, all on white mounts, bounded from Bruges. "Who approaches?" a voice boomed out even before the horses halted in their path.

"The Count of Eu. Godfrey, his brother, and Emma, Queen of England," Willie called back.

"And Edward, rightful King of England," Emma added.

"Inform Lord Baldwin!" the booming voice yelled back and a rider turned his horse and sped back to Bruges.

The others served as their escort into the bustling town. Slop ran on stone-paved streets between the stalls of merchants and a woman squatted to pee in Emma's path and she steered her horse around her. The horse's feet clopped against the stone and obliterated the sounds of voices hawking wares. Heads were bundled in hoods and snow had been pushed away leaving a clear wet path along which they rode toward the house of Flanders.

"Welcome, dear Queen," Count Baldwin greeted her. He was a big man with a wide grinning mouth dominating a clean-shaven chinless face. His skin was a yellow gray marred further by numberless boils. "We must see you warm and dry."

"God thank you, Count."

"It is just one day unexpectedly I hail the Queen of France at my door and upon the next the lovely England." Baldwin touched her wet buttocks as she stepped past him, and it seemed too convenient for accident.

"Bertha? Queen Bertha is here?"

"Yes."

"And the King, Robert?"

"Nay, it is all quite tragical. But we will discourse on all this and also on what you, my dear Emma, be doing in Flanders . . . but after, dear Lady, after you have some dry apparel and some wine."

Attendants were called and they were led to chambers. Emma soon stood naked, drying before a fire in a long, cold room. A large-breasted Flemish woman chattered about the snow and laid out dry wool garments. The coarse material scratched as Emma pulled it on. The color was a pale blue and there was an edging of white needlework. The cloak was a deep purple and Emma felt entirely regal and swept into the great hall.

The court was a mélange of Jews and Venetians, of traders, merchants, bankers, Castilians, of emissaries from the Saxon court . . . someone whispered to her that the dark man in the coarse dress was a Bulgar who kept a bear rather than a mistress . . . there was a Turk, and a bishop from Leon and a giant of a man with a bushy beard, said from Armenia. Standing beside Count Baldwin was Bertha of France.

"My Lady Emma, the sea has swept you in like some goddess of yore," Bertha greet her, kissing her cheek.

"Dragged in. Beaten and bruised by my friend the sea, Queen."

"Queen no longer. If you were betrayed by the sea, I have been traitored by France."

"How is this?"

"I am Bertha, the witch, had you not heard? There are those for these years have worked against me fearing my powers, being powers of demons, of course, over my dear Lord Robert. They finally succeeded. The Pope has annulled the marriage. I am no longer Robert's wife."

"And you accepted this?"

"Did I have a choice? It was that or Robert and I both were to be exiled."

"Good God, Bertha, you anger me! What is the sense of power if you use it not? Where were your armies?"

"Peace. Christ's love does not allow us to lead man against his brother in the name of temporal power. No. *Pax* is the word, Emma. What would be the sense of ruling a kingdom if not ruled as Christ would have it?"

"No man can rule without a sword raised in his arms and you are proof of that, I see. But as to this charge of witchery, surely the Pope—"

"No, the official decree from Rome dissolved the marriage on ground of sanguinity. Yet those behind feared some unnatural powers I supposedly had over the King."

"And what, Madam, without husband or position, do you now?"

"I go where e're I am welcome. I wander the courts until a welcome death o'ertakes me. And you, Emma, I hear the Ironside is dead, why are you not in England with your son?"

"The Dane has stolen our . . . my son's throne. I was aship en route to Rouen to gain an army in my cause, but between the sea and the boy . . ." Emma threw open her arms.

"The boy? What is with Edward, Lady?"

"A fit. He lies neither alive nor dead. We brought him here on a litter. I know not what Richard will say on seeing him thus. My war may well be lost before I have been granted one soldier."

"The poor child."

"The poor mother, I assure you. It was deliberate."

"Deliberate, really, Emma! Think of the poor Atheling."

"Poor, my precious relics. It was quite intentional. Edward could have stopped the fit."

"How?"

"There was a man that served this Queen. Edward's tutor. He had powers—"

"Felim MacBoru?" Bertha interrupted.

"Aye, that is he. He made cures and—"

"I know all this. I know well of MacBoru, but why has he not healed the boy?"

"He is dead, Lady. Alas, the monstrous Edmund had MacBoru's head parted from his body."

"Poor man, but perhaps the luckier he was not burned for sorcery. I fear that death more than I fear life. But the boy, you said he could stop the fits from coming on?"

"Yes, Felim had shown him the way, but the Atheling chose not to and since, these many days, he remains as he is, neither dead nor living."

Bertha did not speak at once and when she did her voice was lowered to barely an audible whisper. "Have me secretly taken to him. And let me be left with him awhile."

"Yes," Emma said, "I remember what you did for Richard. Across the room there is MacBoru's widow, she will keep our trust." Emma called, "Aesval, a word with you."

The former Queen of France followed the heavy Aesval from the hall and Emma joined her brothers and the Count of Flanders, who were learning from the Turk a way in which to break a man's neck using only the thumbs.

"Emma." The count took her by the elbow and led her aside. His voice had a confidential tone. "You know that the weavers of Bruges rely on English wool?"

The question was obviously rhetorical. "Yes."

"This Danish warrior, this Cnute, seems to show little interest in matters of trade I am told." He paused and touched his lips. "If the Duke of Normandy will grant you an army, I will offer you support as well."

Emma did not pause long. "How much support, Count Baldwin?"

"Troops. An army if need be and ships. Say fifty ships easily. They are here ready to sail."

"All this for wool?"

"For continued trade assurances."

"Be certain," Emma pledged. "An army—" she started to ask, but stopped short as she saw Edward in the doorway. He stood by Queen Bertha looking as well as he ever appeared. God, he is ugly. He walked toward her. "I can use that army, Count Baldwin. Indeed, it looks like I can. And give me a ship and I will sail for Rouen on next tide."

CHAPTER 21

Rouen, 1016

GODGIFU, WHO HAD EITHER MOPED OR BEEN ABOMINABLY EVIL DURING Edward's illness, transformed on his recovery to remarkably good behavior. Gone were such deeds as having peed in the soldiers' wine cask and having torn her dress into rags and made knots of it. Emma was delighted with the change. Godgifu clung to her brother, but caused no problems. She was nearly eleven. It was time, Emma realized, to begin seeking a marital arrangement for her. Her bargaining position would be much the better with Edward on the throne. A Saxon match perhaps. Saxony was a good distance and the farther away Godgifu was to be the better for them all.

The voyage was going well. The ships were sound, the sea calm, the weather admirable and Edward was going to be King. Count Baldwin had been generous and with a little maneuvering on her part she could expect a great deal more generosity. He was a good ally and when the throne was theirs it would be well to have him across the channel. Emma was looking forward to Rouen, to seeing Richard. Even the thought of Judith could not distress her. The apprehension that anything else could go wrong had vanished. The sea breezes were left behind as the vessel, its oars beating the water, moved into the mouth of the river. On entering the Seine she felt a sense of excitement. There was no doubt in her mind that with Norman troops they could succeed in driving Cnute's Danes from England. There was a potential superiority in the Norman force that had not been fully put to test. Her anticipation seemed contagious; there was an air of expectancy about the ship. Godfrey, Edward at his side, and Godgifu clinging to her brother, leaned over the rail, pointing out sites to the future King of England. There was certainty in her mind. All was assured. Edward was well. Her brother would be generous. The periodic trees along the bank were leafless, letting the sun reach through. There was no snow on the ground and the air wrapped about her like a warm bedcover. A sense of welcome prevailed as they moored at Rouen and the smells and sounds of the town drifted out to them. The only touch of gloom was the sight of Queen Bertha standing forlorn in the bow. There, but for the Grace of God . . . Emma thought.

It was one of Richard's sons who met them first as they entered the walls of the ducal house. She didn't know which one he was.

"Who are you?" he asked. His tone was demanding and officious.

"Your aunt, the Queen of England."

"I will be Duke of Normandy," he announced.

"Then you must be Richard." Emma moved hurriedly, brushing past him, but he managed to keep at her heels.

"No, I am the younger, Robert."

"But Richard, your brother, is to be the next duke and let us hope not for many years."

"Richard is weak."

Emma did not respond. "Godfrey, tell Edward to hurry. I wish him to enter at my side."

"Madam," the boy said, "you best remember me. It is with me you will have to deal. I will be the great duke."

She looked at him in abhorrence. He was a nasty vain child.

"Richard is scared of his own shadow. You'll see."

Edward came up to her.

"Edward is awful ugly," the boy said. "I hate to look at him."

"Mind your tongue, you insolent boy. You are speaking of the King of England."

"I think not," he said, "I have heard. I am privy to the duke, my father. And I say Edward won't be King."

Emma wanted to hit him, but wiped the anger from her face as an attendant opened the wooden doors and she entered the ducal hall of her brother, smiling, her son at her side. Duke Richard stood at the far end of the long room and at first her mind did not comprehend the strangeness of the trio of men beside him and then realization struck her. The three: Archbishop Wulfstan, Godwin of Wessex and Thorkell's son, the young Dane.

"What—" Emma started to ask as she brushed into the hall, leaving Edward gaping at the door.

Richard rushed down toward her. "Say nothing yet. Good news, Emma," he spoke softly as he embraced her.

"Has Cnute died as well?"

"Better than that, Lady." His voice then changed. "Godwin, will you impart our mission to your Queen and our dear sister?"

"My Lady Emma, Cnute, King of all England, asks your hand in marriage. That you come to him at Winchester as his queen."

Emma simply looked at him. She could not have answered had she been able for there was no ready answer for a question she had never considered. It was no jest, yet it seemed as far removed from reality. She looked about the room. Robert, her brother archbishop, stood at one side of the hall in the dim light. His face seemed a mask and she could not tell whether he found the suggestion as ludicrous as it seemed suddenly to her or if he thought well of it. Cnute was a young man, said to be a handsome man. "A comely man," wasn't that how Godwin had described him? She glanced at Judith. Was it jealousy she read on the so familiarly legible face of her sister-in-law? Godfrey and Willie both looked as shocked as Emma herself was and the nasty little son of her brother had a smirk on his face that said "I told you so." She would let Godgifu loose against this rotten child. She turned around to face Edward, standing between Queen Bertha and Aesval near the door. He began to tremble. Let the fit come. She was so tired of it, so weary of the ugly little monster and his madness. Whether he saw the indifference in her eyes, she did not know, but she saw him tense, watched the tightening of his muscles, and the fit seemed to fade.

"It shall not be," Edward screamed, coming to the center of the hall. "It shall not be."

Emma spoke. "King Cnute has a wife."

"Not a Christian wife," Wulfstan said.

"It seems I have been this journey before," Emma answered. "Ethelred, as well, had 'not a Christian wife.' And I had to deal with his bastard these many years. I think, my lords, I will decline your honor."

"For the sake of peace in the kingdom, my Lady, I urge you reconsider." Wulfstan's eyes pleaded with her as well as his voice. There was a tired resignation in both.

"My Lord Cnute finds you the most beautiful of all the women of this world," Godwin said.

"And how is that, Thegn?" Emma asked. "I have never laid eyes upon him, nor he on me."

"Not so, Madam. The soldier who sat by your fire at my house in Wessex was the King."

Emma for a second time was speechless. She remembered the young beautiful soldier, tall, stooping to get through the door, quiet-voiced, sensuous, and so unlike her image of the great Danish warrior.

"It was, Madam," Thorkell's son said. "That was my Lord Cnute and he was much taken with your beauty, as any man would be."

"There is advantage for us all in this," the duke spoke. "Robert and I have an interest as well. Might we all not wish for peace?"

Emma walked back to the door and faced the Queen of France. "Let me ask you, Lady."

"Put not this on my shoulders, Madam. This decision is yours."

"You are the woman of peace, though, Bertha. How would you choose? The son, or the peace of the land?"

"Do not ask." Bertha's voice was nearly crying.

"I ask."

"Peace," she said, but hardly could she be heard.

Edward shrieked out, "You said you were my friend!"

"I am," the former Queen of France said, "I am, boy."

"You are a traitor!"

"I ask this, my Lord Archbishop," Emma said, ignoring her son and addressing Wulfstan, "what child is to be heir?"

"Any child born of a marriage to yourself and Cnute."

"I would have that written in the marriage contract. Cnute is to disown the heir of his concubine or any others he may sire."

"And," Godwin spoke, "you, Madam, must disavow then as well the claims of your own Athelings Edward and Alfred."

There was a moment of silence in the hall.

"I will so grant."

And then a wail pierced the stillness. Edward. It was a cry which tore the room with its pain, shrill, ripping from his throat, the sound of a wolf being killed.

BOOK TWO

The Parvenu

CHAPTER 1

Rouen, 1017

IT WAS MICHAELMAS AND THE DUCAL HALL WAS A COLLAGE—RICH ROBES OF silk and damask and bright-dyed wool, jewels on chains and fingers reflecting the torchlight in fiery sparkles, fur-trimmed mantles in purest white and deepest black and soft gray and honey brown, the pitch of voices rising to be heard in rowdy tales and off-key songs and tables bent from the harvest of food. A goat wandered among the gowns and was chased from the food and a monk with a harelip related a vision he had beheld of St. Augustine and a knight told of being attacked by four women in the mountains of Castile and of their lewdness and a banker of Bruges with an enormous belly swore he had been robbed by Bulgar pirates and the brother-in-law of Cnute complained of the serat, "What is this ghastly drink?"

"Fermented milk and onion and garlic," he was told, and spit it out and called for wine.

And more torches were lit and the great hall sparkled with the dancing of a bald Italian merchant and the raised silver drink bowls toasting the duke and the pearls the duchess wore in her hair and which dripped down the back of her neck and the white protruding teeth of her daughter Alice.

But in the dark, in a corner half hidden by an arch, Emma's three children remained alone and apart. Edward, wearing an ill-fitting tunic made over from an old one of his Uncle Willie's, sat on a stone rise. He heard, but was not listening, looked, but was not seeing. He was trying to determine how one knew it was the present and not the past or future, and while he fought with the philosophic dilemma, he discovered his hands, empty, and turned and twisted them about as if never having seen them before and continued turning one over the top of the other barely touching them at intervals and enjoying the tingling tactile sensation. He explored one palm with two fingers of the other hand and next gently etched the back of his hand with a fingernail. But how did he know that this was the present and not the past or future? Alfred was stretched out on the stone beside him and Godgifu, looking waifish in a torn gown, was bunched up on the floor and clung to Edward's knee.

"To our guests of the Daneland," the duke said and raised his bowl, "to the son of the Jarl Thorgals-Sprakaleg, Ulf, and his beautiful wife, Estrid, the sister of our brother King Cnute."

"To Ulf and Estrid," the others repeated and drank.

Edward returned to his hands and the guests filed to the long tables. Ulf was a young man, huge with massive hands that looked to tear bears apart, and he sat tearing wings from a roasted bird and his hair was unruly and flaxen and Edward thought he laughed too much and he gave Michaelmas gifts to the duke and the duchess and to the archbishop and to Edward's cousins, Alice and Eleanor and Robert and Richard, and Edward's old grandmother Hilder, who was trying to shoo the goat away.

Ulf spoke and Edward tried to block out the sounds. "Godwin must manage the matters of state, for the King is busy having the Queen Emma."

"Sometimes three, sometimes four times a day," the Lady Estrid added cheerfully.

It was a lie, a horrible lie. Edward could not imagine why the Lady Estrid, who was said to be very often in prayer, would lie so.

"My sister-in-law seems sore used," Aunt Judith said.

"Appropriate words, Lady," Ulf said and laughed, but Judith frowned.

"She is happy," the Lady Estrid said.

Lies, lies, lies. Edward searched his fingernails as if expecting them to sprout fire.

"This Godwin," the duke said, "must be an ambitious man."

Ulf turned to the duke. "He seems not so, your Grace, he has refused an earldom, a small one I admit, but nevertheless a position which would have elevated him to the Witan. 'I'm a simple Wessexman,' he told Cnute and so he has preferred to remain."

"Humble men should be kept under the eye," Archbishop Robert said. "They tend to be frauds."

"There is nothing devious about Godwin," Estrid said. "Though at times he could be more devout and given to God."

"We have report of your fierce piety, Lady Estrid," Uncle Robert said.

"I have two passions, your Grace—God and Ulf."

"I think it is Ulf and God and that's a fact," her husband said. "She and her brother are ample with desire. They must have got the gift from old Forkbeard, for they don't have the same mother."

Judith spoke to Lady Estrid with disdain. "Your mother is Sigrid the Haughty. A pagan I am told."

Lady Estrid didn't seem bothered by her tone. "And alas, there is no Christianizing her I'm afraid."

"They tell a tale of old Sigrid," Ulf began, "when shortly after her first husband, King Eric, died that the young widow was plagued by wooers in Sweden and they refused to go away. She went so far as to burn the houses down that two of them slept in. But the best tale is about how the very Christian King Trygvesson came to Sweden. He went to her bed in the middle of the night and she, thinking he had come to make love, opened her arms to him, but instead of lovemaking he tried to baptize her and she got so angry she bit his ear off."

"She is a hopeless pagan," Estrid said. "She keeps a tree of death on which she hangs dead animals."

"And sometimes dead babies," Ulf added, "and no one knows where she gets them."

No one responded and the table was silent for a moment and then cousin Robert, smiling as sweetly as he could, got up and went over to Estrid and said in a clear voice what Edward knew to be a lie, "I like you, Lady Estrid."

"Thank you, child. I must confess, Duke Richard, your little Robert is an absolutely captivating child."

"A devil," the archbishop said.

"A perfect angel," Estrid argued.

"Lady," it was the duke who spoke. "We do not always find him so, but still, I must confess, he is captivating, our magnificent devil."

"Why don't you take him back to England and drown him?" Edward's Grandmother Hilder said and then stuffed a handful of gravied bird in her face and the gravy ran down her chin.

Judith opened her gift, which was wrapped in red-colored cloth and tied with white cord. It was a large Madonna carved of ivory with tiny jewels inset in the gown. She set it aside without acknowledging it. "Your mother is at Upsala, Lady Estrid?"

"Yes, at the court of my brother."

Ulf opened up his hands in a gesture of expansiveness. "He has the largest testicles of any man on earth."

"I find that accomplishment hardly worthy of noble conversation," Judith said and scratched her arm.

"But it is true, Duchess," Ulf continued. "They are as big as a bull's and the King is proud of them and will show them to man, woman or child who would have a look."

Uncle Robert coughed. "For reasons other than that you have a remarkable family, Lady. Two brothers kings—"

"Three, your Grace."

"Yes, I'd forgot your brother Harold of Daneland."

Her brother Cnute was not the King of England despite what they said. Edward was the King and his mother was going to poison Cnute when she got the chance and the Witan would name Edward their King. Next Michaelmas, when he was King, he would have a rich damask gown trimmed in fur dyed red and wear a necklace of thirty precious stones in a heavy gold chain that hung to his waist and have a crown so weighty that his head would hurt and his mother would sit beside him and he would give her a great gift, some fine relic, perhaps, yes . . . a part of the true cross, itself, and she would give him a ring so large it would cover his whole hand. He turned his empty hands over one another.

"I like you very much," Robert repeated. "You are beautiful."

Lady Estrid beamed. But Edward knew she was not beautiful, not like his mother.

"I have three gifts left," Ulf declared. "Where are the Athelings and their sister?"

"Edward," the duke called.

"I am here," Edward responded softly and peered from around the arch.

"Come here," the duke ordered. "All three of you."

They came into the light and Edward was ashamed for he knew they looked like poor serfs in their ragged clothes and he put his head down.

Lady Estrid stood up and she was very tall. Her hair was brown and turned in a braid around her head and she had long fingers and her nails were chewed. Her feet were large and she wore large red slippers.

"Here, this is for you," she said to Godgifu.

"I don't want it," Godgifu said.

"Open it!" the duke ordered.

Edward took off the cloth wrapping for her as she stubbornly refused to touch it. It was a large seashell, the size of a big bowl, and the inside was a shiny blue and in the middle was a black shape that looked something like a bird in flight.

"It is a black-raven shell," Ulf said, "and very rare and very magic and my sister Gytha found it for me at the sea near our home in Jomburg."

"If you put it to your ear when someone dies," Estrid said, "you can hear the flapping of angel wings as the soul is being taken off to heaven."

"I hope you die so I can hear it," Godgifu said, still not touching the shell.

"Godgifu!" the duke yelled.

"It's all right!" Ulf said. "She is only a child."

"An ill-mannered monster," Judith said.

"For you," Ulf told Alfred, handing him a gift wrapped in yellow cloth. The child opened it and showed Edward the carved wooden ship with the Viking cloth sail and Alfred smiled.

"Alfred loves the sea," Edward said.

Edward's gift was in blue cloth and it was narrow and tied in red. "Be careful, it is sharp," Ulf said as he handed it to him.

Edward slowly removed the cloth, exposing the silver blade and then the wooden and jeweled cross of the knife's handle. It was a splendid knife, fit for a king. "Is it from my mother?"

"No, it is from us," Ulf said. "You must wear it at your waist, beneath your tunic."

"Yes," Edward said, examining the blade with the edge of his finger.

"Have you nothing else to say, Edward?" Judith asked.

Edward turned to Ulf. The man had a slight scar that ran the length of his cheek. His eyes hid nothing and it was hard to hate the man. Edward cleared his throat to make conversation. "If God created heaven and earth what did he do before that time?"

Ulf looked at him a moment and then laughed. "He was probably busy making hell."

"Edward," the duke said in an exasperated tone so much like his mother used.

Godgifu grabbed the shell from the table where Edward had set it and smashed it hard against the stone floor several times until it cracked, broke and fell into pieces. "I hate you all," she screamed and ran from the hall.

"Tomorrow," the duke said, "I am sending the three of you to Falaise. Maybe Godfrey can do something with you."

Edward, the knife stuck at his waist, went out looking for his sister. She sat in the dark on the cold stone of the loggia, blocking the path. The smallest crescent of a moon was visible in the sky above the building opposite. The sounds of autumn insects hummed; otherwise it was quiet.

"I will set fire to this house," Godgifu said.

"It won't burn," he told her. "It's stone."

"I hate it here."

"Tomorrow we were being sent away to Falaise. Perhaps Mother will send for us while we are at Uncle Goddy's."

"She is evil and I hate her."

"You mustn't say that."

"She is evil and I hate her," she repeated, "and she will never send for us."

She would send for them as soon as she had poisoned Cnute. He was certain, somehow. She had killed Edmund and she would kill Cnute as well.

Godgifu sat in the dark and tore her gown some more until the skirt was a shred of rags. Edward said nothing to her, but stood watching. The aura of light moved in the dark toward them and Edward knew by the gait and size it was their cousin Robert.

"Ulf lies," Robert said. "He and the ugly Lady Estrid lied and told you those nasty things about your mother and how the King Cnute puts his pee-pee into your mother four times a day—"

"She doesn't do those things," Edward said defiantly. "She never lets any man touch her there. Never!"

"Ulf lies and says she does. He tells everybody lies. You should kill him, Edward. In the middle of the night you should kill him with the knife he gave you."

Robert ran off. Edward fingered the knife at his waist, touching the jewels in the wooden handle. He stood there in the blackness beside Godgifu until he heard some of the adults leaving the great hall. "I want to see Robin if we are to leave tomorrow. Help Alfred to bed," he ordered his sister and left her there and the ducal house and moved through the dark street of Rouen toward the Church of St. Ouen. A man was lying dead, faceup, in the street and Edward walked around him.

"What is wrong, Edward? Coming here at this time of night?" Robin of Jumieges rubbed his soft blue eyes as he came into the courtyard. In the other hand he held a candle which illuminated his face, the light carving the shadows beneath his high cheekbones.

"You must go to bed with the birds," Edward said.

"I am a monk," Robin reminded him.

"They are sending me to Falaise in the morning. I came to say good-bye."

"And Godgifu and Alfred?"

"They too."

"You must stay together. You must look out for them. They are all the family you have."

"And my mother. She will send for us soon. I know."

"You must not depend on it, Edward. You must rely on no one but yourself."

An old monk, peering with squinting eyes over a candle, came toward them. "In your cell, Robin of Jumieges."

"A friend who is going on a journey has come to say good-bye."

"For an important man one must get from one's bed. It is God's way, for all others our vows do not allow the idleness of company."

"I am the King of England," Edward said.

"Likely, in those rags," the old monk said. "To bed, Robin." He wandered away, his candle disappearing behind a door.

"I must do as he says, Edward, but you look to yourself and keep to your reading."

"Who will teach me now?"

"I will lend you two manuscripts, but you must not tell anyone. They are of the teaching of St. Augustine."

"What if I don't know the words?"

"There is talk of my being sent back to Jumieges and if I am I shall come to Falaise and help you with all the words you cannot master. You must keep a list."

Robin got him the rolled parchments and they parted as Robin blew out the candle and his face disappeared in the dark.

The noise of the ducal house settled into stillness. The other Edward stood in the damp tiny chamber shared with Godgifu and Alfred. Alfred stirred and talked in his sleep, but Edward was barely aware. Cnute was no king at all, not if he left the business of state to a thegn. When his mother poisoned Cnute and he became King, he would have Godwin's tongue cut out and send him to Norway where they said it was terribly cold.

The other Edward stood and only the footsteps of the night guard and the hoot of the owl broke the quiet. Edward slipped furtively from his cell along the loggia until he came to the chamber occupied by the Dane Ulf and his wife and he pressed open the door without a sound. He could feel the pressure of the knife at his waist as he bent over the auras upon the bed and stared into the sleeping face of the giant Dane.

Suddenly the man's eyes opened and for a moment Edward read the fright as Ulf bolted upright upon the straw. The woman never stirred. "Edward," he spoke softly, catching his breath, "you scared me. I thought it was someone come to kill me in my sleep."

"Do you like to climb trees?" Edward asked.

"As a matter of fact I do," Ulf told him, "but not in the middle of the night."

"There is a great oak near where the Robec runs into the Seine. Its branches high up in the tree are so strong they will hold even you."

"Tomorrow you must show me."

"I am being sent to Falaise in the morning."

"I will ask your uncle to let you stay these few days we are here. Do you sword, Edward?"

"Yes, and I am good at it. They say I once knocked Cnute off his horse. You look like him."

"He has a scar on his face, just as I do on mine, but on the opposite side. We gave them to each other as boys when we were at swords, but you and I shall have a go at it tomorrow. And do you play at hazards?"

"I don't know how."

"I will teach you," the Dane said as his wife moved slightly in the bed beside him. "But for now you must sleep, boy."

"Yes," Edward said and started for the door. "Thank you for the knife."

"May you always use it well, lad."

Edward opened the door, but turned back into the room. "Ulf," he asked, "whose idea was it that my mother should marry Cnute?"

"I don't know . . . Godwin . . . I suppose. Most ideas are Godwin's."

"Yes," Edward said and went into the autumn night, closing the door gently behind him.

CHAPTER 2

York, 1017

ON A COLD ADVENT MORNING, GODWIN, HIS BREATH VISIBLE, RODE TOWARD York astride the black mare. The world was barren and seared. Dead. No snow hid the hard frozen earth and ice wiped the streams smooth. Rocks protruded in the narrow road and the horse stumbled over them. Godwin rode alone; his man, a red-headed hunched giant, trudged a mile or so back, and as Godwin looked around he could see Wordig's silhouette visible on the empty moor. Out of seeing, and farther back along the road, moved Godwin's army of Wessexmen.

Godwin took the cold air deep in his lungs. He wore a heavy fur cloak and warm lamb boots and was quite comfortable. In fact, he was well satisfied with the world in general. Emma was happy, occupied with Cnute. Cnute was happy, occupied with his Queen. And with the Queen and King content, Godwin could go about the business of the court and state with little interference. Elgiva, Cnute's whore, or other wife, had been removed from York in anticipation of Emma's arrival and Godwin had been able to rid the court of Ulf for the time being, as well, by arranging to have him escort Elgiva back to the Daneland. Ulf disturbed Godwin. He frequently engaged the King in horseplay and childish games unbefitting the dignity of the royal presence. Godwin was one of the few who had taken a dislike to the generally affable young Dane, for he had no sense of decorum, duty or responsibility and Godwin found it irritating. He was an overgrown boy who had the King climbing trees and swimming in oxen water holes and wasting his time gambling with monks at St. Ultas.

Godwin had worked diligently to make the King's throne more secure. After all, Cnute was an usurper. Emma's Edward had been kept isolated in Normandy, as was his brother, and Edmund's twin Athelings had been literally torn from their mother's arms by one of Godwin's soldiers and sent to the Swedish court, but now Godwin was about to execute the more difficult feat of ending forever the interference and unpredictable trouble which could be instigated by the traitorous Earl Eadric. While Cnute supposedly gathered the Christmas Witan at York to acquiesce to the council and disclaim his right to the throne of Daneland, the true purpose of this Witan was to rid England of the Earl of Mercia. It had been difficult both to convince Cnute of the practicality of that intrigue and to convince him as well that it was a good ploy to pretend to give up his right to the throne of Danes which he insisted his brother Harold had stolen from him. But in the end Godwin prevailed and Harold and the Witan were both to be taken off guard. The Christmas Gemot at York should—

Out of nowhere! His horse nearly bolted and he grabbed tight on the leather. They stood, three hags, blocking his path, looking so alike it was impossible to tell one from the other.

"Godwin is an ambitious man," one of the crones spoke and it didn't matter which for it was no use trying to tell them apart. They changed places like it was a dance.

"Godwin would be King, but he willn't," another spoke, or perhaps the same one.

"Godwin will be great." The voices were shrill and vibrato.

The horse became uneasy with the sound, which had a menacing quality. "Who are you? What do you want of me?"

"We want nothing of you, Godwin, it is you that wants of us." They changed places again. They all wore brown filthy cotterons wrapped with dirty red aprons and despite the cold neither cloak nor mantle. Their hair was all the same, a snarl of gray wads.

"Godwin is ambitious . . ."

"Godwin would be King . . ."

"Godwin will be remembered . . ."

"Who are you?" he demanded, his voice growing angry.

"Sisters. Three sisters."

"Born of the same womb."

"Less than an hour in our ages."

"I am Elgrith, the beautiful one."

"And I be Snurlarf, the mad."

"And alas, I am Gogorunk, the ugly sister."

"And you are Godwin, the pigherder's son, whose daughter will be a queen."

"But Godwin willn't be a king."

"Ah . . . but his seed will steal the crown ere the comet comes a second round."

"This is nonsense. I serve the King, nothing more," he yelled. "Out of my path."

"When pigherders wash the shit from under their nails, the seed of kings will grow there."

"Godwin is an ambitious man."

"Though he willn't be King."

"I don't want to be King!" he yelled as they changed positions once again.

"No worry on that score. Didn't you hear me?" she yelled as if he were deaf. "You willn't be King."

"Your daughter shall be dead, but rise again as if she were air in a pig's bladder." And the crone who said it roared with laughter.

"OUT OF MY WAY! OUT OF MY WAY!"

"Godwin is an ambitious man."

Then they vanished into the ditch.

Wordig came trudging up, grunting and complaining of the cold.

"Did you see them?"

"See who?" Wordig answered with a snarl.

"The three old crones."

"I saw nobody," he grumbled and trudged on ahead.

"You had to have seen them," Godwin said, but he spoke to the cold wind, for while he held back his horse, Wordig was down the road.

Was it his imagination? The spector of Godwin, the magnate, had first crept across his mind in the night to terrorize him as if he were a maid to be raped. He would awake from these night dreams soaked with sweat and his breath gasping the air. What was this lion fear? He saw the men about Cnute: Eadric, treacherous, but floundering in his own indecision; Thorkell, loyal, but constricted by hell and the Christian God; Wulfstan, astute, yet mired in his obsession—England; Ulf, the King's mirror, but careless in youthful enthusiasm; Eric of Northumbria, the venerated warrior, but old and senile with death waiting not too distant at the lintel; Northman, courageous, however doomed by his injudicious mouth; and the others, powerful men, skilled warriors, but not a one without such shortcomings. It was as if they all bore Balin's sword.

If a swineherd's son so easily could become a thegn, how much the simpler for a thegn to rise to chief? He was wiser than the lot of them. Why should he fear? He was the lion in his own lair, the fear that frightened himself. Less than king, he could become anything he wished. He called the lion out to lick his hand. But who then were these three sisters?

Christ! It had grown cold suddenly, he thought, and pulled his fur cloak tighter about him. He passed Wordig by and galloped toward the city, the wind chilling him through. He had never before been to York and discovered that even in the cold winter it reeked of decaying animal flesh and dead urine. It was a large town filled with hunger and pain and there was an air of cruelty and deception, as if lurking behind the mud and timber walls hooded figures waited with daggers thrust from hands. It began to snow and he was welcomed into the archbishop's palace and a roaring fire.

And in the days which followed they came for the Christmas Gemot. Soldiers and clerics and children and wives. With horses and sleds, bundled in skins, bearing gifts and old animosities. They came: Eric, the old man, coughing winter from his lungs; Godric, his ghoulish eyes deep in their sockets, reflecting his dire pronouncements that all the world was doomed to hell; Ranig the Ruthless; Eglaf of the Severn Valley; the revered Thorkell the Tall; Archbishop Wulfstan, his dripping sore nose nearly the color of his robes; Eadric, wearing such arrogance that it masked all perception of his impending downfall; Leofwine, having no thought to being Governor of Mercia, yet destined; Bishop Ethelric, who had a twitch and made a frequent "ta" sound between his lips; Eadulf Cudel, a stranger among them, bald and breathless, spitting phlegm and platitudes, and succeeding his brother Uhtred, discovered but days earlier frozen beneath the ice of the river Tees; Ehtelwerd of Devon, who shared Godwin's conspiracy; and the young men: Ulf missing of course, but Hakon Ericsson, who would raise no sword to gain back the vice royalty of Norway, but vainly preferred to idle his time combing his silken hair, which reached to his waist; Northman, son of Leofwine, whose own mouth would devour him; Harold Thorkellsson with stubbled fingers, futilely gesturing at every question, fearing, perhaps, being indicted by the answers. For days they came, entourages trailing patterns of footprints and trampling paths across the snows of Yorkshire.

The King and Queen arrived and found the comfort of a warm bed. And after several hours Emma appeared in the hall, looking young and fresh, her cheeks red from the journey and her yellow hair shining. She smiled and walked toward the fire and Godwin.

"The trouble with happiness, Godwin, is wondering how long it can last."

"Never fear, Madam, yours shall last. Here, do sit by the fire." Godwin brushed a stool for her.

She sat. "Is the whore a beauty, Godwin?"

"You must not think on her, Lady."

"Is she?"

"She is not fair and has the look of evil. No, Lady Queen. Elgiva is no beauty."

"I were she was dead," Emma said, straightening the folds of her freshly brushed gown.

"Be content she is gone."

"And her son? What of her son?"

"He is a pagan, like his mother."

She waited for a moment. "Godwin, I have been married soon it will be two years. I am not yet with child."

"It is a little beyond a year, Madam, and there is a saying that too often to the garden disturbs the seeds. Enjoy your happiness. There is time to be with child."

"Yes, you are right. Was there ever such a man?"

"Never, Lady."

A young man, frail, with strawberry hair and a short curl of beard on his chin, strummed a lute. His face was finely carved and soft, as if borrowed from a young girl. He had a clear tenor voice which cut through the smoking air of the room. As he sang, the noise in the room stilled. He sang of Ymir the Rime-giant and the beginning of the creation. He sang of how the dripping rime congealed as hoarfrost. He sang of the hermaphroditic Ymir and how he coupled one foot with the other and how was begot a son.

"What is your name, skald?" Emma asked as the boy finished his song.

"Gamol, Lady Queen."

"Well, Gamol, you have a lovely voice. Of whose house are you?"

"The King's mother's, Madam."

Gunnerhild sat in layers of black gown across the room. "I shall make a present of him to you, Queen," the old woman said, but the gift was made without giving or warmth.

"Thank you, Mother Queen," Emma smiled graciously.

"I am not your mother," Gunnerhild told her and turned and talked to Leofwine.

"She doesn't like me," Emma whispered to Godwin.

"She is just old and crotchety," he assured her.

Earl Eric walked over toward them. Despite his age, there was something magnificent in the manner of the great warrior. His hair was like an iceberg in the firelight. He was tall and moved, if slowly, with a grandeur Godwin had never seen equalled. His voice was strong and deep. And Godwin was always drawn in as if expecting drippings of great wisdom to melt from his mouth and yet he seldom made much sense. "Do you know?" he asked.

"Do I know what?" Godwin returned the question.

"Where the Wends are buried?"

"No. Where?"

"If I knew I wouldn't have asked you. Damn fool." Eric wandered off and the Queen laughed.

"You're a damn fool, Godwin," Emma said.

"And I well know it, Lady," Godwin was saying as the King entered.

"The King! The King!"

He looked like a boy. He looked like Ulf. His hair was mussed, but not unbecomingly so, and his scarred cheek had the bloom of winter about it. He made his way across the room, slapping backs and bottoms, laughing, drinking from other's wine cups and leaving a path of pleased faces. They liked their King.

"Maid, you look so lovely that I have quite the urge to rush you to a bed," he told Emma, coming up to the fire and toasting his hands.

"If I had been maid, my Lord, I should have been quite unmaid by you by this time."

Cnute put his warm hands to her cheeks.

"I should not mind returning to the bed, my Lord, but I am afraid we might offend our guests should we depart a second time."

"Damn the guests. This Gemot is Godwin's business. I should leave him to attend the vultures."

"And these vultures, as you call them, would undoubtedly feed upon this poor flesh, my Liege," Godwin said.

Emma gave a nod of her head. "Speaking of vultures, look who but arrived."

Eadric swept into the hall, the shining furs of his cloak reflecting the torchlight. He had the bearing of a king and an arrogance in his carriage that was not quite offensive. There was an unnerving sincerity in his smile, though he did not smile at Godwin as he came toward the fire. Yes, Godwin thought, he is the most treacherous man in England without a doubt. "To kill a bear," as the saying went, "is best done by another bear," and Godwin was ready. Eadric was not as tall as the King, but his manner gave the appearance of greater stature.

"My good King, happy we are to see you again." The man's voice was smooth and waxed like honey.

"We are happy to see you, Lord Eadric, but have learned you arrive not from Mercia but our own Wessex."

"I visited, my Lord Cnute, an old friend near Pevensey, the dying Bishop Aelgstutlf."

"I was not thinking of your visit to Pevensey, but rather your travels in the southwest region, your sojourn into Devonshire."

"There are stirrings in those parts, I was afraid for our Lord King." He smiled at Cnute. "I went to see for myself if there was anything to fear from this pretender in Devon."

"Do forgive me, Lord Eadric, for interrupting," Godwin lied, "but I have tried to reassure the King there is nothing to concern ourselves with from those unarmed peasants and a madman, this Eadwig, who has self-proclaimed himself King."

"I agree, Thegn, the greater threat be the true offspring of Ethelred. Emma's children . . ." He smiled at the Queen. "And Edmund's athelings."

Emma looked up at him. "They say your wife is one of Ethelred's bastards."

"She makes no claim to such, Lady." The smile left Eadric's face and voice.

Across the room a young soldier wearing leather-gartered femoralia and a sale cape, but no shirt or tunic, motioned to Godwin.

"Excuse me, Sire," Godwin said to the King and then nodded to Eadric. "One of my house. Some business of the Gemot, no doubt."

"He seems to be rising in the world," he heard Lord Eadric say as he walked over to the young man whose name was Behi.

Godwin followed the young man from the hall. The soldier's lean build was deceptive; Godwin had seen him exert tremendous strength. And that was necessary for the young soldier's own well-being for he had a need to protect himself.

"At the north gate," the young man said in almost a whisper, and that was all he said.

Godwin nodded and continued to follow.

Like many of Godwin's house, Behi was an outcast. Godwin preferred men with flaws in their moral armor. At some point he had found that if he overlooked whatever their unsocial behavior, they were inclined to be extremely loyal to him. So it was that Wordig could masturbate publicly, and while Godwin might complain, he would never have considered cutting off Wordig's fingers as another master might be expected to do. Behi, too, exchanged unquestioned service, because Godwin overlooked the young man's affinity for taking other men's penises into his mouth.

They walked the narrow street. The rotten-timber and dried-dung houses were pitch black beyond the few open entrances. Voices spoke a dialect that Godwin knew to be Norwegian and the street reeked of slop and strong cabbage and dog excrement and garlic and the corruption of dead rats. Somewhere a baby cried. As they passed the end of rows of hovels and houses they came to the ruins of the old Roman fort.

Ethelwerd was waiting at York gate. From among the carts in Ethelwerd's train a man was delivered, bound and gagged, his face marked with recent cuts and his clothing spotted with dried blood. His arm bones had quite obviously been broken. Godwin seized the man and the slow winding train of carts and carls continued into the town. With the help of Behi, Godwin took the bound figure to an isolated spot near the wall. Behi wiped away the snow to reveal a wooden door into the earth. A rope was tied about the bound man's waist and he was lowered down into the hole where he would find for company not only rats but another prisoner, the battered and tortured envoy of the stout King of Norway. In the beginning the Norwegian had refused to cooperate, but hungered, beaten and his servant dying and being left in the same cell for three days after had brought the envoy around. He agreed in exchange for his freedom to bear testimony against Eadric. Godwin would honor his promise, but he wondered what use the man had left of life. There was but blankness in his eyes.

Godwin returned to the hall. The feasting had started and there was boar and partridge and swan and cow and mead to drink and wine and some bitter draught of the North Country. Godwin never took anything but water or goat's milk with honey to drink. He had learned that a sharper mind could listen to the careless tongues of the imbibers. Some sort of spontaneous dancing had begun and the old man Eric, his white head nodding in rhythm, beat time on the table with a large bull horn. In the middle of his pounding Eric discovered Queen Gunnerhild. "I thought you had died," he said to her.

"Not yet, old man, not yet."

Emma came across to Godwin. "You look like a housecarl about to catch a thief."

"Am I so transparent?"

"Not really. But your face is dressed in a most satisfying smirk."

"I must take care not to give away the plot. Still, I am satisfied. It has been so long since I began this mission."

"Come," she urged. "To the fire."

The singer began again.

"I've learned his mother, a Dane of Guldar's house, was butchered on St. Bice's day," Emma said.

"Whose?" he asked.

"The skald's."

The singer sang of Bari and Boru, of Othin, Vili and Ve. And the noise in the room diminished as the dancers stopped to hear his words.

Wulfstan came toward them. Even walking across the room, his movements exhibited the dignity of his ecclesiastical office. "I will share your fire," he said. "For the older I become, the colder these winters seem to get."

"Do sit, your Grace." Godwin motioned to an empty bench.

"I joy in the Nativity. Yet a Gemot is so difficult in the winter. So many, traveling so far." A large black dog ambled over and lay down at the bishop's feet. "Surely the matter before us, important as it is, could have waited until the warmer weather."

"Perhaps," Godwin suggested, "the King has other matters beside the claim to Daneland's throne to put before us."

"If he does, Godwin, you would know of it. I am uncertain why, but you of all men have the King's ear."

"I am fortunate," Godwin spoke softly.

"Maybe, your Grace," Emma interrupted, "it is because Godwin serves without asking anything in return."

"You will find, if you have not already learned, Lady Queen, everything has its price. And sooner or later the bill is presented." Wulfstan sneezed and wiped his nose on the arm of his red cloak.

Cnute, in a tunic embroidered with small black ravens and a mantle of gray wool tossed over his shoulders, came up behind the archbishop. "And the price of peace is a Dane King, your Grace. That's what it cost you Saxons, isn't it?"

"My Lord King." The archbishop struggled to get up, but Cnute motioned him to stay seated. "We are all Englishmen. We are one land, Saxon and Dane and Norseman alike." Wulfstan looked down and ran his fingers gently across the back of the dog.

"But count around the room. How many Saxons, Wulfstan?" Cnute opened his arms out in a questioning gesture.

"Still," the churchman answered, "those of us Saxons here are men of power. I head the Church. Eadric is certainly the most powerful of the earls."

"That he is," the young King agreed.

"And there is Leofwine . . . and the thegn here. It is rumored if you want a favor of the King ask Godwin."

"He is my trusted aide," Cnute said. "But not all can be so trusted. Should a noble, be he Saxon, Dane or Norse, conspire against me, where would you stand, Archbishop? Still with the peace?"

"With our duly chosen King, my Lord."

"Thank you, Wulfstan. I shall hold you to your word."

The morning rose crisp. The air, like a sharp knife, penetrated the heavy skins in which Godwin had wrapped himself. The early sun was brilliant and the snow crackled beneath the pressure of his feet. He could see the young soldier waiting at the door of the great timbered hall.

"I am ready," he told Godwin as he neared.

Godwin unstrapped a sack tied at his waist. "I give you this with care," he said and withdrew from the bag Cnute's ring. "Show this to each of Cnute's soldiers. It is your authority."

"And should they fail to accept my command?"

"The King says you are free to run a knife through such a man's gullet. Nothing must be given away in advance, no hint. Do not begin until the doors have closed on the opening of the Gemot. Eadric must be secure within and have no chance to escape or give his men any order."

"I understand. And be assured, Thegn Godwin, not a soldier of Eadric's will leave here alive."

Godwin looked at the young soldier, his face shadowed from the sun by Godwin's own figure standing before him. "Behi, you have given me loyal service in all this. What reward shall be yours when this is finished?"

The young soldier said nothing. Yet, his eyes revealed a question.

"Ask," Godwin urged.

"Only this, good Thegn. Should I be sentenced to die, I ask that you will not turn your back upon me."

"I will not let you die, Behi, to this I promise."

"You may have no choice. I do not ask you to save me. I just ask you do not turn from me as others will."

"I understand what you say, Behi, and I will not let you die."

The young soldier took the ring that had been placed back in the sack and tied it to his own cinch and with his head erect turned and marched off. Godwin stood for a moment in the cold watching him trudge through the snow. Godwin went into the great hall.

There was a din of men's voices. They gathered wrapped in furs and layers of coarse winter fabric. Tradition and ritual, pomp and ceremony would play its part, but not all custom would be observed. His Grace, Archbishop Wulfstan, waited not without as was custom, but within the warmth of the hall, and when the conch was sounded and the shivering monks paraded in, feet tracking wet snow, Wulfstan then joined the procession. "The Gemot is called." And the huge wooden doors banged shut.

Godwin watched Earl Eadric. The man's normally ruddy face was even redder from the cold. He was not a large man, but seemed the more so, especially as he was now garbed in an ornate mantle, a tapestry of flowers trimmed in a wide band of ermine. He wore a black soft hat and about his neck was draped a silver chain from which a ruby fell across his chest. He complained of the traffic of East Anglican soldiers into his lands, and there were threats and promises, denials and counterthreats. Earl Eric stood up and shouted. He wanted to war against the stout King of Norway, but his own son, Hakon, proved his greatest opponent as the youth brushed back his silken long hair. Wulfstan blew his nose upon his scarlet sleeve and asked that the discussion of a Norwegian war be set aside. Northman, son of Leofwine, said Cnute favored Thorkell in all things simply because he was the King's godfather and asked that all the nobles be given equal treatment by the King. And Cnute swore at him and told him he would grant his favors to whomever he pleased. And Wulfstan blew his nose again and said the matter they were gathered to discuss was the matter of the Danish throne and they should be about it. The doors opened and an icy wind swept the hall. All conversation ceased, for sessions of Gemot, by custom, were held without interruption. A figure handed a tied cloth sack and whispered something to the cleric guarding the door and then the door was shut again.

"To you," the robed cleric said, in a decidedly Celtic lilt, as he brought the sack over to Godwin, "I am to tell you it is done."

Godwin took the sack and stood. Aware he had become the center of attention, he walked the distance of the long table slowly, piquing the curiosity of the gathered nobles as he made his way around the King to the place at the King's right. He took the ring from the bag and dropped the empty sack on the table in front of Eadric. The earl looked at him more with annoyance than anger or curiosity. Godwin stared back at him as he spoke. "In the name of Cnute, King of Wessex, King of England and rightful King of the North, I accuse you, Eadric, Earl of the Mercians, of treason against the King."

Eadric stood. His small eyes narrowed and he glared at Godwin. "A thegn?" he asked with arrogant disdain.

"In the name of the King," Godwin pronounced.

Eadric turned his back on Godwin and walked from the table. The others sat in stunned silence. The earl threw open the doors and then stopped as he stepped out into the cold. The slump of his shoulders as he turned his head downward indicated he saw defeat. Godwin went over and stood behind him at the threshold. Like a banquet of broken grapes strewn on a white linen cloth, the dead Mercian soldiers stained the snow-covered yard.

Earl Eadric turned and came slowly back into the hall. "I underestimated you, Godwin." His voice was soft. "I truly underestimated you."

Eadric slumped down on the wooden seat.

"Who bears this testimony?" Wulfstan asked.

"I," Godwin answered.

"You are but a thegn. He is but a thegn," Eadulf Cudel pleaded.

"He bears testimony in my name," Cnute said and gave Cudel an angry look.

The doors were opened and a slave of the house of Eadric was led in.

"I will have no slave bear witness against me," Eadric shouted.

"What is your name, slave?" Cnute asked.

"Ourgdel, my Lord."

"Ourgdel, you are now a freedman. Give your testimony."

"I have served in Eadric's house since the waning of the corn moon. I was witness to his meeting with Olin, a man of the King of Norway. I heard him plead of Olin that the Norwegian King raise troops against our true King Cnute. Eadric spoke as to how he would soon be King of all England."

"Lies!" Eadric shouted. "All lies of a slave. Angry because I caught him stealing mead and beat him."

Cnute motioned the slave to continue. "Eadric spoke how he would raise the rabble in support of the one called the Churl-king and when

Cnute was overthrown, he, Eadric, would kill the Churl-king and take the crown by right of his wife's birth."

Godwin smiled at the slave. "The King thanks you for your testimony. Bring in the Norwegian, Olin."

The envoy was literally thrown into the room. His eyes seemed to burn from the lightness of the daylight. His face bled from the bites of rats and the blood wet his ragged beard. His arms were twisted and broken. He looked near death. What had been his clothing was now merely a tatter of dirty rags and he smelled abominably.

His voice was barely audible. "The Earl . . . the Earl Eadric bid . . . me ask my King for ship . . . and for men to war . . . to war against Cnute."

"Speak up!" the old man, Eric, shouted.

". . . he would," he added this time, "be . . . be the King in Cnute's stead."

"Did he say that? Did he say it just that way?" Wulfstan asked.

"He . . . did . . ."

"You are sure? He said he would be King?"

". . . yes . . ."

Eadric hardly looked up. "Norwegians are notorious liars," he mumbled to no one in particular.

"Bring in the other prisoner," Godwin called.

Behi pushed Ethelwerd's prisoner into the room. He was more alive than the last witness, but his clothing was as ragged. What had been a smock was but dirty pieces of cloth hanging from his shoulders. His baggy femoralia were bare threads connecting the tears. His hair was wild and looked as if it must be a bed of lice. Godwin's young soldier removed the gag from the man's mouth.

The man's voice was hoarse, but his words were unmistakably clear. "You are all foul-faced fetuses of a dead goat." He pointed with his bound hands in the direction of the table.

"Even Earl Eadric?" Godwin asked.

"That hind-hole of a skunk."

Wulfstan looked at him. "Who are you?"

"I am the rightful King of England."

"Did Earl Eadric say it was so?" Godwin asked.

"He did once, but now I am told that traitorous dung of a diseased horse denies me." He ran toward the table and yelled out, "I AM EADWIG, SON OF ETHELRED, KING OF WESSEX, KING OF ENGLAND."

"King of Churls," Ethelwerd of Devon, who had brought him to York, said with a laugh. "My Lord, Cnute, this is the peasant, the one called the Churl-king, who claims to be a bastard son of Ethelred the Unready."

"You have heard this churl. Eadric calls him King," Cnute said. "You have heard the testimony of a freedman and the envoy of King Olaf of

Norway. All their testimony bears this message. Eadric is a traitor. I shall take his head. Is there a man who sits this Gemot that objects?"

Swords were lifted from scabbards and set on the table. They pointed at Eadric. He brushed the point of one away. "All lies. Edmund warned me about Cnute. He is a foreigner come to destroy our Saxon land. All of you beware. You may be next."

"Take him out and cut off his head," Cnute ordered. "And get rid of this churl here as well."

Eadric was dragged from his chair by soldiers. "A thegn has done this to me. BEWARE OF GODWIN! ALL OF YOU BEWARE OF GODWIN!"

He was taken from the hall and silence fell upon the room.

Godwin went out into the cold. The bloody bodies were strewn seemingly everywhere across the snow.

Gunnerhild, under layers of black fur, came puffing along the path toward him. "This is your doing, son of the pigherder."

He made no response.

"You need a wife to temper your excesses, Godwin." She continued to trudge toward him, never varying her pace as she tramped through the snow.

"A wife, Lady?"

"An ambitious man needs a wife." She puffed along by him without slowing. "Thorgals-Sprakaleg's daughter will do."

"Who?"

"The lass of Jomburg," he heard her mutter as she went off.

He stood there in the cold. She was just a mad old woman; why did he concern himself about anything she had to say? Thorgals-Sprakaleg, where had he heard the name before? He looked out across the sea of snow patterned with the red stains of dead men. Ulf's father, the Jarl of Jomburg, that was who Thorgals-Sprakaleg was. Ulf had a sister; strange, he had never heard mention of her. The old woman was daft, of course, but he was curious; why did she think Godwin a good match for the girl? Vultures began to gather in the sky. He turned back in the direction of the hall. He was curious, nothing more, but he would inquire as to this lass of Jomburg.

Thorkell came out from the hall just as Godwin was about to enter.

"A day's work, Thegn," the tall earldorman said with obvious sarcasm and swept his hand out in the direction of the dead.

"Excuse me, my Lord," Godwin asked, ignoring the remark, "does Thorgals-Sprakaleg have a daughter?"

The eyes of the old man brightened and his voice was warm as he spoke. "Yes, and a 'freshing maid she is. A delight for an old man to think of on a cold winter's day. She is speckled with freckles and has hair the color of soft fire. She's called Gytha."

CHAPTER 3

Jomburg, 1018

DESPITE THE COLD, GYTHA SAT UPON THE OVERHANGING ROCK, HER BARE feet wet against its wetness; below, water lapped at the rock's underbelly. The froth slipped back into the sea, a darker gray than the dull sky. Hard snow wedged in the crevices of rock and stretched beyond in patches in the hill's shadows. Gulls lapped the air and cawed overhead making endless circles entwined as if linking an invisible chain. Sorgad, the hag, moved among the rocks, clawing the water for fish.

In the bay a ship raised its oars in unison. At Jomburg, land and water met hostilely over treacherous rocks, so the ships moored some distance out. Now from this vessel the striped sail fell leaving a naked mast flying the Hart's Head, the banner of the King, from its top. He would come on such a ship, a banner billowing out. He was somewhat indefinite, varying on the day and the mood, but always he was valorous, of great strength, unequalled beauty and known for such heroic deeds as no other man had yet accomplished. He would carry her off and they would have a splendid wedding.

"Do you know who Havelok was?" Gytha asked the hag.

"Don't bother me with your stories," Sorgad grumbled up to her. Sorgad's ragged gown was wet from the sea, but the water had done little to cleanse it, for the coarse-spun fabric was filthy. Her skin, too, was caked with grime.

"He was the son of the King. The most beautiful man whatever was. Of course, he was a boy first. When his father, the King, died, he left Havelok and Havelok's two sisters in the care of this terrible Earl . . . I can't remember his name . . . who pretended to love the King. But when the King was dead the earl butchered the two sisters and sent—Godard! That's what the earl's name was—"

"I don't care what his name was." Sorgad went back to clawing the water.

"This Godard sent Havelok," Gytha continued unabated, "to a fisherman named Grim and told Grim to kill the boy, promising—"

"Why didn't he kill the boy himself?"

"I don't know, he just didn't. Anyway, promising him he'd make him free and give him great wealth. Well, Grim—"

Sorgad yanked a wiggling fish from the water and she stamped her bare feet in glee upon the rocks and grinned and laughed. She had only two teeth, one bottom and one top in opposite sides of her mouth.

Gytha, who had momentarily stopped speaking to look at the hag's catch, continued, "Grim and his wife, they didn't take to killing the boy, but there was the thought of being free and having great wealth so they got an ax."

Sorgad beat the fish's head against a rock until it ceased to wiggle.

"But when they raised the ax there was this great light about the boy and they knew this was the son of a king and they opened his garments and there right on his shoulder was a king's birthmark."

"That's a dumb story."

"Well, I'm not to the good part yet."

"Don't want to hear it."

Gytha stood up, silent for a time as a small boat was lowered from the ship and slapped toward them through the water. It looked like five, maybe even six, persons in the boat.

Gytha sat down again and wrapped her arms about her legs. She wished her legs weren't so skinny and so freckled. Gytha was covered with freckles. "Anyway, Grim and his wife, Leve, knelt down before the boy and promised to feed and take care of the young atheling until he was older and able to take to sword."

Sorgad took the fish between her two hands and with her long nails pulled it open, slitting the length of fish from the top. She scooped out the guts and flung them onto the rocks. The gulls swooped down, snapping up the pieces and flying away with bits in their mouth to dine in solitude.

"Grim went back to the Earl-what's-his-name and told him how he had killed the boy."

The boat drew closer. There was a man at the oars, two other men, two women and what looked like a child, being held by one of the women.

"But the earl, he laughed in Grim's face and gave him nothing. Not his freedom, nor wealth, but nothing and said if he didn't go away, he would have his head for killing the boy, because the boy was an atheling."

"Serves him right," Sorgad said, "for being a part of such a stupid story."

The boat was closer now. It was King Harold and she recognized her brother Ulf and Estrid, his wife and Gytha's good friend.

Sorgad ate the raw fish, breaking off chunks and managing with her teeth to scrape loose the scales and she spit them from her mouth.

The other woman in the boat with the child Gytha did not know. The child looked to be a boy of four or five and though the woman wore a hood Gytha could see the black hair at the cloth's edges. Some said black hair was the sign that your ancestors were animals, but her own grandfather's father was said to have been a bear and her hair was red and Ulf's was yellow and her father's, though white now, was said to have been once as red as her own.

"She's coming. It is the great whore. WHORE!" Sorgad screamed out at the sea.

"Who?"

"Cnute's whore. I seen her once when I was traveling on the moon."

"You never traveled on the moon," Gytha said.

"You don't know where I go when you are asleep. And I hear things. Talk. I hear lots of talk. I saw a tree once that could talk. And I saw this whore on the moon. And I hear the talk and the talk said the child is not Cnute's, be he think so or not."

"Is she a Dane?"

"Nay, she's a WHORE! A WHORE! WHORE! WHORE! WHORE!"

"Stop it."

But Sorgad continued yelling. The woman in the boat had obviously heard her for she attempted to stand, but Ulf pulled her down and the woman settled for shaking her fists at Sorgad.

Sorgad began chanting:

"Cnute, Cnute tosses Elgiva aside.
Emma, takes Emma to bed, wed and bride.
Elgiva, Elgiva, King threw her from Wessex . . ."

She kept repeating it, like a chant.

"You bitch," the voice from the boat screamed back.

Sorgad contorted her face, grinning like some evil monster, and she pulled wildly at the snarls of her gray matted hair, yelling a fire of repetitive bursts, "Whore-whore-whore-whore-whore . . ."

The woman in the boat stood up and shook herself free from Ulf's attempted grasp and leaped out into a breaking wave. She waded through water that washed up to her breasts, soaking the rich fabric of her deep green gunna and the sable-edged mantle. "Suck a goat's tit," she yelled, "you filthy old bag of horse turds."

Sorgad jumped up and down on the rock:

> "Cnute, Cnute tosses Elgiva aside.
> Emma, makes Emma his—"

But before she could finish the woman from the boat was up on the rocks and had thrown Sorgad down hard upon the flat wet rock and began kicking her in the hips. Though Sorgad yelled out in pain, she managed to intersperse: "Not Cnute's!" "Whore!" "Bitch!" "Toad's piss!" "King's slut!"

"Stop it," the King ordered from the boat.

The woman continued kicking with force in the hag's stomach. "That's for putting the yew branches under my bed and making me drop a dead baby, you sow's vomit."

Sorgad groaned in pain from the kick and Gytha could stand no more. She jumped down on the lower rock, nearly slipping as she landed on her wet feet, but caught her balance and threw her toes into the woman's chin. "You stop hurting her," she cried. "You stop!"

"You little red-headed brat!" The woman took hold of her hair and yanked first to one side, then to the other.

Gytha shrieked and brought her knee into the woman's stomach. At the same time she grabbed at the embroidered neckline of Elgiva's kirtle and tore loose the delicate needlework.

"Kill her!" Sorgad yelled. "Kill the whore!"

In defense Elgiva raised her elbows against Gytha's chest. Though Gytha was only fifteen, her breasts were fully developed, and as the woman dug her elbows again and again into the large rounds of soft flesh, the red-headed girl cried out in pain and knew she would have dark bruises.

"That will teach you to defend this old witch of the water." As she spoke, she shoved a fist into Gytha's side.

The girl let out a cry.

"Enough. Enough!" Ulf pushed back his cowl, exposing his unruly hair, and stood up in the boat as the oarsman maneuvered the small vessel to a mooring between the rocks.

Elgiva turned to look and when she did Gytha shoved her backward. She splashed into the water and came up gasping and yelling obscenities. Her black hair streamed wet down her face and hung against her neck.

The old hag shrieked with laughter, cawed and jumped up and down. She held up three fingers as if blessing the woman who stood waist deep in the water brushing her wet black hair from her face.

The woman attempted to climb back up on the rock where Gytha stood with her feet planted firmly apart, ready to shove her adversary back into the sea, but Ulf leaped from the boat and took a strong hold of the woman's arm and though she screamed and kicked at him, he held firmly on to her and she could not get free of his tight grasp. He forced her to move away from Gytha and the hag and steered her reluctantly to a path that wound up from the sea. King Harold followed scowling and swearing.

All the while Estrid, Gytha's sister-in-law, had sat with the oarsman and the boy in the boat. The boy jumped out and ran after his mother and Ulf. He was a clumsy, awkward child, Gytha thought, but there was the look of Cnute about him. He fell as he ran to catch up.

"Odin piss upon you!" the woman screamed back as Ulf tugged her along.

"It was time someone threw her in the sea," Estrid said as she was helped by the man from the boat. Estrid pushed the hood of her cloak back. Her brown hair was braided and wound in a ring and held by silver combs atop her head. She gave Gytha a peck on the cheek. "Still, I don't know how wise it was."

"High time," Sorgad said. "High time."

"What's she to you, old woman?" Estrid asked.

"She made me drink boar's blood and pee at midnight under a full moon."

"She's crazy in the head," Gytha told Estrid. "A lunatic."

"All lunatics," Sorgad said. "Daughters of the moon. Filled with lunacy. To see in the dark. Light to see ahead."

Estrid tried to get an answer to her question. "Do you know Elgiva, old woman?"

"I know Elgiva and on the morrow I tell you I shan't let her look upon the bier of Harold, son of Sven, King of the Danes."

"Hush, Sorgad," Gytha said. "Such talk is dangerous. Harold is not dead."

"No, but you will be," Estrid told Sorgad, "if you don't watch your tongue. My brother Harold would not find your speaking of his death amusing."

"He shall die," the old woman said.

"So shall we all. To live forever with God in heaven, but the King not yet."

"He will. I saw it in a dream. There will be a comet in the sky and the King will die."

"Quiet, old crone," Estrid commanded. "It is a sin to tell of the future."

"What will be will be. Wait, you'll see."

"Diviners," Estrid said, "go to hell and are made to have their heads on backward so they can't see what lies before."

"All lies," Sorgad shouted. "All lies. And all truth lies before. To see in a dream by the light of moon, what is greater shall be than by sun at bright noon."

The three stood there for a moment, the old crone, the woman and the young maid. Sorgad was bleeding across the face where Elgiva had apparently dug a nail through her skin. She rubbed the blood into the dirt of her cheek with two of her fingers. "Nothing is what has been but what has been willed." But after she spoke she seemed to lose interest in the subject and stepped down lower onto another rock. She dabbed her toes in the water in a circling motion and then began again clawing for fish.

"She's old and crazy," Gytha said as she picked up her old cape made of reindeer hides. She was ashamed of it after looking at Estrid's fine woolen cloak and she rolled it into a wad.

"She'd better watch her tongue lest the King hear her rantings." Estrid pushed the combs tighter into the braided circle of her hair.

"She doesn't mean any harm."

"Where'd she come from?" Estrid asked. "I've never seen her in Jomburg before."

"She says she came from the moon. I really don't know. One day I was here and there was no one. The next day I came and she was here by the sea and she has been here since. Sometimes when it is cold she follows me to father's house and sleeps by the fire, but mostly she stays here by the water."

"Does she never wash?"

"Only what seawater wets her. Sometimes she wears kelp in her hair."

From the small boat the oarsman unloaded bundles wrapped in skins and tied with leather laces. He moved them on up to where it was dry amid the dead grasses. He had enormous feet and left huge tracks across a narrow patch of sand and in the hard snow.

"Is that woman I pushed in the water really Cnute's wife?"

"Not his wife. His concubine."

"Is that why you dislike her, Estrid, because she's your brother's whore?"

"No. I hate her because she will not accept Christ. She is a pagan and worse she flaunts it. She laughs at baptism."

"Is that the reason Cnute sent her away?"

"No. The Queen had her sent away. The Queen and a thegn named Godwin."

"Thegns can't send anybody away," Gytha said as they moved up the hill. It began to mist slightly and Estrid pulled her hood up over her hair, but Gytha kept her reindeer cape rolled in her arms. "What is the Queen like?" she asked. "They say she is beautiful."

"She is Christian. That is the most important."

"But what does she look like?" Gytha looked back at Sorgad still on the rocks.

Before Estrid could answer Sorgad pierced the air with a wail and cried out, "King Harold will die."

"Shut her up," Estrid said. "Harold will be angry enough that Elgiva was pushed into the sea, let alone hearing some old hag prophesy his death."

Slaves came from the compound and carried the bundles away. The oarsman in the small boat rowed back toward the ship for another load.

Gytha hid the next day from Elgiva. There was no comet and no death. There was only the anger of her father. Thorgals-Sprakaleg was a great jarl and descended from a bear. He had white hair and a booming voice and when he yelled Gytha stood in fear. He never struck her, nor had he allowed anyone else to inflict physical punishment on any of his children, yet his voice was like Thor's surely must be.

"What you have done, daughter, is disgrace us before the son of the great Sven the Forkbeard. You have struck down a king's wife."

"Concubine," Estrid reminded him.

"They are the same, Estrid. Don't contradict me," the white-haired man ordered.

"This woman of Cnute's was attacking the old hag." Estrid was not afraid of Thorgals-Sprakaleg. "Gytha was only trying to protect the helpless creature."

"Who is this hag?" Her father looked straight down at Gytha.

"She lives by the sea." Her response was meek.

"It seems," Ulf told his father, "Sorgad had a son. Cnute caught him in Elgiva's bed. She claimed he'd forced himself upon her."

"Now there's a barefaced lie, I'd wager," Estrid said.

"Quiet woman!" Thorgals-Sprakaleg boomed.

Gytha shuddered, but Estrid didn't seem intimidated.

"Cnute," Ulf continued, "had the man's penis cut off and he died."

"The old mother is justly angry." Estrid was speaking to Gytha.

"What know you of mothers?" the old man asked. Gytha had heard him yell before because Estrid had not given him a grandson, or even a girl child.

"It's not because I don't try." Estrid gave him an angry look.

"There's truth enough in that," Ulf said. He paused and rubbed his large hand down the thin scar on his face. "But what is to be done?"

"Upon the solstice fire burn a living snake that has been fed the egg of the raven." Thorgals-Sprakaleg bellowed the pronouncement as if they were all deaf.

"I did not mean about that."

"What is more important than having sons?"

Estrid spoke. "I am Christian. I do not believe in these pagan ways."

"I am Christian as well. But it does no harm to honor the old ways."

"The Lord said, 'I shalt not have strange gods before me.' To do so is to be damned to hell."

"Question me, woman, in my own house?" His eyes echoed the anger of his voice.

"Father, wife," Ulf pleaded for calm. "The problem still remains. What do we do about Gytha? Harold is upset and Elgiva demands vengeance."

"It will all settle down," Thorgals-Sprakaleg assured him. "He is a good boy. Harold is a good boy. Stay from his sight for a few days, Gytha. Stay from his sight." He began to cough and wandered toward the door. "Babies, Estrid, what you need is babies and you wouldn't be so goddamn busy with God."

Gytha kept from Harold's sight and a blizzard came and wiped the old snow with new, and it became impossible to see and the wind howled and blew out fires and Gytha could not go to the sea and it tore against the snow-covered rocks and wiped them clean and her father complained of the cold and coughed and word came that in all the blizzard a ship was in the bay and Gytha bundled up and went out and faced the wind.

It was the King's mother, Gunnerhild.

"What are you doing here, old lady, in the middle of a snowstorm?" Thorgals-Sprakaleg asked.

"I couldn't stand Cnute's wife," she said.

"She's here," the old man told her.

"Who?"

"Cnute's wife."

"No. I mean the other one. The new one, though I hate this pagan bitch as well."

"Why don't you like Queen Emma?" Gytha asked her as she joined them at the fire.

"I am an old woman and the old never need a reason for doing anything. It is their way. But I will tell you this. That woman has no heart, she is cold as a winter in the tundra."

"Estrid likes her."

"Estrid is a young fool. She thinks only of Jesus and the size of your brother's organ."

"I like Estrid," Gytha said defensively.

"And I as well, but she is still a young fool."

"So, Gunnerhild," Thorgals-Sprakaleg asked, "are you going to stay here with us?"

"No. I'm going by land as soon as the sky is visible and visit my brother Boleslav."

"So far," he said, shaking his head. "So far."

"Gytha," the old woman said. "You are getting old and ought to be getting married. You must tend to it, Thorgals-Sprakaleg. You must tend to it. How old are you, girl?"

"Fifteen."

"Yes. You'll soon be past the prime. I told Cnute's man, Godwin, you'd make a good wife."

"Godwin?" Gytha was aghast.

"Yes, Godwin. He's too ambitious. Nothing slows a man down like a woman."

"He's only a thegn. I wouldn't marry him if all the jarls in Jomburg were castrated."

"Considering their age, girl," Gunnerhild said, "they might as well be."

"Well I shan't marry any thegn. I tell you that."

After the feast of the Epiphany had been celebrated and the blizzard had ended, King Harold bid his mother good-bye and she traveled overland to the house of her brother Boleslav, King of the Slavs.

Sorgad was a constant shadow and sometimes as dark and silent, and she followed Gytha down toward the sea. The rocks were slippery and Gytha moved with care over pockets of melting ice. She shook her hair loose. It had become a darker red and the winter had melted some of her freckles away and she was glad. Sorgad gathered shells and stones that had washed between the rocks on the small patches of sand. Gytha, her hide foot bindings getting wet, began gathering shells as well and handing them to Sorgad, who placed them in a pile.

"I will tell you of your future," Sorgad said as they wandered down to the sandy area where the snow had been wiped to the sea.

"I don't want to know my future," Gytha told her. "Besides, you always lie."

"I will tell you anyway." She made a circle of stones upon the sand, then flung the shells into the circle, giving a cry, which sounded like the caw of a sea gull. Gulls came and perched upon the rocks overhead as if to watch. She cawed again and a gull came into the circle of stones. Sorgad lurched and grabbed the bird by the legs. She beat its head against the rock as other birds cawed above, circled and then came to roost again on the rocks. Gytha turned away as Sorgad ripped apart the bird with her hands, spilling blood on the sand. She tore out the entrails and strewed them about the circle. She cawed several times and again the birds circled overhead and returned to the rocks.

Sorgad's eyes were wide and, with her hands extended, she shook her body and shouted, "Gytha, bearer of a king, bearer of a queen—"

"I shall be a queen," Gytha said.

"No."

"You said—"

"You shall be a mother of sorrows. Your daughter shall be Queen of

England. She will bear you nothing. Your son will be King of England, he will bear you pain."

"I am not to be a queen?"

"No."

"How is it?"

"It is the year of pain. A comet shall bear you a year of pain."

"I don't like your silly prediction. Nor your silly comets."

"Ulf's sons shall bear forever the crown of the Danes."

"And mine?" Gytha, despite her supposed disinterest, didn't want to be outdone by her brother.

"Your firstborn shall sit upon the English throne and all your children shall bear you pain."

"Stop it. I don't want to hear any more." She put her hands over her ears, but could not block out the words.

"Your son shall kill Ulf's son."

"No."

"And Ulf shall die a traitor."

"No. NO. NO!"

"And tomorrow there shall come a comet and the King will die."

"Hah!" Gytha laughed. "It is all untrue. You said that before and there was no comet and Harold didn't die. You lied. You lie."

Gytha ran from the beach, falling in a patch of dirty ice. She scraped her knees on the shaded hard ice. "Damn," she said. "Goddamn." She got up and continued up the hill. She could still hear Sorgad shouting, "Pain . . . the year of pain shall be seen in the comet."

Thorgals-Sprakaleg was better, and Gytha's hair was getting darker and her freckles going away and she was glad. His voice was not back to its full boom, but he spoke louder and he sat now with the others at the table in the hall. Elgiva was there with her son, whom she seldom let from her sight. He had black hair like his mother and a habit of hitting the instep of one foot with the heel of the other whenever he was made to stand still. King Harold was there and many of the King's men and Thorgals-Sprakaleg's men and between them they devoured great platters of food and King Harold stuffed food, one handful after another, into his mouth, hardly bothering to chew. It was as if he was afraid someone else would eat it first. Gytha watched him in fascination as boar's grease dripped down his face and into his beard. He was a big man, but not as big as Cnute, and his hair was brown, unlike his brother's. He winked at her and she turned away, embarrassed for having been caught watching him.

Sorgad stood at the entrance to the hall. "There is a comet in the sky," she said.

"Get that woman out of here!" Elgiva screamed. Sorgad fled.

The King turned pale and looked uneasy.

Gytha got up from her place at the long table and ran to the door. "There is a great ball of light in the sky," she said.

"I will not look on it," the King said, and turned his eyes down into the table as if the comet should enter the room.

Thorgals-Sprakaleg went out the door past Gytha. Many of the men, both the King's and her father's, got up to look. She went out and stood beside her father looking into the fiery heavens. Elgiva came and stood behind the doorway.

"Harold is afraid," Gytha's father told her. He spoke softly. "For when a comet is seen a king will die."

"Why?" Gytha asked.

"It is the way of kings," he said.

They did not stand there long outside gazing at the heavens for Elgiva called them from the doorway. "Quick, quick!" she shouted. "The King is choking on a cock's bone." Gytha ran back inside. Thorgals-Sprakaleg came more slowly. Attendants and carls of the King's house slapped his back and the King's face turned blue and his eyes seemed to be popping out of their sockets as he gasped and choked and tried to breathe. And then he gave a spastic jerk, choking and gagging, and he fell facedown on the table.

Sorgad watched from the doorway.

CHAPTER 4

York, 1018

EMMA WAS HAPPY. NOTHING COULD DESTROY THE JOY, NOT THE UGLINESS of the gray York day, nor the January cold, nor that she had seen three rings about the moon on the night last. She watched Leofwine approaching from the other direction. He was Earl of Mercia now. Overhead the headless corpse of Eadric dangled upside down. One foot was roped aloft and the body swung above the church entrance. Emma looked up at him. The wind had ripped open his apparel and his rib cage was exposed, the skin, freeze-dried against the bone, stretched tight, giving the appearance of Eadric having starved to death. At the neck black blood vessels dangled like thin string. From inside the church a sound came like a pig being butchered. It was the Norwegian, she had been told, who had taken refuge there. As Leofwine approached he did not look up at the headless body of the powerful man he replaced.

"There were rings about the moon last night." He spoke in an ominous tone. "And a sow gave birth to a piglet with two heads, but it was stolen by a demon spirit."

"I saw the rings," Emma said.

Leofwine brushed his beard with the back of his hand. "I must be off. I go in search of a dragon."

She stood wondering for a moment as he hurried down the pathway what he meant by that remark.

At the great hall Eadric's head was piked at the door. It had been decorated by the children. Red berries left from Christmas dripped from his beard; knife-carved symbols marked both frozen cheeks; a crown of sharp-needled pine boughs tilted rakishly on his head. Both eyes had been left in their sockets and he seemed to have a look of perpetual surprise.

"Where is Cnute? Where is the King?" Emma asked as she entered the warmth of the hall.

"He is gone in search of a dragon," Godwin told her. "A patch of ground where the deep snow has melted was found to the south of the wall. There was no trace of a fire and so it is thought it was caused by a dragon's breath."

"He must return soon. I have news for him." She went over and kissed Aesval on the cheek and sat down beside her.

"What news?" Godwin followed over.

"It is for the King's ear," she told him and gave him what she meant to be a mysterious smile.

Thorkell the Tall, usually a placid and even-tempered man, came banging into the hall.

"You should have had the Norwegian killed, too," Thorkell said.

"I had no one killed," Godwin said.

"Eadric."

"The King's doing."

"As you wish, but the King then should as well rid us of this madman. I can't pray in peace. He spends the day in the croft and when the spirit moves him he begins this wailing. And he is an ugly sight. His arms are bent like braided metal."

"I'll see he's removed," Godwin said.

"And at night they say he goes clawing the frozen earth, digging for roots. Don't you have him fed?"

"He won't eat what we give him."

"And they say he drinks the blood of rats and one of my soldiers swore he was walking in the dead of night with a giant bear." Thorkell came over to Emma. "There were three rings about the moon last night," he told her.

Thorkell sat down, but he almost instantly fell asleep.

Northman, who had been standing behind sipping from a wine bowl, whispered, as if not to awaken the earl, "It is a strange time, Madam. We are kept at this eternal Gemot like some prisoners of the King, your husband. A mad Norwegian roams York swallowing whole hen's eggs and my father goes searching for a dragon."

"There were rings about the moon last night," she said. Northman was not going to spoil her mood.

"It means, Lady," Northman said, speaking aloud, "the death of a nobleman."

"He is already dead," Godwin said as he turned about and faced the young nobleman.

"And who is next on your list, Godwin?"

The old man Eric wandered in, stamping the snow from his feet. "Cold as the Queen of the North's nipples," he said and shook his white hair.

"Or an earl hanging from a church tower," Northman said.

"Uh . . . uhm?" the old man snorted and went over toward the fire.

"Nothing," Thorkell assured him, opening his eyes. "The boy prattles."

The cry was like the caw of seabirds to the south. Everyone seemed startled at the sound and turned to see the strange figure standing with one of Godwin's soldiers, a shirtless youth with a sale tossed over his shoulder.

"I have heard that sound at Corfe," Emma said.

"This seer," the soldier said, "comes from Devon and insisted on seeing you, Lady. He sees the future in the circles of birds, he claims."

The man was thin as a sapling, his frail arms like spindly new branches. He stood a head taller than Thorkell, Emma would have guessed, yet willowy and loose. His face was gnarled and rough, his skin a gray pallor. But it was his hair that commanded attention, painted with streaks of green dye, the color of stagnant water, as if moss had grown over the wild snarls, and on his forehead drawn with charred stick was the head of a bird. His green gown was caked with soil and despite the cold and snow his feet were bare, his toes twisted and bent. He moved, however, as if floating across a tarn.

Emma was about to speak to him when he cried out again like a seabird, fell forward, prostrate, as if cut down by an ax, and mumbled as he fell.

"He says the Queen is with child," Thorkell said.

"Are you, Lady?" Godwin asked.

"Yes," she replied and smiled. Her secret was out. Well, let them all be happy with her and they could celebrate together when she announced it to the King.

And then the seer mumbled again, this time his words only partially discernible.

"What did he say?" Emma asked.

"He said," Godwin told her, "that the child you carry will be male born."

"And will he be King?" she asked.

The seer, with outstretched arms, rolled and turned his elongated torso on the floor and mumbled. Godwin strained to hear.

"Will he? What did he say?" Emma asked.

The seer leaped up, shook his arms, cawed the cry of the seabirds and then quite distinctly yelled, "Yes, yes, yes." He mumbled more words and more sounds and flew from the hall still mumbling.

Emma smiled. "He did say he would be King?"

"He did, Lady," Godwin assured her.

"Could you understand any of the rest?"

Godwin was not smiling. It was Thorkell who answered, "Not a word, Lady. Not a word."

"Well, my secret is out," Emma said.

"It is good news, Lady," Aesval told her and patted her hand.

"I understood the seer," Northman said. Northman's voice had a rasping, irritating quality. "He said the boy would choke to death."

"Did he, Godwin? Did he say that?" Emma demanded.

"He said he would be King. It was all I heard," Godwin said.

The joy the seer had brought had been destroyed by Northman. Where was Cnute? His arms would drive away Northman's frightening words. She attempted to be cheerful and called for Gamol to sing and feigned a cheerful smile as he began, but the words of Northman hung on her like a gloomy rag of mourning.

And as Gamol finished his song old Eric said, "There is a tide that comes red as blood."

Emma looked at him, perplexed.

"You are a silly old man," Northman said.

"And you," Thorkell told him, "are a silly child. And I suggest you become a quiet one."

Northman gave him an angry look, but said no more. Leofwine's son had small dark little eyes and he moved away from Thorkell, brushing his hand through his heavy beard, and walked over to Harold Thorkellsson, who as usual stood quiet in a corner, looking, saying nothing. "If you keep staring at the Queen," Northman said loud enough for Emma to hear, "perhaps she will pay you some attention. Or has she already?"

Leofwine entered at that moment. "The King comes," he said.

Emma was relieved.

"You should teach your son to mind his tongue." Thorkell spoke to the earl.

"He doesn't listen to me," Leofwine told him.

The King, wearing a sword with a hilt jeweled in blue stones, entered with Archbishop Wulfstan at his side. Emma looked at him and he smiled at her and the coldness of Northman's words vanished in the warmth of that smile. "Leofwine," Cnute said, "has found a place where a dragon has breathed."

"My father is wrong," Northman said.

Emma had been looking at Godwin's young soldier and as Northman spoke he slipped furtively from the hall. How strange.

"What do you mean, boy?" Leofwine asked.

"You have seen this sign of the dragon's breath no doubt by two trees in a valley just beyond the town?" Northman asked.

"Yes," his father replied.

"That is not a place of a dragon, any more than I am a boy, but the secret meeting spot of a pair of sodomizers," Northman told them. His black eyes shined and seemed to Emma to burn with hate. "One of these is this boy who sings so sweetly for us and the other is"—he turned to find the one he wished to accuse had fled—"a soldier of Godwin's house who but a moment ago stood near the door."

"How do you know this?" Godwin asked.

"Because I suspected such uncleanliness, such sins under God between these filthy creatures, so I followed the odious pair to this place. They built a fire and made a shelter of skins stretched upon sticks—"

"There was no sign of a fire having been made," Cnute told him.

"They buried the ashes. Had you looked in the snow, you would have found the char."

"Will you testify to these acts?" Wulfstan asked.

"I shall bear witness to their vileness. I shall before you and God in the Church tell of all this that I saw."

The young singer looked frightened and it seemed all eyes were on him.

"He is my musician," Emma said. "Let me deal with him." She was sorry now the child had not stayed with Queen Gunnerhild. He would have been safely from York.

"No, Lady," Cnute told her. "This is a matter for the Church. Leave this to the archbishop."

Tears filled the young singer's eyes. Emma would wait to give her news to the King at a happier time.

"Take him away," Wulfstan ordered. "If he is proved guilty we shall cut off his penis."

A priest and a soldier led him off. The boy did not cry out.

"And find the other," Northman said. "You must find the other."

"Why, Northman?" Godwin asked. "What is a poor singer and lowly soldier to you?"

"My revenge, you upstart, for bringing down the Earl Eadric. It is not the place of sons of swineherds to decide the fate of earls but earls to decide the fate of soldiers and singers. Each man must keep to his born place in life and you, pigtender, are out of your realm."

"And you, Northman, have spoken quite enough." Cnute was firm. "It was I, not Godwin, who decided Eadric's fate."

"And you, King, are you so blind that you are not aware that the pigherder rules in this kingdom? For he rules you. You are blind, you are blind to the fact that your Queen was the cast-off whore of Harold Thorkellsson."

"ENOUGH!" Cnute was livid. He reached for his knife. Godwin restrained him.

"And whose child bears she? Cnute's or Harold's?"

Cnute said nothing. He simply stared at her and it was a frightening, terrible stare. "Our son," she cried. "In all this I had happy news, not fit for the telling in this place." Emma began to weep.

The knife came from Cnute's hands so fast and slid into Northman's breast and he collapsed with barely a moaned protest upon the floor and the blood soaked his tunic.

"My God," Leofwine said and fell upon his son. "My God."

She looked at Cnute. There was no affection in his face. "Take the Queen to her chamber, Lady Aesval. From us."

"My Lord," Emma pleaded, "Northman's accusation . . . was . . ."

"It has nothing to do with Northman. To your chamber, Lady."

Godwin spoke to the King. "Surely, my Lord, North—"

The King turned angrily on the thegn. "I said it had nothing to do with Northman and his loose mouth. NOW GET THE QUEEN OUT OF MY SIGHT."

The tears would not stop as Emma was helped by Aesval toward the door. "Cnute," she sobbed, but got no answer. She heard him speak to Godwin softly as the door let in the cold air:

"I find, Godwin, the deformed body of a woman, big with child, is repulsive. It is the ugliest thing in this world."

The door slammed shut and Emma stood with the big woman beside her in the cold.

Emma cried and spent the afternoon alone in her chamber and the evening, and Aesval came, but Emma sent her away and waited for Cnute, but he never came and in the middle of the night she dressed warmly and went out upon the cold York streets wandering. How had a day which had begun with such joy ended in such bitter isolation? Again, there were three rings about the moon.

She would have a son now, a beautiful son like his father and he would be King. Edward . . . she had no need for him. She wanted not to be reminded of his conception . . . Ethelred's rotten breath over her body. She could forget his birth and when she had first looked upon his white body and wanted to vomit.

An old woman stood at a corner in the moonlight. She was bundled in winds of soiled rags. Her face, even in the dark Emma could see, was a mass of wrinkled dirt and broken blood lines. "The house of Leofwine weeps," she said.

"Do you know who I am?" Emma asked.

"Aye, Lady, and no one lives to bear testimony against your skald for Northman is dead." She said no more and moved away and Emma saw she was crippled and dragged a foot in a path across the snow.

Emma was suddenly very cold and hurried back toward her chamber house. She heard a wolf cry and she went in, closing out the cold night when rings encircled the moon.

"Cnute, I bear you a son," she cried aloud and then knelt by her bed in prayer, but the specter of Cnute pushing the knife through Northman's garment would not leave her, and after the specter of Edward intruded on her thoughts and she was angered that he encroached on her, now, now when the new heir was within her body. What was to become of Ethelred's sons? She could not concern herself with them. Her strengths must be to the new boy within her. He must be her total occupation, the heir to England. And it was better for this unborn child that Edward and Alfred be given no estates, for then they could not marry and Ethelred's line would be cut. She would see to a husband for the girl, that venomous little girl. She fell asleep still kneeling by the bed.

Cnute did not come in the morning. It was Godwin.

"Do I have the plague, Godwin, that my husband may not visit me?"

"He finds it difficult, Madam."

"And am I to be locked away for my entire confinement?"

Godwin turned away.

"Am I, Godwin?" Emma did not try to hide the panic in her voice.

"The King cannot abide the sight of a pregnant woman. Elgiva was sent away when the boy Svegan was born. You will be welcome to him after the child is delivered of your body. Emma, I am . . ."

He had never called her that before.

"I am sorry," he said. "You are to return to Winchester."

"And Cnute?"

"He goes to the Daneland. Good word has come this morning from Roeskild. Harold died at Jomburg."

"And he goes to take the throne?"

"Yes."

"Elgiva is there."

Godwin didn't respond.

"He goes to the whore."

"He goes to claim a rightful inheritance, the Daneland."

"And you, Godwin? Do you go with him?"

"No, Lady. I go to Rouen to your brother duke to ask that he recognize Cnute's claim to the Daneland and to Paris to ask the same of King Robert and to Brittany and Bruges as well."

"Will the King come and see me before he leaves?"

"He is occupied, Madam, and journeys before the day is too long under way, lest they lose the sun too early at sea."

"I shall not forgive him for this unkindness."

Godwin was gone. And the day went by and Cnute must have left as well, but no one brought her word. It did not matter now. Nothing mattered but the heir, and when food was brought she ate and she rested and that night she stood at the doorway alone and looked up at the three rings about the moon.

CHAPTER 5

Normandy, 1018

GODWIN CAME TO ROUEN BEARING LETTERS. HE TRAVELED WITH A SMALL entourage, a few soldiers and clerics. Among them was Behi. It would do no harm to take him from the country for a while. Duke Richard received him as though he ranked as an earl and assured Godwin that Normandy would recognize Cnute as King of the Daneland.

"And my sister, does she well, Godwin?"

"Splendidly, Your Grace, she is with child, as I reported, and is certain it will be a male heir. She was in good health when last I left her in Winchester and she made the journey from York with no harm to herself or the child. She did ask that I might remind Your Grace that her daughter, Godgifu, should be soon wed."

The duke gestured with an open hand. There was an element of arrogance, perhaps not so much arrogance as pomp, a sense of regality in the movement. The Norman duke seemed far more kingly than Cnute. Godwin was impressed by the distance it set the man apart from the others in the room.

"And her sons?"

"As they have no estate—"

"Yes," the duke interrupted to agree. "Well, let us then concern ourselves with Godgifu. We have made, what I consider, an excellent connection. She is twelve, but developed. She has had her blood I am told. The

Count of Vixen will take her, but he wants her now in the blush of youth."

"Then I am to tell the Queen there has been no need to concern herself that all was happily resolved by her brother duke?"

"Not quite, though I wish it were so. The Count of Vixen does not wish his wife brought to his bed screaming and shackled. He wants her to come willingly and ready. She refuses. The child refuses . . ."

"Certainly something—"

"Nothing short of force and she is of no use to Vixen that way. He's most insistent on that point."

"Someone should reason . . . the high honor," Godwin suggested.

"The only one," the duke broke in, "she will listen to is Edward, her brother, and asking him is like getting something from the Pope. By the time he would consent his sister would be buried of wrinkles."

"Is Edward here?"

"No, he is in the keep of his Uncle Godfrey near Jumieges."

"I shall, with your permission, journey there tomorrow, my Lord."

"You may journey wherever in Normandy you like, but seeing Edward will be to no avail. The boy is, as you will discover, quite mad."

The duke's table was sumptuous and draped in a gilt-edged linen cloth. As they gathered to sit, the duke motioned him near the head. It was a strange seating for a thegn, but at the King's own table, since the Eadric affair, he often sat next to Cnute. And it wasn't as if he hadn't been offered an earldom, for the King had been quite willing to gift him one of those small earldoms carved in The March. But he would wait his time. His goal was set.

"Have you a vow?" Judith, the duke's wife, asked. He noticed she always seemed to be scratching and was digging her nails deep into her arms. As she scraped, she pushed up the fabric of her bliaut and he could see the cluster of red sores.

"A vow, Lady?"

"You drink none of our good Norman wine. Perhaps you would prefer some of that barbaric mead Ethelred was so taken with. I can call for it."

"No, Madam, I take no intoxicant."

"You should," she told him, scratching again. "It wards off the sickness."

At the far end of the table, dressed in layers of black, like a nun, a lady sat apart, isolated by several empty seats from the others at the table and engaged in no conversation with the rest of the party. He had not at first recognized her, but she looked up momentarily and he saw her face more clearly.

"Isn't that Queen Bertha?"

"That is Bertha, yes," the duchess answered, "but she bears no title any longer, and travels from noble house to noble house bothering with her pious pronouncements and begging her food with open declarations of poverty. I find it disgusting."

The younger of the duke's sons had been annoyingly pulling on his mother's cloak. "She should kill herself," he said.

Judith ignored her son's remark. "She is an embarrassment to our house, but as a Christian of charity, I can't throw her out."

"She is a wastrel," the brat said. The boy's name was Robert, Godwin remembered. He was dark-complexioned and healthy-looking, with black hair and sharp brown eyes. Godwin had taken an instant dislike to him on his last visit to Rouen.

"What do you know of wastrels?" his mother asked.

"When I am duke—"

"You won't be duke," she cut him off.

"I will!" he screamed. "I will."

"Robert, be quiet," the duke ordered. "And for God's sake, Judith, stop baiting the boy."

As Judith turned to face her husband, the boy, Robert, who Godwin guessed was ten or eleven, stood behind her and held his tongue out at her. His older brother sat quietly at the table. He was fair, with dull gray eyes. A chained jackdaw rested on his shoulder and occasionally pecked at his light-brown curls. There were two other children, four actually Godwin knew, but the duke's bastard sons, Mauger and William, were unwelcome at a table where Judith dined, while the two girls, Eleanor, who was taller than either of her brothers, and Alice, who appeared to be the oldest, were playing some sort of game with the food. Bits and pieces of fowl and nuts were lined up in a pattern before them. Richard, Eleanor and Alice were all fairer and quieter than Robert. But the darker young son seemed the duke's favorite.

For entertainment a singer sang a bawdy song about a woman whose vagina was so large that she kept a whole feast up there for the army of Rolf to feed upon. There were seeming endless verses. A juggler juggled live trained doves, but one not so trained went flying off and its droppings splattered in the archbishop's plate.

"Goddamn," he swore and dumped the contents of the plate off on the floor and wiped his plate clean again with the hem of his robe. The archbishop sat directly across the table from Godwin. "Damned birds are a nuisance."

"No," Robert, his nephew and namesake told him, "when I become King, I shall let loose a thousand doves in the cathedral for my coronation."

"Over my dead body."

"So be it," the boy said.

"You rascal." The archbishop laughed. "And besides all you wanted before was your brother's dukedom. When did you decide to become a king and a king of what?"

"France. Not that awful England."

"See what he thinks of your country, Godwin?" The archbishop leaned across the table.

"I am pleased he doesn't want it," Godwin said.

"And well you should be, he's a nasty little child. Aren't you, Robert?"

"Nasty as a horned devil, Uncle."

It was obviously a question posed before. "By the way, Godwin, my sister speaks well of you. And I have a gift I want you to have for all your kindness to her."

"Thank you, your Grace. I try to serve both the King and Queen."

"You are rather a phenomenon. Most men of humble beginnings, if you don't mind my saying so—"

"My father was a swineherd."

"—most such men are found in the Church."

"I'm afraid, your Grace, my temperament is unsuited to a religious life. But there are some interests of clerics I do share. I have taken to learning writing."

"*Veritas saepe non scitur quod studium ejus est difficile,*" the archbishop said, leaning across the table toward him.

"*Non sine magno labore veritas inventietur.*"

"I can see, Godwin, you are not cast from the mold of other men—but tell me, have you no ambition? You seem content to remain a thegn."

"I would lie to deny I had no great aim in life, but I am not rushing to gain lands and titles. To gain estate one becomes a vassal of another. At present I need serve only the Lord of Wessex, who by good happenstance is also King of England."

"Obviously you know what you are about. I admire efficiency and the duke, my brother, does as well. Thegn, my door is open to you."

"Thank you, your Grace."

"And see if you can't get the Queen to take some interest in those sons of hers. They are like Bertha down there, creatures without root."

He looked at Bertha, who had left the table and was sitting alone in a dark corner.

"She's a witch," the boy Robert said, coming up to him.

Godwin glared at the child. The archbishop was right, he was a nasty child.

"I do not like you either," Robert said, reading his thoughts. "You are a nasty man who smells of pig shit and when I am duke I shall raise an army and put my cousin Edward on his rightful throne because he's an idiot and will do exactly as I say."

Godwin was usually not sensitive to his humble beginnings; in fact he flaunted his birth, but the boy's remark angered him and he could feel the redness creep into his cheeks. And the worst was the smiling little demon knew precisely what reaction he expected of Godwin. He arose and left the boy, going to the corner where Bertha was sitting.

"Queen," he addressed her.

"I am not a queen, Godwin of Wessex."

"You remember me."

"Yes, you came for Emma's consent to wed your King. I was here then. By your face I could see Robert had gotten to you. There is some good in everyone. I simply haven't found it yet in that terrible little boy."

"He is a monster."

"Waste no thoughts on him. How is Emma?"

"Well, Lady. Big with child."

"Another? I don't wish to sound bitter but she ignores the children she has. Edward particularly."

"I have heard, Lady, he has an ear to your voice."

"Not since the day you made his mother Cnute's betrothed."

"They say both he and you, Lady, have a power to cure."

"They? Who are they? Strange things are said about us all."

"I need Edward's help," he told her, "and it will aid me if I can know everything there is to know about the boy."

"One can know nothing of Edward. He keeps his self to his self."

"But he does have the power of healing?"

"I know nothing of these things," she said, but her eyes revealed otherwise.

"I did not mean to batter you with questions. I am simply anxious to make a good marriage for his sister."

"I had a good marriage once." She spoke bitterly. "Men destroyed it."

"Please forgive my intrusion, Lady." He started to walk away.

"You will find," she said, "Edward even more bitter than I. He was, after all, promised a kingdom. It would be hard enough for a boy of his years to understand that being taken away from him, but worse, his mother has abandoned him. The only solace he has is God."

"God is the solace of us all," he told her as he moved away.

The next day began cloudy and overcast. The horses clomped and stumbled over the remains of the old Roman road. Dead snow, gray with soot, had melted and frozen until it, too, was like rock. A light drizzle wet the riders, Godwin and six others of his own house and two Norman guides in pointed helmets. The land was flat. Vultures circled in the distance and then dropped to earth. In time they approached the spot where the birds hovered and they fluttered and rose, circling the sky. The stench was unmistakable. What was left of the body, picked and pulled by the ugly winged creatures, appeared to have been a young woman.

"She should be buried," Behi said.

They rode on.

Against the flat gray sky a Norman tower stood, square and solitary, its stone grayer than the sky it rose against.

"That is it," one of the Normans said.

There was no sign of life within or without. The tower rose straight some forty feet. There were windows at the top only, but neither at them, nor on the rampart above, was there an indication of anyone within.

"We come in the name of Cnute, King of England, by the grace of the Duke of Normandy," Godwin called out.

There was no answer.

A Saxon soldier pounded against the wooden door.

Godwin followed one of the Normans around behind the structure where they found only pigs snorting the earth between a clap of hovels which stretched beside the marsh. Within one of the dank hovels they found a dead naked baby and an old man. He appeared to be mute and grunted and pointed down the road.

So they rode along the road, the dampness keeping the dust down. Some distance away they came upon soldiers and serfs gathered in a field.

"What is it?" Godwin called over to them, but no one answered him. He called once more and, still hearing no response, dismounted and walked across the field.

"Godwin! For God's sake, what brings—" It was William, the Count of Eu.

"I came to Godfrey's keep hoping to find the boy, Edward. Yet the place was deserted."

"I pray you come bearing news to Edward that they have elected him King. Perhaps then he will vacate the cistern he has chosen to reside in."

"Cistern?"

"Yes, he has decided to emulate some saint or other who lived burrowed in the earth and made the swallows obey him."

"St. Guthlac," Godwin said.

"That is the one. But pray, have they made Edward King?"

"No, I am afraid they have not."

"Pity, that would have gotten him out. Godfrey has ridden to the abbey at Jumieges to get a young monk who seems to have some control over Edward. They should arrive soon. Godfrey and I are nearly at wit's end."

"Is there anything that I can do?"

"Outside of announcing him King, I am afraid not. We must wait now upon this Robin of Jumieges."

Godwin went over to the hole in the earth. Others moved back to make room for him. He peered down, but could see nothing but darkness. He moved back and stood with others waiting.

"You are certain he is in there?" Godwin asked the count.

"Quite," William of Eu responded. "I have had multitudinous conversations with him urging him to come out."

"And what does he say?"

"Christ wants him in that hole. What answer can you have to that?"

"None that's rational, I suppose."

And they waited.

The crowd was a scraggle of ill-fitting rags and dirty faces and blabbering in French and whining brats and cowls burying faces and dogs sniffing each other and noses running and babies chewing on pig skin to keep them quiet and young maids ogling young men and young men ogling the maids and smocks streaked with yesterday's meal and the day's before and a priest expounding parables and hair being picked for lice and they sat and stood and leaned against one another and babes took the tit and others cried for want of it.

"How is my sister?" William asked.

"Getting large with the child."

"Tell her I will come and see him when he's born."

"You're so certain it's a boy."

"I have had word from her. That is what she wants and Emma somehow manages always to get what she wants."

"To that end," Godwin said, "I serve her. She wants Godgifu married. It is why I am here."

"And only Edward can control his sister."

"And," Godwin added, "apparently only this monk—"

"Robin of Jumieges."

"Yes, can control Edward. Who controls the young monk, I wonder?"

"They say he is a sodomizer."

"Is that the hold he has over Edward?"

"Good God no! Edward is aseptic. The mere touch of anyone but Godgifu seems to pain him. The idea of sexual contact sends him into one of his fits. No, there is a strange affinity of comradeship between my nephew and this young monk."

Godfrey and the young monk rode up on one horse. There was something mystical about the young man; his beauty was almost ethereal. His hair was dark and but slightly curled, falling carelessly and clean about his chiseled face. His eyes, liquid, seemed to draw Godwin into their blueness. In contrast to the motley crowd, he was scrubbed and carefully attired in a monk's robe, but he wore no cowl and instead was wrapped in a soldier's chlamys of brown wool with a black satin edging. The robe, too, was not of poor cloth but of good linen. He was not tonsured and his head was uncovered. Godwin saw Behi intently staring at the young monk. He wondered if this Robin, hardly more than a boy, knew how much power he contained in those eyes, because there was still about him an icing of innocence as if the man had no idea of his charismatic explosiveness. He vanished, slipping down into the hole in the ground.

Godfrey, who had acknowledged Godwin with a quick wave of his gauntlet when they arrived, came over to him after helping the young man into the well. "You couldn't have come at a worse time. I'd wager it is about the marriage of Godgifu, isn't it?"

"Yes." Godwin responded. "The duke says—"

"Richard says, 'The Count of Vixen.' I've heard."

"Yes."

"I have tried to reason with Edward. It is for his own good, for his brother Alfred and for the girl, as well, but—"

"Perhaps reason is the last approach one should take with Edward." He was saying it to himself more than to Godfrey.

"What do you mean?"

"The irrational, perhaps . . . maybe he should be approached irrationally."

"I am not certain I understand."

"I think it best I do not see Edward till and if he does arise from the ground. May I wait at your keep?" Godwin asked.

"Of course, I shall send an escort with you."

"I would like to see this monk, Robin, before I talk to the Atheling. And tell Edward I have words and a gift from the Queen, would you, Godfrey?"

"Emma sent Edward a gift?"

"Yes." Godwin mounted the horse.

"I shall be your host," Godfrey said, "when we get Edward out of the cistern."

The Saxons started to ride off following one of Godfrey's own men.

"Behi," Godwin called back and the young soldier pulled alongside him. "I have a strange request. I want you to ride to this monastery at Jumieges. And I don't know how you are going to manage it, but I need you to bring me an ecclesiastical glove. The older and more tattered, and the more elegant the needlework, the better. But I will settle for anything."

"A pair?"

"No just one."

Behi posed no further question. He simply turned his horse about and rode in the direction of Jumieges, his sale flying in the wind.

At the keep of the bastard Godwin waited. The place smelled of horse and men and a strong odor of cooked fish. He stood at the window. An hour had passed since he had parted company with Behi. There was no sign of Edward, nor his uncles, nor the throng that had gathered at the cistern. A single rider appeared below and Godwin went down. He came riding fast, and there was no drizzle to hold the dust and it billowed behind in a screen.

"I had not expected you for many more hours," Godwin told Behi as the man got off his horse.

"I was lucky," he panted. "I had no need to go all the way to Jumieges. I waylaid an unsuspecting bishop on the road."

"Was he unaccompanied?"

"Couldn't have been a very important bishop, only two sour-looking priests which I held at bay with a knife. You should have seen that old man's face when all I asked for was one of his gloves."

Godwin smiled. "Let me see it."

The lean young man handed him the glove. It was tattered and gray and the gilded thread was peeling. Still the gauntlet had an ornate elegance about it. "Perfect," Godwin said, "I couldn't have found a better."

Behi, if his curiosity was aroused, gave no indication.

"I have another task for you. I have asked Godfrey's permission to have a word with the young monk." Godwin saw the look in the young soldier's eyes. "When they arrive with Edward from that cistern, if indeed they ever do, take this Robin of Jumieges to the chamber they have given me up above. Stay with him an hour or so. The young monk is said to be a sodomite." Godwin spoke with indifference. "I want to know what he wants in life."

"Wants?"

"Yes. Wealth? Power? To be the Pope? To control kings? He is obviously no churl. Did you see his garb? What service can Godwin be to him in achieving his ambitions?"

The soldier looked at him rather blankly.

"Don't I make myself clear? All you need to do is your part. And then speak with him. Get him to open up. Men are more apt to be free in speaking of themselves to women with whom they have been intimate and I suppose it holds true with men under other circumstances as well."

The soldier nodded meekly.

"I shall take a walk and leave you alone with him long enough to learn what needs to be learned."

Behi disappeared up into the tower and Godwin returned to the door to wait. The sun had appeared briefly and now dropped to an orange ball sitting near the end of the sky, casting long narrow shadows. They came, riders and men on foot. Edward was immediately recognizable even at a distance. The boy had grown taller and thinner and his white hair fell longer, over his shoulders. There was a grotesque distance, not disdain really, but remoteness, that made him seem less a human rider and more the figure of a ghost.

Godwin slipped out of the tower and made his way in the direction of the marshes. As he moved back toward the hovels he saw the dumb man who had been with the dead baby. The man made the sign of the cross toward him. Godwin moved away. He could hear the riders dismounting and going into the keep. And the serfs came back to their plasters of dung and sticks. Their mundane existences had been lifted by the Atheling going into the cistern, but now they had to return to the tedium. How did they exist? It was a life of birthing, and eating, and working, and copulating, and drinking and dying. There was nothing else. Even Edward's choice of living in a cistern seemed the more interesting by comparison. He looked at the glove in his hands. The needlework was really rather crude, however elaborate. Godwin waited. It could only help that he had remembered the story of St. Guthlac, who had lived on some island in a burrow. And the story went that Wilfred, when visiting Guthlac on the island, had left his glove in the boat and Guthlac, having a peculiar perception, remarked that Wilfred had left the other glove there, but his marvelous insight further revealed to him that a jackdaw had taken it and was hiding it. They went out from the burrow and the saint ordered the black bird resting on a roof of an abandoned cottage to bring the glove to him. The jackdaw flew off and came back bearing the glove in his beak and landed upon the anchorite's shoulders. Guthlac gave the glove to its owner. Edward had obviously decided to emulate the saintly Guthlac.

Godwin looked to the tower. He had walked some distance, so he turned and headed back. The sun had vanished and dusk was beginning to slip in and with it cold was also coming on. He moved a little faster. Before he reached the marsh and the hovels he came to the small stream he had crossed over on his way from the tower. A girl, a young woman really, was beating clothing upon stones to shake loose the dirt. She had no right hand, only the stubble where it had been cut off at the wrist. Perhaps she had been punished for thievery. He looked at her and passed on. People milled about the previously deserted tower; he walked through them, on in and up to the chamber.

After he knocked, Behi came to the door saying, "He wants to be a monk at Jumieges. That is his only ambition."

"Surely . . ."

"Nothing else, he told me, unless it is to be left free of kings and nobles."

"As he says, then," Godwin told him and opened the door and went in. It was a small room, crude with rough-hewn floors, a pile of straw for sleeping and nothing else. The young monk was reclining on the straw. He looked up at Godwin as he entered. He had a disarming smile on his face. "Make me Archbishop of Canterbury," he said.

"Is that what you want?"

"No."

"Good," Godwin told him and smiled. "I am not able to do quite that—"

"Yet."

"Not yet," Godwin agreed.

The young man stopped smiling. "What exactly is it you want me to do?"

"What makes you so certain I want you to do anything?"

"Men either use or abuse me. You don't seem the abusing kind."

"I need your help to make Edward convince his sister that a marriage to the Count of Vixen is a good thing for all concerned."

"One doesn't make Edward do anything."

"But you obviously got Edward to give up his burrow."

"Not by any rational means."

Godwin looked at him. "Strange, I said that myself. I am not following my own advice."

"This marriage—is it really a good thing?"

"Yes, it gives both Edward and Alfred ties to a house, the house of Vixen, the house of their sister where they will be really welcome, not as at Rouen, where they are no better than poor relatives."

"And the Count of Vixen will welcome them as brothers?"

"Who's to say, but the Countess Godgifu will."

"There are only two things Edward is really concerned about, one is being King, the other is being a saint. Will his sister's marriage to the count be of any use to him in the pursuit of either?"

"The wealth and armies of the count can only be an asset in any quest for the throne."

"Yes, of course, I will so tell him."

"You will help?"

"You looked stunned. With me, Thegn Godwin, you see the simple more direct approach is more apt to work."

"You did not enjoy meeting my soldier, Behi?"

He put his head down. "Yes, I enjoyed meeting him."

"That is good, but I shall remember your advice should we have future dealings and be less devious. After you have talked with Edward I shall meet with him."

"Maybe he will not see you."

"I have a gift from his mother."

"He will see you."

Godwin opened the door and then turned back into the small chamber. "How did you get him to come out of the cistern?"

"After hours of discussion and an inventory of saints, I convinced him as a saint he could be as an anchorite, but a king who was a saint could never be a recluse."

"Why did it take so long?"

"Edward mulls things over for a long time before he decides. You will not be able to go back to Rouen with a positive answer until he has given it all careful thought."

"I hope to take him with me."

"I shall go to Edward now," the monk said.

Godwin washed the dirt of the road from his face and hands, brushed his clothes and joined his host in the great hall for the evening meal. Edward made no appearance.

"He is with Robin, the monk," Godfrey said.

The fowl was greasy; the oxen tainted; the bread blue with mold; the curds dry and bitter. He was almost tempted to the wine to wash the acrid taste away for Godfrey assured him it was excellent and both he and his brother, William, drank in quantity. But Godwin maintained his temperance.

There was no sign of Edward appearing. The great hall occupied the top floor of the squared tower, but it was no great hall at all, only a small room with narrow slits that did not seem to let in enough air to breathe and the room was smoky and stifling. There were no minstrels, nor jugglers, nor traveling vagabonds to entertain. There were only several soldiers who sang of a wife of the North named Heljeker whose organ was so huge all could climb in and look around.

As the night dragged on it was apparent Edward was not going to appear and when Godwin found himself the last left awake in the hall he excused himself to his sleeping host and went to bed. The bed straw smelled of mold and the rats seemed in command of the keep once the night had settled in and their constant chewing and gnawing kept him awake. He arose early, tired as if he hadn't slept and he wasn't sure he had. He went below, but there was no sign of the Atheling about. He drank flat water and ate blue bread and made his way to the hall.

Godfrey was awake and Godwin wondered if he had spent the night in the hall.

"He is with Robin yet," Godfrey told him and yawned and stretched. The Norman's clothing was spotted with grease from the night's meal.

"Is he really capable . . . that is, does he have the power to heal?"

"I wouldn't know," the boy's uncle said and in such a manner Godwin knew it was a closed subject.

At last Edward arrived. He more floated into the room than walked, gracefully making his way into the hall and trailing his long garment behind. There was something reminiscent of a painting Godwin had seen of Jesus at Nazareth. The robe, however, was not plain as Christ's had been, but embroidered with strips of delicate flowers in green and gold threads. It also was threadbare in places. In his white hair were streamers of green ribbons falling back over his shoulders. He made a startling and a strange sight.

There was triumph in his entrance like a warrior entering at the city gates and his hands touched in front of him, prayer like, fingers pointing upward. No one spoke perhaps mesmerized by the sight of the youth. He slowly opened his hands, extending them out palms open, fingers spread as if dispensing a blessing, great wisdom or a magnanimous greeting to the crowd. There were but a few servants, Godfrey and Godwin, himself, in the hall and the affectation seemed ludicrous and Godwin stifled the urge to laugh.

Edward moved past Godwin, stepped up on a small raised area at the end of the hall and spoke. "You wished a word with me?" Godwin doubted the Pope, himself, moved with such flourish and pomp.

"Yes, my Lord." The address was a feigned humility that he hardly felt. "My purpose is twofold. As you are the male head of your house, at the bequest of your mother, Queen Emma, and your uncle, Duke of Normandy, and your uncle, Archbishop of Rouen, I ask that you come to Rouen to arrange the marriage settlement of your sister, Godgifu, to the Count of Vixen. My second purpose is to present you with the love of your mother and a gift from her."

"She sent her love?"

"Yes. And a gift."

"It is from her?"

"Indeed, Lord Edward. Are you familar with a St. Guthlac?"

"I am." His eyes lit up and there seemed to Godwin a transfiguration. He seemed less the grotesque monster and more the helpless child.

"Then you know the story of Wilfred and the jackdaw?"

"Yes. Yes." Edward spoke with obvious delight.

"This is said to be"—Godwin handed him the glove—"the very gauntlet the jackdaw brought to Guthlac . . ."

"And my mother sent it?"

"Yes. She had thought to put it with her relics, but decided you would find it of great comfort."

"Those are her great treasures," Edward said. "And she would part with them to no man." He scrutinized the glove, turning it and fingering the needlework. "Once they were stolen by Edmund."

"And he has been punished and is dead."

"AND I SHOULD BE KING."

Godwin was shaken by the outburst, but he spoke softly so as to make Edward have to listen rather than interrupt. "And the day will come undoubtedly when your rightful throne will be given to you. But for now your mother thinks of you, as she is isolated and far away, and sends you this precious gift."

"Yes," he said, "my mother has always loved me very much."

Godwin stepped back.

"I will," Edward said, "journey to Rouen with you. When Godgifu is married, it will be better for us all. The house of Vixen will be open to us as brothers to the count."

"Your mother will be most happy."

Edward, carrying the glove extended out in his open palm, with such care he might be a bishop carrying the Eucharist, left the hall with as much pomp as when he arrived.

"Clever," Godfrey said.

"Who's to know?" Godwin responded and shrugged.

"Yes. Who is to know?"

Later, by the edge of the marsh, he was watching the young girl with one hand slap poorly woven garments against wet rocks.

"You are a charlatan," Robin of Jumieges said as he came up behind him.

"Yes."

"I don't think I like you much, Thegn."

"I did only what I came to do." Godwin wondered why he felt it necessary to justify himself to this young man.

The girl washing clothes pushed leeches from her stubbed arm, which was dotted with points of blood.

"Where did you get the glove?" the monk asked.

"None of your affair." But Godwin smiled and added, "Your Grace of Canterbury."

CHAPTER 6

Jomburg, 1018

GODWIN ACCUMULATED. HE WAS ONLY A THEGN BUT HE HAD GARNERED benefices from the King, gifts from the earls, presents from envoys, tokens from the bishops and valuable remembrances from a grateful Queen. For the year before York, and with much greater success after, he had been gathering wealth. As if an alchemist, he turned plate and coin, silks and stones, gold and furs into soldiers and ships. It was a gamble, but sooner or later the main chance would come. The bankers of Bruges could smell success and they had been willing to lend him, a lowly thegn, sums to build the ships and quarter the army. The ships anchored at Greenwich in wait and the soldiers were serfs and freedmen of Wessex ready to gamble with Godwin on the one main chance. He never voiced his total ambition, as if somehow by doing it, it would be taken from him, but as surely as he was a thegn, he would be Earl of— But he stopped short of saying it; wouldn't voice it not even to himself.

And the main chance came in the pounding at his door in the middle of the night.

"Thegn Godwin. Godwin! Godwin!" It was Behi and the rapping continued and he arose and with a woolen robe tossed about him opened the door and blinked into the torch's light.

"A courier from the King. He awaits in the hall, a Dane. Says the Wends have invaded the Daneland. Cnute readies his army at Roeskild and will sail for Jomburg."

Godwin followed Behi as he talked.

By morning messengers had been dispatched throughout Wessex and the call was out. In Greenwich ships were being loaded with supplies and weapons.

He went to the Queen's chambers.

She was vomiting. "I have morning sickness," she told him, wiping her mouth on a linen. A slave took away the basin.

"I ask your permission, Madam, to sail for the Daneland."

"My permission? Since when have you needed my permission to do anything?"

"Lady, you are Queen."

"Someone should tell my Lord husband. Someone should tell him I'm alive."

"You are the regent. I would not, nor could I, sail without your writ."

"And give me a reason why I should let you desert me, too, Godwin. You are all the civil company I have left. You manage the affairs of government. You are my rock and strength and I will need you ere this heir is born."

"Will be months before the next King arrives from your womb, Madam, and I can well promise to have returned long before then, but better the sooner the Daneland is brought to peace, the sooner your husband the King will return."

"And why should he give up his whore for me?"

"Because, Lady, you bring him pleasure and a son. He will wish to be here for the birthing."

"You keep promising me, Godwin, that when I am shed of this belly, my world will be as it was before."

"It will, my dear Queen. I assure you."

"I doubt that it can ever be, but sail. I can't stop you."

"Thorkell the Tall will be here to aid you."

"Yes, the old man is left with the unpleasant task of tending the Queen."

"And Bishop Wulfstan."

"Go. You are free to go."

But he made her put the order in writing.

At Greenwich, when he was ready to board the flagship, he turned about on the plank and for just a moment was certain he saw those three sisters, those three crones he had met on the road to York. "Godwin is an ambitious man" seemed to float on the wind. But when he strained to see them among the crowd gathered at the dock, he saw nothing of the trio.

Godwin hated the sea. It made him ill, but he never allowed anyone but Wordig knowledge of that fact. Fortunately the sea was relatively passive for a winter's sailing and the thirty-three vessels of his fleet, all intact, had anchored at Jomburg a day earlier than thought possible. Cnute's ships and army had quite obviously not yet reached the stronghold of Thorgals-Sprakaleg's, for the harbor was bare but for surf and the thirty-three ships flying Cnute's Black Raven under Godwin's command.

Godwin, with only an oarsman, put ashore in a small boat. He saw no one as he climbed out onto the black rock. The oarsman elected to stay in the rower.

"Stop!" a voice called.

He looked up to see a sword hanging over his head in the arms of a young woman. She was freckled and red-haired and gave him what he supposed was meant to be a frightening look. "Those are Cnute's ships out there. I see the Raven, but you're no Dane."

"I am a Wessexman." He spoke up to the sword.

"Is that a Wend?"

"No, England," he told her, "I have sailed from England."

"How can I be sure?" She still held the sword. "The Wends are coming. They're coming to ravage and pillage and rape and—"

Appearing from behind a rock below where Godwin stood crawled a hideous old hag. "Not me. They wouldn't rape me. They'd shove me aside, like a fisherman tossing back an old carp."

"Careful, Sorgad," the girl called down to her, "he may be a Wend and Wends do great atrocities even to ugly old women like you."

"He's not a Wend." Sorgad stood up and held out her arms. "He's a great warrior come from the great island across the sea to carry you off to his land where you shall bear the royal blood."

"Are you of the royal blood?" Gytha asked. "Have you the mark about you?"

Instead of answering, he asked her who she was.

"I am the daughter of Thorgals-Sprakaleg. Are you of the royal blood? You don't look much like a king, and you are too old to be a prince."

"I am thirty years old, in good health, think you are a lovely princess and wished you would put down that sword you are holding over me."

She let the sword rest on a rock at her feet.

"Do you know the Queen Gunnerhild?" he asked her.

"Yes," she said. "She is a wise woman."

"She told me I should marry you, that it would temper my ambition. I don't know about that, but I think it might indeed do well to marry you, for you are a delightful young lady to behold."

"Who are you?"

"He is a great warrior," Sorgad said "and would marry you, what more do you need?"

"What great deeds have you done? Who have you slain?"

"Ask me in a week," he told her, "when the Wends are defeated."

"You have done nothing. You are no warrior. Tell me your name."

"He will be father of a queen, think on that, Gytha," Sorgad said with great solemnity.

"Your name?"

"Godwin," he said.

"Godwin. I have heard of you. You are nothing but a thegn, a common lowly thegn. A fraud."

"Marry me," he said and laughed.

"Marry you. I won't even talk to you."

She turned as if to leave her perch on the rock when Sorgad called out, "Ships. More ships come."

"The Black Raven," Godwin said, "it is the King's fleet," and sat down on the rock to wait. She sat silent overhead. Damned if he wouldn't marry her. What started out as a game had possibilities. She not only was young and fresh, oh God was she fresh, but she was of Cnute's house through marriage. He could do worse. Much worse. She looked healthy enough. He looked up at her and smiled.

"I'm not talking to you," she said.

"She's not talking to you," Sorgad mocked and cawed like a bird. "But she will. She will." She came over to Godwin and whispered in his ear. "You must promise me to call the girl Edith." God, but the woman smelled of rotten fish and the sea. "Promise," she urged. "Promise."

"I promise," he said, hoping she would not get so close again.

"What did you promise her?" Gytha asked.

"You're not talking to him," Sorgad said, "so shut up." Two small boats were visible and they rowed toward the rocks, and then behind them a fleet of small boats were lowered as Cnute's army rowed to shore. The King was standing up, balancing himself in one of the boats, and Godwin identified Ulf and Estrid . . . oh, and damn, Elgiva and Cnute's boy, Svegan.

Ulf leaped onto the rocks and climbed up toward his sister, barely nodding to Godwin. "Gytha, how is—"

"He says he's dying," she told her brother. "He doesn't roar."

Cnute looked at Godwin as if surprised to see him, though he had been sent word. "All those ships are yours?"

"Yours, my King, and loaded with an army for you."

"You continually amaze me. What will you be thinking of next?"

"A wife," Godwin told him.

"Now that would amaze me." Cnute put his arm about Godwin as they followed Gytha's and Ulf's lead up the hill. Estrid was running to catch up and Elgiva never bothered, hanging on to the boy.

Gytha reached and took her brother's hand and the simple gesture made Godwin jealous. He was being ridiculous. The pair went in where the old man sat slumped in a reindeer wrap. Godwin stood at the door.

"My son," Thorgals-Sprakaleg said, "Harold is dead, the Wends are rising up in the South and your sister is not wed."

"I am here, Father . . . and the King as well."

"The King is dead. I've told you."

"Cnute, Father. The Wends will be put down, we have brought armies."

"If you can't get her a husband at least make certain the obstinate girl is safe. Her mother saw a hawk eat a white rat at low tide."

Godwin wondered what that meant as he stepped into the hall, followed by Estrid and Cnute.

"The blessing of Christ, Jesus, upon you." Estrid pushed off her hood and leaned over and kissed the old man.

"And Odin, too. I would hope." He looked up at her.

"That is pagan," Estrid scolded.

"When one is dying, it is well to petition all the gods. Who's to know if you have picked the right one? Be certain, leave no one out."

"Don't talk of dying, good friend," Cnute said.

"I am old and have lost my voice. No one listens to me when I can't bellow at them. Even Gytha pays me no mind, any longer. I might as well be dead."

"We'll have you up and roaring," Ulf said.

Godwin walked above in the hills and looked down at the rocks and the sea and the boats from all the ships bringing the soldiers and the supplies ashore and the empty boats returning again for another load.

He could do far worse than Gytha. She was redheaded and freckled and pert and lively. She would not be a dull wife. In thinking of marriage, he thought of himself as well. He was not an unfair-looking man, rather comely he felt. Oh, the glass revealed no rare handsome swain. He had not the charisma of Robin of Jumieges, but God had not been unkind to him. His brown short-clipped hair was clean and his face was not marred by birthmarks or unsightly scars and his teeth were good and he kept them white by rubbing them with bark and he bathed often and seldom had lice. He could read a little Latin, though he didn't sing well, nor have an ear for verse. But he was bright and that overshadowed all deficits, for he would be an earl, that earl, the first earl of the realm, and then it would matter little if he were as ugly as a troll. Yet, she had some crazy notion of what a husband should be. He went inside.

Estrid was of little help.

"What would you want with her?" Estrid had violets tied in the braid atop her head. "She is incurably romantic. She exists in a world of dreams, and dragons, of miracles and wonderments. You're a practical man, Godwin. What need have you for a silly girl? Oh, I love her, but I also know her. Forget her."

"She'll never have you," Ulf told him. The jarl's son was dressed less the peasant and more in keeping with his rank, but he was ganglish and still looked the boy in the fancy-stitched gonelle and bright green hose. His hair was messed and his stance awkward. "She wants a warrior the likes of which never existed, even in the greatest legends."

"Who will never have him?" Cnute asked, touching the scar on his left cheek.

"My sister," Ulf said.

Godwin looked humble; at least he tried to look humble. "I did not mean to presume, my Lord," he said to Cnute.

"Presume what? If you want the lass you can have her."

"Ah," Ulf told him, "but there's the rub, you see. She will not have him. I am sure."

"But Godwin is the greatest of the thegns of this land. He is much more than a thegn. He could be an earl if he wanted. I offered . . ."

"That is not the problem," Estrid said. "Gytha wants a warrior out of some legend. She wants no real man."

Cnute slapped his thigh. "Thorgals-Sprakaleg should take a willow to her."

"It would do no good," Estrid said.

"Then," Godwin announced, "I will simply have to become a warrior of legend."

CHAPTER 7

Jomburg, 1018

THE GREAT HALL AT JOMBURG HAD A HIGH-PITCHED ROOF OF HUGE TIMBERS as if built to last forever. The wood was dark and oiled like ships' beams. The posts supporting the roof ran parallel, six or so feet apart near the center, carved with designs that Godwin thought Celtic. There was a sense of the sea about the hall, with flags drooping like sails where the posts met the pitched roof. The tables had benches on the outside walls only and a fire trough ran the length of the hall in the center of the room between the two rows of posts. Those at the tables on one side sat facing those at the tables on the other looking over the fire between them. Large dried fishes left from last summer's catch hung from the rafters. Yellow and salted, they gave the room a pungent air. Oars of vessels lined the walls and two great figureheads, one a dragon, the other a bear's head, stretched out at each end of the hall.

Queen Gunnerhild arrived at Jomburg. She came by sea and was bounced from the shore in a litter carried by four small men who struggled up the hill with the black-draped sedan. While the men lugging her were hardly bigger than dwarfs, those that escorted her on horseback looked to be giants, and the soldiers that marched beside her, as well as those on horses, were ribboned in black sashes.

"The King is dead!" one of the riders proclaimed, and with that she emerged from the curtained box in layers of black fabric, her face covered with a thin lace of black, and without a word she walked all the way back down to the sea and let out a sharp piercing wail, followed by another and another.

Thorgals-Sprakaleg said, "Someone has killed a lion."

She left the sea and trudged up the hill and was taken to a chamber without a word and was said to have sat there in the dark.

Thorgals-Sprakaleg had insisted upon being brought into the hall. He was carted on a flat litter. The old Danish warrior tried to yell at his bearers, but failed. Godwin followed the litter into the room and behind him lagged Wordig, sullenly. Thorgals-Sprakaleg was laid beside the fire trough and his face reflected the heat of the flames. Godwin saw Cnute, who stood out among Thorgals-Sprakaleg's men, at the far end of the hall. His boyish good nature and his exuberance were like a spring wind in this winter of old warriors. Beside him sat the woman, Elgiva.

"Get that man out of my sight," Elgiva yelled when she saw Godwin enter. Her black hair shook as she moved her head angrily. Her eyes were like fire.

"Godwin, pay her no mind," the King said.

As he moved closer he thought how ugly was her nose. Almost bulbous, it looked enflamed when she was angry, as she was now. For all Cnute spoke of her sexual dexterity, Godwin thought the black-haired, dark-skinned woman was unappealing and she was getting old. Her shrewishness had left lines creasing her face.

"I will not be in the same room with that creature." Elgiva stood up as if threatening to leave.

"Then go," the King told her.

She glared at Cnute.

"Or be quiet. We are not gathered to listen to the caterwauling of some woman."

She slumped back down in the chair, defeated.

"We have received word, Godwin," Cnute said, "that the Wends are encamped within fifteen leagues of here."

"Where do they come from?"

"They have no land of their own. They claim Jomburg as their 'holy place by the sea' and whenever it's left unprotected they gather the dispersed tribes and come on us in force. They are Slavs and mostly scattered about Saxony when they are not at war with us. We will set out at sunrise on the morrow and march halfway and the day next we will complete the distance. Are you provided for?"

"My army is ready, my Lord." Godwin sat down beyond the empty seat left for Ulf.

"As is Ulf's. He will command Thorgals-Sprakaleg's as well. I know the village where the Wends are encamped. It is in a valley. We will take advantage of the high ground overlooking. I want to surprise them for they will have, from all reports, the advantage in numbers."

Elgiva was still sulking and she pulled at her black hair as if to inflict some self-punishment.

"How strong is the force?" Thorgals-Sprakaleg asked in a weak voice.

One of his men replied, "At least a thousand strong, some say, my Lord. Others estimate six hundred or so. None say less than that."

"A Wend is a madman in battle." Thorgals-Sprakaleg spoke with a rasp.

"We shall be outnumbered even at six hundred," Ulf said as he entered the hall. Godwin could sense Ulf was at home here. Gytha was at his side and he was followed by Estrid and a pack of old women. One of them, stout-faced and breathing heavily, carried a box piled with dyed Easter eggs.

"But it is not yet Easter," a gray wisping wife of Jomburg said.

"It will be. It will be. Christ shall be born again," the stout woman proclaimed. "And Thor, too."

"And your eggs will all be rotten," the wisp said and appeared delighted at the prospect.

"And if we are outnumbered," Cnute told Ulf as he came up to the table and sat beside him, "the more reason we must take them by surprise."

"I shall pray for you all," Estrid said and sat down.

Elgiva snorted.

"We shall pray for all, too," a cleric of Jomburg said. "And we will pray for the soul of Thorgals-Sprakaleg, as well."

"I'm not dead yet." The old jarl found some strength when he voiced the statement.

"Of course, my Lord." The cleric flustered about.

"Soon it will be Easter," Estrid said. "They have allegories acted out at the mass in Rouen at Eastertide, Emma told me."

"That is sinful," the cleric said.

"Not in Rouen, Priest." Cnute smiled.

The cleric moved with a slight limp to the low end of the table.

"Nothing is sinful in Rouen, Priest," Ulf added. "The duke tells God what is right and wrong and the Pope as well."

"Ulf, don't talk that way," Estrid said. "I've been to Rouen—"

The King interrupted her. "—and you found the food no better than here. Let's eat. If our host is ready."

Thorkals-Sprakaleg muttered.

Dried fish was served. It was salty and tough. Godwin picked at it. The King pinched Elgiva and she squealed like a young piglet. Estrid looked annoyed. One of the old Jomburg women beat her fish again and again upon the table to break it up and then stuffed the pieces in her mouth chewing and telling some tale of a woman raped by a Wendlander. Gytha left her place and went over to her father after he groaned.

"My father," Ulf spoke, "welcomes you all to his table. He is angered that he may not join us in battle and is not well enough to stand up and speak for himself."

Cups were raised. "To Thorgals-Sprakaleg," the cry went up. "To Thorgals-Sprakaleg. He is a bear."

The boy Svegan threw up.

"What is wrong with him?" Cnute asked.

Elgiva looked angry. "No doubt, upon Thor's chest, someone is trying to poison him." She turned. "Godwin!"

"Don't be stupid," Cnute said. "Why would loyal Godwin poison my son?"

"Because he is in the pay of the Norman whore."

"You are talking about the Queen." Estrid spat the words at her.

"Enough of this. Elgiva, have the boy taken out and washed off. He is covered with his meal."

Elgiva, herself, took ahold of the boy's hand. "If not Godwin, perhaps that witch! Sorgad has put a curse upon him. The boy will die."

Svegan let out a cry. "I don't want to die!"

The old man groaned from his litter, "Of course I am going to die."

"Svegan won't die," Gytha said. "I know what's wrong with him. The house slaves were whispering elvenfolk had emptied the honey pot. I think Svegan's an elf. Are you?"

"Yes," he said and began to vomit again.

Elgiva left with the boy whining and she had to pull him from the hall.

Thorgals-Sprakaleg spoke in a near whisper. "I have just seen a vision."

"What is it, Father?"

"Who are you?"

"Your son's wife."

"Where is Cnute?"

"I am here, Thorgals-Sprakaleg."

"I have seen a vision."

"What was it?" Ulf asked.

"Yes what . . . ?" the old man said and seemed to doze.

"Don't mind Elgiva." Cnute touched Godwin's arm and he nodded his assurance to the King.

A robe of one of the Jomburg clerics suddenly burst into flame as he walked too near the fire. He screamed in terror as Wordig threw him to the ground and smothered the flames with his huge body.

Thorgals-Sprakaleg yelled out, "Oh, God, I must be in hell."

"Hush, old man, it is all right, just a priest burning," one of the women of Jomburg said.

"God be merciful to you," the cleric said, barely able to breathe, "God be merciful."

Wordig only grunted.

Thorgals-Sprakaleg moaned, "I saw a vision."

"Yes, Father." Ulf went to his father. "It was only a fire. A man burning, nothing else."

"No, I saw the armies marching out to meet the Wend. They were small in number. There were no West Saxons, only Danes."

"There will be Wessexmen there a plenty," Godwin told him.

"He is out of his head," the King said.

Godwin spent the night with little sleep. His mind raced. It was to be his moment, his few hours of glory. The details were framed in his head. From these few days nothing again would remain as it was. He would be titled and he would be married. Marriage was entered for the purpose of having sons and daughters. Most men overlooked the worth of daughters, but they should not, they were a valuable commodity. Gytha was now. Her father was dying and wanted her set, so much so, even the swineherd's son would do. But not Godwin's daughter. She could marry a king if he wished it. She would marry well for Godwin would in a short time be, dare he think it, a great earl. Children were essential, for though there might be life eternal with the heavenly father, nothing certain existed beyond the grave save a man's offspring. Like a dead stock of grain, cut from its roots, only the seed was left to germinate. A man could not live forever, yet did through his progeny. And Gytha, healthy like a good brood sow, came from strong stock and she appeared to him perceptive and certainly had a mind of her own and that appealed to him. He didn't want a wife who was dutiful and dull. He would be able to share his world with her. She was yet a child, but she would grow and he would tell her his outrageous dreams and schemes and plots and plans. They could connive together. He would give her lovely gowns and exquisite jewels and they would build a house of stone like the Normans and she would bear him many children, all bright and finding their own places in the kingdom and his children would be his friends and Gytha's. This was his dream and he would share it all with her.

He must have slept, but he was still thinking of her when he awoke.

They marched. And before night fell they made camp. Godwin had learned one thing from the Normans: an army travels best on a good stomach. He ported the huge cauldrons for hot meaty stews, and while the King's troops and those of Ulf's nurtured on dried fish and cold mucky pastes, his men came alive with hot food. Cnute had said, "If you're going to serve your army warm mess, camp away so the smell doesn't drive my men mad." He was glad he had for it made the plan easier to accomplish. The night was cold for it was not yet spring; it almost felt as if it would snow. He shivered, sat in his tent and waited. Across the ravine he could see the tents and fires of both Cnute's and Ulf's camps.

"Behi, call the leaders. Have them assemble in my tent."

They gathered, the sturdy Saxons. Their faces were still ruddy and flushed from the sea. Most had full beards, or at the very least a bushy mustache, and their hair, except for a few balding pates, was full and uncropped, falling to the shoulders. They sat on the floor and stood at the entrance of the tent and they talked and joked as they waited for Godwin to speak. "I give you this," he said to them. "If we do this night what I hope we can do this night, I shall reward each of you with land acreage in Wessex."

An old man spoke. "We know you are familiar with the King, but you are but a thegn."

"If I achieve tonight's goal, I shall be a noble. But I need your help and loyalty."

There were murmurs of assent. An old man patted his leathered foot upon the ground in affirmation.

"Before the moon rises I want all your men to march quietly, no silently, from this place. We will leave the fires burning, the tents standing."

"We are deserting the King?" a thin man with a drip of brown whiskers asked.

"No," Godwin assured him. "We are going to take the Wends ourselves. We will surprise them in the night. Slaughter every last body in that village . . ."

At first no one said a word, then at once they all agreed with a constant of "yeses" and how they were greater than the Danes and would destroy the Wend.

"If there are women in the village?" someone asked.

"Kill everything that moves. The Wends are not only fearsome, they are vindictive, and a survivor will spend a life searching for revenge and breeding new Wend warriors. No one lives. Make that understood among your men. We shall move silently in and catch them in their sleep. Let us lose no soldier if we don't have to. Let them know when this is done should the King stay in Jomburg or Roeskild I will send my army home. Every last man except for Behi here, all of you, can sail for Wessex. And I shall reward all. What plunder there is, after the King's share, will be to divide among them."

The leaders were loud with excitement.

"Less noise," he cautioned. "The Danes are camped but within ear range across the ravine. The village lies to the south on the road just beyond the rise. We follow right along the edge of the river. It is but four or so leagues. You will know it is me riding ahead for the horse has a large white circle on its right flank. Go now and rouse your men."

Behi remained behind. He took off his sale and sat nude from the waist up, his gartered legs propped up on a chest.

"You should eat more," Godwin said.

"Tell me, Thegn, when you declined before, why now do you accept an earldom."

"Because, Behi, this time I shall be offered"—and he whispered the last word—"Wessex."

"But that is a kingdom."

"It was until tomorrow. The seed has been planted. Tonight we harvest the crop."

"Wessex is home. I miss England." Behi put down his feet.

"And I. But I will wed the Jomburg maid."

"I suspected as much. Godspeed you, Earl Godwin."

"Godspeed you, Thegn Behi. For I shall see you are made such if we succeed this night."

"The likes of me a thegn." He picked up his sale. "We shan't fail, my Lord." And he left the tent.

The bearded army moved quietly from the camp. They were nearly three hundred in number. Each man was directed to kill at least two of the Wends, more if he was able. The night was getting colder. And even the march didn't seem to help. Godwin led rather than rode his mount from the camp, lest he be too visible across the ravine. They left no one, only fires burning slowly toward embers and the tents pitched as if they were occupied.

If all went as he had planned, Godwin was not only sure of the earldom, but of Gytha's hand as well. The Wend would be sleeping. All wars should be fought this way. It was much easier on the victor. It was far more economical. Surprise, quickly won and over. He tired of walking and asked for help to get back on his mount. A soldier with a bushy head of hair as pitch as the sky extended his hands together and Godwin stepped up.

Behi, who also rode, came alongside. "The forerider returns," he said.

"What say you?" Godwin asked the rider in a whisper.

"The village is just ahead. The Wends are there all right. I crept in close as I dare. They don't have much in the way of guards posted. Most heads are soaked in strong drink, many are asleep, yet there are enough still moving about." His accent was East Anglican.

"Do they give any indication they've readied for battle or that they know we are supposedly camped a short way from here?"

"I can't tell. The tongue they speak is foreign to my ear."

"But they do not appear alarmed?"

"No."

"Tell the men to slow down, Behi. Let's give the Wend time to get a wee drunker and drowsier before we attack, and counsel them again to silence. I heard a voice or two and laughter earlier. That could be the death of us all now." He turned to the man with the Anglican tongue. "Now, rider, come and describe this village to me. The moon is rising and you can draw with a stick in the earth."

As the man drew in the dirt, Wordig, who had come this distance from Jomburg, from Winchester actually, with barely a word, walked up to Godwin and whispered, "I know the Wends. They are a-feared of the cross and a burning cross in the night puts them in mortal fear."

"How do you know this? How do you know of the Wends?"

"I know," was the only response.

Godwin was certain it would be hopeless to press the man, yet so much hinged on the success of this enterprise. Still, he trusted Wordig explicitly. If Wordig said he knew the Wends, then he did. "What should be done?" he asked the giant.

"Have each man make a cross of sticks. When we get into the village, set each a-burn by torch or campfire there and enter the places where a Wend sleeps. I warrant, not a jackman of 'em will raise a sword."

"Behi, you heard him. Tell the leaders what is to be done."

Behi went back into the night of marching soldiers.

"If this succeeds, Wordig, you are a freedman."

Wordig grumbled off.

The moon was bright as they slipped from shadow to shadow surrounding the village. Each man had made a long-handled cross of dry twigs tied with pieces of green bark. The encampment was a crisscross of two roads with most of the serfs' hovels lined along the roads, though some were back behind others. There were a few distinct voices, and fires burned low outside the huts, but mostly the village seemed dead with sleep.

The signal: two hoots of an owl.

And when it was heard the village became a sea of chaos, of running men and terrifying yells and burning crosses thrown at the feet of dead Wends and hovels going up in flame. There were screeches of pain, of angry oaths of vengeance. The Wessexmen moved and struck and caught those trying to flee from hovels engulfed in fire and women's voices cried out as well as men's, and these were the sounds of death, of annihilation. Godwin saw heads lopped from bodies, bodies burning in clothes caught aflame, arms and legs chopped from massive trunks, of a Saxon soldier sticking his penis into a woman even as he killed her, of children being tossed onto the fires. . . . The stench was horrible. . . . The Saxons seemed to move with the agility of deer. . . . There was no doubt as to the outcome: they had caught the Wend completely unaware, stupified by sleep and strong drink, unarmed and unready to battle and none knew escape and the howls of death grew and the flames of death grew and the sky was lit orange and eerie and Godwin stood visible to the men . . . and then the sounds of anguish began to subside and the fires burned to glowing embers . . . a last hovel caught fire and a dog ran out of it, his fur afire. He howled, pleading for death, and the sound seemed worse than the cries of the men. The first light of morning began in the sky.

Someone screamed out, "Blessed be Jesus Christ!"

Blessed be Christ's cross, Godwin thought.

"We have lost few men." Behi's face and chest were black from the soot. He slumped down on a mound of earth near Godwin. "I will give you the names before we leave this place. There are a few more with blood wounds, but mostly we came out unscathed. It was the crosses. I have never seen such fear in men's eyes as those burning crosses . . ." The sentence fell away and his exhaustion was apparent.

"Rest now. You have earned it."

"None escaped . . ."

A priest came up. "I would say a mass of thanksgiving," he said.

"Do," Godwin said. "Do."

And the priest wandered off. As the daylight crept in Godwin could see all that survived were West Saxons, horses, pigs, chickens and gods; the soldiers and the animals seemed at a loss as what they should do, moving about aimlessly, their bodies unable to slow down. The priest began, amid the dead and mutilated bodies of the Wends, to sing the ritual of the mass and the soldiers gathered about the makeshift altar.

Wordig came wandering by.

"What is that you are holding . . . ?" Godwin asked, but before he finished the question he realized what part of a woman it was. I am glad, Godwin thought, he is not my enemy.

Behi looked up. "Sometimes," he said, rubbing his sooted chest, "the man disgusts me."

Godwin did not reply. The mass continued and he wandered through the destroyed village. Here and there a hut of dung and straw partially remained, but those inside were dead. The smell was the stench of war, familiar, but never pleasing. The earth seemed wet, as if all the blood had seeped from the Wends to it. Heads, apart from bodies, were strewn indiscriminately. A few twig crosses that hadn't burned were tossed aside. Swords and shields never used, jeweled trinkets, some fur skins, a carved piece of tusk and rings with fingers still in them were the meager loot collected and tossed in a heap. Only a single ornate necklace of tiered stones seemed worth the taking and Godwin did. These Wends were nomad warriors not collectors.

The mass ended. "Raise the Black Raven," Godwin called. And the sky became red in the east as the banner of Cnute was unfurled on a tall pole, a totem in the center of the village. A body near the pole screamed out in pain and was released with the slice of a sword.

"And now?" one of Godwin's leaders asked. He appeared tired and his face was wiped with Wend blood.

"Now," Godwin said, "we wait for the King."

And they waited. The sun rose full and bright. It was going to be a warm spring day. Cocks crowed and the morning caw of birds broke the air. At the edge of the village the first ugly bird, the vulture, appeared, circling, but waiting, and then another and another until all the tree branches seemed weighted by the waiting scavengers. How do they know? Godwin wondered.

And then the sound of the King's army. Above on the hillside, as if readying to attack, lined the forces of Cnute and Ulf.

"Raise the Black Raven higher. Let it wave. Let it wave." Godwin commanded.

And a soldier shinnied the pole and raised the banner on a long branch, waving it as if the Raven should lift off in flight. And as he moved back and forth, brushing the branches, the vultures, frightened by the movement, lifted into the sky and circled.

"Go," Godwin told Behi, "tell the King the Wends are destroyed."

Behi rode off up the hill.

"Sound a conch, a victory conch." And the horn pierced the morning air and birds were silent except for the flap of their wings as they turned in circles through the air. A dog sniffed at the blood in which Godwin was standing. He kicked the mongrel away. A cry went up on the hill and Godwin saw Cnute. He ordered his mount brought and was helped up and rode out to meet his King as the armies massed down the hill toward him. The King, next to the rider bearing the Black Raven, rode at the front. Cnute was a magnificent young man, Godwin realized, sitting tall on the black steed. He rode to the place where Godwin had stopped to wait.

"I thought you had deserted," Cnute said.

"I had to do this," Godwin answered.

"I honestly thought you had deserted. It happened once before to me."

"With Eadric?"

"Yes." The King removed his helmet. "How many of them are dead?"

"To my knowledge, all, my Lord."

"It is a great victory. Your victory."

"I did not mean to cheat you of it," Godwin said. "I am your man and it was your honor fought for."

"I am the King. I make the battle plans."

"Yes and my head rests at your sword."

"No." Cnute paused. "I should be glad it is done and Jomburg secured. Though I miss the battle, I suppose. Why so daring a feat?"

"Surprise was the only real hope. They outnumbered us. There could be seven or eight hundred dead here. I don't know. I knew none of my Saxon men would sell out to the Wends, they were strangers and did not know the language, but some of your army and some of Ulf's could have kin here. There could be a spy in one of your camps."

"As always, Godwin, your thinking surpasses mine."

"I only sense—"

"Your name will be ranked with Havelok and Beowolf. You'll be legend, Godwin."

"I care not for that, but do you suppose that the deed will be enough to convince the Lady Gytha I am a legend?"

"That's why you really did this, to win the freckled-faced girl?" But Cnute laughed. "If it isn't enough to convince her then we shall shackle her to you until she relents. I have been cheated out of my battle because a man wants a woman. I can understand that."

"I hope she will be more willing."

"But I can't have you a mere thegn, particularly, Godwin, if you are to wed my kin. And she will have you more easily if you are made an earl."

"You know my feeling on that matter," Godwin said.

"Aye, but I have the answer. I plan to make you Earl of Wessex."

"But . . . my Lord." Godwin feigned surprise. "That is a kingdom."

"It is no longer. And you know my feelings on Wessex as well as I know yours." His horse wheeled suddenly. "And I suspect, Godwin, you would have settled for nothing short of Wessex."

"My Lord . . ." Godwin bowed, newly aware that this boy king must not be underestimated.

Cnute smiled. "We shall in time set out those fiefs and benefices which will be your direct holdings, but they will give wealth enough, I assure. So I greet you, Godwin, Earl of Wessex, son of—"

"A swineherd," Godwin interrupted.

"A swineherd." The King laughed. "Shall you have arms bearing pigs on a pike?"

"I think not, my liege King. And I am deeply honored."

"And well-earned. Now show me this village and collection of dead Wends." A rider approached them. "Ah, here comes your soon-to-be brother-in-law, as well as mine already."

Ulf leaped from his horse. "Tell me what has happened. I thought you had deserted us, Godwin."

"The Wend are all destroyed," the King said. "Brother Godwin has rid us of this menace in the night."

"Cheated of a fight?" Ulf rubbed the scar on his face roughly.

"Neither you nor I have lost a soldier and Godwin but few. We have also not lost a battle and Jomburg is secure. Come, let's see this night's work before the vultures devour the village."

"There is little pillage," Godwin said.

"There never is among the Wends," Ulf told him. "But, Godwin, I am angry to have been cheated so. You should have waited."

"Godwin wanted to be a legend, you fool. He did it to win your sister."

Ulf laughed and slapped Godwin, nearly knocking him from his mount. As Cnute moved ahead, the jarl's son leaped on his horse and followed.

Behi rode up before Godwin started off. "Thegn Godwin—"

"Earl, if you please," Godwin interrupted, "Earl of Wessex, Thegn."

Behi broke into a smile and then slapped his horse and rode ahead, passing the King.

"Make way for the King and the Earl of Wessex!" he yelled out. "Make way!"

In triumph Godwin and Ulf and Danes and Saxons trooped behind the King into the great hall where Thorgals-Sprakaleg's breathing sounded like air rattling through a hollow of a log. Estrid, her brown hair hanging loose, not in its usual braid, was bent over the old man. A shell with water in her hands, she tried to give him drink, but it only wet his lips and seeped to his neck. There were tears creeping into her eyes and she touched his face and dried his neck on the sleeve of her bliaut. She looked up at Ulf. "He has not long."

"Father," he said, leaning over beside her, "the Wends are destroyed."

"You and Cnute have destroyed the Wends!" She looked across the man at him.

"My wife, Godwin destroyed the Wends," he said.

"Godwin has slain the Wends?" Gytha asked from where she was standing above Estrid. Godwin saw her pain. Well, he would not have a wife by force. Cnute could give him the maid, but he would not accept her if she were not willing.

"Indeed," Cnute said. "Godwin and his men alone. They killed all the Wends, every last woman and dog of them. They hit upon them during the night and—"

"The night?" Gytha interrupted. "Does a great warrior destroy the enemy in the night?"

"If he had not, Gytha," Cnute told her, "many of the Danes and Saxons would have died this day and Jomburg not so easily saved."

"Great warriors go out in the sun and die gloriously in battle," Gytha said.

"A warrior," Ulf said to his sister, "kills his enemy any way he is able. There are no rules in war, Gytha."

"There is honor," Gytha told him.

"There is death and living," he said to her. "There is nothing else."

"And Ulf is alive," Estrid said to no one in particular. "Godwin saved us all."

"He did indeed, Estrid," Cnute told her, "and we shall sing of his victory and I have named him an earl."

"But Godwin as usual has declined," Estrid said.

Gytha whispered loud enough for Godwin to hear, "He has rejected being named an earl?"

"Ah, but now I name him Earl of Wessex," Cnute announced.

"What's Wessex?" Gytha asked.

"It was a kingdom. The old Saxon kings come of the house of Wessex," Cnute told her, "but now it is to be an earldom and you, Gytha, shall be a great countess in England, the Countess of Wessex."

"No," Gytha told him.

Elgiva had been standing quietly in the corner with her son, but now she stepped forward. "The man is insufferable. A swineherd's son and he thinks to marry into the King's family. No man is so ambitious as Godwin, no man so corrupt. Gytha does well to disdain the advances of a pigherder's brood."

"I shall wed him," Gytha announced.

Thorgals-Sprakaleg groaned.

The King grinned widely and went over and gave Gytha a kiss. "The wedding will be tomorrow."

Estrid looked at him in alarm. "No. The Church does not allow it and the child must have time to prepare a robe. A splendid robe."

"No, Sister. The old man is dying. His daughter must be looked to. The wedding is tomorrow."

"Yes." Ulf spoke softly as if by whispering the old man would not die. "We shall put him to sea, afloat aboard his best ship."

"He is Christian. Grant him a Christian burial," Estrid said.

"He is Viking as well. He shall have the Christian rite and what is tradition among us." Ulf leaned over his father and kissed his cheek. The rattle of death kept its low even pace like a long-distance runner. Ulf turned to the King. "He is dying. My father is dying."

"He is a warrior of great fame, a man born of a bear, a god among the North. I vow I shall not leave this land ere he recovers or dies." Cnute crossed himself, bent down and kissed the dying man on both cheeks and then kissed Ulf as well.

"Thank you," Ulf said and embraced the King.

"You are my brother since we were children, the first among my men and my sister's husband and therefore my brother double over and we honor your grief."

The dying man coughed.

And on the next evening when the juggler and the lute player and the monkey trained to ride on the back of a horse and the man who walked on the rope pulled over the fire pit and the feasting and the drinking had all finished and the torchbearers gone away and the obscene caws had ended, Godwin found himself alone with his bride.

He removed the neckband from her, touching her shoulders, moving his hands against her pale neck. He started to undress her, but she motioned him away to do it for herself and as she did he pulled his tunic off over his shoulder revealing his bare chest and shoulders.

"CHEATED!" she screamed.

"What is wrong?" he said, trying to calm her.

"There is no cross . . ." she cried in her hysteria.

"What?"

"There is no cross on your shoulder." She would not turn around, nor look at him.

"No," he said.

"I've been cheated. It is the mark of kings and I have been cheated."

"But I am no king."

"Sorgad swore the mark was there. Our son will be a king—"

"Perhaps."

"Never. Not without the mark of kings."

"That is silly fable," he said. "Cnute has no mark—"

"Only a wife would know. I've been cheated. NO!" She ran from the chamber and toward the sea. He put on chlamys and followed. She sat the night on the rocks and he walked above, facing the sea until the night became dawn.

And the day went by and night came again and Gytha sat upon the rocks by the sea and he came and stood above her. He listened to her cry, her tears soft and quiet.

"Why do you cry?" he asked.

"Because there is only one life and I want it to be wonderful."

"But it is," he said.

"In this world there are great men and—"

"And I am a great man," he said.

"But there are signs. In Havelok there are signs. He bore the emblazoned sign of the King. There must be signs to reveal the wonderment."

"Like?"

"Like crosses that glow upon the body."

"My deeds are visible in their actions. Gytha, there is nothing in this world I cannot do if I want to do it. For I am wiser than all men I know."

"Even the King?"

"Treason though it may be, even the King. I say it because you are my wife and what is said between us is sacred."

"But what of signs?"

"Worry about what I am able to do. I killed all the Wends because it meant I could wed you."

"But deeds are not done for such reasons . . ."

"No?"

"No. They are done because they are noble and honored in the doing."

"But better done for purpose," he said.

"No."

They sat in the dark and the moon slipped over the hill, large and round and yellow and the sound of the sea interrupted their silence.

"Sorgad says we will have a son a king and a daughter a queen, but she lied about the cross and I do not believe her."

"We will if I work at it and you as well."

"No, things should be if they are to be. Not for any other reason."

"No, child. Events must be made to happen. It is the way of the strong. I am but the son of a swineherd."

"You are an earl—"

"An earl, son of a—"

"Don't say that."

"But it is so. I am also a great earl and will soon be the greatest earl of all England. I am what I am because I wanted it. I made it happen. If I want a son a king or a daughter a queen it will be made to happen." He took her hand.

"Our son will be King?"

"Yes. If you want it."

"I would wish it so," she said.

He led her from the sound of the sea to the chamber.

CHAPTER 8

Winchester, 1018

THE DEATH OF WINTER HAD PASSED. SPRING CAME TO WESSEX IN SHOOTS OF green grasses pushing through the thawed earth, in early buds bursting pink on leafless apple trees, in a rush of rivers released from icy solids, in churls putting a till to black wet soil and sun-warmed petals floating down from leafed trees and apples forming green and the soil spouting grasses.

And then summer swept in on a murmur of soft wind and the hum of insects. Emma's belly grew and swelled, ripened, and her purple gown swept before her and she tried to remember what her feet looked like.

She waddled. She was ugly. She was obese and old and ugly and her husband was repulsed by her and she didn't blame him and she hated him. She would get revenge. The Wends had been destroyed, but he stayed. "A vow" Godwin wrote; well what of Cnute's marriage vows? Somehow she would get revenge.

She remembered his hands, his big ugly warm hands wrapped at her breast and she hungered. She remembered his toes and his wide knees and the hair curling on his thighs and the way he squealed when she tucked her finger in his rectum and the joy she found in having the wide head of his penis rest between her breasts. She remembered him sitting on the golden horse, riding toward her and lifting her off her feet. She remembered him taking her in the field on the hill beyond Winchester and the soft grass scratching her legs and the weight of his heavy body upon her and the sun drying the wetness of his perspiration on her body. She hungered.

After the pit at Corfe where inedible swill had been poured down to her, she vowed never to hunger again. And yet she was starved for just the slightest touch, the sight of his body.

Anger welled as large as the child within when she thought of those ugly hands upon the black whore at Jomburg and she wanted to rip off her own breasts because he had touched her with those hands, those ugly coarse hands.

Aesval rapped at her door. She could always tell Aesval's rap for it came in frantic bangs. The heavy woman came in. "You need to walk, to get some air."

"Don't nag me. I'm wallowing in self-pity."

"You've a right to wallow."

"You? Quiet, mousy Aesval daring to criticize the King?"

"He ought to have his gonads cut off."

Emma began to laugh. "Aesval, I can't get over you." And Emma laughed more and Aesval laughed as well.

"Do you feel better?" Aesval asked.

"Yes. Better," Emma said and she smiled. "Let's go to the hall."

"Are you up to it?"

"Yes. Let's go hear the news from Roeskild. The report on Thorgals-what's-his-name's dying and why the King isn't coming home today."

They walked across the stone court. Emma occasionally took the woman's arm to steady herself. "The time will come, Aesval, when I shall find a way to cut his testicles off. Not literally, for that would be a waste, but I shall have my revenge on this indifferent husband." She stepped into the sun and the warmth of it felt pleasant against the back of her neck. Despite her belly and the swollen feet, she walked into the hall as the Queen, for as always her demeanor transformed as she entered a crowd. Her face became a mask and her carriage had a sense of haughtiness about it. It was expected and she carried her hands up and to the side, so that she might gesture to those she passed as she walked the length of the hall. "My God, get me a seat," she said as she reached the end where Thorkell the Tall, presided.

It was Harold Thorkellsson with the stubbled fingers who set the chair for her.

"The news from Roeskild?" Emma asked as she made herself as comfortable as her condition would allow.

"Thorgals-Sprakaleg is dying—" Thorkell began.

"Bless me," Emma spoke with extreme sarcasm. "This is a shock. The most surprising news. And next you will tell me the King can't come home because he has a vow not to leave while Thorgals-Sprakaleg lives." Emma felt a pain in her side.

"Yes." Thorkell nodded. "The King states he will return on the jarl's death."

Emma looked over at Archbishop Wulfstan, who stood nearby. "I have it figured out, your Grace. We get the same news from Roeskild each day because the courier has been lost these many months and he keeps going around in circles and delivers the same message over and over. He doesn't look the same because he comes to us in disguises, lest we think him the fool for having lost his way."

"I fail to find the humor in it, Madam, which you do? Cnute was elected by the Witan as the King of England and in England he belongs."

"Should we have chosen another?" Thorkell asked angrily.

"There was the Atheling."

"Oh, yes," Emma said, "and you could have married me to my son. Well, I will say this for Edward, he used to be constantly in my sight." She let out a quick cry. "Nothing," she assured Wulfstan as he moved to touch her. But the contractions had begun.

"Godwin sends his greetings to his Lady the Queen and says he hopes to be home in time for the birthing."

"We had better send word to Godwin to start running." Emma felt another contraction.

"And he says his own lady gets a belly."

Godwin married and now Godwin was to be a papa. Well, thegn's wife, no, no, it is earl's wife. This daughter of Thorgals—God what is his name—was the Countess of Wessex. Well, Countess, I hope your husband doesn't desert you, leave you in Jomburg and come flying off to Winchester. The pains came again.

"The King also reports, and this was pain to him, that his mother has gone mad because of Harold's death and that Gunnerhild went about killing all the chickens for he had choked on a cock's bone."

"Is there any other news from Roeskild?"

"No, my Lady."

The news was the same. Even the singer from France was the same, although the song was new, of an abbess who was bewitched by a devil and made pregnant by a man of the village and verse followed verse and the nuns of the abbey taunted the poor abbess and tattled to the bishop and he was stern, and the singer's voice became stern; the bishop called the abbess to be examined and the singer sang softly of how she spent the night in the bishop's house and how the mother of Christ came and delivered the abbess of her child and took the baby away and "glory" the singer sang in the morning she was examined and found not with child and the bishop reprimanded all the other nuns for their evil tongues. "Bless be to the Mother Virgin Mary."

The pain was becoming more intense, and Emma gripped the arms of her faldstool.

"We must send word with the courier," Wulfstan said, "that the Queen's time is near and for the good of the heir and for the good of all England, the King should hasten to his own land."

"I am afraid, your Grace, it is too late," Emma said, standing up and leaning on the arms of the stool. "It is time you tied this Lady to the bed, for the Queen will this day be about the birthing."

"Madam," Wulfstan said, coming over and taking her arm.

It was summer and she perspired and the pains were intense and there was a fly which buzzed near her head. Her yellow hair was tied beneath a cap and she wore a linen gown but it had been pulled up to expose her vaginal opening to the witnesses who stood at the foot of her bed. Her arms were tied with cords and her legs braced open and she grunted and cried and pushed her pelvis about and the sweat was mingled with tears on her face and she was afraid. Not of the pain, not of the birthing, but a fear hidden inside that she had not let loose before, the horrible fear that this child, this boy, would come out ugly and white, a monster like Edward. And she didn't want to expel the child but keep him within and the beads of moisture on her forehead were sticky and the fly touched her hairline and she wanted to swat it away but her hands were tied. Aesval wiped her brow with cold water and wet her lips with a touch of cool wine. "JESUS!" she screamed out. "I will have revenge." And she saw the face, the kind sweet welcome face, leaning over above her. She focused on the face. "Willie?"

"It is me, Emma. Goddy is here, too. I guess we came none too soon."

"I'm busy today, Willie," she told him and smiled. "We can't go hawking or warring or riding." But then the pain came intensely. "JESUS GOD!"

Godfrey came to the other side of the bed and touched her tied hand. "They've got you in a rather disgusting position. Your blue-veined legs and your swollen opening are about all of you visible to the world at large."

"It's to make sure I don't cheat. It's to make sure what comes out really came out."

"Old Eric down there can't see that far can he?" Willie asked.

"Edward sends his mother his love," Goddy said.

"Please. Please don't talk about him at this moment." The pains were coming one upon the other. "It will be a beautiful boy, won't it?"

Goddy nodded. "Yes. It will be the likes of Robin of Jumieges. Do you remember him?"

"Yes. It will be beautiful like the boy monk." And then she churned and thrust and pushed and screamed, "OH, SHIT! SOW'S BLOOOOOD! OHHHHHH JE-SUS! GOD! JESUS!" . . . and suddenly it was over.

There was silence in the room and then a baby's cry.

"Tell me." Emma looked up at her brother. "Is it all right?"

"Yes," Goddy said and everyone in the room started talking. "It is a boy, fat and healthy."

"Not white, not, not—"

"He does not look like Edward, Emma," Goddy assured her.

"God be praised."

She saw Thorkell the Tall raise his sword to cut the cord. "A babe loose of its mother is a life. A boy free of his father is a man," Thorkell said. "I give the child to my son, Harold. The King would have him the godfather."

"As the King wishes," Emma said weakly.

Harold Thorkellsson took the baby, still bloody, and it cried and he said, "The son shall be called Harthacnut after the father, for this is the King's wish."

"So be it," Emma said and she smiled. "Give him to me."

"Let them wash him first," Aesval said.

"Are you all right, Emma?" Godfrey asked.

"I am fine now. A fat healthy baby boy. He will be my revenge."

"What do you mean, Emma?" Goddy looked puzzled.

"He will be my revenge."

CHAPTER 9

Winchester, 1018

THE SEA WAS NOVEMBER-COLD AND SHE STOOD IN THE BOW WITH ULF watching the water spray at the figurehead, a blue-painted dragon with bright-red eyes. The beast looked more silly than formidable, as he was meant to look. Her shoes pinched her feet. Godwin had had a pair of them made for her of elk when the shoemaker had come to Jomburg early in the summer. Elgiva had more than shoes made, Gytha suspected, for she had seen the young man furtively slipping from the black whore's bedchamber. By Halloween, Elgiva could no longer hide her pregnancy and Cnute shipped her off to Roeskild the moment he learned of it. Gytha wondered if the baby was Cnute's or the young shoemaker's. She looked down into the water.

"What will it be like?"

"What will what be like?" Ulf fended her question.

"Winchester? Wessex? What is it like?"

"Like Wessex, I suppose."

She frowned at him. "What kind of answer is that?"

"What else can I say? A place is like what it is. Jomburg is like Jomburg and like no other." He added pensively, "And I wish to Thor I had stayed there."

"I didn't know you wanted to stay that much. Besides it was Cnute—"

"Yes," he interrupted, "it is always Cnute. I do what he wants. I have since we were boys."

"He is the King."

"He wasn't then. I have no life. I have his life."

She touched his hand. It was large and rough. "That's silly. You have Estrid—"

"His sister. Even my wife is part of Cnute's life. No, I have no life." He took her hand and squeezed it. "And I don't know what is worse, being cast aside by him and left at Jomburg as he should have done with me or constantly being in his shadow. Someone once took me for the King, a thegn near Hastings."

"You look like him." She turned and saw Godwin leaning against the mast watching them. He had a scowl on his face and she wondered why he was so displeased. There were times she felt he was almost jealous of the affection Ulf had for her and the few hours she and her brother spent together.

"I love him," Ulf said, "I hate him."

"Hate Cnute?"

"Sometimes, for he is King and I am nothing."

"You are the son of Thorgals-Sprakaleg," she reminded him. "You are the Jarl of Jomburg."

"And I shall miss my father," he said.

"And I."

Thorgals-Sprakaleg had been put to sea in his ship after a spring and summer and a fall of dying as they all had waited. The King spent his time in Elgiva's bed or hawking with Ulf. Estrid had prayed. And Gytha had spent her time with Godwin and they sat for hours by the sea and talked of what was to be, but sometimes he was bored and she knew he was glad to be returning to his Wessex, to be home before their child was born. She liked him. She was quite surprised, she really liked him. He was mostly patient with her and explained things, though she was certain at times her questions were a silly girl's. But she liked him best at night when she was curled in his arms on the straw.

They arrived in Wessex and it rained, a cold wet drizzle and it was foggy and hard to see and she was damp and ached of the heavy baby in her belly and the trip from the sea overland was rough and she was carried in a litter and tossed about by the bearers as if she were in a gale. They marched toward Winchester. On the third day the sun shone and even though it was November it seemed warm and Gytha was helped from the litter and upon a horse. And the countryside was gold and red, and brown grasses stretched up gentle slopes and they rode near marshlands, still green, and many trees lifted bare branches making cracks across the sky and despite the warmness Gytha could sense that winter waited not too far off and the soil where it had been tilled was black as moonless night. The King rode ahead with Ulf and Godwin; she and Estrid followed and after came an army of clerics and priests and soldiers on horses, in carts and afoot. Lastly straggled the servants and slaves. They formed a long winding train and Gytha could look back down the hill and see the end of it. The brilliant-colored robes of the nobility were a contrast to the muted browns and grays of the servile classes which formed the tail of the snake which wound its way toward Winchester. The sun glistened and Gytha smiled at Estrid. "We are nearly home," she told Estrid. "Home" . . . the word seemed strange to her here.

"But a few furlongs."

Perhaps it was just the idea of finally arriving at their destination, but she felt better than she had for days. In all the tales, Goldborough bore to Havelok fifteen children. Perched on the rock at Jomburg, she had dreamed of the days when she would wed her Havelok and bear him not fifteen but twenty children, all sons, but she wondered now how Goldborough could have stood it. Having vomited her way across the sea and across half of England, she doubted she could stand to go through this again. But one son was not enough. Sons died. Winchester was just ahead. She was excited. It was where her first son was to be born. The Black Raven unfurled in the November wind.

"You should see it in the spring," Estrid said. "It is beautiful here."

The conch sounded as they came close into Winchester. And they were met by another army, this of nobles dressed in fine garments, colors the likes of which Gytha had not seen before, and the people, serfs and freedmen, women with babies at their breasts and straw flowers in their hair, and children carried sticks of ribbons and had ruddy faces and a tiny girl clung to a woman's skirt. Standing before them all was a great girth of a man, an archbishop regaled and carrying his crozier.

Estrid whispered to Gytha, "That is Wulfstan."

"We welcome you, our Lord King." His voice was a chant.

A chorus of monks' voices burst into a thunderous *Te Deum* and shivers ran up Gytha's spine and she felt as regal as Queen Goldborough and raised her head up to be the lovely countess. . . . And she saw her, the woman who must be Emma. She was a great beauty and looked every bit the Queen, standing with haughty pride in grand robes of rust color with embroidered sleeves and her undergown was of gold. Her headdress was a round little cap frosted in pearls and held with a satin gold chin strap. Her yellow hair fell behind. Though the woman stood back from the nobles, the King's eye apparently found her for she looked at her husband and smiled. Her smile made her more the charming and Gytha was certain she would like Emma.

Even in the middle of the *Te Deum* Cnute spoke. "Go get undressed, Queen," he said.

"But my Lord." The archbishop went up to him as the King dismounted. "The business of state."

The Queen smiled and turned and walked back through the throng. "Excuse me, your Grace, my Lady waits."

"But—"

The King pushed into the throng and people touched him and tried to kiss his hands and he vanished in their midst.

"What do we do now?" the archbishop asked.

"We wait," Godwin said.

The *Te Deum* continued. Gytha looked at the faces of the nobles. Among them was Thorkell the Tall, and she felt at home. As a small girl he used to put her on the end of his foot and rock her and sometimes she fell off and would giggle. As the music ended he came to her.

"Gytha child."

"Good old man," she greeted him.

"My friend Thorgals-Sprakaleg is dead and I was not there. He was beholden to Christ and a warrior like the Danes have seldom seen."

"He was a bear," she said, as she had said so often when given the same salutation.

"A bear." He patted her obtrusive belly. "He should have lived to see one grandchild born."

"He almost did," Godwin replied. "He had the longest death I have ever seen."

"Earl Godwin, I salute you. You have stolen the child I had always promised to marry."

"You never came back for me." Gytha smiled at her old friend.

"Come," Thorkell said, "why should we chat here? Let's go in the hall and wait for the King." He led the way off in the direction of the King's compound, the crowd parting as he moved, his helmeted head visible above them all.

Behi helped her from her mount as the archbishop, who Estrid said was Wulfstan, came over to her husband. "After nearly a year away, you'd think the King might find a few moments for his counselors."

Many of the nobles moved off in the direction in which Thorkell was heading.

"After nearly a year, your Grace," Godwin said, getting down from his horse, "he had a great need of his wife and I am glad for her sake, as well as yours and the kingdom's, that he has returned."

"Kingdom, only one kingdom now. For you, and we bless you as is due you in honor, are now Earl of the West Saxon and it is part of the kingdom of England."

"Your England," Godwin said. They stood near the great wooden gates —the archbishop, Godwin, Gytha and Estrid—blocking the passage of those of lesser status behind them. Their horses impatiently snorted and nodded their heads.

"Yes, I am a fanatic on the subject am I not? But I want more than anything to see us as one people, Dane and Saxon, alike united against those from without."

"From without?"

"Olaf the Stout, particularly. Cnute must keep his army strong and here to protect England. England before the Daneland. The Normans, too, should we become weak, will take advantage."

"But the Queen . . . Emma?"

"Yes, as long as she is Queen her brother will keep his place, but mortals die while kingdoms live forever and we must have always the future in mind."

"But if you want a secure land then there must be ships and the army and the bishops oppose the levying of the Danegeld."

"Not I. And the other bishops must be brought to bay. I will be glad of your support. Thorkell would go with the bishops and has been lax in enforcing the King's demand for payment. I am asking the King to journey to Glouchester to meet with an enclave of the Church hierarchy. This was my urgent business."

Ulf, who had been directing the logistics of the entourage, came riding up from behind. "Are the affairs of state so pressing they must be spoken on the wind?"

"Indeed not, Ulf. And my manners are lacking. Your Grace, may I present my Lady, Gytha, daughter of Thorgals-Sprakaleg."

"And sister of the Jarl of Jomburg," Ulf said.

"Gytha," Godwin continued. "This is his Grace of York."

She knelt and kissed his ring. "My blessings to you, Countess," Wulfstan said and raised his hand and made the sign of the cross over her. "And welcome to your new country."

"Make way for the Archbishop of York," a monk cried, pushing aside people standing in the path.

"And the Countess of Wessex," Godwin said and he kissed Gytha on the cheek and took her hand. "Your hand is cold. I should not have kept you so long in the wind."

Winchester was the grandest place Gytha had ever seen. It sprawled everywhere. There were old buildings, the timbers weighted and bent, and new buildings, and buildings being built and they wound in behind one another and were clustered so close together that the higher structures looked to be atop the others. Roofs were of thatch and waddle. The street almost everywhere was of stone.

"That is the monastery down over there." Godwin pointed to rock walls beyond a cluster of trees.

There were winterhouses and summerhouses and kitchens and houses-she-didn't-know-what-they-were and bathhouses and bower upon bower rowed along the stone-paved road that wound up a hill to the great hall.

She entered and it was the most splendorous place she had ever been in and large enough to hold six of the great halls of Jomburg. Even the hall of Havelok and Goldborough could not have been so magnificent. A table went along one long wall and then turned and went along that wall and then turned and went down the other side of the hall and the table was so laden that in places it buckled under the weight. Men talked and there were languages foreign to her ears. There was the English, which she could understand, and her own Norse, of course, and the language of the Northmen, which she also knew most of, but there were many words spoken in the room that were just sounds to her. There were Celts lilting lovely tales she'd wager and there was an envoy of the Pope come from Rome who was a meager little man with hair as black as Elgiva's and whose mouth seemed to be a rapid of words, and there were Slavs, who all claimed to be Cnute's kin, Godwin told her, and there were Burgundians and Franks and Flems and Lothians and a real Jew from Lombardy and the colors of their robes were red and bright greens and pale blues, and one, Estrid told her, was of brocade from Babylon and some of silk and jeweled and others of soft velvets and most dragged after the wearer sweeping clean the floor behind them and many here were said to be heathen and worshiped the Anse gods and Cnute didn't care, but Godwin said the bishops did and were giving him a lot of trouble.

And on one wall was a hanging so large it nearly ran the length of the hall and it told the tale of the Jomburg Vikingland and she saw her father turned in threads and his red beard and great massive body dominated a corner and she was sad as she thought of him. The opposite wall was covered with shields and spears and heavy swords all glistening as torches were carried in to light the room. And Gytha took the place set for her at the table and a skald came and sang in a tenor voice of Sigfrid and Brunhildr. And the talking became a whisper and soon ceased and the young man's voice filled the hall.

As the skald's poem came to an end the King and Queen entered the room and the cries went up. "You must sing that for me sometime, Gamol." The King patted him on the shoulder. "Come now to the tables, everyone. Let us eat before we all suffer of starvation." The King led Emma up to their places at the center. "Do not look so unhappy, your Grace of York. After we eat, then to the business of state. I understand we have a problem to be resolved at Glouchester."

"The bishops—"

"Bishops are the plague of kings," Cnute said.

"I give you no trouble, my liege Lord," the Archbishop of York said.

"Indeed you do not, Wulfstan, and I am grateful for your counsel."

Gytha wondered where Glouchester was and stuck a slice of dried apple in her mouth.

Gytha sat two places from the Queen. "You are Godwin's wife. I must compliment him on his choice."

"Thank you, Ma'am."

"Estrid is my friend and you must be as well, Gytha." The Queen's yellow hair was now hidden beneath a veil of lace.

"Yes, Lady—"

"And you must call me Emma, as Estrid does, and after your child is born—"

"My son."

"So it is to be a son. I told Godwin before Harthacnut was born it was to be a boy. A mother knows."

Godwin poked her and handed her a ripped crust from his bread. She took it and looked at it strangely.

"Dip it in your broth," the Queen told her. "It is a Norman custom which we honor here. Husbands give their wives a crust to dip."

She dipped it in the bowl of hot meat broth and stuck the soggy thing in her mouth. She didn't care for it, nor the custom, she decided. Godwin went back to discussing something called the Danegeld with the archbishop.

"I understand," the Queen said, "you have a seeress in your house. I hold much store by foretellers."

"Godwin insisted she come along. She is nothing but an old crone, as ugly as a dead bird—"

"You have never seen anything ugly, child, until you have looked upon my eldest child by Ethelred. But go on. I am, as I say, much interested in predictors and seers . . . and relics. I must show you my relics. What is this seeress's name?"

"Sorgad. She will miss the sea at Winchester."

"The sea?"

It was Estrid who answered. "She tells the future by reading the circling of the seabirds."

"Ah, then we must send her to the sea, to Pevensey or Corfe."

There were oysters and hams and roasted birds, huge, the likes of which Gytha had never seen, and strong curds and wines from France, was said, and she liked the taste, and they drank salutes from horns and cups and drinking bowls. "To the King! To the King!" And they drank to Thor and Jesus Christ and the Jarl of Jomburg and the Earl of Wessex and the Queen and the Countess of Wessex and she drank each time and thought she liked being called the Countess of Wessex and she drank some more and the cups and bowls were raised to St. Cuthbert and King Boleslav and the Pope and the Emperor and Gytha stood up—"To Havelok," she said—and fell back down in her chair.

"You're not used to this French wine," the Queen said. "You'd better let them take you to a bed."

"Your bro . . . brother"—Gytha stood up again, wobbling and hanging on to the table—"is the Duke of Nor-mandy."

"Godwin," the Queen said over to him. And Gytha remembered no more of the feast.

When she awoke the room was dark. Godwin sat beside the bed on a stool.

"How are you feeling?" he asked.

"Tired," she said.

"And the wine, do you feel bad from the wine?"

"No. It was a great feast, a grand occasion. I shall like it here and the Queen was very kind to me."

"Even if you did get drunk," he said. "But you must take care not to drink so much wine until after the baby is born for you might fall and hurt yourself."

"I will take care," she said. "And you, Godwin, you were greatly honored. They called your name again and again, and drank toasts to you."

"There will come a day when I shall sit first next to the King." His voice seemed bitter and she didn't understand.

There was a rap on the door of the bower and Godwin got up and opened it. Behi stood there.

"Come in," Godwin said.

"My Lord," he said as he closed the door behind him, "I learned something from Gamol which might be of use."

"Yes," Godwin said.

"Is it all right to speak freely here?" Behi looked directly at her.

"You can cut out my tongue, Thegn." She spit the words at him.

"Go ahead," Godwin said, "and learn this as well. Never anger your Lord's wife. She can be your greatest ally or your worst enemy."

Gytha relented and smiled at the young thegn. "Don't worry, Behi, I shall not have your head."

He smiled too, and the tense moment was past. "Thorkell the Tall, in the King's absence, made arrangement for the safekeeping of Eadric's widow."

"I am surprised Emma is not livid over it," Godwin said.

"The Queen does not know, nor the King. Because this Edith, that is said to be the lady's name, is a bastard of Ethelred's and so it was done in the greatest secrecy."

"There is perhaps more here to suspect. Thorkell is himself a widower, after all. He could have plans to wed the lady."

"Lord husband," Gytha said, "how can you suspect honorable Thorkell of ulterior motives, he is a good and Christian man, noble—"

Godwin whispered to Behi, but Gytha could overhear. "Arrange for a spy in his house. We must safeguard the interests of the issue, Harthacnut, from any other claims."

"There is no need to whisper," Gytha said, "besides, I can hear you as plain as—"

"Then hear this as well, Lady," Godwin told her, "you are my wife and what is said to me in our chambers shall be my business and no other man's. Am I understood?"

"Then hear this, Wessex," she answered, "don't try and hide things from me if you want my confidence."

"Spoken fairly," he said.

But she wondered if he meant it.

The next day Gytha felt miserable. It was cold and her nose dripped and the boy in her belly never seemed to settle down as if he had a gut pain from the French wine. Estrid came to see her and found her in bed.

"Up," she said. "You promised the Queen you would bring Sorgad to her."

"I don't remember that."

"I suspect there is a great deal of yesterday you don't remember."

"Who is Eadric?" Gytha asked.

"Why do you ask?"

"I heard his name."

"He was. He is no more. Your husband was responsible for his death."

Gytha dressed and they found Sorgad throwing horse turds at some children who were taunting her. Sorgad was wearing a Norman hauberk and a pointed helmet on her head. She rattled as she walked.

"Come along. The Queen will see you," Estrid said and gave the hag a shove ahead of her.

"It will do no good here at Winchester, though, for she needs the birds of the sea," Gytha said.

"After Emma has had a look at her, she may not want to bother."

Estrid wore pearls wrapped in her braid, which was turned in a crown upon her head, and her velvet red bliaut was laced at the sides exposing the pink chainse beneath. Her hands were lost in the long sleeves that dripped so long they swept the streets. Gytha thought her sister-in-law quite beautiful, though not as beautiful as the Queen, but an elegant lady fit to be the wife of a great jarl like Ulf.

They strolled together. The streets were less crowded this morning. Slop was thrown from bower windows and hogs and chickens meandered along the stone way. A shepherd moved his flock in their path. A priest sat on the road cleaning the dirt from between his toes. A whore raised her skirt exposing a dirty vagina to a soldier. Estrid walked over to the whore and struck the girl across the face. A hawk swooped down and gathered a gray dove in his talons. A thegn drove a slave with a whip along ahead of himself, cursing and calling the man names. A woman approached, offering to sell them her two children for half a dead pig and a loaf of bread. A foreigner from the East doffed his cap and bade them good morrow.

Emma was waiting.

"You have lovely hair," the Queen said to Gytha.

"It is red and ugly."

"It is red and beautiful. So shiny and thick."

"And I have freckles," Gytha added.

"They will go all too soon. Be glad for your youth."

Gytha smiled. Sorgad came into the room.

"Tell me, does she always dress as a soldier?"

"No, Lady," Gytha answered. "Old hag, why are you in such garb?"

"There are seven hills in Rome it is said and seven gates to hell." Sorgad turned from them and faced a blank wall.

"She is mad," Estrid said.

"Yet Godwin tells me she knows the future," the Queen said. "Can you tell my future? The future of my son, old woman?"

Sorgad did not turn around. "Only the birds of the sea see. Only the caw of the gull tells. Only the guts of the dead know—the sea holds all knowing and all telling. There are seven seas and seven gates to hell."

"If I send you to the sea, can you tell this Queen her future?"

"Only if the sea knows the Queen and the birds of the sea have looked upon her often and then can the sea tell the birds. Then can the birds tell Sorgad. Then can Sorgad tell the Queen."

"At Corfe. I will have you sent to Corfe. For the sea knows me well there."

Sorgad stood without speaking facing the wall.

"I'll have my son sent for and show him to you," the Queen said, but before she could call for him to be brought there was a rap at the door and a slave opened it to Ulf and Godwin.

"I was looking for Estrid," Ulf said.

"Now that is unusual. 'Tis she that usually chases for you," the Queen said.

"You make me blush, Emma."

"And well you should, Estrid. But what brings you in search of your wife, Ulf?"

"The King would journey on the morrow to Glouchester. The matter of the bishopries must be resolved and only he will be able to force the matter upon them."

"Yes," Emma said, "and the King would have me travel with him and I shall despite the cold, not having seen him these months."

"And I as well," Estrid said, "shall ride to Glouchester."

"Estrid," Ulf said, "how of my sister?"

"I had forgot. I'll stay here with you, Gytha."

"I am afraid," Godwin said, "you shan't be able to make the journey in the state you are in. It was bad enough reaching Winchester."

"True, but no need for Estrid to stay behind."

"It would be wise if she stayed with you," Godwin said.

"She should be with Ulf. And it is not my time yet. I will be fine. You go, Estrid."

"Are you certain—"

"Yes."

"You will be lonely," Estrid said.

"I shall be fine."

"I shall leave Aesval behind with you," Emma told her. "She has midwifed and will take good care of you."

"And Sorgad," Godwin added, "she will be here with you as well."

"A frightful help she will be," Gytha said.

Sorgad turned and pulled with her bare hands the chain mail apart from the neck to the waist on the right side, exposing a dirty sagging old breast. She raised the nipple between her thumb and finger, offering it to Gytha. Gytha pulled back in disgust.

"Now that's what I call *tétin pour tétin*." Emma smiled.

Gytha did not laugh.

Sorgad spat on the floor in front of Gytha. "Pain, naughty child. You bear pain." In her military garb, ripped to the waist and exposing the one breast, she stamped barefooted from the bower.

Snow fell in the morning as the cortege of riders, impatient horses, litter bearers, monks, carts, bundled nobles and their ladies assembled to depart Winchester. "We shall be gone no more than two weeks," Godwin said, kissing her upon the lips, and then let them lift him to his horse.

"You will be home in time," Gytha said. "Do not fret."

It took two priests to help the Archbishop of York upon his mount. And then the Black Raven fluttered and they were gone.

She returned to her bower and the assembly had barely ridden from Winchester when the pain began.

After the first pangs of agony ceased she yelled for Sorgad. The old woman still wore the hauberk but had unskillfully repaired the damage to the front, lacing it with dried vines. She had removed the helmet.

"Fetch the Lady Aesval. The pain has come."

"We can do this ourselves," Sorgad said.

"No."

"She is West Saxon."

"And I, too, and this boy he shall be a Wessexman as well."

"Pah!" Sorgad stamped her wet feet in quick little steps. "A daughter born of a bear shall always eat the shit of a rabbit." As she went out she hung a spray of dried rosemary over the lintel to help ease Gytha's pain.

The pain came again. Morning turned to afternoon and the snow fell heavier. Aesval sat and sewed and Sorgad chewed on a piece of leather and dug through Gytha's treasures and found one with a runic inscription.

"Where did you learn to read?"

"When the rime giant first made the earth."

"That is nonsense." The pain came again.

"It is written here"—Sorgad laughed viciously—"that Odin shall punish the daughter of a bear who has put this brooch upon her person. Have you wore this brooch? Gytha? Have you? Have you?"

"You are just trying to frighten me. Isn't she, Aesval? Can you read, Aesval?"

"Mercy, no, Countess. But my husband could."

"Where is your husband?"

"Had his head cut from his body. That's how much good reading did him. I keep his head in a chest."

Despite the hurt, Gytha had a sense that all would be well, her son fine. She looked at the large breast in the brown gonelle and thought of her own mother, whom she never knew and always imagined as big and comfortable as this woman Aesval. The Saxon woman's brown hair was streaked with gray and her own mother, she had been told, had hair so blond it was near the color silver.

And the pain came again. And again. And again. And afternoon turned to evening and food was brought, but Gytha ate nothing. And they sat by the fire.

"Tell me of Emma's son. She says he is ugly."

"Ugliest creature I ever saw, save a dwarf once with warts. And the Atheling had the fits, frothing and foaming at the mouth and gagging till you'd swear he was going to choke on his spit. But my husband said he had the gift of healing, just as MacBoru himself did."

"He was your husband?"

"Yes. I will show you his head sometime. Edward, that be the Atheling's name, is white. His skin, his hair like a ghost and pale and he is a strange boy given to standing in the same place for hours at a time as if frozen, yet it could be the middle of summer. I'd wager he's grown. I have not seen him this very long time."

And the pain came again.

"The Queen," Aesval said, "gave me some fine swaddling silk to wrap your baby in."

Gytha dozed. Sometimes she awoke or was she awake most of the time? She was not certain. As she lay there, her eyes at times open, at others closed, her thoughts were of herself. This man-child had made her older. She was not the girl she had been before the battle of the Wends. She was not a child any longer. A candle was kept burning. The smell of rosemary was strong in the room. And the pain came and she cried out. Her mind wandered back to the sea and the waves pounding the rocks and she could almost see the wet black rough surface, crevices filled with water, and the smell of the sea—she could smell the air, almost taste it. She wanted at the moment to be home in Jomburg. The pain came again. The smell of rosemary and burned taper was all she could smell. The sea had gone. The color brown was all she could see as she opened her eyes, brown fabric, so close, so large and she tried to remember where she was and with a passing awareness she realized it was Aesval. The woman sat beside the bed on a bench and she was sleeping, snoring lightly. Gytha edged over toward her and looked down at Aesval's feet wrapped in soft slippers and they seemed so large. The pain came again. Sorgad stood in the distance, her eyes wild watching Gytha and Gytha wanted to shout out and tell her to go away, but it seemed as if it would require too much effort. And the pain came again. She screamed it hurt so and Aesval gave a spastic jerk and sat up, her eyes wide open. Sorgad seemed to smile. Gytha tried to doze again, but the pain came again and then again and the light of morning seeped in between the closed shutters and Gytha shrieked and Aesval sat up and the pain subsided and came again and Aesval bent over her and Sorgad stood at the bed and the sea shells about her neck seemed to roar of the sea and Gytha cried out, she thought not from the pain but from hearing the sounds of Jomburg. And the pain ceased for a moment and she tried to think of the sea when it was serene. "The birds," Sorgad told her, "the birds are circling about so calm." "I can't see them," Gytha groaned and the pain came again. Again and again. She thought of her own mother with the beautiful hair, who died when she had been born. And the pain was excruciating and she didn't want to die as her mother had. She tried to find the sea, the calm sea. And she screamed out. She wished and screamed and pushed and cried out and was torn apart, her insides coming loose, and she tried to expel this thing, and she cried and the pain was horrible and she wished she would die—and then a SHOVE! IT WAS OVER! She ached, but the worst was over and she heard the faint crying and she cried as well and said so softly, "Bring him to me."

And Sorgad came and brought the baby to her and she looked up through her tears at the naked creature and shrieked and shrieked again and again and Aesval bent over her and tried to hush her, but she would not be quieted.

"You witch, Sorgad. You filthy beastly witch," Gytha screamed. "You have cut off his penis."

"It is a girl," Aesval said softly.

"No. No. No. Sorgad has done this evil thing. She has torn the penis off my son."

"Hush, Countess. Next time. There will be a next time."

"No."

"Here, let Sorgad put your daughter to tit."

"That maimed child shall not touch me."

There was a pounding on the door.

"What is it?" Aesval called.

"It is I, Behi. Is everything all right? We heard the screams."

"Go away," Aesval called back.

Sorgad still held the child.

"Take the thing out and kill it. I will have no deformed child for a firstborn."

Sorgad stood like a statue of the Madonna with the deformed penisless baby in her hands.

"Do as I say, hag. Kill the monster. Kill the beast. Cut up the rest of it as you cut off its penis."

Sorgad took the baby away.

CHAPTER 10

Glouchester and Winchester, 1018

GODWIN WAS ANXIOUS ABOUT GYTHA. HE KNEW THERE WAS TIME BUT BABIES were notorious for not knowing when they were to arrive and he fretted and he was annoyed that the affairs of state waited upon a chess game. What he resented most was that Cnute was playing with his brother-in-law, who seemed to have no other duty in life but to entertain the King in boyish pastimes.

The two men sat upon the stools silent, hunched over the table. Ulf should be at Jomburg, Godwin thought, seeing to the fiefdom of his father. And he had yet to grant him Gytha's dowry land near Roeskild on Zealand. Ulf moved a thegn piece.

"Your king is slaughtered," Cnute said and set a bishop in place.

Ulf looked angrily at the board, then kicked over the table and board and pieces went flying. "Lion's dung."

There had been a time not so long back when Godwin would have bent down and picked up the pieces. No longer.

"Raven piss!" Ulf poured himself a cup of drink.

"Do not curse upon the Raven," Cnute said. "You're getting better, Ulf. It is taking longer to beat you."

"I still lose. I always lose."

"Better luck tomorrow. Perhaps, you'll win."

Ulf shrugged his shoulders in a gesture of disgust.

"And now, friend, you'd better go to your wife, before she comes looking for you and has the whole abbey astir."

Ulf grunted, threw his chlamys across one shoulder and with his cup in his hand went out.

"He is becoming melancholy and his temper is getting worse," the King said.

"He does not have enough to keep himself occupied," Godwin said.

"Should I have only that problem. Tomorrow we face the bishops and abbots. How am I to get the money out of them without beating them with a mace? I'll get it, I have no doubt of that, even if I have to burn down every abbey in England to do it, but I'd rather take it with a smile."

"Thorkell's leniency has made the situation more difficult."

"I'm afraid the old man is becoming an old woman in these late years of his. He worries of nothing but his damned soul. I'm Christian, too, but I let it not interfere with my life."

Godwin wondered what Cnute would think if he knew his godfather, the Earl of East Anglia, had granted sanctuary to Ethelred's bastard daughter, Edith. But Godwin would save that for when the time was right. The King was not happy with Thorkell; now he would build on it.

"My liege Lord, I think the problem is not that the bishops resent the levy of the tax, but they see it as the Danegeld of the past, a ransom, money paid to a foreign pirate."

"I am their KING, dammit." Cnute did not at that moment however look very kingly in his tattered coarse gonelle and his cross-laced braies.

"Yes, and we must make them see it."

The King was silent for a moment. He wore soft hide boots and he walked with care to avoid stepping on the strewn game pieces. He went to a small shelf and from a bowl poured wine into his drinking horn, drank and wiped his mouth on the back of his hand. "I have a dream, Godwin, of an empire of the North—of England, the Daneland and a return of Norway. But empires are not made without armies. The host of Danes has been paid off and sent home. And that was well for they were seen as conquerors in this land, particularly in Wessex, but I have only a few thousand men—"

"And the armies of Leofwine and Ulf and myself . . . and the others—"

"Yes. But I need not serfs and peasants, which are fine for short wars and then back to the tilled land. I need mercenaries to wage a campaign of conquest that could take years. I need the Danegeld not to pay an army but to build a select force, a corps of warriors whose only responsibility is as fighters. The old Jomburg Vikings, if you will, a brotherhood, a guild with a code of fraternity. I want only the best men, aristocratic youths bound together by a dedication to battle, their king and each other. I want them a force, strong and deployed from Exeter to Roeskild. One king, one army, one empire. I need the Danegeld, but I will need it again and so would wish the bishops provide their fair share willingly. How do I get it?"

Godwin did not wait long before answering. "Prove to them you are their King . . . Saxon King. Tell them you are reinstating the laws of Edgar."

"No. We are under my law here," Cnute said firmly.

Godwin phrased his words carefully. "What exactly is the law of Edgar that the Saxon is always glorifying, asking to be restored?"

"I don't know," the King said.

"And neither do they. Sheer rhetoric. Edgar was the last of the fit Saxon kings so his rule is a shrine of justice. The law of Edgar, my liege Lord, becomes exactly what you want it to be."

The King looked at him and Godwin realized he had made his point.

"A subject," Godwin continued, "believing he has rights is ever as content as one who has them. It makes for the best rule for a ruler gives away nothing and the subject wants for nothing."

Cnute smiled. "A return to the law of Edgar."

"In fact, my Lord, at the synod, I would but barely mention the matter of Danegeld, making the assumption it is expected and will be paid. Tell the enclave the purpose for which they were called was so you might define the rights of your people, your English subjects."

The King accidentally kicked the game pieces as he moved over to sit down again on one of the stools. "Hail the King." Cnute applauded himself. "Let's determine exactly what I am to say—"

And they went to work.

In the charterhouse at Glouchester the bright scarlet, red, ruby and almost violet brilliant satin and silk, velvet and white linen of the ecclesiastics were a contrast against the gray stone in which they assembled. A *Gloria* was sung and the King entered to the rise of shuffling as the mitered and the tonsured figures stood. And then the King moved with deliberation to the very center of the circular enclosure and fell upon the stone in prayerful supplication. He lay prone, his magnificent frame dramatically positioned before the circle of English prelates and monks. For several minutes he lay there in prayer and then Wulfstan stepped down to him and extended his ornately gauntleted hand and the King rose before the enclave.

Despite the drama of the moment, mirrored in the surprised faces of a few, the bishops and abbots remained mostly hostile.

"My brethren in Christ," the King said.

With the opening he caught a few more off guard and Godwin smiled.

"We are a people at peace. And we are one people, you and I. I did not spare my treasure while war was threatening to come upon you; with the help of God I have warded this off by use of my treasury—the armies that came from over the seas have been paid and sent away. It is time to return this land to the ways of peace. I have gathered you in this enclave to ask your support in returning England to the Law of Edgar—"

The King stopped. First there was the pause of disbelief, then murmurs, smiles, followed by a spontaneous rising of the churchmen, many with crozier in hand. The King, with extended arms, accepted their tribute and then motioned them to sit again. The benches banged and ornate fabrics rustled and the ecclesiastics were seated. The King recited the written words of the charter they had drawn up.

Of all, Wulfstan seemed the most amazed and Godwin watched him in amusement, as the portly archbishop had expected the King to come demanding his Danegeld and instead had disarmed the Church. When the King was finished, the Earl of Wessex, with the other nobles and the bishops and abbots, witnessed the King's charter. Cnute, for all his boyish charm, never seemed less the boy to Godwin.

They were free to return to Winchester and Godwin was glad it had all been accomplished so quickly for Gytha was constantly on his mind. He felt something was wrong.

"You fret too much," Estrid told him. "Having children is a simple matter."

"How would you know?" Cnute asked. "Godwin, I am pleased with what you have accomplished for us here. The Queen and I wish to make a gift of Pevensey to you and Gytha as a belated wedding present. It is a pleasant place, but because of its association with Edmund, the Queen has never been comfortable there. We hope it will bring you some joy."

And the praise was not alone from the King. As they readied to depart, Wulfstan spoke with him. "Your counsel, Earl of Wessex, was well-advised. When there is a question put before our next Witangemot, for now you sit with us, I should much like your view and determination before we convene, so that we might find ourselves in accord. I can be useful to you, Godwin. Today was a bit of genius and I admire you. The King came to Glouchester adamant about the Danegeld and yet he had not to mention the matter." The big man was helped on his horse. "We shall hurry home to the birthing of this child of yours."

It was approaching evening of the third day when they neared Winchester. Winter was attempting to arrive. It was cold and Godwin looked forward to the warm fire. He thought of Gytha and hoped all was well. The trip had given him new admiration for the King; he was wise for his years, listened to advice sensibly and made his own decisions. He held the reins of power firmly. He could be ruthless if the need called, gentle if it did not. Godwin must not underestimate the Dane because he was young. Cnute was King. And Godwin would be the voice in his ear.

Behi met him as he dismounted. "The Lady Gytha—"

"What happened? Is Gytha well?" Godwin pushed passed him.
"Yes."
"What is it then?" He turned back to face the soldier.
"The baby . . ."
"Go on, the baby?"
"It was born."
"Be praised. Take me to Gytha. She is all right, you say?"
"Wait, my Lord. It was a girl."
"So? There will be another time."
"She was so angry, my Lord, that she . . ."
"She what?"
"She ordered the child killed."

Godwin's cloak flew behind him. He nearly shoved a slave off his feet as he ran through the street. "GYTHA!" he screamed. He pushed open the door of the bower. "GYTHA!" She was not there.

"The hall . . ." a slave whispered.

He went into the hall. She sat in a corner in the dark of the great hall. "What have you done?"

"I did nothing," she said.

"You killed our child."

"I had no child."

"You . . . you killed our child." Godwin began to weep.

"I bore a monster without his penis and did as any mother would do who bore a monster. I had it killed."

Gytha, the child of Jomburg, was gone. She looked to him a woman now. A tired woman, almost ill-looking. There were no freckles left on her cheeks, he realized. Her gown was plain and a muted gray and it only made her color look more pale.

Emma had entered the hall at some point, for she spoke now. "If I had had the courage of Gytha."

"She is mad," Godwin said and he stormed by Emma and out into the cold evening air.

He walked through the streets of Winchester. Slaves and servants and children stepped from his path. He walked in no direction but moved aimlessly down the hill and came to the open field near the church. She had to have been mad to kill their own issue, their first child.

"Godwin, son of Wulnoth."

He turned to see the hag Sorgad. "Could you not stop her?" he pleaded.

"I did."

"You . . . how . . . ? But the child?"

"Your daughter lives. She lives. Two arms, two legs, one head and no penis. She lives. She suckles on a wet nurse."

"You do not make rhymes, for just making rhymes, old woman?"

"Nay. Nay, not this day. She lives. In a hovel by the gate. I took her afore 'twas too late. The countess ordered death. The countess thinks she is God. In a hovel by the gate . . ."

"Take me to this hovel."

"Follow," she said. "I will show you the girl you will call Edith."

"Edith?"

"Yes, that is the name of the Queen. She will wed a cloud and bear you empty bowls of fruit."

The hovel was no better than a pigsty. The smell was the same, and though he was raised in a sty, he certainly wanted better for his daughter. She was, after all, to be a queen. But she looked unqueenly. She was tiny and red and cried and had no hair, but she was his daughter and he took the child in his arms.

"I will send soldiers with you. Take the child and the wet nurse to my house in Guildford. One of the soldiers will be the man you know, Behi. The people of Guildford are familiar to him."

"I must seek the dark sea for the Queen, for birds are lonely with their words."

"The soldier will take you to Corfe. But I beg you, when you return give the Queen only words she wants to hear. See what you see, interpret what you will, but tell the Queen only what she wants to know. God go with you, old woman. I am in your debt."

He was too angry to go near Gytha, and when he learned she had gone to the bower, he went instead to the great hall. The woman Aesval was there bearing a shriveled head on a platter as if she were going to serve it as a feast.

"It was my husband," Aesval said, but she seemed both preoccupied and despondent. "He was a man of magic and healing, not a bearer of death like myself. I thought perhaps he could help me find your dead child and bring her back to life. He could do that, you know. And they say he taught Edward the Atheling. Perhaps we could send for Edward."

"Why are you concerned?" he asked.

"Because I should have stopped her. I should not have let her give the babe to the old hag. I cut that cord and the Lady Gytha cut away her life."

"I will tell you this because you try to amend this evil. But my wife is not to know. The girl child lives and is being cared for—"

"The old hag, she—"

"She kept the child. I have seen it and it is safe."

"Thanks be to God."

For two days he did not go near Gytha. He could not look at her. Yet, there was no way to begin building a new heir if he never saw her. He could only pray the next issue would be male.

He found her sitting with Estrid sewing as if nothing in the world had happened. She sat there like any woman at gossip, looking no different, no horror written upon her face, no pain or guilt or even worry about his absence. "Child," he said to her. "What is done is done. It does not make it right, but there are some things which cannot be undone."

It was as if he hadn't made mention of the subject. "Estrid is going to have a baby, Godwin," she said. "Finally, Estrid and Ulf are going to have a baby."

He went away still angry, but he knew he would not stay from her. In five days Sorgad came from Corfe.

"The birds of the sea know the Queen," she said.

And he took her to Emma. "Remember my caution," he warned. "Only what the Queen wants to hear."

"Daughter of Rolf, Queen of England, Queen of England," Sorgad chanted.

"Why do you repeat it?" Emma asked.

"Because you did," she cawed with laughter. Sorgad was draped in fish scales and she wore a coronet of broken egg shells. "And twice you shall have sons kings."

"I shall have another son?" the Queen asked.

"You have another son," Sorgad said. "The birds at Corfe shit at Rouen."

"Harthacnut shall be king."

"Son of Cnute, son of Emma that is one, what of the other, the white birds sing bearing his brother."

"Shall Harthacnut's heirs reign?"

"The blood of Normans reigns in England."

"And Danes?"

"These were Norman birds."

"Who will sit at Roeskild?" Emma fired one question after another at her.

"Norman birds speak no Dane."

"But you are of Jomburg . . . the birds there."

"Say Elgiva must have her womb cut out."

"It would be my pleasure," the Queen told her. "Whose grandchild will sit at Roeskild, Elgiva's or mine?"

"Neither. Estrid's."

"That can't be. You have been too long from Jomburg. You are wrong."

Godwin was worried the old woman would tell the Queen more to displease her and was thinking to get her away.

"I want not to hear of Estrid's children. Tell me more of mine."

"You will be betrayed."

"By whom?"

"By your pet birds who will pluck the eyes from your child."

"Who is this?"

"Time will show you. When darkness falls upon England. But before the comet comes."

"The comet?"

"Yes. Your son an old king will die. And Gytha shall know pain."

"And his heir? The heir to the kingdom?"

"Shall in a year be of your father's blood."

Sorgad said no more. She toyed with the shells on her head.

"It is well," the Queen said and sat when it appeared Sorgad would say no more.

"Come along, old woman," Godwin said, anxious to get Sorgad away lest she mention something of an early death for Harthacnut as previous seers had done.

"Now this, too," Sorgad spoke as she turned about to leave. "Edith shall be Queen."

"Edith? What Edith?"

"The birds repeat at Jomburg, at Corfe. Edith will be Queen. Edith will be Queen. Edith will be Queen."

Emma looked puzzled. "I know her not. What else do you tell?"

"The birds say no more."

Godwin led her away, relieved, but as they were crossing the open yard from the hall he asked her, "Though I believe not in your birds, what tell they to you of the death of Harthacnut that you kept from the Queen?"

"The birds told and I did not tell the Queen. He shall feast death upon his own breath."

"And shall he die young?"

"Yes."

It was the same as the old green-haired seer at York had told.

"And who do you mean when you said one would betray the Queen?"

"You."

"Never!"

"For you are the father of a queen."

CHAPTER 11

The Vixen, 1021

SUMMER WAS DYING. AUTUMN CAME TO THE VIXEN IN PARCHED LEAVES which sifted to the soft earth wrapping the ground and crackling beneath his feet. The flail beat against the grasses and he stood watching the serfs as the seeds of grain were separated from the straw to be used as winter bedding, and in the fields the stubble bristled and the first cold frost came leaving the land singed with a morning white and the birds vanished and the snow gently hid the land.

Edward walked alone. His heavy woolen cloak had been dug out from the packing and smelled of must. The air was damp and clear and the snow wet on his soft leather boots. It was chilly, not cold, though there was no sun and the world seemed empty; there was a solitariness about the gray morning. He was seventeen and should have had wealth and fortune and been loved by a kingdom of people, but instead he walked alone across an open field in a forgotten corner of Normandy. He was isolated, deprived of his birthright, deprived of the love due him. "The King is much loved. . . . Cnute is much loved." That love was Edward's; it had been stolen by a Dane, as had his mother. Cnute called himself Emperor, Drogo said, and would rule the North: England, the Daneland, Norway, Wendland, Scotland, Lothian, Hibernia and even Sweden, Drogo said. And maybe Drogo was right, though Drogo was dumb and Edward didn't like his brother-in-law. Edward should have been the Emperor of the North. Yet, he really didn't want all that, only England, only what was rightfully his. Cnute could have the North, or his son Svegan, or the brat his mother had given Cnute. Harthacnut, what kind of name was that? He was three years old and Uncle Goddy said fat and ugly. Well, it served her right. She was supposed to give Cnute poison and instead gave him a baby. He hoped the fat little monster choked on his rind tit.

A stream ran, breaking a winding path in the snow, coldly washing the rocks, and Edward gazed down into the clear water. He remembered his mother's yellow hair and round brown eyes and soft voice and breasts heaving as she breathed and she walked like a queen. And he must face the truth. She did not love him and inside his belly hurt when he thought about her and he knew he could not stop loving her. Not even God's mother was so beautiful.

His braies were darned but had torn in another spot and the white skin of his leg pushed through as he leaped across the stream. He should have had silken robes and damask stoles and slippers of fine lamb's wool, but it had all been stolen from him. Uncle Willie said Cnute gave money out to visiting Norwegians as if it were cups of wine. And most Norwegians were horrible barbarians, believing in Anse gods and not at all Christian. Edward would not waste his wealth on Norwegians. He would buy fine robes and give alms to the poor and have himself a cloak of shining black velvet. There was no need for fine clothes in the Vixen, for no one ever came here, at least no one of importance, and Drogo sat around and drank and beat Godgifu until she cried and his sister would not let Edward interfere and said it was her punishment for having not killed her mother and Godgifu sent the Queen a poisonous spider, but their mother must never have received it for last Edward heard she went hawking "in a green gown trimmed in fur," Uncle Goddy said, and he was glad she had not died. He forgave his mother for it was not her fault she had gone away. It was Godwin's. It always came back to that for it was Godwin that came to Rouen and took her away. It was Godwin that had kept him from going to Winchester and claiming his throne. Godwin had a son now, a boy called Sven, and Edward decided the best revenge would be to kill Sven, but as of yet he had no plan.

He ran from the stream across the field. It was Martinmas, but there wouldn't be much of a feast. Drogo was too cheap. Edward ran beneath the empty trees and seemed alone in the world for he saw neither man nor as much as a field mouse . . . until some distance, a silhouette against the morning light at first and then as Edward approached, there appeared the most wondrous of men.

Edward was certain it was a saintly vision. The man was a warrior saint, St. Michael perhaps, wearing glistening mail, and despite the chill of the morning wore no coat or sale, and he had massive arms, each encircled in a heavy golden arm ring. A Danish ax hung from his shoulder and it had a silver and gold handle, and his sword was gold-hilted and he wore a helmet overlaid in gold. He was truly an apparition.

"Edward?" the apparition asked.

"Are you a saint?"

"Christ, no. I'm kin."

"Why are you dressed like a saint?"

"I'm a thinglith. I'm dressed like a thinglith."

"What's a thinglith?"

"One of Cnute's imperial officers."

"Go away," Edward said and turned back in the direction of the stream.

"I am going to kill Cnute," the man who called himself a thinglith said.

Edward turned back about and faced him. "Why don't you? Why do you come to me?"

"Because if you are not there when I do it, they will give your crown to Harthacnut."

"And why, fellow, should you want me to be the King? No one else wants me to have my throne."

"Because you are my uncle."

"Uncle? You are older than I. How old are you?"

"Nineteen."

"See?"

"My mother was Edith, wife of Eadric, and she was a daughter of Ethelred."

"Some say so," Edward agreed, but not much really believing it.

"My name is Raglar. Cnute and Godwin killed my father. He was the Earl of Mercia and they took all his lands, which were rightfully mine and left me with nothing. I want my earldom back and will help you become King if you will grant it to me."

"Yes," Edward said. "Yes." He didn't care whether Edith was his half sister or not. Still, it might be a trick, to get him to England and kill him. He was one of Cnute's chosen warriors. "How come, if you are Eadric's son, Cnute has you among his housecarls?"

"He does not know I am Eadric's son. He thinks me someone called Vistar from York, whose father served the Forkbeard."

"And how, after you have killed the King, can we be certain they will support me?"

"Thorkell will and if Thorkell does the others will, all will but Godwin."

"We should kill Godwin."

"Yes," Raglar said, rubbing the gold arm ring as if to polish it.

"And his son."

"Yes."

"And his daughter as well."

"Godwin has a daughter?"

"A girl named Edith my Uncle Godfrey says, but she is kept locked away."

"A monster, perhaps."

"Most likely." Edward paused. "But how can you be so sure Thorkell will be with us?"

"A fortnight ago he married the widow of Eadric of Mercia, my mother. Thorkell is now your brother-in-law, my Lord Edward."

"I never thought to have a brother-in-law so old, nor one so tall." But Edward stopped smiling for it made him kin of Harold Thorkellsson, who had raped his mother in the chapel at Corfe. The more Edward thought on it, the more certain it grew in his mind that it was rape.

"The thingliths will all gather at Pevensey upon the first thaw for a celebration. I will send one of my mother's house to bring you to the sea and across by boat. I have thought it out and we will disguise you under a heavy cowl as a monk, for in any other disguise you would be surely recognized."

"Because I am ugly," Edward said.

"Because you are very recognizable, my Lord," the thinglith said. "We must hide as much of your face and body as can be hid, for it is most necessary that when I kill Cnute you be present to take his crown."

"Yes," Edward agreed. "I will not be cheated another time of what is rightfully mine."

"You must tell no one, particularly your uncles or the Count of Vixen."

"I should not tell the Count of Vixen anything for he is but a drunken idiot. But I must tell my sister for else they will raise an alarm to find me and it may not be so easy if they suspect I have gone to England."

"If you must. But no one else. I leave you now and we will meet in Pevensey. Good-bye, Uncle."

Edward could not bring himself to say nephew to the older young man. "Good-bye," he said and stood watching the golden figure walk across the field.

Godwin should be tortured before he had his head cut off. But Edward would not blind him, nor would he draw and quarter the children. Drogo swore, though, that Godwin was a richer man even than the King. Well, Edward should have Godwin's wealth as well as Cnute's and the return of Wessex was for certain. For it above all lands in England was the realm of kings.

It was as if the thinglith were a vision or a dream, for he came and vanished so suddenly. Edward went back toward the buildings to wait for the spring thaw.

CHAPTER 12

England, 1022

Gytha was nineteen. Though the mother of two sons, and having as well given birth to that other thing, she had kept her waist. With care she put on the chainse. It was fine linen made for her by a Flemish woman with six fingers on each hand. A pattern of flowers was woven into the fabric in the fashion of the craft of Damascus. Over it she pulled the bliaut, a brocade of blue with silver thread, and Gytha laced it up the sides, pulling her small waist to its narrowest. Her hair was more auburn now and but a few traces of the freckles remained. She was proud of her hair now and did not wear the wimple and guimpe but set it off with a small coronet of hammered silver set with blue stones from the Indies. She cinched her waist even tighter with a silver cord and went out into the compound.

Winter had been harsh, but spring came kind and warm and green, gentle rains and soft winds and clear sea air. Pevensey was worn by the sea. Green growth clung to the walls. The smell of fish hung like a net in the air. The constant lashing of the gales left the rot of wood and thatch torn and battered. The Normans built fortresses of stone, like churches, and Godwin said if he dared he would build one here at Pevensey. Godwin was wealthy enough; perhaps no one but she, outside of Godwin himself knew how wealthy. "Care," he would caution her, "your dress is not more elaborate than the Queen's." But she was learning her place.

"Ready this house," Godwin yelled back to the slaves as he came out and joined her in the open of the compound. "Below come the King and Queen. Hurry." They walked together toward the wooden gates to greet the guests.

They came up the hill from the sea, some along the paths, some over the banks. It was an invasion of fine robes and colors like a sprawl of spring flowers. Bishops and skalds and concubines and jugglers and archbishops and spies and thegns and foreigners and countesses and slaves and children and abbots and earls and envoys and seers, they came with retinues of subordinates with their subordinates and their subordinates and so it was how the King and Queen traveled and their host Godwin met them at the gate. The King was flanked by his elitist new guard. They must have been four hundred strong. A vain group, these housecarls, or "thinglith" as the Norse and Danes called them, strutting in marching formation, they glistened in gold helmets and gold arm rings and gold-hilted swords, and disdain seemed as essential to their uniforms of triple-corseleted mail. Estrid and Ulf were beside the Queen.

Godwin gave Emma his arm. The Queen's beauty was fading. She had become, it seemed to Gytha, more pensive and at times melancholy. She did not forget the year of Cnute's neglect. "Revenge," she had told Gytha. "The day will be when I will have revenge." Cnute, of course, went to her bed less now. The court was guested with young women of the noble houses and the King was never lacking in enamored women willing to copulate.

Cnute still looked the boy, hair tousled and a complexion cleansed by the air and sun, but he was less given to horseplay and spent fewer hours with Ulf. Gytha worried about her brother. More and more, he would be drunk, his peasant's garb often soiled and stained, dissipation sapping his youthful looks, his skin sallow and his eyes without their clearness. She went up and kissed him. She looked over to see Godwin scowling. He always scowled when she showed her brother the slightest affection.

The Earl and Countess of Wessex were never to be outdone and they served their guests swan and honey and oysters and eel and oat breads and pigs baked in a frosting of curds and scallions and they fed them lamb brains and tortoise and oranges pirated from a Moorish ship and dried apples and gravied hare and boiled lumpish things made with ducks' eggs rolled in ground meal and fish baked in pies, and the guests ate and their voices sang above lutes, singing of kings and villeins and dragons and Godwin's destruction of the Wends, and there were dancers and tumblers and a wonderment of a man who ate fire, and Gytha sat proudly beside her husband.

She looked about and realized Behi was missing. "The thegn is not here," she said to Godwin.

"Only trouble keeps him away. I am worried," Godwin whispered and then turned and smiled to the King.

It was after the meal that Behi came to them in the hall.

"Please excuse us, my Liege," Godwin apologized to Cnute. "A household matter to attend upon. Gytha and I should be but a moment."

Gytha followed Godwin, who followed Behi from the hall.

"The Atheling Edward is here, my Lord, and in disguise," Behi whispered and motioned them to follow up a flight of narrow stairs. From a window there Behi pointed down into a small court. "There, the monk with the cowl pulled about his face."

"There? That is Edward?" she asked.

"You are certain?" Godwin was looking down at the figure.

"Yes. I saw him up close. There is no doubt. He is a young man, but a boy really, with white skin."

"Has he made contact with anyone?" Godwin asked. "His mother?"

"Only the thinglith known as Vistar."

Godwin moved back from the window. "And we know who Vistar really is. Well, the fall of the house of Thorkell, Behi. 'A tall fall,' as they say. But we'll have to be careful. It is our chance to bring Thorkell down, but there is obvious danger to the King in this, a real danger. Have the man you have watching Vistar or Raglar Eadricsson or whatever he calls himself see if he can get close enough to hear any conversation Raglar might have with Edward."

"I'd do it myself, but Edward might remember me from Jumieges."

"Well, Behi, the world is full of surprises. Gytha and I had best get back to our guests."

In the forenoon Gytha was sitting with Emma sewing.

"I'd rather be hawking," Emma said. Emma always complained about doing needlework, but she was good at it.

"You? Hawking?"

"I've taken to it. I have a natural affinity for it, it seems. At least Wordig thinks I have."

"I never thought Wordig had opinions on anything," Gytha said.

Before Emma could reply they were interrupted by Godwin's arrival.

"Have you come to sew?" Emma asked and offered him her needlework in jest. "Smile, Godwin. Must you look so officious?"

"I am afraid, Madam, the matter I bring you is not one to smile over. To put it bluntly, there is a plot to kill the King and put Edward on the throne."

"You don't take it seriously, I would hope."

"Edward is here at Pevensey."

"Here?" Emma looked completely surprised. Gytha sat quietly, saying nothing as the two of them talked.

"In disguise."

"That's impossible; there is no disguise sufficient—"

"He's wearing a simple cowl and wandering about like a monk," Godwin told her.

"You are going to do something?"

"Yes," he assured her, "and most particularly talk to the King. But I think you should be cautioned of something first, as the old man is a close friend of yours."

"What old man?"

"Thorkell—"

"Be careful, Godwin. Your envy of the old warrior is apparent to me." She set down her needlework. "Your motives are suspect."

"Hear me and decide yourself. Thorkell has married without the King's permission."

"Treason in one of his rank, I suppose, but I think Cnute will overlook it in Thorkell's case."

"To a daughter of Ethelred's?"

She looked at him as if he had hit her. She said nothing for a time and then asked, "Edith?"

"Eadric's widow."

"I don't need to ask if you have proof."

"I have the priest. But that is not the worst. Edward's plot is with Raglar, Edith's son."

"My God. They do plan to kill the King?"

"Yes. I am certain Thorkell is not directly involved. But by his secret marriage he is implicated."

"And what," Emma asked as if it were his decision, "do you want done with him?"

"Banishment should be enough."

Emma nodded in assent and went out with Godwin in search of the King. Godwin was very smart, Gytha thought, to get Emma on his side before bringing Thorkell down. The poor old man, his only crime was that he stood between the King and her husband. Now there was only Ulf. Was he next? Godwin wanted to be the first lord of the realm. After Thorkell only Ulf stood in his way.

That evening was the feast of the thingliths. As their hosts, she and Godwin were special guests at the gathering. Godwin explained it to her. Among the Thinglith Guild were laws of comradeship. A thinglith who failed to care for his horse or a fellow in arms and was found convicted of such an offense three times was given the last and lowest place at the table and became the recipient of bones thrown and he was required to endure such humiliation without a word. Raglar sat at the lowest place and was being pelted with ox bones and goats' bones and elk bones from the meal. Gytha watched as the cowled monk, Edward, slipped quietly in at the door. There were worse crimes than those of Raglar, for if a brother killed another of his brothers, he was either killed, fined forty marks or exiled at the discretion of the ranking thinglith, who was of course the King. As Gamol sang, Raglar got up from his place at the table and as if drunk staggered in the direction of where the King had stood to make a toast.

It was instantaneous. Raglar barely drew his weapon before the King, with one swipe, had removed Raglar Eadricsson's head.

The King claimed the man had made an obscene remark about the Queen's virtue and he threw himself upon the mercy and judgment of his brothers and humbled himself before the fraternal order of guards and confessed his guilt and requested punishment. But by law, he was the judge of such a crime.

Behi and one of his men stood on either side of the hooded figure of the Atheling. He could not move, as they held their knives to his back. The King fined himself nine times the amount customary, three hundred and sixty marks, and added nine more as a gift.

No one knew. No one knew of the attempt to kill the King, nor Thorkell's complicity, nor Edward's presence. The Atheling was quietly escorted from the hall and held until the banquet was ended.

Afterward, in the quiet of their own chambers, Behi came to report to Godwin that Edward had been shipped back to the county of Vixen without being allowed a word to either the King or his mother, who had no desire to see him. "And there is," Behi said sarcastically, "wondrous praise among the thingliths of the King's generosity and magnanimity."

"He is the King," Godwin reprimanded Behi.

"And his gold guards are a pack of simpletons," Gytha could not refrain from adding.

Thorkell the Tall, the Earl of East Anglia, was ordered within the week to leave England. Within a fortnight the court left Pevensey for Winchester. Gytha and Godwin, with their house, traveled with them.

Spring became a warm summer. Cnute spent less and less time with the Queen and consequently Gytha had to spend more and more time with her. Emma was, frankly, looking old. Her figure, and Gytha had seen it unburdened by the great gowns the Queen drowned herself in, was becoming heavy and the flesh hung down from her upper arms. There were tracks of gray in her hair, which she usually wore well hidden by a veil. The lines about her eyes and puffiness developing in her cheeks indicated her years of childbearing were numbered.

For the moment though she had escaped the Queen and sat quietly with Godwin. It was a rare respite. He was bent over a parchment at a small table and she sat sewing tiny pearls on a headpiece.

"You have women to do that," Godwin said, looking across to her.

"I know, but I enjoy it. And I do it right."

He went back to his reading. They sat in silence for several minutes and then he quite surprised her by saying, "You are the most beautiful woman in all England."

"Perhaps the King will take a fancy to me," she teased. "What would you do, Godwin? He has pinched me a time or two."

"Cnute has pinched you?"

"A time or two. But what would you do if he took a real liking to me. He does many of—"

"I'd take you off to the country immediately," he interrupted. "To Pevensey or Jomburg . . . that is good and far away."

"Are you certain, Godwin, for the sake of your own position, you wouldn't let the King have me?"

"Of that I am most assuredly certain."

"You could always become a pigherder, I suppose." He smiled but she had hit a raw edge. He no longer joked about his humble beginnings. "How is your reading going?"

"Not well. I don't know how these clerics manage. It takes me so long to get through one page."

She got up, set down the pearlwork and went over to him. "It's more than most men in your position manage." She touched his hair. He no longer wore it in the short fashion of the Normans and she preferred it long, as it was now. The color of fall grass, it was wavy and full. He was not a handsome man, but he was comely enough.

"They say Edward can read," he told her.

"I should like to meet Edward sometime."

"He came calling at Pevensey."

"Well, you wouldn't let me meet him. All I got was a peek from the window."

"You may have your opportunity. We may have to go to Rouen. Cnute wants assurance the duke won't intervene if he moves upon Norway."

"I don't think I want to go anywhere but home."

"You are tired of Winchester?"

"I am tired of the Queen. She has become irritable and talks mostly about Elgiva. There is nothing I can do about Elgiva. She is regent in the Daneland and it is not my doing. But Emma acts as if—"

She was interrupted by a knock on the chamber door and the entrance of Behi. As usual he was bare from the waist up. He rubbed his hand over his abdomen. "Olaf of Sweden is dead," he said.

"That will change things," Godwin said.

"He is Estrid's brother," Gytha said. "I will have to go to her. They weren't close, but he was her brother."

"It certainly will change things," Behi said. "Word has come from your man at Roeskild that the boy, James or Anund, whatever he is called, has already made a pact with his brother-in-law Olaf of Norway."

"He's a busy little king for just a boy," Godwin said as he got up from the small table where he had been reading.

"Busier yet. He has made an alliance with the Danish jarls to recognize a separate king at Roeskild and not Cnute."

"The choice being," Godwin interrupted, "Elgiva's son Svegan, I suppose."

"Do you believe the Danes actually would put the boy Svegan on the throne?" Gytha asked.

"Yes." Godwin set the scrolled parchment aside. "They are independent enough. It is foolish of them, for Cnute will never let them get away with it and they should see that. I never have understood the way these Danes think."

"I am a Dane," she reminded him.

"And I don't always understand the way you think." He smiled, but she suspected it was the truth. "Well, Behi, we best go to the King and inform him that his eight-year-old son has usurped him."

"The King is"—Behi paused—"resting."

"Behi," Gytha said as if correcting a child, "I know about copulation and I also know the King. Do not mince words. Who is he 'resting' with?"

He looked embarrassed. "The wife of the banker from Lombardy."

"Wait until he gets her undressed." Gytha laughed.

"Why?" Godwin asked.

"Because the ladies whisper, 'She is pregnant.'"

"Serves him right," Behi said.

"My sentiments exactly," Gytha agreed.

"He is the King." Godwin's voice rose. "And who, Behi, are you to be making moral judgments?"

Gytha looked at the lean young man. Any slight reprimand from Godwin left him crushed. "You are too hard on the thegn, Godwin. Don't be such a vicious tyrant." Gytha took a blue cloak from a peg. Even when it was warm she carried her cloak. "Estrid will need consoling. I best go to her."

"She will undoubtedly be praying," Godwin said.

"Yes," Gytha agreed. She opened the door. "I still say Cnute deserves the pregnant Lombard." She quickly closed the door before Godwin could say anything.

The splendors of Winchester had lost their splendor for Gytha and she wished she were at Guildford or Pevensey of any other of the sundry places they called home. Anywhere but Winchester. To her it seemed a coop of intrigue and vain pretense and rank and empty pomp and hypocrisy and the summer stink of a thousand bodies all moving, bustling like chickens pecking for the last kernel of grain. But Godwin was happiest here at the heart of the cluck and the clack. He became restless away from court, as if something might occur without his being able to mitigate or dictate the outcome.

On the walk to the quarters of her brother and his wife, Gytha was flanked by two thingliths. It was an honor these days, if you were of the King's house, as she and Godwin were, to be escorted by these golden-haired men with their golden gear, but Gytha found them a pest, particularly when she walked with Estrid or one of ladies, for they destroyed all chance of gossip.

Estrid met her drenched in black fabric. The shutters were closed and the room was dark. A single candle burned. There was a strong smell of stale fish and urine.

"My brother has died at Upsala," Estrid told her, motioning her into the chamber.

"What is that awful smell?"

"The healer gave Ulf a potion and he spat it out and tipped over the rest of the bowl."

"It smells like piss." Gytha wrinkled her nose.

"I suspect it mostly was."

"Ulf? Is he ill?"

"He has the melancholy." Estrid's voice was weary. "Did you hear me say Olaf is dead?"

"It is why I came."

"I've been praying for his soul."

"What comfort can I offer you?" Gytha asked.

"Only prayer," Estrid said. "Only prayer."

"I shall," Gytha assured her. She never seemed to find the time for prayer that Estrid managed. Perhaps when she got old she would.

The door from the adjacent room opened. Ulf stood in the frame bowing slightly to fit beneath the lintel. He wore nothing but a pair of torn muslin braies. His blond hair was disheveled and his eyes were red and sore. "I've decided to die," he said and looked directly at Gytha.

"Nonsense!" Gytha went over and pushed open the shutters. "Let some light in this tomb. And some air. It stinks horribly. I'd want to die, too."

"We are in mourning," Estrid said.

"Mourning or not . . ." Gytha opened another set of shutters. "Good Lord, Ulf, you look horrid. Get yourself bathed and some fit clothing on."

"Why?"

"Because you are the Jarl of Jomburg. Act like it."

"I am the errand boy to the King."

Estrid spoke up. "You are the King's brother-in-law."

"I am his lackey."

"Ulf," Gytha ordered, "stop feeling sorry for yourself."

"How should I feel?" He ran his hands into his snarled hair and plunked down on a bench. "You say I am the Jarl of Jomburg. Then why am I not at Jomburg? Why do I sit at Winchester waiting for the King to finish his shit so I may wipe his ass for him?"

"There is no need to be so crude," Estrid told him. She looked at the windows. "What will Winchester think with the shutters open and my brother newly dead?"

"What do you care what they think?" Gytha asked. "You are the King's sister." Gytha wrinkled her nose again. She called out, "Fronjarde!"

A serving woman appeared at the rear door as quickly as if Gytha had conjured her, a slave who looked to be underfed, for she was as thin and tall as a bean stalk, yet Gytha knew she ate like a pig. The girl stood nervously rubbing her fingers.

"There is a smell of piss in here, get some water and clean it up," Gytha ordered.

Fronjarde vanished.

"Gytha—" Estrid started to say.

"If you won't take charge of your house then I will. I know you are in mourning, but neither of you, despite Ulf's wishes, is dead yet. Though I have—" She was interrupted by a rap on the door. "Come in," Gytha called out when Estrid failed to answer at once.

Gamol, the Queen's singer, entered. "Lord Godwin said I would find you here, Lady," he addressed Gytha. "The Queen would have you wait upon her."

"And the Lady Estrid?" Gytha asked.

"No, Ma'am, just you. She asks you come at once."

"Ulf," Gytha said, "I will talk with you later, but for God's sake make yourself presentable." She followed the frail Gamol from the chamber. The young man moved like a dancer, delicate and quick.

Emma was waiting on a horse outside the great hall, with two thingliths and another horse, Gytha's own, an ebony mare. Godwin had given it to her and it was said to have once been owned by an Irish chieftain. Gytha did not hide her surprise at seeing the horse.

"I had him brought round. I need a companion for the ride," the Queen said.

Gytha wondered why. The Queen usually rode alone. "Of course, Lady," she said and let one of the thingliths help her on the horse. He was a big man, young, no more than her own nineteen years, and swarthily complexioned. His exposed chest was covered with black hair which rolled over his shoulders and ran down his arms. It was darker than that curled on his helmetless head. He wore wide gold arm rings that emphasized the muscles of his huge arms. She had seen him about before and recalled he was from Brittany. His nose was pugged and his face rather flat. Godwin once had a performing gorilla and the Breton reminded Gytha of the huge animal.

The Queen turned her own horse about, a silver stallion sent as a gift from Robert, the King of France. The Queen's gown was as red as the wine of Burgundy and with sleeves so wide they nearly trailed on the ground. Her head was covered in a pale blue guimpe and her white wimple hid her neck. Despite the age Gytha knew to be buried beneath, Emma looked fresh and young and every bit the Queen.

The horses clopped against the stones of the Winchester street and animals ran from their path and babes were pulled out of the way as the Queen set a quick pace toward the gate. The dark-haired Breton followed, and Gytha rode next. The other guard behind her was a golden-helmeted Dane who often had escorted Gytha and Estrid. Outside the gates Emma struck her horse's flank and he bolted off down the road. The thinglith's horse galloped after, the dark-haired man's sale flying in the dust. Gytha kept a more sedate pace, though she often liked to ride fast, particularly at Pevensey, near the sea. She and the other guard followed the riders to a rise with some trees not far outside Winchester, but when they reached the spot where the horses were nibbling on the summer grass, both the Queen and the Breton had disappeared and Gytha understood why she had been asked to accompany the Queen.

"May I help you down?" the thinglith asked her.

"I will stay a-horse," she answered.

"Is there anything I can do for you, Lady?" The question was suggestively posed.

"Absolutely nothing," she said firmly.

They waited and without further conversation. Gytha was angry. Not because she abhorred or was even upset by the Queen's conduct but, rather, she resented the time wasted. She was worried about Ulf and the minutes could be far better spent trying to console him. Yet, she didn't understand his frustration. Why couldn't he serve the King as Godwin did? Cnute loved Ulf and yet her brother had come to resent his friend. She couldn't discuss Ulf with Godwin, either, for he only threw up his hands and called him wastrel. "He gambles too much. . . . He drinks far too much. . . . He'll never grow up." To talk to Godwin of Ulf was hopeless. In the distance a monk, or some like-hooded figure, trod down the road. Estrid, too, could be more understanding of Ulf. All she seemed capable of was prayer and copulating. Estrid was her dear friend, but Gytha was losing patience with her. She looked toward the trees but there was no sign of the Queen. The world was mad. Here she was, one of the great ladies of the kingdom, waiting in the midst of a field while the Queen copulated. Perhaps the old Queens Gunnerhild and Sigrid had come by their madness from waiting. But Emma had to wait, too, didn't she? She had to wait on the whims of Cnute. He would come to reject her more and more as Emma grew older. Gytha could see that and felt a sudden compassion for the Queen. They came from out of the trees, Emma and the Breton. He was carrying his sale and she her guimpe and wimple.

"Get me from this horse," Gytha said to the thinglith and he lifted her down. As the pair approached from the trees, Emma's face seemed expressionless and the Breton had a look of almost evil satisfaction. "Here," Gytha said, "let me help you with your headdress."

"Leave us for a moment," Emma told the two men. The thingliths led the horses down the rise. The Breton was doing the talking, in whispers, but Gytha could imagine what he was saying and resented the man. "You disapprove of me," the Queen told her as Gytha fastened the wimple.

"No, Lady, I do not."

"Yes. You once disapproved of the way I treated my children, but then you ordered your own daughter killed."

"She was not a daughter. It was a boy whose penis the hag had cut off."

"And," Emma continued as if she had not spoken, "the day will come when your own husband will no longer find you to his liking. Age comes and there is nothing that will hold it back. It is like a flood from melting snows, nothing stops it."

"You are young," Gytha told her.

"I am old. I will get older. I will become ugly. I can have young men like the Breton because I am the Queen, but I cannot have Cnute much longer. Do you know who's in his bed this morning?"

"No," Gytha lied.

"That black bitch, the Lombard banker's wife. She reminds me of Elgiva. Age rushes at me, and I must bear another son before my time is over. For there are two kingdoms and but one son."

"But Harthacnut will rule them both." Gytha adjusted the pale blue guimpe over the woman's yellow hair. The gray was there.

"I think no man can, Gytha. No matter what Cnute's grand schemes of empires be. Harthacnut will rule England. The seers have promised me. But I need have another son for the Danes in Zealand."

"You have Edward."

"He is NOT my son. But I will bear another. One for each throne. And I am plagued by that dirty black whore at Roeskild."

"Godwin believes Cnute will exile her. There is a plot to put her Svegan on the throne. It seems the Danes do want their own—"

"My God, Gytha, why didn't you tell me?" the Queen asked.

"You rushed me from Winchester. Who had a chance to tell you anything?"

"Forgive me. But let's speed back now. That is good news, Gytha." Emma raised her hand, motioning to the men. "The Breton has the finesse of a churl."

Gytha looked at Emma. She felt sorry for the woman. "Emma, do you know what they say about the banker's wife? That she is already months pregnant."

"That is hilarious," the Queen said and smiled. "Cnute must be furious. 'It is the fashion,' that black bitch said of her loose-bodiced gown. Fashion be damned. She was hiding her brat. Thank you, Gytha, for telling me. Thank you for being my friend."

Two days later Gamol came to fetch her to the Queen. Emma was wearing only a plain muslin chainse and her back was to Gytha as she entered the lady's chamber house. The room smelled of camphor. The Queen turned about. Her face was bruised and her eye blackened.

"Emma!"

"Don't tarry long with me. Cnute is unaware that you know of my adultery and there is no need of you to be accused of complicity, but I want you to warn the Breton. The King will have him killed surely. Tell him to flee. I care little for the man, but I don't wish to see him dead on my account."

"How did the King learn of it?"

"I don't know. But as you can see by my face, he did learn. It is better than the treatment Ethelred gave me. He ordered me weighted and thrown in the river."

"At this moment I hate Cnute, Emma. That he should—"

"I will have my revenge. Sooner or later, not for this, but the months of neglect before Harthacnut was born and after when he did not acknowledge I was alive. Better he hits me than ignores me. But the Breton?"

"Of course. Is there naught else I can do?"

"No. Obviously I will not be making an appearance this evening in the hall." The King's anger had left the Queen looking old. Her unblackened eye was red and strained and her hair seemed to have even more gray. Gytha realized for the first time that Emma's oldest child, that Edward, was nearly her own age.

Gytha tried to warn the Breton. He was arrogant and would not listen. "The King will not harm me," he had told her. "I am a thinglith, a brother-in-arms." She urged him to flee. He wouldn't listen. "You are a fool," she had told him.

That evening there was a feast honoring the emissary from the French King. Gytha dressed simply in a gown the color of new grass and let her dark red hair fall loose and put a long string of pearls around her head. The Earl and Countess of Wessex stood with the others awaiting the King and Queen.

"Where is Emma?" Godwin whispered as the King and the Frenchman entered the hall.

She was surprised at times. Godwin could know what was happening at

Rouen and Tunsberg and yet failed to see what occurred beneath his nose at Winchester. She merely shrugged. Across the room she saw the Breton. The audacity of that young man.

It was so quick, and yet she should have expected it. For a moment the King left the side of the French emissary and went over to the Breton.

"What did you say of Earl Eric?" the King asked in a loud angry tone so as to be heard throughout the hall.

"I said nothing. I haven't said a word." There was panic in the Breton's voice. She could see he knew what was about to happen and the arrogance had melted. He looked over at her, his fear clearly visible.

Without a further word, the King lifted his golden-hilted sword and the man's head went flying and hit the wall, splattering down, leaving a red path of blood.

Gytha looked at her husband, who stared at what had just happened in disbelief.

"He was a comrade!" a thinglith called out and the call was picked up by others of the guild. "A comrade! A comrade!"

King Cnute fell to his knees. "I am guilty of a grievous offense," he said. His voice was soft and humble.

"Pevensey and the killing of Raglar," Godwin said.

"Yes," Gytha answered softly. She felt sorry for the dead stupid Breton.

The King was on his knees in the center of the hall. "I have killed a fellow of the brotherhood and must stand punishment. I find myself guilty of this hideous crime and though the fine be forty marks for such a deed, this thinglith, Cnute, will pay tenfold that for his sin."

A cheer went up from the other thingliths gathered about the hall. "The King! The King!"

And the King motioned everyone to the table. During the dinner the body lay on the floor where it had fallen and the head near the wall. Gytha was glad when the feast had ended and she was in her own bower next to Godwin on the straw bed.

"You were not surprised," he said.

"No."

"You knew."

"Yes. It is why Emma was not there. Her face is bruised and she has a black eye."

"He could have killed her," Godwin said.

"Yes. But tell me. Why is it right for Cnute to bed the Lombard banker's wife but not for Emma to copulate with the Breton?"

"Cnute is a man."

"I know. But why is it so?"

"The way of God . . . No. That is wrong. It is the way of man. He who rules makes the laws."

"I should've been born a man," she told him.
"Not you, my sweet. But Emma should have."

Summer was miserable and hot and Gytha longed for the coolness of the sea. Her temper seemed to flare with hardly any provocation. She yelled at the children, the slaves and at Godwin. Worse, they were now going to Lunduntown, where it was even hotter. To pacify Canterbury after having shown favoritism toward York, Cnute had decided the body of St. Elfheah would be removed from Lunduntown to be enshrined at Christ Church.

In the heat of the day Gytha left her bower flanked by two of the housecarls, their gold arm rings flashing the last light of day. From the shadows Sorgad stepped and blocked her path. The stamping feet of the thingliths stopped. Sorgad, who had avoided her since the birth of the monster whom she dressed as a girl and who clung to the old hag constantly like a bad wart on a crippled walrus, flashed her two broken teeth.

"Out of the way, hag," Gytha ordered. Anger welled inside.

Sorgad's hair was snarled with bones, wound and twisted through it. She took a bone in her fingers and rubbed it. It looked to be human. The housecarls shoved her aside with their spears. "Cawed the birds, cawed the birds. Edith will be Queen. Edith will be Queen." Her caw was the caw of the raven.

Gytha heard it and glared at the disheveled mess and remembered only the day when she had been torn by the pangs of birth to be shown the son with its penis gone and she looked at the woman and anger rose red in her face and she screamed, "TAKE HER AWAY AND CUT OFF HER HEAD!" Gytha fastened her eyes closed. "She is a menace . . . A MENACE!" And Gytha held her breath and then opened her eyes. "Wait." She called but the thinglith were gone. And she stood there. There had been no struggle, nor a sound. Sorgad had vanished with the golden guards. Gytha went back to the bower and curled up in a corner and the slaves looked at her and took the children away and she went out and searched for the thinglith, but they all looked the same and she could not find them and she went back to the corner of the bower and curled her knees up to her chin and tried to cry but could not and they came and put the head, the bones still knotted in the hair, upon the table and it leaked blood upon the floor. And Godwin came, but he did not raise his voice, nor hit her. He did not bang his fists against the wall. He said, "What have you done?" And she did not answer. The door closed and he went out.

"A comet will come and there will be a year of pain." When? Gytha wondered. Is it now? The head looked as if it wanted to caw, and Gytha cried out, "Sorgad. Sorgad." And she remembered the black nights by the sea, nights which all looked the same, but she knew they were not, for each day something irrevocable was done and it forever changed the days which followed. And she spent the night huddled in the corner and when morning came the head was gone and she had not slept nor seen anyone take it. It had simply vanished.

They came for her and said, "London, Lady, you must. It is expected of you." So they dressed her and she rode to Wardrobe Palace and the next day they dressed her again, but all the while she was numb and they took her to St. Paul's Minster. And the Queen was there. "God spare the Queen!" The cry went up again and again. "God bless the Countess of Wessex!" another cry went up. But God should not for she had wronged the old crone in a moment of anger. "God save the King! God save the King!" And Gytha saw the King arriving accompanied by his Grace, the Archbishop, and with them was Godwin, and clinging to his hand was the monstrous child Edith whom he named his daughter. "God bless Bishop Ethelnoth!" "God bless the Earl of Wessex!"

She shuddered and did not want to look at the child. Godwin said not a word to her as he came to march beside her. The blast of the conch and drums were slapped and a choir of monks began a roaring anthem and the procession moved behind the archbishop's crozier into St. Paul's.

There were *Paternosters* and *Ave Marias* and the recitation of two litanies and *"ora pro re nobis"* resounded in the church. But while others sang in joy, tears filled her eyes. Sorgad was dead. The saint's body was elevated and borne from the church to Southwark through the streets and flowers were thrown and people knelt in prayer and raised their cups and there were crys and shouting and the selling of food and clomping of horses' hoofs and the blast of the conch and whores went about the crowds trying to sell their wares and it was pomp and chants. Overhead above the Thames seabirds flew in a circle. The body of St. Elfheah was entrusted to the care of the bishops to be taken from Southwark to Rochester. The King and the nobles and clerics marched back to the palace, but the festival had begun and it continued into the noise of the night's carousing.

In the morning the royal household left for Rochester flanked by four hundred guards. Godwin did not address one word directly to her as they rode and she could not get Sorgad from her thoughts.

In tents on the green at Rochester those of the royal house were gowned in splendor and she saw Godwin beneath a tree and he had a new cloak of green with a fur hem. The King was in gold and with armbands twice as wide as those of the thingliths and the Queen stood in a robe of deep purple; a huge stone of red faceted the light and shimmered on her breasts. The Lady Aesval, plump in a satin bliaut of yellow, adjusted the Queen's train. And Gytha stood near a clump of yews and thought of Sorgad. She slipped back beyond the yews and went in search of a priest and at a small stone church surrounded by graves she found a cowled monk praying in the graveyard and she confessed, kneeling in the dirt, her sins and asked of a nun and the monk sent her to the house of seven windows down a path, and there she disrobed and gave her clothing to the poor and put on a sack cloth and the nun helped paint her face and body with ashes.

"Gytha!" The Queen stood staring at her.

"I am in penance," Gytha said.

And during the long march in the procession of elegance from Rochester to Christ Church, when many rode and a few walked short distances, others were borne by litter or on horse, Gytha barefoot trod upon the sharp stones until her feet bled, displaying her shame. Her eyes were tears but she could see Godwin watching and all the way the child walked, clutching Godwin's hand or being carried by him, though servants offered. The body of the saint was carried into Christ Church and Gytha made foot tracks in red blood against the stone. The dead bishop was given his resting place at the side of the altar and Gytha threw herself, exhausted, prostrate at the foot of his tomb. She was picked up in large comfortable arms and realized it was Godwin. "You have done enough penance, Gytha. I will take you home."

He took her to Pevensey and bathed her feet and had them wrapped. "This is Edith," he said, bringing the child into the room. She shrank from the small figure, but then slowly put her hand out for the child to touch and it was warm like fire and she took the girl into her arms and held her.

Godwin was kind and patient, but she could not look about the sea without the birds forming patterns overhead. "May we not go back to Winchester?"

They spent the rest of the hot summer in Winchester and she came to know the child. The four-year-old girl was ethereal, almost as if she were unreal except when Gytha touched her, and she was like a fever. She brought Gytha bruised and wormy apples and a rusted knife with the hilt gone. Things she found she gave as gifts.

Thorkell died in Rouen just as the summer ended. Gytha and Godwin had been with the King when the news came and Cnute cried and went to his chamber. Godwin and Gytha were ordered to bear the body home.

They were met on the banks of the Seine with ceremony and pomp as if they had been a king and queen. To the beat of muffled drums they marched from the river to the stone fortress. Banners flapped in a soft autumn breeze and the Archbishop of Rouen, crozier in hand, led the procession toward the ducal house. His grace, Duke Richard of Normandy and the Duchess Judith met them at the door of the great hall. The duke seemed pale and moved with difficulty as if ill and the Lady Judith scratched as the duke made a welcoming speech declaring his affection for his brother the King of England and his sister Queen, and the great loss that the death of Thorkell, the King's godfather, was to them all. And Godwin read a prepared speech and then the duke called for a chair and asked of his sister and brought his children to meet Gytha. Richard, the heir, light-complexioned, had dull gray eyes.

"You had a jackdaw on your shoulder the last time I saw you," Godwin told him.

"I think Robert poisoned him," the boy said.

"You shall never be able to prove it," Robert said, coming up behind. "And watch and keep care, brother, or you might go the way of the jackdaw." The dark-haired boy cackled a sinister laugh and said to Godwin, "You are the swineherd's son. Beware, Wessex, I plan to make my cousin Edward the King of England."

"Stop it, Robert," the duke said. "The boy is an absolute monster. His uncle, for whom he was named, only encourages him in these outrages."

Gytha was shocked by the child's behavior as she sat quietly watching him. She wore a white gown embroidered with gold thread and the train swept behind, and her sleeves fell like icicles and she was afraid she outshone the duchess and wished she had dressed more simply.

They had brought the child Edith along and she, too, was gowned in white. Godwin presented her to the duke. "My Edith," he said.

"What a beautiful child," Richard of Normandy said. "What a marriage you can make for this one. How old is she?"

"Just four," Godwin replied.

At that moment the bronze doors were slammed open and standing in the sunlight was a tall black-garbed figure with pure white hair. Gytha gasped at the sight of who she realized was the Atheling Edward.

Edward approached, swept, actually, as if he were walking upon water and the doors closed out the light behind him. His cloak was voluminous yards of black wool and he raised his arms, as if to display the fullness, and he reminded Gytha of some giant bat swooping down upon them. He threw back the cloak, displaying a gold pendant the size of a large plate that he wore on a heavy chain.

"His sister, the Countess of Vixen, buys him these outrageous gifts," Judith said with quite obvious disapproval.

Edward came and stood before them. "What has my mother sent me?"

"Love," Godwin told him.

"And a gift?"

"No," Godwin said. "She is angered with you because you tried to kill the King."

"And she should be," Judith said.

"Still," Edward said, "we return our mother's affection."

Edith went up, reaching out to touch the young man, but he pulled back as if she held fire in her hands. She persisted in taking his hand and as Gytha was about to tell her to leave Edward be, he seemed to relax and accept her touch and he took her hand and led her to a seat.

"Now there's a match for you, Godwin," the duke said with a laugh.

Godwin obviously found it less funny. "I think not."

"Strange," Gytha said. "I thought him so much younger. My brother Ulf tells of him. He rather liked the child. But he really is no child is he?"

"Eighteen." The duke coughed and when he stopped added, "Without fortune and without future."

BOOK THREE

The Progeny

CHAPTER 1

Winchester, 1026

IT WAS FOUR YEARS MARKED BY DEATH AND BIRTH, FOUR YEARS DURING which Cnute plotted against fat King Olaf in Norway. It was four years in which Emma plotted to get pregnant and it was four years in which Godwin had succeeded in becoming the first earl of the realm. Elgiva, out of favor with Cnute, was powerless, living in isolation in the North. Emma should have been content. Her son, Harthacnut, was the regent in the Daneland. He was only eight, but for the past three years had been the regent. Ulf was the viceroy, and he, too, should have been content, but Gytha told her that Ulf found the viceroyship only further proof that he was "nothing but Cnute's shadow." But Emma knew she would be satisfied if only she could have another son.

And so she plotted. She would creep into Cnute's chamber just before dawn and slip into his bed, she would watch him make arrangements with this maid or that and then have the girl carted out of town and go to the King's bed in her stead and she poured good wines in the King's cup and urged toasts on the table and the drunken King would haul her off to his bed.

Gytha never had any trouble getting pregnant. She had three sons now, Sven, Harold and Tostig, as well as the little girl, Edith. Estrid had given birth to a third son at Roeskild and Emma had never seen the boy, though he was nearly three.

It was four years marked by birth, but death as well. Leofwine had died in the winter of 1023 at Coventry and they had kept his body outside in the cold, frozen, until Cnute could reach there. And Cnute was readying to invade Norway and he had to postpone it as they went to bury Leofwine. Leofric, the new Earl of Mercia, so proclaimed by the King as expected, seemed little concerned about his father's death. "This is my wife," he told Emma. "This is Lady Godiva." She was bug-eyed, wore no headpiece and her long hair fell nearly to her knees.

Wulfstan died at York in 1024 and Cnute again had to postpone his attack on Norway. The court journeyed overland to York.

"Does no one die in the summer?" Cnute asked as they plowed and pushed the long train of King and followers and hangers-on into Northumbria.

At York, Earl Eric, his hair the color of the blanket of snow which covered the shire, stamped into the great hall from the outside, leaving the door open behind him. Someone closed it. "Goddamn!" he said.

"What, my Lord Eric?" Gytha brushed snow from his mantle.

"It is colder," he said, "then St. Agatha's tit in this damn Glouchester."

"Glouchester?"

"Here in Glouchester," he growled.

"This is Northumbria," Gytha reminded him.

"I thought it was Glouchester." He came over to Emma, buckled his knees and peered up into her face as if trying to determine who she was.

Emma pulled back from him. "You are the Earl of Northumbria. How could you forget such a thing?"

"I was the King of Norway," he told her, "and I learned to forget that." He pinched her rear and complained of a pain in his side.

"You must come to Winchester." Emma moved away from his grasp. "I have this new healer who cuts the pain right out of you."

The requiem chants echoed on the wind as the pageantry blew away and the King's entourage moved toward the sea and sailed for Wessex. The situation in Norway had altered and the invasion was postponed. "Soon," the King said, "we shall march on Norway." And spring came to Winchester as did the old white-haired Earl Eric and the healer cut him open. Eric died. Cnute told Eric's son, the new earl, Hakon, "I shall make you viceroy of Norway," and Hakon nodded and sat combing his hair, blond and nearly as long as the Lady Godiva's.

It was four years punctuated by birth and death, but now Cnute was ready to invade the Northland and Emma had finally managed to get Cnute's baby growing in her womb and growing too well as she bound her waist and hid her figure beneath full gowns, but in the end it could be kept secret no longer and in her seventh month the King did not send her away, but packed up the court, moved to Wardrobe Palace in London and left Emma behind in Winchester.

Alone, except for Aesval, a few loyal members of her house, some slaves and a small squad of thingliths, who Cnute must have culled from his corps in search of the ugliest to leave behind, she was angered and vengeful. She had not forgiven him for the last time he had deserted her and this only increased her determination to get back at him.

She missed Gytha; there was not even anyone to share her anger with for Aesval accepted the world far too stoically and was forever trying to cheer Emma up. Emma didn't want cheering up; she wanted to hate and to hate with vengeance. Gytha, she knew, would have shared her outrage. "You will have a boy," were the parting words of the Countess of Wessex. Yes, she would have a boy, two sons, one to rule the Daneland, the other England. She should have as many children as Gytha bore, dropping them like eggs from a swan, four sons and that daughter which Gytha had rejected. Gytha should not have weakened. Still the child was an interesting thing . . . beautiful, exquisite eyes and delicate hands . . . but young Edith could be a cacophony of questions . . . like Edward, when he'd been young. She was forever asking questions. Edith had asked her once, "Why are butterflies called pretty, but other flies ugly?" and another time wanted to know, "Who tells the sun when day is over, so it will go away?"

She was alone and she had all of Winchester to herself. She went across to the King's chamber. She opened the cupboard. It was bare of his robes and gowns and there was a dead mouse in the bottom. The skins were still left on the straw bed and the room smelled of Cnute and she was torn by her lust for him, for he was still a young man and exciting to her, and her hatred. She lay down on the straw and pulled one of the skins over her big belly and watched the light sift through the window boards and she remembered those early years before Harthacnut was born and how once they had locked themselves in the chamber for two days exploring each the other's body. And she remembered, as well, how he had deserted her for the whore, and though the whore, too, was now in exile, Emma had no sense of empathy for Elgiva. Her hate for the woman had never diminished over the years. She hated her then and hated her more if possible now. Emma was publicly delighted when Godwin produced the shoemaker and the King faced the reality that Elgiva's son, Harold, was not his. Cnute, the cuckold, Emma had whispered to Gytha. The thought pleased Emma as she lay upon the bed thinking how she would scheme to get revenge on Cnute.

She looked across at the chess pieces, readied for an unplayed game on a table in the corner. She looked at the basin where Cnute washed his hands and the wine cup on the shelf and the ivory comb and the padded kneeler near the boarded window. All parts of the room, all parts of Cnute. None enough to save him.

It took a month, but it was resolved. She was in her own chamber resting the day Gamol awoke her. "Lady," he said, "there is a man, Hak of Strangeby, come from Viborg for you."

"Tell him I will walk with him in the field beyond the great hall. I want to speak in the open where we shan't be overheard."

Hak of Strangeby looked like an ancient Viking warrior; he was grizzly and wore skins and a horned helmet and slaps of bark on his feet tied with leather windings.

"Ulf has left Roeskild, Lady, and taken Harthacnut to the ancient seat at Viborg; there the jarls of the Daneland have proclaimed Harthacnute their King."

"I have word from Normandy, you may convey to Ulf. His grace, my brother the duke, supports us in this and will come to our aid and defense should Cnute move against us."

"I had heard, Madam, when I landed at Dover, that the Duke of Normandy had fallen ill."

Emma was upset by the news. She had not heard, but didn't want the man to know. "It can be nothing serious." She smiled. "Or surely I would have been told. No, we can rely on Normandy. Assure Ulf of that."

"He has made, as you suggested, an alliance with Olaf."

"Good. And Sweden?"

The walk was getting a bit much for Emma and she wished there were a place to sit down for a moment.

"Yes, with King Anund, as well. You will sail for the Daneland, Lady Queen?"

"As soon as I am delivered of this burden. My next son," she added as she turned and began walking back toward the hall. "I should be able to travel in a little more than a month, tell Ulf, and shall come to Viborg. Is it pleasant there?"

"Old," he said, "very old."

There was an awkward moment and neither spoke until the man said as they neared the hall again, "Kings Olaf and Anund have sent ships to Scania to protect the Zealand."

"Let's hope they protect it and aren't off for stealing it. Tell Ulf not to trust these Norse too far."

"The ships of Olaf are some four hundred and fifty by count and hold the bay between Scania and Zealand, not a thing can slip past them toward Jomburg, the Wendland or Sweden."

"And the wife of Ulf?"

"The lady of the viceroy supports her husband, Madam."

They had reached the hall and Emma parted from the man called Hak of Strangeby. She only wished she might be there peering in a crack in the door when Cnute was told he had been overthrown by his eight-year-old son.

CHAPTER 2

London and the Daneland, 1026

Two years work destroyed! Godwin was livid. He went to put on his mantle and it tore open at a seam as he roughly pulled it over his shoulders. Damn! Damn! He was so certain that he controlled, manipulated and varied the affairs of the kingdom that something like this seemed impossible. The Dane, who called himself Hak of Strangeby, had but left the chamber and Godwin realized somehow he had lost control.

Two years work destroyed by the Queen and he was not even certain why she had done it. For two years they, he with the King, had struggled in the preparation of the conquest of Norway. "Patience," Cnute maintained. We will use four manners of approach: build an enormous fleet; outwait the Swedes, who are not long on alliances or wars; bribe the earls of Norway; spread harassment and rumor to keep Olaf off his guard. Two years they worked and waited. Waited for the Swedish lords to tire of a readiness to war that never matured and to which they had finally given every indication they had had enough waiting. Cnute had bribed the earls, and when they died, bribed their sons until some publicly supported Cnute and others were ready the moment Olaf fell. Time and again Olaf was led to believe the invasion force was upon him. Ships were sent into the fjords and vanished, rumors were dropped at courts where Olaf had envoys and among the Norwegian earls and particularly among the clergy, who never tired of gossip. A fleet was to be built of one thousand vessels. Seven hundred and sixty-two were already seaworthy. Of those six hundred and eighty-seven were manned and geared to sail. It would take but eight days to get the provisions and crews together. That would be Woden's day after the morrow. And there was little doubt that the King would agree with him, the fleet must sail now.

Godwin in his torn mantle left his chamber and made his way along the drafty corridor of Wardrobe Palace, growling at a passing thinglith as he neared the door of the King's chamber.

Godwin had been informed the King was playing chess with his chaplain, the priest, Stigand. He would never as a rule interrupt Cnute when at women, game, sport or chess. This was an exception. Cnute, as he matured, was becoming more drawn into the pattern of the Christian king and he talked these days of a pilgrimage to Rome and of the Emperor, and what the most Christian King of France bequeathed or built in the way of monastic centers and Stigand advised him on the mores of a most Christian king, and, of course, had all the while his own eyes set upon the miter. But what king's chaplain didn't want a bishopric. And Godwin didn't mind Stigand as long as he stayed within his sphere of advisement, yet he kept a sharp watch on him.

He rapped at the King's door and went in.

"Can it wait?"

"It cannot, my liege Lord."

"Then, Wessex, let's have it. Should Father Stigand be gone or stay?"

"It is an ecclesiastic matter and it may be compromising for him to stay," Godwin lied and the priest made a quick bow and left.

"I take it this is no ecclesiastic matter."

"No, my Lord King. I have thought to compose a hundred prefaces for what must be said, but none changes the cold hard fact and it is this. Your son has been placed on the throne of Denmark as King in your stead by your trusted lieutenant and brother Ulf."

Cnute simply looked at him.

Later, Godwin brought Hak of Strangeby to the King.

"Hak of Strangeby has told me, sire, that the ships of Olaf number some four hundred and fifty."

"How many of the ships are the Swedes'?"

It was Hak of Strangeby who answered. "Maybe a hundred. No more."

"So if we outwait the impatient Swede, that leaves three hundred and if we are able to block those three hundred from getting out Olaf is without a fleet at Tunsberg. With a thousand we could have overpowered them. But we are given no choice. With what we have we will keep them trapped and destroy what we are able. If we can stop Olaf from getting back to Tunsberg we may have time to get the support of the Norwegian earls."

On the eighth day they sailed from the mouth of the Thames. Cnute's new longboat had one hundred and twenty rowers, a mast of gold with a red, blue and green sail which bellowed out like the pregnant Queen. Earl Hakon, the pretender to the viceroyship, the earl overlord of Norway, his long hair flying in the shore winds, was the second in command with a ship of eighty rowers. Godwin sailed with the King. Earl Leofric had been called to London and was told he was the governor of England and advised that the Queen was to be kept confined and not allowed to contact the Duke of Normandy. His wife, bug-eyed Godiva, listened and stood silently beside her husband. Cnute embraced Leofric and the ships set sail. One after the other until there were six hundred and sixty-two longboats moving oar by oar toward Jutland.

He stood with the King at the bow. "I don't think," Godwin said, "you need worry about Richard of Normandy. I have made inquiries. He is quite ill. You will be safe from him for a while."

"That is the only matter of fate in our favor these days."

"I made provisions," Godwin continued to tell the King, "that all messages from the Queen were to be intercepted. And Wordig, who serves her hawking, will keep an additional watch."

"The woman, Aesval—"

"She is being watched also, my Lord."

"She is not harmless," Cnute said. "Emma, one night early in our marriage, told me Aesval was responsible for the poisoning of Edmund."

"Do you believe it?"

"I think so," the King said. He stood staring down into the water. "The Queen is getting old, Godwin . . . and fat . . . and a little mad, I think . . ."

On the fifth day to sea they landed in the Jutland, the King's ship first, and Cnute leaped from the small boat that brought them to shore and he took long strides, in the wind through the high grass, toward the ancient great hall, Viborg.

It was dark and gloomy inside like a robbed tomb and Cnute roared, "WHO HERE SERVES ME?" And a small voice answered. When Godwin's eyes adjusted he saw the only one in the otherwise empty hall was the pathetic figure of eight-year-old Harthacnut.

"KNEEL TO YOUR KING!"

And Harthacnut knelt as his father bellowed and he quaked and he looked up at the King, who stamped toward him, and he started to cry.

"Stop your sniveling. You tell me, insolent boy, who is your King?"

"You."

"You are my King and liege Lord, that is what you say to your father." Cnute spoke more kindly.

The voice was weak. "You are my King and liege Lord."

Behi entered with Ulf at sword's point.

"This knave's zeal," Ulf said, "has outraged his good sense. He escorts the Jarl of Jomburg, brother-in-law to the King, at the point of a sword."

"He must be under a misapprehension," Cnute said, "which we all seem to have, that he thought you the uncle of the King of the Danes."

Ulf said nothing.

Godwin looked at the two men. Cnute angry, the slight scar on his face more visible than usual. Ulf, his counterpart with the same scar, whose expression was one of indifference as if he cared little what Cnute was to do with him or about the Daneland.

"You may explain," Cnute told him.

"The jarls wished a king of their own, not one shared with England who cares more for his adopted country than his native birthland. I thought better to give them your son than to let them find one other of their own choosing."

"Without consulting me?"

"You are there. They are here."

"But the Queen is there and you found time to counsel with her. If she promised you support of Normandy I can only add, since last she sent you writs, her brother Duke Richard lies ill. Danes may expect no help from their cousins there."

"If you are to have my head, then do it," Ulf said.

"No. You are my brother. For my love, for my sweet sister's sake, for the love of this boy, who is your nephew, bears you and because you were led to foolishness by my own wife, I will not."

"It was my doing. My idea. Not hers."

"I am certain," Godwin said quietly, "she allowed you to think so."

"I forgive you," Cnute said. "Gather your ships. We must now chase the Norwegians and the Swedes from Scania and Zealand."

"My ships are mostly at Jomburg. All passage is blocked, but by land."

"Then you will command ships of mine, brother," Cnute said and embraced him, but Ulf was stiff, his expression never changed from stubborn indifference, and it was a strained reunion, one too easily forgiving and the other not willing to accept forgiveness.

"Now we must assemble the jarl lords," Cnute said.

For three days they waited. Cnute paced and tried to indicate to Ulf that their relationship had not changed, but Ulf sulked by the sea and Estrid came to Cnute. "He meant none of it," she said.

"I know," he assured her, but she did not seem assured and went to church to pray.

An old man came bearing the tale that Olaf was preachng Christ and benevolence at Roeskild and asking the Danes to submit to him and word came of English longboats. "And when the fat King was afraid, he was told there were but two merchant ships, and he went back to preaching, but I knew the Great King would come and I told my wife to pack me bread and goat's curds and I will find the King."

Cnute gave the old man a golden coin. "The ships?"

"They lie like a fishnet betwixt Scania and Zealand. No Zealander will submit to a Norse king, my Lord. We are Danes."

On the third day all the jarls but one appeared and Godwin sent an assassin to him and the jarls submitted, causing all to know that Cnute, King of Daneland, was their lawful liege Lord and they went home and gathered their armies to ready for their King.

The King sailed. The Black Raven rode at the fore in the new longboat with the red- and blue- and green-striped sail. Ulf's ship followed and then Earl Hakon's.

"We will wait until the morrow," Cnute ordered to all the ships as dusk approached and they neared the straits. "What ships are able can find shelter in the mouth of the Holy River. I will remain at sea." But all the boats could not sail into the Holy River for above the tidewater the level was strangely low. Word was brought of this to Cnute and he called for an old man who had gone deaf and now his speech made only sounds but who knew the ways of the sea. Even as too many ships juggled for position in the low water some ships ran aground.

And the old man, who couldn't talk, built a pile of broken wood on the deck an then poured water behind and Cnute understood. "It is a trap," he said. "Order them to sail at once into the sea and out of the river." And word was carried to the ships.

"I don't understand," Godwin said.

"I have heard from those who have seen them at Tunsberg. Olaf builds dams. He has dammed the river and that dam will be broken and the ships destroyed. I was a fool not to realize . . ." Then Cnute paced on the deck. He walked, but he never left off watching the mouth of the river and ships began slipping out like bees from a hive. But suddenly! First was the sound. A roar and the thunder of water. Timber. A flood of wood and ships and broken men and water poured from the mouth of the river like a great wave and was devoured by the open sea.

Cnute clenched his fists.

Men were pulled from the sea. One hundred ships were destroyed, or so badly damaged they would never put to sea again. Fifty more were crippled. Over three hundred men were lost. Olaf had built a timber dam upriver and had simply cut it loose upon the anchored fleet.

"We still outnumber them in ships and men. We sail into the straits at first light."

And the sky came up red. But when they reached the straits there were no ships. The Swedish and Norwegian fleet had sailed into the Baltan Sea. Yet, no matter how long they stayed, those ships must pass through the straits to be free.

"We have him," Hakon said, his blond hair flowing from beneath his helmet. "We have won."

"No," Cnute said, "we have not lost, but we have not won. Not yet."

The fleet was left to occupy the straits like a necklace on a war-king, tiers, one upon the other, sparkling in the moon night's water. The King would return to Roeskild and Godwin went with him, as did Ulf.

"We will wait on Olaf here if it takes the rest of my life," Cnute said and sat down on a hard bench as if getting ready for the long siege.

The sea was calm. Harthacnut was sent from Viborg back to Winchester. "Send to King Boleslav for Elgiva," the King told Godwin. "Svegan is twelve; he is almost old enough to sit as regent without a viceroy, but we will call Harold Thorkellsson to sit beside him." Godwin thought of the silent man with the stubbled fingers, dark and taciturn, and wondered what the man might have been had he not met the Queen. And did the Queen have such a hold on him yet that the boy Svegan might not be safe? Who knew what Emma was capable of? Still, Godwin didn't care. Not at this point, either for the Queen or Elgiva's son.

They sat in the first darkness of evening by the sea.

"The sea is so calm the world could hardly know that while we sit here," the King said, "my kingdom crumbles like overdry bread. The sun tonight was like a red ball that sank so deep in the water that it extinguished its fire. Yet tomorrow at precisely the same time as it does each year on this day it will rise again from water in the other direction. The sea holds all secrets."

"Gytha told me Thorgals-Sprakaleg spoke when he was dying of an old Viking legend that the earth was round. Maybe it is and the sun goes under and comes back up again."

"Do you suppose there is another kingdom to conquer there below? I can't manage what I know."

But before Godwin could answer, old Queen Gunnerhild came out to where they sat at the cliff's edge.

"You think me mad," she said.

"Mother, care, the edge of the cliff is loose, you will fall to the sea."

"And who would care? You think me mad."

"I would care," Cnute told her.

"I am mad, but I have seen the root of madness. Power is madness. You dam it like Olaf dams the water. I hear and I know. You think me mad because I mourn Harold, but your brother was not diseased with power like you, like your father. Power is dammed like the water and then let loose in torrents and it destroys everything in its path. If the comet had not killed your brother you would have . . . or Emma. . . . The Normans are the most diseased of all upon the earth and they will spread like a great plague. I am mad. But I see. Poor Ulf, he was content as a boy, now he, too, has been turned into a seething dam, pent and able to fight all but himself."

"Ulf has wronged me, Mother, but I will use him kindly," he assured her.

"It is too late for Ulf," she said.

"Be careful of the edge, Lady," Godwin cautioned.

She stared at him for a moment. "And the likes of you no one cares about, be they mad or sane. You are pig dung turned to rock. The smell is gone and what is left is hardness that doesn't even care for power." She wandered off in the direction of the sun, which had set, but away from the cliff's edge.

Three days later Estrid arrived from Viborg with her three sons. "Harthacnut's gone back," she told her brother. "He goes with my prayers."

Sven and Osbeorn were made to kneel before the King and Beorn the baby was laid before him and Ulf in a monotone declared them Cnute's men.

Godwin thought of his own sons and longed for England and Gytha.

That evening as the sun was setting Queen Gunnerhild was walking on the cliff by the sea and the cliff gave way and she fell down into the sea without even a cry. Cnute saw it from afar and cried for his mother.

Two months they waited. It became like waiting for Thorgals-Sprakaleg to die. Word reached them that the Swedes had disbanded their fleet and had gone, the lords, to their homes. Only the Norwegian vessels lay in the Baltan Sea. They had been seen from Jomburg and by ships Cnute had sent in search of Olaf's fleet.

Ulf stayed from the King. For two months he had barely set foot within the King's presence. "Estrid," Cnute told her, "call your husband."

Later in the day Ulf, sullen and looking lost, stood before the King.

"Do you avoid me, Ulf?"

"I find it safe to stay from your presence."

"I will bring you no harm, brother."

"It is not you I fear, but myself."

"Nonsense. Be my friend again. Tonight come and we shall play chess."

But Estrid came that night to her brother and said Ulf was unwell and they should not be able to play chess.

Godwin sat alone that night by the sea. The birds cawed overhead and he thought of Sorgad and felt sad. He had liked the old woman and he was sad for Gytha, too, because she had loved her. And he remembered the prophecy that his daughter Edith would become the Queen of England and that Emma's son, but not Harthacnut, would be her husband. So Emma was to bear another son and he would be a king as well, according to the birds. But what did birds know of anything or old crones with two teeth? Night fell and the birds disappeared and he went back into the timbered compound at Roeskild.

A messenger came the next morning bringing word that Richard of Normandy was gravely ill and was not going to live. Cnute would not have to fear the boy, the new duke, with his dull eyes. The remainder of the day was like all others at Roeskild, waiting. And in the evening Cnute sent for Ulf to play chess, but Estrid brought word he was ill and should not be able to play.

The morning brought another messenger running from another ship. "The Queen has given birth . . ." he yelled into the wind as he ran up toward where Godwin and the King stood watching the vessel in which he had sailed bob in the sea.

"And?" the King asked.

"It is a girl, my Liege."

Cnute roared and he rolled on the ground laughing and he got up and hit his sides and he rolled again on the ground and the messenger began to laugh and Godwin laughed. "Oh, Godwin, I hurt," he said. And he roared some more and when he could finally get his voice he spoke in spurts between the gusts of laughter. "She did it all for nothing . . . for nothing . . . she didn't have enough sons, save Ethelred's, to go around for her kingdoms . . . poor Emma . . . ah but a daughter, poor daughter . . . Emma will make her Empress of all the Bulgars. St. Irene—has she ever told you about St. Irene? Yes, she tells everyone of the Empress of the Byzantine. That's what Emma would be, the Empress . . ." He stood up and stopped laughing. "She is short one son and she will stay that way. Her body shall know this King no more."

The Queen was near forty. Even if she could have more, her beauty would soon be more faded than it was. The King would shortly have been disenchanted anyway.

"Send word back to Emma," the King ordered the messenger. "The girl is to be called Gunnerhild."

Ulf stayed from the King, though Cnute again sent word to play chess. But once more Estrid brought the word that Ulf was ill.

Each night Cnute called for Ulf and he did not come. On the fourth day Elgiva arrived from the Slav kingdom. Her bulbous nose seemed larger, Godwin thought, and her skin, so dark before, pale olive and blotched and her black hair gray and wadded in mats.

"She is so ugly," the King said.

He called for Ulf for chess, but Estrid came and said he was still ill, so the King went off to the bed of Elgiva, but he came away after a short time and had a cup of wine with Godwin, who sat sipping on a bowl of milk. "She stinks and her body is filthy. She will bear no more children of mine. Still she can stay here with her son after I'm gone. He is getting to be a big lad."

"He looks like you," Godwin said and it was the truth.

The next day was uneventful. Elgiva complained and the King told her if she didn't shut up he would keep Svegan and have her sent back to Boleslav. "You've gotten old and ugly," he said.

At night he called Ulf for chess, but Estrid send word that Ulf was ill.

And the next morning word came to Cnute that King Olaf Haroldsson had gone home by land and was safely back in Tunsberg and the ships were left in the Baltan Sea and would stay forever if Cnute did not sail home. "We go to Winchester," Cnute said.

And that night Ulf came into the great hall. He was dressed in a golden tunic and wore bright green hose and a sale of green was draped over his shoulder. He looked like the Jarl of Jomburg. "Do you wish to play chess?" he asked Cnute.

"Yes, friend, yes," the King said. The King in a muslin smock and cross-laced braies looked the peasant compared to the elegantly attired young jarl. "I am glad you have come, Ulf."

Ulf did not smile and he stood with legs apart, almost defiant, certainly proud. The chess pieces were set up on the table in the center of the hall. Neither man spoke. It was chilly and a fire had been lit in the fire trough and that lighted the room. Stools were brought and the King sat first and then Ulf across from him. Neither man said a word. Godwin sat, too, and wondered why, yet something held him. Ulf had the black pieces; the King, as always, the white. The first move was made, but then neither man stirred, nor spoke. The firelight cast an orange pale over them and in the frozen stillness they looked like wood carvings. A piece was moved, and another and still not a word was uttered. Beneath that calm Godwin sensed the turbulence and there was something frightening in it and he himself wanted to yell out, to break the stillness, but he felt a fool. It was only a chess game. For an hour the only sound in the room was that of the fire and an occasional chess piece being moved. Once Ulf ran his finger along the edge of the scar on his face. Later the King moved a thegn and rubbed the scar on his own cheek and pushed back his tousled hair. Neither moved for some time after that and Godwin knew and was frightened because the silence could not last forever.

Estrid came looking for Ulf, but before she could speak, Godwin put a finger across his lips motioning her to silence. Neither man acknowledged her presence. She looked horrified as she saw the two of them, almost as if she wanted to scream. She stood near the fire watching them. Godwin thought of Sorgad's words that Ulf would die at the hands of the King and he, too, felt the terror. And yet, it was just a game, simply a game, and he felt foolish for being terrorized by nothing. Ulf moved and Cnute quickly retaliated. He then got up and came over to his sister. "Have a cup of wine," he told her, and poured himself some. It was the first time in well over an hour anyone in the room had spoken. Cnute was perfectly natural and Godwin felt all the more foolish.

Estrid shook her head.

"The sea," Cnute said, "you can always hear the sound of the sea." He looked at his sister. "How are your children? I have not seen them these days. You must bring them round to me."

"I can't," she said.

"Why?"

"They are with their grandmother at Upsala."

"She is locked up."

"They are at Upsala."

"Why? You are my dear sister."

"Because they are not safe here."

Cnute went back to the table. Again it was silence. Ulf moved and Cnute countered. The heat from the fire seemed to be getting oppressive and Godwin wanted to get up and leave, but it was as if he were chained. All the while Estrid stood like Lot's wife staring at her husband and brother. Godwin thought of Gunnerhild and the night she fell to the sea and the words—"It's too late for Ulf"—she had said. He put the old woman from his mind and tried to think on pleasant thoughts, of home and Gytha and her beautiful red hair and his children and Edith, his lovely Edith, a *papillon*, but his mind could not escape the room. It was like a prison in which he was fated to be locked with only dark thoughts and it was as if the room was filled with birds and Sorgad and death and a weighty silence.

It seemed hours. Godwin knew it was not near that long, but it seemed endless and neither man moved as much as a finger. Both looked intently down at the board, their faces set with a fierce intensity as if life and death were at stake. The room seemed to constantly grow warmer and it was as if there was no air. It was becoming like a tomb. Estrid stood never taking her eyes from the men and Godwin sat and the only sound was the fire.

And when Godwin thought he could stand it no longer and was ready to yell out, to insist someone speak, Ulf moved a piece on the board, stood up and yelled, "Check! And doom."

Cnute stared at the table, sat for a moment and then rose slowly. His face was twisted with anger and in the firelight the shadows cast by his own features made him look like some mad beast. He spoke with fury. "This is but a game. In life, as well, you would challenge a king, but fail because you are a coward."

Ulf moved from his position and came behind the King and swung the large frame of Cnute about to face him. "Coward? It was not I who was the loser at Holy River. That was a stupid military blunder by a dunce who thinks himself fit to be King."

And then it happened. All that that oppressive silence had been building toward. The knife came from beneath his tunic and slipped from Cnute's hands into Ulf's ribs without warning.

Estrid stood as if she had been waiting for it. She did not cry. She did not move. Ulf slid to the floor.

"What have I done?" Cnute sunk to the stone beside the body. "What have I done?" He touched the chest of the man lying motionless and took his hand and pressed it against the scar on Ulf's face. There was no breath in the man. Cnute's eyes opened with tears.

Godwin stood up and went outside. Dawn was coming. Light sifted over the eastern sky and the sea was visible and overhead the gulls cawed and formed in a circle.

CHAPTER 3

Winchester, 1026

THE AIR HUNG WITH MOLD. IT SEEMED TO EMMA IT HAD RAINED FOREVER. Not soft gentle rain, but water beating against the roof and walls. She was not allowed to leave the chamber. Still, she could see the water rush over the stone street of Winchester, like rapids seeking some endless lower rest. And all the while, she, Queen of England, seething for activity, sat sewing, jamming and retrieving the bone needle through the coarse fabric. Lady Godiva sat across from her with hands as delicate as butterfly wings weaving the thin thread into the cloth. Emma looked at her own hands, the sparsity gone, and round flesh pressing for space against the next finger, the backs of both hands speckled with brown dots and a pleat of lines folding between thumb and finger. They were the hands of an aging woman. She was angered by the youth of the young Godiva. Would she, too, waste her youth as Emma had wantonly spent her beauty on Ethelred, not knowing how precious and short-lived a commodity it was? Godiva, though, was not a beauty, despite the knee-length hair and unmarred skin, her high, carved cheeks and sweet mouth. Her features were overpowered by huge eyes that bugged out, and while they dominated her entire appearance, they seemed empty. She was like an annoying but harmless insect and Emma had the urge to step on her, slap her aside. No, Godiva was no beauty. But Emma knew she, the young Norman, the daughter of the ducal house, had been strikingly beautiful. "Had"—what an ugly, horrid word. She touched her face with her flat hand as if to preserve what was left, but feeling only puff against puff, she knew how much the prettiness of youth had washed away like the water over the stone street. It would leave behind only the erosion lines of time.

"The poor," Lady Godiva said, her voice, as always, weak, barely audible, as if there were no breath beneath it, "it is they who suffer so in this rain."

Emma said nothing. Do you think, Godiva, I do not suffer, sitting here your prisoner, never left from your sight, or Gytha's, or worse, that of your coarse husband's?

"So cold," the tiny voice said. The young woman pulled her cloak over her breasts. "Their fuel is soaked and their children have so little to eat. Still, I suppose, it is God's will. It must be sinful of me if it be God's purpose, yet I want to cry out to them."

Emma still made no response. She stuck the needle into the cloth. Goddamn Godwin . . . Godwin . . . Godwin. She pulled the needle through again . . . Godwin . . . Godwin . . . goddamn. She shoved the needle . . . Godwin . . . She had cursed him for days, yet it was little satisfaction. It in no way resolved her dilemma. She was never left alone except for a few moments to bare her sins to a priest, and not even her own confessor, for he was denied access to her. Instead, she was allowed some masochistic meek creature of Godiva's house, whose very voice seemed to urge her to horrendous lies of vile deeds to satisfy his appetite. She gave him bland mush instead. He was a slimy fellow, much like a fat nightcrawler left behind in the daylight after a heavy nocturnal rain. She never could remember his name. The only other priest they might possibly let her see would be Cnute's chaplain, Stigand, who had been left behind, they said, because he vomited continually at sea. Perhaps Stigand . . . just perhaps. She had watched him looking at her, seemingly not aware that her beauty was fading. Yes, Stigand . . . just perhaps.

"You're smiling," Godiva said, dour dolorous Godiva, the sorrowful mother, *dolce far niente*.

"I was thinking of a confession I once made."

"And that makes you smile?"

"Yes, the sins were horribly wicked." Emma delighted at the discomfort it was giving the bug-eyed woman. "It made the priest shudder."

"I should hardly find that amusing."

"No, I suppose you wouldn't. But there is little else to amuse me now but my past transgressions. I certainly have no opportunity for sin these days."

Godiva responded only with a frown of disapproval. They sat silent, the rain pounding. Emma looked across at the younger woman thinking what a delight it would be to pull each of the knee-length hairs one by one from her head. Scream, let Godiva scream. She punched the needle through the cloth.

The door opened. A cold wet wind cut through her bliaut. Emma did not need to look up. She knew who it would be. "The changing of the guard."

"Pardon?" Godiva set down her sewing.

"She sees us as her keepers." Gytha, dripping from the rain, stood near the door. She threw off her cloak and went to the fire. "And I suppose we are."

"Not at all, Lady Wessex. Not at all." Godiva stood up. "We serve the Queen."

"Jailers," Emma said.

"Well, I leave her to you." Godiva was tall and she moved, fawnlike, across the room. Emma hated her. "The Queen is in a bad humor this morning." Godiva slipped on her cloak, letting the long hair remain beneath, and pulled the hood up over her head. "Until vespers," she said and left.

"The Queen is in a bad humor this morning," Emma mimicked in a little voice. "How should the Queen be?"

Gytha shook loose her red hair, wet despite her hood, and pushed it back from beneath with both her hands.

Emma watched her. "You are pregnant again."

"Yes," Gytha answered. She sat and took from a bag she had brought in with her a child's garment and began repairing a torn seam.

"The Countess of Wessex, the wealthiest lady in the kingdom, more wealthy than the Queen herself, mends."

"I am but a simple Jomburg maid at heart." Gytha smiled.

Emma found it difficut to be angry with Godwin's wife. She watched for a moment as the red-haired woman skillfully repaired the seam. "Gytha, let me send a letter to my brother."

"No."

"My brother—"

"You are not to be trusted."

"You think I did it in spite."

Gytha set the sewing aside momentarily. "I don't know why you did it, Emma. You destroyed two years of Godwin's work."

"Godwin's?"

"The King's."

Emma realized she would get nowhere with her. Still, she persisted. "You know the Dane. You know he will have no king that is not anchored at one of those devilish old halls like Roeskild or Viborg or—"

"Jomburg."

"Precisely. I only did what Cnute was too blind to do."

"You betrayed my husband. Your friend."

"Gytha, it was not against Godwin—"

"He trusted you."

Emma gave up with a sigh and picked up the needle. She thought of St. Irene. Somehow she would not stay here like this. She would find the way. There would be a way of escape. Somehow she would free herself from this confinement. The room was still; only the drone of the rain and the whisper of needles slipping through fabric were audible. Emma felt the eternity in the endless needlework and the more endless rain, which, now and again, varied in its intensity.

The door opened, breaking into her thoughts. Wind and rain swept in with the Countess of Coventry and Harthacnut.

"What is the boy doing here, Godiva?" Gytha asked the tall woman.

"I caught him drowning one of God's creatures in a large pool of water, Lady Wessex." Godiva's weak voice reminded Emma of a tattling child.

"It was only a dog," Harthacnut said and looked over at his mother.

"Careful, Harthacnut," Emma cautioned, "you're liable to get bit. And if you get bit you will catch the fit and die. What have you got all over your face?"

"Berries," he said, smearing the black about his mouth into stains across his cheek. He was a pudgy child and seemed constantly to be eating.

"He stole the berries," Godiva said like some nasty little girl. "From the abbey."

"Well, boy," Gytha said, her expression becoming falsely stern, "you'll have to go to confession now."

"No," he screamed and ran back out into the rain.

Confession. Stigand. It was the only possible way to escape. It would take time; she'd need patience to bring Stigand around. There was his pride, his fear of Cnute, his vows, she supposed, and Lord knows what else to be dealt with, but he could be brought around.

"I'll go after the boy," Godiva said, quite obviously hoping Gytha would make a move to retrieve him.

"Yes," Gytha said, "and put him to bed for his punishment."

Emma should have objected, but her thoughts were more on Stigand. The sooner she got working on him the better. The wind chilled her as Godiva went out. "This evening, Gytha, I should like to go to confession."

Gytha looked at her. It was with apparent suspicion.

"And I don't want that awful little priest of Godiva's."

"There is no one else."

"There must be. I won't have that nasty fat creature."

"Only Stigand."

Emma waited as if reflecting on the matter. "Then send me Stigand. Cnute's henchman, weasel that he is, is better than that worm of Coventry."

Gytha looked at her even more suspiciously.

Emma took the needle out from the cloth and tried not to smile.

In the evening Leofric sat as her guard. As always, she refused to respond, remaining mute. "It is unseemly, leaving me alone with that man," she had told Gytha. "Nonsense," Gytha answered. At first Leofric attempted to speak with her, but he no longer bothered and they sat in silence. She did not sew. She did nothing. He was a big man. The floor was not dirt and straw but built of boards and when he moved the boards moved and creaked under his bulk. She stayed as clear of him as possible for he always smelled of his own excrement.

There was a rap and Leofric responded, creaking his way to unlatch the door. Father Stigand entered. He was a short man, seeming even shorter beside Leofric. There was a cowering deference as he addressed the Earl of Coventry, yet a strange air of pomposity in the same motions.

"What are you doing here?" Leofric asked and scratched his genitals.

"I have come to hear the Queen's confession."

"Well I hope then for your sake she is more talkative in that than she is with me. Her confession might be worth the listening to, if she does speak; my brother Northman, rest his soul, always maintained she was a whore. A whore should be worth the hearing, uh?"

Emma refused to be goaded and said nothing.

Leofric remained standing near the door, making no apparent move to leave.

"Perhaps, if you'll excuse us," the priest suggested ever so humbly.

"Aye. I have my own sins," he said.

As he lumbered out the priest gave him a patronizing bow and a look that said you can trust the Queen in my care. The floorboards creaked and the door closed.

"I was surprised you asked for me, Lady. That is, under the circumstances," the priest added. He had a sparse brown beard which failed to hide his raspberry face to any degree. His eyes were like tiny black pearls, and if they had anything to reveal, Emma found them illegible. Despite this and the fact that she really knew little about him, other than the occasional lewd glance she had caught him giving her, she suspected he was an ambitious man. She wished she had given him more attention in the past.

"With my own priest deprived me, Father," Emma began, "I at least wanted the ear of a fair and just man. You are said to be fair and just."

"One tries, Lady. One tries."

"And loyal to my husband. They say you are Cnute's man. I would have no less."

He looked at her with a perplexed expression. She knew he was not as comfortable as when he had come in. "I am that above all," he said after a moment. "I am loyal to the King."

"Do have a chair there. 'Tis pillowed." She pointed across the room to a chair with a cushioned seat but which had an outrageous back of carved birds whose beaks and wing tips dug into the back of anyone attempting to sit in it. He sat, quickly, however, positioning himself upright, as Emma knelt upon the red-cushioned kneeler next to the chair. "Bless me, Father . . ." He leaned his ear toward her and as he did she was fascinated by the smallness of his mouth, which she had never noticed before. It was totally disproportionate to his ruddy face and she continued to stare at it. "I am accused of conspiring against the King. Of this I am guilty. My sin, if it is a sin, is that I attempted to save Cnute from Godwin."

"Earl Godwin?" His voice was a whisper.

"Yes. He is plotting to take the English throne."

"Godwin . . . ?"

"By occupying the King in the North with a war against both the King's kin in Sweden and with Olaf of Norway. It was his plot to engage the King in such a war, leaving England vulnerable, and then Godwin would return to secure England in the name of the King, while in reality inciting an uprising in Denmark. While the King was busy dealing with the wars in the North, Godwin could claim the throne in England for his own."

"Madam . . ."

"What I attempted to do, when I saw what Godwin was about and saw how great his influence was with the King, was to secure Denmark for Cnute. Well, you know my act as well as I . . ."

"Yes . . ." His small lips barely parted.

"I knew Cnute would never believe me. Not with Godwin whispering in his ear, so I sought to secure the Danish throne through Harthacnut and Ulf in order that the King should be free to return to Winchester and tend the throne of England."

"And Norway?"

"Norway! What does Cnute want with Norway?"

"He spoke to me often of Norway and its conquest."

"I ask you, Father, what possible real interest could Cnute have in Norway? He is a Dane and King of England. Norway is a long way off, a hard and cold and mostly heathen land. These were ideas, ideas of being a northern emperor, put in his mind by Godwin. Godwin is not stupid, he knew no man could govern all three kingdoms at once. You see, Father Stigand, I was only trying to help the King and for it I am punished."

He started to interrupt, but she cut him off, continuing, "I found it impossible with Godwin about to be forthright and was reduced to this subterfuge—"

"Madam—"

"That is my only sin."

"Why have you not told all this to the King?"

"I have been kept from his ear by Godwin. But Ulf understood. He knew. One need only ask him."

"Madam, Ulf is dead—" He stopped as if he wished to retrieve the words.

"Dead . . . no . . ."

"Word arrived but yesterday." He pinched his small lips.

"But Gytha . . . his sister? She said nothing of this."

"The Countess of Wessex has not yet been told. Godwin is sending the Thegn Behi to bear the sorrow to her. I ask you, please, say nothing of this to her." The small lips closed to convey the notion that he regretted having started the conversation.

"How did he die?"

"I have said more than I should."

"Godwin plotted it, no doubt. He hated his brother-in-law. Godwin undoubtedly convinced the King that Ulf was the usurper and must be killed—"

"The King killed him in a rage after Ulf beat him at chess." He spoke quietly.

The rain came harder. For a moment she said nothing, but then added, ". . . still, Godwin . . . You have heard my plight, good Priest. I am not a prisoner of my dear husband, but of Godwin. And I am deprived of my husband. A wife deprived of the instrument of a man is given to lustful thoughts." She could now read the beady eyes and could see that her words were having the desired effect. "When a woman has such emptiness between her thighs, how is she to be fulfilled when her rightful husband is denied to her?"

"God grant you grace." He choked on the words.

"And I have been allowed no word of my family. Not only not hearing of my dear children in Normandy, but my beloved brothers as well." Emma attempted to look near tears.

He said nothing when she finished, but simply looked into what she hoped was her sad face. He whispered when he finally spoke. "I will tell you this much, Madam, for I think it your right to know. Your brother the duke lies ill—"

"Richard—"

"Yes, Lady."

"How ill?"

"Perhaps dying."

"Could you—"

"No, Madam. My orders are quite explicit on that matter. There is to be no communication between yourself and Rouen. Orders—"

"Godwin's orders." She watched him, trying to look as pitiful as possible. "Both you and I are at the mercy of Godwin, Father Stigand. When Cnute wanted you named Dean of Christ Church—"

"Dean of Christ Church?"

"Surely you were aware of that. And you know the last dean, as is not uncommon practice at Canterbury, became the archbishop there. Well, 'twas the Earl of Wessex who urged the King to pass your name by."

"Godwin opposed my being named?"

"I supposed he feared your growing influence with the King."

There was more silence as she watched the small mouth tighten.

"Do you grant me absolution and give me penance?"

"I see little of sin upon your soul, Lady. I grant you absolution." He made the sign of the cross and absolved her with a Latin incantation. "Dean of Christ Church?"

"Yes. Cnute would've had it so. But Godwin, and as is custom the earl of jurisdiction in which the ecclesiastic appointment is to be made, was consulted. His choice prevailed."

The priest stood up, scraping his back against the sharp wing of a bird. "Lady, there is a cleric here from your brother's court. If I can find a way to bring him to you I shall and you may have firsthand word of the duke's health."

"Thank you, kind Priest. You are a true son of Christ."

He turned and went out into the night rain. Emma smiled. It had been easier than she could have imagined. The tale about Dean of Christ Church had been a moment of sudden inspiration. Stigand could be used.

He had barely walked from the room when Godiva appeared, wet and coughing. "It still rains," she said.

A fact which to Emma seemed perfectly obvious and hardly in need of comment. Feigning the necessity of penance, Emma fled any further conversation with Godiva, knelt and plotted. She must get word and have word from Rouen. Better yet, she must reach Rouen. Gytha might be the key. Ulf dead and Gytha not told. Well, there was advantage in that, but she would have to reach Gytha before Behi arrived. Ulf dead! It was strange to think of. All that vibrancy blotted out. She knew Cnute; he would be having great remorse over that deed. She wished she were in Denmark now. How she could use that guilt of his to reach him. And Gytha! Gytha will be ready to kill Cnute. Stigand turned upon Godwin and Gytha turned against Cnute. This could well be the way to her freedom.

Lady Godiva attempted to interrupt with small talk. Emma cut her off and returned to her feigned prayers. Aesval! She would need Aesval. Was she still at Winchester, or had they sent her away? Harthacnut would know. Gytha must be told about Ulf this night before Behi arrived with his Godwin-prepared statement to pacify the daughter of Thorgals-Sprakaleg.

Emma's knees ached, but she refused to be distracted now by any prattle of Godiva's, so she kept her place, head bowed. She was reminded of Edward standing for hours without movement. Ugly child! No, he was no longer a child, a man now. And she became angry as she thought of his age and blamed him, for it made her realize her own years. Yet, she was not too old. She would have another child. Cnute's child. She had had Gunnerhild and would bear another. They told of a woman of Ely who bore a child though she was near seventy, though they claimed it a devil's child.

Yes, she would get free of this prison, go first to Rouen and then to Cnute, and he, weighted by his guilt in killing Ulf, would come to her and give her another baby.

She looked over at Godiva, surprised to see her eyes closed, her head bent forward. Emma had to see Gytha, but Gytha would come no more this night. When Emma readied to retire, serving women of Godiva's house would come and a thinglith would be posted outside her door. Godiva's head bobbed.

Emma bolted up and screamed. "I want my children."

Godiva was jolted by the outburst and nearly fell from her seat.

"I want my children brought to me!"

"But, Madam, the hour."

"Don't 'Madam' me, Countess. I am the Queen. I want my children."

"Lady . . ."

Emma closed her eyes and shrieked, "MY CHILDREN!"

Godiva fled from the room. Emma laughed aloud. A thinglith had already been planted outside her door, but Emma didn't mind. She was not ready to make her escape. Not yet. The rain had stopped momentarily. Emma waited.

In the arms of a dirty servant, Gunnerhild was brought to her and Godiva came behind dragging the young Harthacnut, who was screaming that he didn't want to come. The three tracked mud in upon the floor. Between Emma's piercing screams and now the boy's, Harthacnut's, wails, enough noise had been created and it would produce the desired effect. Emma knew it was but a matter of time; in the interim, she might as well get what information from Harthacnut she could about Aesval. With the crying baby in her arms, she pulled Harthacnut off to a corner. "Boy," she whispered, pretending to coddle the baby, "I want you to tell mother a secret."

His eyes lit up. "Yes," the pudgy child answered.

"Is Aesval in Winchester?"

"That's no secret," he blurted.

Godiva seemed not to have heard and was busy cleaning mud from her bliaut.

"Shsssh . . ." Emma cautioned. "Is she?"

"Yes. In Gordelia's cottage."

"Gordelia?"

"The hag with the hanging neck who lives by the gate. They won't let Aesval out, but sometimes I talk to her through the window. Gordelia chases me away with a stick."

Emma was about to pursue the matter when Gytha burst into the room. "What is this? What is going on?"

"She wanted the children." Godiva was flustered.

"Take them back to bed," Gytha ordered.

"But—" Godiva began.

"Take them out."

The serving woman took the baby and Godiva grabbed Harthacnut and they went out.

"Emma, what is this? Some trick of yours?"

"Yes. I needed to see you. I knew you wouldn't come if I asked."

"I cannot help you. I shall see the other guard posted and we shall all get some rest."

"Wait."

"I will not help you, Emma."

"No. I wish to help you."

"Nonsense. Some ruse."

"I have news for you. Bad news, Gytha. Sit down."

"How would you have news for me?"

"I have, Gytha. It is painful."

"You are a prisoner here. What—"

"Let it be enough, I know. Please, Gytha, sit down. I do not relish telling you what must be said."

"I will not sit and I will not hear your nonsense."

"Dear sweet Gytha, sit."

"No."

"Ulf is dead."

"YOU LIE!"

"Hush, the guard will hear. It is true, Gytha. He is dead."

"NO!"

"Gytha . . ."

"It's a lie. You want to hurt me."

"No, Gytha. He is dead."

"It is one of your games, Emma. You are—"

"Listen to me, Gytha. Ulf is dead."

"No." Gytha's voice cracked and she slumped down on Emma's straw bed.

Emma put her arm about Gytha's shoulders. The younger woman's cloak was wet. "He is dead, Gytha."

"No. Don't touch me," she yelled and pulled away from Emma.

"Please, Gytha. I know the pain, but I am not lying to you." Emma took the other woman's hand. This time Gytha did not pull back from her.

"How could . . . No. You want to hurt someone because you are locked up here. That's it, isn't it, Emma, that's it."

"I wish it were, Gytha. At this moment I wish it were."

Gytha grasped a handful of her own red hair and tugged at it. "It is not true. I would be told before you."

"Behi," Emma said softly, "is being sent by Godwin to tell you. To ease the blow. Ulf was killed by Cnute. The King was in a rage."

"No. Cnute wouldn't. All that business of the Daneland is long past. They were—"

"Over a chess game."

"No. Cnute would not kill his brother. They were like brothers. He would—"

"In a rage. You know Cnute's rages. Remember the thinglith with the black hair."

"Oh, God!" Gytha wept. She turned over and buried her face in the straw and sobbed. Emma put her arm about the woman's shoulders. "Oh, God, Emma. I did so love my brother." And then she tore herself free from Emma's grasp and got up off the bed and yelled out angrily so all of Winchester must have heard, "I shall kill the King."

"Hush, Gytha, hush," Emma said.

A week and a half later, with the help of Gytha, Aesval, Stigand and the cleric from Rouen, Emma, disguised as a nun, fled Winchester with her two children. A Norman ship awaited her at Corfe and she sailed, the clear taste of freedom blowing in the sea wind.

CHAPTER 4

Normandy, 1026

EDWARD KNEW THAT HE WAS MAGNIFICENT. HE WAS SPLENDOROUS. THIN. Tall. The silk mantle, a deep ruby, swept back from his shoulders over the rear of the horse reaching the tips of the black beast's tail. The retinue of the Count of Vixen made its way toward some nameless village. Despite the roughness of the pitted road, Edward sat erect. His mantle was bordered in linen, embroidered in detail as intricate as a monk's illumination. The three riders were apart from the rest, close after the lead soldiers. Alfred, his blue cloak askew, and torn at a back seam, rode between his older brother and sister, Godgifu. She looked somewhat incongruous with her shoulders as massive as a smith's sitting sidesaddle on a small gray mare.

It was a white August day and the sun reflected off the gilded Norman helmet that Edward wore as if a crown. His long white hair dropped from beneath it and melted into the snow-ermine lining of the mantle.

As they wound between the hovels of the village, a scattering of dirty serfs gathered to gape. Edward extended a thin pale hand out as if in a benediction.

"It must be God," a torn-bearded serf with only one eye cried out. "I've seen God."

"Out of my way, turd," Godgifu yelled down as the man reached out toward Edward.

Alfred's horse, following behind the mare, stepped in fresh horse dung and it spattered on the one-eyed man. Alfred was stocky and his thick thighs pressed against the animal. His smile, even now, was never malicious, as he grinned when the dung hit the one-eyed serf in the face. He prodded the horse forward and the village was soon behind them. Alfred looked neither like Edward nor his sister. He had sandy hair, unruly, a flat nose, large ears and a voice deep for his fourteen years.

Edward, just as he was aware of his own image in reaching out to the serfs, could visualize the painting of the three as they must appear moving down the ridge of the slope outlined against the white sky. Like the altar triptych at Bruges, they were the epiphanic three kings. The sun beat down; Alfred wiped the sweat from his brow. In the distance three lone birches burned to indistinction by the hot sun blurred against the colorless sky.

The Count of Vixen, Dreux, came riding up from the rear. He puffed. He was a pudgy man who sat his horse forward and clung to the mane. Sweat ran down his red face. "Edward, if that horse shits on that robe—"

"I hope it shits in your mouth, Drogo," Godgifu said.

The count hated being called Drogo, so invariably Edward and Godgifu made a point of it.

Dreux attempted to pick up the cadence of their horses. "I only want your brother to take a little care of that robe. It cost me a pope's ransom."

"You'd keep us in rags, you miserly fat toad." Godgifu spat in the direction of his horse.

He attempted to pull the animal from her range of fire. "Rags? A duke doesn't keep such dress as Edward."

"The duke's not a king," Alfred said timidly.

"Neither is your brother."

"I am a king, the rightful King." Edward spoke with disdain and trotted the black stallion back directly at Dreux.

The count swung his mount from Edward's path and when out of the way added, "And I'll be a holy martyr."

"Good. Go die and leave us alone." Godgifu galloped away.

Edward followed as Dreux's voice carried after him on the wind. "I don't understand how you can even wear that thing in all this heat." Edward turned as he caught up with his sister to see his brother-in-law had fallen back with the other riders.

The three slowed as they gained ground on the lead riders.

"It is too hot," Alfred said. "I don't understand why we have to go to Rouen, anyway. Drogo promised us we would go to Fecamp." Alfred loved the sea.

"Because Drogo must be in Rouen," Edward explained, "and where Drogo goes Godgifu goes, else he beats her. And where—"

"He'd better not dare try and beat me," she interrupted. "Not any more. I'd kill him."

"Then why must we go?" Alfred wiped at his nose.

"Drogo would have us locked up for the whole time he was gone if we didn't," Godgifu told him.

"There is no sea at Rouen," Alfred said.

"There is no sea in Vixen either," Godgifu said.

"But at Fecamp . . ."

Edward put the reins in one hand and smoothed his mantle. "There is the Seine, Aly."

"That's no sea." At Fecamp or Boulogne or Ryes, Alfred would stretch out nude on the sand and let the breaking waves wash over him. "The sea is my mother."

"Better than that bitch who is," Godgifu told him.

"What is she like?" Alfred did not remember her.

"A devil," she answered.

"Beautiful, like a statue," Edward said.

It was a game they played often.

The horses clomped over the rocks.

Along a barren stretch of the road an old woman, shrouded in a filthy yellow robe, bent and gathered bits of dried horse dung. She stepped back from the road and looked up at Edward as they neared. Her eyes were old and deep-set in hollows of blackness, yet the skin of her face was barely wrinkled and, like a baby's, pale pink. Her voice was hoarse and cracked. "I have seen a king. I have seen a saint."

"Me?" Edward asked, bringing the horse to a halt.

"You," the old woman said. She reached out to him with a piece of dried horse dung. "On the day you are crowned I shall die. Burn this on your fire that day and have a pair of foot skins made from the hide of a heretic. Kneel with them on your feet and pray for the soul of this woman born nearly an abortion and tossed upon the rubbish heap."

Edward took the dung.

With her old eyes she stared into Edward's own. "I was baptized by a mute who made seal-hide slippers for a nun who drank the blood of Christ and had seven toes on one foot." She turned. "St. Crispin was burned in a fire made from horse's shit." She walked away.

"Wait," Edward called.

But she did not look back and moved down into a ravine. He rode to where she seemingly had gone, but when he reached the spot she had vanished.

Edward bounded up the slope and to the road. "She was a vision. You have heard her?"

"What does an old woman know?" Alfred tapped his horse with his heels.

"The ways of the world," Edward answered. "Old women have seen birth and death."

"That is what makes them old," Godgifu said.

The grasses on the slopes burned yellow in the heat. There was a sense of summer ending in the air. The green earth was dying.

Alfred slid out of his cloak and let it fall back on the horse. "It is so hot. I don't know why Drogo has to go to that stink-hole Rouen, anyway."

"The duke is dying," Edward said.

"Let him die." Godgifu relished the idea.

A hawk circled in the white sky. "Uncle Richard frightens me." Alfred ran his hand through the bowl of Norman hair and then shook it loose. "Goddamn, it's hot. It's never hot by the sea."

"The sea is your mother," Godgifu said.

"To be at the sea," Alfred said, starting another game.

"To see at the sea," Edward chimed in.

Godgifu continued the game. "You pee in the sea."

"I do not." Alfred was defensive. "The sea is my mother."

The hawk still circled. Edward sweltered beneath the ermine and silk, but he did not remove the mantle, nor mention the heat.

"Who will be duke?" Alfred asked.

"Your stupid cousin Richard," Godgifu answered, "or his bird."

"Robert killed Richard's bird," Edward told her.

"How do you know?" she asked.

"I watched him." Edward slowed the pace as they again were getting too close to the front riders.

"Someone may have killed the old hag as well," she said.

"You mean the old woman we just saw?" Alfred rode slightly behind her.

"I mean Emma."

"No," Edward said.

"It's true." Godgifu spoke with obvious delight. "Drogo says Cnute has had her locked away. Nobody has heard from her. She may be dead."

"No," Edward said. "If anyone kills her it will be I."

"What's she look like?" Alfred asked.

"Hard and mean." Godgifu pulled on the reins. "Like the blade of a torn-edge sword."

"A stone," Edward said, "a cold precious stone."

And the game continued as the three rode together, apart from the others, toward Rouen. In the white sky the hawk circled.

Death hung at the ducal house. It stifled speech and a hush whispered through corridors. There was impending change and its fear in the quiet.

"I will not go to his bed," Godgifu told Drogo and stamped a large foot.

"Nor I," Edward said.

"Nor me," Alfred's deep voice added.

"He's done nothing for us," Edward said.

"Let him die," the Countess of Vixen told her husband and sat down on the stone floor. "Let him rot in hell."

Dreux left them and went alone to the deathbed of his liege lord. The afternoon crept toward evening. A pot scrubber saw a human skull when he looked in the well. A lady to the duchess had the east door boarded when she saw death trying to come in. Evening fell to night. Emma's children, if no one else at the ducal house, slept.

"Lesson," Edward told his brother in the morning.

"No," Alfred said.

"Yes. You must learn to battle."

"I'd rather sit by the sea."

Edward raised up his arms as if employing the heavens. "You must help me take my throne."

They crossed a field near the Robec where Edward had played as a boy. A large oak spread shade, protecting them from the bright sun. The brothers brandished heavy swords, Edward with skill, Alfred awkwardly. Like a seabird, Edward circled about his brother, who turned about, a captive within the ring. Metal clangs rang in the air and a sword thumped to the earth.

"Pick it up, Aly."

"That hurt," Alfred complained.

"It would have hurt worse if I had whacked your head off. Come pick it up."

Alfred swatted away a fly and picked up the sword. Again with rings of a flat bell the weapons hit against one another. Edward beat upon his brother's sword with heavy blows as Alfred strained to keep hold of it. The weapon fell again. Alfred, with resignation, picked it up before Edward had an opportunity to prod him and he again defended himself against the onslaught of Edward's sword.

"Kill me, Aly," Edward yelled above the ring of the swords.

Alfred grunted and puffed and slashed out at his older brother, who parried his blows. A shape came toward them from the direction of Rouen. Edward looked away as the moving strange form approached. Alfred, with a clanging blow, knocked Edward's sword from his grip and it fell to the dirt. He brought the point of his sharp weapon to Edward's neck. Beads of sweat had wet Alfred's forehead. "You're dead," he said, as he wiped the sweat with his free arm.

"Put it down, Alfred."

"I killed you. You're dead."

"All right, I'm dead, but something very weird is coming toward us."

Alfred turned and looked in the direction of the shape. "It's a horrible beast, Edward. Get your sword." Alfred turned, his weapon ready.

Edward stood and stared as the creature moved nearer. It was human, Edward gathered, or appeared to be. It hobbled in a twisted way, moving as much sideways as forward as it approached. One arm appeared grotesquely large and bent, the other hung down and seemed of normal size. It looked to have one large breast, or the flesh was greatly enlarged on the right side. But it was the head and face which were inhuman.

"Go away!" Alfred shouted and brandished his sword.

"Hush," Edward said and motioned the figure that had stopped with Alfred's outburst to continue forward.

As it came up to them Edward could get a closer look. The face on the creature was of no particular shape, but seemed to be globs of gray flesh. There was a horrible odor about it. Alfred backed away. It had two eyes, but they were not on a line; one, bulging and large, hung down, the other, raised, was nearly closed by the blobs of flesh above it. Its mouth was to one side and it spoke slowly, barely audibly. "Robert wants."

Alfred still held the sword out. Edward brushed it down. "What does Robert want?"

The creature paused a moment. "Ed . . . Edward."

"God, it stinks," Alfred said.

Edward looked at the beast. "Why does Robert want me?"

"Ka . . . King . . . Ehhh . . . Edward." The form grotesquely fell in homage to one knee, nearly tipping over as the awkwardness of his weight was shifted.

Edward looked at it and in the gesture and halting "Ka-king" understood the message. "Where?"

Without stammering: "Follow."

Edward nodded. The creature made some move to get up. "Me," it said and seemed to look at Alfred.

The boy pulled back in terror. "No," he said. "No."

Edward leaned down and helped the hulk of strange flesh to its feet. It lumbered off. Edward picked up his sword and followed. Alfred lagged behind. The white sky burned overhead.

"I've never seen anything so ugly," Alfred said.

The coolness of the narrow street of Rouen felt comforting. They made their way along the stones following the limping figure. Edward jumped aside as a fat naked child peed from a doorway. The two followed beneath the heavy shadow of St. Ouen's. Suddenly, as if some angelic apparition, Robin of Jumieges stood in the path of the grotesque creature. "Evil," he cried out and, holding a crucifix, uttered a Latin incantation. The creature turned and fled down a winding street. Edward started to follow.

"Wait, Edward," Robin urged.

Edward called after the figure, "Come back." It vanished somewhere along the street. He went back to where Robin stood, the crucifix still raised. "He was taking us to Robert."

"Your cousin?" Robin asked.

"Yes."

"I don't know which is the greater devil, Robert or the evil being."

"I knew it," Alfred spoke in his deep voice.

Robin looked at the youth with interest, but his words were to Edward. "Have you no welcome for a friend? Aren't you surprised to see me here?"

"No. I went to Jumieges in search of you. They said you had been called to Rouen."

"To the duke's service, but mostly I am allowed to stay cloistered here at St. Ouen. I serve God and am content. But I am glad to see you, Edward."

"And my brother as well, I see."

"This is Alfred? I would not have known him. But truly I would not have known him."

"He interests you?"

"I have given that up. I serve only God now, as I say."

"I am happy you no longer seek the sins of flesh. Still, if you want him . . . you are my true friend and he is yours."

Alfred stared at them both, and it was obvious to Edward that he did not fully understand, yet he was uneasy nonetheless.

"Those times are past," Robin said. "I was shocked to see you in the company of the devil."

"Surely he is but a harmless poor creature."

"He is a devil, truly, Edward. He came from nowhere. One day he appeared. Your cousin, Robert, gave him a place at the ducal table. The duchess screamed with such fright and young Richard swore he saw horns upon the thing's head, a tail and cloven hoofs."

"He has none of these," Edward said.

"You and I don't see them, true."

"He has them not." Edward was emphatic.

"Nonetheless, he is a devil. Did you not smell the evil of his rotting flesh? He shuns from the cross and the words of Christ. It was how I drove him from the ducal house. They say yet Robert keeps him about and it must be so if he was sent to fetch you. But enough of this ugly monster. How be you, Edward?"

"Not yet King. But a seer on the road to here promised it would be so."

"She was but an old hag," Alfred said.

Robin, despite his protestations, looked at the boy and there was lust in the blue eyes. "You are a handsome lad, Alfred."

"Who be you?" Alfred asked.

"A monk. Your brother's friend, who was but this moment searching him out."

A donkey laden with pots and led by a tinkerer clanged past them.

"You heard I had come and were looking for me?"

"The duchess seeks you out. It is for her I was looking for you. Your sister said you had gone to the Robec to play at swords."

"Not to play, Robin, but to teach this boy," Edward told him. "Two swords we shall raise to my throne. What does Judith want of me? She is a pig."

"Your aunt has been told you learned the healing touch from Mac-Boru. She would have you come touch your hands upon the duke."

"I do not like Judith," Edward said.

"It is not she who is dying, but your uncle."

The foul smell was prevalent before the grotesque figure appeared from around a corner. The three turned to look. Behind the deformed creature walked the duke's second son, Robert. He had grown tall. Edward was surprised how large a figure he now made. He wore neither tunic nor sale and was bare above the waist. Despite his youth, his upper torso was a mass of tight black hair which swirled over his chest and crept over his shoulders, stopping abruptly where it was shaved at the neck. His eyes were black. His cheeks were painted with red crosses. His Norman-cropped curly black hair formed bangs down his forehead.

"My good cousin, King Edward." He smiled like a naughty child.

"You flatter Edward," Robin said.

"I only speak to what is rightfully his."

"And why," Robin asked, "do you keep the devil at your side?"

"Sassy is no devil. Sassy loves me and does my bidding. Don't you, Sassy?"

The figure grunted an assent.

"Is it a man or woman?" Alfred asked.

"Who's to know and who's to care?" Robert laughed. "And who be you?"

"Your cousin, Alfred," Edward told him.

"Well, Alfred, cousin, no matter what Sassy be, it loves me. Sassy is my heart's beauty." Robert went over and kissed the creature hard on its misshapen mouth. "And I love thee as well, Alfred." Robert went over and attempted to kiss him on the mouth. Alfred recoiled in horror at having the same lips near him that had touched the beast. Robert roared, stopped abruptly and turned on Robin. "Why do you stop Edward from coming to me when I have requested? Know you your place, common Priest."

"I come at your mother's command. She would have Edward restore the health of your father. Be that God's will."

"And what has my father ever done for Edward?" He turned to Edward. "Let him die, cousin."

"Robert!" the young monk admonished.

"Let him die. Let another have a turn. You owe him nothing. I shall make thee King of England, Edward, when I am duke."

Robin looked at him. Anger was in the blue eyes. "Your brother Richard will be duke when your father dies, rest his soul."

"NO!" Robert wailed. "No. I shall be duke!"

The creature got down on all fours and with hands pounded the stone pavement. "Duke Robert. D-d-duke Robert. R-Robert D-Duke. Duke," he repeated.

Robert held out an empty hand to Edward. "He has never aided your cause, Edward. Think on it." Robert's voice had returned to normal.

"No, Ned," Robin said.

"Wait but one day and think on it. Ask where was Duke Richard when Cnute stole your throne and your mother."

"And my mother," Edward added pensively.

"Ned." The young priest's eyes pleaded as well as his voice.

"They will come for me and haul me off to his bedside. What am I to do?" he asked Robert.

"I will hide you," Robert said.

"Yes," Edward said, "and Aly as well."

"The duke will die." Robin spoke softly.

"Let him die," Robert said.

The grotesque creature was helped to his feet by Robert.

"Why do you have red crosses painted on your face?" Alfred asked.

"To ward off bad dreams that pursue me."

"I get bad dreams when I eat too much," Alfred told his cousin.

"I eat little," Robert said. "Sassy eats for me."

The figure nodded its grotesque head.

"A less wicked conscience and you would have no such dreams," Robin said.

"Then, Priest, I shall make you my confessor and cleanse my conscience."

"Thank you not," Robin said.

Robert turned. His hair in the back was shaved up to the crown. He motioned for Edward and Alfred to follow. "Stay, Sassy, and see the priest does not follow."

Robin raised the cross, the monster shrank back and then ran on ahead of the three. Edward looked back. Robin stood and then turned and went toward the ducal house. They made their way along the street where the Jews lived and then out into the open, away from the shadows of St. Ouen and into the white heat of the August day.

CHAPTER 5

Rouen, 1026

THE FAINT MALODOR OF DEATH'S CORRUPTION HUNG IN THE AIR, HARBINGER, for the duke was not yet dead. He lay, mammoth, under a swallow of animal skins. Leeches pinned themselves to his cheeks and forehead and one upon the bridge of his nose left red contrasting tracks upon the paleness of his sallow skin. Whispering physicians, with vulturous faces, hovered in long black gowns. The shorter of three turned lard and cracking beetles with some dried powders in a stone bowl and plastered the strong ungent on the duke's neck. They hissed pronouncements. Emma, in the silence and the dim light, explored her brother's blank eyes for some sign of recognition. The room was stifling hot and stank of powerful ungents and the duke's urine. Godfrey came and took her hand. Across the bed, the physicians had stepped back and the large figure of Robert, Archbishop of Rouen, man of decisive action, stood helpless, unable even to determine what to do with his own massive hands, which he nervously rearranged. At the foot of the bed Judith wailed and dug her nails into the torn flesh of her bleeding arms. Her head was bare and her gray hair was oily, dirty and matted to her skull. The windows were boarded, but a thin line of light crept between and cast a streak of pale illumination down on the younger Richard as he stood beside his mother. Emma looked at him. He had an inane expression of pain, not the ache of sorrow, but rather intense discomfort, as if he would be more at home hiding in some closet. He was frail and looked a boy, yet she knew he must be eighteen and they said he had a bastard son. Sitting on the floor near his brother, the second son, Robert, dark and shirtless, toyed with a jeweled knife. He grinned at her and she turned away. There was something evil in him. It was stifling, hot.

Emma let loose of Godfrey's hand and reached beneath the skins and took Richard's swollen hand. She thought his eyes flickered in recognition, but the moment faded. A vulture stepped toward the bed as if to remonstrate, but she glared at him and he slipped back into the darkness.

"Don't touch him." Judith spat out the words.

Emma clutched the hand firmer and made no response.

"Don't you dare touch him," she repeated.

"Hush," the archbishop said.

"It's her son's fault he's dying."

"Harthacnut?" Emma could make no sense of that.

"Edward. Edward's fault." The words came bitter and with rapidity. "He could have saved him."

"Edward?" Emma simply looked at her.

"From MacBoru. He learned from MacBoru. A blind child at Bec saw when Edward touched her."

"Nonsense," Emma said. "He wouldn't cure himself of fits."

"They say he has the gift of healing, Emma." Godfrey's voice was soft.

"Then if he is in Rouen, have him sent for. For God's sake." Emma was impatient with them all.

Judith's second son stood up. Robert was taller and not nearly as slight as his brother Richard. "I can find him," he said.

"You?" Emma asked.

"Edward is my friend. He will come for my sake."

Godfrey turned to Emma. "One thing is certain. It will do no good to force him to come. If he does have the power to heal, we may bring him to the duke's side, but who can make him perform a miracle?"

"He will for me," Robert said.

Emma scrutinized the sincere face of the young man. He did not seem the willful, nasty little boy that he had been, yet there was something evil in his nature. "Go then," Emma said.

The young man stuck the jewel-handled knife into the girdle at his waist and slipped from the room. Judith began the wailing again. It was stifling, hot. They stood. Leeches were rearranged and new red appeared upon the duke's face. A bladder of some animal was brought in and tied above the duke's head with a spray of dried mustard. Judith's wails evolved to soft sobs as if her voice tired of the mechanics of wailing. She scratched. Emma looked at her own aging hands, realizing how much kinder time had been to her than to her sister-in-law. The younger Richard said with urgency, "I've got to pee." And he fled the room.

"The next duke," Emma said with disgust.

"The next duke," the archbishop echoed and shook his head.

The Count of Vixen entered the chamber. "Is he any better?"

The vultures looked disconsolate and in unison nodded in the negative.

"The lady countess? Is she better?" Judith inquired.

"In truth, Madam, she is not ill at all. I have locked her in her chamber. More than all, I did not dare let her loose this day."

"Because I am here?" Emma asked.

"I fear to say, Lady, but she threatened to bring a knife and cut off all your hair and that was the least of her threats. Madam, sometimes I think your daughter—"

"She is no daughter of mine, Sir. I disavowed her years ago. You have undisputed possession of that lady."

"Such a child is conceived in evil," Judith proclaimed.

"At least hatred," Emma answered pensively. "I do not deny it. And how, Sister, were yours conceived?" Emma looked at her. "Did you scratch all the while you copulated, Judith?"

The duchess did not respond, except with wailing.

It was stifling, hot, in the room.

"What will you do now, Emma?" the archbishop asked. "Stay with us in Rouen."

"No. I will go to Roeskild."

"But, Cnute—"

"Will be desolate and penitent over Ulf's death. I know this Dane."

"You are certain"—the archbishop leaned over the dying man with concern for his sister—"you are not going to the falcon's nest?"

"He is a martlet in mourning. I have no doubt."

"You must not go alone, sister," Godfrey advised.

"No. Will you bear me company and courage, Goddy?"

"Hush," Judith said.

"And a small army," Godfrey said, ignoring the duchess.

"Nothing threatening," the archbishop cautioned.

"Just a hint of strength, Robert," Godfrey agreed.

They were interrupted as the body on the bed moved and a rattling in the duke's throat came with each breath. The archbishop turned to one of the hooked-nose physicians, who came forward. The black-gowned figure nodded. "Dreux, fetch young Richard," the archbishop said. "Someone open up the doors. It is the end. Tell Willie it is time to bring in the bastards."

"No," Judith said.

"Yes." The archbishop was firm. "Go, Dreux."

The rattling became worse. Emma leaned over her brother searching for some sign of recognition. There was nothing. The doors were thrown open and in the corridors could be heard the beating of the wooden sticks of death. The rhythm of the paddles was off a beat from the rattling of the dying man. Somewhere in the distant structure of the ducal house the dire chant of a multiple voice of monks began in unison the psalmic ritual.

Harthacnut ran into the room, stumbling on the stone and picking himself up. "I want to see," the pudgy little boy said. "I want to see death."

"Yes," Emma said and took the boy by the hand and led him to the bed. "It stinks in here," he said and leaned over and poked his uncle on the cheek.

The vulture tending from the bishop's side recoiled in horror. "Madam, the boy . . ."

"Don't do that," Emma said and slapped his hand.

The child merely giggled, turned his back on the bed and looked under his arm.

"What are you doing?" Emma asked.

"Seeing what death looks like upside down."

As Emma straightened him up, her other brother, Willie, the Count of Eu, came in with the duke's two bastards. They were tall young men and though not thought to have the same mother looked remarkably alike. Mauger, the younger of the two, had tears in his normally sharp, penetrating eyes. Judith glared as they moved to a corner of the room. William, the older, had a purple birthmark on his neck. The sandy-haired pair had been brought to the court when they were but tots. "These are my bastards," the duke had said and all acknowledged them but Judith. Some rumors had it that their mothers were nuns; the duke never said and the brothers themselves were never told. The secret now would die with the duke.

Godfrey entered, pushing the duke-elect ahead of him into the room.

"Where have you been, boy?" The archbishop frowned.

"He was copulating out in the kitchens with some slut old enough to be his grandmother."

Richard looked down at the floor like a child caught at some knavery.

The voices of the monks drew nearer. The archbishop came around to where Emma stood, and a priest, the duke's chaplain, took his place and began the interminable last rites as the duke's breath rattled, becoming slower and more uneven. The daughters, Alice and Eleanor, came in weeping, accompanied by the ladies of the court. The room was crowded and stifling, hot. Judith's wail became mechanical, continued in an emotionless tone that varied neither in pitch nor tempo. Richard, the next duke, fidgeted and shifted his weight from foot to foot as he made noises with his tongue. Harthacnut chewed a pork rind and kept trying to get up in bed with the dying man. Emma held him in control. Judith suddenly screamed out, demanding Edward save the duke. The beating of wooden death sticks continued in the corridor. The bladder and the mustard weed were cut down and the leeches bottled away as the priest dabbed the duke's forehead with the holy oil. Count Willie came to the foot of the bed and reached down and touched his half brother's foot.

And somewhere in all the commotion and turmoil, Emma found death. The finality of never again hearing Richard's voice struck with weighted force. She was crushed under the pain of the end of life. Heaven and the hereafter seemed remote, unattainable and she knew, was fully aware for but an instant, that there was an end. "*Miserere nobis,*" the monks chanted as they now stood outside the door of the chamber.

Shortly thereafter he died.

The archbishop went over to his nervous nephew and knelt before him. "My liege Lord."

"NO!" Robert screamed out. At what point he had come back into the room, Emma did not know. "I AM THE DUKE!"

"Hush, Robert," the archbishop told him. "Kneel to your brother."

"NEVER! I am Duke."

"You are Count of Hemois. Your brother is eldest and heir."

"No. If you make him Duke, I will kill him. I AM DUKE." He held the knife at his girdle tightly and then yanked it out and pointed it at Richard. "This is for you, Pissy-Rich." His eyes were black and evil.

"Enough, Robert," Godfrey said and pushed the knife downward. It folded in his hand and then the young man let it fall to the stone floor. Richard trembled.

"Where is Edward?" Judith asked as if it might still do some good.

Her son did not respond. "Richard is an idiot," he said, "a frightened hare, and rabbits do not survive the lion." He went over and picked up his father's coronet from the chest.

"Robert . . ." the archbishop yelled at him and he left the room carrying his father's crown.

"Where is Edward? Bring his servant here," Judith ordered.

The cathedral bells began to toll.

"He's got my crown," Richard whined.

"It doesn't make him Duke," the archbishop said. "Stop your crying. You are the Duke of Normandy. Act like it."

The young man moved back with his mother. He wore Norman knee-length breeches and they were still undone at the waist from his escapade in the kitchens.

"When is death coming?" Harthacnut asked.

"Death has been," Emma said and took his pudgy hand.

"It was fun," he said, "but not as much fun as boiling a pig."

"Hush."

"The pig squeals. The duke didn't do much of anything."

Men came bearing basins of water and they began the final washing of the body. Emma turned aside. The beating of the wooden paddles continued. The tolling of the cathedral bells turned to a clamor, announcing a new Duke of Normandy. "My God," Emma spoke aloud, "we all must die."

"When will I die?" Harthacnut asked.

Emma did not answer him. The archbishop placed his arm about her shoulders and led her from the chamber.

And as the cathedral bells rang in joy, in the distance the bells of St. Ouen began their tolling.

CHAPTER 6

Rouen, 1026

A PEACOCK'S SCREECH PIERCED THE DIM MORNING QUIET. EDWARD WALKED through the gray mist; it was damp and clammy against his face. The day would be hot, as the day before had been, and the day before that. Edward wore white: white hose, white slippers, white gonelle. But over it his mantle was blood-red and dragged several feet behind him upon the wet and garbage-stained stones of the narrow Rue St. Amand. He carried a bundle. It looked like rags, but in reality was a coarse-woven peasant's cloak and rolled inside, in a white linen, was the ducal crown.

Out of the light fog the scaffolded cathedral loomed unfinished in his path. He walked along the length toward the front, to the parvis, where his mother had trod upon the burning coals. He remembered and his groin ached. He looked up, away. Gargoyles peered down at him, flashing devilish grins, as if mocking his memory. His mouth tasted of vinegar and oil and sulfur from the paste Godgifu had made for his sore tooth. He had cured near-dead men, but had difficulty managing his own pain. He could stop the fits but little more. He spat the evil taste from his mouth and went into the dark church.

The cathedral was already a noise of activity, a hive of monks swarming at the apse, flitting out into the dark recesses, appearing out of cellular rooms. Long robes swept the floor as sandaled feet slapped from place to place. "This is to be a funeral, idiot," an officious cleric yelled and a pale, pimpled, robed bean pole vanished with an armload of white and gold vestments. A skull on a pole also offended the officious cleric, who seemed in command, and he ordered it removed. A beggar, scratching his genitals with one hand, extended the other to the cleric, who spat into the open, festering palm, ordered someone to see to fresh altar linen and marched into the sacristy. Two chickens wandered, pecking at the stones. A dog nosed toward them, and the hens fluttered brown wings and scurried toward the altar.

Edward, staying in the dark perimeter of the cold building, removed his red mantle. He slipped beneath a rise of wooden scaffolding and carefully unwrapped the crown and rolled it up again, still in linen, this time into the red garment he had been wearing. He put the coarse peasant's cloak on and pulled the hood up over his white hair.

A thin man, a spindle of a man, six feet tall at least, with an elongated face and a pointed yellow beard, came up to Edward and with great mystery asked, "Do you wish to live forever?"

Edward's tooth hurt worse. He simply looked at the man.

"I will sell you, for but a little gold, the secrets of heaven and hell. I am," the man said quite matter-of-factly, "three hundred and forty-seven years old."

Edward sensed something sinister in the creature and pulled back from him. "Go away," Edward whispered.

"Two ducal coins," the man's voice cracked, "and you can live forever."

There was no aura of light about the man. It struck Edward suddenly. There was no aura of light about him at all. "You are dead." Edward spoke with awe.

"Yes," the spindle of a man said and wandered off.

Benches and chairs were brought in and banging and building and wood against stone echoed up into the unfinished ceiling. A fat monk with a sniffling nose draped black cloth anywhere possible: upon gold crucifixes, vases and candle holders, over statues of marbled saints, wooden Madonnas, around paintings of death and resurrection, about the doors, over arches, around windows, on other monks if they happened to stand too still, and even about the neck of the tall thin man who was dead.

Alfred clanged through the big doors and stamped into the church. A snorting pig followed at his heels. The boy brushed his hair back from his face.

"Over here," Edward called in a loud whisper. "Did you find the old healer?"

"Yes. The cure is horrid." Alfred scratched the back of his thigh. "You'd better heal yourself."

"I tried. It does no good. Did you see any sign of Seven?"

"No," Alfred said, "and no one knows anything other than Aunt Judith ordered he be taken out and whipped."

"I'll kill Judith. What did the healer say is to be done?"

Alfred handed him a greasy ball.

Edward made a grimace. "Egggh. What is it?"

"A candy of mutton fat mixed with the seed of sea holly. The old man said you're to put it on your sore tooth, then I am to bring a lighted candle as close to the tooth—"

"You'll set my face on fire."

"I am only telling you what he told me. Burn the candle and hold a basin of water under your chin. The worms in the tooth will escape from the heat of the candle into the water and drown."

"You had better be careful with the candle." Edward looked at his brother with apprehension. "Take one of those from the holder over there. I can rest my chin on the holy-water font." He stuffed the mutton-fat ball into his mouth and gagged on it.

A monk with red hair that stuck straight out from his head and made him look like an insect with red feelers came trotting over to Alfred. "Put that back, boy. Put that back." The monk's voice squeaked.

Alfred, the candlestick in his hand, hesitated.

"Bring it here," Edward ordered.

As Alfred brought the lighted candle toward the font, the feelers on the monk vibrated as he shook his head. "No. No." He attempted to take the candle from the boy.

"Set his hair on fire," Edward said.

Alfred shoved the candle in the direction of the man. He shrank back, looked once at Edward and quietly evaporated into the sea of other monks in the dimly lit expanse.

Edward pushed back his hood and set his chin on the stone rim of the font. "Be careful," he cautioned as Alfred brought the fire near his cheek and held it there. Edward let the fat mix with his saliva and drip from his mouth into the holy water.

"Better?" Alfred asked.

"No," Edward said and spat the remaining fat into the water. It floated in globules.

The thin man who claimed to be three hundred and forty-seven came up to the font. "I am death," he said and stuck his hands in and retrieved the mutton-fat ball, which he ate. He smelled of urine and Alfred and Edward moved away from him.

It began. In the distance, the faint sounds of the clapping boards could be heard.

"They come," Edward said. "It is time." Edward motioned for his brother to pull his hood up over his head and he did the same. The clapping sound grew louder as it neared. Edward led the way out of the dark cathedral. The parvis was crowded. He squinted from the bright August day. "Over there," he said and Alfred followed as Edward walked beneath the scaffolding and stopped near the corner of the building. He stuffed the red bundle under his brown mantle.

The clapping boards grew louder and Edward could tell they turned up the Grand Rue away from the Seine. Soon they were visible and the crowd let out a roar as hundreds of men in black gowns slapped thin pieces of flat wood against one another in a rhythmic death toll. They formed a wall about the parvis, enclosing the crowd. As they moved into position an army of monks, seemingly thousands, marched, chanting a dull, even toneless, *Kyrie*. The great cathedral doors were thrown open and the monks sifted into the dark. Behind them a priest in an enormous black cope bore a gold monstrance, raised high to display the Eucharist to the crowd. A cheer went up for the Eucharist. Four strong young men carried the weighty train of the priest's long cope. Edward watched in awe as the priest moved with such grace across the parvis. Mounted riders, helmeted, and bearing raised swords, followed. The crowd in the parvis applauded and some put their children upon their shoulders so they could see the riderless horse of the duke being led into the church. Ranks of vestmented priests, some bearing burning incense, others holy water and one the great book, walked carefully behind, stepping, here and there, to avoid the horse droppings. A loud roar went up and from around the corner the archbishop, raised high in a chair, was visible as he blessed the throng. Bearing his Uncle Robert in the chair, Edward could see among the young men chosen for the honor, were his cousins, the archbishop's three sons. Edward put down his head as his Uncle Robert was carried near the entrance to the cathedral. The slapping boards continued and then the crowd began to laugh as the mummers wound across the parvis, taunting the skeletal figure of death, which lashed out at them with bony arms.

The crowd became quiet. Under a large canopy the body of the duke, dressed in magnificent splendor, jeweled and ermine-robed, was carried slowly through the parvis. There was no wind stirring and the black ribbons on the canopy hung flat and still. He wore no crown. Yet, for all the splendor, many of the crowd turned their heads away, for already he reeked of death, and as he approached the great doors Edward could smell the disgusting stench.

Behind came the mourners. Edward pulled his hood more about his face. First the new duke, young and frightened, pale in black robes. His mother walked beside him and scratched. Robert followed, arrogant and wearing a magnificent black tunic weighted with a breast piece of red stones set in a gold filigree. He looked toward Edward, who was almost hidden in the cloak, and touched his hand to the hilt of his sword. Edward nodded to assure him all they had planned was ready. Following Robert came the daughters and the bastard sons.

"Where is she?" Alfred whispered.

"There. Just behind Mauger." Edward pointed a finger toward their mother.

"You're certain?"

"Of course I am certain. Don't you remember her at all?"

"She's so old," Alfred said. "And kind of fat."

"She is not. She is beautiful."

Emma, holding the hand of the fat boy in an ill-fitting black tunic, walked between her half brothers, Godfrey and Willie. Beside Godfrey was a striking young man, his son, Gilbert of Brionne.

"I've never seen so many kin at once," Alfred said.

"There's more."

Edward was right. The houses of Brittany, Flanders, Eu, Godgifu and Dreux of Vixen, Mortain, Evreux, Ponthieu, the fearful Montgomeries, and Edward no longer knew who was related and who was not.

"Who was the fat boy with her?"

"It had to be Harthacnut."

"He looked like he was lost, poor waif," Alfred said.

"He ought to be killed. Perhaps I will have you do that," Edward said.

"I won't," Alfred told him.

There were foreign emissaries, and more bishops, envoys and their ladies and sons and daughters, mostly in heavy black and sweating in all the heat and their smell mingled with the smell of the corpse and the smell of the crowd and of the board bangers dressed in black, who continued to pound in a monotonous toll and the mummers still danced about and the crowd would wait until the duke was laid in the crypt and ducal coins would be distributed to the lucky among them and they would jockey for position as the almoners came with bags of gold and they would go home and wait for another holiday.

Edward pushed a monk aside and he and Alfred shoved a path back into the darkness of the building away from the clapping boards and into the din of chanting monks and the smell of the rotting Duke of Normandy.

"I never knew anybody dead to smell so bad," Alfred said.

"It's the heat," Edward whispered.

The corpse was positioned so the light from the big window illuminated him and the jewels about his neck and the many rings on his dead fingers glistened. The ducal family, Emma among them, sat stiffly on chairs to one side of the body. On the other the archbishop was enthroned, his robes covering the arms of the golden chair. The celebrant, still wearing the heavy long black cope, extended his hands out over the duke and the blessing he sang was in a startling soprano voice.

Edward slipped back into an alcove. Everyone seemed to be watching the celebrant and not to notice as he tossed aside the coarse brown cloak and put on his own magnificent scarlet mantle. The monks began the *Dies Ira*. The ducal crown remained wrapped in the white napkin. Holding it, extended before him like an offering, Edward pushed through the crowd. "Out of my way," he ordered. The red robe trailed behind; the mummers became silent as he moved forward. The focus now was on Edward.

"You!" Emma cried as she caught sight of him. "YOU!"

The chanting monks stopped their hymn, unevenly trailing into stillness. The celebrant brought his hands back to his breast and stood silent. The archbishop rose. "What is the meaning of this, Edward?"

Judith extended a finger toward him. "Monster! Devil! You are responsible for his death. You are vile."

Robert, the jewels on his tunic glittering, stood up. With deliberation he took out his sword, watching Edward as he did. Edward stopped, his arms still extended, holding the covered crown. Robert walked toward him.

"No," the archbishop said, "this is not the place for this. No, Robert."

Robert continued toward Edward. The crowd was expecting to see blood, the blood of the white-skinned Saxon. Robert obviously surprised them when he stopped in front of Edward, laid his sword at his cousin's feet and then knelt down in front of him.

Edward roared, his voice echoing in the vaulting above, "I, Edward, son of Ethelred, rightful King of Wessex, King of England, acknowledge you, Robert, son of Richard, to be Duke of Normandy and no other." He threw off the napkin and set the ducal crown down over Robert's black hair.

"Ahhhhhhh." Richard let out a piercing wail and fell upon the stone. It was Emma who moved. As Robert turned, the crown upon his head, and faced the crowd, Emma pushed by him and with her open palm swung hard and struck Edward across the face. He reeled.

The pain of human touch, his tooth, the terrible rebuke of his beloved mother! Tears blurred his vision. The fit, he must ward off the fit. He fought the tears and he fought the seizure which wanted to engulf him. He saw but not clearly. Godgifu appeared from somewhere. She had a knife, he saw the knife. Godgifu lunged. Edward shoved Emma but not quite soon enough and the knife tore into the fabric of her sleeve and red flesh and blood were visible in the tear. He was not even certain why he had stopped Godgifu from killing her. Some soldiers grabbed the screaming Godgifu. Judith was yelling. Robert fled still wearing his brother's crown. There was more yelling. Young Richard cowered on the floor. The archbishop called in vain for order. Godgifu was dragged, screaming obscenities, out of the dark structure. The boy Harthacnut—Edward looked over at him, the child appeared to be laughing. Edward could not take his eyes from this fat half brother. Then the child began clapping. Godfrey went over to Emma. The archbishop was still calling for some semblance of order. Edward turned from Harthacnut and walked through the crowd. He saw Dreux sneak away. Godfrey helped Emma to a chair. When he was clear of the throng, Edward marched defiantly out the big doors.

Outside, the crowd still milled, the mummers wound about in a dance and the board bangers continued their toll. Edward saw Godgifu fighting with her two captors. He went up and drew his sword. They let her fall as they drew their own weapons. He tossed his knife to his sister. As the two men came at him, Godgifu stabbed first one and then the other in the back of the neck. Alfred came wandering out of the cathedral as if it were an ordinary day. "Let's run," Edward told Godgifu. "For God's sake, Aly, come on."

The three started away but were encircled by the mummers, who danced and laughed about them and drew them back toward the soldiers who were being drowned in their own blood. The figure of death hunched over the two men. Alfred was the first to break through the circle. Godgifu and Edward followed. They raced through the narrow streets. Behind them Edward could still hear the sounds of the banging boards.

He led them to the rubble of the old church of St. Gervais and disappeared down some steps into an ancient Roman crypt. The pair followed. It was dark going down the moss-covered broken steps, but once down inside, a shaft of light came down from where the floor in the ruined church above had given way.

"What is this place?" Godgifu asked.

"I found it when I was little. Uncle Robert says St. Victrice may be buried down here."

"It's cold and I don't like it," Alfred said.

"It's safe. I want you to go to St. Ouen and get Robin. Be careful you are not followed."

"And bring some food and wine," Godgifu added.

Alfred disappeared up the stairs.

A stone bench ran about all sides of the room. Edward sat down.

"You should have let me kill her," Godgifu said and traced with her finger crosses which were carved in the stone altar.

"Perhaps you're right," Edward said. "I really don't know what made me stop you. I always defend her, say she's beautiful. She's not; she's a monster. And that fat little beast . . ."

Godgifu went over in the corner and threw up.

"What's wrong?" Edward asked.

"I'm going to have a baby," she answered, wiping her mouth on her sleeve.

"I don't know how you can do it," he said.

"Do what?"

"You know what."

"I do it so you can wear scarlet silk and so Alfred can stuff his always empty gut and so that we all three have a place to sleep. You think I like the feel of Drogo, drunk, crawling on top of me."

"I'm sorry." It was hard for Edward to think of Godgifu being a mother. She wasn't built like a mother, more like a soldier, with her wide shoulders and her heavy arms. "What are you going to call him?"

"Call who?"

"The baby."

"God, how should I know? I simply hope I have him and get it done with, that's all. He'll probably be a horrid little thing and look like Drogo, a short, ugly little Drogo."

"Call him Ralph," Edward said.

"What if it's a girl?"

"It won't be."

They were quiet for a time. Light came through a small window near the ceiling.

"Who was St. Mellon?" she asked.

"Why?"

"He's buried here."

"Really?" He came over and read the stone.

"And over here," she said, "is the tomb of someone called St. Avitien."

"My God," he said and then he looked at her strangely. "When did you learn to read?"

"While you've been hawking. Secretly. I don't want anyone to know. I thought it might prove useful. Knowing what's in a letter, that sort of thing. That little priest from St. Clair-sur-Epte, the one with yellow hair, taught me."

They went about the small crypt reading the names on the tombs.

"Someone is coming," Edward said and they stopped talking.

Alfred came down the steps first carrying food. Robin, his blue eyes trying to adjust to the light, followed with a wineskin.

"I never knew this place was here," the young monk said.

"It is the tomb of saints," Edward said and winked at Godgifu.

"It stinks like vomit," Alfred said.

"You were followed," Edward said.

"I was careful," his brother told him.

"Smell," Edward ordered.

"What is it?" Godgifu asked.

"Sassy. That stink is Sassy. Cousin Robert followed the two of you. He and Sassy are about."

Robert appeared at the bottom of the steps with his sword drawn. "I've got you all. You're my prisoners."

"I knew you were there," Edward told him.

Robert put away his sword. Sassy came into the room, hunching behind him. "What are you doing here with the dead?"

"I think we are not too welcome in Rouen," Edward said.

"We will have to go back to Tosny," Godgifu said.

"I don't think you can go there either. They'll butcher the Count of Vixen with the rest of you, if they can find any of you."

"Poor Drogo," Edward said. "We do get him in trouble."

"Poor old Drogo," Alfred mocked.

"A fart on Drogo," Godgifu said. "I hope they do find him and butcher him."

"No," Edward said, "I might be in need of some new clothes."

Robert looked about the tomb. "Unless you want to live down here with the dead, I think I had better take you all off to Hermois. At Falaise we can make plans to make me Duke."

"What?" Robin asked.

"And when I am Duke, young Priest, who likes young boys, I shall give you St. Ouen. You can be prior there and sodomize with a feast of little monks."

"I want neither to be prior nor any part of you, Robert."

"I shall make you my confessor, Robin."

"No."

"Oh, yes. When I am Duke you will have to do as I say. I shall save up all my sins. I—"

He was interrupted by sounds on the steps. Both Robert and Edward drew their weapons. All eyes were on the steps.

Sassy stood, his crooked arm aloft, as if ready to strike.

"Hello."

It was the fat boy Harthacnut.

"Kill him," Edward said.

"No," Robin said.

Harthacnut looked at Edward. "You are my brother. And you, too." He turned to Alfred.

"Kill him," Godgifu said. "He's the whore's child."

Harthacnut noticed Sassy, who had slipped back into the shadows, for the first time. "A monster. I like monsters best of all, and eating. I like to eat and throw up. I like to throw stones, too, from the parapet, down on chickens and babies, and I like to pee from the parapet—"

Robert interrupted him. "My confessor priest should be obeyed."

"Why?" Godgifu asked.

"The boy will be useful. Would you like to be King of the Danes, boy?"

"I was King of the Danes once," Harthacnut said.

"So you were," Robert agreed. "So you were."

The air was dank in the crowded room. It smelled of vomit and the sound of a rat gnawing could be heard.

"I know where Seven went," Harthacnut said.

"You know what?" Edward asked.

"I know where Seven went."

"What do you know, you fat little—" Edward grabbed ahold of Harthacnut.

He shook free. "Aunt Judith's man, Groggh, sold him to a miller from Bec."

"How do you know?" Edward scoffed.

"I was hiding in the flour when they hauled him off. They beat him and he didn't even cry and they hauled him off—"

"I don't believe you," Edward said.

"I do," Alfred told him.

"Harthacnut will be King of the Danes," Robert said, "and I shall be his heir as well as yours, Edward."

"Why his?" Alfred asked.

"He's as much my cousin as you and Edward are."

Alfred turned the fat boy around. "He really is my brother?"

"Yes," Robert said.

"Half," Edward said, "half brother. His father is a butcher."

"We had best make ready for Falaise. I'll find Dreux and arrange for the horses. We will meet at the Roman Gate after sundown." Robert rubbed the hilt of his sword.

"And him?" Edward pointed to Harthacnut. "What do we do with him?"

"Take him with us, of course," Robert said.

CHAPTER 7

Roeskild, 1026

EMMA AWOKE. SHE WAS ANGRY. THE SEA POUNDED IN THE DISTANCE. THERE was a feel and smell of wetness, mold. Aesval was a shapeless lump upon a pile of straw in the corner. She snored unevenly. Emma got up and, throwing off the light piece of fabric which had covered her, walked across the dirt floor. It was moist against her feet. Aesval stirred. The sea hammered. A discordant matins came from a nearby tree, sounding as if it were just outside the chamber door as angry birds scolded and chattered and screeched. Emma put on a pale green gown of soft material. Aesval opened her eyes; Emma motioned her to go back to sleep. Still barefoot, Emma went outside. The quarreling birds struggled in the tree for dominance, for power. It was a dull wet morning without a sun. She looked to the tree. Some bird, an outsider perhaps, had upset the order. By day's end there would be a new master in that tree, no doubt. A certainty was that it would be no female. Her feet, soaked by wet morning grass, moved in quick steps, long steps, toward the sea. Her gown dragged, becoming soaked at the hem and turning dark green, nearly black. The sound of the birds diminished until she could no longer hear the struggle, but the sea pounded, beating against rock, thrashing and angry, loud and unruly. No man could contain the sea, and in this Emma took comfort.

She had had little other comfort since they had arrived late the previous night. Cnute would not see her, last night, nor ever, she was told by a

Dane, whose dialect she could barely understand. She had asked for Godwin, to be told he "was abed." She had traveled this distance, watched her brother, the duke, die, because her son had refused to save him, been nearly stabbed to death by the vile Godgifu, had to steal Harthacnut back from that devil Robert at Falaise, endured a drenching storm before they reached Bruges, had been attacked by wandering dwarfs in the lowlands, had to ward off the amorous attentions of an Ambrosian friar, only to arrive at Roeskild to be ignored. She was angry. She demanded attention on their arrival, but was shunned by little men, of little power, who would pay for their insolence. The sky, like the sea, was angry. Gray clouds twisted above her.

A figure stood alone, black against the sky, where the land dropped to the sea. Even from afar, the stance, the determined, proud, overbearing manner in which his head was tilted back, told her it was Godwin. She moved angrily toward him.

"Emma," he said as she neared, as if surprised to see her.

He would have been informed of her arrival. She did not smile or make any attempt to be pleasant. "You keep me from my Lord Husband, King."

"No, Emma."

"I was told he would not see me. Who but you would be responsible?"

"He keeps himself prisoner in a dark chamber. His feet are chained together, his arms shackled as well. He speaks little to anyone, calling only for Estrid."

"This is nonsense."

"Yes, Emma, I agree. Ulf was as his brother. But he is the King of England and Daneland. It is nonsense."

"And Estrid?"

"The greater fool. It seems a family affliction. She hides behind the altar in the church. She has been there since the moment her brother killed her husband. 'Ulf' is all she will utter. She stays in the dark and refuses to come out. Food is brought in and she hunches in a place no bigger than her body, like some animal, and she stinks of her own excrement and urine."

"And her children. Who tends her boys?"

"She had them sent to her brother in Sweden before Cnute killed Ulf. I have sent for them in hopes it will bring Estrid out." He looked out to the sea. "I certainly didn't, but I think she knew that Cnute was going to kill Ulf."

"You wanted it."

He turned and looked directly at her. "No."

A seabird circled the sky.

"You wanted him dead."

"No," he said, but there was little certainty in his voice and he turned again to the sea. "And my wife? How is Gytha?"

"Angry. With child and angry."

"You used her anger to get away. You used her."

"Yes." Emma saw no point in denying it. "My brother is dead."

"We were told."

"Normandy is in a turmoil. The boy Richard is too weak. What is to become of Normandy now?"

"What is to become of England . . . or the Daneland? The King sits chained in a cell. I manage the affairs of government, but I have no power."

"You have power, Godwin. I am the one without power."

"But you are a woman." He turned and again looked straight at her. She saw the lines about his neck that had not been there before. He was aging, as well. "It is the law of nature."

"No. It is the law of men. God has given me no less lust for power than say that hideous offspring of my brother, Robert. The boy will yet kill to be Normandy. My failing is that I can understand him. He can't help himself, no more than I."

Godwin didn't respond for a moment. When he spoke, he spoke slowly. "Power, what power did you expect to gain with a revolt in the Daneland? You gained nothing."

"I gained."

"It was futile. A foolish gesture. Did you think Cnute a fool?"

"He is a fool. A man swayed by your machinations—"

"No, Emma. My schemes are always the reflection of Cnute's own mind. I know this King and I use only that. I never place myself beyond his power."

"And you think a man not a fool who can be used by the whore, that dark bitch Elgiva?"

"She is done. Elgiva is long this time not welcome to his bed. It will make you happy to learn she has become old and nagging and tired and ugly. She stinks and her teeth rot in her mouth and she has no hold upon your husband."

It had begun to mist. Emma wiped the wetness from her face.

"Come," he said, "we must go back now for it's going to storm."

They walked together back toward the compound. "I would have helped you, Emma. I would do nothing to betray the King, but I would have helped you."

"And now?"

The rain fell heavier.

"I can't trust you, Emma. I can understand your need, but you lack prudence. Build the power for your children. All the hereafter we have in life is the life of our children." He moved more quickly.

"And of heaven and hell?" Her hair was getting soaked and the water dripped down her neck.

"Sometimes I am not so certain—"

The sky opened up and they ran back in the direction of the buildings. Lightning pierced the clouds and the turbulent sea clashed against the land. They reached shelter as a deafening clap of thunder came like a warning from an angry god.

The rain came heavier through the morning. Emma sat with Aesval and sewed impatiently.

A ship was wrecked, broken against the rocks. Men were helped to the compound. They were of Jomburg and sat about the fire in the great hall. Two of their boats were missing and though Roeskild men braved the storm and searched the coast, the two were not found. The Jomburg men told of an eagle which had been seen the day before. An eagle seen so far from land was an omen of evil. Emma listened to them curse the sea and the eagle, barely able to discern their words, to understand the dialect.

Harthacnut sat on the floor assembling the bones of a fish into the shape of a fish. He was too old for such games. "Get up," she told him, "and throw those bones into the fire."

"I am hungry," he said.

"You just ate."

"The Duke of Normandy said I could eat all I wanted when I am King of Daneland."

"The Duke of Normandy?"

"Robert. He is my cousin."

"Robert is not Duke of Normandy."

"Yes he is, and Edward is King of England."

Emma slapped him across the shoulders, nearly knocking him over. He began to whine. "Your father is King of England and you thereafter."

He stood up, wiped tears from his eyes and glared at her. "And when I am King I will cut off your tits and eat whatever I want." He ran from the room and out into the rain.

"Harthacnut," she called, but he had vanished.

She sent a serving man to find him and take him to his chamber. Damn child! For three days they had combed Rouen looking for him. "He probably fell into the Seine," Judith suggested. "Eaten by a warlock," young Richard announced. "Fallen into a well." "Taken to hell by the Devil."

Emma stared into the fire. A pig came up and snorted at her feet and she kicked it away. She watched the twisted shapes of the flame. Aesval had gotten ill; it was probably no wonder; the fish at high meal had tasted rotten. She hoped the woman would be all right. She must look in on her after a bit.

"We want Cnute!" one of the Jomburg warriors called out and the chant was picked up by others. "The King! Give us the King." The sound of drinking horns banging against the table set up a rhythm. "The King! The King! Cnute! Cnute!"

"Quiet!" Godwin appeared from somewhere. Godfrey was beside him. "Quiet. The King is a man of the Christian God and he is in prayer, atoning for his sins. You are heathens to yell so."

"God have mercy on our souls," one of them said, but others grumbled and complained under their breaths.

Godwin, Godfrey walking with him, came over to Emma. He spoke softly. "This is the great empire of the North. My God, he wants Norway. If he doesn't come to his senses soon, he won't have the Daneland ... and worse, England cannot endure without its leader."

"There is Harthacnut." Emma smiled.

"Careful, Emma, the Witangemot will choose Edward before they will accept another boy King."

Edward was like a disease that had no cure. He plagued her, always there like some open sore, some ugly growth. And like some rotten festering growth, he should be cut away. "Edward should be killed."

Godfrey spoke. "Emma don't talk foolish. I'll say this, Godwin, the envoys at the ducal court conveyed words of anger among the crowns of Europe toward Cnute."

"And what business is it of theirs?" Yet Godwin's voice revealed the importance he placed on the opinion of Europe's rulers.

"Cnute attacked the man who Christianized Norway. Olaf is a Christian brother to these kings."

Godwin's hands turned in a gesture to indicate the hopelessness of the situation.

"If he would attend the coronation of the Holy Roman Emperor," Godfrey suggested.

"I agree the friendship of Conrad would be valuable for both himself and England."

Emma put her finger over the edge of her lips. "And a marriage between the Emperor's son Henry and our own Gunnerhild would form a solid alliance."

"Do you never give up, Emma?" Godwin asked.

"No." She thought for a moment. "Apparently you do."

"All right," Godwin said, "you get the King out of that Godforsaken chamber."

"The coronation will be in Rome, am I right?"

"Yes, Emma," Godwin said.

"You said Cnute called for Estrid."

"Yes, and she's not about to be brought from behind the altar."

"The only thing in the world that will get that woman out from hiding will be one of her children. You said they were sent for."

"Yes," Godwin answered. "But once Cnute is made to come out, how do we get him to Rome?"

"Penance. We buy a priest to convince him that he must visit the chains of St. Peter or some other shrine in Rome."

One of the Jomburg warriors came teetering over toward them. He nearly fell in the fire, and went off into a corner.

"You can bribe nearly any priest in Roeskild," Godwin said.

The sun shone. It was humid and the sea had become drowsy and still. It barely persisted in small waves against the land below the cliff. A bee plagued Emma as she walked in the direction of a stone church. It was dark inside and stank of human excrement. The smell became worse as she moved near the altar.

"Estrid," she called. God, the stink! "Estrid." Emma walked toward the back of the altar. There was an alcove there. Emma turned her face away. Flies buzzed all about the opening in the wall and above the altar.

"It is no use, Lady."

She turned in the dim light to face a priest, a wrinkled little man with a burn scar on his forehead.

"It is no use, Lady Queen. She won't speak."

The priest was bribed easily with the thought of getting rid of the stench from his church and the price of two gold candlesticks, which Emma generously offered. Cnute would be required to go to Rome and prostrate himself before the chains of Peter.

Days passed. The sea remained dull. Emma peered through cracks in the chamber wall, spying upon Cnute, who sat there, his beard unruly, his hair mussed, his skin becoming sallow from the lack of sunlight. A servant washed him and he ate. Yet each time she peeked in, he sat there unoccupied, staring blankly across the dim room. In the center of the room on the floor lay the knife he had used to kill Ulf.

The ship came. They took Estrid's youngest child, Beorn, round-faced, wide-eyed, into the stench of the church. Estrid came out almost at once, but she was filthy and they would not let her touch the child until she had been cleaned up. She was scoured. She cried and spoke and then took the child and rocked him and pressed him against her breast.

"I won't go to him." Estrid had trouble seeing, getting used to the light.

"Then we shall take the child out and have its arms cut off," Emma told her.

The lice were picked from Estrid and her hair combed with a walrus-tusk comb and she went with the wrinkled priest to the chamber where Cnute had chained himself. Two hours went by and Emma waited, not patiently, with Godwin and Godfrey. Finally Estrid emerged, followed by her brother and the priest. Cnute's arms were bleeding from the shackles and chains, which had been removed before they came out. He cried and Estrid cried and Emma smiled and Godwin smiled.

"Would you have really cut off Beorn's arms?" Estrid asked later.

"No," Emma said and wondered if it were a lie.

Cnute gave Estrid a small cask made by the çooper of Winchester and it was filled with gold coins. Cnute spoke with Emma. He was friendly and did not mention anything of the trouble she had caused in Roeskild, but he did not come to her bed. Cnute gave Estrid an iron box filled with sea pearls and though he sat between Estrid and the Queen at the table in the great hall, he did not come to Emma's bed. Cnute talked of his plans to go to Rome for the coronation of King Conrad. He gave Estrid a small casket set with gems and filled with more gold coins. He did not go to Emma's bed. He gave Estrid a little cabinet filled with precious stones, some loose, some set in brooches and neckpieces. Emma sat beside him as he received the Danish lords and envoys to the court, but he came not to her bed. The priest, though the church had been scrubbed by fourteen nuns, still complained bitterly that the smell would not go away. Cnute said they would return to Winchester soon and gave Estrid two cloth sacks of gold coins. He took Harthacnut by the hand and walked along the cliff with him and talked to him of the sea. He did not come to Emma's bed. The stone church burned down and Estrid gave the priest money to build another and Cnute gave Estrid the amount in return.

"Come to my bed, my Lord," Emma finally begged him.

"No, Lady. I find you repulsive. Queen you are, but my wife no more."

"No. I will yet have another son for you."

"Not by me, Lady. For though this hand killed my brother, Ulf, it was you who stirred him to his treason. If not for you, he would be alive."

"My Lord, this—"

"No! I will say no more on it. Never raise the question again or I shall have your womb burned with hot irons."

CHAPTER 8

Falaise, 1026

EDWARD, IN BLACK MANTLE, BLACK TUNIC OVER A BLACK GONELLE, SAT the white horse, a black hawk resting on the back of his extended white hand.

"What you lack, Robert, is a sense of regality."

"How so?" the virile young man asked.

Sassy ran behind them picking up horse turds along the trail and throwing them at serfs bent over in the fields.

"You wear no tunic. A king suffers the heat."

"When I am Duke I will suffer the heat. Until then I will be comfortable." He rubbed the black hairs of his bare chest, beaded with sweat.

They were a contrast as they bobbed along the road on their mounts, the olive-skinned, black-haired young man and the white-haired young man in the heavy black clothing.

It was a hot September day. The sun made prisms in the sky and upon the water in the ditch. There was no wind and the stench of the tanners' hides burned the air as the riders approached. Beneath the flap of skins, hung to keep out the sun, a middle-aged man was yelling. Young men were cleaning skins and girls boiling them in pots and two older women tended the fires.

Robert drew his horse to a halt and Edward stopped beside him; the horses pranced, impatient to move on, as the pair watched. One of the girls pointed at Sassy and another held her nose. Sassy dropped the horse turds and jumped into the ditch and splashed water about. A third young woman leered at the pair of riders and pulled the front of her garment down and exposed a breast to them, pinching the nipple and laughing. One of the middle-aged women tending the fire whacked her across the butt with a wet skin. The girl yelped.

"You can have her," Robert said.

"Who?"

"The girl with the tit," he told Edward.

"I don't want her—or any woman."

"Then one of the boys perhaps. Would you like to mount the tight hole of one of those boys?"

Edward turned his horse away. "You are being disgusting, Robert."

Edward looked back over his shoulder to see if his cousin was following. Robert was smiling at the girl. Edward stuck his heels into the horse and it bolted forward. He heard Robert come up behind him shortly.

"You will never marry?" Robert asked.

"I told you I would not," Edward said without turning about.

"I just wanted to be certain."

"You can be certain."

"That's why I asked you that," Robert told him. "I wanted to be certain. I will be your heir."

"Yes."

"And should I die?"

"Your son."

They rode along together. Sassy tried to keep up, often falling behind, limping after them, jumping in and out of the ditch.

"You'll have to see that I am made King, first," Edward said.

"I shall see to it. And Harthacnut shall be King of Daneland."

There was no response.

"Edward?"

"I suppose, Robert, but rightfully it is mine as well."

"You said you didn't want it."

"I guess I don't."

A bird flew from a branch. Without stopping his white mare, Edward let loose his hawk to have the bird.

"That bird is nothing," Robert said.

"It bleeds as well as the next," Edward told him.

And so they spent the day as if there were not a care in the world, yet Normandy was in chaos. Richard could keep no order. His uncles tried, but the counts were not to be controlled. Bishops and viscounts and clerics and counts were in rebellion and warred against the young duke and each other. Highwaymen and knights were a terror on the open roads. The King of France threatened; the King of England threatened;

Flanders threatened; Brittany threatened; and wise men kept to their keeps.

Edward and Robert left the kill, some not fully dead, tossed upon the grass. The serfs would come and take away the hares and birds for their pots. There was blood on Edward's fingers and he examined it as they rode back in the direction of Falaise. The sun slipped behind the keep, a single tower on the horizon. The sky glowed orange and Falaise became but a dark shadow. It was still humid and warm and the flies bit at the horses' hinds. Sassy made strange noises and kicked the dirt along the road, occasionally throwing a rock into the ditch with his good arm and then yelling as the water splashed up.

She was there wading in the ditch a mile or so up the road from where she had exposed her tit to them in the morning. She looked up at them and gave them that same leering expression.

"Goddamn!" Robert swore. "I think I know how to end the day."

Edward turned his horse away, but Robert stopped.

"Will you come lay with me, girl?" Robert asked her.

She turned her back toward him, raised her skirt over her head and exposed her bare butt to him. Edward stared at the hair between her legs and then turned away.

"Come along, Robert," he said.

"Will you lay with me, girl?" Robert repeated.

"No," she said.

"I am the duke's son."

"I don't care if you are the duchess's spittle. I'll have naught of you."

"Whore!" Robert yelled and reached out to grab her.

She darted from him, leaping out of the ditch; she ran in toward the field. She was laughing and calling him "Black Chest."

Robert turned his horse about and leaped over the ditch.

"Robert," Edward yelled after him, "leave her be."

The girl stood for a moment laughing, looked toward the rider and ran. Robert, his horse nearly stumbling, caught up with her, swooped his arms down and picked her up. She shrieked and yelled and Robert pulled her more firmly upon the horse. He turned back toward the road. She lay across the horse in front of him, her legs dangling and kicking out. He held her at the waist.

"Let her go, Robert," Edward yelled, but his cousin galloped by, the girl kicking and yelling out. Robert raced forward, and Edward, his horse now at a gallop as well, moved to catch up. Sassy was back somewhere near where the girl had been wading. They rode by the tanners' now cold kettles and Robert waved to them, displaying their daughter's rear as he raised up her skirt. One of the girls shrieked out and clapped. The father swore at Robert. As they neared Falaise the vesper chants of monks sifted out across the darkening orange sky.

"What is it?" Albert asked as Robert abruptly dismounted and pushed the laughing, yelling girl ahead of him into the tower.

"Nothing," Edward said. "Nothing."

Edward sat on the parapet. The sun fell and soft night with scattered stars stretched across the sky. The crescent of an early evening moon gave little light. He did not want to listen to them, but he could not help but hear.

"I am a virgin and you shall not have me," the girl defied him. "I'll bite and scream and yell and bite off your penis."

"I want you," Robert said. "I want you more than the sun."

"The sun is set."

"The moon."

"You are a fool." She laughed. "A funny fool—but I will not give in to you."

It had gone on for nearly an hour now. They argued. Robert was a boar, panting and persuading, but she was like a doe and Edward thought of her not coarsely, not as the girl with the tit pushed toward them, but soft and saintly, as her obstinacy made her seem now. Not looking at her, hearing only her voice, she seemed to him a poor virgin, holy and pure. Edward knelt and prayed for the girl.

"I can stand no more," Robert said finally, but he laughed. "What do you want?"

"Too much."

"What is too much?"

"For my family. My father—"

"He's but a tanner."

"He reads."

"I do not read," Robert said. "What does a tanner have to read for?"

"So he will not always be a tanner. Centuries past, my family was said to have served Charlemagne."

"Who is Charlemagne?" Robert cawed with a diabolical laugh.

"Do not make fun of the great Charlemagne."

"What do I care for Frenchmen? I am descended from Rollo."

"A butcher."

"Better than a tanner."

They were silent then.

"What do you want?" Robert asked after a moment.

"That you will do something for my family, my father, my brothers—"

"What? No aunts and uncles?"

"Will you?" she asked.

"And you will lay with me if I do?"

"Yes."

Edward wanted to cry out "NO!" but he remained silent.

"But how do I know that you will keep your word?" she asked.

"Edward," Robert called out, "are you there on the parapet? Do you hear?"

"I am here," he said softly. "I hear."

"Tell her I will keep my word," Robert said. "You can rely on Edward. He is going to be a saint. He is a virgin, himself. Aren't you, Edward? Tell her I will keep my word."

"He will keep his word," Edward said.

"And he will make me, be certain," Robert told her.

"And what will you do for them, my family?"

"Knighthood for your father. Land. A horse. Is that enough?"

"Yes," she said. "Yet, I would not do it just for that. I have seen you often. I want you, Robert of Hermois, as much as you want me."

"Why, you little whore," Robert yelled.

They laughed and panted and gasped and grunted and breathed heavily within the room. All of which Edward heard. His back to the wall, he stretched his legs out to the parapet, against the stone, and listened and wanted not to. And then there came silence and he touched his fingers together and tears formed in his eyes.

The moon gave off so little light. He sat there on the stone floor in the dark and cried.

"I should be the one crying." She stood above him. There was a breeze and her gown drifted lightly in the wind.

"Robert?"

"He's asleep."

They were silent. She stood there. He remained stretched out on the stone.

"Are you crying for me?" she asked.

"Yes."

"Thank you. I can't cry for myself. I never cry."

He looked up at her. The white gown was thin and he could see her breasts moving as she breathed. Her eyes, so blue in the sunlight, were not visible now. The aura about her glowed softly.

"Why did you do it?" he asked.

"I could say it was for my family, and it was that, too. But I have seen Robert since he was a mere boy come here to Falaise and I told my sisters I would have him. They laughed and called me foolish. I knew when you passed by early today you would be back on the same road. I waited hours by the ditch. What were you doing so long?"

"Hawking."

"After he touched me, I knew I would be his."

"I don't understand," Edward told her.

"Have you never wanted to touch, to love, to own, to belong, to—"

"No . . . no." He began crying again.

"Your name is Edward," she said. "He called you that. And I am Herleve, daughter of Fulbert."

"Herleve is a pretty name," Edward said, not knowing what else to say.

"Robert is a pretty name. Robert, son of Normandy."

"The duke is dead," Edward told her and looked into the sky.

"I know the stars. I read them. My grandmother knew of the stars."

"And what do they say?" he asked.

"I should not tell you this—"

"Why?"

"You will laugh," she said. "It sounds foolish."

"Tell me."

"The stars have said I shall conceive a king."

"I shall be a king." Edward looked up into the stars. "The stars, that is it."

"What?" she asked.

"Robert's son. Your son shall bear my crown. The crown of England."

"Where is England?" she asked.

"Not far, an island beyond the sea."

CHAPTER 9

Normandy, 1027

THE PATH UP FROM GRANDMESNIL WAS ROCKY. WITHOUT PENETRATING THE soft leather of his boots, the sharp stones tore into Edward's feet and each step was painful. Herleve, enormous with the bulging child of her belly, leaned on Edward for support and that, too, was painful. The sky was as gray as the stones they trod and Edward hoped it would not rain before they reached Falaise. A hawk circled in the sky.

"A hawk in a gray sky means we will meet a prophet," Edward told as they trudged up the winding incline.

"Is it so?" she asked.

"Always," he assured her.

At the crest of the hill they stopped and looked down at the village below. They had come in search of the anchorite of Grandmesnil to get a blessing for the coming birth, but the anchorite, who had lived in a box for eight years, had died two days before. A servant who brought him water each day had fallen in the well and drowned. While the servant perished from too much water the anchorite of Grandmesnil had died from want of it. "It is the justice of God," the gravedigger at Grandmesnil had said.

They had walked the long distance to Grandmesnil because Herleve had not dared ride, yet the pilgrimage had been in vain and tiring and Edward wished they had not come. Herleve seemed less disturbed and as they moved down the other side of the hill on to a wider road, less torn with rock, she hummed lightly and moved more quickly.

There was a shriek.

They stopped, neither speaking, waiting as if expecting another cry. Edward looked toward the trees where they might hide if necessary. These were dangerous times. Young Richard, the Duke of Normandy, could keep no order, men and knights terrorized the roads and pathways and Edward wished they had remained safely at Falaise. He gripped his knife handle, but there was no second cry and they began to walk again, but more cautiously.

They reached the river Dive. The grass beside the river was lush and long and damp and they sat, matting it, and the sun came out and warmed them.

"I can go no farther," Herleve said. "The child will be born here."

"But you have said nothing—"

"A woman bears her pain in silence," Herleve told him. "For it is joy as well as pain. A woman creates life—"

"God creates life," he interrupted.

"God and woman," she told him. "It is something no man can do."

He saw the pain now on her face, but she did not cry out. "What can I do?" he asked.

"First make some stakes and with tears from my gown tie and stake my ankles. All else is to cut the cord and wash the baby in the river." The gown which he had ripped he tied back about her waist. She was sprawled on a flat stretch of grass.

He staked her legs. He moved back and sat watching the swollen opening of her vagina, red and sore, wet with excretions as it tightened and expanded with the thrust from within. Pain was painted on her face.

"Can I take the pain from you?" he asked.

"I am happy," she said and, though she spoke with difficulty, did not cry out.

There was something tremendously remarkable about life, something incomprehensible, Edward realized as he sat watching those flexible doors waiting for the arrival of Herleve's child. Why did God choose this way, this pain as man's way to life? Even Jesus came like this into the world. How did all this occur? Why? What made this child to be born the person it would become, cruel or kind, beautiful like Robin or ugly like himself? The child would be a bastard and no doubt doomed to ignominy, yet it would be a distinct and unique individual. Would Edward like the child? Or the child, Edward?

And then it appeared, a bloody mess, headfirst, slowly entering the world. How amazing, Edward realized, as he moved toward Herleve and watched as the child slipped out onto the matted grass. He cut the cord with his knife and took the child in his hands. He felt the sensation of blood on his white hands and understood that birth, like death, was a thing of blood. He took the tiny child to the river and washed it and the baby cried and Edward dried the tiny soft body with his mantle and wrapped the infant in it and carried it back to Herleve.

"A boy," he said.

"Yes," was all she said and took the child as he untied her ankles. He took off his tunic and soaked it in the river and gave it to Herleve to clean herself and then sat down beside her as she let the child nurse at her breast.

Edward was not quite certain when he felt the presence of someone watching him, but he slowly moved his hand to his waist and took a grip on his knife and then turned to face the boy up in the tree.

"I am a friend, King of England," the boy said and jumped down.

"Who are you?" Edward still held the handle of the knife.

The boy had one brown eye and one green eye and was short and perhaps not as young as he looked. His face was soft.

"A seer," Herleve said. "The hawk . . ."

"I am called 'the boy from Lisieux' and you are Edward, King of England, and I would serve you and the child. The babe whose binds you cut will be Duke of Normandy."

"He is a bastard," Edward said.

"He is Duke of Normandy." The boy's voice conveyed that the fact was without question. The boy had a streak of white which ran through his hair across his eyebrow and lashes. He was perhaps twelve, Edward guessed.

The boy from Lisieux carried the infant to Falaise, referring to him always as "Your Grace."

"He shall be called William," Robert said and the Archbishop of Rouen came and baptized him and Edward stood as his godfather. Robert was fond of his son and the affection surprised Edward.

Fall came and the baby grew and life fell into a dull tedium at Falaise and Edward wished to God they could raise an army and march on England, but instead they hawked and had at swords. On a day Edward and Robert were going at swords, the boy from Lisieux sat apart watching. Robert was a good swordsman, but Edward was the better. Metal clashed as they danced about one another.

"You are going to lose," Robert said. "You are angry this morning and when you get angry you lose."

"I'm tired of Falaise. We do nothing but hawk, hunt boar and have at swords." He clanged against Robert's weapon with all his strength. Edward was, because of his pale coloring, deceptively weak-looking.

The dark-haired young man nearly lost his balance.

"You say"—Edward hit hard again—"you will be Duke of Normandy, but you are not."

Robert came back hard with his sword. "You are right, cousin." He beat with heavy blows upon Edward's iron. One sharp glance. It fell upon the ground. Edward stood beaten, surprised. "I told you."

Robert turned about, picked up his mantle and walked away. The boy from Lisieux followed and when night fell Edward realized Robert had left Falaise and the boy from Lisieux as well.

It was All Hallow's Eve. Dark spirits were abroad. It was not the wind that howled, but the breath of devils clamoring in the night. In the round tower they sat in a circle, a single tallow burned in the center of the ring they formed, and it enlarged them and cast huge black images of each of them against the stone wall.

"I want to go to bed," Alfred whispered to Edward.

"No," Herleve told him. "When one of the house is missing on All Hallow's Eve, the rest must wait in a circle around the light, else the missing one shall be doomed. The dead walk the roads this night."

Dreux belched loudly and took a sip of wine from the cup before him. "Robert damn well better be duke before this night is over. I've hazarded all on him being duke and I've waited a year. It's long enough."

They were quiet after that. The devils still howled and sometimes the devils' breath slipped through the stones and blew at the flaming tallow, but the fire did not blow out. Sassy grunted occasionally; otherwise there was little sound. Alfred dozed. Dreux fell asleep from the wine as he always did. Godgifu's head began to nod and she, too, eventually fell asleep.

Edward looked over the burning tallow at Herleve. There were tears in her eyes. "It will be all right," Edward consoled her. "He has gone to Rouen. I am certain."

"Yes, he has gone to Rouen," she repeated. "And when he returns Duke of Normandy I will have to be married off to someone else. I've known it always."

There was nothing he could say to console her so they sat the night mostly in silence. Waiting. Waiting for the inevitable return of Robert as Duke of Normandy. It was Sassy who stirred first. He began pounding on the floor. "C-c-coming," he stammered and pointed toward the west. Edward blew out the candle as Herleve awoke the others. "Robert's coming," she said and shook Dreux. And on a cold All Souls' morning, they went down into the first breath of day and stood, wrapped in skins, looking like waiting refugees from some long siege. They stood there before the tower, hearing the sound of the approaching horses. They came like an army, Robert, helmetless, in the lead, his black hair blowing in the wind.

He was breathless as he leaped from his horse. "I am Robert, Duke of Normandy. My brother, Richard, died after severe pains in his guts."

Edward took the reins of his horse as Robert took the baby from Herleve's arms. "They will say," Edward told him, "that you poisoned him."

"They will say," Robert agreed, "but they will follow me. See them. My brother was not Normandy; he lacked the vigor for it."

The hall at Falaise was not meant for so many and that night they were crowded in a room choking with smoke from the fire. Men's bellies were filled with wine and food and they belched and gurgled. There was an air of celebration in the overcrowded hall.

Robert sat on the floor playing hazards with their cousin Gilbert of Brionne. Edward stood above watching.

"What of Richard's son?" Dreux asked. He sat over by the fire, drinking too much wine as always.

"His bastard?" Robert looked up as he threw the dice. "He will by necessity have to be disposed of, I suppose." He looked down at the dice. "You are too lucky in this, Gilbert. It is not good manners to beat your liege Lord."

"I am not used to you being such yet," Gilbert told him.

Herluin, one of Gilbert's men, came over and stood above them. He was tall, neither young nor old, with kind eyes and a soft voice. "My Lord Duke, Richard's bastard is but a babe like your own. Send him to a monastery, perhaps. He has no legitimate claim. He can do you no harm."

"What he says is true, Robert." Herleve, who was standing near the fire, smiled at the young knight. "Spare the child."

Robert looked up at them.

"Vicomte Conteville," he addressed Herluin formally. "What think you of Herleve here?"

"She is a sweet lady, my Lord Duke."

"She is my whore, Herluin, a tanner's daughter, but you may have her for your wife."

"Robert!" Herleve stepped back from him.

"Is there someone in the room you would rather have? Is that it? Point him out. He is yours."

"No one." She bit her lip and put her head down.

"It is time you made a marriage," Robert said. "You knew it would come to that."

"Yes." Her voice was soft.

"But need you have done it this way?" Edward asked.

"Perhaps, Herleve, you should marry the King of England here. You would never tire of his amorous ways. You are lusty, insatiable, aren't you my white cousin?"

"There is no need, Robert," Edward said.

"There is a need for Herleve to marry now. She knows it. For her protection and for my son. Will you have her, Herluin?"

"Yes," he said.

"And you, tanner's daughter?"

"As your Grace wills it."

Robert threw the dice and took some coins from in front of Gilbert.

"The boy?" Herluin asked.

"The boy? Ah, yes, Richard's boy." Robert smiled. "I will give you his life for a wedding gift. Be careful, Herluin, your soft heart will do you in. This is a hungry dog's world."

Edward left the hall.

In the night a terrifying shrill cry broke the sleeping silence. Edward had not been asleep, but had been standing out on the parapet when he heard the sound. A few moments later he felt the presence of someone behind him and turned to see Robert standing there in the dark.

"Did the cry wake you?" Edward asked.

"It was I who cried out. I dreamt I was dying, choking to death. There are devils about this night."

"All Hallow's Eve is past," Edward said.

"I am plagued by a devil spirit. Tomorrow send for that priest of yours."

"Robin?"

"Yes. He has fled St. Ouen and is said hiding in Jumieges."

"And if he won't come?"

"I shall have him killed. I am Duke of Normandy now and he is a subject. Like the rest, he will do my bidding. He will be my confessor. He shall carry the weight of my sins."

Edward was silent. An owl hooted nearby.

"Cheer up, cousin, before long we will invade England and kill the Dane."

"Will you marry?" Edward asked.

"I would rather spend my life with Herleve, but yes I will marry, as is my station, to a lady of royal blood and have legitimate heirs as becomes a duke. But promise me, should I not live so long—"

"You are but a child. Speak not of death—"

"Death haunts me. Do as I ask. Promise. See to William, see the boy is made my proper heir if I have no other. Promise?"

"On my oath. I will see to it." Edward leaned over the stone wall. "Must you treat her like a whore?"

"It is what she is. I am Duke. You are King. She is a whore."

Edward suddenly noticed the boy from Lisieux was there on the parapet in the dark.

A star fell in the sky.

CHAPTER 10

Winchester, 1027

OUTSIDE, THE FIRST SNOW FELL WHITE UPON THE GROUND AND THE AIR WAS crisp and invigorating; indoors, in the King's chamber, the air was heavy with disease and its cures.

"He has urine in the eyes," the physician from Countances said, and plastered Cnute's face with rabbit dung and bay leaf. The King coughed and hacked and closed his eyes, shutting back the yellowed eyeballs.

Gamol sang softly in the dim corner, not for the King, who breathed with strenuous unevenness as he attempted sleep, but because Emma wanted it. She could not have endured sitting here in the pallor of the chamber without some distraction. Gamol sang of a Roman named Coriolanus, but it was not this Roman who intrigued Emma but his mother, Volumnia, and the power she exercised over her son. There was grandeur in the noble mother, a towering spirit. She saved Rome, but it was at the cost of her son's life.

"Go away, Emma," the King said and Gamol stopped singing. "I want Estrid. Send Estrid to me." He closed his yellow eyes again.

Estrid came and was closeted with her brother. Emma, her fur tightly about her neck, paced the courtyard and wet flakes of snow moistened her face and melted on the cobble. What was Cnute giving his sister now? Her concern was legitimate for it was her son's inheritance which was being diminished by the constant gifts of land and treasure, which Cnute made almost daily to his sister. Many of the royal lands had already left the King's demesne and become Estrid's property. The giving had to cease. But it would not, Emma was certain, as long as Estrid remained at Winchester. Emma had to get her away. Emma paced as the snow fell in wet globs against her blue mantle. How? Cnute would never let Estrid leave. Not as long as he lived. As long as he lived . . . she tasted the snow on her lips . . . how long was that? A seer from Glouchester, a tall dirty man wearing only an equally dirty loincloth, had said the King would live yet seven years, but he also told her the King would bear twelve more children and kept rambling on about a red lion that would be King and she had sent the old fool, who read the future in a circle of rocks, away in disgust. There was another seer that had come from Normandy, a boy. She had not seen him yet, but he was kept hidden in the cellar.

Estrid came out from the King's chamber house tightening her plain brown cloak.

"What did he grant you today?" Emma tried to hide her irritation, but was uncertain whether or not she succeeded.

"Lands in Devon, wherever that be," her sister-in-law replied on the wind and scurried into another chamber out of the cold and wet.

Emma went to the cellar. It was cold and dark and smelled of vinegar. The boy was led by an aging monk out into the little light which sifted from a dirty window. "You may leave us," she told him.

"I keep to the boy." His voice was as old as his appearance.

"I told you to go," she ordered.

The monk creaked up the wooden steps. The boy was handsome, but perhaps no more than eleven or twelve. He had one brown eye and one green eye and a streak of white which ran through his black hair, struck across his eyebrow and through his lashes. The color of his eyes and the streak of white gave him not a freakish look, as she had expected, but an aura of mystery, a sense of hidden powers. "Are you afraid of me?" she asked.

"No." He looked directly at her.

"You are from Lisieux." It was more statement than question.

"Yes," he told her.

"I put you in the cellar for I don't want anyone to see you. I must know how long the King is to live. No one else is to be told what you tell me."

"I will have to see the King." His French seemed more Burgundian than Norman, she thought.

"Before you see anyone, you will tell me why you came to England, what you are doing here."

He looked at her without replying.

"Perhaps," she suggested, "you have come from Edward to kill me or were sent by him to spy on us."

"Who is Edward?"

"A young man who lives in the house of the Norman duke. He has white skin and his hair is white—"

He interrupted. "I saw who you mean once. He rode with the duke. And I stood close enough to his horse to read his hand. He will die soon, this young man."

"Now that is cheery news, seer. But you have yet not answered my question. What are you doing in England?"

"I had a vision in which you called for me to come and look into the King's hand to tell you of his time of living."

"And death . . ."

"Yes." The one brown eye and one green eye looked directly at her. There was a strange angry passion, as well as vision, in those eyes, yet she trusted he spoke the truth.

"How do you read the future—the bowels of birds, the stars, branches upon the earth, the entrails of rodents . . . ?"

"I have to see the King."

"Yes, you said that, but what instruments of divining will you require?"

"The hands. I will find the King's future in his hands."

Emma sent the physician away and no one was about except the thinglith who stood guard at the King's chamber. She led the boy in. "The King has urine of the eyes," she told him.

Cnute's eyes were closed and he seemed asleep.

"I must be left alone with him," the boy said.

Emma hesitated, but went out as the boy sat down on the edge of the bed and opened the King's hand. Outside in the entry room, Emma waited with the thinglith, a swaggering sort, as they all were, bare-chested, with wide gold armbands and his hair creeping out from beneath his gold helmet. Neither Emma nor the guard spoke.

There was suddenly a yell, cursing and screaming. It was Cnute. The thinglith pushed open the door.

"This little bastard tried to kill me," Cnute said and he held the boy's wrist. There was a knife, a jewel-handled knife in the boy's hand. Emma recognized the weapon. It was one Goddy had given Edward on his saint's day.

"Edward is the rightful King of England," the boy said.

His head was hung at the door of the King's house in Winchester and people came to see the head of a boy with one green eye and one brown eye. He looked to be smiling and his hair had a silver streak which ran through his eyebrow and over his lashes and they marveled, these people who came to see the head. On the opposite side of the door was the head of an ancient monk.

Godwin was angry with her. "Emma, would you please tell me when you bring creatures like this into Winchester. My spies could have told you that he served Edward. His name was Clau. He was the bastard of some Burgundian monk and was raised in Lisieux by a vintner's wife. He was found by Edward and was part of Robert's house at Falaise."

Estrid, who had been walking with Emma, gave Godwin a curious smile. "Do you know the innermost secrets of us all, Lord Wessex?"

"The eye but watches where it must, Lady," he said.

Emma took Estrid's hand. "You have great wealth, Sister, and you keep it too carelessly in your rooms. You should be grateful that someone keeps an eye to things, knows who cleans your chambers, attends your needs."

"Do you, Godwin?" Estrid asked.

"I have no need. Emma does such a thorough job of it."

"Emma! Do you spy on my people?"

"I don't spy, merely keep a tender watch over your welfare."

They reached the King's chamber. There was a new physician come from Palermo. "He has urine in the eyes," the doctor said as if telling them something new. He gave Cnute a draught of rose water and wormwood and explained to them all what it was. The King did seem improved and he gave Estrid a gold and bronze pendant set with a great green stone and the chain was carved of ivory. Emma had often admired it for it was said to have come from a Persian queen and she was angry, but hid her feelings beneath a smile.

That night, late, after Aesval had left Emma's chamber with Gunnerhild in her arms, there was a rap on the door.

"It is Beatrice," the voice said quietly.

"Come in."

The woman entered. She was a pale little woman with tiny beads for eyes, no chin and she attended upon Estrid. She was also one of Emma's spies. Beatrice wore several layers of a heavy brown fabric. She was always complaining of the cold, even in the heat of summer. She had a fur skin about her shoulders. "I waited until you were alone."

"You have news," Emma said.

"Yes. Disturbing, I'm afraid. Tonight I saw a thinglith go to her chamber. I don't know his name. I've seen him about. Northumbrian, I think, has a deep scar on his shoulder. I went into the little cupboard in the room next, where we had made the hole in the wall. He sat beside her and they talked. And then he tried to touch her. He tried to get his hand beneath her gown, but she pushed him away and when he asked why all she said was, 'God,' and then he left."

"Well." Emma looked at Beatrice, who was rubbing her tiny hands together. "No harm seems to have been done."

"But that was not all. I was about to leave when Lady Estrid took a tallow from a drawer and went back to her bed. She raised her gown and stuck the tallow up between her legs and then"—Beatrice began talking faster—"she shoved it in and out as if it were a man's penis. I couldn't watch any longer . . . I . . ."

"It is well you told me."

"I thought you should know."

"I think Estrid needs a husband."

"Yes." Beatrice looked down at the floor.

"The chests? Did she give the thinglith any coins or jewels from the chests or the little casket the King gave her?"

"No. She gave him nothing."

"Thank you, Beatrice."

The tiny woman left. Estrid needed a man. Quite obviously she needed a man. Care must be exercised, however. Estrid being in the state she was in—well, any man could easily get his hands on all that wealth, any man at all. What Estrid needed was a husband who was already rich . . . titled by necessity, considering her rank. And one far from Winchester, far from Cnute's treasury. What lord? A king? But there were no kings for the having. An earldorman, but who was there? Or . . . or . . . oh . . . that would be funny . . . a duke? Emma laughed aloud at the thought.

Early the next day she called for Godwin.

"The King is much better today," he said.

"Estrid needs a husband," she told him.

"Why do you say that?" he asked.

"You know well Cnute's insatiable needs. Hers are no less. She needs a man. I am a woman, I know. And Estrid is a Christian who abhors the ways of sin. She needs a husband."

"What are you up to, Emma?"

"I am up to nothing. I am stating fact. The fact is if we don't find her a proper husband, she is liable to find one for herself, not so proper. I will only hint, there is a certain thinglith, a Northumbrian—"

"He went to her chamber. Bye the bye, your spy, the woman Beatrice, is not particularly subtle."

"She's effective," Emma told him and smiled. "The topic is Estrid. She needs a man to her bed. She needs to be wed."

"And, the candidate is—"

"No less"—she paused and then dropped it like a heavy weight—"than the Duke of Normandy?"

"Emma, you're not serious." He started to laugh and then stopped. "You are serious."

"Robert."

"Why would you do that to Estrid? He is a child, and an insane child at that."

"He is going to raise an army and invade this island."

"He can attempt. He would hardly succeed."

"Perhaps," Emma said, "but he has cousins in Flanders, in Brittany. Why, the King of France supports his every move and the Pope is his friend."

"When Cnute goes to Rome."

"But he hasn't gone yet and with his health may never go. Robert could be neutralized so easily by a marriage. Edward and his foolish claim would be forgotten. Without Robert to help him we would never have to worry about that ugly child again."

"Why," Godwin asked, "would Robert want her?".

"She is attractive enough, beautiful actually, and wealthy. One brother is King of England, another King of Sweden. One of her sons by right is the Earl of Jomburg and, as they are young, she will control. Robert needs an heir . . ."

Godwin said nothing for a moment. "Let me think on it," he said finally.

The snow fell and covered the ground. Late that night, Emma, shivering in the cold, went to pray with her sister-in-law.

"You should marry again," Emma suggested.

"Yes," Estrid said and continued praying.

"We shall have to find you a husband . . . a handsome husband . . . a virile husband . . . a lusty husband—"

"Emma, really. I am at prayer."

"Pray for a husband—a rich, young, titled lord of a mighty kingdom."

Estrid forgot her prayers momentarily. "And where am I to find such a beast who is also, as you say, handsome and virile?"

"I know just the young man," Emma teased, keeping it light, making a game of it.

"Who?"

"The Duke of Normandy."

"Emma! He is a baby. A child. Oh, a delightful child if I remember, but—"

"A child no more."

"A mere boy—"

"No boy, I can assure you. Dark, hair as black as a moonless night, youthful, lean, hair upon his chest, body as lithe as a young stag, spirited, powerful, bright eyes which sparkle—a Viking." Emma wondered what he really looked like now. She hadn't seen the monstrous boy since her brother's funeral. "Sits a horse like a king, I'm told, puts his eyes to a woman and it makes her melt."

The next morning Emma arose early. The stone street was a sheet of ice and she walked with care, bundled to keep out the cold. Gytha was surprised to see her. The Godwin household was a menagerie. There was the little girl, Edith, who must be about nine, Emma thought. She was a polite little thing, quite pretty and given to religion. She took after her Aunt Estrid there. She seemed more quiet than shy. The boys were anything but quiet and there were enough of them, Sven and Tostig and Harold and Gryth and Leofwine, and the new one a baby with a stumped foot. He was called Wufnoth and he seldom cried. Estrid's boy Beorn was there as well.

"How do you stand it?" Emma asked Gytha.

"I rather like the noise," she said, looking somewhat like a child herself.

Sometimes it was hard for Emma to realize how young Gytha really was. She'd had her first child when she was barely fifteen and that was less than ten years before.

"I have thought on it," Godwin said.

"And?"

"I can see the practicality of it. I suspect it will do Estrid no great good, but you're right it neutralizes Robert. The yeas outweigh the nays."

Gytha threw up her arms and picked up Leofwine from the floor. "The two of you. That poor woman. The boy is vile, for God's sake. He killed his brother."

"Poooh," Emma said.

"He killed his brother," Gytha repeated.

"There is no proof to that," Godwin said. "That is a supposition."

"You're horrible, both of you. You'll destroy that poor woman. Hasn't she been through enough?"

The weather got worse. The King got better. Two days later Emma went to his chamber. He was out of bed and sitting in a chair. In earlier days he would have been playing chess, but since Ulf's death, he played no more. The pieces no longer sat upon the table in the corner, but had been put away. Cnute motioned for her to sit.

"Godwin has discussed it with me. I am opposed." He rested his arm on the table.

"Then we should perhaps talk of something else. The weather, perhaps?"

"Don't be silly . . . but Estrid married to that horrid child?"

"She needs to be married to some man. She craves a man's penis. I could tell you things. I won't, but she needs a man."

"But not that devil."

"He is Normandy," she reminded him.

"They say he poisoned his brother."

"Nonsense. You saw Richard, he was a sickly thing, given to playing with birds. No. That is all but an ugly lie." She looked at Cnute; he looked better, but he still appeared tired and the eyeballs were still a yellow cast. "Normandy is a threat. Edward is the young duke's friend. That boy of Lisieux would never have been able to have reached England so easily without the duke's help. A year ago at Richard's funeral, Robert acknowledged Edward to be King of England."

"I am not afraid of either of them."

"But I am. You are going to Rome. What if Normandy were to attack."

"We are strong."

"But without you here . . . and you will be gone a long time."

"You make it sound much more dangerous than it is."

She had only one throw of the dice left and she tossed it out. "Estrid wants it. She wants to marry Robert. You are depriving your sister of happiness and she has so little. She has nothing really since Ulf . . ." Emma didn't need to finish.

Cnute looked properly beaten. "I will do this much," he said quietly. "I will talk to my sister."

Emma hurried away to find Estrid, to prepare her for her conversation with Cnute.

CHAPTER 11

Rouen, 1027

IT WAS IRONY, EDWARD SUPPOSED, BUT HE WORE THE TRAPPING OF DEATH before the deed. His garments were shreds of black rags. Sitting on the slow-moving jackass, he suspected he was a picture of some grotesque stone carving. He had stained his legs and feet, his arms and hands and his face with a mixture of pine resins and charcoal. It gave his skin a refulgent gray hue and it made him feel almost as unreal as he knew he must appear. If he looked death, he was in harmony with the landscape for the world about him was a place of death, sere and ungrown. The earth was encrusted brown, barren and without snow and the trees dug with pricking fingers into the sky as if scratching for blood. Let it rain blood, the blood of the ambitious, of kings on stolen thrones and queens who exchange their sons for reechy kisses. Blood perchance for tears will fall, Edward thought. He stared into the hazy, but for a moment perspicuous, sky. It was as if God supported him. This incisive awareness was but a fleeting instant, but in that brief puncture of time Edward understood that his actions were not some self-fulfillment but transcended self and were in the order of divine destiny. It was God's insistence and he was fated to be King of the English and nothing must stand between him and the throne, not Cnute, not his mother.

His mind forgot his body. He was cold and forgot to feel it. He was hungry, but gave no thought to his fast, his growling and gurgling stomach no reminder of the emptiness. So intense was his self-communion that he was quite startled to see Rouen on the horizon.

Despite the midmorning hour, there was a moon, a dull sliver in a dull sky. It had gone full cycle since Robert had ordered him banished to Falaise. Robert had made the cold and flat pronouncement of his intent to wed Cnute's sister and Edward had screamed loud, piercing, cutting, knifing wails. He refused to be consoled. Robert's reassurance that nothing had changed and England would still be invaded and Edward made King were hollow. Edward screamed and raged for two days and in the end Robert had sent him away. Robert and his ugly old bride-to-be could stand helplessly and watch as Edward killed Cnute and his mother. Edward conjured visions of the deed and smiled as he pictured Robert standing there in magnificence, helpless, impotent, staring at the bleeding pair, their crowns toppled from their heads as they fell. And Godwin . . . Godwin would not stop him this time. Edward had kept his own counsel. There was no Ragner as there had been at Pevensey. He had not even told Godgifu of his intent. Godwin would be able to do nothing but watch the usurper and his queen die on the gray stone floor of the great ducal hall.

She was beautiful and he did not want to kill her. He only wanted her love, for her to recognize his right. He would never marry; he could make her a greater queen than either of her husbands had. Ethelred had put her in the pit and it was said Cnute cast her aside and took other women to his bed. Edward could make her a great queen, but he knew if he let her live and killed Cnute, she would force the Witangemot to put that ugly child Harthacnut on Edward's throne. Even if he wanted to let her live, he could not. Not now, for he understood it was the will of God that he be King and she stood in his way. Their red blood would puddle on the stone and they would make gasping noises and Edward would stand above them and stare down into their dying eyes and smile. He was determined and he was disguised. His white skin was hidden beneath the stain and his white hair he had dyed with woodwaxen, giving it the color of straw. If none came too close, they would not recognize him, even Robert. The repugnant smell from a pigsty ahead along the road gave him the idea of how he would keep others at bay. As he reached the stone enclosure of the pen, he got down off the jackass and climbed over the short wall. He smeared his ragged clothes with pig dung and the stench fumed up into his nostrils until he thought he would gag, yet he continued to cake his rags and skin with the noxious excrement. As he swiped his hand down into the soft dung a huge sow with dangling nipples snorted at his feet. He climbed back over the wall and onto the ass. The smell of the dung sickened him, but he knew if it sickened him, it would sicken others as well and none would approach too close and there would be less chance of being identified.

At the ducal house he was turned away by a soldier repulsed by his smell. "Out of here, you pile of pig shit," the soldier yelled and pushed in the air in Edward's direction but was careful not to touch him.

"Tell the English Queen this," Edward said. "I am a seer come with a great wonderment for her."

"She'll not see the likes of you. Now get away with you."

"She will see me. Tell her but this. 'I know her to bear a brown spot on the right of her belly.' Tell her a seer comes bearing great wonderment."

"I will tell her and as well of your stink. Away with you."

Edward wandered off a short distance and sat down and leaned against a wall. A doctor of the ducal house came scurrying by, but tarried long enough to spit on Edward as he passed.

It was nearly dark when the guard yelled out to him. The guards and house servants made a path for him, mocking him, as he entered the courtyard. Good, none recognized him and Edward was not in the least disturbed by the taunts. He was shown into the ducal hall, pretending not to know the way.

"Good God! What a stench!" one of the Montgomeries said as Edward came into the crowded hall.

Edward moved into the center of the hall. Tied from his waist and dangling down on his upper thigh were a pair of crows. Buried into the birds and hidden by the feathers were sharp knives with tiny handles, one each for Cnute and his mother. They sat at the dais at the end of the hall, near where Robert stood. The woman, who must be Cnute's sister, was standing with him. Edward was happy to see that both Cnute and his mother were wearing crowns. It was as he pictured it.

"My Jesus, you stink," Robert said to him without the slightest sign of recognition. "Some kin of yours, Godwin?"

Godwin did not smile. His daughter, the girl Edith, held on to Godwin's hand. Edward saw the recognition in her eyes. "You should not do this," she told him.

"I come bringing a message to the Queen," Edward said, making his voice raspy and deep.

"You should not do this," Edith repeated.

"Quiet, child," Godwin told her.

"How know you I have a brown spot on my belly?" His mother looked directly at him without any sign that she knew who he was.

Edward remembered her nude body in the chapel at Corfe. "The crow has the answers." He looked straight into her eyes and imagined he remembered being born. She was beautiful, fatter than she had been and there were signs of age on her face, particularly about the eyes, yet she was still beautiful. The beautiful must die as well as the ugly, he thought. He did not look at Cnute. He sensed everyone was watching as he carefully took the birds from his waist and held one in each hand. He put the birds together, head to head, and with no one being able to see the breast side of the birds held close to his chest, he pushed the handles deep into the birds until the knife points were thrust well out of the birds near the throats. Holding the birds such, he began a nonsense chant and moved in the direction of Cnute and his mother.

"You must not do this," Edith repeated, but no one paid her the slightest attention.

Edward knew he was the focus of every eye in the room. He began dancing about, the crows held in his hands; he lifted and dipped the hands as if the birds were in flight. He continued the nonsense words, letting the tempo increase, faster and faster as he moved closer and closer to the sitting figures of Cnute and his mother.

"What message have you for me?" his mother screamed. She seemed enraptured by his movement and the chant as well.

Perhaps it was the smell of the pig dung, but he had not noticed the smell of Sassy in the room and he was startled suddenly when the grotesque figure tapped him. "Ed . . . Ed . . . Ed . . . ward . . ." the voice stammered.

"Yes," Robert yelled. He sprang forward. "It is Edward."

Edward lunged in the direction of his mother and Cnute, the birds extended, driving the knives toward them, but it was too late. The terror of recognition had lifted them from their places and they moved back and the birds struck into the air and Edward felt the grasp of the guards' tight hands upon his shoulders and the birds and knives fell clanging to the floor.

"Take him to a cell," Robert ordered.

"Kill him," Edward heard his mother say.

"A cell," Robert repeated.

Edward screamed with vehemence as he was dragged from the room. And he screamed for hours after in the small dark cell in which they locked him. But his voice finally tired and the screaming ebbed and evolved to sobs and then silence. Even God had deserted him. Why? Why if God wanted him to kill Cnute and his mother, and he was certain it was God's will, had God prevented it?

There was no window in the tiny cell nor cracks in the heavy wooden door and Edward didn't know if it was still daylight or if darkness had fallen. With so little air in the room the stench of the pig excrement was nauseating. He tore off the black rags and threw them in a corner, but his skin was still caked with the dried pig dung and he picked at it as he sat naked in the dark. He thought his head might burst with the pain of failure, and yet, despite the pain, he did not sense that a fit would come to relieve the anguish. Why had God left him? He felt slightly dizzy and it reminded him he had had nothing to eat or drink. The pain in his head began throbbing and he cried out in anguish. And then the other Edward, who had not come to him for well over a year, came and took command and the pain vanished. Edward forgot the solitary darkness and the stench. The air became soft and he heard singing and knew it was angels and bells sang as well, not harsh and pounding, but dulcet, touching, a sweet unfamiliar melody. And then slipping in before his eyes, vanishing and returning, Edward saw clearly the head of Felim MacBoru. He was not pale like some apparition, but his face was full of color and warmth, his hair unruly, as it had been when he was alive. There was no body and the head did not speak, but the eyes did, mollescent and empathic, and Edward found much comfort in seeing his old friend, if only an apparition. The face would drift before him, so clear and discernible, and then slip away and return again. And so Edward sat naked in the center of the room, the other Edward, in control, for an indeterminate time.

A slight rap at the door. The pain returned, along with the stench. The other Edward disappeared and the apparition of MacBoru's head as well. Edward could hear the chains, which lashed the door, being undone. There were men's voices and then a soft gentle voice. "It is I," she said. It was Godwin's child, Edith.

"I am naked," Edward said.

"So God made us," the child said.

The door opened and the torchlight was blinding and Edward, forgetting his nakedness, stood there, his eyes closed against the bright light.

"Fire this candle," the young girl ordered, "and put the basin and food on the little table and begone. Take the torches and begone."

Edward sensed the guards hesitated, but heard them leave and opened his eyes. The candlelight, though softer, still was hard to bear after the darkness. He squinted and looked at the child.

"The duke let me bring you some water warmed by the fire and a clean robe." She pointed to the basin.

"Thank you," he said and went to the basin. The water was warm and gentle, but seemed ineffectual against the dried, coated dung.

"Use this," the child said. "It is called soap."

It was harsh against his skin, but in its lather the excrement and some of the stain vanished as well.

"You should not have tried to kill them," she said.

He looked at her. Her words were so terribly old for one so young. She could be no more than nine, he was certain.

"God wanted it," he told her.

"God does not want us to kill," she said.

"God wants me to be King," he said and then added, "and saint, as well."

"Saints do not kill their mothers," she said with great wisdom.

And Edward understood why he had failed. The child was right. Saints did not kill their mothers. He could kill Cnute, but not his mother.

His body was raw with the scrubbing. Although usually obsessed with modesty, Edward did not find the child's presence discomforting. When he finished washing, the water ugly and brown, he dried with the cloth beside the basin and then took a brilliant red robe which she extended to him.

"There is some wine, a piece of mutton and some bread there," she told him. "You should eat."

He took a sip of wine from the bowl and bit on cold meat. "I shall still kill Cnute," he told her.

"He goes to Rome in the morning."

"But the wedding?"

"The emperor's coronation is on Easter Sunday and the wedding cannot be held until Lent is over. The King—"

"Cnute," he corrected her.

"And his chaplain, Stigand, go on to Rome. The Queen and Papa will stay here with Aunt Estrid for the wedding." She had small brown hands and Edward wondered how they stayed so tanned after the dark of winter.

"Your aunt is old."

"Yes," she agreed. "She is a silly goose. She wants Duke Robert so he can make babies in her. I've heard her talking with the Queen. I shall never let any man make babies in me. I shall never marry."

"Nor I," Edward told her. He looked at the delicate child. She reminded him of a butterfly. "Your name is Edith."

"Yes. And my friend is the gray wolf." She told Edward about a gray wolf in Winchester who followed her about. Edward ate and told Edith about a man he had met traveling from Falaise. The man lived in a hovel in the ground and when Edward asked for a bite of bread and some wine, the man told him he had none. Edith suggested when Edward was freed from the chamber, he should send some food to the man in the hovel.

"Yes," Edward agreed. "It is what saints do."

And they talked about saints until a serving woman came and took the child away.

Edward was kept in the chamber through the next day. Though his body was clean, he could not escape the smell of the pig dung which hung in the room from the rags tossed in the corner. That night he was given a fresh robe and taken by the guards to the great hall. He had been uncertain of the time when the door had been first opened, but the ducal house was silent and he knew the hour to be late. The great hall at Rouen was hung with the heads of dead young Richard's followers, wrinkled, discolored, wizened, unidentifiable men of little consequence who had served the young duke in his short reign. There was a woman's head among the collection. It belonged to Richard's mistress, the kitchen woman, the mother of his bastard.

Robert stood alone in the hall, posing, as if letting Edward absorb his lofty presence. He scowled and walked toward the fire. His black hair glistened from the flames. The hall smelled of stale cooked fish and the shrunken heads. The young duke toyed with a gold necklace which fell to his chest. "You should not try to kill my guests. It darkens my name as a host."

"I shall not try again to kill my mother."

"Kill her if you wish, just don't do it when she is my guest, nor anyone else who is made welcome under my roof."

"I have no interest in killing anyone but Cnute."

"He is gone to Rome."

Edward joined him at the fire. "Then your house shall be at rest and I will keep to myself."

"Then I need not lock you up like some prisoner."

Edward looked at him. The anger had left the dark young man's face. "May I return to Falaise, then?"

"No, wait until after the wedding night. Then I shall leave the bride here, and you and I shall go to Brionne. She is old and I have little interest for this Lady Estrid."

"Then why do you marry her?"

Robert ran his hand through his hair. "She is said to be laden with money. I was reminded she even has a brother King of Sweden. All of which impresses me immensely, as you can imagine." Robert cynically raised the corner of his lip to match the sarcastic tone of his voice. "I care not a whit for Sweden; I don't even know where the damn cold place is."

"They are using you. They would only have you wed her for assurance that you won't raise an army against Cnute."

"It won't matter what they think. I shall raise an army when we are ready to put you on the throne. All I need from her is an heir and her wealth."

"There are other women," Edward said.

"Name me one daughter of a king, of age to grant me an heir, who does not have a husband, and mark you, Estrid is the daughter of a dead king. I shall marry this old woman, have my heir and throw her out.

Edward stirred the fire with an iron and sat down near it. Perhaps Robin had been right, Robert was mad. Certainly this marriage was madness.

Edward was not taken a prisoner but was allowed instead to go to his own chamber. He had settled into a fitful sleep when suddenly a piercing scream rent the silent night air. It was the horrible nightmare of dying which plagued the young duke in his sleep and he had suffered with the horrid dream almost nightly since the death of his brother Richard.

Edward lay awake in the darkness of the chamber and the second scream tore the silence. He got up from his bed and looked out between the cracks of the boarded window and watched a night snow as it fell. Again, the scream cut the night's quiet. Edward waited by the window. The young duke did not cry out again, yet Edward did not return to his bed, but stood the night peering out at the snow.

In the weeks that followed, Edward either stayed in his chamber or rode in the countryside, avoiding the guests from England except for the child, Edith. Occasionally from a window he would see his mother or Godwin or the Lady Estrid, but he avoided any direct confrontation with them. He heard of Godwin's anger that the marriage was not to be a grand ceremony in the cathedral but a private wedding in the chapel on Easter Monday. The moment the wedding ceremony was over, Godwin and the Queen were to sail for England, if the tide was with them. Robin was ordered to perform the ceremony. He had no choice but to obey the duke though he had told Edward, he felt sorry for the lady and tried to refuse. And so it took place on the morning after Easter. There was no feast and Edward watched from a window as the English sailed on the afternoon tide while Robert and his bride stood at the edge of the river and waved good-bye.

That night Edward sat alone in the great hall watching the fire. He heard the footsteps and looked up to see Robert at the door.

"You are to be in your marriage bed," Edward said.

"Oh God, Edward. She is old, she stinks and her teeth are yellow and . . . and I couldn't . . ."

"An heir, Robert. You—"

"She made me ill. The smell made me ill. Her body made me ill. And I told her so. I told her she was a filthy pig and I never wanted to see the sight of her again."

"Your marriage—"

"Will never be consummated. I will take an oath on it. I want to go to Brionne."

"In the morning?"

"No. Now."

The shriveled heads looked down on them. The woman among them seemed to be smiling in the firelight.

CHAPTER 12

Winchester, 1027

EMMA COULD NOT GET ESTRID FROM HER THOUGHTS. SHE TRIED TO CONVINCE herself she had not been responsible and yet she knew she was and the guilt hung on her like a torn garment that she was forced to wear. Even as she lay in bed with the man, Estrid kept creeping into her mind. Robert was said to have locked Estrid away and kept her a virtual prisoner.

"What are you thinking of, my sweet Lady?" the man next to her in bed asked. She responded only with her eyes. The man was, in a sense, a present from Cnute. A German, he had come from Rome bearing good news of Gunnerhild's betrothal to Henry of Germany. Gunnerhild, in her cradle, could hardly have understood the elation it gave Emma. Someday the infant would be Empress of the Holy Roman Empire. Emma ran her fingers down the spine of the man. He was not a youth, nor old either, thirty-five perhaps. He had a strong, deeply brown back and his hair, cropped above the shoulders, was jet black. He seemed more Latin than German. She ran her hand gently over the curve of his butt and moved her fingers into the hairy crevice and then stuck a finger into the anal opening. He moved slightly. She had not asked him his age. He was a large man and seemed more a soldier than the cleric that he was. He was a strenuous lover and seemed at times insatiable. He had begun to doze. She moved her hand up to his shoulder and she gripped it at the curve. He stirred, then turned, opened his eyes and smiled.

"I should leave soon," he said.

He had come to her bed for the twenty-two nights he had been at Winchester, but he always slipped away in the early morning light.

"Where do you go?" she asked.

"To pray. And to write."

"And what do you write?"

"I am writing a book," he said, "about the lives of the saints of Saxony."

"And where do you learn of these saints' lives?"

"In my head. Some stories have been told to me, some I have known since a child, but most are revealed to me."

"Revealed?"

"Yes. God reveals all to us. All learning comes to us through revelation. God tells me of what I am to know of each saint. It is the same with all knowledge. I wrote a book upon matter once."

"Matter?"

"Yes, the essence of all that is."

"What is the essence of all that is?" Emma smiled.

He kissed her and then lifted his body atop hers, keeping his weight upon his own arms and knees. "Much too complex to explain simply, but I will say this—all matter is basically the breathing of angels." His penis was hard and he gently put it inside her as he moved his fingers lightly over her breasts. "Angels' breath freezes like ice," he said pumping in and out, his own breathing becoming intense.

She clung to him. She hung herself about his neck and shoved her body up to meet his and he continued on and on until she was sore from the rubbing. Finally, he allowed his orgasm to seep into her, thrusting hard, gasping, and then with a heavy breath pulled himself free. "Each time an angel breathes, matter is formed," he said. "This has been revealed to me." He smelled musky and good and she pushed her hands through the heavy mass of shiny black hair.

"You're a pleasant woman," he said, "and solid."

"Like angels' breath," she told him.

He got up and put on the coarse gown of the monk. "May I come back tonight?"

"Yes," she said and watched him slip out into the gray morning light. She crawled up, bolted the door and went back to the bed. It was chilly and she pulled the skin around her. She might have dozed; she wasn't certain. Yet, she seemed awake when she heard the knock on the door. "Who is it?"

"Godwin."

She got up, threw on a cloak and opened the door. "You saw him leave," she said, motioning him into the room.

"I saw no one," he said and sat down without being asked.

Godwin was a liar, she thought.

"The King is come," he told her.

"He is here at Winchester?"

"Not as yet, but will be by morning." Godwin put his hand to his forehead. "And in good time, too."

"Norway?"

"It sits above us like an avalanche ready to break loose."

"I shall dress now," she said.

"There is no haste. It will be several hours. I only wanted to forewarn you. Get your sleep. Have you had any sleep?"

"I thought you saw nothing."

"My question was rhetorical."

"I'll dress," she said and as she opened the door to let him out she saw the bare-chested Thegn Behi waiting outside for Godwin. His sale was thrown over his shoulder and he smiled knowingly at her. There was something arrogant in his manner, and she found herself more and more disliking him. Perhaps it was simply his preference for the beds of men to hers. She closed the door and went to her cupboard.

Emma dressed like a Queen in a deep forest gown of heavy soft wool banded with embroidered linen. It seemed tight at her waist. She tucked her hair beneath a pearled net and picked up stranded pearls to wear about her neck. They were a saint's day gift from Estrid and she set them aside.

All of Winchester seemed gathered at the gates and Emma joined them. She went and stood near Gytha and they talked. The children ran about, Godwin and Gytha's children. There seemed so many of them. A large butterfly danced in the air and then rested on the girl's, Edith's, arm. She stayed so still it remained there. Edith smiled up at her father and Godwin grinned back.

"The King!" someone shouted. And the cries went up, "The King! The King!"

And the butterfly flew away.

Clerics burst into a roaring anthem, but it was almost drowned out in the shouting. The King, the Black Raven flying, was flanked by an army of stately riders in golden helmets as they rode toward the gate. The King was gold, dazzling, brilliant gold. His sale was gold and clipped at the neck with a giant gold brooch and he wore huge golden armbands and a gold helmet set with a ring of red stones. Yet for all his splendor, Emma thought he looked unwell. The yellowness had returned to his eyes, she realized. She greeted him amid the cries of the throng, but he returned the greeting with a coldness she had not expected and turned and began walking up the stone street. It was to Godwin he spoke. "What of Norway?"

"Crucial, my Lord. As soon as these festivities are ended I would you would closet yourself with me and the Lord Hakon."

But even as Godwin replied, Emma hurried to catch up to Cnute and she took his arm. He smiled, but it was at the crowd, and when he spoke to her it was through his teeth. "Lady Queen."

"What is wrong, my Lord?"

He removed her arm from his own. "What is wrong, Lady, is that with your infernal meddling"—all the while he continued waving and smiling to the crowd—"my unhappy sister is now kept a sobbing captive in Rouen . . . unwed in actuality, unwanted and untended. It is your doing. This marriage was arranged at your instigation."

Gytha looked over at him. There was obvious sorrow in her eyes. "Can you now not rescue her?"

"For the present," Cnute told her, "I can do nothing. Not until the question of Norway is resolved. I cannot expose my flank. Robert, I can fight. Will fight. But in one direction at a time."

"That is nonsense. She is your sister." Gytha made no pretense of smiling.

"Lady, enough."

"You butchered her husband and now—"

"Gytha!" Godwin ordered. "Shut up!"

The King turned his back to her and moved up the hill. Emma hurried to keep pace. Godwin ordered Behi to keep Gytha back from the King. He, too, then hurried to keep abreast of Cnute's long strides.

"Tell me as we walk," Cnute said to him, "of Norway."

"Erling has defeated Olaf at Tunsberg."

"Your word of this reached me in London. They will want to make Erling their king, these fickle Norwegian magnates."

"Yes," Godwin agreed. "I am worried on that, too."

"What do you suggest?"

"This, my Liege," Godwin lowered his voice. "I have a soldier, a spy in Olaf's camp. Let him kill the Lord Erling."

"And Olaf will be blamed." Cnute smiled. "We will meet on it ere this business be ended."

Godwin slipped back into the crowd. Cnute's strides seemed to Emma to get even longer. She started to ask him a question about the Norway problem, but he cut her off short and gritted through his teeth about her "infernal interference" and she tried to explain, but he would hear nothing she had to say.

"If you should as much as open your mouth to me about any subject of state," he told her, "I shall have your head placed on a pike outside my door."

They reached the great hall and a feast was begun. A magician performed an act of great marvel. He had a large piece of iron bent into an arch and with it he raised swords and pots and helmets into the air as if they were glued to the iron and it took two men to pull one sword away from the powerful magic of the iron arch. The King smiled at the wonder of it and those in the court "aahhed" and "ooohed" that such a thing was.

Cnute arose and cheers went up and then he stood at the table and told them all of the wondrous reception the Emperor and the Holy Father had given him . . . of the splendor of Conrad's Easter coronation and of the love which now bound Conrad and his brother Cnute . . . and how the infant Gunnerhild was to be united in marriage to the imperial heir Henry . . . Henry, but a child, yet already King of the Germanies. Cnute was telling them of further blessings which the Pope sent to his people of England—

"Tell us of Estrid!" Gytha was on her feet facing the King. Only Godwin stood between them at the long table.

The King was angry. "Lady, I bid you sit."

"Tell us, King, of your sister shunned even on her wedding night by the Duke of Normandy, locked up in a chamber in Rouen and left to the company of rats. Tell us of this glory, King Cnute."

"Countess of Wessex, I will warn you no more—" He was calm.

"Tell us how my brother died and now how you treat his widow—"

"She is my sister!" he screamed. He took a deep breath, but he was quite visibly livid.

Emma looked across at Gytha, whose face was fired to match her red hair.

"Butcher!" Gytha yelled.

"Godwin! If you do not get her from my sight I will have her chopped up and set before you for your next meal."

Godwin and Behi removed a screaming Gytha from the hall, and before the feast had ended, Gytha and her brood were packed off to Pevensey, Behi as their escort.

In the afternoon, when the feast had run its course, Cnute told his lords they would gather in his chambers. "We will speak of Norway now," he told them.

"I am sorry for what Gytha has done," Godwin said.

"Wives"—Cnute looked directly at Emma—"should bear their fruit and then, like the vine, be left in the garden alone to wither. They serve no other purpose."

Father Stigand, who had, despite his propensity for seasickness, gone with Cnute to Rome, was called to join the lords in counsel. So, Emma thought, the little priest with the tiny mouth, beady eyes, raspberry cheeks and little brown beard was to be closeted with the great. Well, Emma saw there were ways to learn what was the business of state even if the King would shut her out. Godwin and his infernal loyalty to the King would be useless, but Stigand, who had helped her once, could be brought around. Cnute would not shut her off so easily. Emma called for Wordig and went hawking.

That night she sent word to Stigand that she had need of his counsel. She was nude upon her bed when the knock came upon her door.

"Who is it?" Emma called.

"Father Stigand."

"Come in. It's unbolted."

He entered in the darkness. He was an inept lover. On again, and quickly off again. He had spindly legs and a soft roll of fat around his waist. His breath was like stale grease.

"You are such a great pleasure," Emma told him.

"You poor woman. Not one whore, but two the King has brought from Rome."

"Yes," she said. She was quite dumbfounded. How had she overlooked two women in Cnute's entourage entirely? "And you, poor man, you must be exhausted. The long trip and now all the business with the Norwegians to resolve."

"Hakon will be leading a force north, of course," he said.

"And Cnute—" She let him interrupt.

"Will not be going, naturally."

"Naturally," she agreed. "He told me he felt more needed here," she lied as if Cnute shared every confidence with her.

"I think it is less that and more, though he would say that to comfort his wife, of course, that the Norwegians are such fickle creatures, who's to know what they'll do next. The three should reach here on the morrow."

"The three?"

"Kalf Arnesson, his wife, Stig, and her brother, Thor the Dog."

"Lovely woman . . ." Emma hadn't the vaguest notion who he was talking about.

"You are so kind to everyone, Emma. I may call you Emma?"

"Of course." She looked at his tiny mouth. "Poor Cnute, it seems there is nothing he can do to help his sister."

"Nothing. Not until the danger from Norway is absolved. I must go now though, Emma. I have my evening office yet to say."

"Come to me in about three days," she said. "We must not be seen together too often or it will be dangerous for you."

The priest put his robes back on and left. Emma sent for the German.

"He's gone," the serving woman told her. "He's gone back to Saxony."

Emma tried to sleep, but Estrid kept crowding her mind as she would nearly doze. There had to be something she could do for her. She had meant to get Estrid out of Winchester, but she had not meant to bring this living death upon her. Finally she fell asleep.

Had she known, she still could not have prepared herself for Stig, wife to Kalf Arnesson. Stig was a virtual giant. She not only was toweringly tall, but big-boned and fat. She wore some sort of skirt made out of lamb's hide, nothing on her legs or feet, and the skirt came no lower than the top of her knees. She had enormous breasts with long nipples, all quite visible through the coarse-weave blouse-like thing she wore from the waist up. Her hair was brown and she had it stranded into two long braids. She carried a sword, unsheathed, through the rope tied about her waist. Kalf was shorter but broader than his wife, a flaming red-haired man with a ruddy face, scarlet ears and a scraggle of a beard with a space where the hair wouldn't grow midway down the right side of his face. Thor the Dog looked more to be Thor the Bear and was bigger than either of the other two. Emma assumed that in all that hair somewhere there existed a human being. He wore braies tied with leather straps and an apron about his waist, but he wore nothing above. The hair, however, covering his upper torso was so thick and long, it looked as if he were wearing a hair shirt. He loomed; he occupied a room, and though he was terrifying to look at, Emma soon found him a gentle sort of man and considerate.

Emma found Stig less gentle. She came that first evening to the feast given in their honor bearing several huge rather old-smelling fish. She declined to eat any of the prepared food and, instead, scaled and cleaned the fish and cooked them on sticks over the fire. She insisted Kalf and Thor, though they had eaten heavily of the banquet food, eat the fish as well. After, she went out and got a large earthen tub, heated water and did her laundry by the fire. She washed the blouse-thing she had been wearing and so sat bare-breasted while her laundry dried by the fire.

During the course of her visit, Stig managed to kill a cow belonging to the abbey, two goats belonging to villagers, chickens wandering loose on the streets, assorted doves, an abbey pig and a thinglith's horse.

Emma tried to avoid the woman as much as possible and kept to her chamber. Estrid's plight occupied more and more of her thoughts. She had to do something, but first she had to determine exactly what was the lady's condition and decide who could be trusted to help. When they were in Rouen, the priest, Robin of Jumieges, had seemed more than sympathetic toward Estrid, and although Robert's confessor, he did not appear on the best of terms with him. Perhaps—yes, Robin might help. Godwin watched her and she would have to be careful that he did not fall upon her plot. The beautiful young priest from Jumieges was said inclined toward men. She could send Gamol and tell Cnute he had been taken with some disease and that she had sent him off to be cured. Care, she must proceed with care, take her time and be cautious.

But another problem nagged at Emma and it was one which would not wait upon time. She had missed her second menstrual and she would need to pay a visit to the old hag who lived near the gates. Emma had not been to Cnute's bed since he first discovered her pregnant with Gunnerhild, and were she found pregnant now, he would certainly have her killed. Before the day was over she must get some herbs from the old hag at the hovel near the gate.

Emma was about to call for Gamol when a thinglith came and informed her that the King wished her to attend upon their guests in the great hall.

"You are negligent and not giving proper attention to our guests," Cnute told her, his voice soft and friendly but his eyes hard.

Emma gritted her teeth and walked across to where Stig was milking a cow she had brought into the hall. "Do you well, Lady Stig?" Emma asked.

Stig grinned. "I once trained a kid goat to lick my ass after I shit," Stig told Emma. She had sharp fang-like teeth. She was also once again doing her laundry and her nipples and bare breasts pressed against the cow as she tugged upon the cow's teats. The sword kept getting in the way and she removed it. "I'm going to kill Olaf with this sword," she told Emma as she set it aside with a clang. "Olaf had my father hung by the testicles for calling on Woden to end the drought."

That afternoon Emma escaped from the Norwegians. Together with Aesval she made arrangements for Gamol to get to Dover and for a six-rower to take him to Rouen. Then, but not confiding in Aesval, she paid her visit to the old hag who lived in the hovel by the gate. The old woman had only one tooth, a fang which dug into her lower lip. She smiled displaying the fang, and for the price of two chickens and a hunk of smoked pork gave Emma a bowl of gray, mortared powder. The hovel stank of dead rats and Emma was glad to escape it.

Two weeks passed and Stig had her menstrual period and wore a goat skin quite visibly tied between her legs. The goat's head and horns bounced along the ground as it dangled down from between her legs. The sight made Emma fully aware of her condition. The bitter powders given her by the old hag at the hovel by the gate had as yet done no good.

"If you want to unbear the child, ride a brown horse," Stig whispered to her, but Emma pretended she had no idea what the woman meant. Emma was concerned, however, that her condition would be visible before long and she had to get away from court and Cnute.

"I would visit the Countess of Wessex," Emma told Cnute.

"You will go nowhere until our guests from Norway have departed," he told her.

She went back to the old hag who lived in the hovel by the gate for more powders, but they did no good.

"A brown horse. Ride it at least ten leagues," Stig grinned and whispered. Emma was becoming alarmed.

And then word came from Norway. Lord Erling had been killed.

"Olaf did it," Stig said.

But Emma knew it was Godwin's spy that had killed him.

"I shall kill Olaf," Stig announced and the Norwegians loaded their train and readied to depart for the North. Stig whispered to Emma as she bid them good-bye, "A brown horse. Remember, it must be a brown horse."

The train had barely gone from sight when Emma went to Cnute. "May I journey to Pevensey now to visit the Countess of Wessex?"

"The better from sight," he said. "At least you won't be interfering in our business with Olaf. Go."

Emma sent for Aesval and the Lady Beatrice and they readied for the trip. She had word sent to Gamol to return to Pevensey.

"Where's my horse?" Emma asked as the train prepared to depart.

"A sore shank, my Lady Queen," the hostler told her. "I brought this mare about for you."

Emma was helped upon the brown horse and the train moved off. The sun was hot and they rode east away from it and the day cooled and became night and crickets patterned an endless song against the stillness. It was a dark night of clouds with but a few patches of stars and as they neared the sea a fog came in and ate up those.

"Lady Queen," one of the soldiers suggested, "we should stop and seek shelter hereabout for the road is barely visible and I fear the night."

"Well, I fear it not and we shall continue," Emma told him. And so they rode through the dense mist. A wolf howled and Emma shivered. There was something anxious in the cry of the wolf. Trees appeared out of the haze, strangely twisted and seeping water from their leaves. The sound of a furious sea cut the thick fog. "Are we near?" Emma asked.

"Perhaps seven leagues or so, Lady," a soldier answered.

He had barely spoken when the pain came. Jesus! Oh God! Emma could hold it back no longer and screamed out. They helped her from her horse and she felt the aborted mass between her thighs, wet and like slime and her insides felt like they had all come out. Jesus! Maria! Lord God! The pain! She tried not to cry out again, but could not stop herself.

"What is it?" one of the soldiers in command inquired.

"The Queen is taken with a pain in her belly. The pork at morning meal was perhaps bad," Aesval told him. "Take the men away and I will tend her."

"Can she be moved?" Emma heard the same soldier ask and stifled a scream. The pain was unbearable.

"We shall see," Aesval answered. "Go away." Aesval took the aborted mass from between her thighs and, concealing it, buried it in the damp soil. She then stripped large tears from her bliaut and stuffed the fabric between Emma's legs to soak up the blood. "Can you make it to Pevensey on a stretcher?"

"The brown horse . . ." Emma answered.

"Can you make it?"

"Yes." The pain was subsiding.

They made a stretcher of branches and skin covers which were among the packings of the train. Emma was bounced and tossed about as the soldiers carried her on the litter in the dark. She tried not to think of the pain and instead thought of Estrid and of her pain. Although there was as yet no light she could sense the dawn. She cried out as the men carried her down an embankment.

"You are too rough," she heard a voice say. "I will carry the Queen down the hill." He took her in his arms and she realized it was Wordig. She hadn't remembered he was even in the party. He carried her gently down the slope and she was put back on the litter. "But a few more miles," Wordig assured her.

It was a cold gray dawn just inching its way in from the east. Doors banged and shutters opened. Emma didn't open her eyes but she could hear the sounds. "The Queen," a voice called out.

And then she heard Gytha. "The Queen? What of the Queen?"

"She is here, my Lady. She is here."

Emma opened her eyes and looked up with relief to see Gytha leaning over the litter.

"She is bleeding," Beatrice said.

"My God! How came she to be hurt?" Gytha asked.

Aesval whispered to her.

"Take her to the chamber there . . . across . . . the next room. I will call for the physician," Gytha told them.

In midmorning Gytha came in to see her. "Go have some breakfast, Aesval, I will sit with the Queen." When Aesval was out of earshot she added, "Now, Emma, what is all this about?"

"I came for two reasons. I sent Gamol to Rouen to find out where and how Estrid is being held. And if possible will try to arrange her rescue."

"Emma, do you think—"

"Yes. Will you help me?"

"Of course," Gytha told her. "Do you have a plan?"

"We can do nothing until Gamol returns."

"Behi is here," Gytha told her. "He will help."

"He doesn't like me much. Can he be trusted?"

"Yes," Gytha assured her, and after a moment added, "But you said there were two reasons for coming."

"Isn't the second apparent? I was certain if I spent one more day at court someone would find me out, report me to Cnute. It would be obvious to anyone that it's not his child."

"Obviously. Whose was it?"

"I am not certain."

"The German priest?"

"How did you know about the German priest?"

"Everybody knew about the German priest."

"Oh, Lord. Yes, it was probably his."

Emma spent a quiet week and a half recuperating. She told Gytha of all the gossip of court, of the strange Norwegian visitors, of Olaf fleeing to Russia, of the important news and the trivia.

"Oh, Emma," Gytha admitted, "it gets lonesome at Pevensey."

"Even with your brood?"

"Even with my brood."

At the end of the week Gamol arrived from Rouen. They plotted. Estrid was being kept a prisoner in the crypt beneath the rubble of St. Gervais. Emma and her brothers had played there as children and she knew it well.

"There are two guards at all times," Gamol told them. "Men loyal to the duke. They cannot be bribed, I'm told."

"But killed?"

"Yes. A woman of the duke's house takes the lady's meals to her. Her sister was the poisoned duke's mistress, whose head it's said hangs in the ducal hall. The woman can be bribed."

"And Robin of Jumieges?"

"He will help us."

Two days later Emma, Behi, Wordig and Gamol set sail in a small rower. Emma had no doubt that they would succeed. The sea was gentle.

CHAPTER 13

Rouen, 1028

THE HOUR WAS BUT PRIME, YET THE POUNDING AT THE DOOR PERSISTED. Edward got up from his prayers.

"The duke," Gilbert of Brionne said, "the duke will have us in the great hall."

Gilbert looked washed and scrubbed and his hair, for Gilbert at least, was in place. Edward wondered how, at such an ungodly hour of the morning, he could look the picture of composed pleasantness.

"Let me throw on a tunic." Edward pulled the loose-fitting linen over his head and pulled the thin white hair out from where it was caught beneath.

"He is mad, Edward. I think our cousin, Robert, is quite mad. Did you hear him screaming in the night?"

Edward straightened the loose braies he was wearing and cross-gartered them with leather laces. "He screams every night. He dreams he's dying."

"He's mad, that's what."

"Do you think I should have changed into something more respectable?"

"There's no time. He's raging about something and wants us there. One of the priests says he thinks Robert's possessed. And others whisper—"

"There are those who would whisper anything." Edward folded a mantle over his arm and followed Gilbert from the small chamber.

"I think"—Gilbert turned back to him—"he has nightmares because he poisoned his brother."

Edward followed him along the arched loggia. "What on earth does one have to do with the other?"

"God is punishing him," Gilbert said.

"God punishes us by sending us to hell. Not with nightmares."

Gilbert didn't respond and they walked in file toward the great hall, moving swiftly.

Each morning it seemed to Edward there were fresh heads hung in the hall. There were new shriveled faces this morning. Edward wondered where they came from. Robert was pacing at one end of the long room.

He turned to them. "Well, cousins, we take our time."

Despite the early hour the room was fairly crowded. Men parted as Edward approached the duke. "We came at once." Edward felt cross and he was further irritated by the tone of Robert's voice.

Robert stopped pacing and threw up his arms in disgust. *"Divortium Procurator.* This legate of Rome, this papal puppy, talks to me of *Divortium."* Robert pointed to a thin dark-haired man in cardinal's robes who stood near the corner. The man had a blank look of indifference. Robert's finger punctured the air in the man's direction and he yelled, "No woman in the history of mankind has ever divorced her husband."

"The woman"—the legate spoke Latin with a decidedly Italianate dialect—"does not seek such a suit; her brother, the King of England—"

"The King of England is over there." Robert shoved an arm back in Edward's direction.

"I am the King of England," Edward announced.

"—Daneland and Norway," the legate continued unabated, "asks that the marriage be declared null—that the marriage was never consummated and therefore did—"

"Oh, I rode the old mare," Robert yelled. "I'll tell you, Roman priest, she stinks like a sow too long in the pen, but I held my nose and rode her. I could tell you how I plowed that rotten pasture, how—"

The legate ignored him. "And consanguinity. The woman claims your blood within the fourth degree."

"She's a damn Jutland heathen; what blood have we in common?"

"And she accuses you of adultery, naming a tanner's daughter—"

Robert laughed. "The tanner is a knight for all that now."

"And she claims to be one of fourteen God sibs who stood to your baptism."

"She's old enough for a fact, but she wasn't there. All lies. She is a greater sinner; she not only lies, but she kills. This is the greatest of sins. She killed two of the men attending on her. A sinner true enough, but a sinner I shall keep as wife. Tell the Pope she is my property, my chattel and I will have her back. Her estates are mine; and this was but part of her dower. The gold I was promised to wed this Danish pig has not yet been delivered. I shall go to war for it. Tell the Pope that. And that I sue for what is mine. And tell him divorce is against the nature of God. Matrimony is a sanctified state, broken only by death. The woman is my chattel by Norman law, by Roman law and by God. And by God, I shall not give her up."

Robert turned his back to the legate, walked through the men and strode from the room. Edward and Gilbert followed. As Robert reached the outside he leaned down over a bench.

"What is wrong?" Gilbert asked.

"My head," Robert said. "My head is killing me."

"Here." Edward put his hands over his cousin's black hair, pulled slowly, his arms aching until the aura moved upward. With it a black ball was formed. Edward drew it out, pulling it like a stone from a thick gruel. He tossed it aside and then took several deep breaths. "Is it gone?"

"The pain is gone. I know not how you do that, Edward, but it is a miracle."

"The legate did this to him," Gilbert said.

They made such a contrasting trio, standing there under the loggia, away from the morning sun, the dark-haired and dark-skinned young duke, the count from Brionne with his brown unruly shock of hair and sun-gold skin and the pale white albino with his pink eyes and white hair. There was nothing to suggest their kinship.

"It was not just the legate. I have not slept the night. Robin has tried my patience and withholds absolution from me until I give up claim to my lawful wife. I know he helped her escape and I shall have his head for it."

"Yet, he is my friend," Edward said.

"He is a traitor. And my cousin Alan has sent me this lovely gift which arrived this morning from Brittany. A sculpture, an effigy of my head, or so the letter did read. I opened the box to find the head of a dead pig."

" 'Tis but your mother's doing," Gilbert said. "Pay no mind."

"Alan is my man and, damn Judith or not, he will kneel to his lord. After I destroy England, he is next—"

A monk scurried by carrying a dead squirrel on a white cloth. "The fourth in a week," he scolded. "Someone is poisoning the squirrels."

The three hardly looked at him.

"And to break my day further"—Robert slumped down upon a bench with a thud—"some petty French nobles give us trouble in Vixen."

"Do we go to put them down?" Gilbert asked.

Edward reached to touch his sword, but realized he was not wearing it. "I ache for a fight."

"Good, but we'll leave Vixen to Dreux; we are invading England."

"When?" Edward's eyes lit up. This was news.

"Three days hence."

"You have a fleet?" Edward asked.

"I have seven ships that will be ready."

"Seven ships!" Edward turned away. "Lord! Robert, that is not invasion, that isn't even a visit."

An old serving man with a limp, in a torn tunic, and a black puppy at his heels came up to the duke. He pulled the cloth back on a basket he was carrying. "Will you have some bread and wine, my Lord?"

"Yes." Robert reached into the basket and took out a loaf of bread. "Edward?"

"No . . ."

The old man took a silver cup from the basket and gave it to Robert and from a skin poured a deep red wine into it.

"Don't fret so, Edward," Robert said after sipping from the cup. "Seven boats of Norman men will be enough to destroy Winchester. Gilbert, take some wine." Robert handed him the cup. "Cnute and his thinglith, I've learned, are in York. Winchester lies unprotected. And there is rumor that Olaf is marching from Russia toward Norway—"

"But seven ships!" Edward stared out into the courtyard. The grass was long. Sheep or goats should be let to graze.

"Cnute's move to York was sudden and I have had no time to raise an army. And why do we need one? There is no one to strike back at us. We'll go in and raze Winchester."

"I'll be a king without a—"

"You can always build a new Winchester. We'll loot it well. There is a great wealth there I am told. The Rome of the West they call it. And prisoners . . . for slaves . . . Estrid and the Queen." Robert snorted with delight. "You shall have Emma for your prisoner and you can get up every morning and have her tortured before breakfast. That should brighten your day, Edward. We'll fight like the Dane. Like old Rollo did. It's in my blood. We'll strike and pull back and strike again another day and pull back—"

"And how does that get me England?"

"With the wealth of Winchester, I'll raise you a great army."

"Godwin?" Edward asked. "Where is Godwin?"

"With an army at Pevensey."

"Not with the King?" Gilbert again took the wine cup from Robert. "What's to keep Godwin from burning Rouen while we burn Winchester?"

"Surprise. No one will expect this." Robert was enraptured with the plot. "I have talked to no one of this until now."

"Winchester is far from the sea, Robert," Edward told him.

"I know Winchester is far from the sea. Where is the best point to land if we want to surprise them at Winchester?"

"Corfe, I suspect," Edward said. "But seven ships?"

"Christ fed the multitude. . . . Have a little faith, Edward . . . a little faith." Robert handed the serving man the empty wine cup. "We shall sail in three days hence. The fleet will be at Boulogne—"

"Fleet?"

"Seven ships, then. But let's to the hawks and not a word of this to anyone."

That night there was a thunderstorm. Edward had been asleep, but he remembered clearly getting up and putting on his mantle and going outside onto the loggia, just beyond his chamber door. He looked out into the dark courtyard. It was the dead of night and raining heavily; still there were sheep wandering in the open court nibbling the grass. Edward stood back under the arches in the shelter from the rain; yet it sifted upon his face. Lightning cracked open the sky; still the sheep neither huddled nor sought refuge beneath the portico. Monks came, shrouded in black hoods, their faces hidden, and they carried on their shoulders a board with a body upon it. And the body had no aura of light like the monks. They moved, the monks and the bier, out into the open under the heavy rain. Lightning opened the sky again, and Edward saw the body was that of a dark-haired man and he went out into the rain and up to the corpse which was dry despite the pouring rain and he saw that the young man was dead and realized it was Robert. He was wearing black hose and breeches and a black tunic with a breast of seashells. On his head was a coronet made of tiny tapers. One of the monks lit the candles and despite the rain they blazed and then they carried him away until even the blazing candles could not be seen. And then more shrouded monks came bearing another corpse. This was Cnute and he was dressed in a gown of gold coins. He wore no crown and his hair was tied in knots. And then the monks and the body they bore vanished. A third body was brought fourth. It was dressed wearing his own fine scarlet mantle and when he approached with horror thinking to see himself, he saw that it was Alfred, but he had no eyes and his sword was broken in half. The body, like the others, vanished and Edward went back into his chamber. He knelt down upon the cushioned kneeler.

The rain ceased and the sun arose and Edward dressed and stepped out onto the loggia. The grass was clipped and short and he knew what he had witnessed in the night had not been simply a dream.

It was but evenings before the planned sailing. Robert gathered the cousins and knights of his court and revealed his plans to march upon Winchester. The archbishop protested it was folly, but Robert ignored his uncle and rallied his men.

"I have a new sword," Alfred said.

"You aren't going, Aly." The dream or vision weighed heavily on Edward.

"I shall."

"No." Edward was firm.

"I shall ask Robert."

An old man, filthy and naked except for layers of kelp, still wet and making mud of the dirt on his legs, suddenly appeared in the room. Everyone ceased talking. He moved toward Edward and then stopped directly before him. "Like a giant candle, the mast will dance with fire and a great storm shall rage upon the sea. It is a sign from God that Edward, son of Ethelred, a saint and King-to-be, shall never take England by the sword."

Robert leaped to his feet. "What say you, old man?"

"St. Edward shall never take England by the sword."

"Saint, is it now?" Robert tossed a large bone at the old man's head. The man ducked and the bone fell upon the stone. "Is this some of your doing, Uncle?"

"I have no truck with these mystics. Some madman who can't even find his clothes." The archbishop went back to his plate of food.

The old man started out, a piece of wet kelp dragging behind, stopped, turned and spoke. "A flaming mast shall be the sign of God. Heed it, Robert, Duke of Normandy."

The doors clanged behind the old man. For a moment there was silence in the hall and then everyone seemed to be talking at once.

They sailed. Robert had allowed Alfred to come despite Edward's pleadings and he was in the duke's ship. Edward commanded the troops of one of the seven ships; Mauger, William, Gilbert, Richard of Evreux, Ralf of Gace, cousins all, the rest. Foolish, Edward thought. We are foolish and we shall all be killed. Edward led his soldiers in prayer. The vessels were small and overcrowded and the ship Edward commanded was no larger than the rest. But the sun shone and it was a beautiful clear day, the sky and the sea both brilliant blue. There was a good wind as they rounded from the port at Boulogne.

They were half an hour to sea. The sky was clear and then out of nowhere came the storm. It was sunny bright one moment and the next black as night. The wind, so strong and helpful, became violent and angry, tearing at the vessels, tossing the water relentlessly against the small ships. There was no controlling direction; they were being driven back toward the Norman coast. Gale rains soaked them and water filled the deck. Edward struggled to keep the vessel ahead and the ship behind in his view. Robert was directly afore with the most experienced helmsman of the seven aboard, so Edward urged his own helmsman to do little more than stay within sight of the lead ship. The rain came more intensely and at times it was hardly possible to see those on the ship, let alone the other vessels. For hours, which seemed days, the sea tore at the small ship. Was this the death of which the vision foretold? If it was, what of the corpse of Cnute?

"The mast! Look to the mast!" someone shouted and Edward looked up to the top of the mast where flames danced in the storm. Men fell to their knees in prayer and Edward knelt and the flames disappeared and came again—a ball of fire which moved about the top of the mast like a halo. Edward, down upon his knees, heard the voice as if brought in upon the wind: "Edward, saint, shall sit upon the throne of England, but not by the sword."

Edward stared up at the mast. "Do you see?" he asked.

And all hands yelled that they saw.

"And did you hear the voice?"

But no man had heard the voice.

The voice came again: "Edward, son of Ethelred, shall sit at the hand of God and upon the throne of England, but he shall not attain his birthright by the sword."

"Did you hear the voice?" he asked again.

But no man had heard the voice.

The fire came again and then vanished. The storm ebbed, disappearing almost as quickly as it had risen. The gale winds became a breeze and the rain stopped, but the sun remained hidden. It was near dusk and they moored together. All seven ships were saved. The commanders conferred on the deck of Robert's vessel.

"We saw at the mast a strange fire sent from heaven," Robert said.

"And on our ship as well," Gilbert said.

And the others all saw the fire.

"And did you hear the voice?" Edward asked.

"I heard nothing," Robert said.

Nor had the others.

"The voice spoke to me and told me that I would not gain England by the sword, yet I would be King."

"It is a sign we should turn back," Ralf of Gace said and Edward sensed a sigh of relief among them all.

"Think you it is so, Edward?" Robert asked.

"A sign," Edward said.

"My starsman tells me," Robert addressed them all, "that we have come around Contentin and that Jersey lies ahead. We shall night in Jersey and on the morrow go to Dol and bring Cousin Alan to his knees."

Dol was a far easier conquest than Winchester. None seemed to regret the change. Alan was not brought to his knees; he literally waited upon them. The ships must have been sighted earlier for the Count of Brittany greeted his Lord of Normandy and cousin upon his knees on the shore. Alan had flaming red hair and spoke perfect Norman, though Edward could understand hardly anyone else among these strange-tongued Bretons. Judith had fled her son and Robert laughed at his mother's fear and Alan laughed and all the cousins laughed and they formed a circle and made a pact and each cut into his finger. For Edward the pain was almost unbearable. They let the blood fall into a golden cup and then the cup was passed among them and they drank signifying their unity.

It was late into the night and they marched in the darkness to the church at Dol. The sanctuary light burned. Robert stood before them in the dimness.

"And if I should die you shall bow down to my heir and make him your man, save Edward, who is King of England." Robert took each by the hand and each answered, "So I vow."

And when he came to Edward he said, "And Edward shall make my heir his heir."

"And so I vow," Edward said.

Robert took the golden cup and from it spilled three drops of the red blood upon the altar, staining the white linen cloth.

A gray monk came banging into the church and started screaming in that strange Breton tongue at them.

"Kill him," Robert yelled.

As Ralf of Gace drew out a knife, the gray monk fled and they laughed and sat on the stone floor and found wine and drank.

CHAPTER 14

Winchester, 1030

EDITH WALKED. SHE NORMALLY SKIPPED BUT THE TITMOUSE SAT ON HER shoulder and she was afraid it would fly away. She was alone. She was not supposed to be alone, not after what happened on Wodensday, but she was not scared. God would look after her. God told her so. She saw God. Everyone thought God was an old man with white hair, but Edith knew better and told no one. God was an eagle, a giant golden eagle and he lived in the sun.

A crone sat cross-legged on the stones in the middle of the street going up the hill. She was mashing berries into a stone bowl and her fingers were stained and blue. "May your piss be free from sin," she greeted Edith.

"And yours, Old Mother," Edith said as she stepped around her.

"Here," the old woman said, handing her a dried bean pod, "put this between your bed and the door and death shall pass by your house."

"Thank you," Edith said, taking the pod. "I shall tell God of your kindness."

"Tell Godwin. That would be of better use," the old woman said. She called after Edith, "Tell your father."

The titmouse stayed on her shoulder.

She came to the square unafraid. The man's head was there on a pike. She was not sorry he was dead. On Wodensday he had followed her up the narrow little street behind the cooper's where the heathens once lived.

They were all gone now, driven away, and the thatch was blown from the roofs and only the walls of empty hovels remained. At the end of the winding path was a stone fence. It was here she came often to meet the gray wolf. It was near the stone fence that she turned on Wodensday to see the man behind her. His braies were pulled down and he had his thing in his hand and it was big and hard and ugly and he moved toward her and she could feel his breath like the smell of a dead rat upon her.

"Let me put it where you pee-pee," he said.

The gray wolf came and stood beside her and the man backed away, still holding his large hard thing in his hands. The gray wolf ever so slowly moved toward the man until he was pressed against the mud wall of one of the empty heathen hovels and his thing had gotten shriveled and small. Edith ran to the King's house and found her father. Now the man's head was on a pike. He died because he had sinned. "For man shall be punished for sins of the flesh." Edith knew what that meant and she also knew no man would ever touch her, ever . . . ever. Edith would bring no man to sins of the flesh. She had vowed so to God on a hot day when she lay on the hillside beyond the walls of Winchester and her brothers played in the stream below. The golden eagle came down and perched in a tree and she knelt down and made that vow. She was not afraid of men like the dead man whose head was on a pike for the golden God of the sun would look out for her.

The gray wolf was not there today in the narrow street. He did not always come. She knew he was sent by God. She had brought him a piece of cold mutton, which was in her pocket. She never ate mutton, but saved her piece for the gray wolf.

The titmouse pecked at her ear and she giggled. She turned and went back down the path to the stone street. A girl was squatting in the way. Red urine ran over the stones, down, away from the girl. Edith was only twelve and had not yet had her flux, but she knew what it was and was not afraid to see the red urine.

A thinglith, high up on his horse, waved to her as he clomped by. His name was Dorgalag and he was from York and he let her brothers play with his gold-handled sword.

Edith made her way toward the King's house, but it was not a house at all. It was a ramble of buildings inside a spiked fence. She went through the gates. A thinglith stood to each side. Her mother didn't like the thingliths and called them names, called them "fancy fools" and "pompous pigs," but they were mostly good to Edith and her brothers, and one, who was called Igedmor, brought her back holy water from Rome when he went with the King and a feather from a giant condor he saw captured in the North.

One of the thingliths smiled down on her as she went through the gate.

"Where did you get the bird, child?" His gold armbands shone in the sun.

"From God," she said. "He came from God."

"How do you know it's a he?" the other thinglith, who had curls of red hair that hung to his shoulders, asked.

"Because if it were a mother bird it would have had to stay in the nest," she said quite assuredly and went on into the courtyard moving between chickens and priests, pigs and Italians, whores and Norwegians . . . and there were mummers there and she stopped to watch. She turned when she heard the great piercing shriek that came from the hall and ran quickly inside to see what was happening.

Standing in the middle of the great room was the largest woman Edith had ever seen and she didn't have any clothes on. She wore nothing at all and her huge breasts were the size of near full-grown pigs and they hung down and had long nipples like sticks at the ends. Between her legs was not hair like most women, curled and in a patch, but it was straight and hung down like she ought to wear combs in it. Edith thought it looked quite silly, still she didn't laugh. It was all rather amazing. The woman was holding a great iron sword over her head and she let it drop with a clang to the floor.

"I am Stig," the woman cried out, "and I have killed Olaf with this sword and the sun went out."

The King sat on his chair at the end of the hall and Edith thought he looked surprised. The Queen sat next to him and she was just shaking her head. And on Cnute's other side her father was standing, but she couldn't see his face very well for he was whispering something to the King.

A cry went up. "Hail, Stig. Hail, Great Stig!"

And the titmouse flew away.

"I have killed Olaf Haroldsson and even the sun was afeared of me," the woman yelled and she took her breasts in her hands and raised them so the nipples were pointing out and then she almost sang, "And I've nursed death."

Edith felt a hand on her shoulder.

"What are you doing here?"

She turned to face her mother. Her mother was young, much younger than the Queen, and was pretty and had bright red hair.

"I came to watch."

"You were told to stay at home with your brothers. You know what happened on Wodensday."

Edith took the woman's freckled hand. "God and the gray wolf will take care of me. Besides, the man with the hard thing is dead. I saw his head in the square."

"Oh, child . . . sometimes . . . well . . . now that you're here stay in the hall and don't leave until either I or your father go."

"Did that woman really kill King Olaf?"

"She says so," her mother answered.

"They say Olaf was a saint," Edith told her.

"I think not. At least don't let Cnute hear you say such. He doesn't . . . Oh, Emma is beckoning to me. Now, Edith, you mind and don't leave the hall without one of us. Do you understand?"

"Yes, Mum."

Edith wandered about the big room. She could tell the languages and dialects even though she didn't always know what the words meant: an Italian in elegant clothes, tall and bald . . . and over there a Norman . . . they weren't welcome much at Winchester, she knew that . . . she thought of Edward and when she went to Rouen . . . he had long white fingers and white hair and she knew he must be a holy saint . . . there was a Flem . . . and a Celt . . . and more Norsemen than she could count. She did not see the titmouse anywhere. The woman called Stig went about telling people in a loud voice how she ran the sword through Olaf and how it became dark as night and Edith followed her about and the woman still didn't have any clothes on and she didn't even seem to notice and no one else paid much attention either. Yet Edith wanted to fetch her a skin to wrap around her waist to hide the long hair which hung from between her legs. She went away from Stig.

"How old is the lad?" she heard the bald Italian ask a Norseman.

"Cnute's son Svegan?"

"Yes."

"Sixteen, I think, or thereabout."

"A man then."

Edith stood and listened to them.

"He's not Emma's son?"

"No, he's the black whore's . . . Elgiva she's called."

"And he," the Italian asked, "is to be King of Norway?"

"No," the Norseman corrected him. "Regent. Svegan Cnutesson is to be regent."

Edith did not remember Svegan Cnutesson. Only his brother, Harold. She hated Harold. He was her age and mean and he had skinny feet and he pulled the legs off her rabbit, alive. She had heard a man whisper, here in this very hall, that Harold wasn't Cnute's son at all. She hoped he wasn't, that his father was a devil, and took him back to hell. The devils lived in the North it was said . . . in the cold where the sun never shone. Harold came from the North.

The Norseman was now telling the Italian about Harold. "Ah . . . but you see . . ."

"And you say," the Italian whispered, "that he looks nothing like Cnute?"

"Nothing. But he looks like a shoemaker in Roeskild. Cnute ordered the man brought to him, but he had disappeared."

The Italian spoke still more softly. "And Cnute calls this child 'son'?"

"No longer. They say Godwin has convinced him the boy is the son of the vanished shoemaker."

"Where is the child? With his mother in the North?"

Now the Norseman leaned over to the Italian and Edith could barely hear him. "Not so far north, not as far north as the King would like. Cnute doesn't know, but Leofric—"

"The Earl of Mercia."

"Yes. Has had the boy brought to Coventry. Cnute would be angry if he knew. You can—"

A table of food was carried into the hall and Edith turned to watch and forgot the Italian and the Norseman. It was carried by four men and filled with meats and curds and honey and wine and loaves and a great pudding. Edith never ate meat, nor bird, nor fish, not the flesh of any animal. "It was wrong to eat God's creatures," she said and her mother did not make her. She ate only what grew from the ground or what animals gave willingly like milk and curds and birds' eggs, although she was not always certain about the eggs.

"Butterfly, what are you doing here?"

Edith turned about to face her father.

"Papa," she said.

Her father was the most handsome man in the great hall . . . in the world, perhaps. He bent and hugged her. He was kingly. He could be King if he wanted; she was certain. He was more kingly than Cnute. She had heard men say in the great hall, "Godwin thinks he's King."

"Olaf is dead," he told her.

"He is a saint they say."

"Ah, child, you may be right. Olaf will probably come back to haunt us all. He'll come popping up out of his grave like a cork in water."

She laughed.

"Anyway, the King is happy. Do you remember his son Svegan?"

"No," she told him.

"He will be regent of Norway. He's a good lad . . . much like his father, in lots of ways."

She looked at him with great seriousness. "I remember Harold."

"You can forget Harold. The King no longer calls him son. Poor Harold shall be left to ignominy in the North. A shoemaker's bastard he is."

"He is at Coventry."

"No, child—"

"I heard them say. Two men say he is with the Earl of Mercia—"

"You heard?"

"Yes."

"From whom?"

"The Norseman with the great nose told the Italian in the pretty robe . . . the man over there." She pointed.

"Edith, I was going to send for someone to take you home, but you could help Papa, I think. Would you just wander about this room and listen and later you can tell me everything that you heard?"

"You didn't know Harold was in Coventry?"

"I did not. And it is of great importance to the realm. Will you be Papa's spy?"

"Yes. Can I stay long?"

"Until I leave, if you wish."

"What if Mother wants me to go?"

"Leave her to me. Now off with you, master spy, and learn what you may learn."

She heard lots. Not much of it made much sense.

"There's a fire raging on the moor," a Yorkman told a Dane.

Then the man with the birds nesting in his hair was brought in. He had no legs and was carried on a board by two dwarfs, both with large feet which flapped when they walked. The man without legs had wads of gray hair, snarled and wound, twisted and dirty, and two sparrows were nesting in it. The dwarfs stopped before the Yorkman and the man without any legs rapped on the board. "I have sparrows nesting in my hair," he said, "and they peck at my brain."

"Go away," the Yorkman said.

The man on the board wore only a short tunic and where his legs ended there were shrivels of loose skin and deep scars. He had red pubic hair and a tiny penis. Edith followed the dwarfs carrying him and they stopped again, this time before Lady Beatrice of the Queen's house. "I have nesting sparrows in my hair and they peck at my brain," the man repeated.

"I have nothing for you," Lady Beatrice said and walked away.

The man's tunic was filthy and bird dung dripped down the front. The man motioned for Edith and when she came over he raised his tunic and displayed his navel, which, while the skin was dirty, had been brilliantly painted with designs of birds encircling his belly button. "I have nesting sparrows in my hair and they peck at my brain."

The Queen was crossing toward Father Stigand and the man without any legs motioned the dwarfs to move. They stopped directly in her path. "I have nesting sparrows in my hair and they peck at my brain." He displayed his navel for the Queen.

"And do the birds tell you anything?" the Queen asked.

"They tell me this, Lady Queen—a fat shote was made a crown of golden grain and he strutted about in his crown and he ate, as shotes will eat, anything, and a white crow—"

"Crows aren't white," the Queen said.

"This crow is not like other crows; it has white skin and white feathers and tiny pink eyes. And the shote and the crow were brothers for they had the same mother. And the white crow ate the crown of the shote and then started to eat the shote and pecked and picked until the shote's head was empty and it died and then the white crow took the farrow pig's tail and made its own crown."

The man without any legs fed a seed to one of the birds in his hair.

"And what must I do to save the shote?"

"You must kill the white crow," the man without legs told her.

And Edith understood. Harthacnut was the fat shote and Edward was the white crow.

"I will do as you tell," the Queen said. "And what will you have of me?"

Edith realized the Queen was saying she would kill Edward.

"I will have food for myself and my bearers and some seeds for the two sparrows that nest in my hair and peck at my brain."

The Queen ordered food and wine brought. She turned, noticing Edith. "Edith, dear child," the Queen said and touched her hand.

Edith recoiled as if she had been burned.

Father Stigand came over to the Queen. "The Archbishop of Winchester is dying," he said.

"I think," the Queen said quite deliberately, "that I shall have Edward killed."

"I said Aelfsige is dying."

"I heard you," the Queen told him. "You want to be Archbishop of Winchester, of course?"

"Yes."

"Then you will see Edward is killed."

"I am a priest," he said. There was a look of terror in his eyes.

"And you want to be an archbishop," she told him and walked off.

"A fire . . . a strange interminable fire burns across Devon," a bald man with a necklace of seashells said.

"And in Sussex . . ." a woman responded.

Edith realized the Queen meant it. She had to help Edward, get word to him, but how? She was but a child, who could she turn to? Papa would not help her in this, nor her mother. She walked about the hall listening, trying to determine what to do about Edward and all the while searching for the titmouse.

"The world is coming to an end," the Lady Aesval told the great Italian cardinal in his red robes. "It is burning up. There is said to be fire everywhere."

Edith's eyes were getting heavy and she sat down in a corner to think how she might help Edward, but she fell asleep.

She didn't wake up until the next morning at home, but she was the first up. All her brothers were still in bed. Sven usually was up before them all, but not this morning. Her brother Sven was bad, they said, and he was always getting into trouble, but he meant no harm and he loved all the animals and he was good to her and to his brothers and would hit anyone who picked on them. He was bad at his lessons and Papa made him learn to read, but he didn't really learn. He was good at swords and was learning to ride . . . only Mama always worried about him falling. Tostig followed Sven everywhere and sometimes he was just as bad. Papa called the two of them his "vile Vikings" and said they would come to no good. Harold was different. He was always so serious and told Papa he wanted to learn how to read. He never seemed to laugh and collected things and hid things like a pack rat. Papa said he would be wealthier than all the men in England before he was twelve. Harold said he was going to be King, but Papa told him to hush and not say such things. The baby cried and Mama's white dog pushed open the door and went in where the baby had been sleeping.

That day Edith went back to the great hall to spy for Papa. On the way she went up the narrow street to find the gray wolf. He was waiting for her and she gave him the mutton and the bone. "It's wrong to eat flesh," she told him; the gray wolf paid little heed to her and kept eating. She never petted nor touched him for she sensed he didn't like that. She merely stood and talked to him. Once a man came and threatened to kill the wolf and Edith told the man if he didn't go away she would bite his leg off.

"Who are you, you little bitch?" the man said and picked up a big stick.

"The daughter to my Lord of Wessex," she said, looking straight at him, and he dropped the stick and ran away.

The gray wolf finished the mutton and disappeared behind the empty hovels. Edith went on her way to the great hall. Big wreaths of rosemary were hung at the gates. They were hung to ward off the sickness of red sores. "Who has the red death?" she asked one of the thingliths at the gate.

"The Archbishop of Winchester," the guard said and scratched his bare stomach.

That night at home her parents were speaking of the bishop, who was taken out of Winchester to die.

"Stigand will be archbishop," Edith said.

"What do you mean?" Papa asked.

"The Queen told Stigand he would be archbishop."

"Where did you hear this?" her mother asked.

"At court. I went to court to spy for Papa."

"Godwin, do you have this child spying for you?"

"She can hear things. Like Stigand being Emma's choice for the vacant see."

Edith looked at her father. "They say Stigand sleeps with the Queen."

Her mother came over to her and put her hand beneath her chin and turned her face up. "What do you mean sleeps?"

"That he puts his pee-pee in hers, I guess."

"That does it." Her mother threw up her hands.

"Gytha, please . . ." Papa said.

"I say this child goes to court no more. No more. Do you hear me, Godwin?"

"I hear," Papa said. But he didn't actually forbid her to go.

The next day Edith stole away to the King's house.

Edith sat on the steps between the King and Queen.

"You must admit, Cnute," the Queen said, "I seldom interfere in the problems of state."

You could tell by his voice he was being snotty. "I am grateful, dear Queen, so grateful. How do you manage?"

"I have found the Church my occupation. As you won't grant me wifely privilege, what is left but God?"

Edith looked back over her head at the Queen. Emma was smiling at the King.

"What do you want, Emma?" The King sounded bored.

"For myself nothing . . . for the Church . . . well?"

"Well?"

"Aelfsige is dying, the bishop's seat will be vacant and I would have it for . . . but, I suppose you've already decided to give it to your chaplain . . . to Stigand."

The King said nothing for a moment and then told her, "Yes. Precisely that."

"Then I will ask nothing," she said and arose and walked away.

It didn't make much sense to Edith. After all, hadn't the Queen told Stigand she would help him? She went across to where the priest was examining a dead bird. "It is arranged," the Queen told him.

"Arranged?" He looked at her as if he didn't know what she meant. He was really stupid. Even Edith knew what the Queen meant.

"You will be named Bishop, Archbishop of Winchester."

"You . . . you are certain?"

"Quite."

"Thank you, so much Em . . . dear Queen. How can I possibly repay you?"

"By having Edward killed, Father Stigand, by having this albino monster eradicated. He goes to Brionne often I've learned. Have him killed by the priest there."

Edith felt helpless. There was no way of getting a message to Edward. There was only one Norman in the entire room and she didn't know at all who he was. That night Edith had trouble sleeping. Someone surely could help her.

Papa was very angry the next morning. Her mother told her it was because Olaf's body was said to have arisen out of the ground and, no matter how many times they buried it, the coffin kept floating up out of the earth. And there was said, her mother told her, to be no corruption and his nails and his hair kept growing. All the Norse were calling him "Saint."

Edith slipped from the house and went back up toward the King's house. She forgot to stop and see if the gray wolf was there near the empty hovels. It was early when she reached the hall and neither the King nor Queen was there. Papa was there and he pretended not to see her.

"There are more fires." A little monk with a frenzy of brown hair scurried about the room. "It is the end of the world. I know it. God's judge—"

"Don't be silly," Papa said.

The monk looked hurt, as though he was going to cry.

The tall, balding Italian came in. He was dressed in a magnificent green tunic that nearly covered his feet it was so long. "There's a dead chicken in the doorway," he said.

"And what would you have me do with it?" her father asked, giving the man a look of disgust. She knew that look well.

Edith saw the Norman she had seen several days before. At least she might determine who he was. He was standing alone when she went over to him. "I am Edith, daughter of Godwin," she told him.

"Yes, I know," he said.

"Who are you?" she asked.

"My name is Herluin."

"But who are you?" Edith asked him.

"An unpopular fellow," he said. "I am here as Duke Robert's envoy."

"Do you know Edward?"

"The Queen's son. Yes," he said.

"I am his friend," Edith told him.

"As am I," he assured her.

"Then tell him please that Father Stigand has been asked by his mother to have a priest kill him at Brionne."

"Child . . . ?"

"It is true," she said. "Please tell him. I heard the Lady Queen talking to Stigand, here in this hall." Edith walked away for fear her father would catch her talking with the Norman.

She had but moved across the room when Father Stigand entered, followed by half a dozen or so monks. "Is the King here?" he asked.

"Does he look here?" Her father was in a bad mood.

"I am to be Bishop of Winchester," Stigand said.

"You might have the decency to wait until Aelfsige is dead." Her father turned his back on the priest. "Winchester, though in Wessex, is out of my jurisdiction."

"Not like Canterbury, hey?"

"What do you mean by that?"

Stigand cleared his throat. "Well, you did block my appointment to being named Dean of Christ's Church?"

"I did nothing of the kind. To my knowledge you were never under consideration for that post at any time I can remember."

"Oh. I was under the impression I had been."

"Don't believe everything the Queen tells you."

"I just thought . . . anyway . . ." And then he spoke very quickly: "Do you know there is a dead chicken in the doorway?"

Her father looked at him a moment and then smiled. "I thought it would make for interesting conversation." And then angrily added, "Yes, I know there is a dead chicken in the doorway."

"You don't need to shout," Stigand said softly.

"I need to shout!"

The King came in, followed by the Queen.

"Why do you need to shout, Godwin?" the King asked.

"Because my liege Lord, the dead King of Norway has risen from the dead."

"You mean that business about him floating up out of the ground?"

"Precisely that business. Do you know what is being made of that business? It is going to destroy your regency. They are saying, all those Northmen who wanted you as King, that Olaf was a saint. Elgiva will have a civil war on her hands."

"And so, Godwin, what do I do about it?" The King went up and sat on his chair.

The Queen walked across the room to where Stigand was standing.

"How do you fight a dead man?" Papa asked the King.

The King was silent for a moment. "Do you know, Godwin, there is a dead chicken in the doorway?"

Edith wanted to laugh. She wandered around and listened and she heard something from a monk that had come from Coventry that made her want to cry. She couldn't tell Papa. She just couldn't. She listened and moved about, but all the time thinking about what the monk from Coventry had said.

She was quiet on the way home and Papa was angry so he didn't seem to care. Her mother was waiting at the door when they arrived.

"You are using the child, Godwin. I thought she was forbidden to go to the hall," she said.

"She is helping me, because she can."

"Godwin—"

"I am tired. It has been a horrid day. I should have known a dead chicken in a doorway was a bad omen."

"Since when are you disturbed by omens?"

He went to bed.

Edith sat beside her mother. She began to cry.

"What is it, butterfly?. What is wrong?"

"I couldn't tell him," Edith said. "I couldn't tell him."

"Tell him what?"

"About Behi."

"What did you hear about Behi?"

"A monk from Coventry said Behi was in the service of Earl Leofric and that Cnute was going to die of urine of the eyes and they were going to make Harold King of England."

"You are certain that is what you heard?"

"Yes."

"That will break your father's heart."

"I know," Edith said.

"You are a good child. Perhaps you shouldn't go to the court for a while. Still, one can't live one's life sitting on a rock in Jomburg."

CHAPTER 15

Winchester, 1034

EMMA LOOKED AT THE FIGS FROM IBERIA. THEY WERE DRIED AND WRINKLED and ugly. She pushed them aside and avoided looking at her own reflection in the silver plate. She felt old and ugly and her world was falling apart. It had been nearly four years since the dwarf had told her the parable of the shote and the white crow and yet it would not leave her mind. The crow seemed to pick at her brain, just as it did at the shote in the dwarf's tale. Every bite Harthacnut stuffed into his fat cheeks reminded her and he gorged himself like a gelded shote. "Gelding," the word blistered in her head like a festering burn. What if Harthacnut were a gelding? NO! Yet, he was sixteen and showed no indication of reaching puberty. She had secretly brought in doctors, trying to keep the fact from Godwin's knowledge, and the doctors shook their heads and gave no hopeful whisperings.

"Strawberries," Harthacnut demanded in a high-pitched voice and a serving man poured strawberries onto his plate and the boy shoved them into his mouth, smearing the red stain on his chin and above his lip.

A young man who claimed to be an abbot from Fecamp had come and he told Emma that for a ring and three gold coins he would transform Harthacnut from childhood to manhood and so Harthacnut at the hour of midnight on a cold winter's night was stripped and laid on the floor in the center of Emma's chamber and the abbot cut up a white cat he had buried alive three days earlier and the bits of cat flesh and skin he dipped into the cat's blood and laid the red wet pieces in a circle about a screaming Harthacnut, who dared not move for fear of touching the flesh of the cat encircling him, and Emma looked at the billowing fat of her naked hairless son, his genitals nearly lost in the fat from his stomach. She had little confidence in the abbot's magic as the young man from Fecamp mumbled incantations and assured her that by morning Harthacnut would be a man and able to sire a brood of offspring. Morning came and Emma had dozed in the night and the abbot had vanished with the ring and three gold pieces and Harthacnut remained as hairless and unmanly as before, terrified within the circle of cat flesh.

Harthacnut yelled out for more strawberries and, when told they were gone, cursed and pounded the table.

Emma needed not only the assurance that a son of her blood would rule England, but that the bloodline would continue after. She sensed eternal life and immortality in that stream of blood to follow her and she must be assured of it before she died. She did not want to think on death, not on her own death. Cnute was dying and had been for nearly three years. The urine in the eyes slowly drained him of his strength until now he lay mostly out of his head in his stinking chamber. He would give her no more sons. The white crow haunted her. That aberration of her womb, Edward, would never rule, on that she was adamant. He, in his ugliness and monstrous appearance, not only lacked the towering grandeur of her Norman ancestry, but was the child of Ethelred. She hated Ethelred almost as much in these long years beyond his death as she had when she had borne his insulting manner and grotesque children. She had tried to have Edward killed and each time failed, the last the failing of Stigand's inept efforts. She feared the oracles for the seers found amid the entrails of dead beasts or the appearance of birds the signs of Edwardus Rex. Yet she could not think of the ugly white thing, and Lord, he was nearly thirty now, as anything of herself. He would not rule! Harthacnut was her only hope and she looked over at him, his face red with anger as he beat against the table, and Emma longed to bear other sons.

Estrid turned to Gytha and spoke. Emma listened without saying anything. "Cnute is better; I am certain of it," Estrid said. "He smiled at me this afternoon as I knelt praying at his bed. He did not speak, but he smiled. I am sure of it."

Cnute could not live much longer. Harthacnut would come of age soon; Emma told herself it would be soon, for there were Elgiva's brats to contend with now as well. Emma had created the problem, she realized that, but she had feared Godwin's accruing power. It was Godwin, as the King lay incapacitated in his chambers, who made the decisions, who wielded the arm of might. Godwin's power seemed to wax in proportion to the waning Cnute's physical condition. Emma came to fear that he might take the throne for himself or make his own son King and so she had poisoned Leofric's mind against Godwin, pointing out the wealth Godwin had accumulated and making him see Godwin's ambition. But that implanted infection came back to haunt her as Leofric amassed an army at Coventry and swore to put Elgiva's son, Harold, on the throne. Cnute had denied Harold, damning him as the shoemaker's issue, but Leofric knew only that he needed a weapon to bear against Godwin. She had tried to reason with Leofric, but the earl insisted Harthacnut would be ruled by Godwin. Twice Emma had gone to Coventry, but without success.

Emma looked over at Godwin's son Sven, only a year younger than Harthacnut, big and healthy, not big and fat. He reminded her of Ulf when he'd been young, something boyish and mischievous, but Ulf had lacked the sensuality of this boy. There was something of an animal about Sven and a cruelty, not evil in a deliberate sense, but almost as an animal might be cruel, unthinking and with an innate need to satisfy its own urges. Perhaps it was the lips, always slightly open as if begging to be filled. At fifteen he had seduced one of Cnute's Italian whores and had killed a monk from Glouchester over a priest's wife. Emma wondered what the boy would be like in her bed. She was staring directly at him and he smiled. There was nothing coy in Sven Godwinsson's smile. It was broad and Emma was embarrassed, as if being unmasked of her thoughts.

Emma chewed on a greasy pork bone. Sven was still smiling. At times she despised youth, perhaps only because it was an insolent reminder of her age. When her eyes had been soft blue and her hair yellow, how would Sven have looked at her then? He took an oyster from the shell, opened his mouth and let it slide down his throat.

There were three Svens among these youth, all named after the great Forkbeard and all bearing some kinship to one another. Besides Godwin and Gytha's Sven, there was Estrid and Ulf's boy Svegn, and Cnute and the whore Elgiva's Svegan, who Emma had not seen since infancy. Estrid's son was a lanky fifteen-year-old with a narrow, sculptured face, high cheekbones and wide eyebrows, chestnut like his cropped ruffled hair. He had insolent eyes, a deep brown with long dark lashes. There was no doubt he was a beautiful lad, but she sensed he hated her. His tone seemed always as insolent as his eyes. Whenever she looked at him, he seemed to be watching her, as he was now, and he made her uncomfortable, as if he could see into her head and knew precisely what she was thinking.

Godwin said something to her. "What did you say?" she asked him, having been engrossed in the condition of her teeth.

"I was talking about Norway."

"I'm sorry," she apologized. "Please go on."

"I was saying that it is not just the canonization of Olaf threatening, but my people at Tunsberg tell me that Olaf's son is being brought from Russia."

"Olaf has a son?" Emma was genuinely surprised.

"Yes, by a whore. His name is Magnus."

"Even saints have whores, it would seem." Gytha leaned around Godwin as she spoke.

"No doubt," Godwin said, "the Norse will want to make him King of England as well as Norway. One more contender to contend with."

"Cnute will get better," Estrid said. "I know it."

"If God were only so generous," Godwin sighed.

Cnute would get no better. He had been dying for three years and he would get no better. Of that Emma was positive. Harthacnut would soon be King. What if he could bear no children? Emma amused herself with the thought of wedding this Magnus Olafsson and putting him on the throne. Three husbands she would have, and all kings of England and each younger than the next, for certainly Magnus must be a young man. It was, of course, but foolish musings, yet she was not yet fifty and could bear more children. Was Magnus lean and handsome, she wondered, sensual like Sven Godwinsson or was he insolent like Estrid's Svegn? What if Cnute could give her another child? She came to a decision.

After the meal in the hall, as on other nights, she crossed the court toward the King's chamber house, the dutiful Queen inquiring as to her King's health. There was a full yellow moon and the blind boy with the bald spot on the side of his head was milking a goat in the center of the courtyard.

She went up the steps into the King's chamber house. She toyed with one of her relics, which she had put on a small iron chain and wore about her neck. It was the tooth of St. John Chrysostom. Cnute, teasing her, once whispered in her ear as she stood playing with the tooth as she did now, "What if that is not his tooth? What if that didn't come from the mouth of Chrysostom?" "Of course it did." "But what if it didn't? What if it belonged to an old woman with a devil inside her?" Cnute had taunted her in a sinister voice. But she had not doubted, ever, about her relics. "I know it is the tooth of St. John Chrysostom, just as I know there is a God . . . or a devil." He had blown in her ear as he then asked her, "And what if there is no God?" But that had all been in days when they were young and Cnute had dared, with his heathen Danish ways, question God. He had grown older and afraid of God and dying and hell. So afraid of God. The whores barely left his bed, her ladies reported, than he called for his confessor to free his soul of mortal sin.

A thinglith stood just outside the door of Cnute's bedchamber. "How is he?" she asked.

"Coughing and having pain," he told her.

Emma went in. The room reeked of excrement and impending death, herbs and a lack of sun. A doctor with a shaved head and a pointed nose stood on one side of the bed. On the opposite stood a priest with a dirty face and he wore a badly soiled robe. The doctor shook his head and the priest opened up his hands in despair, both looking at Emma with the incompetence of their respective abilities apparent in each face. Emma stood at the end of the bed. The King had big feet; even though they were hidden by the throw, it was obvious the King had big feet. He was forty years old and going to die. She must take advantage of the little time which was left. His eyes were closed. He was wasting away toward death and she realized she didn't hate him anymore. She simply didn't care. The big muscles of his arms were yellow flab and his once tousled blond hair was long and thin and matted and he was nearly bald on top. He sweated and occasionally coughed while she stood there, but otherwise gave few indications of life. This was the Emperor of the North, a rotting shell of greatness.

"You will leave now," Emma told the doctor and the priest, "for I am going to join the King in his bed."

"But, Lady," the doctor said, and the priest looked alarmed.

"Go away," she ordered.

They left, but reluctantly. They would report what she had done, and so when she became pregnant it would be a matter of public record that she had slept in Cnute's bed.

But struggle as she might there was no arousing him, and though she tried to get his penis inside her vagina, the soft piece of flesh could not be made hard enough to penetrate. He smelled of death and urine and sores and excrement and his breath was foul, yet she worked the night through attempting to excite him. She brought his hands to her body but they fell away limp, as if unaware of her presence. The only signs of life were his irregular breathing and the hacking which rattled from his throat and at times she thought he might choke to death. Toward morning he urinated on her and she got up and cleaned herself off. She was exhausted from her vain night's work and it was an effort to get dressed.

Before she left the chamber Emma went up to the head of the bed. She bent and whispered in his ear, "There is no God, Cnute."

She went out into the damp morning air. Perhaps Magnus of Norway would prove more virile.

Weeks passed and the King's condition remained unchanged and Harthacnut gave no indication of becoming a man. Somehow what had seemed but a jest, the idea of marriage and an alliance with Magnus, became to Emma a plausible solution, and why not? She could bring him the throne of England; he could bring her the arms to ensure it; together they could create an heir. She shared her idea with no one but Stigand, however.

A dove monotonously "coo-cooed." It was a dull morning. The early air was cool and heavy with moisture. Emma walked in the direction of the hall and when she reached it paused in the doorway, her eyes adjusting to the even darker gloom within. Godwin came into focus at the far end where he seemed to be instructing Gytha's nephew in the use of a dagger, showing the boy how to block a thrust with his forearm. The hall otherwise was empty and the man's voice echoed.

"Does Svegn Estridsson have enemies at such a tender age?" Emma let her skirt drag and walked toward them.

"All men have or will have enemies." Godwin lowered the weapon.

"Even Lord Godwin?"

"You've seen to that, Lady Queen."

She looked at Svegn. He really did have insolent eyes. She stifled the urge to reach out and strike him.

"I'm interrupting," Emma said and turned, began to walk away, and then spoke clearly, her back still to him. "I simply came to tell you that I'm going to Caledonia."

The dagger fell with a clang to the stone floor. "You're going where?"

"Caledonia—"

"Nobody goes to Caledonia."

"I am."

"Emma, the King is dying. Magnus' followers are dragging Olaf out of the grave and turning Norway into chaos and threaten to invade the Daneland. Leofric is at Coventry with the boy, Harold, waiting for the King to die so he can bring us to a civil war . . . and you are going—"

"To Caledonia." Emma went toward the door. It had started to rain and she threw her hood up and it caught in her hair and she adjusted it. The wind came up and blew the rain and she tightened her cloak about her, yet it, and her gown, dragged in the wet and a dead goose lay in the street and the water running down the street diverted around it as if it were a down island and when she neared the minster it began hailing.

Bishop Stigand stood just inside the arched door waiting. "Here is the messenger," he said and literally pushed a Clunaic monk toward her. He was a young string of a man with fingers like nervous sticks. His robe was soaked and hung on him like a limp rag on a pole.

"The blessings of St. Columban upon you." His voice was hoarse and full of breath. "The very blessings."

"He has traveled far," Stigand said.

"And with news?" Emma loosened the cinch on her soaked cloak.

"And with news," Stigand echoed.

"You are from Malcolm's court?" Emma hid a smile behind her hand as it suddenly struck her that someone stretched on the rack must look a great deal like this elongated man.

"No, my Lady. Actually, I serve Thorfinn Sigurdsson."

"The Earl of Orkney?"

It was Stigand who explained. They would meet the bishop at Stromness in the Orkneys. ". . . and also . . ." Stigand did not say the name but Emma knew full well who he meant.

"But we will go to Scone first?" Emma assumed the answer.

"Yes, as planned, with a full retinue." The raspberry-faced bishop tweaked his wisp of a beard with his thumb and finger. "We will go to the Orkneys in secrecy with only a few who can be trusted."

They decided they would go north by sea from London and Emma looked forward to being at sea again and free. Sometimes she thought she should stay always at sea; it seemed the only time she was happy.

Godwin, sullen, stood with the others at the gates as they readied to leave.

"Do not," Emma ordered Harthacnut, before she mounted her horse, "under any circumstance leave Winchester while I am away and do exactly as Godwin advises."

"I shall do as the King commands," the fat sixteen-year-old told her and belched.

"The King is unable to command," she said.

"Then I shall rule." His tunic was greasy and food-stained. There was a particularly large stain where his belly pushed out at the waist.

Behind him stood Svegn Estridsson and Godwin's Sven. Estrid's boy was smiling without opening his mouth and it irritated Emma. Damn him.

"Let's hear it for fat King Harthacnut," Sven Godwinsson yelled.

Harthacnut belched again.

"That's enough, Sven." Godwin scowled at him. "Harthacnut will do as I tell him."

"I will do as I want," he said and tossed the chicken bone away.

Emma reached up, he was considerably taller than she was, and with her open hand whacked him hard and the boy went reeling and began to whimper. "You will do as you're told." Emma mounted the black mare with the help of Sven Godwinsson and raised her arm as a signal to depart.

"Foolish," she heard Godwin say as she led off.

The sea was calm and they sighted a great white whale which one of the rowmen told Emma was God in disguise and that to kill the white whale was to kill God. It spouted and lumbered through the water, leaving a white path behind, and then vanished. Emma stood aft letting the spray dampen her cheeks as she watched the water trail behind much like that left by the whale and they were but a few days at sea when they reached the Firth of Forth. To the larbord was Lothian-Northumbria, and as they drifted up the firth, Emma could see the tower of St. Giles clearly visible high above. But they landed on the opposite shore and traveled by horse and foot northerly in the direction of Scone.

Malcolm was ancient. His hair was as white as chicken feathers and stuck straight out on both sides of his head. "Women," he said as Emma was presented, "should stay at home."

"Father doesn't mean that," Duncan said.

"Father means it," the King told him and added, "I'm going to bed if nothing more exciting than this is to happen today." He got up. His chair was a large stone and he rubbed his behind as if it were sore from sitting. He was a tall man and he shuffled as they led him from the hall, continually brushing aside the slaves who tried to aid him as he walked.

The hall at Scone seemed almost Viking, Emma thought, with tables running in a row along each of the long walls and a fire burning in a trough down the center. A carved sea serpent was mounted the length of one wall; the paint on it had peeled and flaked. A full-sized Christ, crucified, hung above the entrance. Stigand told her in times of crisis it was said to drip blood from the wounds.

"You must pay no heed to the King," Duncan told her. "He has lost his wits."

Duncan had prepared a feast of roasted porpoise and a tangy root boiled in sour wine and sheep innards mashed in a grainy meal and goats' hearts stuffed with tiny fish and a barley drink which made Emma lightheaded.

"I am Gruoch, wife to MacBeth." The woman stood behind Emma. She was of average size, but had enormous hands.

"Duncan is a most gracious host," Emma said, not knowing what else to say and attempting to be pleasant.

The woman raised her enormous hands to her brow. "Do any of Kenneth's grandchildren bear more right to the throne than another?"

Emma simply looked at her, having no idea what was the expected response.

"I am the granddaughter of Kenneth," she said and shook her hands at the ceiling and wandered off. Emma felt a kinship for the woman, for she, too, suffered the frustration of the powerless.

After the meal, Emma's dwarf entertained the host on the harp and the timpan and Duncan's musicians played the pipes and a girl from Persia swallowed a dagger and a mime gave battle to a dragon and Duncan stood and MacBeth, Stigand and Emma went with him to a small chamber.

"You will said to be on a hunt with MacBeth and his lady; instead you will go by boat to Strongness." Duncan sat down on a creaky bench. "May I ask, Queen Emma, why you are doing this?"

"The canonization of Olaf will bring down the viceroy in Norway. Svegan is controlled by his mother, the whore Elgiva. I will do anything to see her destroyed. I pretend no other reason. And why do you help me, Lord Duncan?"

"I work to unite the Picts, the Celts, the Bretons and the Angles into one Scottish realm. To my south is the leviathan England ruled by the great Cnute. To the north is the leviathan Norseland ruled by Cnute's son as regent. I am like a tasty morsel set between the jaws."

"We have like aims," Emma said.

MacBeth folded his arms. He was a melancholic sort of man with deep-set eyes and a large belly. "Friends are people with the same enemies," he said. "It does seem strange to me that in this instance then that enemy is your own husband, Lady. I am not certain I do see your purpose. To destroy your rival, Elgiva, you would destroy your husband."

"Cnute is ill, Lord MacBeth. He will not live long. I want a secure England for my son, nothing more. What needs he with these excursions into that formidable north country? It is cold and barren and the people eat little besides fish." She never mentioned Magnus. First she would meet him, see if he would make a proper husband and king and then broach the subject.

They left word that they had gone hunting and vanished from Scone.

The boat came into the Scapa Flow. The tall rocks of Hoy grew straight up out of the water. They floated beneath and made their way with care through the deep and landed on the large island. It was a brilliant day and fall blooms covered a section of the hill.

They were escorted by two soldiers wearing sharks' teeth about their necks and brought to the longhouse of Thorfinn Sigurdsson. There, to Emma's amazement, sat Stig, her breasts exposed, doing her laundry at the fire. Her husband, Kalf Arnesson, greeted her warmly and behind him stood the mild Thor the Dog. Emma was baffled.

"I don't understand," Emma told Kalf.

"Olaf is a saint," he said.

"But . . . but . . . to put it quite frankly your wife was the one who killed him."

"And how else could he be a saint but somebody killed him?" Stig asked from across the room.

"And Cnute? Your fealty owed Cnute?"

"And yours, Cnute's wife?" Thor smiled.

"I oppose Elgiva and her bastard," Emma said.

"As do we. As do we." Kalf nodded. ". . . ah, his Grace."

Bishop Grimkell entered the room. He was a tiny man with little eyes and bushy eyebrows. His cheeks were ruddy and his hair streaked brown and honey. He had a soft melodic voice. "Lady Queen." He bowed.

"Your Grace." Emma returned the courtesy, presenting Stigand.

"And what brings your gracious Ladyship to the Orkneys?" he asked as if having no idea.

"The canonization of King Olaf, your Grace."

"Ah . . ." His voice floated in a low register. "That is a matter for my holy see, that is my concern. Not yours. Not a presumptive determination to be made by Christian well-wishers, but an investigative matter to be resolved upon the evidence of miracles. A matter for the see—"

"No less," Emma said, "but how goes the investigative procedure?" And where was Magnus? She expected him to be with the bishop. Despite her words she had very little interest in Olaf's canonization, nor even in the downfall of Elgiva at this moment.

"Well and not so well. The evidence is substantial. The sun vanished from the earth the day upon which he was killed and—"

"I'll swear to that," Stig yelled out. "Dark as the deepest hell, it was."

The bishop continued, ignoring her interjection, and melodically spoke. "Four times his body rose from the grave. Popped right up out of the ground. The coffin was as if it had been newly planed, the wood unchanged by the moisture of the earth. It was opened and his hair had grown long and his nails like sharp knives. His body was nearly as good as when he was alive. Of course he was dead."

"Yet," Emma said, "you said 'well and not so well.' To me it seems—"

"Ah, to the layman, to the layman." Bishop Grimkell shook his brown and honey-colored hair. "The evidence was presented before the regent—"

"Svegan."

"Yes, at Nidaros. I had cut some hair from the body of Olaf and I tried to burn it in the holy incense, but it would not burn. Now Svegan was impressed, but the lady, his mother—"

"A whore—"

"The lady, his mother, was not."

"The final decision is the regent's," Emma said.

"Yes," the bishop agreed.

"You are wrong," Emma told him. "The final decision is the King's and I bring you a document with his seal giving you the authority that should your investigation find conclusive evidence that indeed St. Olaf is a true saint of the mother church, he is to be canonized." Emma handed him the forged document.

"I will have it read to me and see if it is in order."

"You will find it in order," Emma assured him.

"Magnus will be indeed happy. He loved—"

"We understood that he was to have made the journey with you," Emma said, hoping her voice didn't betray the anxiousness.

"Oh, but he's already here."

It was Stig who spoke up. "Kalf is his keeper."

"Keeper?" Stigand asked.

"Guardian," Bishop Grimkell said.

"He is beautiful," Stig yelled. "The son of a saint, but that I could have nursed him with these breasts."

"Would you like me to bring him in to meet you, Lady Queen?" Kalf asked.

"Very much indeed," Emma assured him. Emma was flustered. She was not young anymore and she knew no longer beautiful, but she was a queen and would soon be a widow. She could bring him the kingdoms of Norseland, England and the Daneland. All she wanted was an heir, an heir from a virile young man, not an albino ugly monster, nor an obese undeveloped creature who could bear nothing, but a son; she wanted a son who would be the son of Rollo the Viking, and that raging blood that ran in her could wrench through his body and make him a wolf among men. She wanted a king for a son, a real king, not some half-formed misgotten creatures. She wanted—

The door opened.

Emma gasped.

"How old is he?" Stigand asked.

"Ten," Stig said. "He's ten. My little beauty is ten."

"I never dreamed he was so young." Emma's voice was almost panicked.

It was Bishop Grimkell who spoke. "Well, the Pope . . ."

"Yes," Kalf added, "Benedict is only twelve."

"Yes," Emma said and looked at the floor. She had made this entire journey for nothing.

CHAPTER 16

Winchester, 1034

ANGER RAGED IN THE HEAVENS. A DEAFENING SHARP CRASH OF THUNDER was followed by a swelling roll and then another crackling blast as if the sky were being rent apart. Rain fell heavy on the thatch and in the corner dripped to the floor in a monotonous rhythm. Wind tore through the cracks in the walls. It was not the infusing sounds which occupied the room, however, but the silent omniscient presence of death, malingering, as if waiting for the exigible moment, seeming to expect the calamitous state of Cnute's empire to disintegrate further and wanting not to be precipitous in the event conditions might worsen. Godwin wondered if they could.

Stinking and sweating, yellow-skinned, matted hair, eyes—the eyeballs a gray-yellow—occasionally opened but without a flick of recognition, Cnute, with tired breaths, was slipping toward death. The King's large hands, the nails tucked with black, were soft from disuse, his cheeks puffy, the scar on the left one wider and more pronounced because of it, and beneath the linen cover, Godwin knew, sores festered, grown large from the King's immobility. And all the while Death, its skeletal face indifferent, waited in a dark corner of the dim room.

Godwin stood at the foot of the bed.

When he died, would the empire die with him? Leofric, with the shoemaker's bastard, sat at Coventry waiting for the breath on this bed to cease. Harthacnut was the heir designate; it was written in Emma's wedding contract, any son she would be delivered of was to be King. But with Cnute dead, who was to order the Witangemot to accept the fat, inept, dull-witted boy? He resembled some eunuch of a Turkish potentate, or at least what Godwin pictured one to look like. Harthacnut, King—what a horrid thought! Yet the alternatives seemed worse. Elgiva's son Svegan was an amiable enough young man and appeared capable with far more sense than erratic Harthacnut, but he was tied to his mother and Elgiva hated Godwin. She had never forgiven him for the incidents at York. That had to have been twenty years or longer ago, and supporting Svegan was a gamble. Godwin would lose whatever influence Emma had at the court of the Holy Roman Emperor and elsewhere on the continent. Only if Cnute lived and Svegan was taken from Elgiva would that be a viable choice, and Cnute was dying. Time was slipping away in the breaths of the large man on the bed before him.

Thunder shook the chamber.

The shoemaker's bastard, Harold, was out of the question. And Emma? Who could predict what Emma would ever do? She would not support any claim of her son Edward that he could rely upon. How would Leofric stand on Edward? It was a possibility. Edward must be thirty years old. He was strange and obstinate as his mother, yet Godwin sensed he might be able to control Edward. His obstinacy appeared more channeled than Harthacnut's total unpredictability. But Edward on the throne did not excite Godwin. The wind whistled and one of the candles in the room blew out. There was Emma's other son, Alfred, and in Hungary one of Edmund's athelings still lived. And always haunting Godwin were the prophecies of Sorgad, which again and again he told himself were nonsense: Edith would be a queen and one of his sons a king. Nonsense.

Cnute still breathed, but the question of succession needed resolve. In Norway, Elgiva had alienated the Norse nobles and would be driven out by the ghost of the sainted Olaf. In Caledonia, Emma plotted what? In Coventry, Leofric had an army and a narrow-faced black-haired boy who resembled a shoemaker. In York, Siward waited to follow the lead of Coventry. In Rouen a hungry Normandy was at the call of its capricious duke, who had no business in the affairs of England, yet had decided the pale Edward should be its King. If the strong-willed Archbishop Wulfstan were yet alive the decision would be easier resolved. Godwin had not thought of Wulfstan in years.

He turned from the bed and picked up his cloak from a bench, a dun, coarse cloak, and he pulled the hood forward over his head and stepped out under the eave, but the hood offered little protection. Despite the fact it was midmorning, it was near night-dark. The courtyard was flooded like a shallow lake and it formed a river as it ran through the gates and down the slope of the street. No thingliths were posted and the courtyard remained empty except for a dog, who huddled, his coat dripping, near a wall. A quick stab of lightning split the sky in an erratic zigzag. A terrifying drum of thunder followed. Godwin ran from under the eave, getting soaked as he sped toward the great hall.

The messenger from Scone stood trying to dry himself by the fire. Godwin tossed off the soaked cloak and joined him, warming his hands. The man had only one arm; the other had been cut off when he'd been caught stealing.

A serving boy came with some warmed wine.

The messenger was nearly bald, yet Godwin knew him to be barely twenty-five. He had narrow, sharp gray eyes.

Godwin handed him a cup of the wine. "Well, Undger?"

"I cannot make hare nor hides of it," the messenger said and took a drink of wine. "At Scone there was a noble named MacBeth—"

"Yes, I know who he is," Godwin said.

"The Queen and Bishop Stigand were decided to go hunting with this MacBeth and his lady. Yet, no one else that had traveled all that way with them was invited. Well, I followed them. They was on horseback, but so was I, so I dasn't get too close and stayed out of sight. But instead of going north which they said was the way to Lord MacBeth's lands, they went to the east and the sea. And there was a boat waiting for them and since my horse don't take to walking on the sea, I could follow them no more. One thing is certain, it were no huntin' they were going."

"I wish to God I knew what Emma was up to."

The messenger held out his cup for more wine and Godwin filled it from the wooden pitcher.

"Was there anything unusual about the boat, or the men on the boats?"

"No," the one-armed man said, "except they wasn't Scots I don't guess. They was dressed more like Norsemen, though I can't tell. None of 'em, Scot or Norse, is what you'd call civilized."

It was less than an hour later Godwin stood in the doorway and watched the old blind monk cross the courtyard. With a stick poking the way, he shuffled barefooted through the water. His clothing was soaked as if he had been wading to his neck in the river.

Suddenly it struck—a sharp shaft of lightning! Godwin was certain he saw it as it hit the old blind monk, who toppled to the ground. A deafening clap of thunder drowned the old monk's cries. Godwin ran out to him and didn't take the time to slip on his cloak, which he dropped in the doorway. He reached down to see if the old man was alive.

"I can see light," the monk gasped. "Jesus in heaven! I can see light."

Godwin struggled to get the old man up. He had him to his knees when the monk cried out again. "I can see shapes. You are Godwin, I know from the smell of you, but I can see the shape of you before me

... and now clearer ... your face ... I can see your face." He reached up and touched Godwin's face. "Merciful God, I am going to see again."

They stayed there in the rain, the old monk on his knees, and Godwin, being drenched, stood over him.

"Come," Godwin urged. "Come out of the rain."

"I want to see the King," the old man said. "I want to see the King."

"He is dying," Godwin said.

"It need not be," the monk said.

Godwin helped him to his feet and led him to Cnute's chamber. The King lay like a caught fish in the bottom of a boat—not dead, but not a flap of life left either. They were a pair, Godwin and the old monk soaked to the skin.

"I can see Cnute Svenson." He went up and touched the King's hand. Cnute's body jolted as if he had been struck by lightning and he shook and then his breath eased and the King opened his eyes and looked at Godwin and Godwin was aware that the King recognized him, and despite his skepticism knew it was a miracle. The King was weak and he tried to speak and his voice faltered, but Godwin knew the King was alive.

The doctor came with his leeches hungry for blood and Godwin over the "No's" of the doctor sent him away and the King motioned the doctor away as well with his hand.

"How ... how ... long?" Cnute's voice was barely audible.

"Months," Godwin told him.

And the King slept.

In the morning the King said, "You ... you ..." But Godwin told him that it would all wait and he must rest and Cnute slept and in two days time, though he had little strength, was able to sit up in bed for a short while. St. Clerish, they already were calling the old monk who saw the sun rise and set and sat on a hillside watching the stars. "To see is to be," he said. And he saw the world from daylight to dark night.

The sun had reasserted itself and air was let into the King's chamber, but there was a fall chill and Godwin sensed winter would come early. The King was weak, but alert. "Your eyes," the King repeated, "your eyes ..."

"What of my eyes?" Godwin asked.

"They are ... troubled ..."

"They will be fine now. The problems existed because of your illness. Everything will be fine now."

"Tell me ... tell me of ... them."

"In a few days, when you are better."

The sun shone. It stayed cool. In a few days the King was stronger. He was sitting up in the bed bolstered by several rolled skins. His color had improved little, but both his face and his hands revealed that he was recovering his strength.

"The Queen," he said, "I have not seen the Queen." His words were slow and soft.

"She has gone to Caledonia, my Liege," Godwin told him.

"Why?"

"I wish I knew. I am certain Emma is up to something, but I have been able to learn nothing."

Cnute looked at him for a moment before speaking. "This is why you have looked so troubled?"

"No, my Lord. I have been troubled by the Earl of Mercia. Leofric has the boy Harold—"

"Elgiva's son?"

"Yes, the shoemaker's bastard in his keeping—"

"He is not my son. You agree, do you not, Godwin?"

"I have seen him, my Lord. He is not your son. Yet, Leofric would have him your heir and refuses to acknowledge Harthacnut."

"What purpose—"

"Against me . . . he thinks I would rule England by ruling Harthacnut."

Cnute's voice indicated he was tiring. "But surely he didn't expect to make that bastard I have disavowed King?"

"He did."

"You would not have stood for it."

"I may have had little choice," Godwin said. "He and Siward, who stands with him as usual, have built up enormous armies."

"I did not die . . ." Cnute paused and breathed deeply. His large hands began shaking slightly. "I will bring them . . . down . . . I am so tired . . . but there is more to . . . to this . . ."

"Yes and we can discuss it when you are feeling more rested."

The King closed his eyes as Godwin left the chamber. Harthacnut was sitting on a bench with the slave Wede, a bitty, elfish man who prepared superb dishes for the King's table. The King's son was plucking a chicken and intermittently sucking on a hardened honey ball on a twig.

"He should have been a cook," Wede said of the boy.

"Yes," Godwin responded truthfully. "He should have been a cook."

In the afternoon, Godwin, though not tiring Cnute with all the details, informed him of how Olaf popped out of his grave and the impending canonization and the move to make Olaf's son Magnus the King.

"Then we must move our armies against the Norwegians."

"Yes, my Lord, but if we do that we leave ourselves at the mercy of Leofric."

"What do you suggest?"

"That you disarm Leofric by naming your son Svegan the heir to England."

"I must admit, Godwin, I don't take much to Harthacnut. He came to see me today. There is something wrong with the boy. He eats too much and his voice drives me mad. The boy is not a man, Godwin. He is sixteen and not yet a man."

Godwin touched the King's white fingers. "You should sleep now. We can talk more later."

It snowed during the night, but it melted with the morning sun. The air was cold and it was only October. As Godwin went out, he saw Edith coming up the hill. He waited for her. It was not just a father's pride; they were beginning to speak of her beauty. She was not beautiful the way Gytha was, pleasant and fresh and freckled, but in a more exotic and mystical way. Her quiet, penetrating green eyes seemed to house some special secret. Her skin was gold yet from the summer sun and her hair was not red like her mother's but a deep auburn, almost black. She was sixteen and ripe for marriage, but she had a fascination for the Church which disturbed Godwin. He also hated to lose her to any man and made no issue of the necessity of marriage. But it would have to be faced.

"Good morning, Papa."

He kissed her cheek. "You have been to the church?"

"Yes. To pray for the King."

"Would you like to see him, go with me this morning?"

"Yes."

They started up the hill.

"I had a dream," Edith said. "I dreamt a deep snow covered the earth. A wounded raven flew through the sky, dropping blood upon the snow. And then the sun came out and melted the snow and the blood vanished with it."

Godwin listened and said nothing. They continued up the hill. Suddenly a man, his gonelle filthy and torn, leaped out and blocked their path. He had a knife and turned it about and waved it in a threatening way. He had large jowls and deep bags beneath his eyes.

The man's voice shook. "Your son . . . your son has taken my woman."

"Care," Godwin said. He fingered the knife hidden beneath his tunic.

"He . . . he came and took her there in my house." The man's eyes were like a cornered rat's. "I shall take your daughter. I shall—"

The man stopped his threat in midsentence for a gray wolf appeared from out of nowhere. The wolf snarled and began backing the man away. There was terror in the man's eyes, and the wolf leaped and its teeth bit into the man's neck. It was instantaneous. The man was dead. Godwin had never seen an animal kill a man so quickly. The knife lay on the cobble. The wolf vanished.

Edith took her father's hand. "I have not seen the gray wolf for almost a year." Her voice was surprisingly calm.

Godwin was shaking. They walked on up the hill, leaving the dead man where he'd fallen.

Cnute was propped up in the bed. Svegn Estridsson stood at his side. Though quite obviously getting stronger, the yellow pallor remained. Edith stayed back in the shadows and Cnute looked around Godwin to see her.

"She should be married soon," the King said.

And Godwin nodded. He tried to get thoughts of the man killed by the wolf from his head.

"Estrid's boy—"

"I am no longer a boy, Uncle," Svegn interrupted the King. "When you were my age, Mother said you led an army into England for Sven the Forkbeard."

"You do not interrupt the King, Svegn," Godwin admonished the fifteen-year-old.

Svegn looked angrily at Godwin. "I am Jarl of Jomburg. I should be in the Daneland."

The King looked pensive. "Your father said that to me once. As I started to say, Godwin, our nephew here wishes to take an army into the Daneland."

"The regency in Norway is collapsing," the boy said.

"Where do you get your information?" Godwin asked.

"I listen. Kalf Arnesson has turned traitor."

"Is that true, Godwin?" the King asked.

"Yes. I just learned this morning. I must say, nephew, you get your information surprisingly fast. Anyway, my Lord, it is what I came to discuss with you this morning. I have learned Kalf Arnesson has Olaf's son, Magnus, in his care. He was on the Orkneys, but has since returned to Norseland. Olaf is certain to be canonized and Kalf is rallying the Norse magnates around the boy."

"How can Olaf be canonized without my proclamation?"

"They have forged your writ apparently and claim to have your approval."

"I shall deny it."

"Yes, but it won't matter by then. The Norse are determined to make the boy, Magnus, their King."

"Why? Why have they turned against me?"

"Elgiva has not helped. She has done her utmost to alienate them. Your son is completely ruled by her."

"Women are the curse of nations. They should all be locked in towers, let out at night, stuck with a penis and locked up again."

Godwin looked back at his daughter. Her eyes flashed angrily; there was a bit of Gytha's temper in her and he was afraid she was going to speak violently to the King, but she remained silent.

"And," Godwin continued, trying to get the subject back to Norway, "the Norse are as unpredictable as a storm at sea."

"They will invade the Daneland," Svegn said.

"Yes," Cnute agreed. "You may go to the Daneland, boy, and have your army, but know you this, Svegn Estridsson, your cousin shall command it and you shall be his lieutenant."

"My cousin?" His voice was quizzical.

"The heir."

"Harthacnut?" He hid neither his astonishment nor his displeasure, "Jesu in torn braies!"

"You should not blaspheme, Svegn," Edith said to her cousin. It was the first time she had spoken since coming in.

Godwin was delighted with Cnute's decision to send Harthacnut out of England.

Svegn excused himself and, not happily, left the chamber.

"The King of the Scots is dead," Godwin told the King.

"Old Malcolm?"

"Yes. The Queen sent us word. Duncan is named King at Scone."

"Have you determined why Emma went to Caledonia?" the King asked.

"No, I am baffled. It makes no sense."

"When she returns, I want her locked away. She is meddling again, we can be certain. I warned her." He coughed. "Women have no business in the affairs of men."

"Women—" Edith started to say.

"Should keep their mouths closed," Godwin interrupted her and gave her a stern look of warning.

Edith was quiet and looked down at the floor.

Five days later Leofric arrived in Winchester. He came well bundled against the cold and well armed with troops. Cnute left his bed and chamber and, buried under warm furs, stood in the courtyard to greet him in an attempt to display his health and vigor, but his skin and eyes still had the yellow cast. He coughed and his hands shook.

Leofric's horse seemed restless as the earl dismounted and handed the reins to a soldier. "We are happy to find our liege Lord from his bed."

"And living, Leofric," Cnute said, "living, and I intend on living awhile longer." Cnute was carried in a chair into the hall. The rest followed. It was cold and damp inside and the King coughed more. He looked like what he was, a man who had gotten up off his deathbed. "My Lord of Mercia," he said, "what grievance do you bear us that you should deny our rightful heir?"

"I do not wish to see the son of a swineherd King."

"If you refer to the Earl of Wessex, and I assume you do, as he readily admits his sire was a swineherd, he is our counsel and seeks to my knowledge no greater office. Is that so, Godwin?"

"It is so, my Lord."

Leofric spit into the fire. "He has been King these many months you have laid ill."

"He has administered, as he does when I am in good health, my government, nothing more, but what has this to do with the lawful succession?"

"He will be the King in all but name should Harthacnut be your heir."

"Harthacnut was named my heir, supported by the rights of primogeniture as is stated in my marriage contract to the Queen. This matter has been agreed upon by the Witangemot and is in keeping with an ordered Christian succession. Why do you question it?"

Leofric stood, his feet planted apart. "Harthacnut is not capable of assuming the duties of a king and would abdicate that responsibility, I am certain, to those under whose influence he fell."

"Specifically me, you imply?" Godwin asked.

"Most specifically."

"And instead," Cnute said, "you propose to make as King the son of a shoemaker."

"Your son, my liege Lord, as the Lady Elgiva does rightfully testify to—"

"A man knows his sons, Leofric. The shoemaker's bastard is not mine. Svegan is my son, Leofric. Do you believe that?"

"Yes, my Lord."

"And would you if I should ask acknowledge him as my heir?"

"Yes, my Liege."

Cnute stood up with difficulty. "Then hear you all. I name Svegan heir to England, Daneland and Norway. We have heard the Earl of Mercia pledge us his fidelity." Cnute turned and was helped from the hall.

Leofric stood looking dumbfounded.

Godwin made his way down the hill to his house. A lame woman, who carried a bundle of fagots, called to him, "God bless you, my Lord. God bless you." He acknowledged her with a smile.

Tostig met him at the door. "The brown goat died," he said. Tostig had been freshly shorn and Godwin rumpled his short hair and went into the house.

They had a quiet supper. As quiet as a supper could be with that brood and Estrid's there as well.

"What is going to happen to the Queen?" Edith asked.

Godwin held a beef bone in his hand. "What do you mean?"

"When she returns. Sven heard she is on her way back," Edith told him.

It was Gytha who answered. "She ought to be locked up."

"She will," Godwin said. "No husband wishes to be disobeyed, but particularly not a king. Cnute forbade her to interfere in the business of state."

"It is because she is a woman," Edith said. "If she were a man—"

"Women are women," Estrid said. "Men have their place and women theirs."

"And theirs is servile," Edith told her.

"If you want to get along," Gytha told her, "you'd better accept that fact. I do as your father wishes. Is that not so, Godwin?"

"Most of the time." He laughed. "Most of the time."

"No man is going to order my life," Edith said and lowered her fist onto the table.

Sven pounded his. "Hah," he said. And then her brothers and cousins each did the same. "Hah . . . hah . . . hah . . ." It went down the table to the littlest one.

"I mean it," Edith said. "The King has no right to stop Queen Emma, no right—"

"Treason," Beorn said. "We shall have Edith beheaded for treason."

"For treason. For treason," they all yelled and pounded on the table with drinking horns and bones.

"Mercy," Estrid said, "what a noisy trial."

CHAPTER 17

Bruges, 1035

EMMA STOOD ON THE PARAPET AND STARED IN THE DIRECTION OF THE SEA, but saw nothing but the blackness against darkness and the shadows of the land upon the deep night. Death must be like this. Dark. Winter had not yet vanished and it was cold. A chilling wind came, now and again, and tossed her cloak behind her and bit at her face. Death. On New Year's Day a baby had been found dead in the baptismal font. "It will," a young nun declared, "be a year of death." That afternoon the young nun was found dead in the streets of Bruges with a crucifix buried in her vagina. Count Baldwin's young wife, Eleanor, had told Emma of the nun. It had been years since the death of her father, Duke Richard, yet Eleanor was in mourning. But Emma came to learn it was not her father she mourned, but her brother Richard, the inept young man who had been poisoned by his brother. She was married in black and gave birth to her child, Judith, wearing black. Eleanor, perhaps, was pretty; who was to know? Perhaps, under all that black. Strange. When Eleanor was but a child, Baldwin had wanted to marry her. "I know Baldwin. He shan't have her," the duke had said and now, after all these years, here she was his wife. Emma realized, thinking on it, she was not particularly fond of her niece. She was grateful to Baldwin, however, for his hospitality.

She had fled England in the dead of winter and would be a prisoner there yet had it not been for Godwin's daughter, Edith. Winter had raged in early like a feral tyrant, savage as it smothered the last vestiges of life beneath its weighted shroud. Her lengthy train of mounted soldiers and bundled servants had stumbled toward Winchester fighting the angry wind and trenchant cold. Edith, unidentifiable beneath the bundles of woolens and furs when Emma first saw her on the rise with her brother Harold, had come miles out from the city to warn her. The King was not only recovered, but was going to lock Emma in a keep, Edith had said, as the morose Harold, perhaps thirteen, sat his horse in the turbulent silence. "God thank you, child. But why have you come out in this blizzard to warn me? Why have you done it?" Emma had asked her. "The King thinks women but brood sows. And that is wrong," Edith had responded. And on that cold bitter morning Emma had learned her son Harthacnut had been sent to Roeskild in the Daneland. Any thoughts of joining him were short-lived for Edith had told her Elgiva and Svegan had fled Norway after Olaf's canonization and were at Roeskild as well. Emma had wanted to reach out and touch Edith, to squeeze her hand, but the cold and bundles of clothes had made that impossible, so she had simply thanked her. And again she heard Edith's parting words, spoken into the wind as Emma had turned toward the sea: "I shall pray for you, Lady Queen."

Emma stared again into the shadows of the deep night. She heard no footsteps, but only the sound of a pebble falling, long, from the parapet. Someone was there. She did not turn about and contained a moment of panic with a slow careful breath. She could sense that somebody had moved, was standing directly behind her.

"I should push you off." The voice was ominous.

It took her a moment to realize who it was. She did not turn about. "Why don't you?"

"The great God in heaven knows you've tried often to kill me," Edward said.

"You meddle in the affairs of England."

"I am England."

"You shall never be."

He was silent for a while and then walked over to the parapet and stood beside her gazing down into the same blackness. "You should not have cast me aside. You would not be here in exile for I would have made you the great queen—"

"You? You would have made nothing of me, nothing of yourself and nothing of England for you are but a mad, irrational—"

"Irrational?"

"Uncontrollable, unmanageable."

"That is the problem, isn't it? You couldn't control me as you tried to do with Cnute, as you think you can do with Harthacnut. You are right, Lady. I am as unbendable as the sword of Edgar. It is my strength you oppose. It is—"

"It is your ugliness. Your white ugliness I despise."

"It is my tenacious will, the iron of my blood—"

"What blood?" Emma laughed at him. "You have no blood, the diseased sap of Ethelred is all that drips through your veins."

"The blood of Edgar and Rollo—"

"No."

"Yes," he screamed at her and for a moment she thought he just might push her off the parapet.

"If you could see your reflection, deep down in the water below, you would see no Norman warrior, only a dead branch fallen from a rotten tree."

"I am from your womb." He spoke softly.

"Never," she told him. "I dug you out from a sow dung pile and wiped you off and gave you to a wet nurse to breast. You didn't come from my womb. I never had such an abortion."

"Lies. All lies. You say these vile things because you know even when I become King you won't be able to rule me. Never, Mother."

"I am not your mother."

He came close to her and she could see his face in the dark. There was no joy in his face, only pain. "Mother," he repeated.

"Why don't you push me off? If you weren't such a weakling you would push me off."

He was silent again and walked over to the parapet away from her and into the darkness. "I had a fit, but four days ago, and St. Olaf—"

"You lie," she interrupted without even waiting to hear what he was going to tell, knowing only that it would be distasteful.

"—and St. Olaf told me to lay down the sword for I should be King of England and build a great abbey to St. Peter and be, myself, called St. Edward, the—"

"Rubbish!"

"So you see, Mother—"

"Don't call me that. I am not your mother."

"So you see, Mother, I shall be England and there is nothing you can do to stop it. So why should I seek your death?"

She looked at him, barely able to perceive his face in the black. She could attempt to push him off, but he was a large man, and she knew she would only lose in the scuffle. "Why have you come to Bruges? Why do you want to haunt me like some pale ghost?"

"It was I who brought Baldwin his lovely young bride, Eleanor—"

"Who could tell if she's lovely under all those black veils?"

"She wears it for her dead brother and she says she will wear it until his death is avenged."

"His murderer is Robert."

"There is no proof."

"He is a monster."

He cleared his throat. "I have come to Bruges to stand as godfather to Count Baldwin's new daughter."

"They name her after that vile old Judith. I hope the child doesn't grow up to be so stupid and full of sores. The women—" But Emma stopped. She realized Edward was no longer there and she was talking to the darkness.

CHAPTER 18

Rouen, 1035

THE SPRING WAS STILLBORN FROM A BARREN WINTER, COLD AND DRY, WITH little snow, and that dissolved by wind and not the earth. Trees remained bare and budless; they scratched against a mooned sky like skeletal fingers of an untended corpse. The night was leaden in its oppressive stillness. Yet Edward watched. Eerie shadows twisted in the moonlight. Mute werefolk, Loki and evil spectral shapes sifted through the dry air. These were creatures of autumn; spring should have arrived in soft rains. Edward stood at his chamber door, immobile, waiting for the latent wail to shatter the deep night. Darkness was abroad in the gray-yellow luminescence, more felt than seen. The air begged voicelessly for water, choking. And then for the fourth time since bed, Robert's screams tore through the stone silence of the ducal house.

Edward hurried along the arched loggia in the direction of the cries. Robert sat naked on the stone tearing at his black hair. He had ripped the thin linen cover into shreds and the rags surrounded him. The inhuman sound of his voice was difficult for Edward to block away, but he concentrated on the aura, obliterating the contorted face and demonic writhing of Robert's body. Each time seemed to become more difficult and Edward pulled strenuously to draw the darkness. It seemed boiling hot and he at last grasped the wad of blackness in his hands, his arms aching from the strain, and he flung it aside and fell upon the stone.

Edward lay there and listened as Robert's breathing returned to normal. "I can stand it no more, Edward." His voice was pain. "I really cannot stand it any longer. Each time now it becomes worse."

"I know." Edward got up. He was still weak, but helped his cousin to his feet and got out a soft linen from the cupboard and slipped the young duke's arms into it.

"What am I to do?"

"I have no answer," Edward told him, tying the cinch about Robert's waist.

"What am I to do?"

Edward made no reply. The oppressive silent night again engulfed them. Robert slumped down upon the straw bed. Edward stood at the chamber door staring into the diabolic stillness, wondering if it would ever rain again. He heard as Robert began weeping, not loudly, but soft tears. And the words, when they came, were barely audible. "I killed Richard."

Edward turned and faced him. "Someone had to," he said.

"Cain. I dream of Cain. He stands over me with an ax, dripping blood in my hair and it mats and dries like parched clay and then he chops open my chest and takes out my heart. 'For my brother, Abel,' he says, 'I need your heart for my brother, Abel.' And then devils come with blue faces and they have stubbled bloody feet and they begin cutting me into small pieces and feeding me to a dead bird, forcing open the bird's beak and shoving my bits of flesh down the gullet until there is nothing left but my head with bloody matted hair and then they pull out my eyeballs and there is nothing but the darkness and pain, the horrid pain of death."

In the years of the nightmares Robert had never explained before. "Devils come" was all he had ever said. Priests had tried to drive the demons away. None succeeded. And now the dreams came more and more often, sending the Duke of Normandy into fits of madness.

"Sleep now," Edward said, "lie down and try to sleep. I'll sit here in the room beside you."

"I must not sleep," Robert told him. "Cain will only return. There is only one way to stop the dreams beyond never sleeping and that is to do as Robin says."

"Go to Jerusalem?"

"Yes."

"And I shall go with you, Robert."

The young duke didn't answer for some time. He seemed to be planning, to be engrossed in his decision. "No, you must stay behind to look after the bastard. He is all of me I leave. You must look to him. I don't trust the others as much as you. And should I not return, you will keep your promise."

"He shall be heir to England's throne," Edward said. "But why would you think you would not return? It is but a pilgrimage to the Holy Land and many a man has made that journey."

"I sense I shall not come back. It is why I've been so reluctant to leave. Yet I cannot go on being tortured by these devils." Before Edward could remark, Robert added, "I have made up my mind. Call Osbern to have them assemble in the hall. The decision is made."

"Now?"

"Yes."

"In the middle of the night?"

"Yes."

It was the deep of night and a sea of confusion. Half-dressed, dressed, and dressing viscounts and soldiers, clerics, emissaries, and the keepers of the house, kin and knights scurried through the loggia. As if the night, too, were aroused, its silence was broken. An owl hooted. The archbishop was irritable and grumbled as he tightened his waist cord, nearly running head on into the red-headed Count of Brittany, who was rubbing his eyes with his fists.

The great hall was a blaze of torchlight.

Edward followed the archbishop into the room. His grumbling uncle, as he walked through the door, transformed himself into the imposing apostle of Rouen. He gestured with open hands and made his way to the duke at the far end of the hall, smiling patronizingly and appearing as if it were midday and there was nothing uncommon in their being here. Edward was not to be easily outdone. He had put on a magnificent white and gold robe with a long train. Waiting until Uncle Robert had reached the steps where the duke stood with the King of France, Edward, his hands together, slightly open and fingers pointing up, moved grandly, as a king who one day would be canonized ought, the train sweeping the stone as he made his way gracefully through the parted throng.

Duke Robert, himself, was splendidly attired in a silver mail hauberk over a crimson gown. He wore the polished ducal coronet and in his hands held a large gold crucifix. There were four chairs on the raised area. Two monks, at the motion of the duke's free hand, escorted the archbishop to the chair apart. The duke then led the way, followed by Henry of France and Edward, to the other chairs. Henry, who looked rather shabby in a simple green robe, sat to the duke's right, Edward to the left.

A hymn of penance was sung by the monks of St. Ouen, who had been dragged from their beds, and the bells of St. Ouen and the cathedral rang out, which must have perplexed and alarmed the sleeping citizens of Rouen as they clattered in the middle of the night. While the monks sang, Edward studied the sea of faces. Godgifu was there, wearing, as she had taken to wearing, a bronze- and pearl-handled sword in an embroidered scabbard which hung loose from her waist. Nobles and knights complained, including her husband, Drogo, but the duke, at Edward's behest, had granted permission to her. "Sinful," old Osbern snorted. Where was Alfred? Edward scanned the room. Godfrey, Uncle Godfrey was there. When had he arrived? But where was Alfred? The hymn ended.

Robert arose. "The land is parched and God neglects us. Famine has come upon us like a bloody sword and your duke is plagued with dreams because he has sinned." Two monks came and slipped the hauberk off . . . "I beg the forgiveness of Jesus" . . . and the crimson gown . . . "and shall atone for my most grievous offense against the living God" . . . a hair shirt was put on him and then the robe and hauberk were donned again. Robert, with the dignity of his ducal role, walked down the steps and into the throng until he stood before Robin of Jumieges, and then, falling to his knees, looked up at him and said, "Priest, I free you from the burden of my confession. You shall no longer have to carry the weight of my sins. I have asked his Grace, the Archbishop of Rouen, to name you to the vacancy at Jumieges." Robin looked more baffled than anything else and Robert got up and took his hand and was going to lead him away, but the monk got tangled up in Godgifu's sword. "No man is allowed to wear a sword in the hall," Osbern had said more than once, unhappily. Robin was untangled and led before the archbishop. It was Robin's turn to kneel. The duke stood behind his uncle, and the heavy archbishop came to his feet with difficulty and in imposing tones spoke in Latin and named Robin to be Abbot of Jumieges and gave him a crozier and a chair was brought for the new Abbot of Jumieges and he sat beside the great archbishop.

A pig, a large brown sow, came snorting into the hall and snooped about.

Robert returned to his own focal position and knelt upon a yellow cushion placed before his chair and faced the mass of Normans, and speaking in a loud clear voice proclaimed, "I go to the Holy City, to Jerusalem, to seek forgiveness and atone for the suffering I have brought to the living Christ." A priest came and put the Eucharist in his mouth. The archbishop again arose and came over and blessed him and then turned about and blessed those in the room. Edward gave credit to this Norman house, for without any preparation the show and dignity of the occasion were magnificent. Much of the credit of course belonged to Osbern, the old steward.

A herald tapped a golden pole and heads turned to the rear of the hall; standing in the door in brilliant dress was the seven-year-old William. His entrance was timed perfectly. He walked the length of the hall, not as a child who had been awakened in the middle of the night, but with the arrogance of his father and a great presence of authority. Edward could read the satisfaction in Robert's face as the boy slowly approached, came up the steps and stood beside his father.

"Know you all," Robert said, "this is your liege Lord in my absence. To him is your allegiance and fealty bound. Into his hands I put your welfare. Should the merciful God take me from you and we meet again no more in this life, this is my heir, this is Normandy, to him are you bound as his men."

Chickens, probably awakened by the bells, came into the hall pecking at the stone floor in search of crumbs.

With some difficulty, Archbishop Robert got down on his knees before William and then all the men in the hall, save Henry, King of France, and Edward, came in file and knelt, and someone had to wake the Viscomte Quasiment Bovin.

When all had acknowledged young William as their Lord, Robert took his son and led him to where Henry, King of France, Lord over Normandy, sat in his green gown. Edward noticed it was torn at the seam.

Father and son knelt before their King. "My liege Lord, Henry, who is France, true Christian and defender of all his people, we are your men and pledge ourselves to your service as your vassals and in turn beg your protection." Robert kissed the feet of the French King and motioned William to do so as well. Henry took the hands of the young lad and helped him up. "William will have our protection, Robert. You have served your King. Your King shall be as faithful to Normandy. We ask the King of England here to bear witness to our pledge and remind us should we at any time be remiss in our duty."

Edward stood. "I so bear witness."

The priest who had given Robert communion was scurrying at the bottom of the steps with a chalice and he fell, spilling the round wafers on the stone. And while he was lapping them from the floor with his tongue, Robert brought William over to Edward. The boy smiled up at him. They were friends. "Of our cousin, Edward, King of England, and we recognize no other, we ask protection of young Normandy, who is heir and is to be England as well as Normandy." There were murmurs in the hall from among those who apparently found the fact surprising that William was heir to England as well as Normandy. The priest was still trying to consume the holy wafers from the stone.

An anthem was sung and chickens fluttered with the noise and scooted from the hall. As the roaring voices ceased, the soft rain could be heard. Silence fell over the hall as they all listened and then, as if finally realizing what it was they heard, a clamor broke loose and there was applause and cries of joy and many ran out and Edward could feel the coolness of the rain as the doors opened and an oppressive weight seemed lifted from Normandy.

Tables were being carried in and the cock crowed and with the dawn came a morning feast, all somehow arranged by the skillful employment of the old man Osbern.

Godgifu came over to Edward, her sword swinging at her side. "Make

Robert take Drogo to Jerusalem with him. A skinny rabbit dead from the famine was found in Drogo's bed. The man with no right ear, who bears the water to clean the privies, says it is a sign the Count of Vixen will die on a journey."

"Can I have a sword like Googoo's?" William asked. He had called her that since he had been very young.

"I'll have to teach you how to use it first," Edward told him.

"Soon?"

"After your father is gone."

"I shall be a great warrior," William said. "It is in my blood."

Gilbert, who had been out in the rain and whose hair was wet and plastered against his forehead, came toward them, smiling, dripping water from his fingers.

"Have you seen Alfred?" Edward asked. "He was not here."

"He's left Rouen," Gilbert answered.

"Left Rouen? Why?"

"Kalf Arnesson and the Norse have attacked the Daneland. Albert left early last evening with a small band to fight for Harthacnut."

"He said no good-bye."

"He knew you'd try and stop him."

"And I would have. The fool could be killed for the likes of that fat pig."

Behind him he heard a voice: "Norway has invaded the Daneland."

Outside, men were taking off their tunics and like small children running from the loggia into the rain. Edward stood beneath the arch and watched. A snake scurried beneath his feet and he recoiled. He loathed snakes. Herleve came up to him. "I have lost my son."

"Robert will be gone a half year, the most, perhaps much less," Edward assured her.

"No. Herluin quite by accident killed a sparrow. An old woman with only one eye was passing. She took the bird and with her teeth split it open and emptied its entrails upon the ground. 'The duke will journey to the tomb of Christ and die.' That was a month ago at Conteville before we came back to Rouen."

Edward said nothing. To deny the oracles was wasted breath. Robert, too, had sensed the finality of his pilgrimage.

"The Daneland has been attacked," he heard someone say to someone else behind him.

For two weeks the ducal house readied for Robert's pilgrimage. The spring came in a continual pleasant rain. The famine would end. Seeds would be planted and grow. Edward was horrified by the number of snakes which suddenly appeared and he always left his chamber cautiously.

"There is a woman in Meules who hunts them and eats them," Osbern said. "I will have her brought to Rouen."

The nights were quiet and the duke slept without terror. Robin had gone. Edward would miss him. With a simple good-bye, he had gotten on his horse, the crozier being borne by a monk riding with him.

"I shall yet make you Archbishop of Canterbury," Edward said.

"It is a long time in coming." Robin laughed and rode away in the gentle rain.

Green grass appeared; buds tipped the trees. And still the careful rain fell. The duke rode from the parvis with as much fanfare and festival as the weather would permit. He handed out ducal coins. And many came despite the rain. The Jew of the yellow house was to ride as his guide, but it was a small party of only twenty-eight, including the Count of Vixen. Drogo had not wanted to go, but could find no legitimate excuse to refuse Robert.

"I think the journey foolish," the archbishop said and blessed them.

"The famine . . ." Robert shrugged.

"The rains are here now," the archbishop reminded him.

And Edward sensed Robert would have liked to climb down off that horse and forget it all, but he held the horse's reins taut and told his uncle to take care of the boy. To Edward he said, "Protect William."

Edward promised and the twenty-eight riders, Robert at their lead, clomped through the streets of Rouen and toward the Seine gate and the bridge.

Months were washed away by the rain. Only occasionally did the sun appear. Word was sent back that Robert had reached the Holy Sepulcher and that God was blessing and protecting them. Soon they were to start home.

Outside the great hall the woman of Meules, whose dirty gray hair hung in clumps to her waist, was beating the head of a snake against the stone arch of the door. It was her method of killing them and then she ate the snakes raw. Edward hated the sight. "It will be a year of death, mark you that," she told Edward.

The hall was dark and the fire smoky, but he went in to escape her. The heads, shriveled and dried, looked eerie in the dim, pallored light. He coughed and sat on the steps. What would happen, he wondered, if Robert didn't return? These Normans were difficult enough for Robert to contain; how was a seven-year-old boy supposed to do it? A rat gnawed on something in a dark corner. He could not see the rodent, only hear its constant chewing. In England they said Cnute was well again, but he didn't do much to save his empire. The Norse had named the boy, Magnus, King and denied all claims of Cnute. Cnute's son Svegan and his mother were said fled to the Daneland. When Edward became King he would give little concern to either the Norse or the Daneland.

Someone came in. Edward looked up to see Eleanor, the Countess of Flanders, in her black robes, hardly visible in the dim light, black against black.

Before he could ask she gave him the answer. "Old Baldwin died. I came home to see Rouen while Robert is gone."

"I'm sorry about Baldwin," Edward said. "We had not heard. When was the funeral? We should have been told."

"He was an old man." She came over and sat beside him. "When we were children we used to play in here when it was dark like this. Richard complained a rat was going to kill his bird and Robert killed the rat with his bare hands."

"I remember," Edward said. The rat had squealed as Robert wrung its neck.

"I didn't stay after the funeral. I felt unwanted there." Eleanor looked up. "All these awful heads. They weren't here when we were children. God may forgive Robert for killing Richard, I never shall. You all hated Richard but he was good to me. He used to let me play with his bird. But he let no one else."

"He was a failure as a duke," Edward said.

"He didn't have the cruel spirit for it. Yes. He was kinder than the rest of us. He had a boy, you know."

"Yes, the son of the kitchen woman. Her head's up there."

"How horrible," Eleanor said. "I have been to see the boy. He's in a monastery. His name is Nicholas. Robert will probably kill him."

"No. His life is a wedding present to Herleve and Herluin."

"I shall wear black until Robert is dead."

Edward changed the subject. "Another Baldwin is count?"

"Yes. But the old man was good to me and left us well provided for and just as well, his son is parsimonious. There is a fat dowry arranged for Judith. It's up to you as her godfather, Edward, to make a good match for her when she comes of age."

"I shall. Is she with you?"

"Yes," she said. "May we go? These heads . . ."

Spring warmed to summer. The sun shone on fields of flourishing grain. Wild animals returned to the countryside and life came to Normandy again. It was July. Edward took young William hawking. A Norwegian falcon sat erect on the boy's wrist as they rode through the open country beyond Rouen. The boy was bright and determined and, like the swording, he quickly mastered any skill he was taught and so took to hawking with ease. They rode far into the country and spent the day and there was a sense of room and cleanliness away from the buildings and the stink of human excrement and the rats and the snakes which pervaded Rouen. No matter how often he bathed or washed during a day, Edward never felt quite clean in Rouen.

Toward sunset the pair, their kill hung across William's mount, rode back in through the gates of the city. As they reached the ducal house, Edward sensed something was wrong. There was a peculiar stillness, and as he walked down the empty loggia, William following, he knew. Eleanor came toward them. She was wearing a brilliant yellow gown.

"You are Duke of Normandy, boy," Edward said and touched William's shoulder lightly. "God have mercy on you."

CHAPTER 19

Bruges and at sea, 1035

HE TOOK LITTLE STEPS. HIS GOWN WAS SHODDILY WOVEN. HE HAD BURIED HIS father with such parsimony it was disgraceful. Baldwin, the fifth, was decidedly not a splendorous count. His thin hair was somewhere between a pale red and dun, parted in the middle and hanging long at each side of his face. "You are welcome in this house," he said, wiping the running nose of his tiny daughter Matilda off on his sleeve. Matilda was an obdurate child with large freckles and delicate hands.

Emma knew what the Count of Flanders said was a lie and Baldwin knew Emma knew it was a lie and it was understood she would leave. Emma's household was small; she had traveled with fewer than fifty, and two of those had died.

Emma looked down from the parapet. Horses were copulating just below near the wall. Old Baldwin's young widow, Eleanor, had taken her small daughter and fled to Rouen before the lid was hardly on the coffin. Eleanor was like her mother; she scratched. No one knew because she drenched herself in all those layers of black fabric, but Emma had caught her scratching one day when Eleanor thought she was alone. They said old Judith was at Rennes. She was probably scratching yet. It was daylight and sunny and she was not alone; a Flemish soldier stood some feet away. His skin was burned dark from the August sun. Yet, she recalled the black night when she had been alone in this same spot. Edward could have killed her. She would not be obligated to him because he was too cowardly to act. She would not be in his debt. On a day clear like this the sea was bright in the distance. She had to leave; she had to go from Bruges.

She could not go to Winchester; Cnute would lock her up.

She could not go to Roeskild; Elgiva had fled there from Norway.

She could not go to Rouen; Edward was there.

She could go to Germany, where her ten-year-old daughter was Queen. But what would she do there?

It was time to act, but she needed to find out what was happening at the English court. She sensed something was very wrong. Why hadn't Cnute come down hard on the Norwegians? They named a new king and he did nothing. They attacked the Daneland; he did little. Duke Robert's death left Normandy on the verge of chaos, but he made no attempt to intervene that she had been made privy of, although she was privy to little enough these days. Her news of England came from occasional travelers and emissaries. She learned little more than gossip: Gytha had gone to Pevensey a week ago; Bishop Stigand had installed new bells at the cathedral and was not in the King's favor. Hardly matters of import. She had no spies at Cnute's court. But something was wrong. Where was the power of the splendorous imperial Winchester? Stigand, if out of favor, would be of little use. There was really no one with an ear to Godwin and the King who could tell her what she needed to know. Gytha would tell her nothing, Gytha—

It struck her—Edith. Edith apparently missed nothing. Edith helped her flee in the cold of winter. Edith shared something with Emma that perhaps no other woman understood. Edith resented the dominance men took over women. Edith was disturbed by that and rebelled. Yes! Edith. Edith could be trusted. She would ask Baldwin for three ships. He would probably offer one. She would settle for two.

The meal was spare: a salty fish, a watery gruel, badly molded bread and a bitter wine. He knew how to get rid of his guests.

"Your daughter is coming to visit," Baldwin said, brushed the hair back from his face and puckered as he put down his wine cup.

"The Queen of the Germans?" Emma knew full well who he meant.

"No, the Widow of Vixen."

Count Dreux had died at Bithyrian Nicae, as had the Duke of Normandy, and both of the same affliction, a constant purgation of the bowels.

"I am leaving," Emma said. Let him think it was because Godgifu was coming. "I will need three ships."

"My dear, Queen Emma, as much as we endeavor to be a gracious host"—he broke off a piece of moldy bread—"we simply do not have three ships to spare."

"Less than two and I shan't be able to leave," she said. It was in her voice. It was her final offer.

"Will I get them back?"

"Yes." She took a fish bone from her mouth, thinking, but not for a while.

The two ships were barnacled and had badly patched sails, missing oars and rowmen, but Emma was grateful for anything that would get them to sea. With little preparation they sailed. The salt wind tasted upon her lips and was exhilarating. The ship rolled upon the crests of water and she was free. Just off the coast a whale was sighted and there was a clamor to the portside to view it. And then land disappeared behind them and the channel settled into a rolling calm.

Aesval came up beside her, getting her sea legs with difficulty. She was terribly heavy and Emma noticed how much she was aging. At times she was even cranky, but the sea, or perhaps just getting away from Bruges, enlivened the heavy woman's spirits, too. Emma wondered how old Aesval was. She had never asked.

"And after Pevensey?" Aesval asked.

"I don't know. Caledonia, perhaps. Gruoch, MacBeth's wife, is an ambitious woman. She might be of value. So much depends on what we can learn at Pevensey."

"If anything," Aesval said.

"I am afraid that might well be the truth. I am not at all certain the girl, Edith, will be there."

"If Gytha is, the child most likely will be as well," Aesval assured her.

"Still"—the ship rolled over the swells—"she is attached to her father." Emma was silent for a moment. "Do you ever get tired of this? How many times have we been locked up, exiled or fled?"

"Life is never boring," the older woman said.

Emma laughed. Aesval had changed over the years. She was no longer the country Saxon girl, backward and content with her place. She had become the lady of the court and yet there was still beneath it all that acceptance of one's fate.

They landed four or five miles up the coast from Pevensey. "Flemish nuns," they told a peasant woman who waited on the shore. The woman said her name was Grythgourd and told them she'd had a dream in which a famous abbess came by sea and granted her a wish.

"I am a famous abbess." Emma smirked. "What is your wish?"

"To have a large black pig with a white spot and a goat without horns."

"I will grant your wish," Emma said, "but you must first go to Pevensey and get the names of all the children of the Lord Wessex who are there, and tell me if they ever go down to the sea alone."

Grythgourd went to Pevensey and Emma sent a man servant in the opposite direction to buy a black pig with a white spot and a goat without horns.

The sun began to sink at the edge of the water and they gathered large clams and oysters and caught a great sturgeon, and Lady Beatrice, who had stopped throwing up when she got off the ship, was bitten by a large spider and they made a driftwood fire on the beach and the rowmen went swimming and dove from the ship into the water and one of her ladies, Marzgrth, sang about a man who had a penis growing at the end of his nose and how he "pissed when he caught a chill" and grew a yellow beard. In her nun's black robe, she sang and danced about the fire, throwing small bits of wood into the flame. A rowman from Brittany played the bagpipes and another strummed upon the harp.

And the peasant woman returned first.

"I have learned what you wanted to know," Grythgourd said.

"What is the answer?" Emma asked.

"Where is the large black pig with the white spot and the goat without horns?"

"He shall be here with them shortly."

"When I have my wish, I will tell you."

"You try my patience," Emma said.

It was nearly dawn when the man returned. He herded a pig and led a goat.

"Where have you been?" Aesval scolded.

"Have you ever tried to find a black pig with a white spot?" he said and wandered off.

Grythgourd examined both the pig and the goat carefully.

"Well?" Emma looked at her.

"The children are there"—and she counted on her fingers—"Edith, Sven, Harold, Tostig, Gryth, Leofwine, Wufnoth and Gunnhildr." The woman had only one finger left, for she was missing the middle finger on her right hand.

"My Lord, she's had another," Emma said. "And do they go to the sea?"

"Nearly as to every day, they say, except the little ones now, the ones Wufnoth and Gunnhildr."

"Edith?"

"She tends them, but sneaks off to pray as oft as not. She climbs to a place up above on the rocks."

"You were told this?" Emma asked.

"I saw. I can describe the place to you," Grythgourd said.

"Do."

Most stayed at the ships. Only Emma and five of the women, including Aesval and Beatrice, made their way along the coastline. Emma led. Their black skirts billowed out in the sea breeze as they filed along the water's edge. Terns ran before them and large-winged seabirds cawed and circled overhead. The country this distant from Pevensey was unfamiliar to Emma, yet she led anyway. Sometimes they stayed along the rocky beach, other times they walked above at the edge of cliffs, which fell off into the sea. The morning sun had risen high and the heavy and hooded robes they wore for disguise became unbearably hot. Aesval puffed some distance behind as Emma set the pace. The sea sprawled blue as the sun dazzled across it and Emma came to the reefs. As it was unfamiliar country, she turned inland slightly, through a meadow.

Emma approached the rise described to her by Grythgourd. "You stay here," she told them. "I'll see her alone."

It was a steep and difficult climb. The path sometimes seemed to go straight up and she clutched on to the rocks with her small hands. She tore the black skirt on a jagged edge. She continued the steep ascent and stopped, breathed with difficulty and pushed on again. There was a rocky beach below and she could see Godwin's other children there. They ran in and out of the water, splashing and yelling and she thought of her own brothers, of Robert and Richard and Godfrey and Willie and how they would play on the banks of the Seine. So long ago and Richard was dead. Lord, the finality in that word.

Emma reached the flat plane at the top. Edith was there, nude and praying. Emma stood for a moment watching, envious of the girl's taut breasts and narrow waist. The child's skin seemed almost without a blemish and it was golden-tanned by the sun.

"Edith, child."

The girl swung around, startled obviously. "Lady Queen . . . what?"

"I came to see you, child. To see if you will help me again."

Edith stood up. Her legs were like a golden statue's. Oh God, to be young and beautiful again. Emma simply looked at her.

Edith appeared not embarrassed, but seemed to sense the curiosity. "I come to God, who lives in the sun, so that I might feel his touch upon me and I am blessed and warmed by his power." Edith slipped her gown over her head and sat down on a rock. "You wish my help. How may I help you, Lady Queen?"

"Because I am a woman, I am the chattel of the King. Like his horse, but not treated as well, I am bid to do as he demands without question. And because I acted as a person, and not as property, by visiting the dying King Malcolm, I am either forced to live in prison in England or wander the earth." Emma was conscious of her every tone and gesture.

"You are not safe in Bruges?"

"The old count is dead. The new one does not welcome me."

"Where will you go?"

"It is why I have sought you out, Edith. I do not ask you to betray your father"—Emma watched her words carefully—"or grant me any confidence of Godwin's. I ask you only to tell me of that which I would have learned at Winchester had I been there. I would like to join my son at Roeskild." She knew the answer, but asked the question regardless. "It was you, dear child, who first told me that Elgiva and her son had gone there. Have they left Roeskild?"

"No, but they won't be there much longer. I perhaps should not be telling you this but . . . well, you know, of course, that the Earl Leofric is opposed to Harthacnut being heir."

"Yes," she said, "he would have the shoemaker's bastard a king, but surely Cnute will not have any such nonsense from Leofric."

"The Earl of Mercia has raised a large army and Papa says he refuses to accept Harthacnut as Cnute's heir—"

"But Cnute, no doubt?"

"Has compromised. Svegan is to be made heir instead of Harthacnut," Edith said rapidly, spitting it out.

Emma was careful. She tried to keep her voice from betraying her anger. "And your father?"

"Papa is worried about Elgiva. He says she hates him, but . . ."

"But what, Edith?"

"Harthacnut is my friend, but . . . well . . . they, my brothers say . . . even though he's seventeen . . . he can't . . ."

"Copulate," Emma finished the sentence and slumped down on a rock. "But he will, Edith. He will outgrow this."

"I never shall do it," Edith said.

"Certainly, you will."

"Never. My body is for no man. Only God. I will be no man's property."

Emma looked at the young girl. She would change her mind. Yes, as she grew older, she would discover how pleasurable a man could be. Emma turned and looked down at the children running on the beach below. "And Leofric. Will he accept Svegan?"

"Yes. Svegan is to be brought to Winchester."

Emma paced for a moment. The anger welled within her. "And the King's health?"

"They say it's good. But it's not. Mama says he's dying. Papa says that's silly. But he gets very tired and his skin and eyes are still yellow. I pray for him, almost every day, but he is dying."

"And your mother is well?"

"You have not seen her?"

"No. I came to see you, child. I think it best your mother doesn't know. She would tell your father and he would tell the King and I would never reach Roeskild. When Svegan leaves for Winchester, Elgiva will leave, too, and I will be able to go to the Daneland—"

"But Svegan probably won't be brought to England for another month. Where will you go until then, Lady?"

Good. A month. That should be enough time. "Caledonia, to Scone, perhaps," Emma said. "I'll find some place to welcome me for a short visit." Again she looked down at the children playing below. "I understand your mother had another child—"

"A girl, Lady Queen, Gunnhildr, named for the King's mother."

Poor mad Gunnerhild, who fell into the sea; perhaps young Svegan would fall into the sea. Emma continued to make small talk lest she appear too anxious to get away and she was terribly anxious to get away and be en route to Roeskild.

Edith showed her the gold necklace set with a cluster of tiny black pearls. "Edward sent it to me," the girl said.

"Edward?"

"Your son, Lady Queen."

How strange, Emma thought, and she looked at the sun and realized that she had better be getting away before it got dark and too late to reach the ships and she walked slowly and climbed slowly until she was certain she was out of sight and then fled down the steep hill, hurrying, falling, picking herself up again, in an effort to reach Aesval. She was out of breath when she came to where the women waited. She walked aside with Aesval as they began the long march back to the ships. "Corfe haunts us again. Thank God, we've come before it was too late." She stopped for a few moments, looked up at the seabirds overhead and said softly, "Elgiva's son, Svegan, must be killed."

The sails billowed to the North. The sea air was cold and Emma wrapped herself warmly and stood at the fo'c'sle. The water was turbulent and Lady Beatrice vomited the entire journey. They lost the second ship for a while in the North Sea, but it caught up with them before they anchored off the Daneland.

Aesval dressed as a nun and made ready to sneak into Roeskild. She took with her two men of Emma's house, Stopard the crude and Wilkert, a cask-maker with short stubby legs. They were disguised as monks and Wilkert waddled like a duck in his robes. They were searching for no particular news, simply to listen and hear what could be heard. As much as she loved the sea, it was a relief to get to shore for a bit, and though Emma didn't dare go with them into Roeskild for fear of being seen by Harthacnut or Estrid's Svegn, she did go as far as the beach and sat watching the birds from a cluster of rocks up just above where the waves swept the shore. It was pleasant and the sun was warming and she felt sleepy and was nearly dozing when she saw him.

She spotted him walking on the beach, a boyish carefree walk, and she wanted to call out to him, "Cnute . . ." But it was not Cnute and she knew who the figure on the beach must be, so young and full of exuberance as he ran and tossed pebbles across the waves. Oh God. He was the young soldier who had come to her on a cold night in a chamber at the house of Thegn Godwin. He was a laughing young King climbing trees with Ulf on the hills outside Winchester. He was the young lover in her bed. Emma's chest ached and she crept behind the rocks and cried. Where had youth gone? When had she died? She stayed there until her eyes were dry and when she came back out Svegan Cnutesson was gone.

"We'll have to work quickly," Aesval said on returning. "The young man and his mother sail for Elmham in eight days and are to wait there for the call to come to Winchester."

"We let them sail," Emma said.

"Why?"

"I've changed my mind."

"You saw him." Aesval repeated, "You saw him."

"Yes. I saw him."

"I saw him as well. I thought it was young Cnute. He is twenty-two they tell. Older than the first time you set eyes upon Cnute."

"You understand, Aesval? Nothing is to be done."

"I understand," the heavy woman said. "I quite understand."

A small boat came out from Roeskild. Emma, Aesval, Wordig, Beatrice and a few of the others who might be recognized stayed out of sight. The young man with the insolent eyes, Svegn Estridsson, and a party of Danes came aboard. "Who are you, Norse? What are you doing anchored about these waters?"

The steersman had his instructions. He spoke with a strong Flemish accent. "We are from Bruges, priests and nuns, bound for Armagh. We are waiting for our third ship to find us and we'll move on."

"We'll be watching," Estrid's son said. They snooped about and left.

Emma decided they might as well wait the eight days for Elgiva and Svegan to sail and then make themselves known. She didn't know what she would do now, but she knew the young man could not be killed. Stopard and Wilkert, in their disguises, went into Roeskild to keep abreast of the news, but it was felt Aesval might be discovered and she did not accompany them. Harthacnut told Stopard he looked like a Winchesterian he knew, but Alfred rushed him on and Harthacnut left, pursuing the matter no further. There was great fear in Roeskild that the Norse would attack and they were very suspicious of the Flemish ships and thought they might be spies for the Norse. On the fourth day Stopard and Wilkert returned early. It was the waddling Wilkert who spoke. "Svegan Cnutesson has been killed. A knife in his back."

"Aesval," Emma screamed.

Aesval had been aft when the men returned. "You have not seen me leave this ship, Lady Queen."

"I did not want him dead." Emma slumped down on a keg. "Such a young man, full of life."

"They suspect it was his Norse mistress," one of the men said.

"And she's disappeared," the other told her.

"Aesval," Emma asked. "Did you?"

"No," Aesval said and walked away.

It was Wordig who suggested that they should slip away in the night. "They may come looking for the Norse mistress and search the ship and we'll be undone."

Emma agreed. "We can go to Caledonia for a while and come back."

They raised anchor. There was a body hooked on it. A light was brought over.

"Who is it?" Emma asked.

Stopard said quietly, "Svegan Cnutesson's Norse mistress."

The body was thrown back in the sea and they set sail.

CHAPTER 20

Winchester and Shaftesbury, 1035

THE WIND RAILED AGAINST WINCHESTER LIKE AN OFFENDED TYRANT, venting its rage in desultory bursts. It eructed, an aroused dragon chewing thatch in gluttonous gulps, rooting up trees and battering them against defenseless hovels that caved beneath the weight and it exhaled a swirling breath of dirt and withered leaves that formed a brown fog, and then it died. It breathed no more. And all that remained was the debris of its terror. Godwin looked up into the sunless sky. Day was ending. A tree stood, its torn white sinew exposed. The dismembered branches blocked the entrance to the King's chamber house. A layer of dirt, twigs, leaves and thatch was scattered across the cobble of the courtyard. A dead pigeon was being examined by a snorting fat sow and Godwin stood and watched and then moved on toward the great hall.

It was cold and empty inside. The fire had been left untended and was but a scatter of embers. He stretched out on the steps. Above him was the King's chair, the green cushion torn at the seam and feathers creeping out. Like a thread being spun from a full tuft, the King's power had been attentuated and Godwin wondered if it could be restored.

He deluded himself no more. The King was not well. After the miracle of being touched by the lightning-struck monk Cnute regained a measure of strength, but the old stamina and vigor were missing. His skin and eyes were still tainted by the urine color. He still required long periods of rest. His voice lacked force. What spirit he had seemed to develop was broken when the lad, Svegan, was killed. But the death of Cnute's son was not just a blow to the King, but had struck at what Godwin had been working toward as well and that was an ordered acceptable succession. Like a crack of lightning, it ended. Svegan Cnutesson was killed. His father mourned and Godwin felt like he was playing in one of Cnute's chess games minus the most important playing piece.

It was October. It was cold. It had gotten dark while he sat there. Godwin was about to get up when the door opened at the far end of the hall. It was Gytha. He recognized her steps before he ever saw her in the last remnants of daylight.

"I want to go home." She walked toward him in even, slow steps. "To hear the sea." She looked tired. Too many babies, he wondered? Yet there was still no gray in her red hair.

"We will go home permanently after Shaftesbury," he said and sat up straight.

"Not that I wouldn't wish it, but you can't leave."

Her gown was simple and unadorned, a lush green. Despite the babies she had kept her figure.

"Let Leofric advise the King for a while. I'll go home and play the spoiler . . . sit at Pevensey and plot." He laughed. "We could invite Emma to come visit us and stir up trouble."

"You're not serious." She smiled and sat down on the steps beside him and put her hand over his knee.

"I am very serious about going home for good."

"You'd die not being in the center of things. You'd shrivel up and die, Godwin."

"I'm tired, Gytha. You're tired. I can see it in your eyes. We need a rest."

"Perhaps. But you won't be happy with nothing to do. And what of the succession?"

He touched her fingers resting on his knees. "I thought all was settled. The older Harthacnut got, the worse he got. He really is an abhorrent fat mass."

"Not so loud, these walls undoubtedly have ears," she cautioned.

"Still, it's true." But he lowered his voice. "I doubt he will ever be able to sire a child."

"If our Sven only had the same problem." She threw open her hands.

"I don't know what to do with that boy," Godwin told her.

"You'll have to take him to Shaftesbury with you. I can't handle him anymore."

"In a locked box," he said and gently touched the back of her neck. "I'll keep him in a locked box."

"The first woman that came by he would talk into breaking the lock and she would let him out and he would have her."

Sven had become a real problem. In the past three months he had not only gotten three women pregnant, but had killed the brother of one of the women and the husband of another. "We should give him to the Queen for a present."

"Have you any news of Emma?"

"She's left Roeskild and gone back to Bruges."

"I heard." She pushed a stray red hair from her face. "But why?"

"Svegn Estridsson doesn't like her and asked Harthacnut to tell her to go, so the unpredictable regent ordered it."

"Poor Emma."

"Poor Emma, indeed." Godwin stood up. "Poor the rest of us. Emma is like a gale at sea. You never know where next will be the strike, if at all. Do you know I sometimes feel she was in some way responsible for Svegan Cnutesson's death?"

"That's nonsense."

"I know it," he said. "Yet, whenever I've had trouble, Emma is somewhere in the pot."

"It seems to me," Gytha said, "Harthacnut has suddenly become commanding. I can't imagine Emma—"

Godwin interrupted. "He's obstinate. He scares me at times. He gets something in his head and there is no discouraging him. Sometimes his ideas are foolish and dangerous."

Gytha stood up. "By the way, you'll have to talk to Edith. She ran nude again through Winchester."

"Oh Lord."

"Looking for the gray wolf, or so she said."

He put his arm about her. "It is time we went home, Gytha. Past time. I'll play important earl, be Leofric for a while."

"And should I ride through the streets of Pevensey nude like Godiva did at Coventry?"

"I don't think you'll need to. Edith would do it for you."

"Talk to her, Godwin."

"I will." He kissed her on the forehead.

They walked the distance of the dim hall without speaking. Godwin kept his arm about her.

"Why Shaftesbury?" Gytha asked at the door.

"You should have a cloak," he said and took off his and put it around her. "Leofric wouldn't come to Winchester or Glouchester and Siward won't go where Leofric won't go . . . and I urged the King not to leave Wessex. So it is Shaftesbury."

"You'll have to take Sven."

"In a locked box," he repeated.

And they made their way along the dark street.

Two weeks later winter threatened. The ride to Shaftesbury was cold and uncomfortable. Godwin was bothered by a swelling in his foot. He, like the King, had to be helped to a chamber when they arrived. "You stay about where I can keep watch on you," he told Sven. Sven smiled as only Sven could smile. Godwin dozed; when he awoke Sven had vanished. Their host, though, was one of Godwin's thegns and he saw that Sven was locked in for the night. Godwin was told Leofric had arrived and had the boy, Harold, with him. The plan was simple. The Witangemot would meet in the morning. The King would name the shoemaker's son his heir and take him to Winchester. Godwin would give up his post as first counselor. Leofric would be offered the job and would most assuredly accept. Cnute promised Godwin by Christmas Leofric would be brought under control and the shoemaker's son butchered, perhaps Leofric as well. The journey had wearied the King. His face seemed more yellow than usual and he was breathing with some difficulty after the trip.

Godwin was brought some goat's milk and he settled, his leg still bothering him, in a chair by the fire. There was a rap at his door.

"Enter," he called without getting up.

Thegn Behi stood beneath the lintel. Young Behi no longer looked so young. Despite the cold, he was bare-chested, his sale, as always, back over his shoulders.

"Come in, Behi," Godwin said.

"I wasn't certain I'd be welcome." He came into the room, but only a few steps. "I owe you an explanation."

"You owe me nothing," Godwin said.

Behi didn't speak. He simply stood there for a moment. It was awkward. "You could have seized my lands."

"You earned your lands. I'm not a vindictive man. You were with me long enough to know that." It wasn't the truth. Godwin had been furious. He had saved the sodomizer's life in York. What he got in return was treachery. Why had this trusted young man, whom he had made a thegn and given lands, turned upon him? The disloyalty he didn't understand, but he didn't wish to display enough concern to listen to Behi's explanation. Godwin had raged and been prepared to have Behi killed, his lands confiscated. It was Gytha's good sense that had prevailed. "There will come a day, Godwin, when you'll need Behi. Keep him in your debt."

"I thank you, but I should explain."

"No," Godwin said. "Let it lie. How is the boy?"

"Harold, you mean?"

"Yes."

"You won't like him," Behi said.

I never have, Godwin thought.

Behi continued. "He is willful and headstrong, like his mother. But the Earl of Mercia seems to be able to control him."

"And you?"

"I am very fond of him."

So that was it. Why hadn't he guessed? For lack of anything better, Godwin said, "Yes."

Behi put his head down. "Why did you accept him, my Lord of Wessex?"

How formal, Godwin thought. A simple "Godwin" or "Wessex" in the old days. "For England. I have always put England first. I still believe Harthacnut is the legitimate heir, but I don't wish to see England torn again by battling earls. And I am tired; I look to Pevensey and a rest."

"You look well, my Lord."

"Old," Godwin said, "I'm getting old."

"And the countess?"

"Gytha is fine."

The conversation became awkward; two people with nothing to say to one another, making useless talk.

After Behi left Godwin went to bed. He was awakened in the night to be told by a messenger that the Norse had launched a massive fleet against the Daneland. Thank the good Lord, this would be the last night his sleep would be interrupted like this. Tomorrow he would be freed of the burden.

On the way to the gathering of Witangemot, he met Bishop Stigand. The man seemed to scurry and he carried his crozier like a weapon, poking ahead of him as if a pack of mad dogs was approaching. Godwin followed him into the hall. The great hall at Shaftesbury was far from great: a straw floor matted by the filth of time, high walls which let the cold sift through. It was a narrow ugly room with a door which rattled in the wind. In one corner alone at a table sat Siward, the Earl of Northumbria. He had long gray hair which hung in his face and a bushy beard. Earl Leofric sat on a stool cracking nuts in his teeth. With him was his ward, Harold. The boy had grown tall. He had a long nose and a thin face. He did not stand still and kept moving his open hands about in a strange pattern. His feet were bare, long and narrow and his toenails had been dyed a deep purple. They said he could run faster than a deer on those narrow bony feet. His dark eyes constantly seemed to be shifting. Godwin would not have recognized him but for the coal-black hair and the narrow face. He was sixteen, Godwin was told. He looked younger. He no longer resembled the shoemaker and, except for the hair, looked little like his mother, either.

"You are staring at me, Lord Godwin. I don't think I like it," the young man said. His voice was brittle.

"Yes, I was," Godwin said without apology.

The King was carried in a chair. He looked extremely ill, worse than Godwin had seen him in months, and simply nodded to them in passing and seemed to have little interest in either the boy or the proceedings about to take place.

"What is wrong?" Godwin asked the doctor who walked behind the King bearing a crucible containing the ashes of a cremated bear.

"His eyes are filled with urine," the doctor whispered. "I think he is going to die. I think the King is going to die."

Godwin slumped down on a bench. He said nothing. What was going to happen now? What if the King died? What if Cnute died?

The King spoke little beyond the required formalities and those in a voice cracking with a rattle in his chest. He stared blankly ahead as the first phase of their plan was put into effect: the boy Harold was pronounced heir and the Earl of Mercia named the new chief counselor.

Bishop Stigand asked him to call the Witangemot to a close, but Cnute didn't respond and Godwin realized the King was dead.

BOOK FOUR

The Anointed

CHAPTER 1

Londuntown, 1042

It was a blistering cold day in January. There was no snow, but cakes of frosted ice, pillowing or flat, rough and even, floated in the Thames. Edward watched as a young boy with yellow hair, perhaps nine or ten, retrieved dead fishes and placed them in a circle on the cold frozen mud of the shore.

The sky was bleak and empty and the air raw as an open sore, painful and sharp. England was in rebellion. Fat Harthacnut was King, mad, worse even than the now dead Harold before him, and Edward did not care. There were few he cared about: Sassy and Godgifu and Edith and Eleanor's child, Judith, and Herleve and Robin and Herluin and the young duke, William, and Tostig and Godgifu's Ralph and the servant Seven, if he still lived. The rest were dead: Alfred and Gilbert and Robert and MacBoru and Uncle Goddy—all dead.

Edward stood above in the dead grass of the embankment, his eyes intent upon the boy below as he took stones, dug them from the hard earth and laid them on the fishes. He next built a fire in the center of the ring and stepped outside the circle of dead fish. A seabird, a large tern, swooped down toward the fish, but instead dove directly into the fire; the bird cawed and was no more. The yellow-haired boy then moved back into the circle and stood looking into the fire.

It was sudden. "Edwardi Rex!" he called.

"I am here," Edward answered as if he were expecting the boy to call him and yet he had given it no thought.

"Until the eighth of the month, eat no flesh but that of fish," the boy ordered.

"The eighth of what month?" Edward asked.

The boy didn't look up at him. He leaped over the dead fish and ran along the shore and disappeared. Edward stood there. The fire died and seabirds came and ate the dead fish and the rocks fell upon the hard mud and Edward sat down on the dead grass and thought about the eighth and he sat in the sharp cold for hours and then slipped down the bank and gathered the stones.

He was gathering stones when he heard Edith calling him and looked up toward the bank to see her, her hair blowing in the wind.

"It's Tostig," she called down to him. "He can't breathe."

He scurried up the embankment. Edward owed Edith and Tostig his life. Tostig had been but a boy on the day six years ago when Alfred and Edward had landed in England with troops to drive Harold from the throne. It was young Tostig and Edith who had met Edward on the Dover road and warned him that they had been betrayed. No one had warned Alfred and now Alfred was dead.

"No," Godwin said as Edward followed Edith into the Godwin chambers at Wardrobe Palace.

"Yes," Gytha said and pointed in the direction of the room where Tostig was gasping for air. And Edward went into the room and gave his friend back his breath. Tostig laughed and Gytha cried and Godwin thanked him and Edith gently touched his hand. It was warm and friendly in the room and Edward drank a hot wine and sat by the fire.

Edward knew he would be King and waited for the eighth of the month. He was used to waiting. He had waited so many years. Cnute had been King and he had waited and then Harold Harefoot had been King for five years and he waited and now Harthacnut was King and he still waited but he knew he would be King and he treasured the ball of dried horse dung the old woman seer had given up so many years ago to burn on his fire the day he was crowned.

Harold had become King by force of Leofric and Siward, but he had ruled without Cnute's treasure, for Emma had gone to Winchester ahead of Harold Harefoot and absconded with it to Bruges. Baldwin the Fifth welcomed her because of all the treasure and she stayed in Bruges those years with forty thingliths and countless servants in her household. All that treasure Emma brought to Harthacnut and in less than a year in his own reign he had exhausted most of it.

The earls and thegns and clerics had, Edith said, cheered when Harold died from excessive opium use on March 17, 1040, and had been joyed to have a new King. But now they had come to hate Harthacnut, perhaps even more than the shoemaker's bastard. When Harthacnut arrived in England he had traveled at once to Westminster and had Harold's body exhumed and thrown into a fen. But Edward didn't mind Harthacnut's extravagance for he gave Edward gifts for being his brother. On a single day he gave Edward twenty-seven new robes. He also gave gifts to Beorn Estridsson and his brother Osbeorn. When the treasure was spent, Harthacnut levied taxes. He had a greater number of thingliths than even Cnute had in his guard and he started to rebuild the King's compound at Winchester which Harold had burned to the ground when he discovered Emma had gone off with the treasure.

The eighth of February came and Edward dressed in a new white gown. At court they spoke of Donalbain going to Northumbria to plead for an army to raise against MacBeth, for Duncan was dead and Donalbain swore it was Gruoch who had killed him, but Northumbria was more concerned with its taxes and did little for the dead King's son. Edward wore a red sash and pointed red shoes and the stones which the boy had placed on the dead fish Edward had set into a neck chain and he wore it and it hung heavy upon his chest.

"That is an ugly neck chain," Harthacnut said.

Edward did not reply.

Tostig came into the King's hall and told them stories of the sea and of a great sea monster which ate ships and the Queen said the story was silly, but Tostig told of how a woman at Degannwy had seen the monster and that it was green and as large as sixteen ships and rose and fell from the water and spit fire and devoured, whole, a ten-rowman Norse ship, but Emma said all Celts lie and you couldn't believe a thing they said and Tostig went off to bed and one by one they drifted away and the King, who had been eating during the entire evening, belched and was carried off to his bed and the fire turned to embers and Edward was the last to leave the hall and the eighth had ended and nothing had happened.

Sometimes Edward missed Normandy even though it had become a difficult land for him after Robert had died. He missed William, whom he had taught to sword and hunt and the ways of battle. But he had became a poor relation, often being cast from one keep to another. Godgifu was a widow with few rights and there was little she could do for him. It was his Uncle Robert, the archbishop, who held the duchy together until his death. But there were always plots to kill William, and Walter, Herleve's brother, often had to flee with William in the night to save his life. Others loyal to the duke were killed. Alan of Brittany was poisoned. Even Gilbert, his dear cousin Gilbert, was eventually killed. Uncle Robert's bastard, Ralf of Gace, more and more drove others away and took over the responsibility of guarding and tutoring the young duke until there was no one but him to advise William. Edward was driven off like the others, but by then Godgifu had remarried and was the Countess of

Boulogne and Edward went and lived with her and her husband, Eustace, and Eustace gave him coin to build a shrine at Boulogne to St. Olaf in memory of Alfred. Poor Aly, he meant no harm to anyone. Edward built the shrine near the sea, which Alfred loved so much. The sea was his mother, he used to say.

The eighth of March came. Edward put on a new silk white robe and wore green soft shoes and a golden cinch. A great fire swept Londuntown in the midmorning and they fled with the King to Greenwich and some muttered as how they should have put the King in the fire and Edward thought of his dried horse turd and his white robe became black and sooty from the fire before they ever escaped the town.

"That is an ugly neck chain," Harthacnut said.

Edward did not reply.

The King's house at Greenwich was cracked and drafty and Edith brought Edward a rib bone, but he refused. He ate only the flesh of fish. He drank some wine with the King, but Harthacnut spilled half of his on his tunic, and Godwin didn't join them. Godwin never drank wine and these days he sat glumly as if waiting for something to happen, but nothing good came of the waiting and England became more angry with its King and government and Godwin seldom gave the King advice and had asked to go to Pevensey, but Harthacnut insisted he stay and tend to the affairs of state. The sun set and they rode for Londuntown, for word had come that the fire was out and Wardrobe Palace had not burned but that St. Paul's had a hole in the roof. A seer predicted the next fire that came would destroy the entire church. The eighth ended and nothing had happened.

They trooped back into Londuntown to be greeted by indifferent faces and piles of offal at every doorway. A dead horse was left rotting on the cobble. A crone with a bald head and lumps of flesh as large as walnuts called down obscenities on them as they passed. At Wardrobe Palace they were greeted by dank and musty air and stale darkness.

Harthacnut's tax became more oppressive, and here and there revolts against it were heard and they became more and more vociferous. The people of Worcester refused to pay it. Harthacnut stammered and stuttered in his high-pitched voice and sent two thingliths to deal with Worcester, Rogion with the big nose and Clemor the Brute. They rode to Worcester and were attacked by a mob and ran, finding refuge in a monastery. Yet, someone there betrayed them. The mob came and dragged the two thingliths, cursing and screaming, whining and pleading, out against the protestations of the abbot and they tied them to horses and whipped the horses and they were dragged through the streets, their heads beating against the cobbles. They yelled out and screamed and their backs hit upon the stones and they were swung from side to side and their heads hit posts and corners of buildings until their blood left a trail behind them and when the horses came to a stop the pair were dead. All this and more were related to the court by the abbot.

Harthacnut launched an army of thingliths upon Worcestershire. The monastery was leveled by torches until only a blackened foundation remained. The monks were castrated. In the town and the surrounding country, women's breasts were cut off and men lost arms and legs if not their lives. The town was not simply burned, but the people were boarded inside their houses and hovels before the torches were set. Some reported they could hear the screams all the way to Glouchester.

Edward smiled as the magnates of England assembled armies. Edward knew Godwin and Emma plotted and that Emma sent a man to steal Godgifu's son, Ralph, and bring him back and make him King. Edward sent a message to his sister. Godwin plotted with Svegn Estridsson, who was Harthacnut's regent in the Daneland. Edward sat waiting, rocking back and forth on the edge of his stool, silent. Edith came to court nude, except for a black ribbon she wore about her waist. "For the dead of Worcester," she yelled and screamed a litany of obscenities at the King. He laughed and chewed on a leg of mutton. Edward continued to rock back and forth in silence.

From Boulogne an envoy came bearing a gift for the Queen, a large silver casket, and when Emma opened it she screamed and dropped the casket and the head of the man she had sent to steal Ralph rolled out on the floor and a large snake crawled from the silver box also and hissed and wound its way through the hall as servants screamed and ran from its path and it coiled and darted its fangs into a pot boy and he died.

Harthacnut laughed and told his mother, "You owe me a new pot boy."

The eighth of April came and Edward put on a new white mantle with tiny embroidered red crosses and he wore red hose and red shoes and a red *bonnette* with a white feather.

"That is an ugly neck chain," Harthacnut said.

Edward did not reply and went down to the river. He picked field flowers with soft red petals and yellow centers and the sharp thorns pricked at his fingers and he took them to Edith, who sat by the riverbank. Beside her was a gray wolf. She took the flowers and smiled and told him not to touch the gray wolf for the wolf did not like to be petted and Edward did not. They sat and sometimes talked, but mostly in silence looked down at the Thames. There had been a rebellion in Glouchester and a soldier of the King's had been stoned, but the King was not told for fear he would raze Glouchester as he had Worcester and they talked about the King.

"I will be King someday," Edward told her.

"Yes," she agreed.

And they baked fish over a fire down on the mud and they ate it and drank wine and the day ended and nothing had happened.

And the next day Edward and Edith and Tostig rode to Guildford.

"This is where it happened," Tostig said. "We, Edith and I, were tied with hemp and brought in by Behi. He called us informers and Papa got very angry and told him to cut us loose and so he did."

"They waited then, Papa and Behi and all the men for Alfred and his soldiers to come," Edith related. "And when they came they were taken prisoner and Behi said to Alfred something about 'being the pretty one' and hadn't the monk Robin been taken with him. Papa wasn't really paying any attention and Behi screamed and yelled out, 'Well, he won't want you anymore.' It was then he poked Alfred's eyes out and Alfred let out a terrifying wail. It was like a sharp knife cutting the air. I grabbed Papa's knife that he had used to cut our bindings and stuck it deep into Behi's chest."

"No one seemed to move," Tostig said. "They just stood there looking."

"I did as the gray wolf would have done," Edith said.

"The blood leaked from his red sockets and down his cheeks. It was awful to look at," Tostig said. "And all the while Behi lay there on the ground still breathing with the knife sticking in his chest and none of his men daring to do anything for fear of Papa."

"And then they took Alfred to Ely?" Edward asked.

"Yes," Edith told him. "And he died there from poisoning in the eyes. I have seen the green spot on the floor where his face rested and left a stain."

"I thank you for killing Behi," Edward said.

They rode back toward Londuntown. Edward said little. He was thinking of Alfred and the games they had played and Alfred stretched out on the sand by the sea, calling the sea his mother.

On May eighth a horrible thunderstorm struck and clouds broke apart and rain beat the cobble and lightning zagged from the heavens to roofs and burned thatch, but the rain put out the fires and an old man with a club foot was struck by lightning and he smelled as if he had been burned. The King was ill from something he had eaten and Edward went to visit him. The room smelled of vomit and sweat and dirty linen.

"Where did you get that ugly neck chain?" Harthacnut asked and vomited.

Edward did not reply and went back to his chamber.

He sat the day long in a new white surcoat and silver helmet and the rain fell and leaked into the chamber. Word came that the young Duke of Normandy was taken by his Uncle Walter into hiding with peasants after the Burgundians nearly trapped the boy duke at Pont-Athou. Tostig came and sat awhile with him.

"Siward is said ready to march on Londuntown," Tostig said.

"Let him march," Edward told him.

"And the King?"

"When they kill him I will be King," Edward said.

And Tostig left and the rain continued and Edward knelt on a red cushion in prayer and the day ended and nothing had happened.

On June eighth the sun was white-hot and a dry wind blew and Edward scurried from the chapel to his chamber to dress for the celebration. It was but prime and yet so hot, like standing before an open oven. Harthacnut sat, overlapping a stool in Edward's dim chamber. He spilled wine as he put the cup to his mouth and it dribbled down his fat chins. "Look what I got you brother," he said and pointed.

The slave from Orkney held up a white silk gown with white sleeves and linen cuffs embroidered with gold martlets. The slave set the gown aside and displayed a golden-colored mantle of soft wool.

"From Bruges." Harthacnut slopped some more wine. "It was made by the weaver who has no arms and weaves with his toes. Put it on. Put it on."

"I must bathe first," Edward told him.

"You wash too much," the King said and tipped over his wine cup. The slave filled it again and wiped the floor. "I must have some breakfast. Come to me when you're dressed. You shall ride Cnute's golden stallion today." As he stood up, a wooden box that had been buried in the folds of his gown fell from his lap to the floor.

"What's that?" Edward asked.

"A gift Mother sent you. Don't open it. It is a poisonous spider. Don't accept gifts from Mother," Harthacnut cautioned as he went out. The slave left the garments and followed.

The streets of Londuntown were nearly empty as they rode toward Lambeth. There were no churning crowds, only a few occupied Londuners bearing baskets or babies in the dry wind. Emma rode behind in the procession.

"I feel safer when I can see her," Edward said, as he, sitting magnificently upon the golden stallion, rode beside the King through the narrow streets.

"Beorn is back there with her," the King reminded him.

A hawk hung in the hot sky.

"Why don't you take off that ugly neck chain?" Harthacnut asked.

Edward did not reply.

At Lambeth the feast was held in a grove of trees behind the house of Osgot Clapa. Corn was thrown at Gythana and Tofig the Proud, and the bridal pair ran out into the grove. Tables were set in long rows and buckled under the weight of the food and the King began eating his way the length of one of the tables. He was smearing gravied swan about his mouth as Edward turned about to face the host and the Earl of Wessex.

"Congratulations, Osgot. A fine daughter," Godwin said.

Osgot raised his wine cup. "She's got big lungers. Tofig said he married her for her big lungers. Your own daughter there"—Osgot directed the wine cup toward Edith—"should be getting married, Lord Godwin."

Edward looked across at Edith, who stood with her brother Harold. Dressed in a pale blue gonelle, she looked like the soft-colored illumination of a saint—a virgin, he thought.

"I have it in mind, Clapa. I have it in mind," Godwin assured him.

"A king, no less, is good enough for her. She is a beauty, your daughter is," Osgot told him and cupped his wine to his lips.

"You are perhaps right." Godwin stood looking at Edith.

Edward moved in the direction where she and Harold were.

A drunken guest was complaining, perhaps a little too loudly, about the horrible taxes. Yet the King seemed not to have heard. Another said more quietly that Leofric and Siward were massing armies in the North and would come and free them all.

Harold Godwinsson never seemed to smile. He looked like his father, a little taller perhaps, but only slightly. His hair was sandy and he had cold gray eyes which tried to look inside Edward when he talked with him, but Edward never revealed himself to Godwin's second son. He trusted Harold and liked him, but he was not a friend as Tostig was, or Edith; there was a distance between them and Edward never attempted to cross the barrier. Harold dressed as an earl's son ought, yet he was plain in his attire and the only slight hint of ostentation was a large red jewel sewn into his cap. At his waist was a small skin bag in which he kept the nipple cut from the breast of a nun at Guildford who had tried to seduce him when he was fifteen. He had shown it to Edward once. "She prays more now," Harold said, but he neither smiled nor laughed when he said it.

The King gorged himself on jellied fawn, legs of rabbit, crushed oranges and pomegranates and pushed stuffed oxen ears into his face and honey-filled breads and horse cheese and lamb's tongue and pig's feet and great salted pork rinds and glazed heron and he gulped and burped and never moved from the tables.

The bride and groom danced.

"I shall never marry," Edith said to Edward as he came and took her hand. The neckline of Edith's gonelle was cut low and her breasts cleaved together and were golden and soft and Edward gazed at them.

"Papa would wed you to that fat pig," Harold said and tossed his head in the direction of the King, who at the moment had spilled a bowl of something dark and it oozed down the front of his gown.

"I will marry you, Edith," Edward said, "and you shall be my Queen and virgin and we shall dedicate ourselves to God and all His holy ways."

"Yes." Edith smiled. "I shall marry you, sweet Edward, and no man can touch me."

"And just when do you plan on becoming King?" Harold asked.

"On the eighth," Edward said.

"The eighth of what?"

Godwin's appearance interrupted them. "Harold, dance with your mother." The earl ignored Edward and turned to Edith. "Butterfly," he said, "we shall dance." He led Edith away.

The musicians played and the dancers danced. The Queen danced with Osgot Clapa and kept slapping at his hands as he attempted to rub them across her butt each time the partners joined together. Edward watched Edith's breasts as they bounced in the tight gonelle and her auburn hair tossed in the dry wind. Godwin puffed. Gytha swung about with her son Harold, and the bridegroom, Tofig, danced with his fat mother-in-law, who sweated and heaved and stumbled once and had to be helped to her feet by a struggling Tofig. Finally he willed her off on the man who had been complaining of the high taxes and joined his bride at one of the tables where they fed each other oysters from the shells and giggled and drank wine and Tofig dropped an oyster between Gythana's big breasts and began searching for it with his tongue and the bride giggled more.

All the while Harthacnut ate. Edward went over to him where he was stuffing roasted finches in his mouth.

"I hate that ugly neck chain," Harthacnut said.

Edward did not reply but took some fish and ate it and handed Harthacnut a brown roasted seabird. The King chewed and spit out bones and then with a gulp he began to choke. He grabbed at his throat and the bird fell on the ground as Edward stood there watching him. Harthacnut choked and coughed and Edward reached down and picked up the bird and held it out as an offering to the choking King.

"The King is choking!" someone yelled out. "He's caught a bone!"

Harold ran over. "Edward, aren't you going to help him?"

"No," Edward replied and watched the King gasping and heaving and bending over and trying to suck in air.

"Today is—"

"The eighth." Edward completed Harold's sentence.

The King was turning blue and he fell to the ground in a fat heap of greasy gown as he struggled to breathe and suck the air and the guests gathered and stood about doing nothing.

Emma came flying with the host, Osgot Clapa, behind her. "Do something!" she yelled and bent down over him.

But no one moved. They stood there as if mesmerized by the efforts of the King to breathe. "Please," Emma pleaded and looked at the circle about her. But there was nothing that could be done and the King made spastic jerks of his neck as he tried to breathe. And they stood about in disbelief as the King lay upon the ground before them dying.

"No!" Emma yelled out, but it did no good. Harthacnut ceased to breathe.

"He is dead," Harold said.

The guest who had been complaining of high taxes said, "*Deo gratias.*" Mostly the guests just stood doing nothing, not knowing what could be done, seemingly not even understanding what had happened.

"Who will be King?" the bride asked.

"I am," Edward answered.

And the guests seemed to understand this even less and looked at Edward as if he were a stranger in their midst.

Emma looked up from the ground at him in horror and then she screamed and screamed as if she had been bitten by a great wolf.

CHAPTER 2

Winchester, 1042

AESVAL WAS DYING.

The window boards were closed and Emma sat in the silent dim and listened to the hot August wind rustle early fallen leaves and dried twigs over the cobble.

Carah-with-the-hawk-on-her-breast banged into the room.

"Quiet." Emma's voice was soft, but angry.

"I'm sorry." The girl was breathless and looked down at Aesval and then in an excited whisper added, "There's a lion been seen by the grist."

"There are no lions in Winchester. Get to your pots."

Aesval was bloated like a pig's bladder blown up with air. Red blotches burned on the puffy skin of her face and arms. Emma touched the woman's forehead; it was aflame.

Pots banged in the next room.

"Hush," Emma said.

Carah-with-the-hawk-on-her-breast was from Clontarf and claimed her grandfather had been Brian Borumha, but all Celtic slaves claimed to be descendants of some great clan chief or another—Malachi or Niall Glundubh.

Aesval called again weakly for Edward.

"The doctor will be here again soon." Emma tried to hide her anger at the dying woman for asking for Edward—Edward, who went about calling himself King—well, he wasn't King and he wasn't going to be

King. And he couldn't cure the sick, no matter what they said. Even Godwin believed that fable. Edward was a monster and had let Harthacnut die and she should have fed him to the pigs on the day he was born. This was Godwin's house and Edith went about telling a tale that Edward saved Tostig from dying here. Edith would go to hell for lying.

The doctor came and Bishop Stigand as well. The doctor was a Norman from Sicily with powerful enormous hands and a scar across his forehead. He touched Aesval with a big hand.

"She is dying," Emma told the bishop.

"It's the most amazing thing." Stigand rubbed his little brown beard. "A lion is loose in Winchester. I came with four guards."

Carah-with-the-hawk-on-her-breast came from the other room. "The birds say if a queen looks upon a lion she will bear a son as powerful as a lion."

The Celtic slave was said to have powers to know because the brown mark of a flying hawk was spread across her right breast.

Emma opened the window boards. The day was burned from August heat and the street deserted, barren all the way to the top of the hill where the reconstruction on the King's house had been halted. Emma closed the boards and went on out into the sun. Flanked by Stigand's four guards, their spears drawn, Emma walked up the baked street. The heat was intense and perspiration beaded at Emma's hairline. On each side of the street black shadows offered hiding and she looked carefully from side to side as they walked up the hill. A window board banged and Emma turned quickly and saw nothing; there was a dryness in her mouth and she had both fear and determination as they moved closer to the charred beams intermingled with new raw timbers, not yet darkened by time, of that what was and was yet to be of the King's palace.

It came without a sound. A lion stood in the gates before her. It stood and stood and then leaped and the spears, all four, drove through the air and struck the lion and it fell with a cry. The guards, who looked like a matched set of chess pieces they were so similar in their swarthy appearance, picked up their spears and drove them through the lion, raising the beast on their spears from the stone.

Emma heard the approaching rider and turned to face that young bull Sven Godwinsson on a gray sweating horse. "Are you all right, Lady?" he asked. The rider was sweating as well.

"The Queen," she said, brushing past him and hitting his calf with her elbow, "is disturbed by neither man nor beast."

A crowd gathered behind her, clamoring about the rider and the guards. Emma walked quickly to get out of the sun and away from the flat-nosed son of the Earl of Wessex. She reached Godwin's house. Carah-with-the-hawk-on-her-breast had opened the window boards and was looking out. "He reminds me," she said to someone inside, "of King Cnute."

He looks nothing like Cnute, Emma was about to say when she heard Stigand inside and stopped just before the door.

"There's been gossip," Stigand was saying, "that he is Cnute's son and not Godwin's at all. That he is Gytha and Cnute's."

Emma stepped into the room. "Who?"

Stigand turned away and faced Aesval in the bed. He was obviously embarrassed. "Only silly gossip, Lady, only idle chatter."

"That Sven Godwinsson is not Godwin's son at all?" Emma questioned him. "But an heir to England?"

"Not a truth in it. I can assure you," Stigand said.

Carah-with-the-hawk-on-her-breast closed the window and went to the door and stood. "There is an old crone from Meath, who lives in a shallow dry well, just beyond the minster. Take the lion's teeth to her, Lady Queen, she'll tell you what you want to know."

Emma looked at the Celtic girl and then to the figure on the bed. "The Lady Aesval?"

It was the Norman doctor from Sicily who answered. "She calls for the King."

"He is not the King," Emma declared and went out. "Give me all the beast's teeth," she told the guards.

Stigand came over to the door. He spoke softly to Emma. "She will be soon in the hereafter."

Emma thought of what Aesval's husband, MacBoru, had once told her: "The only hereafter is the life our bloodline lives beyond our tomb." Emma's children were all dead: Harthacnut, Alfred and Gunnerhild. The other two abortions of her womb were some demon issue that had inhabited her body. They were not hers at all. But she had seen the lion. She would bear another child. She was fifty-seven but she would bear another.

Sven came riding up and he spoke as he climbed off the horse and handed away the reins. His voice was deep. "My father will reach here on the morrow, but he bid me tell you Lyfing has accepted Edward as King."

"Lyfing is the biggest idiot in England." He was Bishop of Worcester, Devon and Cornwall and his voice counted.

"I have other news," he told her.

"I will grant you an audience in an hour," she said and turned her back on him. She took the teeth and started to walk toward the minster.

"What should we do with the carcass?" one of the guards asked.

"You may have it," she answered.

And the four who looked alike began to quarrel.

The old crone who lived in the shallow dry well was leading a goose by a gold cord around in a circle.

"The goose will get dizzy and die," the old crone said, "and I will eat it."

The air was stifling hot.

"Why don't you simply wring its neck?" Emma suggested.

"The goose will die when I get hungry." The old crone wore a thin open-weave gown and her sagging flesh, gray and dirty, was visible. She had very little hair, pure white, and wore a red-dyed string with a tiny bronze bell on it which tinkled as she walked in a circle. "I sang for the Pope once."

Emma opened her hand and displayed the lion's teeth.

"A queen who sees a lion will get a large belly." The hag put all the lion's teeth in her mouth and then blew and spat them all within the circle formed by her walk with the goose as a round track in the dust. She stopped walking in the path and went and examined the teeth. "The brother of a man who dies a king will fill you with a juice as white and thick as an abbess's milk and if it is a child—"

"What do you mean 'if it is a child'?"

"—you shall call him Groumbert. For a queen who sees a lion will get a large belly. Send me a white cat with thick fur and only three legs as a gift."

"I will," Emma promised.

Emma walked slowly back. Suppose Sven Godwinsson was Cnute's bastard? He looked a little like Ulf . . . perhaps . . . Cnute. He certainly didn't resemble Godwin. Not like Harold did. What if he was Cnute's son?

Emma walked faster.

Aesval was plastered with poultices and the doctor from Sicily shook his head negatively and looked appropriately forlorn. The bishop had gone; she had wanted to question him further about Sven Godwinsson's parentage. Emma took Aesval's fat swollen hand. The woman made no sign of recognition. There was only the constant rasping breaths, uneven and hollow thrusts of wind. She would put it to Sven and she knew where to find him. She let loose of Aesval's hand and went out the back in the direction of a dingy hovel. It was down a slight slope and she stepped about the offal and human excrement piled in the path. She found the flat-faced young man where she expected to find him, atop Carah-with-the-hawk-on-her-breast, his bare ass in the air pounding away. Emma toppled Sven off the girl with one furious clout and then started lashing out at the Celt, who escaped Emma's blows and ran, exposing her hawk to the streets of Winchester.

"Perhaps, Madam, you are only jealous it was not you." He smiled.

Despite the urge, she did not strike him, but stood calmly. He wore a long shirt, but his big legs and genitals were bare as he sat on the dirt floor bending over his knees.

"Perhaps," she said. She tossed him his braies and he slipped them on. "How would you like to be King?"

"Of what?" he said, lacing his legs with leather straps.

"Of England."

"Why not Emperor of the North?"

"I am serious, Sven."

"I know what I am and what I am not. I am the son of a wealthy earl, but I am also the grandson of a pigherder. Why do you play games with me?"

"Suppose you were not Godwin's son?"

"But I am."

"Suppose you were Cnute's?"

He stood up. "That's ridiculous."

"Cnute told me once in anger that you were his son," she lied.

"I don't believe it."

"It is true," she told him and took his hand and led him toward the bed of Carah-with-the-hawk-on-her-breast. "You see, Sven, if you claim the throne and marry me—"

"MARRY YOU?" He pulled his hand free.

She sat on the bed and rubbed her hand over his heavy thigh. He smelled like an animal. "To marry the widow of the King, just as Cnute did in marrying Elthelred's widow, secures the throne for you."

He did not attempt to get free of her roaming hand. "But you are so old."

"But still able to bear fruit. I looked at a lion today and a queen who looks at a lion shall conceive. A seer told me I will give birth to a boy who is to be called Groumbert." Emma ran her fingers over his genitals. His penis began to harden.

"You are so old." He wrinkled his face.

"But still able to have children. John the Baptist, well, his mother was in her eighties. Did you know that?"

He didn't respond, but simply looked at her in an odd mixture of disgust and lust. She helped him undo his leather laces and out of his braies. She raised her gown and lay back on the bed.

"I am really Cnute's son?" he asked as he roughly pushed his penis between her thighs.

"Yes," she said and pulled him down on her.

She left him asleep in the hovel. He was brutish and rough, inept and clumsy, yet she had been satisfied and it was not just his youth. She would have him again and she would bear his child and no matter that he was not Cnute's son, she would make him a king and their son an heir. She went in and sat by Aesval. The woman moaned occasionally, but mostly it was the rasping breathing which broke the silence. The afternoon came and Sven apparently still slept and Emma had Carah-with-the-hawk-on-her-breast found and whipped and the girl cried out curses in that strange language.

Evening came and the heat subsided little. She had ordered a large meal, but though Sven ate heavily it was mostly roast ox and goat's milk and a little dark bread and she picked at the other delicacies, the pruned mallard and soured eel, the baked finches and herbed venison.

She toyed with a raw oyster. "We will rebuild Winchester," she said and sucked the oyster from the shell.

He drank milk from the cup and it left a white moon over his mouth. "And drive Magnus from Norway."

"Groumbert shall be viceroy in the Daneland." She leaned over to him and with her tongue licked the milk from above his lip.

He wiped his mouth on his sleeve. "Who is Groumbert?"

"Our son," she reminded him and opened her mouth wide and dropped another oyster in. She stirred her finger in gravy in her bowl and licked it, rubbing her finger over her teeth. "Normandy is weak."

"Yes," he agreed and chewed on a rib bone. "The duke is young and Normandy could be taken. We'll raise a large army and"—he smiled maliciously—"I'll have lots of concubines."

She threw an oyster at him and he ducked. "Bastard!"

"So you tell me," he said and smiled more pleasantly.

It was his damn smile that got her and she laughed. She drank some wine and set down the cup. "We'll have Edward beheaded."

"No," he said and he was serious.

"Yes."

"No. Edward saved my brother Tostig's life."

"That's nonsense."

He ignored her and went back to his rib bone. For the moment she dropped the subject.

They spent the night in Emma's bed and were still there when the guests arrived before prime. She heard Godwin's voice.

"Oh, Jesu!" Sven said.

"Never mind. He has to know sooner or later."

Together they entered the room where the dying Aesval still rasped and moaned. Godwin was there and Gytha and their son Harold.

"I gave you credit for better sense than this, Emma." He looked directly at her and stood very much the Earl of Wessex. He was even dressed finer than usual. Gytha's face seemed as angry red as her hair.

"We are going to be married," Sven announced. "I am going to be King."

"Sorgad prophesied I would have a son who would be King. Little did I think it would be so easy." Godwin spoke sarcastically. "All you need do is say 'I am King.' Are you mad, Sven?"

Sven simply looked at him.

"I will tell you something, son—"

"I am not your son."

"You are not my son," Godwin mocked him.

"Mother had me by Cnute—"

"Oh, Emma," Gytha cried. "You've done some foul things in your time and I've witnessed most of them, but this is the most evil. I have never in my life known any man but Godwin and to poison my son with these horrid lies . . ."

"Why, Emma?" Godwin slumped on a bench.

"Sven and I are going to have a son."

"Emma, you are fifty-seven years old." Godwin raised his voice. "You are barren."

"I am not," she screamed at him. "I saw a lion and a seer has told me I shall bear a son." Emma was losing control of herself and she stopped and took a deep breath.

Sven stood looking foolish and she was angry with him for saying nothing more.

"Your womb, Emma, is as empty as your heart." Gytha went over to Aesval.

"Do you realize, Sven," Godwin spoke to him and his voice was controlled, "that even if some believed this foul lie that the Earls Leofric and Siward, along with the Church in the North, would never allow anyone as closely connected with Godwin and the house of Wessex to make any claim to the throne. They'd destroy you, me and your brothers."

"And the whore Queen, as well, I hope," Gytha said, looking directly at Emma.

Aesval moaned and called for Edward.

Harold, who had stood silent, said, "I will ride to Westminster for him."

"You will do nothing of the kind," Emma told him. "That monster shall not come near here."

"You'd let the poor old woman die," Harold said.

"Edward is a fraud," Emma screamed. "Don't any of you realize he is a fraud and trying to steal England from me?"

"When you are more rational, Emma, I will discuss the realities of England with you. The Church, at an alarming rate, is accepting your son—"

"He is NOT my son."

"Edward, then, as King of England."

"I am going to have another child." Emma went over and stood in front of Sven. "Sven, your father was Cnute."

Gytha turned from Aesval and crossed the room. She raised her arm and struck Emma hard across the face.

Emma reeled and fell to the floor. Her cheek stung. "I am the Queen! No one strikes the Queen and lives."

"I shall never say another word to you, whore!" Gytha turned and went out the door. The morning hot air swept into the room.

"Sven," Godwin ordered, "take your mother to Guildford."

"Sven," Emma cried, but he was out the door and gone. Godwin stared at her and said nothing. It was as if the doctor had been waiting for the air to clear as he came in and began examining Aesval and putting fresh poultices on her face. The herbs had a strong pungent scent.

Godwin arose. "I shall be at the minster conferring with Stigand. Our one hope is to generate support for Svegn Estridsson. When you've got yourself under control, send Harold for me and we can talk."

Godwin did not apologize for Gytha slapping her, nor say any other word of consolation. He simply walked out into the bright sunlight. Harold sat. Emma sat. The doctor fussed over Aesval. Abraham's Sara was ninety it was said and St. Elizabeth was eighty. Their children were great men. Harold got up, went out and rode off. Emma barely noticed.

She had a servant find a large, white long-furred cat. A leg was cut off and it was sent to the old crone. And Emma sent messengers. One to Magnus with terms of a marriage and a promise to honor Harthacnut's pledge of succession. She sent another man to Roeskild offering marriage to Svegn Estridsson. She was not too old to bear England an heir. The pot girl, the Celt, had run off and Emma went out and began scrubbing pots herself, but a serving woman came and led her away and so she sat on a stool next to Aesval and told her stories about the saints and when she was a little girl at Rouen and she told Aesval about being kept in the pit at Corfe, but, of course, Aesval knew that story.

It was midafternoon she guessed when Godwin came in. At least it was much warmer and the perspiration ran from Aesval's forehead.

"Where's Harold?" he asked.

"Gone off," she said.

"Where?"

"I don't know. Gone off and never said good-bye."

"Emma, are you all right?"

"Nothing's wrong with me . . . morning sickness, perhaps. I'm pregnant, you know."

He came over to her, but did not touch her. "Emma, we all have to grow old."

"No," she told him. "We can die."

Godwin ordered some wine brought into her and handed it to her.

She sipped. It was very warm wine. "I want to marry Sven."

"You can't, Emma. Put it from your mind."

"I am going to have his baby. It will be a bastard now. Do you want that? Do you want your grandson to be a bastard?"

"You are not going to have a child, Emma."

"Yes."

"You are beyond your time."

"No."

"Listen to me. If you want to stop Edward we must be united in our efforts to put Svegn Estridsson on the throne. True, his claim is through the female line, yet he is able and liked. He is Cnute's nephew."

She did not tell him that she had also sent a marriage proposal to Svegn Estridsson. "And your nephew . . ."

"Gytha's," he said. "Gytha's. But it will be an objection some will raise against him as a choice."

She made no response.

"Are you with me?"

"I will give England another heir."

He walked out, saying nothing further.

Emma sat the night with Aesval. She told stories to her of the old crone and Sorgad and the boy with the one green eye and the one brown eye and the streak through his hair. She told her how Edmund was poisoned and how she first met Cnute. Aesval didn't stir. She told her of Magnus of Norway and how he would want to marry her and of how Svegn Estridsson also would want to marry her.

A raven perched on the sill of the open window and she remembered that when Cnute had died she had planned to have all the ravens poisoned and she had forgotten it in all her troubles with the shoemaker's bastard.

"They are spirits of his dead ancestors," she told Aesval, but Aesval didn't answer, didn't stir. "Once Cnute gave me a spring daffodil for between my legs. But he hated me when I was pregnant and would hate me now because of it. He's dead and rotting in his grave. I'm pregnant, Aesval. I'll make no secret of it. No. Of course everyone would soon see the signs anyway. But I shan't tell who the father is. No, I shan't tell. Not even you. You won't be able to drag it from me."

It began to rain and the raven flew away.

Rain and darkness and she sat there talking to Aesval, but Aesval was in a mood and didn't respond. She was getting grumpy in her old age. There was rain and darkness and the drone of her own voice. Dawn came to the window first and then the housecarls, so many housecarls. They were Harthacnut's thingliths. She recognized the faces, but he was dead. She was certain Harthacnut was dead. He had choked to death at Osgot Clapa's daughter's wedding and Edward . . . oh they said Edward could cure the dying, but Edward had done nothing for Harthacnut. Edward was a fraud. And they expected him to save Aesval? Emma took the woman's hand. It was so cold and stiff. Her fingers wouldn't move and were bent as if she were clutching the air. He stood in the door. Edward, vile Edward. "What do you want here? Go away!"

He stood.

"Come along, Madam," Harold said.

She didn't budge.

"It is as the King commands, Lady," Harold told her and literally pulled her up out of the chair.

But there was no King. Harthacnut was dead and Sven would be King, or Svegn Estridsson . . . or Magnus, perhaps. Whichever she chose as her husband. They led her outside. Bishop Stigand sat on his horse and his hands were tied.

"Why are your hands tied?" she asked.

But they shoved her by him and he only looked frightened and didn't answer.

Godwin came. "Where have you been?" he asked Harold.

"To fetch Edward. But the old woman was already dead." Emma did not know who they meant. Certainly she was neither old nor dead. She was helped upon a horse, but she didn't understand why or where she was going.

"Why are the bishop's hands tied?" Godwin asked.

"The King is—"

"The King?" Godwin questioned.

"The King," his son continued, "is charging him with treason for having violated the body of the Queen, his mother."

"And she?"

Harold went toward the house. "Is being taken to a nunnery."

Who was being taken to a nunnery? Emma wondered.

"I take it," Godwin said, "you have joined forces with Edward."

"It is expedient. I would suggest you do the same," Harold said.

Emma listened but was not certain at all what was going on. She must look to Aesval. Aesval was ill, wasn't she? So stiff and cold, the old woman was. "I can't travel," she told a soldier. "Godwin, tell them I can't travel. I'm going to have a baby."

Godwin said nothing and Stigand said nothing. Stigand sat there, his hands together; they were tied for some reason, and she couldn't understand. He said nothing.

"A queen looked upon a lion," she told the soldier and smiled.

CHAPTER 3

Winchester, 1042

There were at least three hundred soldiers, Godwin surmised. Stigand, his hands bound, his head bowed, simply sat the horse.

"He is a bishop," Godwin said. "You can't do that."

Edward came out of the house; men followed him carrying the body of the dead woman. "Stop me." He went over and climbed up on the gold stallion. He wore a long multicolored mantle which he pushed back over his shoulders.

Emma was ranting about a lion and he suspected she had gone mad. A baby; she kept insisting she was pregnant. Mother and son, he looked at one, then the other. They were both mad. I will raise an army of thousands and stop him, Godwin thought.

The corpse was laid gently in a cart.

"We'll be in Londuntown, Lord Wessex," Edward said and turned his horse toward the gate and the procession began to move away.

Harold was making certain the body of Aesval was properly covered. Godwin watched him. Sometimes Harold was an enigma, hard as stone and gentle as wool.

"He had come to save her life," Harold told him. "The King rode all that way to save the old woman's life."

"He's not the King."

"You're getting old," Harold said. "See it for what it is—both the archbishops, Canterbury and York, support him. Devon supports his claim, and the Bishop of Glouchester and old Ethelstan at Hereford as well as the Bishop of Ramsbury—"

"The Church—" Godwin started to interrupt.

"And the Danish stillers and most of the reeves and the abbots and the people of Londuntown cheer him—"

"And what of the earls? They are all that matter, really."

"Siward and Leofric are cautious, I admit, but they'll come around. There are no sons of Cnute living. There is one son of Ethelred alive, Edward. This is no weak claim. This is the house of the great Edgar, direct and indisputable—"

"And the Earl of East Anglia?"

"Will support him." Harold mounted his horse.

Godwin shook his head. "Harold Thorkellsson will never—and besides which he's in Rome. I don't think—"

"Harold Thorkellsson is dead."

"What?"

"Harold Thorkellsson was killed by highwaymen in Normandy as he was coming home. I am to be East Anglia now."

"You are to be an earl?"

"Yes."

Had he underestimated Edward this much? "He killed Harold Thorkellsson."

"No. He was killed by highwaymen in Normandy."

"You are not even the oldest son."

"Edward recognizes that. Sven is to be given an earldom carved from the west. It might do Sven some good to battle the Celts. It'll keep him out of some unsuspecting husband's bed."

"You think to be East Anglia simply like that?"

"Yes. And I'll tell you a secret, father. But it must remain a secret until Leofric and Siward are brought to knuckle and firmly in the King's camp. Edward knows it would only alienate both of them, but the King is to marry your daughter. And she is more than willing."

Harold left him standing there and he was certain his mouth was agape. Godwin watched him as he rode quickly to catch the others.

Sorgad . . . the white bird . . . the white bird . . . she meant Edward . . . "the other son" . . . Edith will be Queen. He had not really believed it until now, not with Harthacnut . . . "and she is more than willing." Godwin stood there and it began to rain again. His cloak was getting soaked and he went into the house. A raven came and perched on the windowsill. He watched it and the bird watched him. Godwin had sorely underestimated Edward. This almost ghost creature with the white skin, strange eyes and thin white hair had a political acumen that had escaped Godwin. Yet, was it so surprising? He had survived. He had survived

Ethelred and Edmund and Cnute and Harold and Harthacnut and the Normans and disease and Emma . . . mostly he had survived despite Emma. And now this strange man was making his second son Earl of East Anglia. Had he arranged for highwaymen to kill Harold Thorkellsson? Edward knew Normandy and it would be to his advantage and there was enough reason to suspect he hated Harold Thorkellsson, who was said to have lain with his mother at Corfe. Perhaps Edward survived, but would all survive him? Yet Gytha swore he had saved Tostig's life in this very house. They said he could have saved Harthacnut as well. That was no loss. Edward had survived, but so had Godwin and he was not ready to leap for any supposed winner quite so quickly. Svegn Estridsson's claim was legitimate. The country had endured Harold and Harthacnut; it did not need another of that ilk. Svegn Estridsson was a bright and competent young man. He was a grandson of Sven the Forkbeard and . . . he was his wife's nephew. No, Godwin would approach the precipice with care. He was not about to jump off into the deep.

At dusk the rain had ceased. Godwin walked up the hill. The street was quiet, not like in the days when this had been the center of an empire and Moors and Lombards and Turks and Slavs and Norse and Persians had mingled in colorful robes and strange tongues up and down the hilly street. Glorious Winchester with vain thingliths parading bare chests and golden armbands had faded into the quiet of a herder calling his hogs. Godwin didn't go into the ruins of the compound where old charred frames burned by Harold stood next to half-built raw timbers raised at Harthacnut's order; instead he went back down the hill.

He reached the house and the rain started again. In the middle of the main room a girl sat cleaning pots. "Who are you, child?" he asked.

"I am called Carah-with-the-hawk-on-her-breast." And she exposed a round tit and showed him the birthmark.

"They have all gone," he told her. "It is only myself and a few of my soldiers down at the minster that are left."

"The Queen?"

"Gone to Londuntown."

"She beat me." The girl displayed a whelp mark on her back. "I come from Clontarf," she said in a lilting voice. "Me grandfather be Brian Borumha, and I am cursed," she said, "by the sorrows of Deirdre."

"And who is Deirdre?" Godwin asked, knowing full well he was about to hear a legend.

"Surely you heard, now, of Deirdre of the sorrows?" Carah-with-the-hawk-on-her-breast had a voice that sounded like a harp. "She was the daughter of Felim the Bard. And King Connor, he would marry her, for she was a great beauty, she was, oh, a great lovely beauty. She was the loveliness itself, now would you have. But she ached for Naorie and he was handsomeness itself, would you, and he, after all, had pressed her hand and so he stole her from King Connor's palace and took her across the sea to the land of the Picts, and his two brothers, oh fine young men they were indeed, Ainnle and Arden, went along. Deirdre was happy, happy just bein' with Naorie, but he and his brothers, as men is like to do, longed for Erin and would be home. King Connor, he sends word that he will forgive them and for them to come home, for surely it is sad, now, to be away so long. Ah, and do I not know that." Carah-with-the-hawk-on-her-breast looked about wistfully as she interjected the remark. "And Deirdre, now, she was no fool, that girl was not indeed, and she warned Naorie not to return, that King Connor would kill him sure, but he so longed for the isle and the touch of the sod and they sailed. But, it was as Deirdre had said and they no more than touched their feet upon the green land than Connor's men killed Naorie and his brothers. Deirdre, she was so stricken with grief, she fell to the ground and drank the blood of her slain lover and then went to a rock and beat her skull against it until she was dead."

Godwin sat silent for a moment.

"It's a lovely story," he said. "You would go home, girl?"

"Ah, that I would, but I wear these." And she displayed the black iron slave anklets.

Godwin called a soldier and had the ankle bands cut off. "Go home now," he told her.

"Which way be it?" she asked.

"Follow the setting sun," he told her. "You'll come to the sea. And take some bread and meat and wine. And I'll give you this coin," he said.

And she took some bread and a leg of mutton and a skin with some wine and left.

Godwin sat in Winchester for a week, thinking, and then he journeyed to Guildford and his wife.

Estrid had come to Guildford in his absence. She sat at a spinning wheel, her foot pumping furiously. "Magnus has attacked the Daneland again," she told him. "You may pray for my son." Estrid had large dark bags beneath her eyes.

"He will not leave the Daneland, then?"

"He will not. But he will still be the King of England and the Daneland as well."

"That may not be easy," Godwin told her. "These English want their King amid them."

"There is danger at Roeskild. The King must be there."

"There is danger here and the King must be here."

The wheel spun faster. "He will not leave. Not now."

"Then Edward will take the throne."

It was a warm day, yet a cool breeze sifted through the old dark room. The two women both spun. Godwin watched his wife. She said nothing, but moved forward now and again and let the thread from her hands. Finally she spoke. "Tell him, Estrid."

"I intercepted a messenger from Winchester. That old bitch has asked my son Svegn to marry her." Estrid laughed. "That tired old hag thinks she can have the likes of my son."

"And mine," Gytha said.

"And Magnus of Norway, I've learned," Godwin told them. "Poor Emma—"

"Poor Emma?" Both women spoke at once.

"She's mad."

"I want Emma's head borne me upon a silver platter," Gytha said.

"Yes," Estrid agreed. "The gall of that decrepit old sow to ask King Svegn to marry her. I will see her boiled in a stew, that dried-up old crone."

"I'll provide the pot for the executioner," Gytha told her.

Godwin left them arranging Emma's demise.

Two days later he went to Londuntown. The two women were still damning the Queen when he got on his horse.

Godwin was made immediately aware that Edward had the full support of the Londuners, who had hated Harthacnut, and he was in residence at Wardrobe Palace above the Thames. "The King" they all called him, all these strange Londuners. Glouchester was Glouchester and York was York, but these strange folk in Londuntown were controlled by no one and they had a collective mind and force that Godwin never quite knew how to deal with.

The great Earl of Wessex, as they referred to him, these men of Edward's, was escorted ceremoniously into the hall, the old smoky hall of Wardrobe. Torches burned, but the room was without proper ventilation or light. Edward occupied the King's chair and standing near him were Godwin's sons Sven and Harold and Tostig, his nephew Beorn and the Bishop of Londun and a young man with sea-blue eyes who was wearing the abbot's robe and held a crozier. The young man came toward him and spit at Godwin's feet.

"You killed the Atheling Alfred," he said and banged his crozier against the stone floor and marched from the hall.

Godwin realized after the young abbot had left who he had been. Robin of Jumieges. He had been but a monk. Godwin looked at his sons. None of the three had come to his defense.

"Pay no need to Robin, Lord Wessex," Edward said. "My brother Aly was dear to him."

Godwin knew that he had an enemy at court and one with whom, sooner or later, he would have to deal.

"Why have you come, my Lord of Wessex?" Edward asked him and stood up and walked down to him and took his fingers lightly. His touch was so strange, like the touch of an animal after rubbing its fur.

"I have come to you, Edward, son of Ethelred, to support your claim to the throne of England."

A cheer went up in the hall. The loudest voices were those of Godwin's sons.

Edward smiled. "You must then, my Lord Godwin, present me with a greater gift than you gave my brother Harthacnut."

"I shall, sire, when the Witangemot is met," Godwin said and knelt and kissed the red-shoed feet of the white-skinned man. "I would ask of you," Godwin said, rising, "that you free the Bishop of Winchester in faith of your goodwill."

Edward, who had sat during the foot kissing, arose. He wore a magnificent green robe which trained behind him down the steps and he took Godwin's hands and raised him up. "The Bishop of Londun has already begged such of me and Stigand went off to Winchester early this morning."

"And the Queen?"

"The Queen will be freed from the wooden box in which she is kept when she comes to her senses. I ask no more of her than that she promise to quit trying to have me killed. It is annoying if nothing else. She also goes about saying she is having a baby."

"She is old," Godwin said.

"And out of her head," Sven, his son, added.

He asked to see her and was taken to a chamber where Emma was nailed inside a coffin.

"Emma?" he called softly.

"Is Aesval dead?" she asked, her voice muffled inside the box.

"Yes," he said.

"Edward couldn't have kept her from dying."

"She was old, Emma. We all have to die."

"My daughter Gunnerhild died. She was only a child and she gave birth to a brat and it poisoned her womb. She was to have been an empress, but she's dead."

"And you'll die if you don't come to your senses. Die inside this box."

"Svegn Estridsson is going to come. I am going to marry him."

"He will not have you, Emma. He thinks you are old and ugly."

"That is unkind."

"Youth is unkind, Emma. Youth is unkind, simply by being there, being there reminding us of vitality . . . and we call it beauty . . . and somehow try to consume it, thinking it will make us young again. But it is gone, Emma. Youth is gone and there is no finding it."

"I was beautiful once," Emma said. ". . . and Magnus? Magnus will not come either?"

"No, Emma. No one will come. Edward will be King and we, you and I, must accept what is."

"I hate him so."

"Why, Emma?"

"You don't see his ugliness, but always I see that horrid face looking down at me from the croft at Corfe, judging me, accusing me for the sins of the flesh. He is my judge. If he is dead, then, there is no one to judge. I will find acceptance. I will find acceptance in youth, in the eyes of your son or nephew as I needed acceptance from Harold Thorkellsson. I saw in his eyes the lovely Emma."

"He is dead."

"Harold?"

"Yes," he told her.

A sobbing, gentle crying came from the box.

"You must," he said, "for your own sake, acknowledge Edward as the King. It is your blood."

"No. It is evil blood. I can stay in darkness," she said.

"You will die in this box," he said. "For me, for your old friend's sake, live, Emma, live."

"I am old."

The Witangemot met. Leofric was there, and Siward. The two old men talked with Godwin and sighed with relief and wished only for peace, quiet and less taxation. Leofric smelled and looked tired, and Godiva, bug-eyed, stood beside him. She was getting older as well. They named Edward their King. And Godwin presented the new monarch with a ship with four more rowsmen than that given to Harthacnut.

Edward rose before the Witangemot. "I will wait until Easter to be crowned," he told them, "for our reign is dedicated to Him, our savior, whom we wish to please and emulate. We ask the blessing of Jesus Christ and all the holy saints upon us and all the people of this land."

Godwin remembered when Cnute gave such speeches, but there was a difference when Edward spoke. Godwin realized the man was in total earnest.

Edward continued, "We enjoin you to be free from sin and to rejoice with us at his resurrection when we shall be anointed with the holy oil."

There was something alarming about Edward, almost frightening, and Godwin was never quite comfortable around him. It seemed not to bother his sons, however, especially Tostig, whose praise of Edward was carried to extremes. Edward, in turn, had an affinity for the young man and related to Tostig better than to either Sven or Harold.

They left the hall after the Witangemot. A blind man was led up to the King. Edward touched him for but a moment and then fell as if in pain.

"I can see," the man cried out. Edward was helped to his feet. "I can see!" the man repeated. He fell to his knees before the King. Edward, with great pomp, extended his right hand and lifted the man, who was gazing at Edward's face, to his feet. "A saint," he cried. "My first sight is of a holy saint."

Edward smiled and led the way down the Londun street. The others followed. "To St. Paul's," Edward cried out.

Godwin looked back. Emma, who had been convinced by him, to swear allegiance to her son, stood apart. She pulled a veil over her face and walked back inside Wardrobe Palace.

CHAPTER 4

Londuntown, 1043

IT HAD RAINED DURING THE NIGHT AND THE BRUSH WAS WET AGAINST HIS face as he broke through it. In the distance he could hear the sound of the river, the Thames, and the only other sound was that of men trampling through the thicket. The long grass and dead leaves were wet against his shoes and leggings. A bird was roused from its nest and fluttered up from the grass and into the trees. Water dripped as the bird flapped into the leaves.

A deep snort. A squeal. Edward saw the bristled boar. A huge gray wiry mass of fear and anger that sensed the danger started to run and then veered about, charging directly at Edward. They were alone, one on one, and Edward let the spear fly. It snapped into the animal's head. The boar choked on a loud hollow breath which seemed to well out of deep inside and then it fell, twisting, its legs giving spastic jerks, and then stillness and only the sound of the river. The boar died. He approached it as he heard the rustle of leaves as the others came and stood about and Edward took his knife and cut through the bristly hide and he plunged both of his hands deep inside the animal and felt the wetness of the boar's blood. He took his hands from inside and looked at them and let the blood drip and seep from his fingers. He rubbed the red fingers of one hand into the palm of the other, being careful not to spill blood on his tunic. The boar was taken away and a basin of cold water was brought to Edward and he washed his hands, gently moving them in the basin of water, until the water had turned red. A servant extended a soft rag of wool and Edward dried his hands carefully.

Two days earlier he had killed the hart. Never had he seen an animal bleed so. His hands had been drowned in its blood. And such red blood, such a brilliant red it had been, so much life draining from the antlered proud creature. He had killed the hart with an arrow set in a long bow and he could almost hear the sound of that arrow yet, stinging through the air. The hart had not made a sound, not a gasp nor cry, only the sound of its weight falling upon the ground into a pile of brilliant red blood.

Robin came up and stood behind him. Edward looked back up at him. The monk's look was one of disgust. "I wish you wouldn't do that."

"Why?" Edward looked back down at the dead boar.

"It sickens me."

The trees drizzled dead wet leaves that fell, rather than floated, to the ground. Despite the wetness, they still rustled as Edward walked toward a fallen tree.

"You must not bait the Earl of Wessex," he told Robin.

"He is responsible for Alfred's death."

"Behi killed him."

"Godwin was there; he could have stopped it."

"In time all will be dealt with. I learned from watching Harthacnut and his horrid failures as a king. Restraint in the exercise of power can be a wondrous thing. It keeps the world off balance."

The sun came out. The wet brown and red leaves sparkled as it struck. It was a red sun, brilliant blood red and ready to set. He still saw no reason for the sun to set in the west and rise in the east. The Norse legend of the world being round made no sense. You couldn't stand on a ball, even one as wet as this earth was now. Yet, how did the sun get back around to the east? Edith said God was the sun, and if that were true then, as God could be everywhere and anywhere, no other explanation for the sun was needed. Still, Edward was not certain at all that God was the sun, though he knew from the fits that God was a great white light.

They came into a small clearing. Beorn was sitting on a rotten log. He was rubbing his hand gently over his crotch. The boy seemed to have a continual erection. Edward thought of Harthacnut, who had been unable to achieve any erection at all. Edward had, more than once, found himself with an erection, but he controlled his vile thoughts and on one occasion, when the hardness persisted, he ordered a barrel of cold water be brought him and he sat in it for two hours and on a cold snowy winter day when he had been plagued with a growth he went out and stood to his waist in an icy river.

"Beorn," Edward said as he came up to the rotting log, "before the snow I want you to go to Roeskild for me. You may tell your brother I am celibate and sworn to such and that if he relinquishes any claim now to the throne, I will make him my heir."

The round-faced, lazy-eyed young man agreed and continued sitting on the log rubbing his erection. Robin was watching him intently.

Edward turned and walked in the direction of the horses. Robin followed.

"You don't intend on making Svegn Estridsson your heir?"

"A lot of good it did Magnus that Harthacnut promised it to him. No. His claim at the present is an annoyance and this assures him I will make no claim upon the Daneland."

"You relinquish the Daneland?"

"Not yet, but I shall in time."

"And your heir?"

"Still remains Robert's son. I vowed it years ago."

"The bastard of Normandy."

"The Duke of Normandy," Edward corrected him. "For the while that choice shall not be voiced. I think these Saxons and Danes might not take too kindly toward it."

Robin got up on his horse. "I don't argue your choice of a Norman. Of course I am all in favor of it, but why such loyalty to Robert? What did that devil ever do for you?"

"He was my friend," Edward answered, "as were you. I have had so few friends in my life. I do not forget them."

Edward was aided upon the horse. He took such attention and being waited upon for granted. In a short time he had learned not to do for himself, as he had been required to do for so many years.

"And is Harold Godwinsson your friend?" Robin asked as he took his reins and turned his horse toward the trees.

They rode under the trees in the flickering afternoon light. "He is useful."

"Mightily useful to earn an earldom."

"There was no one else to give it to and it earned me the backing of Godwin, which was essential if I was to be King."

They moved along side by side through the dense woods. A rabbit appeared and vanished. It was a peaceful time of day and the low sun lit the tall trees from beneath. The horses clomped through the deep leaves and wet brush.

"There are those who whisper that you had Harold Thorkellsson killed."

"And why would I have had Harold Thorkellsson killed?"

Robin didn't respond at first and when he answered he spoke softly and slowly. "Because he fornicated with your mother. It is told you saw." Robin stopped his horse. "Did you see, Edward?"

Edward turned his mount away from a thicket. "I saw a man . . ." The words were barely audible and inched slowly from his tongue. ". . . with only two fingers on one hand, there before God in His holy place . . . take his hard penis . . ." And he clinched his fists and shook them to the heavens as he screamed. ". . . and stick her!"

And the trees echoed. And Edward slumped and took the reins again and rode quickly from the darkening woods.

That night a feast of boar was held in the hall. It was served with a brown gravied sauce and a hundred cooked apples and around the great platter on which it was carried was a ring of stuffed quail. Edward sat the center place as a king ought. There was noise and talk and singing and jugglers. To his right was the Earl of Wessex and the Countess Gytha and beyond sat Godwin's son Harold. To Edward's left was the Abbot of Jumieges and the Lady Estrid, who styled herself Duchess of Normandy. The Queen sat near the corner at the far end of the table, at her own request. She was buried in black veils. Near her on the floor, leaning against the wall, was Sassy.

"I have decided on a course of action," Edward told Godwin and ate delicately of the pork. "I am a simple man, as you know. I grew up in poverty and know the value of wealth. I am a man of peace who wishes to pursue no wars against his neighbors. Vigilance, aye, but no war. So I have reached the conclusion that I can live quite royally on the benefices of my holdings. It is my intent, therefore, that not only will Harthacnut's rowmen's tax be abolished, but I intend to end Cnute's gilder tax as well."

It got the proper response. Godwin was stunned. His coronation would be a success.

Edward sat through the meal accepting Godwin's praise for the wisdom of his decision and listening to a skald sing of Sigfrid and Brunhildr. At the end of the song, Edward rose, thanked God for his blessing and, with a whirl of fabric, swung about and walked from the hall in great majesty.

He sat alone in his chamber, a chamber where Ethelred had slept many a drunken sleep, and he gazed into the fire. He took out the horse turd from the casket in which he kept it and toyed with it in his hand. He had gone back once in search of the old woman who had given it to him, but he had never found her. It was well being King. All his life, thirty-eight years, he had lived to be King and yet . . . there was something unsatisfactory in it. Henry of France had told him, "Being King is not being much, Edward." But Edward had not believed him then. Now he thought perhaps Henry was right. There was something not here, something missing, yet he couldn't say what it was. Henry had found it lacking, and Robert, pious King Robert, had believed a serf as much a man as was a king. And Bertha, Queen Bertha, had been a holy saint. And Emma . . . his own mother, unlike Henry's sainted Bertha, was a whore. Still,

Jesus forgave the Magdalene and healed her of evil spirits. He would attempt to forgive his mother. It was his obligation, if he was to be a saint, to emulate Jesus.

The next evening at meal, he placed her between Godwin and himself. She kept buried in her veils, refused to talk, let alone say a kind word, though she addressed him a few times in outrage and anger. Gytha would not talk to the Queen and acted as if no one sat there.

"You must speak to the Queen, Lady Wessex," Edward admonished her.

"I shall not." Gytha was defiant. "That old hag seduced my son."

"But Christ forgave Mary Magdalene."

"She was not such a great sinner as Emma," Gytha said.

The next evening Edward placed her on the other side. Lady Estrid walked in the hall, saw her and refused to come to the table.

Edward gave his mother a golden brooch in the shape of a seabird and she promised to wear it on her back where she didn't have to look at it. For Christmas he built her a new house at Winchester, but she rode all the way to Winchester and wouldn't set foot inside the door. Spring came and he had oranges sent from Iberia and made a present to his mother of them, but she cut holes in them and squeezed the juice onto the floor until they were dry and then threw the empty peels at the skald as he sang.

Godgifu and the Count of Boulogne arrived before the coronation and sat at the great table and Godgifu leaped up on the table and took her husband's sword and ran at Emma with it. Edward pushed his mother out of the way. "No!" he yelled at his sister.

"Yes!" she screamed. "I'm going to kill the old sow."

Edward and Eustace held Godgifu and Archbishop Stigand led Emma from the room and Lady Beatrice ran behind. Emma was cursing and Godgifu yelling and the skald began singing and the jugglers juggled and Sassy leaped up and down. Edward was worried about his mother.

Godgifu was settled as if nothing had occurred, eating blueberries and staining her fingers, and Edward sat uncomfortably and watched. Finally he leaped up and told Godwin, "I must go to the Queen."

"She'll be fine," Godwin said and pulled his chair back for him to sit. "Sit and eat your dinner. You can go to her later."

And then Gytha made a strange remark, at least for her. "I think," she said, "the King should go to his mother."

"No . . ." Godwin was saying, but Edward turned from the table and went down the corridor in the direction of the Queen's chamber. Lady Beatrice was outside the door.

"You can't go in there," Lady Beatrice told him.

"I am the King," he said.

She blocked the door. He didn't even know why he was so persistent on going in, perhaps it was just that she had tried to keep him out. He shoved her aside and threw open the door. There was the spindly legged Bishop Stigand, his bare buttocks up in the air, *sticking the Queen*. Edward was suddenly at Corfe and his mother was on the floor, her face strained with lust and the Dane with his penis in her. Edward screamed, "Whore!" And then felt the light of God and knew he was having a fit.

Less than two weeks later on April third, Easter, in the year 1043, he was crowned most majestically by two archbishops, York and Canterbury, at the minster in Winchester. The preparations had taken months, for Edward wanted no flaw, not an unaccounted-for butterfly, marring the proceedings. Psalms broke the air and Edward entered, not as his ancestors, wearing the crown, but his white head bare. His robes were purple and ermine-trimmed and beneath the simple white tunic he wore the chain of stones. The horse turd was carried before him on a cushion by his nephew Ralph—and the joyous chorus rang out.

His mother was absent from the church. He would not have her spoil his day.

His sister, the Countess of Boulogne, broad-shouldered and wearing a gown of gold, entered carrying a silver dagger held out before her eyes as if bearing a crucifix.

Edith was in the minster at the front. In time, when appropriate, and the earls to the North secured, she would be his Queen. She sat quietly on a purple-cushioned chair in an open-weave dress which allowed her pink skin to be visible against the white fabric. She wore a band of spring flowers like a halo on her head. She smiled and he returned the smile.

He bore the rod and scepter and the choir sang out, "*Vivat Rex! Vivat Rex!*" Robert should have been here, but Robert was dead and Edward tried not to think on that or other sad thoughts on this day. Ralf of Gace came to represent the young Duke William. And the King of France sent his brother and the Emperor an envoy. But these men meant nothing to Edward. More important were the friends that were there: Sassy sitting alone, as no one would sit with him, and Robin was there carrying his crozier, and his nephew Ralph, who had carried the turd, and his goddaughter, Judith, Eleanor's girl . . . but MacBoru could not be there, nor Aesval, nor the blind pigherder, nor his servant Seven, nor Uncle Goddy. . . . Herleve was there and her husband. The chorus of monks sang out and the bells were rung and clamored and clamored.

And while they were still ringing, the ceremony ended, Edward, accompanied by the Earl Siward, the Earl Leofric, the Earl Godwin, the Earl Sven and the Earl Harold had the Bishop of Winchester arrested for having carnal knowledge of the Queen mother. All his lands were confiscated and fell to the majesty of the crown.

And Emma was ordered to a nunnery.

CHAPTER 5

Westminster, 1045

THE THAMES WAS PACIFIC, LIKE THE DAY. WATER LANGUISHED AT THE shore. There were no boats visible, but a fish leaped and broke the stillness. Land birds chattered and scolded, unseen in the trees, while gulls floated silently above the river. A few feet back from the shoreline was a low embankment, eroded and topped with long grass. Clusters of small pink blooms, here and there, breathed above the bending grass. Edith picked bunches of the flowers as she intermittently ran along the bank. She wore nothing on her feet and an occasional rock or sharp twig would nip at her callused soles. The monastery bells in the distance ordered the monks to their midmorning labors. She wore only a thin linen gown and she felt the air warm upon her flesh. She jumped down from the low bank to the pebbled beach and pulled the linen up over her head and tossed it on the ground. The sun struck her. His warmth, she always thought of the sun as God, fell upon her breasts and the gentle heat crept through her skin and into her soul. She picked up the flowers from where she had dropped them and then lay down on the small stones, scattering the pink blossoms over her naked body. She combed her long straight hair with her fingers. It looked almost red in the sunlight. She lay still, letting God smother her. Heat caressed her feet and calves, her belly and hips, and soothed her forehead and cheeks. She closed her eyes and listened to the kind water and the scratch of insects across the grass. There was no evil here. There was no passion on a soft warm morning, only

God's enveloping love. She opened her eyes and watched a cloud, as white and silent as a swan, swimming without rippling the sky. A heron swooped, long legs trailing over the edge of the water, on the far bank. She closed her eyes again and gave herself to the gentle warmth of God and she ebbed into a state of deep consciousness, as if her soul had somehow left her body to hover above the naked woman with auburn hair lying still upon the pebbled beach.

"Make yourself chaste!" the voice commanded.

She was less startled than annoyed by the intrusion into her private communion with God. She opened her eyes and looked above to see the robed figure standing on the bank above. He had turned away, as if not to look at her. She stood up. "I am as God made me." She was neither embarrassed nor ashamed of her body. Still, the Bishop of Londun did not look at her. She slipped on the plain linen gown.

"It is a sin to—"

She interrupted. "Sin is not the soft day, but the dark hard night of men."

He was the bishop, yet he wore simple monastic robes. "Do you preach theology to the Bishop of Londun?"

"I preach truth to you, Robin of Jumieges." She climbed up on the bank as he extended a hand to her.

"It is sinful to lead men to carnal desires by the wanton display of your flesh, just as much as if you had a passion yourself."

"I am not accountable because man is a lewd animal."

He looked at her with his deep-blue eyes. "I am a lewd animal," he said. "I fight always to keep my lust embedded deep within me. Sometimes my knees ache from the stone as I cry out to God to deliver me from my shame. And mine is not even a natural lust."

"No lust is natural," she told him. "No man need be a beast."

He took long strides as he walked ahead of her. "I do not know what it can be to be like you . . . to feel nothing . . . to not be aroused . . . to sense nothing, as you and Edward do."

"We sense God." She bent down and plucked a yellow rose from its thorny vine and pricked her finger. "Why am I following you?" She caught up with him.

"The King is returning. Your father would have you present."

"Why do you hate him?"

"Who?" he asked, but she knew he understood what she meant.

"My father."

"The Earl of Wessex is. He exists in power. He has no strong convictions and shifts like a fire in changing winds, from Cnute to Harold to Harthacnut to Edward. He survives without loyalty to any man or to God."

"That's not true." Yet, in truth, she sometimes wondered if her father ever considered God at all. "He is loyal to the King."

"Any King," Robin said.

At St. Paul's, the miter on his head, dressed in embroidered vestments, he was the middle-aged shepherd of Londun, but here, his blue eyes melancholy, wearing the simple garb of a monk, he seemed but a lost boy, Edith thought. Her father loathed him and called him that "Norman turd" when he was being kind and much worse when he wasn't. He had been furious when Edward had given him the See of Londun. It had been over three years since the King's coronation and for three years Robin and her father had agreed on nothing.

His strides were so long she had difficulty keeping up and was out of breath when they reached the abbey. Thorney Island housed St. Peter's and the unpretentious house of the King and not much else. St. Peter's, sometimes called the Westminster, was a small monastery of nine monks, but the King had promised to build a magnificent new abbey here modeled after St. Mary's at Jumieges. The Bishop of Londun was in full accord with the King's grand plan and, consequently, Papa was opposed. "There's no worse location in England," Papa had told Edward.

Her parents stood near the entrance to the little garden where her brother Wufnoth raised flowers. "Nobody grows flowers," Godgifu, the King's sister, had told them. "They grow in the fields." Yet Wufnoth grew the largest flowers anyone had ever seen and he knew the names and could tell everyone when he planted them what color they would be. "He has a gift," Mama always said. Wufnoth was born with a club foot and he limped and dragged his foot when he walked and he spoke seldom for he always stuttered. But he could sing without stuttering and sometimes Edith would climb the tree above his garden and lie back against the trunk and listen to him sing while he dug in the dirt between the flowers. There was a fence of stone which he had built all around the flowers and it had a wooden gate where her parents, the Earl and Countess of Wessex, now stood.

Papa spoke to the bishop. "You did not have to fetch her like some housecarl. I suppose you wanted to be the first to tell her."

"I haven't told her," Robin said.

"Tell me what?" Edith asked.

"You are to be married within a fortnight. To Edward. You are to be Queen of England," her mother said.

Edith smiled.

"You don't seem surprised," Papa said.

"I always knew I was to be Queen," she said.

Robin smiled. It was one of the few times she had seen him do so. Edith went over and knelt at his feet.

He made the sign of the cross over her. His blue eyes were gentle. "May God protect you always, child of the gray wolf."

But Edith knew she was no longer a child. She was twenty-seven years old and about to be married to the King of England.

Oars dipped and swept the no longer still water of the Thames. Birds circled and cawed. Thirty-two ships anchored at Thorney. The golden cross on the King's blue flag dropped limp on the mast. The quiet in the shadows of the summer day was broken by the sounds of men and horses as they poured from the ships. The King's white beard nearly disappeared against the white of his robes as he stood, splendid in the sun, and waited to be escorted from the water's edge. Edith stayed in the shadows of a hanging willow and watched as the King, in a sweeping gesture, made the sign of the cross and then, with the two boys bearing the train of his white robe, he came up toward the abbey.

"You have routed Magnus." Papa knelt on the ground before the King.

"We have sent Magnus back from our seas flying against a north wind," Edward said and extended his hands.

From the abbey the monks came bearing a man on a stretcher and he was set before the King and Edward bent down over the man, not quite touching him, and kept drawing with his hands and then pulled his arms back with a jerk as if flinging something from his hands. Edward slipped to the ground exhausted, but for a moment, and then he arose as did the man on the stretcher, crying out that he was cured, and he fell to his knees before the King. Such things happened often.

Edward moved around the man and went toward the hall, preceding the others into the darkness. It was a small musty little hall of hardly any consequence. "The new hall will be large and bright," Edward had promised. Edith slipped quietly in a side door and hung back in the darkness.

"I met with Leofric at Elmham." The King was speaking to Papa. "He broached the subject first. 'You must marry,' he kept saying. 'You're not a boy, now.' I told him I had considered it. Well, you know how he hates the influence of my Norman friends. He would as soon kill our good Bishop of Londun here as look at him—"

So would Papa, Edith thought.

"So I told him I could find no one suitable. There was, I suggested, my cousin Eleanor's daughter, Judith. 'No, No,' he insisted. 'You must marry an English woman.' 'There is no one,' I said, 'but Godwin's daughter.' 'Then marry her, sir. Marry her. She's a sainted woman. They say she is.' I looked at him as if the idea had never really occurred to me before. 'I'll think on it. Yes, I'll consider it,' I told him." The King laughed. He was unusually boisterous and in good humor. "Tostig was my hero, Godwin. Your son was our hero. Where is Tostig?" Edward called.

Edith watched as her brother went up to the King. He was the tallest of the Godwin children and had her own deep auburn hair. He was a cross between Sven's rowdiness and mischievousness and Harold's reserve and moodiness.

"We shall marry him to Judith," the King said. "A hero deserves no less than the cousin of the Duke of Normandy and the daughter of Flanders."

Exactly what Tostig's heroics were the King did not explain.

"And where is Edith?" Edward called out. "Does she not come to greet her soon-to-be husband?"

"I am here," she said. Before entering the hall, she had slipped into a green silk gown and had pulled her uncovered hair back tight behind her head. She had quickly pinned a tiny crown of pearls in her hair.

Edward took her hands. She was, she knew, one of the few people he ever touched. She knelt down and he raised her up. "Will you be my wife?" he asked.

"Yes," she said.

"I am not a young man."

"You are a saint."

He led her to a chair. Papa beamed. Mama looked proud. Harold almost smiled.

"As a wedding gift, Edith, I grant you your wish, whether it be the new abbey at Wilton you would build or the water drained from the Thames, if that be your pleasure."

"What I want you will not grant me," she told him.

"I shall," he said.

"I want the freedom of Queen Emma."

Papa came over to her. "No. She is safe in a convent and the kingdom is the safer for her being there. Leave it alone."

"She is a fornicatress," her mother said.

The King looked at Edith.

"Christ forgives us our sins," Edith said.

Robin came from the back of the hall. He walked slowly and carried his crozier. "It is not often, Sire, that I stand in agreement with my Lord of Wessex, but for the safety of England and the sanity of us all, I say keep the whore locked up."

"I knew," Edith said, "I should not be granted my wish."

"The whore refuses to have me as her son or King. I gave her her freedom once only to find her fornicating with the Bishop of Winchester. What can I do but keep her locked in the company of good and chaste women?"

"I could talk with her," Edith pleaded. "If she was not willing to accept you as her son and her King, I should not beg her freedom. If she is not willing to these terms then I would never ask for her liberty again."

"No," Papa said.

A roar was heard. At the door stood a man as black as char. He held an iron leash and at the end of the leash was a man on all fours with golden hair and a golden beard and it gave him the look of a lion with a brilliant mane. The man on the leash turned his head about and roared again.

"Why do you keep him chained so?" Edward asked the man.

"Because, my Lord of England," the black man said, "to be a saint one must love all beasts."

"To be a saint," Edward said, "one must love everyone, man and beast."

And the hall fell silent and then Edward repeated, "One must love everyone and forgive everyone. For this is the goodness of which the Jesus spoke."

Edith knew she had won.

The man who looked like a lion roared and the man with the charred skin held the leash taut.

Her parents were both angry with her. She could see it in their faces and they barely spoke to her. Her brother Harold lectured her on the responsibility to the sovereign.

"Sometimes, Harold, you are a bore," she said.

Sven laughed. Wufnoth limped in with a large white flower which he gave to her. "For the new Queen," he stuttered.

The King was happy. "Tostig," he called. "Have the hawks readied. It is a fair day for fair game."

CHAPTER 6

Wales, 1045

EMMA ORDERED TWO BATHS A DAY, NOT THAT SHE WANTED THEM, BUT THAT the nuns had to bear the water up a steep hill from a well far below. The abbey, which did not even seem to have a name, was set in barren land beyond Shrewsbury in the domain of Gruffydd ap Llewelyn. It was land where the wind howled and a dragon was known to live. Few moments passed in any day that Emma did not think of Edward and her hate grew and she nurtured it, cultivated it. She refused to rise when the nuns rose, to pray when they prayed, to eat when they ate. She wore her scarlet wool and her yellow linen gowns until they were rags, but she refused to don the black robes they thrust at her. She woke in the night so she could scream and awake them all. She slept in her cell when they attempted to clean it in the day—and she knew that the abbess knew that the fortunes of kings rose and fell like the heat of a day and that Emma, the Queen, yesterday, might well be Emma, the Queen, tomorrow. Eleven times she had escaped. She had bribed and bought, cajoled, slandered, dug and clawed her way to near freedom and once almost reached Shrewsbury.

"We will pray for you," the abbess would say and Emma would sit sullen or wail or beat against the door, depending on her mood. And the abbess would say to the nuns, "This is our cross, sisters. God has asked us to bear this great punishment."

Edith, the daughter of Godwin, came upon a black horse with a white mane and white tail and with forty soldiers and her brother called Gryth.

And Emma heard one of the nuns, the tired one with the boils on her arms, say, "Surely they've come to cut off the head of the old hag."

And Edith walked with Emma on a barren knoll.

"Certainly, child, there were better things to wish for," Emma said after hearing Edith's story of her betrothal wish.

"Nothing could please me more than to know, Lady Queen, that you were not shut in here like a caged bird."

"I hate with such a passion," Emma said. "I detest Edward with a fury which years have enlarged like a swell beneath the skin."

"He is a true saint, Lady Queen. Your womb has gifted this world with a true saint. And all you need do is kneel before him and say, 'I am your mother and you are my son and King,' and like a true saint and with his gift of touch all will be healed."

"Leave me, child, here to pray awhile." Emma watched the woman, a beautiful woman with long dark hair, move as stately as a queen down toward the abbey. How could she expect to give up all that hate? She did not pray; she weighed—weighed the hate against being free—and she thought and the hate welled up in her, swollen by the years of being in this godforsaken place and she thought of freedom to be away from this horrid place and these horrid nuns with their endless prayers and black gowns—and she thought of Edward, ugly and white, pale and useless, of his eyes watching her at Corfe, of finding her with Stigand, of always judging and she hated him, and she thought of Corfe and Winchester and being free to walk upon the streets, to see a lion or ride a horse—God, what she would give to ride a horse or to hawk—and she thought of Edward standing in the dark at Bruges, not having the guts to push her from the battlement. There was only one possible answer: freedom with pretense and revenge. Edward was going to marry and marriage meant heirs and heirs would allow her Norman blood, as much as she hated the thought of it being handed through that horrid creature, to flow in an heir and when it did she would kill Edward and place the boy on the throne. She looked down at the abbey, a prison box in the middle of a wasteland. God never heard these nuns, for surely he never knew this abbey in the midst of hell existed. She would pack her relics and leave the rest. There was little of worth. She would give her scarlet rag to the nun with the boils on her arms.

"God bless," the abbess said, and ordered water fetched for the Queen's bath.

Edith smiled. Emma was genuinely fond of the girl. She was a girl no longer, Emma supposed, yet she thought of her as that little girl whom Gytha had abandoned at birth. How long ago? The world had been full of hope then. Well, there would be hope again. Edith would bear a son and that son would be made a king. Emma would see to it. She bathed and dressed in a fresh white gown that Edith had brought for her and Edith, herself, brushed her hair. It was gray but for a few yellow strands lost in the ugly gray and she buried her hair beneath a wimple.

"It is a long ride," Edith told her as they made ready to leave.

"The farther this place is from the world, the better," Emma said.

The nuns all smiled. They would offer prayers of thanksgiving on this night, Emma thought as she took the reins of the horse. How wonderful to sit a horse again.

"God bless you and pray for us," the abbess said.

Emma spurred the brown mare and galloped off. The last thing she heard was the abbess calling on the wind, "Remember us to the King . . ." The other horses galloped after and they began the long ride to Westminster.

Westminster was an ugly little place, an island full of bugs and the King's house was totally inadequate. Emma complained of the house and her own accommodations, but no one seemed to listen. She had been brought before the King, gritted her teeth and done what she had agreed to do and that was that.

The days were warm and unpleasant, sultry, and the air seemed forever to promise relief in a beating rainstorm which never came. An occasional shower did nothing to alleviate the humidity. She hated Westminster. Gytha ignored her and her only real friend was Edith. Edith smiled and was happy and spent her days with Emma or lying nude upon the bank of the Thames. That horrible Robin of Jumieges had been made a bishop by Edward. Edward made just about anyone a bishop who had enough wealth. Edward sold ecclesiastic titles like a Flem selling cloth at a fair. And they called him a saint! Cnute never did that, not even Ethelred stooped that low. A saint—they should call him St. Gelder. She began also to suspect Edward was mad. The day before there had been an execution. A man accused of stealing a silver cup from the abbey was hung. He dangled there on a limb of a large oak tree and Edward, who had stood with the rest of them watching the life being choked from the man, went up and with his jeweled knife cut open the man's side. Then he stuck his hands into the bleeding wound and took them out. "Christ had a wound stricken in His side," he had said. He let the blood drip from his hands. A servant came with a basin of water and Edward turned his hands over and over again through the water and then dried them on a towel. Yes, he was mad.

It was an ugly little room in which she sat. Hardly better than the nun's cell she had been imprisoned in off in Wales. She had a straw bed, a chair and chest in which she kept her relics and there was little else. She thought about getting up out of the chair and going for a walk in the garden of the boy Wufnoth. It was pretty there, and smelled sweet with flowers. He was a strange child with a limp and he couldn't talk plain. No, it would be hot in the sun, so she sat immobile in the cell.

There was a weak rap at the door. She got up and opened it. A young man stood there. Perhaps he was only a boy. He was a skinny thing with a weak chin. She hated a weak chin.

"The King sent me," he said.

"Who are you?"

"Ralph of Mantes. Your grandson."

"How could I have a grandson so ugly?" she asked. She didn't invite him. He came in anyway.

"How could I have a grandmother so old?" he responded.

Insolent brat. He looked more like Drogo than Godgifu. Whatever she might say about his horrid mother, at least Godgifu had a chin. God, how she hated a face without a chin. Emma had once wanted to make this little monster the King. He wasn't as ugly as Edward, certainly, but he was an unpleasant-looking thing and his skin was blotched and he had a face of pimples.

"Do you want to be King?" she asked.

"No. I should hate it."

"When you address me, call me Lady Queen."

"I should hate it." He paused and added pointedly, "Lady Queen."

"Why?"

"Because it is dangerous. I don't wish to die."

"You lack your mother's spunk, boy."

"I am a man." He went over and sat on the straw bed. "She hates you."

"And I hate her."

They called him Ralph the Timid. He certainly wasn't afraid of her. "And I call her the afterbirth of my aborted son who lived. What do you think of that?"

"I think you are angry."

"Go away," she said. "You have no chin and they say you are a coward."

He got up off the straw. "I only came to see you because the King made me."

He left.

At last the court left Westminster and moved to Wardrobe Palace. It was an old and ugly place, but it was cooler than at Westminster. She remembered Ethelred and his terror of candles. In the hall she stood off in the corner, like Harold Thorkellsson used to do. He had been murdered in Normandy on his way from pilgrimage to Rome. The old faces at court were gone and the new ones which surrounded Edward seemed mainly Norman or Godwin's sons or nephews. The faces were young and they ignored her and in the large, dank hall she was as alone as she would be in a cell at Westminster or in Wales.

Edward entered. He always entered after they were gathered and with a silly pomp, his gown being borne behind him. He wore ridiculously impractical robes made from yards of cloth and on the hottest days drenched himself in furs and wool. He was mad; she was certain of it.

There was a commotion and Estrid was escorted in by her son Beorn. Emma had heard she had arrived in the early hours of the morning. Beorn took her before the throne.

"Magnus," she said without bowing or any other courtesy, "has invaded the Daneland."

"We welcome you to our court," Edward said. "I am certain you wish to acknowledge your King properly."

Estrid made a slight dip of the knee in what she apparently hoped would be accepted as recognizing the King's fealty. "Magnus has attacked the Daneland," she repeated.

"So you have told us, Lady." Edward stood up. "But England cannot be left unprotected for Magnus might strike here as easily."

"So you will not send an army to Roeskild?"

How Emma wished he would dare go to the Daneland. She'd even make that weak-chinned Ralph a king while he was away.

"No, Lady. I have no army to spare."

"Then what," she asked, "is to happen to the Daneland?"

"That is the problem for the Daneland to resolve."

"Edward—"

He interrupted her with a raised voice. "You will address me as a king. I have no force to send to Roeskild. Let Svegn fight his own battles."

"You are—"

"Enough. I have other business."

Beorn came and led her off into the corner where Emma was standing as the King began conferring with the Bishop of Londun. Estrid was crying and her son was begging her to hush and she swore at Edward and he told her to be quiet unless she wanted them all to lose their heads. She kept on crying and he left her as if to disavow her and she went on crying and her face was red and puffed.

Emma smiled and went up to her. "Let me marry your son and I will make him King of England."

At first Estrid was ready to strike out at her and then she caught the grin and couldn't help herself from smiling as well. She took the cloth Emma handed her and wiped her eyes.

"He's a monster," Estrid said.

"Yes, a horrid creature. I have been telling you that for years."

"The Daneland will fall," Estrid told her.

They stood silent for a moment, examining one another. She has gotten

older and even fatter, Emma realized. It was Emma who finally spoke.
"Did you pray for me while I was in prison?"

"I did not."

"You always pray for everyone, Estrid."

"Prayers were of little use to you, Emma."

"I always manage to outdo God," Emma said.

"Or try." The anger and vindictiveness were gone. They were two old women struggling to stay alive in a world ruled by young men.

The weather turned slightly cooler.

St. Paul's was crawling with cats, striped cats and black cats and spotted cats and white cats. They angled beneath statues and sat in alcoves and crawled above the altar and around the cloister, all oblivious that a king was to be married this day.

One brushed by the hem of Emma's gown. For the wedding she had had the nuns of Wilton make her a bliaut woven from the wool of the blessed sheep of Hereford. The sheep came from the Holy Land and were said descended from those very flocks tended by the shepherds who came to the baby Jesus on Christmas. Barren women who wore wool from those sheep grew large and gave birth to healthy boys. Just perhaps.

The Bishop of Londun petted a cat and a monk placed the miter on his head and another handed him his crozier. Preceded by twenty priests and incense smoking in his path, the bishop marched through the nave as a chorus of monks shouted a joyous Latin hymn, only to be drowned in the sound of the clanging bells.

Estrid, who still styled herself Duchess of Normandy, was the first of Edith's family to enter. At the door she was complaining of Edward's refusal to aid the Daneland. With a dour look, she was escorted by the Thegn Osgot Clapa. Her sons followed: Osbeorn, inappropriately shirtless with a gilt-colored sale over his shoulders and sporting an outdated Viking helmet with horns. His legs were bare and leather-laced. Unnecessary, Emma thought, as little as Emma cared about this wedding as far as Edward went, at least Osbeorn, for his cousin's, Edith's, sake could have shown some sense of propriety. Perhaps she was getting old. Such ill-mannered gestures never used to disturb her. Beorn, his brother, round-faced, pleasant and plainly dressed, carried the King's mace. Gytha followed him in the procession escorted by the Earl of Northumbria. Grumbling Siward, like Hakon before him, never let his wife from home. She stayed in York. "Where she belongs." Gytha wore a boxy headdress trimmed in pearls. To hide the gray, no doubt, Emma decided. Her children followed by age. God, what a brood. The Earl Sven, still with that damned enticing smile, was followed by the Earl Harold, who never seemed to smile, who was followed by Tostig, who was followed by Gryth, who was followed by Leofwine, who was followed by the limping Wufnoth and last came their youngest, the daughter Gunnhildr, who was escorted by a thegn they called Odda of Deerhurst, who was himself said descended from some bastard or another of Ethelred's. She couldn't remember which. He had a large hook nose with bushy hairs hanging from it. He was a favorite of Edward's. There was no accounting for the King's choice in friends.

Leofric and Godiva arrived at St. Paul's late and the ceremony waited upon them. He was drunk and the bug-eyed Godiva, her hair still trailing to her buttocks, smiled insipidly at Emma and they walked, the Earl and Countess of Mercia, through the nave.

The King's family was to enter next, and Godgifu, who had been kept apart from Emma in a locked chamber at the rear, was now escorted, or more correctly held back, between two guards as she came into the apse. The two burly thegns, Beorhtric the Ugly and Ordwulf the Black Fox, each held tightly to one of her arms. Godgifu spit in Emma's direction, but did little else to disrupt the parade.

Emma waited. Heads turned to the back of the cathedral. "Who's to escort me?" Emma asked. She was irritated. Perhaps it was Edward's intent to insult her and let her walk through the nave alone. Well, she wouldn't go. Despite the fact that it was Edith's wedding, she wouldn't go.

"A moment, Madam," a monk said. "But a moment."

The young man entered from a side chamber. He was tall, pleasant-looking and wore a brocade mantle and a crown.

He offered her his arm.

"Who are you?" she asked as she took the arm and entered the nave with him.

"Henry," he said. "The King of France."

Emma felt the warm wool press against her belly as she walked statelily through the nave, the Queen Dowager of England on the arm of the King of France. A cat skidded across in her path. Emma sat in the hard chair next to the young King. Where was his wife, the Lady Anne, daughter of Taroslav?

The monks stopped trying to outdo the bells and then the bells ceased. A herald stepped to the altar. "The Viscomte of Conteville and his lady bear the sword of the King's dead brother Alfred."

Emma turned to see the man dressed in black bearing the sword raised straight before him. The lady walked at his side.

"Is she?" Emma started to ask.

"The mother of the Duke of Normandy." The King of France spoke softly.

The sword was placed on a chair next to Emma. Alfred? She hardly knew what he looked like. She remembered bringing him back to Corfe as a baby. MacBoru's headless body had been in a chamber upon a bed. Alfred peed a great deal as a baby. He was said to have loved the sea.

The herald again stepped to the altar. "The Baron of Leiptz, envoy of Henry, Emperor of the Romans and widower of the King's blessed sister Gunnerhild bears the sword of the King's beloved and dead brother King Harthacnut."

Beloved, indeed! What did Edward do to help him from choking to death, and his blessed sister Gunnerhild? Edward had never even seen her. The sword was placed on the chair next to the chair on which rested the sword of Alfred.

The chorus of monks yelled out again in another loud Latin chant.

Godgifu was escorted next, burly shouldered in a mammoth red gown and a cape of red fox tails. She was marched through the nave, a thegn pressed at each side. She sat, one thegn, two swords and the King of France apart from Emma.

Count Eustace, with greasy black hair and dark eyes, fingered his trimmed beard as he followed, and behind him marched the chinless Ralph of Mantes.

There was a pause. The monks sang and heads turned back to seek the delay, but nothing occurred and then a murmur loud enough to be heard above the monks rippled through the nave. Emma turned. My God! It was her brother Richard. Not as she had last seen him, old and dying in his bed, but as he had been at eighteen, vital and full of youthful strength. Richard was dead. Yet, he was Richard, a ghost perhaps, and he walked alone, not with any pomp, but with an innate regal simplicity. Only Richard had such a carriage, that posture of being totally in command. He was magnificent, yet taller than Richard had been, perhaps a little broader in the shoulders. But the face, the almost-smile, the commanding presence—they were all Richard. He wore a simple soldier's hauberk. His hair was cropped short in the Norman way and fell in bangs over his forehead. He came and sat next to her. He reached over and touched her hand.

"Queen Emma," he said.

"You are William," she said.

"Yes, the bastard of Normandy," he answered.

"I remember once," she told him, "when my brother Richard came back from fighting in Poitiers. There was dried blood on his hauberk."

"The blood on mine seldom has the time to dry, it seems."

The bells clamored and the monks yelled louder in Latin in the battle to be heard. Edith came, not carrying her crown, but a bunch of white flowers. What a strange thing to carry, Emma thought, still they were pretty. Her dress was white and the weave so open you could see her golden skin beneath. Her dark hair was pulled tight behind her head, clasped, and then fell on her gown in a tail. Godwin walked with her and bore her crown.

Emma turned from Edith and looked at the young brown-haired man next to her. He was rougher-looking than Richard had been, his skin pocked in places. His nose was flat, like her brother's had been. He looked nothing like his dark father. There was none of the evil about him that had been so apparent in Robert.

Edward was preceded by six boys wearing mantles of swan's down and carrying candles. Six more boys followed bearing his ermine train. All twelve were of near the same age and looked quite alike and later Emma was told they were all bastards sired by the abbot of Bury St. Edmund's. The King wore his heavy crown and carried the scepter and rod. Edward's pomposity was a total contrast to the unobtrusive dignity of the young Duke of Normandy, who sat beside her. The King seemed to float more than walk over the stone floor. When he reached the altar, he set aside the scepter and rod. A blind man was brought to him. Edward gave him sight. A lame man was brought to him and made to walk again.

Show, Emma thought. All for show.

"How does he do it?" the young Norman duke asked her.

"By trickery, no doubt," she told him.

The marriage vows were so abbreviated they were hardly vows at all. The long pledges of progenizing the world were peculiarly omitted. The crown was placed on Edith's head, her fingers were anointed with holy chrism and her forehead blessed. The mass followed. Emma brushed a cat away from the folds of her skirt.

"Why did you come?" Emma asked the duke during the offertory.

"I am Edward's heir." He spoke matter-of-factly.

Emma looked surprised. No one had told her. Perhaps no one knew. "But now the marriage. Edward will bear sons."

"Some marriages never bear fruit."

"It is wrong to say that here in this place, on this day," Emma told him and quickly blessed herself.

At the wedding feast word arrived that the Daneland had fallen to Magnus. Svegn had fled to his cousin's court, to King Anaud's court at Upsala.

"Coward!" Estrid yelled and stormed from the dingy smoky hall.

"She must stop calling herself the Duchess of Normandy," the eighteen-year-old William said.

William's fool, Gall, who had come to England with the young duke, paraded as if he were the duchess, swinging his hips in a mock of Estrid's walk.

"She'll die soon," Gryth Godwinsson told the duke.

Two days later, Emma packed her relics, gathered her new gowns, kissed her daughter-in-law, bade her multiply and fled to Winchester.

CHAPTER 7

England, 1047

A THICK GRAY SMOKE CHOKED A BURNING FIELD OF GRAIN AND HUNG THE air with a heavy pallor. Serfs beat the flames with rags and boards. Godwin and the others rode on, leaving behind the smell of burning grass stained invisibly upon their dress. It was a long ride to Dover and Godwin's aching foot was swollen and his bones sore. Harold rode ahead, two soldiers behind. The road was narrow in places and bordered by stone fences and at other times widened as it crossed open fields. They forded streams and once they stopped and Godwin took off his leather slippers and the water felt cool against his feet. Going through the forests was slow and they watched for cutthroats. Always Godwin watched back to see they were not being followed, that some rider of the bishop's house was not behind them.

Two years and no heir to the throne. Godwin suspected why.

Christmas had been spent at Glouchester and Easter at Winchester and Pentecost at Oxford and Michaelmas at York and still no heir. And they went again to Glouchester and in the spring to Winchester and the King to please his mother released Stigand from a cave in Cornwall and he celebrated mass as the Bishop of Winchester, but he was broken and bent and bald and his spindly legs barely held him up and his raspberry cheeks had pallored from living in the cave so long, and he was wrinkled and sad.

"She is not with child," Emma told Godwin.

"No," he said, but said no more.

Later, as they walked away from the unfinished buildings of the King's house, she asked, "Did I tell you the Duke of Normandy claims to be his heir?"

"No," Godwin told her and in honesty it was the first he had heard of it.

"Who else is there?" she asked.

And the court returned to Westminster, where it spent most of its days, and the King and Queen knelt for hours in the chapel and prayed. Godwin criticized the Queen for frequently going to pray naked as a child and the King said, "She is the Queen and may do as she wishes."

It was a calm two years and Godwin sensed that beneath the smooth shell was hatching a dragon. Work had begun on the King's great abbey on Thorney Island and it was where the Queen liked to be best and Edward obliged the Queen. Godwin, to please his daughter, attended to his public prayers with greater regularity and had been sent a special blessing from the Pope for his efforts. Clement the German was Pope. Benedict, the boy, had sold the papacy to Gregory the Reformer, who had died, and now the German sent his blessings. But there was no heir. No heir, save the bastard of Normandy, which no doubt pleased the Bishop of Londun. Visitors came to Westminster, not like the days of imperial Winchester, but they came. Spytihnev, the son of Bretislav of Selesia, came and Godwin's son Wufnoth gave him a basket of yellow flowers and Spytihnev took them to Edith's chamber and tried to rape her, but the gray wolf appeared and Spytihnev fled to Prague. Edith said God punished Bretislav for having such a son for shortly after the Emperor of the Holy Romans drove Bretislav's armies from Crackow and Prague.

Other visitors came, too, and Hamon Dentatus, the Norman Lord of Thorigny, paid his respects upon the King and Queen and also to the Bishop of Londun, but he met Godwin alone by the Thames.

"Are you aware your King has named William the Bastard as his heir?" Hamon asked and tossed a pebble skimming across the river.

"I have heard such a tale, but the King is newly—"

"Two years, Godwin," the Lord of Thorigny interrupted. "Two years is not newly married and no sign do I see. I suspect, Lord Godwin, you have no more wish to see the tanner's grandson King of England than we to see him Lord of Normandy."

"It is true," Godwin said. "Why do you broach the subject?"

"The Viscount of Contances, Neal of St. Savior, and Naldolf, the Viscount of Bayeux, have joined myself and Grimbald of Plessis to support the legitimate blood claim of Guy of Burgundy. There will be a revolt."

"And what do you wish of me?" Godwin asked.

"That you keep Edward from coming to William's support with arms."

"That may not be possible if William asks Edward for help. I do not control this King. The Bishop of Londun exerts a far stronger influence."

"We need but little time for William will be dead quickly. You can help, too, when Guy of Burgundy seeks Edward's recognition."

"I will keep your counsel and do what I am able," Godwin assured him.

Hamon Dentatus sent another flat pebble skimming over the water.

A feast was prepared for Hamon at the bishop's house in Londun, and Godwin made the journey with the King and Queen. Edward was fond of fish and there was giant sturgeon and white fish and oiled baked shark and tender sole and salted kippers and tough scrod and Hamon ate little.

"I am told," Robin said, "that the duke's stepfather has founded an abbey at Bec and given up the world."

"Yes," Hamon said. "Herluin has become an abbot."

"Admirable. I am told he has given up the flesh and that his wife, Herleve, the mother of the beloved duke, has joined him as a sister in Christ and they have taken vows of celibacy," Robin continued.

"That is admirable," Edith said.

"Admirable," Edward concurred.

"But they already have sons, do they not?" Godwin asked, knowing full well that they did.

"Yes," Hamon said, "two sons."

Later in the evening Hamon told Godwin, "I despise fish."

Within a week word reached Westminster that Guy of Burgundy was in rebellion against the duke. The Bessin and Contentin had revolted in support of him.

"If the duke seeks our help," Edward told his counselors, "we will send it."

The assassination of William that Hamon had said would occur had better happen soon. Godwin had his spies in Normandy and one of them, Breslin, who was a soldier in the house of Grimbald, had arranged to meet with him. Harold and the two trusted soldiers rode with Godwin.

At Dover, Breslin was tired and drank wine. The sea beat against the chalk shore as he talked. "William was at Valognes, Neal's own country. He was bow hunting," Breslin said. "Grimbald insisted on the pleasure of killing William, himself, but somehow the duke's fool, Gall, found out and warned William and when Grimbald reached Valognes the young duke had fled. The duke was said to have crossed the Douve and Vire at ebb tide, but when Grimbald reached the place the water had risen. The duke next went into Bayeux, but learned that it, too, was traitor's country; however, he was helped by Hubert of Nye and his sons. They gave him fresh horses and provided themselves as his guard and escorts and helped him to reach Falaise. He is safe in the tower at Falaise. At least for the time."

"Will he survive?"

"His life seems charmed." Breslin's tone was one of resignation. "It is told a star sat in the heavens the night he was conceived and was never seen again and that he wears it in his heart. Yet, the great houses of Normandy now stand against him and though he may endure the siege at Falaise without help from France or England I cannot see how he can survive."

"It would have been easier if he were dead," Godwin said.

Harold spoke for the first time. "At least the King of France has nothing to gain by a strong Normandy and should be glad of the rebellion."

Breslin was sent back to Normandy. Godwin and Harold returned to Westminster.

"You have been gone these days," Edward said to Godwin on his immediate return. "We have had need of your counsel." The Bishop of London stood at Edward's side. "Normandy is in rebellion against its duke and rightful lord. If we were able I would rush to his aid but at the moment in the west Gruffydd ap Rhyddech has raised arms against us and until I have put down the rebellion I have no army to send. I have sent word to the King of France, our brother Henry, reminding him of his sworn oath to Robert. For Robert helped Henry gain his throne; now he must support the son."

To Godwin's amazement, Henry did. At Val-es-dunes in a great battle of cavalry, of mounted knights, of shields, and swords and lance Henry fought at William's side. Twice the King of France was reputed knocked from his horse only to ride to victory. And Hamon Dentatus, the man who hated fish, died at Val-es-dunes. The rebellion against the duke was at an end.

Godescalc the Wend came to England. Emissaries and petitioners, moneylenders and merchants, spies and flatterers came and went. There was a calm, yet Godwin sensed that beneath a great underground of ire was churning. And still England had no heir. It was after Godescalc came that a series of events began to plague Godwin. His first error was in sending Earl Sven and Ralph of Mantes to quell the Welsh uprising.

In the North, in the Daneland, better things were happening. Magnus rode his horse on a quiet day and Svedger the Crude told how a hare ran in its path, the horse spooked and bashed Magnus's head against a tree and the young King of Norway died and joined his sainted father in the hereafter and Olaf's brother, half brother more correctly, Harold Hardrada became King of the North and King Edward acknowledged him and there was an opening of the earth in the Midlands and twelve people were devoured in the chasm and there was no heir in the making in England. Grimbald was taken prisoner by the Duke of Normandy at Rouen and put in fetters and the pirates of the North, Lothen and Yrling, made raids upon the English coast and fled to Bruges with their booty and were given sanctuary by Baldwin. Godescalc, the bushy-haired Wend, predicted terror in the offing and shook his head.

And there was no heir and Godwin no longer could contain his impatience. He was near sixty; he wanted to live to see his grandson and the future King of England. Emma had come from Winchester at the King's behest to plead with Baldwin not to let the pirates find sanctuary, nor sell their booty in Flanders as they were doing. Emma sent a personal plea to Baldwin.

"It will soon be three years," Godwin said, "and we have seen no inkling of an heir."

The answer he had been avoiding was given him by his daughter. "We are chaste. The King and I have dedicated our flesh to God."

"No!" Emma yelled. "I will not hear it! You will bear sons. It is your duty."

"Never," the King said.

The Bishop of Londun stood. He was smiling. Emma leaped at him. She held a knife. "This is your doing, Priest."

But he grabbed her wrist and twisted and her face echoed the pain and the knife fell to the floor and she was dragged from the hall.

Godwin had assumed the day could get little worse when the Bishop of Worcester, Eldred, arrived. He had a pained look about him. He certainly was not smiling.

"The Earl at Hereford—"

"What has Sven done now?" Godwin asked.

"He has committed a breach of morality beyond the limits of God's forgiveness. He sent for one Eadgifu, the Abbess of Leonminster, and had her kept with him awhile. She is with child and he tried then to marry her." Bishop Eldred belched and added, "He is a seducer of a consecrated virgin."

Edward arose. He went past Godwin without looking directly at him. His face was contorted and Godwin assumed it was anger, but as he turned about in front of the bishop it seemed almost a horror or deep pain. "And the ecclesiastical punishment?"

"Death," the bishop said and did not look at Godwin.

Godwin and Gytha left the hall. A light snow was falling.

"What do we do now?" Gytha asked.

"Try to save our son," he told her.

CHAPTER 8

England, 1047

EMMA WAS SPRAWLED FACEDOWN ON THE HARD FLOOR WEEPING. SHE HAD beat her fists against the stone until they were bleeding and raw. Life would leave her and there was nothing behind, no piece nor particle. Harthacnut, her hope, her child of love, had died a man with the genitals of a child and, like a child, fat and hungrily gorging himself until he had choked. Emma sobbed and her chest rattled with her grief. Edward, for forty-five years, was there like an open sore festering and vile and finally it would kill her. She sobbed more softly, her sagging breasts pressed against the stone and her eyes focused on a pair of bare feet, large feet, ugly feet, of a man and she had heard no one enter the chamber. Her eyes traveled up the length of a big man in a battered hauberk and were drawn to the face, the eyes really, enormous eyes, deep set in dark shadows pulling her in and she was spelled by them. About his face, a large coarse face, pitted, and though shaven, stubbled, was a frame of hair like turns and shavings of iron which sprouted in all directions. He extended a huge hand with dirty nails and dirt between the fingers.

"I am Godescalc, son of Uto." The voice was soft, but low like the long strings of a harp. He had skin so tanned it was almost black, but it was his eyes which commanded attention.

She yet didn't speak, being drawn in deeper by the eyes.

"I've come to bear you comfort and help," he said.

She let him raise her up, her bones sore from lying on the floor.

"I want to go home," she said, her eyes never leaving his.

"I will take you to Winchester, Queen. I was there when King Cnute first wed you. I was there a thinglith, who stood watch at your door. I was there when Winchester was the Rome of the North. I was there when the great treasures of Cnute were hidden in locked rooms."

"I do not remember you," she said.

"I have changed much since my youth. Then, I had not seen so much evil. For many years I was a prisoner of the Duke of Saxons."

"I have been a prisoner." She found a solace in his eyes.

Quietly Godescalc assembled the people of her house. They were few in number now, old slaves and worn soldiers. She had never found Wordig. Without a word of leave or parting, they rode in the night from Westminster. Emma rode an old horse and Godescalc the Wend was at her side. A light snow fell. They rode south and west, passing outside the walls of Londuntown, dark and ominous, in the night. The snow continued to fall, but it came lightly and wet and it was not freezing and as the sun came up the snow was sucked up by the ground until the earth seemed parched.

Smoke drifted from the roof of the Queen's house in the old compound at the top of the hill. Had some sprite seen her coming and made a fire? They entered the warmth of the room and there by the hearth, stretched out as if it were his house, was Sven Godwinsson, rough and smiling like an impish boy. But he was no boy. He was nearly thirty and his hairline had begun to recede.

"Surprised?"

"What are you doing here?" She wanted to sound angry.

"I've come to visit the beautiful Queen."

"She is dead. The Queen who lives here now is ugly and old—"

"No—"

Godescalc interrupted. "He seduced the Abbess of Leonminster, a consecrated virgin, and is under death warrant of the King."

"The part about the death warrant I didn't know, though I suspected." He stood up.

"Did you seduce the abbess?" Emma asked.

"Would I ever yield to the beauty of a woman?"

Emma laughed. She knew she should not be delighted to see him, but she was.

"Will you help me?" he asked.

"Why?" she said.

"Because I will make passionate love to you and give you a baby."

Emma could not laugh about it. "I am sixty-three years old. God grant I could have a baby, but I am barren, old and ugly."

"You are not ugly," he said and took her wrinkled hand.

"I have good teeth." She laughed.

Godescalc came about and stood directly in front of her. His eyes said, "Look at me," and she did, staring intently into the dark pits of his eyes. "You need not be barren," he told her in a soft voice. "Do you know the Slavonic God, Radegart?"

"No," she said.

"He can help."

"But I am Christian."

"As am I," Godescalc's deep voice assured her, "but Radegart will hear you. A woman, an ancient woman of Kiev, who was a hundred and four, asked the god to help and she bore twins who became giants."

"What must I do?"

"When you have found a virile man, I will make a potion in a bowl and you will sit and take in its smoke and then lie together. When the man falls asleep, you will rise from the bed and take a handful of magic seeds and bury them in the cold earth and in the spring your belly, like the seeds, will grow and bear."

"I am virile." Sven laughed.

"You should not laugh," Emma told him.

"Will you help me?" he asked. "I will give you that belly."

"I would help you even if you didn't," she told him. "Bruges is where you need to go."

"But will Baldwin let me stay?"

"He will if I ask."

He smiled, that damnable smile. "And I will give you a big fat baby boy."

"Harthacnut was enough. I want no more fat ones," she said, laughing.

He touched her hand again gently.

"When the child is born," she said, now convinced it could be done, "I will come for you. We will wed and conquer England. You and your son shall be kings."

Godescalc went to the door. "Tonight I shall bring you the potion," he said and left.

"There is something evil in him," Sven said.

"He is kind and will help," Emma assured him.

Sven came over to her and kissed her. It had been years since the rough lips of a man had been pressed hard like that upon her own. "Tonight," she told him in a whisper.

"May I sit with you now?"

"Yes. I will tell you the news of court." Emma had not felt so young in a long time.

It was late when Godescalc came, long past dinner. He crushed an herb into a bowl and, fanning it, let it smolder and the smoke was pungent and sweet and made Emma giddy. She laughed and her words were slow and sometimes she could not remember the word she had but just said and Godescalc left and Sven, speaking slowly, suggested they go to Emma's bed. And in the night she buried the magic grain in the cold earth.

Emma provided Sven with gold and horses and ships to be waiting at Corfe. He fled and she endured the winter and the Pope died and the German Bruno, Bishop of Toul, became Leo the Ninth and Stigand, timid, came to visit and suggested it would be well if she made her peace with the King and Queen and she said "no" and he didn't come to see her again and Beatrix, the daughter of her dead Gunnerhild and the Emperor Henry, who had remarried, was ten years old and named the Abbess of Quedlinburg and would be a virgin and bear no seed and Emma screamed and Godescalc dug holes in the earth, the cold hard frozen earth. One of the Iberians, Muluk Al Tawai'l'f, came to Winchester looking for King Cnute and she sent him to the minster to Cnute's tomb and laughed at her joke and Svegn Estridsson proclaimed himself King of the Daneland and Edward was busy fighting Baldwin, Emma was told, and did not concern himself about the new King of the Daneland for Edward was angry with Baldwin for continuing to give sanctuary to the pirates and now to Osgot Clapa, who had been exiled, and to Sven Godwinsson.

Godescalc came each day and she relied on him more and more and he brought her the news and tended to her affairs and when he was not with her she knew he dug beneath the cobble or in the hard earth or underneath buildings and when the King commanded her to Winchester he sent word she was ailing and unable to travel and the court moved to Glouchester for Christmas, but Emma stayed, playing ill at Winchester, and her belly began to grow and Godescalc brought her herbs and they made her float and have dreams of colors and shapes. Gytha came. Sven had sent her word of Emma's help and she thanked Emma for being so kind to her son.

"You've grown plump," Gytha said.

"Yes," Emma told her. She was pleased and surprised at the woman's friendliness, but Emma didn't tell the Countess of Wessex that she was pregnant and going to bear her a grandson. No, she kept that to herself. Not yet was she ready to tell them.

"And how is Sven?" Emma asked.

"Well and anxious to be home, but the King will not hear upon that."

"Baldwin is a good host."

"Only because you pay him to keep Sven and you mustn't," Gytha told her. "Godwin and I can tend to that."

"No," Emma said. "I wish to."

Gytha left and the court returned to Westminster and Godescalc gave Emma great comfort and peace as she looked into the depth of his eyes and she breathed the smoke of burning herbs which he fixed for her and her belly grew so large that there was no longer any use trying to hide the truth and she was certain it would burst and spring arrived and the court came to Winchester for Easter.

Emma stood waiting at the top of the hill; in the distance was visible the King's progress as it approached.

"There is a great treasure buried here at Winchester," Godescalc said.

"No," Emma told him. "There is none."

Her huge belly protruding, she met the King and Queen.

"You have been ill. You have a growth," the King said.

Behind the King and Queen walked the Countess of Wessex, the earl and Harold.

"I am with child," Emma said as she led the way through the courtyard.

"Nonsense," Gytha said. "You are too old."

"No. I am going to have a child."

"It is as the Lady Wessex says," Edward told her. "You are too old."

"I bear the son of Sven Godwinsson."

"Lord, not that tale again," Godwin said. "Enough of this rubbish, Emma. You need the care of a doctor."

Harold laughed.

"It is not funny, Harold," Godwin told him.

"She may be possessed of some devil," Edith said softly, but not softly enough.

"I am possessed only of Sven Godwinsson's seed."

"And how came you by that, Lady?" Edward asked.

"It is I who saw him safely to Flanders."

"If this is true—" Edward began.

But Godwin interrupted him. "Of course, it is fable. She is an old woman. And I think quite mad."

But the King was not convinced and Stigand was brought around and made to confess that Sven had indeed been at Winchester in the winter and that Emma had provided his escape to Bruges and the bishop was taken out and publicly flogged for having failed to tell the King and Emma was sorry for her old friend, even if he was a coward and weak.

The grain Emma had planted in the night sprouted and grew green from the earth.

Edward took Emma away to Westminster when the court left and Godescalc was left behind digging holes in the ground. Edward was angry and he brought the forces of Europe against Baldwin. He called upon the man he spoke of as his brother, the German Emperor of the Holy Romans, and he ordered the Pope with the Emperor's help to excommunicate Baldwin and he, the Pope, did and Baldwin rather than burn in hell acquiesced and the pirates were given to Edward, but Sven and Osgot Clapa fled with the pirates' ships to the Daneland.

Emma didn't care about any of it. She sat alone in the dark cell. The

Queen Edith came to comfort her and Emma turned her chair about so that her back was to the woman.

"You must see the folly if you persist, Madam," Edith said, but Emma kept her back to her. "Jesus forgives all. Confess your carnal sins and give yourself up to chaste ways. It is the joy of the virgin mother."

Emma turned about and spat at the woman's feet.

Edith pushed back her dark hair and tried to get Emma to look directly at her, but Emma avoided that.

"Go away, you barren traitor," Emma said.

But the Queen sat and Emma sat and finally Emma called for a basin and she urinated in it and that didn't make Edith leave so Emma took the basin and dumped it over into Edith's lap and though the Queen got up and started out, even on parting she kept urging Emma to repent.

And the hot summer sun baked the grass along the Thames and Emma looked out at it and wondered why her child had not been expelled from her womb. And Emma sat in the court and listened. The Godwins, because Sven had bedded the nun and the King's mother, were losing power, but the more they lost the more Robin gained and she disliked him more than she did all of the Godwins together.

The court readied to go to York for Michaelmas.

"What do we do with my mother?" the King asked.

"She is having no baby," Harold said. "She is over her time."

"Of course, she is having no baby," Gytha said. "She is far too old."

Piss on Harold, Emma thought. "I am having your brother's child!" she yelled at him.

"I have sent for a physician from Syracuse to examine her," Harold told the King.

And Emma yelled, "NO!"

But the King said, "Yes."

And the little Greek from Syracuse stuck his nose all about her and his fingers and she bit him on the arm once and then he took a willow stick wrapped in wool and dipped it into blood from a pregnant sheep and smeared it between her legs and into her vagina and told the King that there was a devil inside.

The Bishop of Londun was sent for. She was fettered to the stone floor and exorcised, but the swelling didn't go away and the Bishop of Londun lost favor because of it and the Godwins gained.

"I have it from a spy in the bishop's house," Harold told the King, "that Robin has had sodomous relations with your nephew Ralph of Mantes."

Emma smiled and rubbed her belly. Nothing like a good fight.

The Queen came and tried to speak with her again, but Emma held her hands over her ears and wouldn't listen and Edith gave up and went away.

The Bishop of Londun swore before Edward that he had no sexual relationship with Ralph the Timid. The spy testified against him and her chinless grandson Ralph of Mantes didn't even seem to comprehend what the charge was about and the court traveled to York and the Bishop of Londun was left behind angry and in disgrace. Emma was forced to ride a horse and was in deadly fear of having a miscarriage.

She arrived in York, sick, exhausted and angry. She began to fear for she was so long past her time.

Michaelmas was the time of magistrates and greasy goose. One of the magistrates told of a case brought before him of a youth of the house of Graystock. "The youth was riding near the rye upon a warm day when from the rye, rippling like a sea, there arose a little red man and as the youth watched the little red man grew bigger and bigger." The magistrate stuffed his mouth with goose, as Emma watched the feasting from a corner of the hall.

"Go on," someone urged.

"Well, the apparition came up to him and took his bridle and led him into the rye, where many beautiful maidens sat, and one of them, the most beautiful among them, ordered he be taken from his horse and they did and tore at his skin and flesh and then the lady ordered he be flayed alive, but instead she cut open his skull and took out his brain and left his skull empty. He was put back on his horse and driven from the rye field."

"What happened to him?"

"He came to me a raving madman, begging me to rid him of the little red man who kept pursuing him. But no one ever saw the little man nor the maidens and he sailed for Brittany in search of saints."

Another magistrate told of a similar case and the King and Queen sat amid them and ate goose. Emma left the hall.

She wandered about York, which was a vile town of a thousand wooden houses and vile-smelling Scots and wild Norsemen and where the streets ran with urine and slop and the children crawled with lice and sores and she asked a child where she might find a Jew. And the boy, no more than six, whose blond hair was so filthy it looked gray, pointed to a house midway down a narrow alley.

The Jew had a great beard and wore a high cap and grated his teeth as he bit his fingernails.

"How much do you wish to borrow?" he asked.

"I wish to borrow nothing," she said. "I seek potions to bring my baby out."

"You're too old—"

"I am with child," Emma told him.

"I am a usurer, not a witch. You want Jochim Jochim, the physic. Go to the end of the mews and ring the bell."

She rang the bell. "I am Jochim Jochim. I do not treat gentiles." He slammed the door shut.

She rang again. "I am the mother of the King."

"I do not treat the mother of the King." And again he slammed the door.

"I shall," she yelled through the door, "see that the King orders all the Jews in York slaughtered."

He opened the door. "What is your complaint?"

"I am with child."

He examined her and felt her and looked in her mouth as if he could see all the way down to her womb.

"You are not with child," he said.

"I am."

"You have hysteria," he said. "I saw it once in an old lady at Marntz. The baby is in your head and it's made your belly swell."

"That is nonsense. Give me a potion."

"I can give nothing to help. Forget the baby. It will go away."

"Give me a potion," she said, "or I will see all the Jews in York are dead by morning."

He gave her a potion and it tasted evil and made her vomit. Sick as she felt, she put on a cloak and went to the hall and Tostig Godwinsson was pleading that his brother Sven be allowed to return to England and Edith, too, urged the King to let Sven be welcomed home.

"How say you, Harold?" Edward asked.

"I say it is the King's decision," Harold responded.

"You are horrid," Gytha said.

And they waited and the King decided that Sven should be allowed to come home and plead his own case and Emma was getting sick again and she went up and vomited in Edith's lap.

Emma lay in the bed ill, hoping to God she would either die or expel the baby. The witch came in without knocking. She held a knife in her hand. Her gown was a flowered silk that was frayed and at the waist torn and also at a seam and it was stained but a dress that a great lady would have worn once at a king's feast and Emma didn't look at the woman, only the dress, which fascinated her.

"I came to kill you," the witch said, "but I have changed my mind for you are a hag and have an enormous belly and men would look at you and spit if you didn't make them vomit to see your breasts like empty sacks and your skin like dried figs."

Emma looked up at the witch. Her hair was like the nest of a martlet and her face was creased with filth. She stank and her teeth were black particles. "You are the ugliest being I have ever seen," Emma told her.

"Look in the silvered glass," the hag said, "and you shall see worse. I came to kill you, but far greater the pain to let you live and foul the world with your vile ugliness and let all who look upon you scorn you." She set the knife in the middle of the floor and went to the door. "Elgiva gives you a death worse than death."

Emma hadn't even known it was her.

The sickness went away, but her belly stayed and the baby stayed within it.

Sven Godwinsson came with safe conduct assured; he knelt before the King and said, his face as honest as if he were telling the truth, "I did not have carnal knowledge of the Lady, Queen Emma."

"Liar!" Emma yelled out.

"I beg to come home." Sven spoke penitently.

"Liar!"

"I beg my lands be restored."

His lands had been carved upon between his brother Harold and his cousin Beorn.

"It must be given proper consideration," Harold said.

"No consideration is necessary," Beorn announced. "The answer is no. He can't have anything back."

"Liar!" Emma yelled at Sven.

"No!" Beorn was firm.

Edward arose. "We will put it before the Witangemot at Christmas."

"Liar!"

Sven never looked in her direction.

"You must do something about your mother," Edith said and looked kindly. Bah! Emma knew it was all pretense.

"She is quite mad," Gytha said.

That night Godescalc came to her room.

"I will take you to Winchester," he said.

"Yes," she told him. "I will have the baby at Winchester. My people . . . awake my people and we will go now."

"We'll get your people later," he said and she looked into the deep eyes. "I'll take care of you."

"Yes," she said.

They began the long ride from York and he talked of the treasure at Winchester and she told him there was no treasure.

"There must be. All that great treasury, where did it go?"

"They took it all from me," she said. "Edward took it all." Or was it Harthacnut. So long ago.

"No, it is buried at Winchester," he persisted.

Twice they lost their way and Emma was hungry and they stopped and asked for food from a serf at a hut where a baby was wailing. The serf told them to go away and would give them nothing and Godescalc ran his knife through the serf and they took moldy bread and left the baby crying in the arms of a girl who huddled in a corner in the dirt.

They came to Winchester finally. It was night, but Godescalc did not take her to the Queen's house but a hovel that had little thatch left and had once belonged to a cooper who died of the pox. Emma remembered and did not want to go in.

He looked in her eyes. "It is safer," the voice like a harp said. "They will come for you at the Queen's house. No one will find you here."

The place was cold and she could see little in the dark, but could hear the rats and thought of her prison in the barren hills and wanted to run, but the eyes, even in the darkness, sent her into the hovel and she lay upon the straw and slept.

In the morning she awoke and she was fettered and she screamed out, but Godescalc came and held his hand over her mouth and whispered, "Where is the treasure of Winchester?"

And when he removed his hand, she said, "There is none."

He ripped her gown and twisted her breast until she thought he would twist it off and her scream must have been heard in all of Winchester, but no one came.

"Where is it?" he demanded.

But she could only shake her head.

Sometimes he brought ants and put them all over her and sometimes he would smile and speak softly and give her water or some bread and one time some wine and other times he would hit her or peel back her fingernails with his large hands until she would faint from the pain, but always he would ask, "Where is it?" And then go away to dig and she would be alone. Days folded into one another, but she was never certain and at one hour she touched her belly and realized it was shriveled. There was no baby there. There had never been any child there. She was too weak to yell any more and, even though he no longer put a rag in her mouth, she could only gasp painful breaths and there was no voice. At times when he twisted her breasts until the pain was beyond sensation she could cry nothing and always he asked the same question and his eyes had become so clouded she could hardly find them any longer. Brief lucid moments would come and she knew there were soldiers in the street and she sensed they were looking for her, but could cry nothing but dry breaths.

He came to her in one of those moments when she understood and that was when the pain was the worst and he began pulling pubic hairs as if yanking weeds from a patch of garden. It was at such a time that she thought she saw another figure behind him and then she was certain she did and an ax was raised above his iron hair and she saw it fall and the bleeding head of Godescalc came down between her bare legs and she was moist from the blood. It ran from his open skull, or was she menstruating? The figure, still holding the ax, spoke. He had a raspberry face and tufts of beard and she knew him but couldn't remember who he was. And he spoke and she knew the voice and couldn't answer and the body of

Godescalc was pushed off from her and the head picked up and removed from between her legs and she was carried out by the figure who had dropped the ax and she could still feel Godescalc's blood between her legs and Emma knew she was dying.

She was washed and she even knew she wore a thin clean robe, but she knew little else. Once when she awoke she somehow thought she was in the minster, but she fell away again. Was she dying? She saw the sun just before the rattling began in her chest and she knew for certain life was slipping away. She had heard that sound in others and she did not want to die; more than heaven itself, she ached to live. She fell away again, but before she did she knew a priest had touched her with the holy oils. The ritual of death. God! She did not want to die. Now she sensed she was apart from her body, lucid, and could look down at herself in a white gown. It was a room at the minster and a small cross hung on the wall and Bishop Stigand was there.

And then Edward came.

He hurried, pushing into the room, and he leaned over and called to her, but she wasn't there. And then he began pulling from her and she felt herself, not large and apart any longer, but in her body, and there was a struggle as Edward pulled and drew the pain from her and it was gone, all the pain and anguish and misery and she was weak.

And the King, her son, ugly and deformed, with his white skin and strange eyes, leaned over and kissed her on the mouth and she was not repulsed, but said softly, "There is a God."

And Edward smiled.

Edith, who must have been in the room all the time, came over and took her hand. "The sun is shining," she said.

CHAPTER 9

Glouchester, 1048

BEFORE THE FIRST LACY FLAKE OF SNOW FELL, THOUGH THE AIR WAS BITING cold in the early mornings, an eerie red cloud swept across the land and seventeen oxen died and a nun hanged herself in a bats' cave and a chicken laid a black egg and four deer were seen walking backward across the moors. An earthquake shook all of England and the Abbot of Abingdon arose, as red in the face as the red cloud, and in a voice that shook like another earthquake rolled his eyes and stormed his hands at heaven and proclaimed that an evil walked among them, the evil of an earl who had despoiled a consecrated virgin, and until the evil was removed the wrath of the Lord would be smitten upon them. And the earthquake had split open the brown and worn ground and devoured trees, and seven sheep, and a man who lived upon the tweed. And in the see of Lichfield a church was shaken to rumble. It was reputed that Sven Godwinsson had once stopped there to pray. Godwin doubted Sven had ever stopped anywhere to pray. But the snow came, falling in white heavy pillows that buried the dead brown earth, and the evil in the land passed away as did the Abbot Athelstan of Abingdon. He stood ranting at the heavens one bitter cold morning, his feet bare, when he fell forward and hit his head on an iron crucifix. And the wrath of God fell no further and the court moved to Glouchester for Christmas. The King gave his mother disputed ecclesiastic lands in Sherborne and Selsey and Rochester, which the sees surrendered. To the Bishop of Londun, Edward made a gift of silver mail and twelve white horses and a broad sword with an ivory handle, and for Christmas, Godwin received from the King a vial of holy water from Jerusalem. The winter wind of chance was politic in its shift and Godwin needed no vane to see the direction in which it blew was ill. A cold winter lay ahead.

A miracle. Edith viewed as wondrous the change God had wrought in the Queen Mother. "The joy of God's eternal love."

Godwin, his soft leather shoes wet, his feet cold and aching, stood to the side in the drafty hall at Glouchester, clutching his vial of holy water in a gloved hand and wishing he were at Pevensey by a warm fire. He was sixty years old and at the moment sensing all sixty of those years.

Other gifts were distributed. Gytha was given an ivory comb by the King and Harold a silk cap with a blue feather. Ralph of Mantes was deeded a shire in the Midlands.

"A surprise!" the King announced. "Our beloved mother"—he called her that now—"has prepared a Christmas present for us all, a very special gift."

Mummers dressed in bright gowns came dancing in; one was a tall skinny fellow with a bald top and bushy shocks of carrot hair in clumps on each side of his head. His nose was running in a long string and he flicked it away and announced in a deep voice, "The first Christmas ever. To Bethlehem." The "very special" surprise was Edward's "beloved mother" portraying the Virgin Mary. The tall skinny fellow with the carrot hair became her Joseph and he led her across the hall riding an uncooperative gray ass that balked and brayed and stopped dead in the center of the room and Joseph lugged the pregnant Mary over to the manger of straw piled near the throne. Emma was stuffed to look pregnant and Godwin with pain thought of her accusation against Sven. But the stuffing was tossed aside as she was delivered of the Christ and a young lamb was used as the baby Jesus and the chinless Ralph of Mantes came as the first of the wisemen and presented Emma with a gift of jewels and Edith gave Emma a gold cross and the King set before his mother an ebony-handled dagger and others came with coins and gifts and Godwin realized the same was expected of him, so he gave Emma a vial of holy water from Jerusalem.

The mummers vanished and a Yule log was hauled into the room, trailing wet and snow behind, and warmed wine was served, but Godwin took none and was standing alone at the side of the hall when Emma approached.

"My dearest old friend, my stalwart anchor of our state, I hope God has been your companion," Emma gushed at him.

He was taken aback and said nothing.

"And your treasure of a wife, our gossip and our friend, how is the lovely Countess of Wessex?"

"She is just across the room, Emma. Why don't you ask her?"

"Tut, Godwin. Tut. You must call us Lady Queen. My son, the joy of my existence, insists I be so addressed."

"Gytha is across the room, Lady Queen," he told her. He was nauseated by this new Emma "which God had wrought."

Lamb was served at the meal and Godwin wondered if it were the same lamb of which Emma had been delivered as the virgin mother. Six varieties of fish were also served, while a skald sang the story of St. Edward the Martyr, and the Christmas celebration finally ended and Godwin with Gytha escaped into the blinding snow and Godwin breathed deeply of the cold air, glad to be free of the hall. His lips stung and the snow flurried, so that at times they were barely able to see. His leg was acting up again and the pain shot up into his thigh. He damned the cold and the snow, but at least the court seemed to forget Sven for a while. There appeared no further indication of God's wrath upon the land and perhaps it had been buried beneath the white, cleansing snow.

He turned back to Gytha and spoke in the wind. "God, even God, has forgotten Sven, perhaps."

She caught up to him with effort and clung to his arm, her breath visible as she spoke. "Even in jest, Godwin, that is a horrid thing to say."

It was warm inside and there was a fire. He took off his wet shoes. His foot was swollen. He rubbed fish oil on it and it stank, but it felt less sore and he sat nursing his foot by the warmth of the fire. Gytha went to bed and he sat looking into the flames. It had been a terrible day, a terrible Christmas. There was no doubt: the Godwins were out of favor; the Normans were in command.

The New Year came; the Witangemot gathered and were made welcome by the King and the Queen and by the King's "beloved mother."

"You must be careful," Godwin cautioned his daughter, "or Emma will hold sway over your husband."

"I am happy to see them loved after the years of hate," Edith said. "Emma is my friend."

"Emma is no one's friend."

The King and his Queen and his mother received the earls. Godwin and Gytha were still first, as always, but their reception by Edward was cool; however, Emma was overly florid. Next was Harold, looking sullen, and then came Siward, getting old and without his wife as usual, and behind him was Earl Leofric, whose realm had been extensively diminished by grants to Beorn and Ralph of Mantes. Leofric smelled and was drunk and steadied by Godiva, whose gray hair fell past her waist. She wore a heavy black woolen gown, as she was in mourning for an aunt who had died on the moors beyond Tadcaster. Godiva, in a dolorous voice, told how her aunt had wandered, before the snows came but in the bitter cold, in search of a magic mushroom promised by an anchorite to restore her youth. The aunt had been gored to death by wild goats. Beorn was next after the Earl and Countess of Mercia and Sven was there but not presented, for as yet he had not gotten back his earldom, and the chinless nephew of Edward, Earl Ralph, was last in rank.

The archbishops of York and Canterbury were presented together, lest a fight ensue, as it was wont to do between them. The Bishop of Londun, to Godwin's displeasure, followed third among the clergy.

"He must be nearly fifty," Gytha whispered, "and he hasn't got a gray hair on his head."

His eyes were no less blue, but there was a coldness in them in recent years and hardness. He seldom smiled and found humor in little, but no man had the King's ear, at least at the present, as did Robin of Jumieges. Harold had been a fool to start that business about sodomy and the Earl Ralph. In the end Robin had been vindicated and the King apologized by giving the bishop a large grant of land in Northumbria and Harold found himself less in the King's favor. Harold, he hoped, had learned from the experience. He'd better make certain henceforth that he had the facts when making a charge against one of the Bishop of Londun's influence. Harold sulked in the corner as Robin was kissed on the cheek by the King, who seldom even touched anyone. The Normans were in favor now and Harold was on the outside. Bishop Stigand of Winchester was honored with the fourth position among the churchmen. He was held in great esteem for having saved Emma's life. Yet, Stigand was old and his hands shook. And the other bishops, one upon the other, paraded before their King. Grimcetel of Sussex was dead and Hecca, the new bishop, wore no shoes and walked with a little leap and presented the King with a piece of the thorn which had crowned the Christ. And the King gave the relic to Emma.

"My son spoils me with his generosity and I shall treasure this most among my relics for it came from him who is my pride and was touched by the head of the dying Christ."

Lord, who could believe her?

The abbots acknowledged their King and the thegns and reeves and the hall was crowded and stank of bodies and they sat to eat at long tables and the hall was so filled with tables that there was no room for the skalds and jugglers and mummers and musicians, so they performed on the tables and the guests tried to eat as men stamped in their food with dirty feet and kicked food into their laps and spilled over their wine cups and one mummer tripped over the greasy boiled pig and Godwin was tired and wished he were in his warm bed and out of the crowded stinking hall.

The King wore his heavy crown and after the meal he arose, balancing it on his head, extending his arms in great splendor, the cuffs of his golden gown dripping in a bowl of brown broth, and he spoke in almost a monkish chant. "God is gracious to us, he has given us our mother."

And Emma stood, a bit tipsy from the wine. Her voice was loud. "We thank God, our great protector and his saints, but we thank also the Bishop of Winchester for saving us from the terror of a horrible heathen who entered our head through our eyes and took control of us, and most we thank the King, our gracious Lord and magnanimous son, for the gift of life. Old animosities must be put aside, and grievances forgotten. I beg you all forgive me for any past injustice to your noble persons. I particularly seek and implore the Bishop of Londun for his blessings."

There was no doubt now where Emma stood. She had joined the Normans. God help England if Edward died as suddenly as the shoemaker's son or his half brother. Harold Hardrada would loose an army from Norway, Svegn Estridsson from the Daneland and William from Normandy. Godwin thought he might gag as Emma went over, knelt and kissed the ring of the Bishop of Londun, who graciously blessed her and lifted her to her feet and kissed her gently on the forehead. Emma beamed. Godwin looked at Gytha. There was fire in his wife's eyes.

The "beloved mother" returned to her place and stood beside the King. "I hope God's wisdom shines upon this Witangemot and that its decisions are wise decisions. I hope Earls Beorn and Harold may keep their lands and that you rid this kingdom of any evil within it!"

God! Why hadn't he seen it! This was her game. It was Sven she was after. It was revenge she wanted, pure and simple, and she wanted Sven Godwinsson's head and she was about to get it. Gytha started to get up, as if to speak, but Godwin gently nudged her down and with a nod of his head motioned for her to keep quiet. Damn! Why hadn't he seen it? It was so obvious. Emma had not changed at all, only sides. She had not only gone over to the Normans, but was going to make certain the Godwins were destroyed in the process.

Sven was doomed. The rest of the family would be made to suffer as well. Was Edward really fooled by all that newfound sincerity and love? Emma was as vindictive as ever, perhaps worse, only her tactics had changed. The Witangemot was to meet in the morning. Sven was best to flee tonight . . . but the storm? Godwin looked about for his son, but he was gone. He had been standing near Tostig when the Queen made her pronouncement, but Tostig, too, had vanished.

On their way out of the hall Godwin and Gytha stepped around Odda of Deerhurst, who was vomiting in the doorway. Light from the hall cast a yellow glow out into a thick curtain of falling snow. It came heavy and they tightened their cloaks about them and Godwin took his wife's arm as they moved out into the deep snow.

"Wait!" A voice called.

Godwin turned about. Beorn was trudging through the snow after them.

"Let me help you. You old folks will never make it alone." He was smiling and his breath was visible as he spoke.

"I feel old," Gytha said and gave her arm to him. He took Godwin's arm as well and walked between them.

"It's a regular blizzard," Beorn said and led them back to the little house.

It was warm and light inside. Tostig was by the fire.

"Sven?" Godwin asked.

"He went ahorse toward the sea and his ships. Gryth is off the shore near Bristol."

"Sven was expecting this, then?"

"Yes. 'Emma will find a way to get even,' he told me."

"How will he make it to Bristol in this?" Gytha asked.

"He will make it," Tostig assured her.

It continued to snow during the night and in the morning Godwin and his sons dug themselves out and went to the hall and the gathering of Witangemot. It ruled against Sven and ordered his exile, but Sven was not present and Godwin complained of his bad foot, excused himself and came back to the little house and sat in out of the snow by a bright fire reading from the Book of Job. He was able to read better and better over the years, and faster, but in the last months his eyes had been getting weaker and he read with more difficulty.

"If you get your head any closer to those manuscripts you'll fold up inside," Gytha told him.

He only snorted and continued reading.

Edith entered. She stamped the snow from her soft leather shoes.

"You wanted to see me, Papa?"

"I am concerned for your family and hope you are as well," he said.

Gytha looked at her and not pleasantly. "We are honored," she said sarcastically, "by a visit from her royal person."

"I am concerned as well, Papa," Edith told him, ignoring her mother.

"Your brother Sven!" Gytha spit out the words.

"He sinned mortally against God. He can expect no more than he got. His case—"

"The lady of Leonminster—" Gytha started to interrupt.

"Was a virgin dedicated to God by a vow," Edith broke in.

"She is a woman like any other." Gytha threw up her arms.

"Not all women."

"No, not you and your holy prancing," Gytha said.

"Enough," Godwin said, "but your holy ways are precisely our problem. It is the succession that disturbs me. Sven is less the victim of the King than the victim of his own brothers and his cousin and doesn't concern us for the moment—"

"Sven—"

"Be quiet, Gytha. What I want to know is, why this sudden friendship between the Bishop of Londun and Emma?"

"Edward has asked his mother to love and accept his friends who helped him during his difficult years in Normandy. He said few were good to him then and he owes so much to those who cared and looked out for his benefit."

"That being Robin, I suppose?" Godwin asked.

"Yes, and Emma admits she has treated him most unjustly."

"Emma plays games," Godwin said.

"No," Edith insisted. She took off her headstrap and shook loose the dark auburn hair. It was wet from the snow. "Emma has really changed. She has walked barefoot in the snow as penance for the wrong she has done her children."

"It probably hurt no more than walking on hot coals," Godwin said.

"Did you ask me to come here only that you might have me listen while you vilify the Queen Mother?" Edith asked.

"No. I would like you to tell me who the King's heir is."

"William of Normandy."

"Tell me, Edith, in all your chastity, don't you find that choice immoral and against the nature of God?"

"I see nothing immoral in that he should befriend the son of a man who helped him when no one else in the world cared if Edward was alive. He thinks of William as his son."

"Well, he is not. He is a bastard. He was, my pure and holy daughter, conceived in mortal sin, the worst of carnal desire, out of wedlock, in lust . . . the lust of a man and woman with no commitment to God!"

"STOP IT!" Edith yelled. "Stop it, Papa, please!"

Godwin was sorry he had done that and wanted to reach out and touch her, but he was angry and he did not.

"One of your brothers should be the King's heir," Gytha said.

When the court moved to Londuntown, Godwin and Gytha decided to go to Pevensey. Harold could handle whatever interests they had at court; in fact, even in his diminished stature he held greater sway with Edward than Godwin did at the present.

"Tostig, it would be kind of you if you'd accompany us south," Godwin told his son. "Your mother worries I can't handle the staff on such a trip."

"Edward needs me here," Tostig said.

It was Beorn who decided to make the trip with them. "You are getting too old to travel alone like you do," he said.

"You make me sound dottering. Besides, I have an army of soldiers and servants."

"But that's precisely the problem. You can't manage so large a household. Some of them steal you blind, I've noticed. You need family along to look out for your interests."

Was he getting that old?

Godwin liked the round-faced, big-eyed young man better at times than his own sons. Beorn was respectful and thoughtful. He managed his lands well, controlled his army and, while never one of the King's favorites, he was well enough liked and rewarded by Edward. Beorn was a good young man, so different from his father, and he looked neither like him nor Estrid. He was better to Gytha than any of her own boys and teased her and when she was in a bad mood could make her laugh.

Beorn sat a huge chestnut mare and ordered the train about as they readied to depart. The snow swept across before them in drifts and carts and sleds and pack horses and mounted riders readied to leave Glouchester. They would spend the night in Guildford and journey to Pevensey the following day.

The riders moved and Godwin covered his face and as the train moved slowly to the east Godwin's thoughts were on his children. The family was drifting apart. They were so different, all of them. Edith had taken sides with the Normans. Harold would look out for Wessex and the Godwin interests and he was a good enough manager, as good as Beorn, but he cared less for people and was moody and he irritated Godwin frequently. Godwin wondered if Harold had spies in Godwin's own household as he had in every other house in England . . . and as for Sven. He was a loss.

They forded a frozen river, the horses plunging through the ice. The son of a Wendish slave woman was carried away by the current through the broken ice and Beorn rode after the child and handed the wet screaming babe to his mother.

"He'd been better off dead than a slave," the mother said.

Beorn was soaking wet and Gytha ordered him to change into dry clothing, but he scoffed and said he would be fine until they reached Guildford.

They rode and Godwin continued thinking of his children. Tostig was selfish and irresponsible and would rather hawk with the King than work. Gryth was hardly ever on dry land, big lumbering Gryth with hands as large as pots. He loved the sea and was born too late, perhaps. He should have been a Viking adventurer with Rolf or Sven the Forkbeard. Godwin suspected at times he was a pirate, but as long as he didn't disturb the English ports and confined his activities to the continent Godwin didn't examine Gryth's whereabouts too closely. Leofwine preferred the Daneland and stayed with his cousin the King at Roeskild. He was twenty years old and Godwin hadn't seen him since he was seventeen. And then there was Wufnoth. Poor Wufnoth, who would never walk nor talk straight. He was born a cripple and Godwin worried about what was to become of him after he and Gytha died. His brothers ignored him, though Edith looked after him. He must talk to Edith when they were on better terms about Wufnoth.

The wind howled and the snow blew and an old servant named Nestria, who tended the goats and watched Gytha's gray dog, died and they carried her body back to Pevensey to bury her and three young slaves ran off and Beorn's soldiers captured them and Beorn had them whipped, despite the snow and cold.

They spent the night in Guildford and it was clear and a ring was seen about the moon and one of the goat tenders claimed to have seen Nestria walking in the night. It snowed again the next day and they plowed through the drifts toward the east and the sea.

When they reached Pevensey they were cold and tired and Sven was waiting and Godwin was not surprised. He had five ships offshore and Gryth was with him. Gryth was the biggest of Godwin's children. At twenty-three he towered over his father. He was clumsy as a lummox and Godwin wondered what kind of sailor he could be, continually falling over himself. Sven smiled, as only Sven could smile, and charmed his mother and she was happy to see him, but when she went to bed Sven began to curse Beorn and demanded that he return his stolen lands.

"Enough," Godwin said. "It is not Beorn's doing. You can't go about raping nuns and the King's mother and not expect to rile the Church and Edward."

"I didn't rape either of them."

"I'm certain you didn't," Gryth told him. "It's Emma's doing. All the old whore's doing." Gryth had obviously been listening to Sven.

"Next you'll be denying you even laid with the Queen Mother," Godwin said.

"Do you really think I'd stick it to that old hag?"

"I believe you'd lay with a shepherd's favorite ewe, even if it was poxed, if you were in the mood."

Sven threw up his arms and then he smiled again and went over to Beorn. "I'm sorry, Cousin. I really am. I know it isn't your fault." Sven could be so damn charming when he wanted to be. He gave Beorn that I've-been-a-bad-little-boy look and Beorn smiled but still looked a little wary of his repenting cousin. Sven tossed his arms over the round-faced young man's shoulders and Beorn stiffened perceptively.

"Come, Beorn," Godwin urged. "Forgive him. You've got the lands, you can afford to be generous."

Beorn smiled and took Sven's hand, but Godwin sensed there was still a distance there.

They ate. Godwin drank his goat's milk and felt ready to join Gytha in retiring for the night. The three young men sat about drinking wine and filling each other's cups until they were all quite drunk.

"We've got to sail," Sven said and stood up and wobbled.

"Perhaps you should wait until morning," Godwin suggested.

"Too dangerous. Got to sail tonight." He sat down again.

"There's nowhere like the sea, Beorn," Gryth said and he was quite drunk also. "Remember once when I tried to shove you out of the little boat that Harold had built."

"I saved you," Sven said. And it was true. Sven always looked out more for Beorn when they were little than he did his own brothers. "I got to sail. Come on, Beorn, I'll show you the fleet, my sleek thirty-rower most all."

Beorn hesitated.

"Go ahead, Beorn," Godwin told him. "See them off and I'll wait here by the fire until you come back."

The young men left and Godwin sat by the fire. His foot was better, but he was getting old and his body was falling apart. Tomorrow it would be his neck or back or the other foot that ached. Every man should have a second chance, a second life, but Godwin couldn't think of what he would do different. He put another small log on the fire and it raised the embers. "Fire comes from the sun," Edith had told him once.

"Where are the boys?"

He looked up to see Gytha. "They aren't boys, they are men, and Beorn went down to see Sven's ships."

"You're too hard on Sven, Godwin."

He grunted.

"You should go to bed," she said.

"I will when Beorn comes back. I'll just wait here so that I know Sven and Gryth are safely to sea."

"He's a good lad, Beorn."

"Yes," he agreed. "I'll seek his help in protecting Svegn Estridsson's claim to be Edward's successor. I suspect he will be wanting to travel tomorrow."

She kissed him on the cheek. "I dreamt of Behi the other night. He had picked one of Wufnoth's flowers for me and the boy became so angry he killed him."

"Poor Wufnoth. I doubt he would ever kill anyone."

She touched his hand and left. One thing he would never want to change in a second life would be wives. Even now he felt lust for Gytha. He couldn't understand men like his son, Sven, who could stick a penis in a wet hunk of bread and find satisfaction. In all the many years of their marriage, he not only had never touched another woman, not even a slave, but never remembered having any desire to.

Godwin dozed and he jolted upright, aware he had slept for some time. The fire had died and it was cold in the room. There was no indication Beorn had returned and Godwin felt strangely apprehensive, and yet the young man had only gone down to the sea with his cousins. He tossed on his cloak and walked out to the gate. "Has Lord Beorn returned?" he asked the guard.

"No, my Lord. He went down to the sea with Earl Sven and his brother and he hasn't come back yet."

"Fetch me a warmer cloak, a fur," he said, "and rouse a guardsman to go with me. I will go down to the water."

Godwin wrapped the fur tightly about his shoulders and walked in the direction of the cold sea. A guardsman, a young man, followed him through the snow. The sea was black and empty and Godwin got the horrible sinking feeling that he had sent Beorn to his death. There was no evidence, only the knowledge in his heart that Sven had killed his cousin.

Twelve days later Beorn's body was found buried in a deep grave up the coast at Dartmouth.

Godwin stood before the King. He was the first. He held his gauntlet and dropped it on the floor before the King. "I declare Sven Godwinsson *Nithling*," he said, and his son was no more. And they came, Harold, and then one by one every noble and cleric and reeve and soldier of the land and spoke the word. *Nithling*—Sven Godwinsson ceased to exist.

Godwin sat in the room alone with Harold afterward.

"You drink too much wine," Godwin said.

His son ignored the remark. "I am having the body brought to Winchester to be laid beside Cnute's."

"I killed him," Godwin said.

"After all, the King was his uncle."

"I killed him."

"Will you be quiet!" Harold yelled.

Godwin stood up. "I am Lord Wessex."

"You are an old man, Papa, and if I waited for you to do anything it would never get done. Somebody has to take charge. The family is fading. We are at low tide, thanks to Sven. It is because of him and only because of him that Emma works against us. Now he has committed this greater crime. Your son—"

"He is not my son."

Harold turned the wine cup at his lips again. "Do you know that the King has chosen the Duke of Normandy as his heir?"

"Of course."

"Well, I'm surprised. Credit it to you for keeping abreast of events. Did you know also that the little poop of a duke is infatuated with the runny-nose brat of Baldwin's . . . what's her name?"

"Matilda. Yes, I knew."

"I have sent three nuns to instruct Matilda in the horrors of bastardy. Consequently she continually refuses his advances and her father has been bought with certain trade provisions—"

"Your weaving venture in Flanders."

"Yes. I back a merchant who imports fine Flemish weavings. Still, William persists in the romance. For the life of me I can't understand how any man can have such an infatuation for a maid."

Godwin thought of the young, freckled girl at Jomburg.

"I plan to meet William in East Anglia and I will have the maid there and see what kind of bargain can be struck."

"It's a ridiculous and preposterous scheme," Godwin said. "Far-fetched."

"I don't see you doing anything," Harold told him.

The weather was horrid. The worst winter in years and the frozen air bit at Godwin's face and the wind blew through his cloak as if he were wearing none. The body in all the cold was brought from Dartmouth. Estrid came from Roeskild and would speak to neither Gytha nor Godwin, but kissed Emma on the cheek.

Estrid looked old and haggard and her eyes were red from crying. She no longer had herself called Duchess of Normandy, but had them announce her as Queen Dowager of the Daneland. Her son had married the granddaughter of Hakon, and Estrid raved about her daughter-in-law's kindness in front of the Godwins, but did not speak directly to either of them. She ignored Queen Edith, along with the rest of the family.

They stood in the cold minster as Beorn was laid in a tomb beside that of his King uncle.

"Did you know, Godwin," Emma asked, "that our cousin of Normandy, William, has abducted the Count of Flanders' daughter and married her in Rouen?"

CHAPTER 10

Westminster, 1050

STONEWORKERS HACKED AND CUT, CHISELED AND THE NEW ABBEY BEGAN TO rise and in the old hall Edward sat. Eadsige, the Archbishop of Canterbury, had died, and as usual, Harold was trying to tell him what to do.

"You shan't," Harold said.

"Oh, but I shall, my Lord of Anglia. I shall."

A workman outside yelled and another hollered back.

"There is a limit to how much of these Normans your subjects will endure."

"Harold, there is a limit to how much of you I will endure."

Edward went out and with pleasure watched them haul the stones and raise each up and the hods of mortar and the masons set the stones in place.

Father Grunght, a gift from the emperor, was a mason's bastard and he supervised the building. "It is well going, spacious Graciousness," he called down from his perch. "Well going." He talked strange, but he was a fine architect.

And Edward moved out of the sun and went into the old church. The Queen was not there yet, and Edward knelt against the edge of a broken stone which was particularly uncomfortable, but of course a penitent choice. A painting of St. Edward the Martyr climbing out of his grave hung over the altar. Edward watched a mouse chewing a large nut in the corner. Edward stuck his tongue out and said, "Boo," and the mouse left the nut and ran away. A monk scurried and lit tapers. A door banged and Edward turned, expecting to see his lady, the Queen. It was his sister.

"You came," he said, delighted to see her. "You came."

"I came, but I will not talk to her."

"I don't ask you to talk to her. I just ask you not to kill her." He stood up. "It is important for Robin that all is at peace."

"I will obey your request," Godgifu said. She was forty-two, but had not the slightest wrinkle. "Your eyes are bad."

"They've been sore again," he told her. "And Eustace?"

"With me. He came with me. She will try and kill me."

"No." He looked at her. "She loves you like a mother."

"A mother snake."

"She has great remorse for the past."

"Could I believe the hag of Normandy had remorse for anything?"

Edith came into the church. She was naked except for an open robe, which she threw off on entering. "I am sorry I am late, Edward. My brother Harold detained me."

Edward didn't look at Edith and spoke to Godgifu. "Harold is more important than the King."

Edith, if she noticed the affront, pretended not to. "He told me of your intent to make Robin the Archbishop of Canterbury."

"Yes, Godgifu and Eustace have come for the investiture and hopefully—"

"It is wrong—"

"The King does no wrong!" Edward suspected they could hear him well up where stones were being raised in the new abbey. "Do you interrupt your King?"

"No, my Lord." Edith spoke softly and looked at the floor.

"Hopefully the Duke of Normandy and his bride will join us at Canterbury for the celebration. We'll have a small private feast after the public gathering." Edward turned upon Edith suddenly. "What do you mean it is wrong?"

"He is Norman, my Lord. Robin is Norman."

"Of course he is Norman. Do I need you to tell me that? And what is wrong with being Norman? My mother is Norman. Should I banish my mother, throw her out of England because she is Norman? You irritate me, Queen. More and more you are becoming party to the affairs of your brothers and your father and less and less to those of your King and husband. You berate me for naming my kin, William, as my heir—"

"He is a child born of sin."

"A child of love, Edith. I stood on the parapet outside the room in which Robert and Herleve lay upon the night that baby was conceived."

Godgifu came over to him. "I never knew that, Edward."

"Yes. His mother, William's mother, is a woman of great love, who loves God and now serves him at Bec."

"He was born of lust," Edith said and knelt down on the hard stones.

"The Bishop of Londun is named to the Archdiocese of Canterbury. William remains my heir designate and there is not a thing you or your meddling family is going to do about it." He motioned for Godgifu to precede him from the church and left Edith kneeling, naked, on the stone.

Edward's blue and yellow banner of martlets and the cross unfurled before them and the court made its way toward Canterbury. Harold had been instructed to remain at Westminster.

Just beyond Rochester the strangest sight Edward had ever seen stretched along the ridge of a hill. It looked, but could not be, like a painting from the Holy Land as riders on camels stood in a silhouette against the sky.

"What? What? Look at that!" voices yelled out. "See." Someone pointed and many got down off their horses and stood looking and Edward knew it was not some holy vision that he alone was witnessing.

"Send a soldier, send four soldiers over to see what in God's name these camels are doing in our realm!"

Four riders were dispatched and when they returned a Moorish-dressed man riding a bounding camel followed. "He claims to know you, my Lord," one of the four soldiers said.

The camel smelled horrid and had large calluses on its legs and chest and it stood taller than any of the men about and it had one large hump on which sat a man of middle age who looked nothing like the ancient Magi in the painting at Glouchester. Edward certainly didn't recognize the man, but though his skin was tanned, he didn't look a bit Moorish and was far too fair. The camel made a honking noise and curious servants and slaves fled and Edward's soldiers, also, gave the animal distance. The man in the Moorish garb nudged the humped animal with his legs and the camel fell to its front, callused knees and then its back legs folded down and the man sank to the ground and got off and came before Edward and knelt on the ground.

"My Lord," he said and looked up into Edward's face and still there was nothing familiar-looking about him.

"I don't know you," Edward told him.

The man stood up. He was tall. "You gave me life, my Lord. I am the one who in his boyhood was called Seven."

"My old friend—"

"And servant—"

"The boy who fell through the roof at Corfe."

"Yes, and who you gave life and straight bones, my Lord. And now you are, as you said always you would be, the King of England."

Edward got down off his horse and looked into the eyes of the man in amazement. "But you? What of you?"

"I am a merchant of the desert, my Lord. These camels come bearing gifts for you, who gave me life—fine cloth and spices and jewels of the ancients and books of secrets from the East and sturdy slaves and perfumes and the camels themselves."

"Seeing you again is gift enough," Edward told him. "I looked for you and learned you had been sold to a miller of Bec, but though we tortured the miller, he swore he knew nothing of you."

"It was the miller of Conches, not Bec, but he beat me and sold me to a butcher in Tincherbrai who killed dogs and sold the meat as ox and lived in a house full of flies and he accused me of having raped his wife, who was as ugly as a dead oyster and had only one eye, and when he came at me with a huge ax I threw a knife at him and killed him. And his wife, with the one eye, traded me to the steward of Mortain for two bags of corn and the steward kept me locked in a cupboard at night for fear I would run off, but once when he got drunk he forgot about putting me away for the night and I fled and was on my way to look for you when I was attacked by highwaymen and they tied me and taught me how to steal and then gave me to a Venetian moneylender for some red velvet cloth and he showed me how to cheat a man out of everything he owns and I finally cheated the moneylender and was ready to return to Normandy in a fine ship and a great wealth aboard when we were set upon at sea by Moorish pirates. I was taken to the desert and taught to milk camels and learned to live without wine, and sometimes with little food, but all the moneylender had taught me stood me well and soon I owned much of the desert caravan traffic and sold and bought many camels and goods and I have been to Bagdad and seen the Bosporus and knelt in Jerusalem, but now I come back a wealthy man to serve you, my Lord."

He had gathered a crowd as he had told his tale and they posed questions and asked about the wonders of the world. Only Edith sat silent on her horse.

"Are you a Christian?" Robin asked. "Are you still a Christian, Seven?"

"Most of the time," he said. "But there are times when it is better to be something else."

They talked for three hours and had a feast there in the open field near Rochester and then Seven continued on toward Westminster with his caravan and gifts and Edward's court moved again toward Canterbury. As they neared Thegn Waglork's manor not far from Canterbury two women at the manorial oven fought over a loaf of bread. Edward sliced the air and the loaf in two with his jeweled sword, nearly snipping off the women's fingers. "The wisdom of Solomon," he said.

There was the great service at Christ's Church and then a public feast, but after Edward and Robin's select guests assembled at the archbishop's palace. Robin planned a new palace of stone which would have eighty-seven chambers, four privies, five chapels, a grand hall and a tapestry the length of twenty-six men. For the present they gathered in a private room in the old, timbered house.

"Welcome to my home," Robin said. Robin, who a few years earlier had not a gray hair on his head, now had snow-white hair.

"I promised it to you once," Edward said and smiled.

"Yes, Edward, and I will call you that again, just for this day, my day. But you promised it to me in jest."

"Perhaps," Edward said. "Perhaps."

It was a quiet family meal with the friends of the archbishop and no one else invited. Edward wore an enormously long-trained gown of white, with huge red flowers embroidered down the front, and four lace capes, one upon the other, and a chain of bronze and a heavy Celtic cross while the Queen wore a plain blue gown and a sullen expression. The Duke and Duchess of Normandy were dressed simply. The King and Queen of France came and the Count and Countess of Boulogne and the dowager queens of England and the Daneland, both getting older, grayer and fatter. None of the Godwins were invited. Emma and Godgifu did not speak, but they did not attack one another either. Anne, the Queen of France, the daughter of Jaroslav, King of all the Russians, blew her nose on the cowche covering the table, said she was sorry, but it was better than dripping in the food and told tales of Kiev and a dwarf at her father's court who could throw a knife fifty lengths and hit a man a fingernail above the nose, right between the eyes. She held up a sheep's gonad, cooked in prunes, and said, "What the hell is this?" And they all laughed and she slipped it down her throat and they told her and she pretended to gag and quickly swallowed finch eggs and a goblet of wine.

Estrid tactfully spoke of no unkindness of the Duke of Normandy's father and related the story of a mad swan on the Seine who used to attack virgins in Rouen and William said there were no virgins in Rouen for all women there were ruined and Emma threw a piece of tripe across the table at him and he ducked and it hit a painting of the Annunciation behind him. Edward picked at the pike and sturgeon and salmon and plaice and nibbled at the trout and laughed and Emma, waving a lobster shell in the air, told a story of when she and her brothers, then but children, were playing near old Rolf's tower when a man with a big nose and a little beard tried to rape her and how her brother Robert, the late Archbishop of Rouen, had beat the man to death with large rocks which he pounded at the man's head as he clawed at Emma and Emma complimented Robin on the doe cooked in cherries and held a dainty morsel of snipe on her fingers which she licked across her tongue. Edward dug his dagger into the quinced pasty of drake and dug crab meat from a shell. They all "ooohh'd" as the peacock was carried in, its feathers fanning out on the platter, but one of the pickled pears surrounding it fell off in Emma's lap and she tossed it in the air and Anne the Queen of France farted and excused herself and said that it must be the English air. The Archbishop of Canterbury told of a snake that bit the Abbot of St. Ouen on the butt and how it, his butt that is, swelled and how he sat, the abbot that was, on a sharp rock and the poison seeped out and it made him well again. Woodcock was served buried under figs and chopped eel and horse's liver. Anne of France tipped over her wine and blotted it with her napkin and swore in Russian and they all laughed and Henry of France told of finding his mother's grave in the south of Poitiers. He began to cry and Anne said, "There, there." And Emma said, "I knew her. I knew Bertha. A veritable saint, she was." "Indeed," the Dowager Queen of the Daneland agreed. A dessert of jellied sturgeon eggs was served with a horse's curd and dates. The young Duke of Normandy told of how his grandmother's scratching in the next room at Rennes had awakened him just before someone crawled in and tried to kill him and he screamed and Walter came and took him to a peasant's house. Matilda whirled the leg of a braised stork in the air and said she was damn glad they hadn't. She wiped her mouth with a piece of trencher.

"Is she still living? Is Judith still alive?" Emma asked.

"At Rouen now," the duke said. "She is seventy-two."

"And scratching," Emma added.

"And scratching," he laughed.

"Walter?" the King asked. "Is Walter still with you?"

"Yes," William said, "and old Osbern. But Sassy died, as you know. After he came back from your court he seemed lonely and one day he was alone, all alone, and he fell over and his head was so large. And you know he could never lie down, well, there he was lying down alone on the floor and it killed him."

"Perhaps he lay down deliberately," Godgifu suggested.

"Perhaps," William said.

"I am certain not," Edward said.

They told stories of the past, but Edith told nothing and sat quietly eating a placid piece of plaice. Count Eustace drank too much and swore too much and fell off his chair and Emma said he was a bore and Godgifu took out her knife, but Edward raised his arms and Emma shut up and the knife disappeared. After dinner an old skald by the name of Gamol, who had once belonged to Queen Emma, sang of the romance of Havelok.

"That is my mother's favorite story," Edith said.

"Your mother always was an incurable romantic," Emma said.

Edith excused herself and left the room.

"What is wrong with the Queen?" Emma asked.

"She is a Godwin," Robin answered snidely.

"What's a Godwin?" Anne of France wanted to know.

"A disease that makes you a glutton for power," Edward said and he was serious when he spoke.

Later in the Queen's chamber Edward stormed at Edith and called her names and accused her of spoiling Robin's dinner.

"You insulted my father," Edith said. "You appointed a bishop in Wessex—"

"Not just any bishop. Canterbury," he yelled.

"Without consulting him and you ate a meal in his earldom without inviting him to sup."

"I appoint who I wish and eat where l will!"

Edward stormed off to his chambers. He ran into a drunken Eustace, who said he was looking for his horse.

It was only the next morning that Edward learned that his brother-in-law, wearing mail and with forty-two of his men, had ridden into Dover. They demanded wine at a freeholder's house and were refused. The freedman was killed and by morning twenty of Dover and nineteen from Boulogne were dead. Eustace and his wounded men returned to Canterbury.

Edward ordered Godwin to appear from Pevensey.

"I want the Burgess of Dover punished," Edward yelled at the Earl of Wessex.

"Let the magistrates of Dover be assembled before the Witan. Let them defend themselves in the English custom of law and justice. If they are found guilty, let them be so punished as the Witan deem. If they are found free of this charge let them go in peace but—"

"I am the King! They will be punished," Edward declared.

"No, my Lord," Godwin said.

"Do you stand against your king?"

"I stand against injustice," Godwin said and left.

Edward was in a rage. The Godwins had been building for this, amassing wealth and power. Well, as Robin so often cautioned him, the Godwins had to be stopped. He called for the Archbishop of Canterbury.

"What do I do, your Grace of Canterbury?"

"Call a Witangemot away from Wessex and have the murderer of your brother Alfred called before it, and let the murderer and his sons be exiled and their lands confiscated."

The Witangemot was held at Glouchester.

Godwin came with an army. Harold came with an army. Outside Glouchester, Sven, the *Nithling*, was said to hold another army as well, and his brother Gryth lay at Bristol with ships, but the Witangemot was not intimidated and the armies of the King, of Leofric, of Siward, of Ralph, of the archbishops and the bishops lay in ready.

"Call the Lord of Wessex to stand before his peers," a herald cried out.

Godwin stood in the charter house at Glouchester. Harold, Gryth and Tostig were at his side.

"Tostig, my friend," Edward asked, "do you stand with these traitors?"

"I stand with my father and the justice of England."

The Archbishop of Canterbury read the indictment. "Godwin, Earl of Wessex, you are charged with sedition and corruption of the King's peace. You are his man and have denied your liege Lord. His vassal, you were ordered to bear upon the Burgess of Dover for wrongdoing against the kin of our anointed sovereign and you denied the King's right to adjudicate and to bring punishment to the guilty. A kingdom where wanton disobedience of its people is allowed is a kingdom without order."

"And a kingdom without justice is no kingdom at all," Godwin said.

Robin ignored him. "You are further charged with an act of treason in that you did willfully encourage your son Tostig to wed the daughter of Flanders, who bears allegiance to another monarch—"

"The King encouraged that marriage," Godwin said.

"The King granted no approval to those nuptials. Your wife, the Countess, is charged with slander against the King's Lady, the Mother Queen, Emma. You and your son Harold, the Earl of East Anglia, are further accused of encouraging simony and interfering in matters ecclesiastic and of selling benefices and bishoprics against the papal directives of Leo, the Holiness of Rome—"

Godwin interrupted again. "The King who has sold more bishoprics than a fishmonger at a fair accuses me thus?"

"The King is not on trial here."

"On the other hand, he sometimes gives them to incompetents."

Robin ignored him and continued unabated. "You are also accused of usurping the authority of the King and showing yourself not subservient to our precious sovereign, but plotting to overthrow his rule in consort with your nephew, the self-acclaimed King of the Danes. . . . You have heard the charges. So do you answer?"

"I have investigated the incident at Dover, the results of that inquiry are contained here, written. You will find me vindicated in the name of seeking justice for the citizens of West Saxony. To the other charges, they are so asinine that I will not belittle myself to answer."

"Lock them in the antechamber," Robin ordered. "We will deliberate upon such evidence as is presented."

Edward said nothing.

The Godwins were escorted out.

The deliberation was tedious. Edward was bored and he paid little attention. He wanted to get back to Westminster and the work on the abbey. They haggled. They argued. They called each other names. The bishops of Wessex, all except for Canterbury, opposed any guilty verdict.

"He is guilty," Edward finally said.

The Witangemot agreed.

"Bring in Godwin, Earl of Wessex!" the herald called out.

The Godwin men did not appear. Instead the Queen, Edith, stood at the door. She held keys in her hand. "They are no longer here."

"Take her to a nunnery and have her locked away." Edward was furious. "Her lands, as all lands of the Godwins, are to become property of the crown."

A gray wolf came up and stood beside her at the door.

CHAPTER 11

England, 1052

THE ABBEY AT WILTON WAS NOT THE PRISON EMMA HAD BEEN LOCKED away in off in barren hills. It spread on a rise beside the river Wye in the See of Hereford. Stone, it wandered pleasantly on the opposite shore above the banks of the thawing stream. Bits of ice floated and were trapped by fallen branches or clusters of rock. Winter birds made noise in branches of sparse trees. On northerly slopes a few patches of snow, hard and cemented to the earth, were reminders that the dead season was not ended. Yet, in the warmth of the sun there was a hint that spring was waiting.

The horses clomped over the bridge. The riders were mostly strangers to her, young women and young soldiers. The familiar women of Emma's house, her spies and companions, had mostly died or were too dottering to go about any longer. Beatrice had coughed herself to death in 1050 and Lady Ethna had fallen in a tub of goat's milk and drowned. Only her falconer, old Wordig, who she had finally found, still rode with her. The Bishop of Devon had gotten word to her. Wordig was sharing a cave with four chickens and a tamed rabbit in Cornwall. Close at her side, he muttered constantly, and she paid little attention.

A nun, her head on crooked, stiff-necked, shuffled obliquely down a corridor. "Here," she said and pointed to a door.

Edith was naked, kneeling in prayer. Her deep auburn hair fell loose over her bare shoulders and strands dipped down over her breasts. The cell was light and pleasant and Emma recognized Edith's own bed and chairs from Westminster. Edith should have felt at home here, for as a child she had been sent to Wilton to learn weaving and stitchery and other accomplishments expected of a daughter of an earl.

"Would you?" Emma asked and pointed at her nudity.

Edith put on a plain black robe and shook and straightened her hair.

"Why have you come?" Edith asked.

"To try and help you as you helped me," Emma told her.

"I will not denounce my father or my brother."

"I have convinced Edward that such should not be necessary. All he asks is that you accept his choice of successor and so announce to the court."

"I could never. To do so would condone adultery, to say I saw no sin in wanton carnal pleasure. Lady, it is God I must choose over freedom."

"Edith, you take favors from petitioners who would have the King or your father or brother's ear. Do you not find that slightly immoral?"

Edith appeared more perplexed than offended. "Of course not. I am given gifts by friends who would have me plead their cause. It is a prerogative of being a queen. You did it, I'm certain."

"Yes, but I never professed to sanctity, nor did I do it to the extent to which you managed to carry it, an art, I perceive."

"That is because you were a whore." There was no kindness in Edith's voice.

Emma refused to be insulted. She could hardly deny what she had been.

"Who should succeed the King?" Emma asked. "You will give your husband no heirs."

"Nor is it the King's wish to have carnal knowledge of any woman," Edith said.

"Then who is to succeed?"

Edith simply looked at her.

Emma shook her head. "There is my grandson, Ralph of Mantes, the most inept soldier in England. The Welsh whisper 'boo' and he flies from Hereford all the way to Dover. There is Svegn, the King of the Daneland, Harold Hardrada of the Northland and William, the King's kin and cousin. There is no one else."

"There is Harold Godwinsson."

"What possible claim can the house of Godwin have to the throne?"

"We are a powerful family."

"You, and your would-be-king brother, are the grandchildren of a pigherder."

Edith turned her back on her.

"Edith . . ." Emma pleaded. But her daughter-in-law refused to turn about. "Come to your senses. Dukes die and dukes are born. Agree to the succession and come home to your husband at Westminster. Spring is coming and soon the flowers will be in bloom." But who would tend Wufnoth's garden? The crippled young man was in exile.

Edith made no response.

Emma was led away by the nun with her head on crooked and they rode from Wilton, the women shaking their heads and gossiping and Wordig muttering and Emma reached Winchester sore from the ride.

Still, the next day she decided to go hawking. Edward had sent her a new peregrine and it was brilliant and warm for the fifth of March.

"It's no good about," Wordig told her.

"We'll go to the sea," she said.

"It's a long way to the sea," he said.

"You're just getting old," she told him. "Ready the hawks and none of the gossips to spoil the hunt. Just you and I."

She dressed in a deep green gown and wore a cloak of black wool, which was warm enough without restricting her movements. She drank some wine and stuffed some dry bread into her face.

"You're not going hawking in Lent." Lady Maud was offended.

"I certainly am," she said.

The cloak had a fur trim about the collar and she fastened it securely and was helped to horse. For an old hag of sixty-seven, she sat a horse damned well, she thought. Wordig, muttering, followed and before leaving the city gates she rode first by the minster for a quick prayer. Always helped the hunt. She didn't get off her horse, rather nodded in the direction of the church usually and blessed herself. The bishop was near the main door lecturing a cleric. Probably on the evils of his lice, Emma guessed. Stigand hated lice.

"Your Grace," she called to him without getting down.

He waved to her.

"The court will be coming for Easter," she said.

"I should hope, Lady Queen. I should hope. It is tradition." The raspberry-faced man came toward her. He was considerably younger than Emma, but she decided he looked much older.

"Odda Deerhurst has been named an earl and Elfgar, the son of Leofric and that bug-eyed Godiva is named to East Anglia in place of horrible Harold. They'll both be here."

"No Godwins. It'll be strange, a strange Easter without any Godwins," he said.

"It's of their own doing," Emma answered. It would be Easter without Gytha, the daughter of Thorgals-Sprakaleg, and her brood.

"How's the building coming?" he asked. "I don't get up the hill much."

"It'll never be imperial Winchester," she said, "but they've started work again now that it's warming. I best be to the hawks."

"On the knoll?" he asked.

"No, we'll go down to the sea and we needs be off."

"A long way," she heard him say as she started to ride off.

The day became even warmer as it pressed toward afternoon and the sea was calm and glistened blue in the sun. The Isle of Wight seemed closer to the shore on such a day without even a slight gauze of haze. The new falcon was restless.

"A bit skittish," Wordig said, "but we'll settle it down."

A woman trampling the fields in long black gowns and holding them up to keep from stepping on the layers of fabric came toward them. Emma held her hawk.

"Out of the way, woman!" Wordig yelled.

The woman ignored him and plowed toward them, pushing and stumbling over her clothing. She was breathing hard as she reached them. The woman was white-faced, not translucent, like Edward, but opaque white. Her eyebrows were either shaven or nonexistent and her sockets looked like those of a skull dug from a grave with eyeballs dropped in. "Death is coming," she said. "I'm the serpent of these fields and death is coming. I can smell a storm."

"It is clear as an empty pot," Emma said.

"You had best go. A fog the weight of iron brings death. I know. I am the serpent of the fields."

"Be off with you," Wordig told her and raised his hand in the air as if he meant to strike her, but did not.

"Death is coming like a storm at sea," she said and stumbled off over her hems.

Emma let the bird wing. It rose and circled and then vanished in a fog that came out of nowhere.

"Damn!" Wordig swore. "We'd better head out of this."

"The bird?"

"It'll find us when we get free of the fog."

They moved slowly, not certain of their direction, and for a few moments Wordig was lost from Emma, but then he reappeared and moved to stay closer to her when suddenly his horse spooked. Its front hoofs raised in the air and Wordig went falling backward off the beast. His head hit a rock. A snake rustled away and Emma leaped down from her own horse as quickly as her old body would allow and went over to help him. He was dead. Just like that, he was dead. His neck had snapped and his head wobbled free when she touched it. The old woman with the white face and the eye sockets of the dead had warned them. Emma struggled and pushed and turned trying to get Wordig on his horse. His head kept flapping about. He was heavy and she pulled and lugged and she thought she was going to die herself from the effort and she stopped to get her breath. She lugged again. For such an old man he weighed a great deal. His head was like a flower ready to break from the stem and wiggled about. She could hardly breathe and her heart pounded and she was getting dizzy, but she finally was able to lift him across his horse. She waited until her breath was more settled and then brought her own mount over to a rock and with a struggle climbed up on it. "Death is coming," the old woman had said and Emma, holding the reins of Wordig's horse, led the animal, having no idea in what direction she was headed. Tears filled her eyes. The fog got no less and between the tears and the fog she could see very little. Wordig nearly slid off the horse and she leaned over and pushed him back on. Her horse stumbled over broken trees and through long grasses and at times she could hear the sea and she knew she was getting no closer to Winchester. She went down into a vale and came to a stone fence and it began to rain and she followed the road that wandered beside the stone fence but met no one and the dimness of early evening began to crowd in around the fog and the fog began to lift and the terrain began to look familiar and she realized she was near Corfe.

Tugging the reins of the horse bearing the dead man, she turned up the hill toward the old compound. The burned-out buildings had long fallen and moss grew on old stone foundations. The little house Godwin had built for Sorgad—how old was Edith? Thirty-four, she must be thirty-four, and that was the age of the house—and that was all that was still standing. Emma eased down off her horse. She was stiff and sore from the ride and the tenseness of her body. She pushed her foot against the creaking door and it opened, scraping the dirt of the floor. It was gloomy and dark inside. She went back and the rain drizzled and soaked her hair and it dripped down onto her face. She struggled to get Wordig off the horse and she dropped him, his head flapping loose, and she took his arms and dragged him into the darkness of the house.

She needed to make a fire and she was hungry but there was no food and she thought of all the feasts and the strawberries and goat's cream that she had left sitting on plates and her mind was crowded with platters of roast doe and boiled salmon and herbed kidneys and figs and mutton pie and curds and spiced wine. Emma left Wordig in the dark and walked in the rain out to the point. It was still light enough to see and she walked the long way over wet dead grass until she had reached the point and the sea. She loved the sound, though the sight of the water was mostly lost in the fog. The seabirds cawed and appeared and disappeared into the mist and the sea tore at the rock below as if trying to beat the rock into sand and the darkness of night was crowding over the point when she saw the wolf standing at the edge of the trees. My God! she realized and her breath caught up in her throat for she knew. She had come to Corfe to die! She panicked and ran, wetting, soaking her dress as the rain came heavier. Stumbling, her breath lodged in her throat, she ran and ran toward the little house. Somehow the little house promised safety, yet there was no one there, only the body of Wordig. Yet she struggled to reach the hut and it was almost as if her hand could touch it as she fell a few feet before the door. She tried to crawl and realized she had no feeling in her right side and she had trouble knowing where she was and she could hear the seabirds and she was a young bride at Corfe. She was going to have a baby—a son, a beautiful son, who would be heir to England and she would be the great Queen and her father stood beside her and he gave her a great sword and yet it was so light and she raised it and she seemed to be walking, and a young man came and knelt before her. He was the most beautiful young man she had ever seen. "I am your son," he said. "I am the King." She took his hand and raised him up and he came and sat beside her. He had yellow hair the color of wheat straw and he had a scar on his cheek and his voice was low and soft like the touch of fur. "We will rule forever," he said. A great army assembled as they sat in chairs in a sunny meadow and the sound of the sea seemed always present. The child Edith came and gave Emma a butterfly of soft silver and it perched on the back of Emma's hand as if it were a peregrine ready to strike. And men came and knelt before them, all dressed in white and gold. Wulfstan was there, and old Eric with snow-white hair, and her brother Richard, and Baldwin, and her grandfather and they spoke of her beauty and the beauty of her son. He led her through the meadow and the sun shone on his yellow hair and he smiled at her and she felt warm and comfortable— But why if all this was so, was she alone, lying in the mud, the rain hitting the back of her neck as she tried and could not reach the door to the hut—and wasn't that a wolf standing over her?

CHAPTER 12

England, 1052

THE HALL WAS CALIGINOUS AND SMELLED OF WHALE OIL. THE TORCHES HAD been lighted and smoked and Edward coughed and looked at the silent blurred figures standing about the hall, still and indistinct shapes—there, a cowled figure of a monk, his face vanished in the shadow of his hood . . . a sense of indefiniteness to his being. The shrouded atmosphere of the hall was not broken by the drone of some reeve of some northern shire reciting an accounting of grievances against the Normans in Edward's government in a sombrous voice.

Suddenly Edward shot up from the chair and wailed the long piercing screams of a wounded wolf.

"My Lord—" The Archbishop of Canterbury ran to him.

Edward shrieked.

And the hall at Westminster was filled with wide-opened eyes. They stood silent, blurred except for the eyes, the room was filled with eyes, and he shrieked and he was for no reason acutely aware of the smell of men, stale dirty men, who were only adumbrative shapes and penetrating eyes. He shrieked and shrieked and shrieked and fell, sinking to the floor, and he sobbed. His voice was muffled in his hands. "My mother is dead!"

Robin stood over him. "But how—"

"I know. I know."

The shapes were there. Men moving now, yet as indistinct as their silent tongues. There was ripping pain in his chest and his gut twisted in an emptiness. There was no fit overtaking him, nor sign of one, only the pain and twisting inside his hollow self. The terror of Emma's death and he knew with certainty it was fact.

The reeve stood silent.

The dwarf, who claimed to eat horse turds and sang in the middle of the night, waddled into the hall on his short legs. "A crow fell dead from the sky." And he threw the dead bird down near the King's right hand and waddled out again.

"She said to me once, 'Just for joy I would like to take a knife and hack off Gytha's hair,' and I gave her a gift of a gold-handled knife, it was set with four red stones and a green stone. But she never whacked off the countess's hair." Edward thought on it and rubbed the stone of the floor with his open hand. "We will ride to Winchester tonight."

"It is dark, my Lord, and cold," Robin told him. "In the morning . . ."

Edward got up. "The Queen is dead and we will go to her." He reached down and picked up the dead crow. One of its feet had been torn off by the dwarf. He dropped it again on the stone of the floor.

The night was Stygian and Edward could sense the evil abroad in the murky blackness. Robin was beside him on a nervous horse. A fog would drift in and then vanish as it came. A cry from somewhere carved the troublesome night and a hound bayed to an eclipsed heaven. A hundred riders rode behind them in the pitch, or Edward assumed they were still there by the clomping of the hoofs in a melancholy rhythm.

"Emma, daughter of Normandy, loved me as if I were one of her precious relics," Edward said to Robin.

Robin held tight on the reins of his horse. "She tried to kill you."

Edward looked at him angrily and then smiled. "She did not succeed for, in truth, she loved me." Edward peered out, trying to discern the horizon. "Once in Corfe when I was very small I touched her breast."

"How you forget," Robin said. "The man at Brionne came with poison from the Queen."

Edward ignored him. "I dreamt once that Harold Thorkellsson—do you remember the Earl of East Anglia?"

Even in the dark Edward could see the look on Robin's face. He was perplexed by something. "Of course," he answered.

"He had only two fingers on one hand, I don't remember which hand, and I dreamt he was nude, copulating with the Queen, my mother, on the floor of the Corfe chapel. . . . There is no chapel at Corfe anymore . . . there is hardly anything at Corfe anymore."

"How do you know she is dead?"

"The floor at Corfe in the chapel must have been very hard. My filthy brother Edmund burned it down. Do you remember when we were young and Edmund was alive?"

"Most of Edmund's people believed Emma poisoned him."

"Aesval poisoned him. Didn't you know that? Edmund cut off Mac-Boru's head. I should've been King then but—"

"But your mother married Cnute."

"Yes, you see Ethelred with the mean eye was cruel to my mother. I saw her pain. Sometimes she would cry, other times she would yell at me or Godgifu or Aly—"

Robin wore no helmet and his white hair stood apart in the night's blackness.

"—but she was in great pain," Edward said.

A bat swept across the low sky and with great speed turned in the air and swept above again.

"She was in great pain, but she loved me—"

Robin's horse beat his hoofs against the earth. "She married Cnute."

"Are you jealous that Cnute did not choose you instead, boy of Jumieges?"

"That is not called for, my Lord, this is long since behind me." Robin spurred his horse and rode ahead.

The fog swept in again. The desolate call of a bird cracked in the obscure haze. Edward caught up with Robin. "You may call me Edward, Robin. We are friends of childhood and I know your sins as if I had been your confessor."

"A friend does not say such unkind things to another friend."

"I was jealous of you. I—"

They stopped. A dead horse and rider, pinned beneath a fallen tree, blocked the road. "It's one of Godwin's spies," Robin told him. "I recognize the man."

"Even in this dark."

"Yes. Look at the birthmark on this face."

They rode around the fallen tree and dead rider and horse. The man did not smell, so Edward surmised the accident had probably been but hours earlier.

"Why would you be jealous?" Robin asked.

"Because you, like Mother, feel something for others, are somehow pleased by a slight touch or even the sight of another being. I am aroused by nothing . . . far deader than Emma of Normandy, even in her death."

"How can you be so certain?"

"She is dead."

Daylight was still hours away and the murky night seemed to get deeper and blacker. Robin's horse became more skittish and Edward was certain he heard witches crying in the distance. Trees close to the road took ominous shapes of black shadows against a black sky.

Someone called out that a manor lay just beyond the bend, but it was dark and reeked of stagnant water and they passed on by and the fog again enveloped them and they slowed and made their way carefully along the dark road.

And they rode for a long time in quiet. The sound of horses and the occasional voice of man were all that interrupted the bleak night and gradually the light of day drifted in with a morning fog and as it lifted Winchester sprawled on the distant hill, a gray silhouette against a gray sky.

"I shall grieve for forty days—"

"And England?"

"Should grieve with me."

"Godwin will tear us to pieces."

The streets of Winchester were morning-quiet. A man with a limp led a goat on a long rope and chickens scattered and picked and a pig was driven by a tall man with a crooked pole, and a woman with no arms screamed out for alms and a priest kicked her out of the way and sped down the hill. People looked up to see the King, but there was no pity, nor surprise, nor horror. There was not the look of death about the town. The cobble was broken in many places and grasses grew up between the stones and the horses going up the hill left a trail of horse manure to be washed away in the next rain.

Lady Maud, a big woman with one large breast and one small one, met them in the courtyard, the chicken flew out of her way and a dog tied to a door handle barked at her.

"The Queen—" Edward's voice was urgent as he rode up to her.

"Went hawking on yesterday morn, my liege Lord—"

"And—"

"She did not return. I sent two soldiers in search thinking there must have been an accident, but they returned this morning and found no trace of the lady."

"Did she go alone?" Edward's horse stamped about, being made nervous by the barking dog.

"No, my Lord. Wordig. Her hawker, Wordig, was with her."

Edward turned the nervous horse about.

"Christians do not hunt in Lent," Lady Maud said softly.

But not softly enough. Edward swung back and with his riding leather struck the woman across the face. "My mother is dead, you old pig." He rode off and the riders followed. Part way down the hill the old raspberry-faced Bishop of Winchester came running toward them on wobbly legs.

"His heart will give out," Robin said.

The bishop came puffing and trying to get his breath. "I . . . I . . . heard . . . you . . . 'd come . . . my . . . Lord." He panted and took a deep breath. "I'd . . . heard you'd . . . you'd come."

"Have you seen my Lady Mother?"

He took a deep swallow of air. "Not since yesterday, past prime. It was hawking she was bound to with that old falconer of hers, the man what plays with his genitals in the confessional."

"She did not return," Robin told him.

"Was she going to the knoll?" Edward asked.

The smith came up, his face as cool as his morning fire. He had obviously heard the question. "No good hawking there this time a year, my Lord. No good. I'd wager it was to the sea they went."

"It was," Stigand said. "The Lady Queen said it was to the sea they were going."

Edward heard no more. He struck his horse and the others followed. They rode south. The way got muddy, as it must have rained in these hills during the night. Trees were spotting buds and water dripped from them.

They met a man along the road who was wearing a shoe on one foot only and carrying a bundle of fagots on his back.

"Have you seen a lady and her falconer?" Robin asked.

The man made no reply.

"I asked have you seen a lady and her falconer?"

The man looked at him.

"Are you deaf?" Edward spoke in Saxon and raised his hand.

"No, me Lord, I don't speak no Norman French, only me Saxon."

Robin looked at him with disdain and spoke in perfect Saxon. "And who is your lord, Saxon peasant?"

"Me Lord Godwin, your Grace. The precious Lord Godwin."

Edward suspected that had the bishop his crozier handy he would have struck the man with it. "Have you seen my Lady Mother and her hawker?"

"No, I ain't seen a body, save yourself but let me see"—he counted on his fingers—"eight days now. I sell sheeps' gonads to a Breton by the sea and me neighbors won't have the talk with me."

They rode off.

"Insolent bastard," Robin swore.

A few miles later he added, "Do you know those Bretons sell sheeps' testicles as oysters?"

They searched. They reached the ground above Wight, where the land looks out to the sea, and soldiers went down below, but there were no signs that the Queen had been there.

They searched the day and spent the cold night sleeping by the fire.

"Do you ever long for home?" Robin asked.

"This is my home," Edward reminded him.

At daybreak the search began anew. A piece of black cloth was found torn on a branch. What might be blood was discovered nearby on a rock. A ways beyond, the thicket had been trampled by horses. They followed the trail of the horses and it seemed to go about in circles, but finally they found where it led away and down into a vale.

"Yes," Edward said after they rode for over an hour, "we are near Corfe. The Queen would have gone to Corfe."

The seabirds circled, but the vultures were on the ground and they rose as the riders approached and there in the yard was the body of Emma, her face down in the mud. Edward picked her up. She was stiff and cold and heavy and Edward looked at the wrinkled face and matted gray hair and was amazed at how old she looked. He wanted to wipe the mud from her face but his hands were not free. Pushing open the door to the small house with his foot, he carried her into the blackness and even before his eyes had adjusted and he saw him it was obvious from the smell of corruption that he had found Wordig. He set her on the floor and slumped down beside her and took his sleeve and wiped the mud from her face. There was life. There was death. The two were insular. He had come to realize that she had believed that somehow she could live on through her bloodline; but she was wrong. There was life. There was death. There was finality in that. He was alone. Edward knew he was very much alone. The world of sound and sight and smell existed around him, but he was apart, as if a circular chasm separated him. It was as if man's aura, which was so visible to him, was like a shield which isolated and kept one being from another. He had told Robin he had been envious of him and his Queen Mother's ability to reach out to touch, to feel, but did they really? Perhaps, in the end, they were as distinct and separate and alone as himself. Edward moved his foot. It was strange that Wordig had begun to rot so soon, but the hideous odor was undeniable. To survive from that decay was all that there was and Edward would survive. Armies of Godwins would flood over England and the Normans would be drowned or flee to higher ground, but Edward knew he must survive the flood and if he was careful could do it without letting the country be washed by a red tide of blood. Distance, he must create distance, and if there was no stopping the Godwins then let them come. Edward would survive. Outside was the sound of voices of men, but it was apart from him. He sat in the blackness. Beyond the voices of men was the caw of the seabirds and he knew they circled in the air, never staying long on the earth.

The soldiers came and wrapped the bodies, but the stink of putrefaction could not be contained in cloth. The sacked bodies were each packed on horses and Edward rode between. The sun shone warmly, but it only made the bodies stink the worse and Robin and the others rode apart. Distance. Death created distance.

The merchant Seven came to Winchester with a gift of damask, yards of damask, and a gown of white was sewn for the Lady Queen, and she was laid in a coffin of cedar and the lid was pegged on, but the cedar could not battle the smell of death and Emma stank. Edward sat for four days with the boxed, reeking body of his mother while he waited for the nobles and the bishops of the North to descend on Winchester, and he took little water and no food, yet his bowels had moved, at least once, he knew, and he had peed himself frequently. None came about. Distance. He sat with his mother remembering the years of wanting to be King and wondering why and thinking that the anticipation was more interesting than the fact.

At Robin's insistence, he let himself be taken away and bathed and draped himself in layers of black robes so long that when he knelt they spread eight feet or more in a circle and no one could get near him. The hall filled and voices complained in Norman, Danish and Saxon that the Queen stank. Siward was there, but he was getting old and had hurt his leg and walked with a stick and he had left his wife in York, but this time not by choice, for she had died. Leofric and Godiva and their son Earl Elfgar complained not only of the smell, but of the Normans, and so did Odda of Deerhurst, whom Edward had made an earl when the Godwins had been exiled. Ralph of Mantes had built a fortress of stone in Herefordshire and Leofric whined that he "wanted no goddamn Norman castles in England" and suggested that "if Godwin were here . . ." Time, Edward thought; it is only a matter of time. Poor, frightened Ralph and his stone tower—he had found a way to keep the Welsh from butchering him and Leofric resented that the chinless man wanted to stay alive. Survival. Every man finds his own survival.

Archbishop Robin led the cortege, sprinkling holy water and looking back as if he feared some Saxon might stick him with a knife, his blue eyes alert, his white hair mostly buried beneath the miter. The cedar box was carried on the shoulders of six tall houseguards. Edward had picked the most virile-looking men that he could find, knowing his mother would have liked that. He followed behind, wearing his crown and trailing the yards of black gown over chicken dung and horse turds down the cobbled street of Winchester. Godgifu had sent a messenger. "I am not well, not able and not a hypocrite." Ralph of Mantes walked after Edward carrying the mace. There were just he and Edward; the rest of Emma's blood had been spilled. Alfred, Harthacnut and Gunnerhild were dead. There was that child, a woman now, of course, Beatrix, locked away in some German abbey somewhere. For all Emma's passion there was little evidence left.

Stigand cried and celebrated the mass.

"He knew the Queen carnally," Ralph said, as if telling him of the weather.

"That is more than I did," Edward said.

Ralph looked at him in horror and pulled his arm back away from Edward. Distance.

Edward had her buried in a tomb next to Cnute. Harthacnut was there and so was Beorn. Harold was lost in a fen. Edward wondered if Harold was really Cnute's son. There was no one to say any longer. The dead were so soon forgotten and that disturbed him. Only saints were alive and visible. To die a saint was to defy death.

A stone Emma, an effigy, was placed atop the real Emma. "I go to Westminster to mourn for forty days," Edward announced and the crowd parted as he walked through the minster trailing black fabric over the stone. He had sent for one of his camels and a man in a burnous stood tending it. Edward exchanged his crown for a black cowl, climbed on the camel and, as it stood, his gown, despite the height of the animal, dragged along the ground. The camels were scoffed at and despised and no one offered to accompany him. Distance. He rode with only the company of his soldiers, north, toward Westminster.

He spent the daylight hours kneeling in the chapel, the dark hours in bed. Each day was the same. He spread the circle of black gown and created space over which no one could trespass. For him to hear and pay attention to intruders in his grief, the voice had to be loud, and if it was loud he'd hush it and remind the voice it was in the presence of the living Jesus and invading his private sorrow. Edward never looked up to see the faces belonging to the voices.

The voice was Robin's. "Gruffydd ap Llewelyn has burned Leonminster and Ralph sits in his tower at Hereford doing nothing." Robin never spoke too loud and never sought an answer. He only delivered succinct and salient messages and went away.

The days passed.

Robin came and went bringing bad news. "Harold with his brothers have landed in the west and have joined the Welsh fighting on the border."

Edward straightened his black gown, making certain it formed a pleasant circle about him. He liked black almost as much as he liked white. He took little food, sometimes a bit of fish in the morning or a pinch or two of bread, and no wine.

The days passed.

Robin went to the chapel but stood at the door and yelled, "Saxons are deserting and any day now Godwin will land at Sandwich."

A cleric came. He had a stuffed nose and spoke with a nasal voice. "The Archbishop of Canterbury is fled to Normandy. Godwin marches through Wessex and the people cheer."

Edward knelt, not moving or giving any indication that he had heard. It would soon be over and it would be bloodless.

The days passed.

Godwin and his sons came to the chapel. Edward could tell by the bluster and the walk that it was them and Edith was with them, but he didn't look up.

"We demand a Gemot be called and our lands and titles be restored," Godwin said.

"We want our lands," Sven Godwinsson, the *Nithling*, said.

The cleric came and told them, "The King is in mourning for forty days and will not talk. Come back when the time is ended."

"Ridiculous," Godwin said and stormed from the chapel. His sons tromped out behind him, but Edith didn't leave. He didn't hear her walk away.

"I would talk with you," she said.

He made no response.

He could tell she had removed her clothing and knelt somewhere near and he could hear her breathe and wished she would go away and leave him alone. He thought of the young girl who had touched him in Rouen, and the older child, who had saved his life, and the young woman with the lovely breasts and the golden skin who lay nude upon the banks of the Thames, but she was none of these. She was a Godwin and thirty-four years old and obstinate and had defied him and had decided to support her family in opposition to him. Her chastity was a fraud. She was simply afraid of a man and like him was cold without any passion. There was no virtue in that, for there was no temptation. He knew more than anyone. She was a fraud. Her goodness a sham.

And at the end of forty days . . .

Edward called a Gemot and there was such interest and so many came that it was held outdoors before Wardrobe Palace in Londuntown. The Normans had fled and the people cheered and Godwin, looking tired and ill, laid his ax at Edward's feet and promised him fealty. Edward still wore the black robes of mourning and sat beneath a canopy of black hung with black ribbons and presented Godwin with a precious skull said to be St. Neot's.

The Gemot gave the Godwins all they asked and Edward left the town and went to Westminster.

He sat watching the masons. The stones were cut and chiseled and he listened to the noise of hammers against the rock and the sounds of the men and the German priest who ordered them all about and the Queen came riding from Londuntown on a black horse.

"You say nothing to me," Edith said and was helped from the horse.

"I have nothing to say to you," he said.

"You sent me off to a nunnery and humiliated me."

"You earned no less."

"I am the Queen."

"You are a Godwin."

"I honor my father—"

"But not your husband and King." He got up from the stone on which he had been sitting and walked in the direction of the chapel.

"You must make public amends to me." She followed after him.

"When you accept William as my rightful successor."

She followed him inside, into the cool of the chapel. "Never. To do so is to condone unchaste ways."

"You are a fraud, a barren fraud as cold as hoarfrost."

"And you are not better," she said in a spiteful tone.

"You are an idolatress believing the sun is God—"

"It is God."

"Pagan!" He swung about and looked straight at her.

"You are no saint and you never will be a saint," Edith said vindictively. "You sell bishoprics."

"You," he said, "sell men the privilege to petition me. That is a sin."

"No greater sin than dipping your fingers in the blood of a dead man."

"Or running about nude, displaying your body to entice men to unclean thoughts. Displaying your tits like—".

"Or hypocrisy!" she screamed.

"Yours or mine?" he said calmly.

"You hypocrite!" she yelled and a piece of plaster fell from the ceiling of the chapel.

Edward left early the next morning dressed in the brown rags of the poorest monk. He walked to Londuntown and through the streets looking for the lame and making them walk, looking for the sick and making them well and looking for the deaf and making them hear and looking for the blind and making them see.

And an old man said, "I should have stayed blind. I had no idea my wife was so ugly." And Edward walked on to the well of the saints and drank of the water.

At dusk he went by boat to Westminster.

"Where have you been?" Harold asked.

But Edward didn't tell him. In fact Edward said nothing to Harold at all and went out to where Wufnoth was tending his flowers and Edward asked him the names of blooms and Wufnoth told him and pointed out the different colors and how they should be raised.

And Sven, who had been *Nithling*, came to court, but Edward called him a murderer and walked out of any room which Sven entered and Edith suggested Sven make a pilgrimage to Jerusalem to be made clean and Harold agreed and Sven didn't really want to go but Godwin said it would be politic and Sven sailed for the Holy Land.

Tostig came with Edward's goddaughter, Judith and Edward greeted them warmly and they ate together and played at hazards and went hawking and Judith kept him abreast of the gossip and Edward and Tostig hunted boar and on a cold morning they killed a many-pointed hart and the winter came and the court moved to Glouchester for Christmas and Edward gave no gifts to any of the Godwins except Tostig and Wufnoth and word came that Sven was dead at Lykia and Gytha wept and Edith wept and Edward realized he had one less Godwin to deal with.

Spring came and the court went to Winchester and Edward sat by his mother's tomb and Bishop Stigand came in and wept and went away and the weather warmed and they returned to Westminster and Edward sat on a stone and watched the masons.

Harold, not wearing his usual air of demanding authority, came up to him. "My father is ill. Would you come to him?"

"No," Edward told him.

"Please."

"No."

Edward spent the next day sorting his mother's relics and he found the jeweled knife which he had given her in among her treasures. He slipped it into his own girdle and put the relics away.

Harold came again and pleaded with Edward and Edward refused and Gryth came and Edward said, "No."

Harold asked him a third time. "No!" Edward said. "Let it be final."

"He is dying," Tostig said.

"I will not go to him," Edward said.

"I understand," Tostig told him, but there were tears in his eyes.

Wufnoth brought him a large, white, beautiful flower.

"So early in the year," Edward said.

"Ye-ye-yes," the young man stammered. "M-m-my fa-fa-father—"

"No," Edward said.

The Queen did not ask.

Godwin died in the afternoon.

Gytha raged and stormed and he could hear her coming and he touched his mother's jewel-handled knife at his waist. She banged open the door of his chamber and screamed at him, "You are the most vile filthy human on the face of God's earth. You are not better than the turd of a dying seabird."

He looked at her and said nothing. She was old and haggard and her eyes were red from crying and her hair was an uncombed jungle of red and gray.

"Your mother hated you. She hated you and with reason. You are a monster and monsters should be destroyed at birth. Emma wanted to toss you to the pigs. The world is damned because she didn't do it. You are evil and cruel and you sit judging the world and you judged your mother and made her a whore. She was a *whore*—"

Edward took out the knife.

"You made her a whore, you monster—you ugly monster!"

He grabbed her by the hair and held her hair as she screamed and then he took the knife and whacked and grabbed another handful of hair and whacked again and again until her head was a stubble of red-gray and he let loose and she fell to the floor sobbing.

He stood, out of breath, fighting a fit, seeing the evil blackness in Gytha's aura and when she stopped crying she looked up at him and said softly, so very softly, "You will die, too."

EPILOGUE

Westminster, 1066

It hadn't been worth much—life. Pain, there had been years of pain. There was pain at this instant and he cringed and would have cried out, but his voice was gone. At times the pain was so severe he disappeared and thought he had died, but he would float back and see them. There was no pounding. They should get to work. No. The abbey was finished. Christmas. That was over. The dedication was over and he saw none of it. He lay, then as now, unable to move. Had the New Year come? It didn't matter. Heaven would probably be a disappointment, too. The pain struck; he escaped and returned. There were leeches crawling at his neck and he screamed to have them off, but no sound came. Was his mother in heaven? Would she reject him there? Would it start all over? He was more afraid of heaven than dying. If it were over . . . if death was the close, then there would be peace. There was more to go through. He had wanted a special place—to be a saint. What if saints were only made by men? What if Olaf was no more than Ethelred with the mean eye? The pain came, but not so sharp. That had been important, that drove him to life and now death—to be King . . . to be a saint. But King was an empty crown and he was afraid sainthood would come as shallow.

This time the pain drove him to leave and he was gone and gone and when he returned Stigand was touching his hands with something oily. Wash my hands! he tried to command. In blood. Dip my fingers in blood.

Edward wanted to laugh . . . extreme unction administered by Stigand. But his credentials were not in order. . . . No . . . Rome had balked. . . . It was not funny. What if he was not let into heaven because Stigand's credentials were not in order? Seven years ago the raspberry-faced bishop finally got his pallium . . . but from an antipope! A king should be granted . . . a saint should be granted . . . the last sacraments by someone in better stead with the church. No, it was not funny. Harold wouldn't even let Stigand baptize his bastard son. Stigand was the Archbishop of Canterbury and Harold wouldn't even let him baptize his son. Harold breathed over the bed. Edward always recognized Harold, even when Edward's eyes became too dim to see, for Harold's breath was like a dragon's fire. Where did expressionless Harold get all that fire? Harold's voice was like stale milk on a lukewarm day . . . ah! but there was passion in his breath. Harold, efficient, dull and uninspiring Harold. He lacked Godwin's vitality. Harold would name himself King and Edward envisioned the bells turning and twisting their shapes and at his coronation pealing flat dull thuds. Harold's *Te Deum* would be a flat dull thud. But the Godwins would prevail. Sven was dead. The sinner made a pilgrimage to Jerusalem and it killed him. Sven should have known it would kill a sinner like himself. Just as well, Sven, just as well. If you had stayed about, your brother Harold would probably have killed you. You're dead. Makes Harold the oldest. What if Sven was in heaven? The pain knifed his chest. All the Godwin passion was manifest in Sven, there was none left for Harold. Kings died and kings came after. What's it for? For Harold? Why be King if it was all for Harold? Old Malcolm was King at Scone and died and Duncan became King and MacBeth's wife, Gruoch, the daughter of Boite, took her big hands and drove a knife clean through Duncan . . . to have big hands like Gruoch and dip them in a king's blood . . . and then Malcolm the next Malcolm killed MacBeth and so it went. Siward helped Malcolm, of course, but Siward was dead now and the Godwins gave his son the tiny, tiny earldom of Huntingdon and divided the rest of England among themselves. Harold, the great Earl of Wessex, was big brother, but Gryth and Leofwine . . . there was a pain now, a sharp pain in his right leg which shot from the toes to the knee . . . great earldoms those brothers had, and Tostig, the only decent one in the lot, had been Earl of Northumbria, but the Northumbrians despised him and drove him out.

The flaming breath leaned over him. Like a vulture. Like a vulture. Would Harold pick the back of his skull away?

Edward drifted off.

It was the Queen's voice he heard when he came back.

"Is he dead yet?" she asked.

Edward could see. Harold shook his head. Edward tried to talk, to tell her how mean she looked, but nothing came out. Edith was forty-eight years old and there was not a gray hair among the deep auburn, but her eyes had gotten mean and she rarely spoke to him after Godwin died. Sometimes she would sit naked on the bank by the Thames and he would come by and talk to her of saints and God and she would look at him with cold eyes and say nothing.

The leeches were gone. Thanks to God. The doctors were gone as well. Perhaps Harold would strangle him. That would be senseless. He was dying. Still, Edith was holding his mother's knife, the Queen Lady Emma's knife with the jeweled handle. There was no pain now. He felt euphoric.

"I took the knife from Mama," Edith said. She was going to cut his hair off.

"She must not be allowed to desecrate him. Everything in order and everything proper. He wants to be buried here in the new abbey and he shall be buried here in splendor."

Thank you, Harold.

"And when the miracles begin?" Edith asked in a tired voice.

"Miracles will be fine. He was a West Saxon King. The people will remember he was a Wessexman."

One by one the possible successors had been eliminated. The Normans were driven out and the Witangemot resolved that no Norman should succeed to the throne.

"Ralph is descended from the line of Cerdic of Wessex, from Thor himself, and Alfred the Great. Though the cowardly Ralph never displayed much of Thor's wrath. 'Through the female line,' the Godwins protested, but Ralph was not disqualified, but he died suddenly, too suddenly Eadward the Atheling, they called one of Edmund's twin sons, who for so many years had lived at the court of Stephen in Hungary. The bishops invited him to England. His brother was dead, but he was alive, if not a young man, and had children and he came to England, but was not allowed into Edward's presence. 'He is ill,' Harold had said. 'A danger to you. When he gets well, then he'll visit.'" Suddenly he died. Too suddenly.

There was no pain at all now. Edward floated.

He thought of Leofric and Godiva. Was Godiva alive or dead? Edward couldn't remember. Leofric was dead. Elfgar his son had been Earl of East Anglia, but he fought with the Welsh king against Edward and lost his earldom, but he was given it back only to die. Harold made Elfgar's son Edwin the Earl of Mercia and another son Morcar an earl as well and told everyone it was Edward's doing. Harold ran the kingdom and Edward had gone about becoming a saint and now there was doubt. Had all the cures and miracles and fasting and prayers been for naught? What assurance, but the word of man, was there that heaven existed? Edward's body began to shake and he had no control and his breath began to rattle.

"Am I to be your heir?" Harold's breath was fire above him.

"He said yes. I heard him say yes," Edith said.

Edward could see no longer and his body jolted as if struck by lightning and he heard Gytha's voice: "There's a comet in the sky. And when a comet is seen, a king will die."

"He named me his heir," Harold said.

"Papa should have lived," Gytha said. "The prophecy of Sorgad will be filled."

For only a moment Edward could see. There was a gray wolf lying down on the foot of the bed.